Fifty Readings in Philosophy

FIFTY READINGS IN PHILOSOPHY

FOURTH EDITION

Donald C. Abel

St. Norbert College

McGraw Hill

Connect
Learn
Succeed™

The **McGraw·Hill** Companies

Connect
Learn
Succeed™

FIFTY READINGS IN PHILOSOPHY, FOURTH EDITION

This book is printed on acid-free paper.

1 2 3 4 5 6 7 8 9 0 DOC/DOC 1 0 9 8 7 6 5 4 3 2 1

ISBN 978-0-07-353580-7
MHID 0-07-353580-x

Vice President & Editor-in-Chief: *Michael Ryan*
Vice President & Director of Specialized Publishing: *Janice M. Roerig-Blong*
Editorial Director: *Beth Mejia*
Executive Director: *Mark Georgiev*
Sponsoring Editor: *Jessica Cannavo*
Director of Marketing & Sales: *Jennifer J. Lewis*
Project Manager: *Erin Melloy*
Design Coordinator: *Margarite Reynolds*
Cover Designer: *Studio Montage, St. Louis, Missouri*
Buyer: *Nicole Baumgartner*
Media Project Manager: *Sridevi Palani*
Compositor: *S4Carlisle Publishing Services*
Typeface: *10/12 Palatino*
Printing: *#45 New Era Matt Plus, R. R. Donnelley & Sons*

Library of Congress Cataloging-in-Publication Data

Fifty readings in philosophy / [compiled by] Donald C. Abel. —4th ed.
     p. cm.
Includes bibliographical references and index.
ISBN 978-0-07-353580-7 (acid-free paper)
1. Philosophy—Textbooks. I. Abel, Donald C., 1948-

B29.F5314 2012
100—dc22

                                                    2011013182

About the Author

DONALD C. ABEL is professor of philosophy at St. Norbert College in De Pere, Wisconsin. He holds a B.A. in philosophy from Gonzaga University, an M.A. in philosophy from Tulane University, a Ph.L. in philosophy from St. Michael's Institute, an M.Div. in theology from Loyola University of Chicago, and a Ph.D. in philosophy from Northwestern University. He is the author of *Freud on Instinct and Morality* (1989), *Theories of Human Nature: Classical and Contemporary Readings* (McGraw-Hill, 1992), and *Fifty Readings Plus: An Introduction to Philosophy* (McGraw-Hill, 2nd ed., 2010). He is the editor of *Discourses*, an electronic database of philosophy readings that is part of *Create*, McGraw-Hill's online resource for creating customized textbooks. Professor Abel has received two awards for excellence in teaching and an award for outstanding scholarship. He is a member of the American Philosophical Association, the American Catholic Philosophical Association, and the Society for Ancient Greek Philosophy.

Contents

Preface

Fifty Readings in Philosophy is designed for an introductory course in philosophy that uses primary texts. The readings are from classical Western philosophers, contemporary authors writing in that tradition, and feminist authors. These readings were selected on the basis of their cogency of thought, clarity of expression, historical significance, diversity of views, and accessibility. They are organized into seven thematic chapters: the nature of philosophy, philosophy of religion, theories of knowledge, philosophy of mind, free will and determinism, ethics, and political and social philosophy.

This fourth edition of *Fifty Readings in Philosophy* features eight new readings, three new translations, the conversion of endnotes to footnotes, and updated biographies of living authors.

The new readings are:

> Peter Carruthers, *The Case for Physicalism* (complete)
> James Giles, *The No-Self Theory: Hume, Buddhism, and Personal Identity* (selection)
> John Hick, *An Irenaean Theodicy* (selection)
> John Locke, *Of Identity and Diversity* (selection)
> Anne Phillips, *Multiculturalism without Culture* (selection)
> Plato, *Apology*, translated by R. E. Allen (complete)
> Marya Schechtman, *Personal Identity and the Past* (selection)
> Galen Strawson, *The Impossibility of Ultimate Moral Responsibility* (selection)

The new translations are:

> Paul-Henri Thiry, Baron d'Holbach, *The System of Human Freedom*, translated by Donald C. Abel
> Plato, *Republic*, translated by C. D. C. Reeve
> Jean-Paul Sartre, *Existentialism Is a Humanism,* translated by Carol Macomber

Because most beginning philosophy students need assistance in reading primary texts, *Fifty Readings in Philosophy* incorporates editorial features that enable students to read the works with greater understanding and benefit:

- *Chapter introductions.* Each of the seven chapters begins with an overview of the topic and states the basic points made by each author in the chapter. The overview focuses on fundamental questions intended to generate the students' interest. The brief summaries of the authors' positions show students the diversity of views on these questions and will encourage students to enter into the ongoing philosophical dialogue and to formulate their own views on the topic.
- *Self-contained chapters.* Each of the seven chapters is an independent unit; neither the chapter introduction nor the readings within the chapter presuppose familiarity with any prior section of the book. It is therefore possible to read the chapters in a different order or to omit some of them.
- *Length of readings.* Each reading is long enough to present a self-contained argument, but not so lengthy that students lose track of the author's main point.
- *Self-contained readings.* Each reading, together with its headnote, is a self-contained unit. The headnote provides enough background for students to understand the selection even when the author builds on or criticizes a theory presented earlier in the chapter. This feature enables instructors to vary the order of the readings or to omit some of them.
- *Headnotes.* Each reading begins with a headnote that gives a biographical sketch of the author and a brief overview of the reading. The biography helps place the reading in a personal and historical context; the overview, which guides students through the main arguments but is not so detailed as to serve as a substitute for reading the text itself, enables students to approach the reading with greater confidence.
- *Explanatory notes.* Notes explain terms and references that are likely to be unfamiliar to beginning students. For this edition, endnotes have been converted to footnotes for greater convenience.
- *Retention of original headings.* To help students better understand the context and organization of each reading, all the original headings and subheadings of the book, chapter, or article are included. This format also makes it easier for students to locate excerpts within the original complete work. When the original text contains no headings, I have inserted some headings in brackets to make it easier for students to see the main divisions of the reading.
- *Contemporary translations.* All the translations used in this anthology are by contemporary scholars whose work reflects the latest scholarship and the modern idiom. Since the only published translation of Holbach's *The System of Nature* is the dated (1835) and sometimes inaccurate version of H. D. Robinson, I made a new translation of the excerpt used in this book.
- *Stylistic modernization of classical British authors.* To make the selections from Hobbes, Locke, Berkeley, Hume, Paley, and Wollstonecraft more accessible, I have revised archaic punctuation, capitalization, italicization, and spelling.

For the first time, an online supplement of author-written additional pedagogical material for *Fifty Readings* is available to students and instructors. The *Online Learning Center Website for Fifty Readings in Philosophy,* www.mhhe .com/abel4e, contains:

- *Outline with Study Questions* for each reading. The outline, which follows the reading's headings and subheadings, shows students the basic structure of the reading. Each point in the outline is followed by one or more study questions that ask about the material presented in that section.
- *Questions for Reflection and Discussion* for each reading. These questions, in contrast to the study questions, are designed to stimulate personal philosophical reflection on the points made by the author. They are suitable for classroom discussion and for paper topics.
- *For Further Reading* for each reading. A separate annotated bibliography is available for each reading. The entries include commentaries on the text, critical studies, and works on the topic by other authors. Additional works by the author are sometimes included. The annotations usually refer students to one or more specific sections of the work cited (with page numbers).
- *Logic and Argumentation.* This formal study of reasoning can help students understand the readings more fully, reflect more carefully on philosophical issues, and write more effective papers. Section I presents the essentials of logic and argumentation, Section II illustrates these principles with examples from the readings in the book, and Section III shows how these principles can be used in writing a philosophy paper.
- *Glossary of Philosophical Terms.* A glossary containing 175 entries gives concise definitions of key philosophical terms used in the readings, as well as in the editorial apparatuses for these readings and in the essay on logic and argumentation. The glossary also includes additional terms that students are likely to encounter in other philosophical literature.

I wish to thank Nicole Bridge, Mark Georgiev, Debra Hash, Jessica Cannavo, Erin Melloy, and Nikki Weissman of McGraw-Hill Higher Education, and Lori Bradshaw, Dhanya Ramesh and Kreeti Saravanan of S4Carlisle Publishing Services, for their dedicated and excellent work on this new edition of *Fifty Readings in Philosophy.*

Authors Richard Dawkins, John Hick, James Giles, Nancy Holmstrom, Anne Phillips, the late James Rachels, Stuart Rachels, Marya Schechtman, Galen Strawson, and the late Richard Taylor kindly provided me with biographical information for use in the headnotes. In addition, Penelope Mackie supplied information about her late father, J. L. Mackie.

I appreciate the thoughtful suggestions for revision given by my St. Norbert College colleagues Leanne Kent and Joel Mann, by Diane Legomsky, a specialist in Greek philosophy, and by the reviewers of the third edition, namely, Charles Ackerson, St. John's University; J. C. Berendzen, Loyola University; John Berteaux, California State University–Monterey Bay; Mark Christensen, Lourdes College; Linda Dayley, Western Connecticut State University; Erik Jackiw, Mt. San Antonio College; Ian MacKinnon, University of Akron; Alan Nichols, Georgia Highlands College; and John Santiago, College of DuPage.

Students in my introductory classes at St. Norbert College have contributed to this book by their helpful comments on various readings that I have used in the classroom over the years. Finally, I would like to thank the publishers (listed at the end of the book) who granted permission to reproduce copyrighted material.

Donald C. Abel

Fifty Readings in Philosophy

CHAPTER 1   What Is Philosophy?

The ancient Greek thinkers who explored fundamental questions about the world and about human existence called themselves *philosophoi,* "lovers of wisdom." They took time to stop and wonder about such things as the nature of the universe, the purpose of life, and the meaning of "good" and "bad." In their search for wisdom, they were not content to rely on answers provided by religious and cultural tradition; they used reason and evidence gained from their own experience to formulate new hypotheses. Although not all the Greek philosophers thought it possible to find the ultimate answers to their questions, they all believed that the very activity of seeking wisdom is highly worthwhile. The philosopher Socrates was so convinced of the importance of philosophizing that he declared: "The unexamined life is not worth living for a human being."

The Greek conception of philosophy as the "love of wisdom" is still valid today. Philosophy now, as then, begins with the realization that we know very little about the most important things in life. Philosophers continue to ponder basic questions about the universe and human existence. They are aware of the answers provided by common sense and by authority (religious or secular), but know that such answers can be partially or entirely mistaken. Philosophers are "skeptical" in the root sense of "taking a close look" (*skepesthai* in Greek) at an idea before accepting it. They seek answers based on reason and experience, realizing that any proposed answer (including their own) is tentative and subject to debate. In fact, practically every major philosophical question is still energetically disputed, even after centuries of debate. The lack of definitive answers in philosophy may seem frustrating until we come to see that the value of philosophizing lies not so much in the theories it produces as in the very activity of seeking wisdom. To engage in philosophy is to expand our mental powers, deepen our understanding of fundamental issues, and thereby enrich our lives.

The readings in this book present the reflections of classical and contemporary philosophers on seven basic topics. The readings in Chapter 1 deal with the nature and value of philosophy. (Paradoxically, to ask what philosophy is, is itself a philosophical question, because to understand the nature and importance of the search for wisdom is itself a part of wisdom.) The balance of the book presents differing—and often opposing—views on six topics: the existence of God and the rationality of religious belief (Chapter 2), the nature and grounds of human knowledge (Chapter 3), the relation of the mind to the body and the existence of the "self" (Chapter 4), the existence of free will (Chapter 5), the nature and requirements of morality (Chapter 6), and the nature of political authority and its relation to contemporary social issues (Chapter 7).

Chapter 1, "What Is Philosophy?," contains two readings—one from Plato and one from Bertrand Russell. In *The Apology,* Plato, who was present at the trial at which Socrates was convicted of impiety and the corruption of youth, reports what Socrates said at his trial. In the course of defending himself against the charges brought by Meletus, his primary accuser, Socrates asks Meletus questions. Meletus's responses contradict themselves, and this demonstrates Meletus's failure to consider these important accusations seriously. In his conversations with fellow Athenians throughout his life, Socrates used this method of questioning his interlocutors' thoughts about a certain topic to make them aware of their implicit assumptions, to point out inconsistencies in their views, and to lead them to think more coherently and deeply about the topic. Socrates and Plato believed that this dialectical ("Socratic") method of inquiry—whether used in conversation with another person or in an interior dialogue with oneself—is the path to wisdom. (Plato's *Euthyphro,* which is Reading 11 in this book, is an extended illustration of Socrates's use of this method.) In the second reading, Russell presents his views on the value of philosophy. He argues that philosophizing enriches our mental lives. This enrichment comes not from attaining definitive answers to questions (because practically all philosophical questions remain undecided) but from teaching us to question our own beliefs and to see that there are alternative ways of viewing reality. Russell holds that philosophy helps us see the world more objectively by liberating us from our tendency to interpret everything in terms of how it affects us personally.

Plato and Russell would agree that philosophy is the love of wisdom, but—not surprisingly, given the controversial nature of philosophical questions—not all philosophers would. And even those who do agree would almost certainly have different views about what "wisdom" is and what it means to "love" wisdom. To illustrate the diversity of opinion among philosophers about the nature of philosophy, this introduction concludes with a series of brief quotations from a variety of well-known thinkers from Plato to the present. (Whether one considers these thinkers *philosophers* depends, of course, on how one defines philosophy!)

> The feeling of wonder is the mark of the philosopher; philosophy has no other beginning than this.
>
> —Plato
>
> Philosophy is the cultivation of mental faculties.
>
> —Marcus Tullius Cicero
>
> The beginning of philosophy is the recognition of the conflict between opinions.
>
> —Epictetus
>
> Philosophical decisions are nothing but the reflections of common life, methodized and corrected.
>
> —David Hume
>
> Philosophy is the unusually stubborn attempt to think clearly.
>
> —William James
>
> Philosophy . . . has its origin and value in an attempt to give a reasonable account of our own personal attitude toward the more serious business of life.
>
> —Josiah Royce
>
> The proper method of philosophy consists in clearly conceiving insoluble problems in all their insolubility and then in simply contemplating them.
>
> —Simone Weil
>
> Philosophy is a battle against the bewitchment of our intelligence by means of language.
>
> —Ludwig Wittgenstein

Philosophy [is] the endeavor to discover by systematic reflection the ultimate nature of things.

—Brand Blanshard

To philosophize is to act in such a way that one steps out of the workaday world.

—Josef Pieper

The main concern of philosophy is to question and understand very common ideas that all of us use every day without thinking about them.

—Thomas Nagel

Apology

Plato

Plato was born in Athens in about 428 B.C.E. As a youth he associated with Socrates, a philosopher who constantly challenged fellow Athenians to think about virtue and to improve their souls. Plato's initial interest was in politics, but he soon became disillusioned, especially when, under the democracy that was restored after the rule of the "Thirty Tyrants," Socrates was arrested on false charges of impiety and the corruption of youth, convicted, and condemned to die. After the execution of Socrates, Plato moved to nearby Megara for a time and may have traveled to Egypt. In 388 he visited Italy and the city of Syracuse in Sicily. Returning to Athens, he founded the Academy, a school devoted both to philosophical inquiry and to the philosophically based education of politicians. Plato spent most of his life teaching at the Academy (Aristotle was his most famous student) and writing philosophical works. He made two more trips to Syracuse, in 368 and 361, apparently with the intention of turning the city's ruler, Dionysius the Younger, into a "philosopher-king." (If this was indeed his purpose, he failed.) Plato died in Athens in 347 at the age of 81.

Most of Plato's works are written as conversations between Socrates and one or more interlocutors on some topic concerning morality. His best-known "dialogues" (the name by which his surviving works are known) are the *Euthyphro, Apology, Crito, Phaedo, Meno, Symposium,* and *Republic.*

Our reading is the *Apology*, Plato's report of the defense speech (*apologia* in Greek; hence the title "Apology") and of the two brief additional speeches Socrates gave at his trial. Since Plato was present at the trial, we can be confident that his report is substantially accurate.

In his defense speech, Socrates responds to the charges of Meletus, his primary accuser, that he corrupts the youth of Athens and is impious. Before addressing these official charges, however, Socrates answers the "earlier" charges—three longstanding prejudices that arose against him as he tried to fulfill his God-given mission of urging Athenians to care about the good of their souls. He explains to the court (1) that he does not pursue natural science, (2) that he neither professes to be a teacher nor charges fees for his conversations, and (3) that he is wiser than others not because he has positive knowledge, but because he—unlike those he questions in his conversations—knows that he does not know. Socrates then defends himself against Meletus's official charges of the corruption of youth and impiety. He does so not by continuing to speak directly to the jury, but by using his customary method of conducting a conversation in which he questions his interlocutor. Using this dialectical ("Socratic") method, in the course of questioning Meletus he shows that Meletus's responses are contradictory and that Meletus has not considered his important accusations seriously. (Plato's *Euthyphro,* Reading 11 in this book, shows Socrates using this method of inquiry to lead the priest Euthyphro to think more coherently and deeply about piety.) Socrates thus conducts his defense without ever claiming to know precisely what corruption or piety are.

The jury of 501 found Socrates guilty by a vote of 280 to 221. In the Athenian legal system, when someone was convicted, the accuser would propose a penalty and the convicted person would propose a counterpenalty—and the jury would have to choose one or the other. Meletus had proposed death; Socrates, in his second speech, proposes what he considers a fitting penalty for his conduct.

The jury chose the death penalty. In his final speech, Socrates reflects on the manner of his defense and addresses separately those who voted against him and those who voted for acquittal.

[DEFENSE SPEECH]

[Introduction]

To what degree, Gentlemen of Athens, you have been affected by my accusers, I do not know. I, at any rate, was almost led to forget who I am—so convincingly did they speak. Yet hardly anything they have said is true. Among their many falsehoods, I was especially surprised by one: They said you must be on guard lest I deceive you, since I am a clever speaker. To have no shame at being directly refuted by facts when I show myself in no way clever with words—that, I think, is the very height of shamelessness—unless, of course, they call a man a clever speaker if he speaks the truth. If that is what they mean, why, I would even admit to being an orator, though not after *their* fashion.

These men, I claim, have said little or nothing true. But from me, Gentlemen, you will hear the whole truth. It will not be prettily tricked out in elegant speeches like theirs, words and phrases all nicely arranged. On the contrary: You will hear me speak naturally in the words that happen to occur to me. For I believe what I say to be just, and let no one of you expect otherwise. Besides, it would hardly be appropriate for a man of my age, Gentlemen, to come before you making up speeches like a boy.[1] So I must specifically ask one thing of you, Gentlemen. If you hear me make my defense in the same words I customarily use at the tables in the agora[2] and other places where many of you have heard me, please do not be surprised or make a disturbance because of it. For things stand thus: I have now come into court for the first time, I am 70 years old, and I am an utter stranger to this place. If I were a foreigner, you would unquestionably make allowances if I spoke in the dialect and manner in which I was raised. In just the same way, I specifically ask you now, and justly so, I think, to pay no attention to my manner of speech—it could be worse, it could be better— and look strictly to this one thing, whether or not I speak justly. For that is the virtue of a judge, and the virtue of an orator is to speak the truth.

[Statement]

First of all, Gentlemen, it is right for me to defend myself against the first false accusations lodged against me, and my first accusers; and next, against later accusations and later accusers. For the fact is that many accusers have risen before you against me. At this point they have been making accusations for many years, and they have told no truth. Yet I fear them more than I fear Anytus[3] and

---

[1]As Socrates states a few lines later, he was 70 years old when he was tried; Meletus, one of his accusers, was a very young man. [D. C. ABEL]

[2]*agora:* the marketplace in an ancient Greek city. [D. C. ABEL]

[3]At the trial, Meletus gave the main speech accusing Socrates; Anytus and Lycon gave supporting speeches. [D. C. ABEL]

those around him—though they too are dangerous. Still, the others are more dangerous. They took hold of most of you in childhood, persuading you of the truth of accusations that were in fact quite false: "There is a certain Socrates . . . a wise man . . . a thinker on things in the heavens . . . an inquirer into all things beneath the Earth . . . making the weaker argument stronger. . . ." Those men, Gentlemen of Athens, the men who spread that report, are my dangerous accusers; for their hearers believe that those who inquire into such things acknowledge no gods.

Again, there have been many such accusers, and they have now been at work for a long time. They spoke to you at a time when you were especially trusting—some of you children, some only a little older—and they lodged their accusations quite by default, no one appearing in defense. But the most absurd thing is that one cannot even know or tell their names—unless perhaps in the case of a comic poet.[4] But those who use malicious slander to persuade you, and those who, themselves persuaded, persuade others—all these are most difficult to deal with. For it is impossible to bring any one of them forward as a witness and cross-examine him. I must rather, as it were, fight with shadows in making my defense, and question where no one answers.

Please grant, then, as I say, that two sets of accusers have risen against me: those who now lodge their accusations, and those who lodged accusations long ago. And please accept the fact that I must defend myself against the latter first. For in fact you heard their accusations earlier, and with far greater effect than those that came later.

Very well then. A defense is to be made, Gentlemen of Athens. I am to attempt to remove from you in this short time the prejudice that you have been long in acquiring. I wish that this would come to pass if it were in some way better for you and for me, and that I might succeed in my defense. But I think the thing is difficult, and its nature hardly escapes me. Still, let that go as pleases the god; the law must be obeyed, and a defense be conducted.

[Refutation of the Earlier Accusers]

Let us then take up from the beginning the charges that have given rise to the prejudice—the charges on which Meletus in fact relied in lodging his indictment. Very well, what do those who slander me say? It is necessary to read, as it were, their sworn indictment: "Socrates is guilty of needless curiosity and meddling interference, inquiring into things beneath the Earth and in the sky, making the weaker argument stronger, and teaching others the same." The charge is something like that. Indeed, you have seen it for yourselves in a comedy by Aristophanes: a certain Socrates being carried around on the stage, talking about walking on air and babbling a great deal of other nonsense, of which I understand neither much nor little.[5] Mark you, I do not mean to disparage such knowledge, if anyone in fact has it—let me not be brought to trial by Meletus on such a charge as that! But, Gentlemen, I have no share of it. Once again, I offer the majority of you

---

[4]Aristophanes (about 450–388 B.C.E.), who satirizes Socrates in his play *The Clouds.* [D. C. ABEL]
[5]Aristophanes, *The Clouds,* lines 219–234. [D. C. ABEL]

as witnesses, and ask those of you who have heard me in conversation—there are many among you—to inform each other, please, whether any of you ever heard anything of the sort. From that you will recognize the nature of the other things the multitude says about me.

The fact is that there is nothing in these accusations. And if you have heard from anyone that I undertake to educate men, and make money doing it, that is false too. Once again, I think it would be a fine thing to be able to educate men, as Gorgias of Leontini does, or Prodicus of Ceos, or Hippias of Elis.[6] For each of them, Gentlemen, can enter any given city and convince the youth—who might freely associate with any of their fellow citizens they please—to drop those associations and associate with them, pay money for it, and give thanks in the bargain. As a matter of fact, there is a man here right now, a Parian, and a wise one, who I learn has just come to town. For I happened to meet a person who has spent more money on Sophists[7] than everyone else put together: Callias, son of Hipponicus. So I asked him—for he has two sons—"Callias," I said, "if your two sons were colts or calves, we could get an overseer for them and hire him, and his business would be to make them excellent in their appropriate virtue. He would be either a horse trainer or a farmer. But as it is, since the two of them are men, whom do you intend to get as an overseer? Who has knowledge of that virtue that belongs to a man and a citizen? Since you have sons, I'm sure you have considered this. Is there such a person," I said, "or not?"

"To be sure," he said.

"Who is he?" I said. "Where is he from, and how much does he charge to teach?"

"Evenus, Socrates," he said. "A Parian. Five minas."[8]

And I count Evenus fortunate indeed, if he really possesses that art, and teaches it so modestly. For my own part, at any rate, I would be puffed up with vanity and pride if I had such knowledge. But I do not, Gentlemen.

Perhaps one of you will ask: "But Socrates, what is this all about? Where have the slanders against you come from? You must surely have been busying yourself with something out of the ordinary. So grave a report and rumor would not have arisen had you not been doing something rather different from most folk. Tell us what it is, so that we may not take action in your case unadvisedly." That, I think, is a fair request, and I shall try to indicate what it is that has given me the name I have. Hear me, then. Perhaps some of you will think I joke; be well assured that I shall be telling the whole truth.

Gentlemen of Athens, I got this name through nothing but a kind of wisdom. What kind? The kind that is perhaps peculiarly human, for it may be I am really wise in that. And perhaps the men I just mentioned are wise with a wisdom greater than human—either that, or I cannot say what. In any case, I have no knowledge of it, and whoever says I do is lying and speaks to slander me.

---

[6]Gorgias, Prodicus, and Hippias were Sophists—itinerant teachers who, for a fee, taught Greeks how to succeed in practical affairs. [D. C. ABEL]

[7]*Sophists:* See footnote 6. [D. C. ABEL]

[8]*minas:* units of value roughly equivalent to the wages for one day of labor. [D. C. ABEL]

Please, Gentlemen of Athens, do not make a disturbance, even if I seem to you to boast. For it will not be my own words I utter; I shall refer you to the speaker, as one worthy of credit. For as witness to you of my wisdom—whether it is wisdom of a kind, and what kind of wisdom it is—I shall call the god at Delphi.

You surely knew Chaerephon. He was my friend from youth, and a friend of your democratic majority. He went into exile with you, and with you he returned. And you know what kind of a man he was, how eager and impetuous in whatever he rushed into. Well, he once went to Delphi and boldly asked the oracle—as I say, Gentlemen, please do not make a disturbance—he asked whether anyone is wiser than I. Now, the Pythia[9] replied that no one is wiser. And to this his brother here will testify, since Chaerephon is dead.

Why do I mention this? I do so because I intend to inform you the source of the slander against me. For when I heard it, I reflected: "What does the god mean? What is the sense of this riddling utterance? I know that I am not wise at all; what then does the god mean by saying I am wisest? Surely he does not speak falsehood; it is not permitted to him." So I puzzled for a long time over what was meant, and then, with great reluctance, I turned to inquire into the matter in some such way as this.

I went to someone with a reputation for wisdom, in the belief that there if anywhere I might test the meaning of the utterance and declare to the oracle, "This man is wiser than I am, and you said I was wisest." So I examined him—there is no need to mention his name, but it was someone in political life who produced this effect on me in discussion, Gentlemen of Athens. I concluded that though he seemed wise to many other men, and most especially to himself, he was not. I tried to show him this, and thus I became hated by him and by many who were present. But I left thinking to myself: "I am wiser than that man. Neither of us probably knows anything worthwhile; but he thinks he does and does not, and I do not and do not think I do. So it seems at any rate that I am wiser in this one small respect—I do not think I know what I do not." I then went to another man who was reputed to be even wiser, and the same thing seemed true again; there too I became hated by him and by many others.

Nevertheless, I went on, perceiving with grief and fear that I was becoming hated, but still it seemed necessary to put the god first. So I had to go on, examining what the oracle meant, testing everyone with a reputation for knowledge. And by the Dog,[10] Gentlemen—I must tell you the truth—I swear that I had some such experience as this: It seemed to me that those most highly esteemed for wisdom fell little short of being most deficient, as I carried on inquiry in behalf of the god, and that others reputedly inferior were men of more discernment.

But really, I must display my wanderings to you, which were like those of a man performing labors—all to the end that I might not leave the oracle untested. From the politicians I went to the poets—tragic, dithyrambic,[11] and the rest— thinking that there I would discover myself manifestly less wise by comparison. So I took up poems over which I thought they had taken special pains, and

---

[9]*the Pythia:* the priestess of Apollo, whose major shrine was at Delphi. [R. E. ALLEN, TRANSLATOR]
[10]*by the Dog:* a humorous oath; the Dog is the Egyptian dog-headed god, Anubis. [R. E. ALLEN]
[11]*dithyrambic:* relating to *dithyram,* a kind of lyric poetry. [D. C. ABEL]

asked them what they meant, so as also at the same time to learn from them. Now, I am ashamed to tell you the truth, Gentlemen, but still it must be told. There was hardly anyone present who could not give a better account than they of what they had themselves produced. So presently I came to realize that poets do not make what they make[12] by wisdom, but by a kind of native disposition or divine inspiration, exactly like seers and prophets. For the latter also utter many fine things, but know nothing of the things of which they speak. That is how the poets also appeared to me, while at the same time I realized that because of their poetry they thought themselves the wisest of men in other matters—and were not. Once again, I left thinking myself superior to them in just the way I was to the politicians.

Finally I went to the craftsmen. I was aware that although I knew scarcely anything, I would find that they knew many things, and fine ones. In this I was not mistaken: They knew things that I did not, and in that respect were wiser. But, Gentlemen of Athens, it seemed to me that the poets and our capable public craftsmen had exactly the same failing: Because they practiced their own arts well, each deemed himself wise in other things, things of great importance. This mistake quite obscured their wisdom. The result was that I asked myself on behalf of the oracle whether I would accept being such as I am, neither wise with their wisdom nor foolish with their folly, or whether I would accept wisdom and folly together and become such as they are. I answered, both for myself and the oracle, that it was better to be as I am.

From this examination, Gentlemen of Athens, much enmity has risen against me, of a sort most harsh and hard to endure, so that many slanders have arisen, and the word is spread that I am "wise." For on each occasion, those present think I am wise in the things in which I test others. But very likely, Gentlemen, it is really the god who is wise, and by his oracle he means to say, "Human nature is a thing of little worth, or none." It appears that he does not mean this fellow Socrates, but uses my name to offer an example, as if he were saying, "He among you, Gentlemen, is wisest who, like Socrates, realizes that he is truly worth nothing in respect to wisdom." That is why I still go about even now on behalf of the god, searching and inquiring among both citizens and strangers, if I think some one of them is wise; and when it seems he is not, I help the god and prove it. Due to this pursuit, I have no leisure worth mentioning either for the affairs of the city or for my own estate; I dwell in utter poverty because of my service to the god.

Then too the young men follow after me—especially the ones with leisure, namely the richest. They follow of their own initiative, rejoicing to hear men tested, and often they imitate me and undertake to test others; and next, I think, they find a large number of people who think they have some knowledge but know little or nothing. As a result, those whom they test become angry at me, not at themselves, and say, "This fellow Socrates is utterly polluted, and he corrupts the youth." And when someone asks them what it is he does, what it is he teaches, they cannot say because they do not know; but so as not to seem at a loss, they mutter the kind of thing that lies ready to hand against anyone who pursues

---

[12]The literal meaning of the Greek word *poiētēs* (poet) is "maker." [D. C. ABEL]

wisdom: "things in the heavens and beneath the Earth" or "not acknowledging gods" or "making the weaker argument stronger." The truth, I suppose, they would not wish to state—namely, that it has become quite clear that they pretend to have knowledge and know nothing. And because they are concerned for their pride, I think, and zealous and numerous, and speak vehemently and persuasively about me, they have long filled your ears with zealous slander. It was on the strength of this that Meletus attacked me, along with Anytus and Lycon—Meletus angered on behalf of the poets, Anytus on behalf of the public craftsmen and the politicians, and Lycon on behalf of the orators. So the result is, as I said to begin with, that I should be most surprised if were I able to remove from you in this short time a slander that has grown so great.

There, Gentlemen of Athens, you have the truth, and I have concealed or misrepresented nothing in speaking it, great or small. Yet I know quite well that it is just for this that I have become hated—which is in fact an indication of the truth of what I say—and that this is the basis of the slander and charges against me. Whether you inquire into it now or afterwards you will find it to be so.

[Refutation of Meletus]

Against the charges lodged by my first accusers, let this defense suffice. But with regard to Meletus—the good man who loves his city, so he says—and my later accusers, I shall attempt a further defense. Once more then, as before a different set of accusers, let us take up their sworn indictment. It runs something like this: "Socrates is guilty of corrupting the youth, and of not acknowledging the gods the city acknowledges, but other new divinities." Such is the charge. Let us examine its particulars.

It claims I am guilty of corrupting the youth. But I claim, Gentlemen of Athens, that it is Meletus who is guilty—guilty of jesting in earnest, guilty of lightly bringing men to trial, guilty of pretending a zealous concern for things he never cared about at all. I shall try to show you that this is true.

Come here, Meletus. Now tell me, do you count it of great importance that the young should be as good as possible?

"I do."

Then come and tell the jurors this: Who improves them? Clearly you know, since it is a matter of concern to you.[13] Having discovered, so you say, that I am the man who is corrupting them, you bring me before these judges to accuse me. But now come and say who makes them better. Inform the judges who he is.

You see, Meletus, you are silent; you cannot say. And yet, does this not seem shameful to you, and a sufficient indication of what I say—namely, that you never cared at all? Tell us, my friend, who improves them?

"The laws."

But I did not ask you that, dear friend. I asked you what *man* improves them—whoever it is who in the first place knows just that very thing, the laws.

"These men, Socrates. The judges."

---

[13]Here and throughout the following passage there is a running pun on the name Meletus that can be preserved in translation: The name may mean "he who exercises care or concern." [R. E. ALL

Really, Meletus? These men here are able to educate the youth and improve them?

"Especially they."

All of them? Or only some?

"All."

By Hera,[14] you bring good news! A large number of benefactors! But what about the audience here? Do they improve them or not?

"They too."

And members of the Council?

"The Councilors too."

Well then, Meletus, do the members of the Assembly—the ecclesiasts— corrupt the young? Or do they all improve them too?

"They too."

So it seems that every Athenian makes them excellent except me, and I alone corrupt them. Is that what you are saying?

"That is exactly what I am saying."

You condemn me to great misfortune. But tell me, do you think it is so with horses? Do all men improve them, while some one man corrupts them? Or quite to the contrary, is it some one man or a very few, namely horse trainers, who are able to improve them, while the majority of people, if they handle horses and use them, corrupt them? Is that not true, Meletus, both of horses and all other animals? Of course it is, whether you and Anytus affirm or deny it. It would be good fortune indeed for the youth if only one man corrupted them and the rest benefited them. But the fact is, Meletus, that you sufficiently show that you never gave thought to the youth; you clearly indicate your own lack of concern, indicate that you never cared at all about the matters in which you bring action against me.

But again, dear Meletus, tell us this: Is it better to dwell among fellow citizens who are good, or wicked? Do answer, dear friend; surely I ask nothing hard. Do not wicked men do evil things to those around them, and good men good things?

"Of course."

Now, is there anyone who wishes to be harmed rather than benefited by those with whom he associates? Answer me, dear friend, for the law requires you to answer. Is there anyone who wishes to be harmed?

"Of course not."

Very well then, are you bringing action against me here because I corrupt the youth intentionally, or unintentionally?

"Intentionally, I say."

How can that be, Meletus? Are you at your age so much wiser than I at mine that you recognize that evil men always do evil things to those around them, and good men do good, while I have reached such a pitch of folly that I am unaware that if I do some evil to those with whom I associate, I shall very likely receive some evil at their hands, so that I do such great evil intentionally, as you claim? I do not believe you, Meletus, and I do not think anyone else does either. On the contrary: Either I do not corrupt the youth, or, if I do, I do so

---

[14]*Hera:* the sister and wife of Zeus, the chief Greek god. [D. C. ABEL]

unintentionally. In either case, you lie. And if I corrupt them unintentionally, it is not the law to bring action here for that sort of mistake, but rather to instruct and admonish in private; for clearly, once I learn, I shall stop what I unintentionally do. You, however, were unwilling to associate with me and teach me. Instead, you brought action here, where it is the law to bring those who need punishment rather than instruction.

Gentlemen of Athens, what I said is surely now clear: Meletus was never concerned about these matters, much or little. Still, Meletus, tell us this: How do you say I corrupt the youth? Or is it clear from your indictment that I teach them not to acknowledge gods the city acknowledges, but other new divinities? Is this what you mean by saying I corrupt by teaching?

"Certainly. That is exactly what I mean."

Then in the name of these same gods we are now discussing, Meletus, please speak a little more plainly still, both for me and for these gentlemen here. Do you mean that I teach the youth to acknowledge that there are gods, and thus do not myself wholly deny gods, and am not in that respect guilty—though the gods are not those the city acknowledges, but different ones? Or are you claiming that I do not myself acknowledge any gods at all, and teach this to others?

"I mean that. You acknowledge no gods at all."

Ah, my dear Meletus, why do you say such things? Do I not at least acknowledge Sun and Moon as gods, as other men do?

"No, no, Gentlemen and Judges, not when he says the Sun is a stone and the Moon is earth."

My dear Meletus! Do you think it is Anaxagoras[15] you are accusing? Do you so despise these judges here and think them so unlettered that they do not know it is the books of Anaxagoras of Clazomenae that teem with such statements? Are young men to learn these things specifically from me, when they can buy them sometimes in the orchestra[16] for a drachma,[17] if the price is high, and laugh at Socrates if he pretends they are his own—especially since they are so absurd? Well, dear friend, is that what you think—that I acknowledge no gods at all?

"No, none whatever."

You cannot be believed, Meletus—even, I think, by yourself. Gentlemen of Athens, I think this man who stands here before you is insolent and unchastened, and has brought this suit precisely out of insolence and unchastened youth. He seems to be conducting a test by propounding a riddle: "Will Socrates, the wise man, realize how neatly I contradict myself, or will I deceive him and the rest of the audience?" For certainly it seems clear that he is contradicting himself in his indictment. It is as though he were saying, "Socrates is guilty of not acknowledging gods, and acknowledges gods." Yet surely this is to jest.

Please join me, Gentlemen, in examining why it appears to me that this is what he is saying. And you answer us, Meletus. The rest of you will please

---

[15]Anaxagoras (about 500–428 B.C.E.) was a Greek philosopher also accused by the Athenians of impiety. [D. C. ABEL]

[16]*orchestra:* the circular space in front of the stage of a Greek theater. [D. C. ABEL]

[17]*drachma:* a unit of value worth a hundredth of a mina (see footnote 8). [D. C. ABEL]

remember what I asked you at the beginning, and make no disturbance if I fashion arguments in my accustomed way.[18]

Is there any man, Meletus, who acknowledges that there are things pertaining to men, but does not acknowledge that there are men? Let him answer for himself, Gentlemen, and not make interruptions. Is there any man who does not acknowledge that there are horses, but acknowledges things pertaining to horsemanship? Or does not acknowledge that there are flutes, but acknowledges things pertaining to flute playing? There is not, my good friend. If you do not wish to answer, I'll answer for you and for the rest of these people here. But do please answer my next question, at least: Is there any man who acknowledges that there are things pertaining to divinities, but does not acknowledge that there are divinities?

"There is not."

How obliging of you to answer—reluctantly, and under compulsion from these gentlemen here. Now, you say that I acknowledge and teach things pertaining to divinities; whether new or old, still at least I acknowledge them, by your account. Indeed, you swore to that in your indictment. But if I acknowledge that there are things pertaining to divinities, must I surely not also acknowledge that there are divinities? Isn't that so? Of course it is—since you do not answer, I count you as agreeing. And divinities, we surely believe, are either gods or children of gods? Correct?

"Of course."

So if I believe in divinities, as you say, and if divinities are a kind of god, there is the jesting riddle I attributed to you: You are saying that I do not believe in gods, and again that I do believe in gods because I believe in divinities. On the other hand, if divinities are children of gods, some born illegitimately of nymphs[19] or others of whom this is said, who could possibly believe that there are children of gods, but not gods? It would be as absurd as believing that there are children of horses and asses (namely mules) without believing there are horses and asses. Meletus, you could not have brought this indictment except in an attempt to test us—or because you were at a loss for any true basis of prosecution. But as to how you are to convince anyone of even the slightest intelligence that one and the same man can believe that there are things pertaining to divinities and gods, and yet believe that there are no divinities or gods or heroes[20]—there is no way.

[Digression: Socrates' Mission to Athens]

Gentlemen of Athens, I do not think further defense is needed to show that, by the very terms of Meletus's indictment, I am not guilty; this, surely, is sufficient. But as I said before, a great deal of enmity has risen against me among many people, and you may rest assured this is true. And that is what will convict me, if I am convicted—not Meletus, not Anytus, but the grudging slander of the

---

[18]*accustomed way:* the dialectical ("Socratic") method; see the headnote to this reading. [D. C. ABEL]

[19]*nymphs:* in Greek mythology, minor nature goddesses. [D. C. ABEL]

[20]*heroes:* minor local deities. [D. C. ABEL]

multitude. It has convicted many another good and decent man. I think it will convict me, and is there no danger that it will stop with me.

Perhaps someone may say, "Are you not ashamed, Socrates, at having pursued such a course that you now stand in danger of being put to death?" To him I would make a just reply: You are wrong, Sir, if you think that a man worth anything at all should take thought for danger in living or dying. When he acts he should look to one thing: whether what he does is just or unjust, the work of a good man or a bad one. By your account, those demigods and heroes who laid down their lives at Troy would be of little worth—the rest of them, and the son of Thetis[21] too; Achilles so much despised danger instead of submitting to disgrace that when he was intent on killing Hector his goddess mother told him, as I recall, "My son, if you avenge the slaying of your comrade Patroclus with the death of Hector, you yourself shall die; for your death is fated to happen immediately after Hector's.[22] Achilles heard this and thought little of the death and danger. He was more afraid to live as a bad man, with friends left unavenged. "Let me die immediately," he said, "exacting right from him who did the wrong, that I may not remain here as a butt of mockery beside the crook-beaked ships, a burden to the earth."[23] Do you suppose that he gave thought to death and danger?

Gentlemen of Athens, truly it is so; wherever a man stations himself in the belief that it is best, wherever he is stationed by his commander, there he must I think remain and run the risks, giving thought to neither death nor any other thing except disgrace. I would indeed have done a fearful thing, Gentlemen of Athens, if, when the commanders whom you chose stationed me at Potidaea and Amphipolis and Delium,[24] I remained there as others did and ran the risk of death; but then, when the god stationed me, as I thought and believed, obliging me to live in the pursuit of wisdom, examining myself and others—I would have done a fearful thing, I say, if, at that point, I left my post through fear of death or of any other thing. That would have been dreadful indeed, and then in truth might I be justly brought to court for not acknowledging the existence of gods, for willful disobedience to the oracle, for fearing death, for thinking myself wise when I am not.

For to fear death, Gentlemen, is nothing but to think one is wise when one is not; for it is to think one knows what one does not. No man knows whether death is not the greatest of all goods; and yet men fear it as though they well knew it to be the worst of evils. Yet how is this not folly most to be reproached—the folly of believing one knows what one does not? I, at least, Gentlemen, am perhaps superior to most men here in this; and if I were to claim to be wiser than anyone else it would be in this, that as I have no satisfactory knowledge of things in the Place of the Dead, I do not think I do. I do know that to be guilty of disobedience to a superior, whether god or man, is evil and shameful.

---

[21]*son of Thetis:* Achilles, the greatest Greek warrior in the war against Troy. [D. C. ABEL]
[22]Homer, *Iliad,* Book XVIII, lines 94–96, paraphrased. Homer (9th or 8th century B.C.E.) was a Greek epic poet. [D. C. ABEL]
[23]Ibid., Book XVIII, lines 98–104, paraphrased. [D. C. ABEL]
[24]sites of battles where Socrates fought with conspicuous bravery. [R. E. ALLEN]

So in contrast to evils I know to be evils, I shall never fear or flee from things that, for all I know, may be good. Thus, even if you now dismiss me, refusing to do as Anytus bids—Anytus, who said that either I should not have been brought to trial to begin with or, since brought, must be put to death, testifying before you that if I were once acquitted your sons would pursue what Socrates teaches and all be thoroughly corrupted—if, with this in view, you were to say to me, "Socrates, we shall not at this time be persuaded by Meletus, and we dismiss you; but on this condition, that you no longer pass time in that inquiry of yours or pursue philosophy; and if you are again taken doing it, you will die"— if, as I say, you were to dismiss me on that condition, I would reply that I hold you in friendship and regard, Gentlemen of Athens, but I shall obey the god rather than you, and while I have breath and am able I shall not cease to pursue wisdom or to exhort you, charging any of you I happen to meet in my accustomed manner: "You are the best of men, being an Athenian, citizen of a city honored for wisdom and power beyond all others. Are you then not ashamed to care for the getting of money, and reputation, and public honor, while yet having no thought or concern for truth and understanding and the greatest possible excellence of your soul?" And if some one of you disputes this and says he does care, I shall not immediately dismiss him and go away. I shall question him and examine him and test him, and if he does not seem to me to possess virtue, and yet says he does, I shall rebuke him for counting of more importance things that by comparison are worthless. I shall do this to young and old, citizen and stranger, whomever I happen to meet, but I shall do it especially to citizens, inasmuch as they are more nearly related to me. For the god commands this, be well assured, and I believe that you have yet to gain in this city a greater good than my service to the god. I go about doing nothing but persuading you, young and old, to care not for body or money in place of, or as much as, excellence of soul. I tell you that virtue does not come from money, but that money and all other human goods, both public and private, come from virtue. If in saying this I corrupt the youth, that would be harm indeed. But anyone who claims I say other than this speaks falsehood. In these matters, Gentlemen of Athens, believe Anytus, or do not. Dismiss me, or do not. For I will not do otherwise, even if I am to die for it many times over.

Please do not make a disturbance. Gentlemen. Abide by my request and do not interrupt what I have to say, but listen. Indeed, I think you will benefit by listening. I am going to tell you certain things at which you may perhaps cry out; please do not do so. Be well assured that if you kill me, and if I am the sort of man I claim, you will harm me less than you harm yourselves. There is no harm that Meletus or Anytus can do me; it is not possible, for it does not, I think, accord with divine law, that a better man be harmed by a worse. Meletus perhaps can kill me or exile me or disenfranchise me, and perhaps he and others too think those things great evils. I do not. I think it a far greater evil to do what he is now doing, attempting to kill a man unjustly. And so, Gentlemen of Athens, I am far from making a defense for my own sake, as some might think; I make it for yours, lest you mistake the gift the god has given you and cast your votes against me. If you kill me, you will not easily find such another man as I, a man who—if I may put it a bit absurdly—has been fastened, as it were, to the city by the god as to a large and well-bred horse, a horse grown sluggish because of its size, and in need of being roused by a kind of gadfly.[25] Just so, I think, the god has fastened me to the city. I rouse you. I persuade you. I upbraid you. I never stop landing on each one of you, everywhere, all day long. Such another will not easily come to you again, Gentlemen, and if you are persuaded by me, you will spare me. But perhaps you are angry, as men roused from sleep are angry, and perhaps you will swat me, persuaded by Meletus that you may easily kill me. Then will you continue to sleep out your lives, unless the god sends someone else to look after you.

That I am just that, a gift from the god to the city, you may recognize from this: It scarcely seems a human matter merely, that I should take no thought for anything of my own and endure the neglect of my house and its affairs for these long years now, and ever attend to yours, going to each of you in private like a father or elder brother, persuading you to care for virtue. If I got something from it, if I took pay for this kind of exhortation, that would explain it. But as things are, you can see for yourselves that even my accusers, who have accused me so shamefully of everything else, could not summon enough shamelessness to provide witnesses to testify that I ever took pay or asked for it. For it is enough, I think, to provide my poverty as witness to the truth of what I say.

Perhaps it may seem peculiar that I go about in private advising men and busily inquiring, and yet do not enter the Assembly in public to advise the city. The reason is a thing you have heard me mention many times in many places, that something divine and godlike comes to me—which Meletus, indeed, mocked in his indictment.[26] I have had it from childhood. It comes as a kind of voice, and when it comes, it always turns me away from what I am about to do, but never toward it. That is what opposed my entering political life, and I think it did well to oppose it. For be well assured. Gentlemen of Athens, that if I had attempted long ago to enter political affairs, I would long ago have been destroyed—to the benefit of neither you nor myself.

Please do not be angry at me for telling the simple truth. It is impossible for any man to be spared if he legitimately opposes you or any other democratic majority, and prevents many unjust and illegal things from occurring in his city. He who intends to fight for what is just, if he is to be spared even for a little time, must of necessity live a private rather than a public life.

I shall offer you a convincing indication of this—not words, but what you respect, deeds. Hear, then, what befell me, so that you may know that I will not through fear of death give way to any man contrary to what is right, even if I am destroyed for it. I shall tell you a thing that is tedious—it smacks of the law courts but is true. Gentlemen of Athens, I never held other offices in the city, but I was once a member of the Council. And it happened that our tribe, Antiochis, held the Prytanate[27] when you decided to judge as a group the cases

---

[25] *gadfly:* a fly that bites livestock. [D. C. ABEL]

[26] The suggestion is that Meletus lodged his accusation of acknowledging new (or strange) gods because of the sign. [R. E. ALLEN]

[27] *Prytanate:* a body of 10 officials (each one chosen by lot from each of the 10 tribes) who presided over the Council. [D. C. ABEL]

of the ten generals who had failed to gather up the bodies of the slain in a naval battle[28]—illegally, as later it seemed to all of you. But at the time, I alone of the prytanes[29] opposed doing a thing contrary to law, and cast my vote against it. And when the orators were ready to impeach me and have me arrested—you urging them on with your shouts—I thought that with law and justice on my side I must run the risk, rather than concur with you in an unjust decision through fear of prison or death. Those things happened while the city was still under the democracy. But when the oligarchy came, the Thirty[30] in turn summoned me along with four others to the rotunda and ordered us to bring back Leon the Salamanian from Salamis so that he might be executed, just as they ordered many others to do such things, planning to implicate as many people as possible in their own guilt. But I then showed again, not by words but deeds, that death, if I may be rather blunt, was of no concern whatever to me. To do nothing unjust or unholy—that was my concern. Strong as it was, that oligarchy did not so frighten me as to do something unjust, and when we left the rotunda, the other four went into Salamis and brought back Leon, and I left and went home. I might have been killed for that, if the oligarchy had not shortly afterward been overthrown. And of these things you will have many witnesses.

Now, do you think I would have lived so many years if I had been in public life and acted in a manner worthy of a good man, defending what is just and counting it, as is necessary, of first importance? Far from it, Gentlemen of Athens—not I, and not any other man. But through my whole life I have shown myself to be that sort of man in the few public affairs I've engaged in, and I have shown myself to be the same man in private. I never yielded to anyone contrary to what is just—not to others, and certainly not to those slanderously said to be my pupils. In fact, I have never been a teacher to anyone. If, in speaking and tending my own affairs, anyone wished to hear me, young or old, I never begrudged him; nor do I discuss for a fee and not otherwise. To rich and poor alike I offer myself as a questioner, and if anyone wishes to answer, he may hear what I have to say. And if any of them turned out to be useful men, or any did not, I cannot justly be held responsible. To none did I promise instruction, and none did I teach; if anyone says that he learned from me or heard in private what others did not, you may rest assured he is not telling the truth.

Why is it, then, that some people enjoy spending so much time with me? You have heard why, Gentlemen of Athens; I told you the whole truth. It is because they enjoy hearing people tested who think they are wise and are not. After all, it is not unamusing. But for my own part, as I say, I have been ordered to do this by god—in oracles, in dreams, in every way in which divine apportionment ever ordered a man to do anything.

These things, Gentlemen of Athens, are both true and easily tested. For if I am corrupting some of the youth, and have corrupted others, it must surely be that some among them, now grown older, if they realize that I counseled them toward evil while they were young, would now come forward to accuse me and exact a

---

[28]*naval battle:* the battle of Arginusae, 406 B.C.E. [D. C. ABEL]

[29]*prytanes:* members of the Prytanate (see footnote 27). [D. C. ABEL]

[30]*the Thirty:* the "Thirty Tyrants," oligarchs who ruled Athens for a year. [D. C. ABEL]

penalty. And if they were unwilling to do so, then some of their relatives—fathers, brothers, other kinsmen—if their own relatives had suffered evil at my hands, would now remember and exact a penalty. Certainly there are many such men I see present. Here is Crito, first, of my own age and deme,[31] father of Critobulus. Then there is Lysanias of Sphettos, father of Aeschines. Next there is Antiphon of Cephisus, father of Epigenes. Then there are others whose brothers engaged in this pastime. There is Nicostratus, son of Theozotides, brother of Theodotus (Theodotus is dead, so he could not have swayed him), and Paralus here, son of Demodocus, whose brother was Theages. And here is Adeimantus, son of Ariston, whose brother Plato is here; and Aeantodorus, whose brother is Apollodorus here. I could name many others, some of whom at least Meletus ought certainly have provided in his speech as witnesses. If he forgot it then, let him do it now— I yield the floor—and let him say whether he has any witnesses of this sort. You will find that quite to the contrary, Gentlemen, every one of these men is ready to help me—I who, according to Meletus and Anytus, corrupt their relatives. Those who are themselves corrupted might perhaps have reason to help me; but their relatives are older men who have not been corrupted. What reason could they have for supporting me except that it is right and just, because they know that Meletus is lying and that I am telling the truth?

[Conclusion]

Very well then. Gentlemen. This, and perhaps a few other things like it, is what I have to say in my defense. Perhaps some of you will remember his own conduct and be offended, if when brought to trial on a lesser charge than this, he begged his judges with tearful supplication and caused his children, along with other relatives and a host of friends, to come forward so that he might be the more pitied—whereas I shall do none of these things, even though I am, as it would seem at least, in the extremity of danger. Perhaps someone with this in mind may become hardened against me; angered by it, he may cast his vote in anger. If this is true of any of you—not that I expect it, but if it is—I think it might be appropriate to say, "I too have relatives, my friend; for I am not, as Homer puts it, 'of oak and rock,'[32] but born of man, so I have relatives—yes, and sons too, Gentlemen of Athens. I have three sons—one already an adolescent and two of them still children. Yet I have not caused any of them to come forward here, and I shall not beg you to acquit me." Why not? Not out of stubbornness, Gentlemen of Athens, nor disrespect for you. Whether or not I am confident in the face of death is another story; but I think that my own honor, and yours, and that of the whole city would suffer, if I were to behave in this way, I being of the age I am and having the name I have—it being thought, truly or falsely, that Socrates is in some way superior to most men. If those of you reputed to be superior in wisdom or courage or any other virtue whatever are to be men of this sort, it would be disgraceful; I have often seen such people

---

[31]*deme:* a unit of local government. [D. C. ABEL]
[32]Homer, *Odyssey,* Book XIX, line 163. [D. C. ABEL]

behave surprisingly when put on trial, even though they had a reputation to uphold, because they were persuaded that they would suffer a terrible thing if they were put to death—as though they would be immortal if you did not kill them. I think they cloak the city in shame, so that a stranger would think that those among the Athenians who are superior in virtue, and whom the Athenians themselves judge worthy of office and other honors, are no better than women. These are things, Gentlemen of Athens, that those of you who have a reputation to uphold ought not to do; nor if we defendants do them, ought you permit it. You ought rather make it clear that you would far rather cast your vote against a man who stages these pitiful scenes and makes the city a butt of mockery, than against a man who shows quiet restraint.

But apart from the matter of reputation, Gentlemen, it does not seem to me just to beg a judge, or to be acquitted by begging; it is just, rather to teach and persuade. The judge does not sit to grant justice as a favor, but to render judgment; he has sworn no oath to gratify those whom he sees fit, but to judge according to law. We ought not accustom you, nor ought you become accustomed, to break you oath; it is pious in neither of us. So do not expect me, Gentlemen of Athens, to do such things in your presence that I believe to be neither honorable nor just nor holy, especially since, by Zeus,[33] it is for impiety that I am being prosecuted by this fellow Meletus here. For clearly, if I were to persuade and compel you by supplication, you being sworn as judges, I would teach you then indeed not to believe that there are gods, and in making my defense I would in effect accuse myself of not acknowledging them. But that is far from so; I do acknowledge them, Gentlemen of Athens, as no one of my accusers does, and to you and to the god I now commit my case, to judge in whatever way shall be best both for me and for you.

[COUNTERPENALTY SPEECH]

I am not distressed, Gentlemen of Athens, at what has happened, nor angered that you have cast your votes against me. Many things contribute to this, among them the fact that I expected it. I am much more surprised at the number of votes either way: I did not think it would be by so little, but by more. As it is, it seems, if only thirty votes had fallen otherwise, I would have been acquitted.[34] And so far as Meletus at least is concerned, it seems to me, I am already acquitted—and more than acquitted, since it is clear that if Anytus and Lycon had not come forward to accuse me, Meletus would have been fined a thousand drachmas for not obtaining a fifth part of the vote.

The man demands death for me. Very well. Then what counterpenalty shall I propose to you, Gentlemen of Athens?[35] Clearly something I deserve, but

---

[33]*Zeus:* the chief Greek god. [D. C. ABEL]

[34]The vote of the 501 jurors was 280, guilty; 221, not guilty. [D. C. ABEL]

[35]Under Athenian law, the prosecutor proposed a penalty, and the convicted defendant a counterpenalty. The jury was required to choose between them without alteration. The usual practice was for convicted persons to propose a penalty as heavy as they could bear short of that which the prosecutor demanded, in hope that the jury might accept it. [R. E. ALLEN]

what? What do I deserve to pay or suffer because I did not throughout life keep quiet, and yet did not concern myself, as the multitude do, with money or property or military and public honors and other offices, or the secret societies and political clubs that keep cropping up in the city, believing that I was really too reasonable and temperate a man to enter upon these things and survive? I did not go where I could benefit neither you nor myself; instead, I went to each of you in private, where I might perform the greatest service. I undertook to persuade each of you not to care for anything that belongs to you before first caring for yourselves, nor to care for anything that belongs to the city before caring for the city itself, and so too with everything else. Now, what do I deserve to suffer for being this sort of man? Some good thing, Gentlemen of Athens, if penalty is really to be assessed according to desert. What then is fitting for a poor man who has served his city well and needs leisure to exhort you? Why, Gentlemen of Athens, nothing is more fitting for such a man than to be fed in the Prytaneum[36]—yes, and far more fitting than for one of you who has been an Olympic victor in the single-horse or two- or four-horse chariot races. For he makes you seem happy, whereas I make you happy in truth; and he does not need subsistence, and I do. If then I must propose a penalty I justly deserve, I propose that—public subsistence in the Prytaneum.

Perhaps some of you will think that in saying this I speak much as I spoke of tears and pleading, out of stubborn pride. That is not so, Gentlemen of Athens, though something of this sort is: I am persuaded that I have not intentionally wronged any man, but I cannot persuade you of it; we have talked so short time. Now, I believe if you had a law, as other people do, that cases involving death shall not be decided in a single day, that you would be persuaded. But as things are, it is not easy in so short a time to do away with slanders grown so great. Being persuaded, however, that I have wronged no one, I am quite unwilling to wrong myself, or claim that I deserve some evil and propose any penalty of the kind. What is there to fear? That I may suffer the penalty Meletus proposes when, as I say, I do not know whether it is good or evil? Shall I choose instead a penalty I know very well to be evil? Imprisonment, perhaps? But why should I live in prison, a slave to men who happen to occupy office as the Eleven?[37] A fine, then, and imprisonment until I pay it? But that comes to the same thing, since I have no money to pay it. Shall I then propose exile? Perhaps you would accept that. But I must indeed love life and cling to it dearly, Gentlemen, if I were so foolish as to think that, when you, my own fellow citizens, cannot bear my pursuits and discussions, which have become so burdensome and hateful that you now seek to be rid of them, others will bear them lightly. No, Gentlemen. My life would be fine indeed, if at my age I went to live in exile, always moving from city to city, always driven out! For be well assured that wherever I go, the young men will listen to what I say as they do here. If I turn them away, they will themselves drive me out,

---

[36]*Prytaneum:* a public hall where the prytanes (see footnote 25) and other honored citizens, such as victors in the Olympic Games, received meals at public expense. [D. C. ABEL]

[37]*the Eleven:* police magistrates chosen by lot and charged with oversight of imprisonment and executions. [D. C. ABEL]

appealing to their elders; if I do not turn them away, their fathers and relations will drive me out in their behalf.

Perhaps someone may say, "Would it not be possible for you to live in exile, Socrates, if you were silent and kept quiet?" But this is the hardest thing of all to make some of you believe. If I say that to do so would be to disobey the god, and therefore I cannot do it, you will not believe me because you will think that I am being sly and dishonest. If, on the other hand, I say that the greatest good for man is to fashion arguments each day about virtue and the other things you hear me discussing when I examine myself and others, and that the unexamined life is not worth living for man, you will believe what I say still less. I claim these things are so, Gentlemen; but it is not easy to convince you. At the same time, I am not accustomed to think myself deserving of any evil. If I had money, I would propose a fine as great as I could pay—there would be no harm in that. But as things stand, I have no money, unless the amount I can pay is the amount you are willing to exact of me. I might perhaps be able to pay a mina of silver. So I propose a penalty in that amount. But Plato here, Gentlemen of Athens, and Crito and Critobulus and Apollodorus bid me to propose thirty minas, and they will stand surety for this amount. So I propose that amount. You have guarantors sufficient for the sum.

[FINAL SPEECH]

For the sake of only a little time, Gentlemen of Athens, you are to be accused by those who wish to revile the city of having killed Socrates, a wise man—for those who wish to reproach you will say I am wise even if I am not. And if you had only I waited a little, the thing you desire would have come of its own initiative. You see my age; you see how far spent my life already is, how near to death.

I say this, not to all of you, but to those of you who voted to condemn me. To them I also say this. Perhaps you think, Gentlemen of Athens, that I have been convicted for lack of words to persuade you, if I had thought it right to do and say anything to be acquitted. Not so. It is true I have been convicted for a lack—not a lack of words, but lack of bold shamelessness, an unwillingness to say the things you would find it pleasant to hear: weeping and wailing, saying and doing many things I claim to be unworthy of me, but things of the sort you are accustomed to hear from others. I did not then think it necessary to do anything unworthy of a free man because of danger; I do not now regret so having conducted my defense; and I would far rather die with that defense than live with the other. Neither in court of law nor in war ought I or any man contrive to escape death by any means possible. Often in battle it becomes clear that a man may escape death by throwing down his arms and turning in supplication to his pursuers; and there are many other devices for each of war's dangers, so that one can avoid dying if he is bold enough to say and do anything at all. It is not difficult to escape death, Gentlemen; it is more difficult to escape wickedness, for wickedness runs faster than death. And now I am old and slow, and I have been caught by the slower runner. But my accusers are clever and quick, and they have been caught by the faster runner, namely evil. I now take my leave, sentenced by you to death; they depart convicted by truth for injustice and wickedness. I abide by my penalty, and they by theirs. That is no doubt as it should be, and I think it is fitting.

I desire next to prophesy to you who condemned me. For I have now reached that point where men are especially prophetic, when they are about to die. I say to you who have decreed my death that to you there will come quickly on my dying a thing far more difficult to bear than the death you have visited upon me. You have done this thing in the belief that you would be released from submitting to examination in your lives. I say that it will turn out otherwise. Those who come to examine you will be more numerous; and I have up to now restrained them, although you did not perceive it. They will be more harsh inasmuch as they are younger, and you will be the more troubled. If you think that by killing you will hold back the reproach due you for not living rightly, you are profoundly mistaken. That release is neither possible nor honorable. The release that is both most honorable and most easy is not to cut down others, but to so prepare yourselves that you will be as good as possible. This I utter as prophecy to you who voted for my condemnation, and take my leave.

But with you who voted for my acquittal, I would be glad to discuss the nature of what has happened, while the authorities are busy and I have not yet gone where, going, I must die. Stay with me, Gentlemen, this space of time; nothing prevents our talking with each other while we still can. To you, as my friends, I wish to display the meaning of what has now fallen to my lot. A remarkable thing has occurred, Gentlemen and Judges—and I am correct in calling you judges. My accustomed oracle, which is divine, always came quite frequently before in everything, opposing me even in trivial matters if I was about to err. And now a thing has fallen to my lot, as you yourselves also see— a thing that some might think, and do in fact believe, to be the ultimate among evils. But the sign of the god did not oppose me early this morning when I left my house, nor when I came up to the court room here, nor at any point in my argument in anything I was about to say. And yet in many places, in other arguments, it has checked me right in the middle of speaking. But today it has not opposed me in any way, in none of my deeds, in none of my words. What do I take to be the reason? I will tell you. Very likely what has fallen to me is good, and those among us who think that death is an evil are wrong. There has been a convincing indication of this; for the accustomed sign would surely have opposed me, if I were not in some way acting for good.

Let us also consider a further reason for high hope that death is good. Death is one of two things. Either to be dead is not to exist, to have no awareness at all; or it is, as the stories tell, a kind of alteration, a change of abode for the soul from this place to another. And if it is to have no awareness, like a sleep when the sleeper sees no dream, death would be a wonderful gain. For I suppose that if someone had to pick out that night in which he slept and saw no dream, and put the other days and nights of his life beside it, and had to say after inspecting them how many days and nights he had lived in his life that were better and sweeter, I think that not only any ordinary person but even the great king[38]

---

[38]*great king:* the King of Persia, a proverbial symbol of wealth and power. [R. E. ALLEN]

himself would find these days and nights easy to count in relation to other days and nights. If death is that, I say it is gain; for the whole of time then turns out to last no longer than a single night. But if, on the contrary, death is like taking a journey, passing from here to another place, and the stories told are true, and all who have died are there—what greater good might there be, my Judges? For if a man once goes to the place of the dead and takes leave of those who claim to be judges here, he will find the true judges who are said to sit in judgment there—Minos, Rhadamanthus, Aeaicus, Triptolemus, and the other demigods and heroes who lived just lives. Would that journey be worthless? And again, to meet Orpheus and Musaeus, Hesiod and Homer—how much would any of you give? I at least would be willing to die many times over, if these things are true. I would find a wonderful pursuit there, when I met Palamedes, and Ajax, son of Telemon, and any others among the ancients put to death by unjust verdicts, and compared my experiences with theirs. It would not, I think, be unamusing. But the greatest thing, surely, would be to test and question there, as I did here— who among them is wise? Who thinks he is and is not? How much might one give, my Judges, to examine the man who led the great army against Troy, or Odysseus, or Sisyphus, or a thousand other men and women one might mention—to converse with them, to associate with them, to examine them? Why, it would be inconceivable happiness, especially since they surely do not kill you for it there. For they are happier there in other ways than men are here, and they are already immortal for the rest of time, if the stories told are true.

But you too, my Judges, must be of good hope concerning death. You must recognize that this one thing is true: There is no evil for a good man either in living or in dying, and the gods do not neglect his affairs. What has now come to me did not come of its own initiative. It is clear to me that to die now and be released from my affairs is better for me. That is why the sign did not turn me back, and I bear no anger whatever toward those who voted to condemn me or toward my accusers. And yet, it was not with this in mind that they accused and convicted me. They thought to do harm, and for that they deserve blame. But this much would I ask of them: When my sons are grown, Gentlemen, exact a penalty of them—give pain to them exactly as I gave pain to you, if it seems to you that they care more for wealth or anything else than they care for virtue. And if they seem to be something and are nothing, rebuke them as I rebuked you, because they do not care for what they ought, because they think themselves something and are worth nothing. And if you do that, both I and my sons will have been justly dealt with at your hands.

But it is already the hour of parting—I to die and you to live. Which of us goes to the better lot is unclear to all but the god.

The Value of Philosophy

Bertrand Russell

Bertrand Russell was born in Trelleck, Wales, in 1872. Both his parents died when he was young, and he and his older brother were raised by their paternal grandmother. Russell received his initial education from governesses and tutors. In 1890 he enrolled in Cambridge University, where he studied mathematics and then philosophy, receiving his degree in 1894. Russell was a fellow at Cambridge from 1895 to 1901 and a lecturer in philosophy from 1910 to 1916. In 1908 he became a member of the Royal Society. After his lectureship at Cambridge, Russell supported himself by writing and giving public lectures. On the death of his brother in 1931, he became Earl Russell. He moved to the United States in 1938, teaching first at the University of Chicago and then at the University of California at Los Angeles. He lectured at the Barnes Foundation in Philadelphia from 1941 to 1943. The following year he returned to England, having been invited to become a fellow again at Cambridge. In 1949 he became an honorary member of the British Academy and received the Order of Merit. The following year he was awarded the Nobel Prize for Literature. Russell died in 1970 near Penrhyndeudraeth, Wales, at the age of 97.

Russell's numerous works include *The Principles of Mathematics* (1903), *Principia Mathematica* (coauthored with Alfred North Whitehead; three volumes, 1910, 1912, 1913), *The Problems of Philosophy* (1912), *Our Knowledge of the External World* (1914), *The Conquest of Happiness* (1930), *An Inquiry into Meaning and Truth* (1940), and *A History of Western Philosophy* (1945).

Our reading is the final chapter of *The Problems of Philosophy*, "The Value of Philosophy." Russell argues that, although philosophy does not enhance our physical well-being, it greatly enriches our mental lives. This enrichment does not come from providing definitive answers to philosophical questions, for practically all philosophical questions remain undecided. For example, no one has ever proved—or is likely ever to prove—that the universe has or does not have a purpose. For Russell, the uncertainty in philosophy is an asset rather than a liability: By teaching us to inquire about the universe and to question our ordinary beliefs, philosophy liberates us from the prejudices of common sense, culture, and custom. Although philosophy does not provide definite answers about how things *are*, it broadens our mind by showing us many different ways that they *might be*.

A further value of philosophy, according to Russell, is its ability to free us from our instinctive tendency to interpret everything in terms of self. By attempting to see the universe as it is, rather than simply perceiving how it affects us, we enlarge our self by leaving behind (as much as is possible) our hopes and fears, our preconceptions and prejudices. And when we enlarge our self, we also enlarge the sphere of our actions and affections.

[INTRODUCTION]

Having now come to the end of our brief and very incomplete review of the problems of philosophy, it will be well to consider, in conclusion, what is the value of philosophy and why it ought to be studied. It is the more necessary to consider this question, in view of the fact that many men, under the influence of science or of practical affairs, are inclined to doubt whether philosophy is anything better than innocent but useless trifling, hair-splitting distinctions, and controversies on matters concerning which knowledge is impossible.

This view of philosophy appears to result, partly from a wrong conception of the ends of life, partly from a wrong conception of the kind of goods that philosophy strives to achieve. Physical science, through the medium of inventions, is useful to innumerable people who are wholly ignorant of it; thus the study of physical science is to be recommended, not only, or primarily, because of the effect on the student, but rather because of the effect on mankind in general. This utility does not belong to philosophy. If the study of philosophy has any value at all for other than students of philosophy, it must be only indirectly, through its effects upon the lives of those who study it. It is in these effects, therefore, if anywhere, that the value of philosophy must be primarily sought.

But further, if we are not to fail in our endeavor to determine the value of philosophy, we must first free our minds from the prejudices of what are wrongly called "practical" men. The "practical" man, as this word is often used, is one who recognizes only material needs, who realizes that men must have food for the body, but is oblivious of the necessity of providing food for the mind. If all men were well off, if poverty and disease had been reduced to their lowest possible point, there would still remain much to be done to produce a valuable society; and even in the existing world the goods of the mind are at least as important as the goods of the body. It is exclusively among the goods of the mind that the value of philosophy is to be found; and only those who are not indifferent to these goods can be persuaded that the study of philosophy is not a waste of time.

[PHILOSOPHY'S QUEST FOR KNOWLEDGE]

Philosophy, like all other studies, aims primarily at knowledge. The knowledge it aims at is the kind of knowledge that gives unity and system to the body of the sciences, and the kind that results from a critical examination of the grounds of our convictions, prejudices, and beliefs. But it cannot be maintained that philosophy has had any very great measure of success in its attempts to provide definite answers to its questions. If you ask a mathematician, a mineralogist, a historian, or any other man of learning, what definite body of truths has been ascertained by his science, his answer will last as long as you are willing to listen. But if you put the same question to a philosopher, he will, if he is candid, have to confess that his study has not achieved positive results such as have been achieved by other sciences. It is true that this is partly accounted for by the fact that, as soon as definite knowledge concerning any subject becomes possible, this subject ceases to be called philosophy, and becomes a separate science. The whole study of the heavens, which now belongs to astronomy, was once included in philosophy; Newton's great work was called "the mathematical principles of natural philosophy."[1]

---

[1]Isaac Newton (1642–1727) was an English mathematician and physicist. His *Philosophiae Naturalis Principia Mathematica* ("The Mathematical Principles of Natural Philosophy") was published in 1687. [D. C. ABEL]

Similarly, the study of the human mind, which was, until very lately, a part of philosophy, has now been separated from philosophy and has become the science of psychology. Thus, to a great extent, the uncertainty of philosophy is more apparent than real: Those questions that are already capable of definite answers are placed in the sciences, while those only to which, at present, no definite answer can be given, remain to form the residue that is called philosophy.

This is, however, only a part of the truth concerning the uncertainty of philosophy. There are many questions—and among them those that are of the profoundest interest to our spiritual life—that, so far as we can see, must remain insoluble to the human intellect unless its powers become of quite a different order from what they are now. Has the universe any unity of plan or purpose, or is it a fortuitous concourse of atoms? Is consciousness a permanent part of the universe, giving hope of indefinite growth in wisdom, or is it a transitory accident on a small planet on which life must ultimately become impossible? Are good and evil of importance to the universe or only to man? Such questions are asked by philosophy, and variously answered by various philosophers. But it would seem that, whether answers be otherwise discoverable or not, the answers suggested by philosophy are none of them demonstrably true. Yet, however slight may be the hope of discovering an answer, it is part of the business of philosophy to continue the consideration of such questions, to make us aware of their importance, to examine all the approaches to them, and to keep alive that speculative interest in the universe that is apt to be killed by confining ourselves to definitely ascertainable knowledge.

Many philosophers, it is true, have held that philosophy could establish the truth of certain answers to such fundamental questions. They have supposed that what is of most importance in religious beliefs could be proved by strict demonstration to be true. In order to judge of such attempts, it is necessary to take a survey of human knowledge, and to form an opinion as to its methods and its limitations. On such a subject it would be unwise to pronounce dogmatically; but if the investigations of our previous chapters have not led us astray, we shall be compelled to renounce the hope of finding philosophical proofs of religious beliefs. We cannot, therefore, include as part of the value of philosophy any definite set of answers to such questions. Hence, once more, the value of philosophy must not depend upon any supposed body of definitely ascertainable knowledge to be acquired by those who study it.

[THE VALUE OF PHILOSOPHY]

The value of philosophy is, in fact, to be sought largely in its very uncertainty. The man who has no tincture of philosophy goes through life imprisoned in the prejudices derived from common sense, from the habitual beliefs of his age or his nation, and from convictions that have grown up in his mind without the cooperation or consent of his deliberate reason. To such a man the world tends to become definite, finite, obvious; common objects rouse no questions, and unfamiliar possibilities are contemptuously rejected. As soon as we begin to philosophize, on the contrary, we find . . . that even the most everyday things lead to problems to which only very incomplete answers can be given. Philosophy, though unable to tell us with certainty what is the true answer to the doubts that it raises, is able to suggest many possibilities that enlarge our thoughts and free them from the tyranny of custom. Thus, while diminishing our feeling of certainty as to what things are, it greatly increases our knowledge as to what they may be; it removes the somewhat arrogant dogmatism of those who have never travelled into the region of liberating doubt, and it keeps alive our sense of wonder by showing familiar things in an unfamiliar aspect.

Apart from its utility in showing unsuspected possibilities, philosophy has a value—perhaps its chief value—through the greatness of the objects that it contemplates, and the freedom from narrow and personal aims resulting from this contemplation. The life of the instinctive man is shut up within the circle of his private interests: Family and friends may be included, but the outer world is not regarded except as it may help or hinder what comes within the circle of instinctive wishes. In such a life there is something feverish and confined, in comparison with which the philosophic life is calm and free. The private world of instinctive interests is a small one, set in the midst of a great and powerful world that must, sooner or later, lay our private world in ruins. Unless we can so enlarge our interests as to include the whole outer world, we remain like a garrison in a beleaguered fortress, knowing that the enemy prevents escape and that ultimate surrender is inevitable. In such a life there is no peace, but a constant strife between the insistence of desire and the powerlessness of will. In one way or another, if our life is to be great and free, we must escape this prison and this strife.

One way of escape is by philosophic contemplation. Philosophic contemplation does not, in its widest survey, divide the universe into two hostile camps—friends and foes, helpful and hostile, good and bad—it views the whole impartially. Philosophic contemplation, when it is unalloyed, does not aim at proving that the rest of the universe is akin to man. All acquisition of knowledge is an enlargement of the self, but this enlargement is best attained when it is not directly sought. It is obtained when the desire for knowledge is alone operative, by a study that does not wish in advance that its objects should have this or that character, but adapts the self to the characters that it finds in its objects. This enlargement of self is not obtained when, taking the self as it is, we try to show that the world is so similar to this self that knowledge of it is possible without any admission of what seems alien. The desire to prove this is a form of self-assertion, and like all self-assertion, it is an obstacle to the growth of self that it desires, and of which the self knows that it is capable. Self-assertion, in philosophic speculation as elsewhere, views the world as a means to its own ends; thus it makes the world of less account than self, and the self sets bounds to the greatness of its goods. In contemplation, on the contrary, we start from the not-self, and through its greatness the boundaries of self are enlarged; through the infinity of the universe the mind that contemplates it achieves some share in infinity.

For this reason greatness of soul is not fostered by those philosophies that assimilate the universe to man. Knowledge is a form of union of self and not-self; like all union, it is impaired by dominion, and therefore by any attempt to force the universe into conformity with what we find in ourselves. There is a widespread philosophical tendency towards the view that tells us that man is the measure of all things, that truth is man-made, that space and time and the world of universals[2] are properties of the mind, and that, if there be anything not created by the mind, it is unknowable and of no account for us. This view . . . is untrue; but in addition to being untrue, it has the effect of robbing philosophic contemplation of all that gives it value, since it fetters contemplation to self. What it calls knowledge is not a union with the not-self, but a set of prejudices, habits, and desires, making an impenetrable veil between us and the world beyond. The man who finds pleasure in such a theory of knowledge is like the man who never leaves the domestic circle for fear his word might not be law.

The true philosophic contemplation, on the contrary, finds its satisfaction in every enlargement of the not-self, in everything that magnifies the objects contemplated, and thereby the subject contemplating. Everything, in contemplation, that is personal or private, everything that depends upon habit, self-interest, or desire, distorts the object, and hence impairs the union that the intellect seeks. By thus making a barrier between subject and object, such personal and private things become a prison to the intellect. The free intellect will see as God might see, without a *here* and *now,* without hopes and fears, without the trammels of customary beliefs and traditional prejudices, calmly, dispassionately, in the sole and exclusive desire of knowledge—knowledge as impersonal, as purely contemplative, as it is possible for man to attain. Hence also the free intellect will value more the abstract and universal knowledge into which the accidents of private history do not enter, than the knowledge brought by the senses, and dependent, as such knowledge must be, upon an exclusive and personal point of view and a body whose sense-organs distort as much as they reveal.

The mind that has become accustomed to the freedom and impartiality of philosophic contemplation will preserve something of the same freedom and impartiality in the world of action and emotion. It will view its purposes and desires as parts of the whole, with the absence of insistence that results from seeing them as infinitesimal fragments in a world of which all the rest is unaffected by any one man's deeds. The impartiality that, in contemplation, is the unalloyed desire for truth, is the very same quality of mind that, in action, is justice, and in emotion is that universal love that can be given to all, and not only to those who are judged useful or admirable. Thus contemplation enlarges not only the objects of our thoughts, but also the objects of our actions and our affections; it makes us citizens of the universe, not only of one walled city at war with all the rest. In this citizenship of the universe consists man's true freedom, and his liberation from the thralldom of narrow hopes and fears.

------

[2]*universals:* realities corresponding to general concepts or terms. [D. C. ABEL]

[CONCLUSION]

Thus, to sum up our discussion of the value of philosophy: Philosophy is to be studied, not for the sake of any definite answers to its questions, since no definite answers can, as a rule, be known to be true, but rather for the sake of the questions themselves; because these questions enlarge our conception of what is possible, enrich our intellectual imagination, and diminish the dogmatic assurance that closes the mind against speculation; but above all because, through the greatness of the universe that philosophy contemplates, the mind also is rendered great, and becomes capable of that union with the universe that constitutes its highest good.

Philosophy of Religion

Religion plays an important role in the lives of the vast majority of human beings. Adherents of religion are aptly called "believers" because their commitment to their doctrines is based on faith. But could one's faith be misplaced and mistaken? Is it reasonable to accept doctrines on faith? Can some religious beliefs, most of all the belief that God exists, be supported—or even *proved*—by strictly rational argumentation? These are some of the questions addressed by the branch of philosophy called the philosophy of religion.

Because the fundamental doctrine of practically every religion is that there is a God (there are exceptions, such as Theravada Buddhism), the central question of the philosophy of religion is whether God's existence can be proved. Relying on reason and experience rather than faith, can we show that there must be a Supreme Being? Can we show that this Supreme Being is (in some sense of the word) a *person?* A second major topic in the philosophy of religion is the "problem of evil." Let us suppose that there is a personal God (whether or not this can be proved) and that God is all-good and all-powerful. How then do we account for the existence of evil? If God is all-good, God would presumably want to eliminate all evils in the world, such as human and animal suffering. If God is all-powerful, God would presumably be able to eliminate all evils. Yet there is abundant evil in the world. This problem of evil has led some philosophers to claim that we can prove that God does *not* exist. A third major topic in the philosophy of religion is the connection of faith to reason. Is it reasonable to accept religious beliefs, or does faith lie wholly outside the realm of reason? Can there be legitimate *non*rational grounds for accepting claims that cannot be decided rationally?

Our readings present a diversity of views on each of these three topics. The first group of readings, "The Existence of God," includes arguments both for and against God's existence. Anselm presents what is now known as the "ontological argument" for the existence of God. He defines God as "something than which nothing greater can be thought" and claims that once we admit that such a being exists in our understanding, we must also admit that it exists in reality—for if it existed only in our understanding, it would *not* be something than which nothing greater can be thought because a being that also existed in reality would be greater. Thomas Aquinas rejects Anselm's ontological argument and formulates five succinct proofs of his own. He argues that there must be a first mover, a first cause of change, a necessary being that is its own source of necessity, a being that causes the perfections in all other beings, and a being that directs natural beings toward their goals—and he concludes that God is each of these five things. David Hume presents a fictional dialogue in which three characters discuss the validity of various proofs for the existence of God. In the next reading, William Paley sets forth the "argument from design": Just as the existence of a watch indicates the existence of an intelligent artisan, so the existence of the infinitely more complex works of nature implies the existence of an intelligent Creator. In the final reading in this section, Richard Dawkins argues that the scientific theory of cumulative natural selection can explain the origin of complex organisms without recourse to an intelligent designer.

The second section, "The Problem of Evil," contains three readings. Augustine contends that the evil that we suffer is God's just punishment for our evildoing, and that evildoing consists in our freely choosing to misuse our free will. J. L. Mackie argues that the various attempts made by theists to reconcile the existence of evil with the power and goodness of God are unsuccessful because they end up limiting either God's power or God's goodness. John Hick argues that the existence of evil is necessary if human beings are to fulfill their potential to love God freely and to achieve the most valuable kind of moral goodness.

The final section, "Faith and Reason," has two readings that discuss religious belief. In Plato's *Euthyphro,* Socrates uses his method of questioning (the dialectical, "Socratic" method) to lead the priest Euthyphro to reexamine his notion of what piety is. Blaise Pascal contends that since we are unable, in this life, to know whether God exists, we must make a "wager" and either believe or not believe—and that it is more reasonable to lay down our wager on the side of belief.

A. The Existence of God

READING 3

Proslogion and Exchange with Gaunilo

Anselm

Anselm was born in Aosta, Italy, around 1033. Despite objections from his father, who wanted him to pursue a career in politics, Anselm joined the Benedictine order, entering the monastery at Bec in Normandy, France, in 1060. He became prior of Bec in 1063 and abbot in 1078. As abbot he made several trips to England to inspect the lands that William the Conqueror had given to the monastery. Anselm made many friends in England and in 1093 was appointed Archbishop of Canterbury by William Rufus (son and successor of William the Conqueror). Anselm subsequently became involved in a series of controversies about the authority of secular rulers in ecclesiastical matters, strongly defending the autonomy of the Church. He died at Canterbury in 1109.

Anselm's major works are the *Monologion* ("Soliloquy," originally entitled "An Example of Meditation on the Meaning of Faith"), the *Proslogion* ("Discourse," originally entitled "Faith Seeking Understanding"), and *Cur Deus Homo* ("Why God Became a Human Being"). Our readings consist of (1) the section from the *Proslogion* in which Anselm presents his "ontological argument" for the existence of God, (2) an excerpt from a short work by Gaunilo (a monk contemporary with Anselm) that criticizes the ontological argument, and (3) a section from Anselm's reply to Gaunilo. (The term "ontological argument" is not Anselm's; it seems to have been coined in the 18th century by Immanuel Kant.)

Our reading from the *Proslogion* begins with Anselm's declaration that he believes that God is "something than which nothing greater can be thought." But does this God exist? Not everyone thinks so; the fool in the Book of Psalms, for example, says in his heart that there is no God. Anselm observes that the fool nonetheless understands what it is whose existence he or she is denying. And since whatever someone understands exists in the understanding, God exists in the fool's understanding. To exist in the understanding, of course, is different from existing in reality. Anselm then points out that to exist in reality is greater than to exist only in the understanding. But this means that it is self-contradictory to deny that God exists in reality: A person cannot consistently say that "something than which nothing greater can be thought" does not exist in reality, because if this being did *not* exist in reality, the person *could* conceive a greater being—namely, one that exists not only in the understanding but also in reality. And then the being that, by definition, is that than which nothing greater can be conceived, is one than which a greater *can* be conceived—an obvious contradiction.

Gaunilo, in his brief work "On Behalf of the Fool" (namely, the fool in the Book of Psalms who says that there is no God), contends that the ontological argument is invalid because this type of reasoning leads to obviously false conclusions. One could prove, for example, that a perfect island exists because it wouldn't be perfect if it existed only in our understanding. Anselm responds to Gaunilo's objection by denying that the ontological argument can be applied to an island or to any other finite being. For the only being whose nonexistence cannot be thought is the being than which nothing greater can be thought, and only God fits this description.

PROSLOGION

Chapter 2. That God Truly Exists

Lord, you who grant understanding to faith, grant that, insofar as you know it is useful for me, I may understand that you exist as we believe you exist, and that you are what we believe you to be. Now we believe that you are something than which nothing greater can be thought. So can it be that no such being exists, since "The fool has said in his heart, 'There is no God'"?[1] But when this same fool hears me say "something than which nothing greater can be thought," he surely understands what he hears; and what he understands exists in his understanding, even if he does not understand that it exists [in reality]. For it is one thing for an object to exist in the understanding and quite another to understand that the object exists [in reality]. When a painter, for example, thinks out in advance what he is going to paint, he has it in his understanding, but he does not yet understand that it exists, since he has not yet painted it. But once he has painted it, he both has it in his understanding and understands that it exists because he has now painted it. So even the fool must admit that something than which nothing greater can be thought exists at least in his understanding, since he understands this when he hears it, and whatever is understood exists in the understanding. And surely that than which a greater cannot be thought cannot exist only in the understanding. For if it exists only in the understanding, it can be thought to exist in reality as well, which is greater. So if that than which a greater cannot be thought exists only in the understanding, then that than which a greater *cannot* be thought is that than which a greater *can* be thought. But that is clearly impossible. Therefore, there is no doubt that something than which a greater cannot be thought exists both in the understanding and in reality.

Chapter 3. That He Cannot Be Thought Not to Exist

This [being] exists so truly that it cannot be thought not to exist. For it is possible to think that something exists that cannot be thought not to exist, and such a being is greater than one that can be thought not to exist. Therefore, if that than which a greater cannot be thought can be thought not to exist, then that than which a greater cannot be thought is *not* that than which a greater cannot be thought; and this is a contradiction. So that than which a greater cannot be thought exists so truly that it cannot be thought not to exist.

And this is you, O Lord our God. You exist so truly, O Lord my God, that you cannot be thought not to exist. And rightly so, for if some mind could think something better than you, a creature would rise above the Creator and sit in judgment upon him, which is completely absurd. Indeed, everything that exists, except for

---

[1]Psalms 15:1 (14:1 in some versions); Psalms 53:1 (52:1). [D. C. Abel]

you alone, can be thought not to exist. So you alone among all things have existence most truly, and therefore most greatly. Whatever else exists has existence less truly, and therefore less greatly. So then why did "the fool say in his heart, 'There is no God,'" when it is so evident to the rational mind that you of all beings exist most greatly? Why indeed, except because he is stupid and a fool?

Chapter 4. How the Fool Said in His Heart What Cannot Be Thought

But how has he said in his heart what he could not think? Or how could he not think what he said in his heart, since to say in one's heart is the same as to think? But if he really—or rather, *since* he really—thought this, because he said it in his heart, and did not say it in his heart, because he could not think it, there must be more than one way in which something is "said in one's heart" or "thought." In one sense of the word, to think a thing is to think the word that signifies that thing. But in another sense, it is to understand what exactly the thing is. God can be thought not to exist in the first sense, but not at all in the second sense. No one who understands what God is can think that God does not exist, although he may say these words in his heart with no signification at all, or with some peculiar signification. For God is that than which a greater cannot be thought. Whoever understands this properly, understands that this being exists in such a way that he cannot, even in thought, fail to exist. So whoever understands that God exists in this way cannot think that he does not exist.

　　Thanks be to you, my good Lord, thanks be to you. For what I once believed through your grace, I now understand through your illumination, so that even if I did not want to *believe* that you exist, I could not fail to *understand* that you exist.

Chapter 5. That God Is Whatever It Is Better to Be Than Not to Be; and That He Alone Exists Through Himself, and Makes All Other Things from Nothing

Then what are you, Lord God, than whom nothing greater can be thought? What are you, if not the greatest of all beings, who alone exists through himself and made all other things from nothing? For whatever is not this is less than the greatest than can be thought, but this cannot be thought of you. What good is missing from the highest good, through which every good thing exists? And so you are just, truthful, happy, and whatever it is better to be than not to be. For it is better to be just than unjust, and better to be happy than unhappy.

GAUNILO'S REPLY ON BEHALF OF THE FOOL

. . . I am offered the . . . argument that [something than which nothing greater can be thought] necessarily exists in reality, since if it did not, everything that exists in reality would be greater than it. And so this thing, which of course has been proved to exist in the understanding, would not be greater than everything else. To that argument I reply that if we are to say that something exists in the understanding that cannot even be thought on the basis of the true nature of anything whatever, then I shall not deny that even this thing exists in my understanding. But since there is no way to derive from this the conclusion that this thing also exists in reality, there is simply no reason for me to concede to him that this thing exists in reality until it is proved to me by some unassailable argument.

And when he says that this thing exists because otherwise that which is greater than everything else would not be greater than everything else, he does not fully realize whom he is addressing. For I do not yet admit—indeed, I actually deny, or at least doubt—that this greater being is greater than any real thing. Nor do I concede that it exists at all, except in the sense that something exists (if you want to call it "existence") when my mind tries to imagine some completely unknown thing solely on the basis of a word that it has heard. How, then, is the fact that this being has been proved to be greater than everything else supposed to show me that it exists in actual fact? For I continue to deny, or at least doubt, that this has been proved, so that I do not admit that this thing exists in my understanding or thought even in the way that many doubtful and uncertain things exist there. First I must become certain that this thing truly exists somewhere, and only then will the fact that it is greater than everything else show clearly that it also subsists in itself.

For example, there are those who say that somewhere in the ocean is an island that, because of the difficulty—or rather, impossibility—of finding what does not exist, some call "the Lost Island." This island (so the story goes) is more plentifully endowed than even the Isles of the Blessed with an indescribable abundance of all sorts of riches and delights. And because it has neither owner nor inhabitant, it is everywhere superior in its abundant riches to all the other lands that human beings inhabit. Suppose that someone tells me all this. The story is easily told and involves no difficulty, and so I understand it. But if this person went on to draw a conclusion, and say, "You cannot any longer doubt that this island, more excellent than all others on earth, truly exists somewhere in reality. For you do not doubt that this island exists in your understanding, and since it is more excellent to exist not merely in the understanding, but also in reality, this island must also exist in reality. For if it did not, any land that exists in reality would be greater than it. And so this more excellent thing that you have understood would not in fact be more excellent."—If, I say, he should try to convince me by this argument that I should no longer doubt whether the island truly exists, either I would think he was joking, or I would not know whom I ought to think more foolish: myself, if I grant him his conclusion, or him, if he thinks he can establish the existence of that island with any degree of certainty, without first showing that its excellence exists in my understanding [precisely] as a thing that truly and undoubtedly exists, and not in any way like something false or uncertain.

ANSELM'S REPLY TO GAUNILO

. . . I said that if [something than which nothing greater can be thought] exists only in the understanding, it can be thought to exist in reality as well, which is greater. Therefore, if it exists only in the understanding, the very same thing is both that than which a greater *cannot* be thought and that than which a greater *can* be thought. Now I ask you, what could be more logical? For if it exists only in the understanding, can it not be thought to exist in reality as well? And if it can, does not the one who thinks it, think something greater than that thing is if it exists only in the understanding? So if that than which a greater *cannot* be thought exists only in the understanding, it is that than which a greater *can* be thought: What more logical conclusion could there be? But of course that than which a greater cannot be thought is not the same in anyone's understanding as that than which a greater can be thought. Does it not follow, therefore, that if that than which a greater cannot be thought exists in any understanding at all, it does not exist only in the understanding? For if it exists only in the understanding, it is that than which a greater can be thought, which is absurd.

But, you say, this is just the same as if someone were to claim that it cannot be doubted that a certain island in the ocean, surpassing all other lands in its fertility (which, from the difficulty—or rather, impossibility—of finding what does not exist, is called "the Lost Island"), exists in reality, because someone can easily understand it when it is described to him in words. I say quite confidently that if anyone can find for me something existing either in reality or only in thought to which he can apply this inference in my argument, besides that than which a greater cannot be thought, I will find and give to him that Lost Island, never to be lost again. In fact, however, it has already become quite clear that that than which a greater cannot be thought cannot be thought not to exist, since its existence is a matter of such certain truth. For otherwise it would not exist at all. Finally, if someone says that he thinks it does not exist, I say that when he thinks this, either he is thinking something than which a greater cannot be thought, or he is not. If he is not, then he is not thinking that it does not exist, since he is not thinking it at all. But if he is, he is surely thinking something that cannot be thought not to exist. For if it could be thought not to exist, it could be thought to have a beginning and an end, which is impossible. Therefore, someone who is thinking it, is thinking something that cannot be thought not to exist. And of course someone who is thinking this, does not think that that very thing does not exist. Otherwise he would be thinking something that cannot be thought. Therefore, that than which a greater cannot be thought cannot be thought not to exist.

Treatise on God

Thomas Aquinas

Thomas Aquinas was born in Roccasecca, Italy, around 1224. After receiving his initial education from the Benedictine monks at Monte Cassino, he studied at the University of Naples, where he encountered members of the Dominican order. Attracted to the Dominicans, he joined the order despite opposition from his family. He was trained in philosophy and theology in Paris and in Cologne, Germany, under the Dominican Albert (later known as Albert the Great). After being ordained a priest, Aquinas pursued advanced studies in theology at the University of Paris, receiving his degree in 1256. He taught for a few years at the University of Paris and was then assigned to teach at various Dominican schools in Italy. Aquinas returned to the University of Paris in 1268, but four years later he went back to Italy to establish a new Dominican house of study at the University of Naples. He died in 1274 at Fossanova, Italy, while traveling to Lyons to serve as a papal consultant at the Second Council of Lyons.

Aquinas's major works include *Summa Contra Gentiles* ("Comprehensive Treatise against the Gentiles"), *Summa Theologiae* ("Comprehensive Treatise on Theology"), *Disputed Questions* (summaries of debates he conducted on various topics as a professor of theology), and detailed commentaries on the principal works of Aristotle.

Our reading is from the section of Part One of the *Summa Theologiae* known as the "Treatise on God." More specifically, the reading is the second "question" (topic) of this section, "On the Existence of God." This question consists of three "articles" (subdivisions). The first article asks whether the existence of God is self-evident. (If God's existence is self-evident, there would seem to be no need to formulate a proof that God exists.) Aquinas contends that God's existence is self-evident *in itself* but not *to us.* A proposition is self-evident in itself if the subject implies the predicate. Since God *is* existence (as Aquinas argues elsewhere), the term "God" implies "existence" and God's existence is therefore self-evident in itself. But God's existence is not self-evident to us because our limited human minds are incapable of grasping the full meaning of the term "God."

Since God's existence is not self-evident to us, Aquinas proceeds to ask, in the second article, whether the existence of God can be demonstrated (proved). He explains that God's existence can be demonstrated by reasoning from effects that we experience, back to God as their cause. In the third article, Aquinas presents five proofs that God exists, based on five kinds of facts that we experience. (1) The fact that there are things in motion implies that there is a first mover that is not itself in motion—and this first mover is God. (2) The fact that there are series of efficient causes (agents that bring things into existence or impart change) implies that there is a first efficient cause—and this first cause is God. (3) The fact that there are possible beings (beings that can not-exist) implies that there must be a necessary being (a being that *cannot* not-exist) that is its own source of necessity—and this being is God. (4) The fact that there are beings with different degrees of various perfections (for example, of goodness) implies that there is a being that is the cause of all these perfections—and this being is God. (5) Finally, the fact that natural beings without intelligence act for goals (for example, plants act to grow and reproduce) implies that there is an intelligent being that directs natural beings toward their goals—and this being is God.

Note that Aquinas begins each article by formulating objections against his own view. Then, after setting forth his own position, he responds to the objections he raised.

QUESTION 2. ON THE EXISTENCE OF GOD

First Article. Is the Existence of God Self-Evident?

I proceed in this way to the first article: It seems that the existence of God is self-evident.

Objection 1. Things of which we possess knowledge by nature, are said to be self-evident to us, as is manifest in the case of first principles. But, as Damascene says in the beginning of his book, "All are by nature endowed with knowledge of God's existence."[1] Therefore, the existence of God is self-evident.

Objection 2. Things that we know as soon as we know terms, are said to be self-evident, and the Philosopher in the *Posterior Analytics* attributes this to the first principles of demonstration;[2] when one knows what a whole is, and what a part is, one immediately knows that every whole is greater than one of its parts. But when one understands what the term "God" means, one immediately grasps that God exists, for the term "God" means that than which nothing greater can be signified. What exists in fact as well as in the intellect, however, is greater than what exists in the intellect alone. And so, since God exists in the intellect as soon as we understand the term "God," it also follows that God exists in fact. Therefore, the existence of God is self-evident.[3]

Objection 3. The existence of truth is self-evident, because one who denies the existence of truth admits its existence: If there is indeed no truth, it is true that truth does not exist; if, on the other hand, something is true, it is necessary that truth exists. But God is truth itself, as John says: "I am the way, the truth, and the life."[4] Therefore, the existence of God is self-evident.

On the contrary, no one can think the opposite of what is self-evident, as the Philosopher makes clear in the *Metaphysics*[5] and the *Posterior Analytics*[6] concerning the first principles of demonstration. But one can think the opposite of the proposition that God exists, as the Psalm says: "The fool has said in his heart, 'God does not exist.'"[7] Therefore, the existence of God is not self-evident.

I answer that something may be self-evident in two ways: in one way, in itself but not to us; in the second way, in itself and to us. For a proposition is self-evident because its predicate is contained in its subject's essence, as

---

[1]John Damascene, *On the Orthodox Faith* (a Latin translation of *Pēgē Gnōseōs* ["The Fountain of Wisdom"]), Book I, Chapter 1, Section 3. Damascene (about 675–749) was a Greek theologian. [D. C. ABEL]

[2]Aristotle, *Posterior Analytics*, Book 1, Chapter 3. Aquinas regularly refers to Aristotle as simply "the Philosopher." For a biography of Aristotle, see p. 331. [D. C. ABEL]

[3]This argument, now known as the "ontological argument," was first formulated by Anselm in his *Proslogion*. Anselm (about 1033–1109) was an Italian theologian and philosopher. For a biography of Anselm and the text of his argument, see pp. 34–38. [D. C. ABEL]

[4]John 14:6. [W. P. BAUMGARTH AND R. J. REGAN, TRANSLATORS]

[5]Aristotle, *Metaphysics*, Book III, Chapter 3. [W. P. BAUMGARTH AND R. J. REGAN]

[6]Aristotle, *Posterior Analytics*, Book I, Chapter 10. [W. P. BAUMGARTH AND R. J. REGAN]

[7]Psalms 15:1 (14:1 in some versions); Psalms 53:1 (51:1). [D. C. ABEL]

in the proposition "Human beings are animals," for "animal" belongs to the nature of "human being." Therefore, if all know the proposition's predicate and its subject's essence, the proposition will be self-evident to all. This is evident, for example, in the case of the first principles of demonstration, whose terms are general notions that everyone knows: being and nonbeing, whole and part, and the like. If, however, some persons happen not to know the predicate and the subject's essence, the proposition will indeed be self-evident in itself but not to those who do not know the predicate and the subject. And so it happens, as Boethius says in his book *De Hebdomatibus*, that only the wise have certain general and self-evident notions, such as "Incorporeal things do not exist in a place."[8]

I say, therefore, that the proposition "God exists" is in itself self-evident, because its predicate is the same as its subject; God is indeed his existence. . . . But because we do not know what God is, the proposition is not self-evident to us but needs to be demonstrated by things more known to us and less known as regards their nature—namely, by effects.

Reply to Objection 1. We are by nature endowed with knowledge of God's existence in a general way, with a certain confusion—namely, insofar as God is the happiness of human beings, for human beings by nature desire happiness, and they by nature know what they by nature desire. But this is not to know unconditionally that God exists, just as to know that someone is approaching, is not to know Peter, although Peter is the one who is approaching. For many deem riches to be the perfect human good, which is happiness, but certain others deem sensual pleasures the perfect human good, while still others deem something else the perfect human good.

Reply to Objection 2. Perhaps someone who hears the term "God," does not understand that it means that than which nothing greater can be thought, since some believe that God is a material substance. Even supposing that someone understands that the term "God" means what we assert (namely, that than which nothing greater can be thought), yet it does not thereby follow that such a one would understand that what the term means, exists in the real world, but only that it exists in the intellect's apprehension. Nor can it be proved that God really exists unless one grants that there really exists something than which no greater can be thought, and this is not granted by those who hold that God does not exist.

Reply to Objection 3. The existence of truth in general is self-evident, but it is not self-evident to us that a First Truth exists.

Second Article. Can We Demonstrate the Existence of God?

I proceed in this way to the second article: It seems that we cannot demonstrate the existence of God.

---

[8]Boethius, *De Hebdomatibus* ("On Groups of Seven," also known as *How Substances Can Be Good in Virtue of Their Existence without Being Absolute Goods),* Point 1. Boethius (about 480–524) was a Roman politician, philosopher, and theologian. [D. C. ABEL]

Objection 1. The existence of God is an article of faith. But we cannot demonstrate what belongs to faith, since demonstration causes knowledge, while faith concerns things that are not evident, as the Apostle [Paul] makes clear in the Letter to the Hebrews.[9] Therefore, we cannot demonstrate the existence of God.

Objection 2. The means of a demonstration is something's essence. But we cannot know what God is, but only what he is not, as Damascene says.[10] Therefore, we cannot demonstrate that God exists.

Objection 3. If one were to demonstrate the existence of God, this would be only by his effects. But his effects are not proportioned to him, since he himself is infinite, and the effects are finite, while there is no proportion of the finite to the infinite. Therefore, since we cannot demonstrate a cause by an effect that is not proportioned to its cause, it seems that we cannot demonstrate the existence of God.

On the contrary, the Apostle says in the Letter to the Romans, "The invisible things of God are visible when understood through the things that have been made."[11] But this would only be the case if we could demonstrate the existence of God through what he has made, for the first thing that we need to understand about something, is whether or not it exists.

I answer that we demonstrate in two ways. One is by means of a cause, and we call this a "demonstration why" something is so, and it is by means of what is first without qualification. The other is by means of an effect, and we call this a "demonstration that" something is, and this demonstration is by what is first as to us, for we proceed to knowledge of a cause through its effect, because the effect is more manifest to us than its cause is. But we can demonstrate the existence of a particular cause from any of its effects—provided that the cause's effects are nonetheless more known in relation to us—because effects depend on their cause, and so a cause necessarily preexists whenever an effect is posited. Therefore, since God's existence is not self-evident in relation to us, we can demonstrate his existence by means of the effects known to us.

Reply to Objection 1. God's existence and other such matters that natural reason can know about God, as the Letter to the Romans says,[12] are not articles of faith but preambles to the articles, for faith in this way presupposes natural knowledge, as grace presupposes nature, and as perfecting presupposes something perfectible. Nothing, however, prevents someone who does not undertake a demonstration, from accepting as an object of faith something that in itself can be demonstrated and known.

Reply to Objection 2. When a cause is demonstrated by means of its effect, we need to use the effect instead of the cause's definition to prove that the cause exists, and this happens especially in the case of God. This is so because, in

---

[9]Hebrews 11:1. [W. P. BAUMGARTH AND R. J. REGAN]

[10]John Damascene, *On the Orthodox Faith*, Book I, Chapter 4. [D. C. ABEL]

[11]Romans 1:20. [W. P. BAUMGARTH AND R. J. REGAN]

[12]Romans 1:19. [W. P. BAUMGARTH AND R. J. REGAN]

order to prove the existence of something, we need to take as the means of demonstration what the term means, not what the object is, since the question "What is it?" logically follows the question "Does it exist?" We posit names of God, however, from his effects. . . . Therefore, when we demonstrate the existence of God from effects, we can take as the means of demonstration what the name "God" means.

Reply to Objection 3. We cannot have perfect knowledge about a cause by means of effects unproportioned to their cause, but we can nonetheless clearly demonstrate the existence of such a cause by any one of the cause's effects, as I have said. And so we can demonstrate God's existence by means of his effects, although we cannot perfectly know him according to his essence by the effects.

Third Article. Does God Exist?

I proceed in this way to the third article: It seems that God does not exist.

Objection 1. It seems that God does not exist: If one of two contraries is infinite, the other would be completely destroyed. But we understand by the term "God" something infinite—namely, something good without limit. Therefore, if God were to exist, we would not find anything bad. But we do find bad things in the world. Therefore, God does not exist.

Objection 2. More sources do not accomplish what fewer sources can. But, supposing that God does not exist, other sources seem capable of accomplishing everything evident in the world, since we trace things of nature back to nature as their source, and we trace things of free choice back to human reason or will as their source. Therefore, we do not need to posit that God exists.

On the contrary, the Book of Exodus says in the person of God: "I am who am."[13]

I answer that we can prove in five ways that God exists.

The FIRST and more evident WAY, moreover, is the one we take from motion,[14] for it is sure and evident to the senses that some things in this world are moved. But everything moved is moved by something else. For an object is only moved insofar as it has potentiality for that to which it is moved, while something produces motion only insofar as it is actual. To move something, certainly, is only to bring it from potentiality to actuality, and only an actual being can bring something to actuality. For example, something actually hot, like fire, causes wood, which is potentially hot, to be actually hot, and thereby moves and changes the wood. The same object, however, cannot at the same time be actual and potential in the same respect but only in different respects; for example, something actually hot cannot at the same time be potentially hot, although it is

---

[13]Exodus 3:14. [W. P. BAUMGARTH AND R. J. REGAN]

[14]*motion*: a change from a state of *potentiality* to a state of *actuality*. A being has a *potentiality* for receiving a new quality if it can receive it but has not actually done so; it is brought from potentiality to *actuality* when it receives the new quality. In Aquinas's terminology, motion includes not only change in location (locomotion) but other kinds of change as well (such as a qualitative change from cold to hot, to use Aquinas's example). [D. C. ABEL]

at the same time potentially cold. Nothing, therefore, can produce and undergo motion, or move itself, in the same respect and in the same way. Everything that is moved, therefore, needs to be moved by something else. Therefore, if the cause of a motion is moved, the cause itself needs to be moved by another, and that other by another. But this regress ought not to be endless, because there would thus be no first cause of motion and so no other cause of motion, since second causes produce motion only because the first cause moves them. A stick, for example, only causes motion because a hand moves it. Therefore, we need to arrive at a first cause of motion, one that is moved by nothing else, and all understand this first cause of motion to be God.

The SECOND WAY is by considering efficient causes. For we find that there is an order of efficient causes in the case of those sensible[15] objects, and yet we do not find, nor can we, that anything is the efficient cause of its very self, because such a thing would thus pre-exist itself, and this is impossible. But we cannot regress endlessly in the matter of efficient causes. This is so because, in all ordered efficient causes, something first causes something intermediate, and something intermediate causes something last, whether the intermediate things be several or only one. But the effect is taken away if its cause is taken away. Therefore, there will be nothing intermediate or last if there be nothing first in the case of efficient causes. But if we should regress endlessly in the case of efficient causes, there will be no first efficient cause, and there will thus be neither a final effect nor intermediate efficient causes, and this is clearly false. Therefore, we need to posit a first efficient cause, and all call this cause God.

We take the THIRD WAY from the possible and the necessary, and the argument proceeds as follows. We certainly find in reality kinds of things that can exist and can not-exist, since we find that certain things come to be and pass away, and so can exist and can not-exist. But it is impossible that all such things always exist, because what can not-exist, at some point of time does not exist. Therefore, if everything can not-exist, there was a time when nothing really existed. But if this is so, nothing would also now exist, because something non-existent begins to exist only through the agency of something that does exist. Therefore, if nothing existed, nothing could begin to exist, and so nothing would now exist, and this conclusion is obviously false. Therefore, not every being is something that can not-exist, but there needs to be something necessary in reality. But everything necessary either has or does not have the ground of its necessity from another source. There cannot, however, be an endless regress in the case of necessary things that have the ground of their necessity in another source, just as there cannot be an endless regress in the case of efficient causes, as I have shown. We need, therefore, to posit something that is intrinsically necessary, that does not have the ground of its necessity from another source, but that causes other things to be necessary, and all call this intrinsically necessary being God.

We take the FOURTH WAY from the gradations that we find in reality. For we find in reality things that are more good and less good, more true and less true, more excellent and less excellent, and similarly in the case of other such things.

---

[15]*sensible:* able to be sensed. [D. C. ABEL]

But we say "more" and "less" about different things as they in various ways approximate what is most; for example, an object is hotter if it more approximates what is hottest. Therefore, there is something that is most true and most good and most excellent, and so being in the highest degree, for things that are most true, are beings in the highest degree, as the *Metaphysics* says.[16] What we call most in a genus,[17] moreover, causes everything belonging to that genus; for example, fire, which is hottest, causes everything hot, as the same work says.[18] Therefore, there exists something that causes the existing and the goodness and whatever perfection of every being, and we call this cause God.

We take the FIFTH WAY from the governance of things. For we see that certain things that lack knowledge—namely, natural material substances—act for the sake of an end.[19] And this is evident because they always or more frequently act in the same way in order to achieve what is best, and hence it is evident that they reach their goal by striving, not by chance. But things that lack knowledge, do not strive for goals unless a being with knowledge and intelligence directs them, as, for example, an archer aims an arrow. Therefore, there is a being with intelligence who orders all the things of nature to their ends, and we call this being God.

Reply to Objection 1. As Augustine says in his *Enchiridion,* "Because God is the highest good, he would in no way allow anything bad to exist in his works were he not so all-powerful and good as to act well even with respect to what is bad."[20] It belongs to the infinite goodness of God, therefore, to permit bad things and to bring forth good things from them.

Reply to Objection 2. We also need to trace things produced by nature back to God as their first cause, because nature, by reason of its fixed end, acts at the direction of a higher efficient cause. Likewise, we need to trace even things done by free choice back to a higher cause that is not the reason and will of human beings, since things done by free choice can change and fall short. We indeed need to trace everything that can change and fall short, back to a first source that cannot change and is intrinsically necessary, as I have shown.

---

[16]Aristotle, *Metaphysics,* Book II, Chapter 1. [W. P. BAUMGARTH AND R. J. REGAN]

[17]*genus:* category. [D. C. ABEL]

[18]Aristotle, *Metaphysics,* Book II, Chapter 1. [W. P. BAUMGARTH AND R. J. REGAN]

[19]*end:* goal. [D. C. ABEL]

[20]Augustine, *Enchiridion,* Chapter 11. Augustine (354–430) was a North African theologian and philosopher; for a biography, see p. 74. [D. C. ABEL]

Dialogues Concerning Natural Religion

David Hume

David Hume was born in 1711 in Edinburgh, Scotland. His family wanted him to become a lawyer, but he found himself more interested in liberal arts than law. After three years at the University of Edinburgh (1723–1725), Hume withdrew to study literature, history, and philosophy privately at home. His intensive study took its toll on his health, and in 1729 he nearly had a nervous breakdown. In 1734 Hume went to Bristol, England, to take a job as a clerk for a sugar company. But he disliked the life of commerce and soon resigned his job. Hume then lived in France for three years, studying philosophy. In 1744 he applied for a position in moral philosophy at the University of Edinburgh. Not chosen for the post, he spent the next several years in various occupations in England and abroad. Hume lived in Edinburgh from 1751 to 1763 and then went to Paris, where he served as secretary to the British Embassy for three years. Upon his return, he first lived in London but then moved back to Edinburgh, where he died in 1776.

Hume's major works are *A Treatise of Human Nature* (three volumes, 1739–1740), *An Enquiry Concerning Human Understanding* (1748; originally entitled *Philosophical Essays Concerning Human Understanding,* but renamed in the 1758 edition), *An Enquiry Concerning the Principles of Morals* (1751), *History of England* (six volumes, 1754–1762), and *Dialogues Concerning Natural Religion* (published posthumously, 1779).

Our reading is from the *Dialogues Concerning Natural Religion.* "Natural religion" refers to truths about God that can be known by reflecting on the phenomena in nature; it is contrasted with "revealed religion," which derives its doctrines from divine revelation. The three participants in Hume's fictional discussion about natural religion are Cleanthes, Demea, and Philo.

Our selection begins with Cleanthes defending natural religion. He argues that the world is an intricate machine, composed of many lesser machines, and that just as artificial machines are produced by intelligent agents (human beings), so the natural world must be the product of an intelligent being (God). Demea rejects this argument because it is a posteriori (based on experience); he thinks that only an a priori argument (one in which the conclusion is deduced from abstract principles and does not depend on experience) can indubitably establish God's existence. Philo proceeds to give his reason for rejecting Cleanthes' argument: The argument is based on the questionable analogy between the world and an artifact. Conscious design plays a role in human production, but it is rash to conclude that the universe as a whole is the product of conscious design. Knowledge comes from experience, and while we have seen the manufacture of artifacts, no one has witnessed the origin of the world.

Demea then presents an a priori argument for God's existence. He asserts that whatever exists must have either a cause or a reason for its existence. But since no series of *causes* can extend back infinitely, there must exist a being that has its *reason* for existence in itself. This being, which necessarily exists, is God. Our selection concludes with Cleanthes' objections to Demea's argument.

PART II

. . . [Cleanthes:] Look round the world; contemplate the whole and every part of it. You will find it to be nothing but one great machine subdivided into an infinite number of lesser machines, which again admit of subdivisions, to a degree beyond what human senses and faculties can trace and explain. All these various machines, and even their most minute parts, are adjusted to each other with an accuracy which ravishes into admiration all men who have ever contemplated them. The curious adapting of means to ends, throughout all nature, resembles exactly, though it much exceeds, the productions of human contrivance, of human designs, thought, wisdom, and intelligence. Since therefore the effects resemble each other, we are led to infer by all the rules of analogy that the causes also resemble; and that the Author of Nature is somewhat similar to the mind of man, though possessed of much larger faculties, proportioned to the grandeur of the work which he has executed. By this argument a posteriori,[1] and by this argument alone, do we prove at once the existence of a Deity and his similarity to human mind and intelligence.

I shall be so free, Cleanthes, said Demea, as to tell you that from the beginning I could not approve of your conclusion concerning the similarity of the Deity to men. Still less can I approve of the mediums by which you endeavor to establish it. What! No demonstration of the Being of a God? No abstract arguments? No proofs a priori?[2] Are these, which have hitherto been so much insisted on by philosophers, all fallacy, all sophism? Can we reach no farther in this subject than experience and probability? I will not say that this is betraying the cause of a Deity. But surely, by this affected candor, you give advantage to atheists which they never could obtain by the mere dint of argument and reasoning.

What I chiefly scruple in this subject, said Philo, is not so much that all religious arguments are by Cleanthes reduced to experience, as that they appear not to be even the most certain and irrefragable[3] of that inferior kind. That a stone will fall, that fire will burn, that the earth has solidity, we have observed a thousand and a thousand times; and when any new instance of this nature is presented, we draw without hesitation the accustomed inference. The exact similarity of the cases gives us a perfect assurance of a similar event and a stronger evidence is never desired nor sought after. But wherever you depart, in the least, from the similarity of the cases, you diminish proportionably the evidence; and may at last bring it to a very weak analogy, which is confessedly liable to error and uncertainty. After having experienced the circulation of the blood in human creatures, we make no doubt that it takes place in Titius and Maevius. But from its circulation in frogs and fishes, it is only a presumption, though a strong one, from analogy, that it takes place in men and other animals. The analogical reasoning is much weaker when we infer the circulation of the sap in vegetables

---

[1] *argument a posteriori:* an argument based on experience (literally, in Latin, "from what comes later"). [D. C. ABEL]

[2] *proofs a priori:* arguments in which the conclusion is deduced from abstract principles (literally, in Latin, "from what comes earlier"); contrasted with a posteriori proofs (see footnote 1). [D. C. ABEL]

[3] *irrefragable:* irrefutable. [D. C. ABEL]

from our experience that the blood circulates in animals; and those who hastily followed that imperfect analogy are found, by more accurate experiments,[4] to have been mistaken.

If we see a house, Cleanthes, we conclude with the greatest certainty that it had an architect or builder, because this is precisely that species of effect which we have experienced to proceed from that species of cause. But surely you will not affirm that the universe bears such a resemblance to a house, that we can with the same certainty infer a similar cause, or that the analogy is here entire and perfect. The dissimilitude is so striking that the utmost you can here pretend to is a guess, a conjecture, a presumption concerning a similar cause. And how that pretension will be received in the world, I leave you to consider.

It would surely be very ill received, replied Cleanthes, and I should be deservedly blamed and detested, did I allow that the proofs of a Deity amounted to no more than a guess or conjecture. But is the whole adjustment of means to ends in a house and in the universe so slight a resemblance? The economy of final causes?[5] The order, proportion, and arrangement of every part? Steps of a stair are plainly contrived that human legs may use them in mounting: and this inference is certain and infallible. Human legs are also contrived for walking and mounting; and this inference, I allow, is not altogether so certain, because of the dissimilarity which you remark. But does it, therefore, deserve the name only of presumption or conjecture?

Good God! cried Demea, interrupting him; where are we? Zealous defenders of religion allow that the proofs of a Deity fall short of perfect evidence! And you, Philo . . . do you assent to all these extravagant opinions of Cleanthes? For what other name can I give them? . . .

You seem not to apprehend, replied Philo, that I argue with Cleanthes in his own way; and by showing him the dangerous consequences of his tenets, hope at last to reduce him to our opinion. But what sticks most with you, I observe, is the representation which Cleanthes has made of the argument a posteriori; and finding that that argument is likely to escape your hold and vanish into air, you think it so disguised that you can scarcely believe it to be set in its true light. Now, however much I may dissent in other respects from the dangerous principles of Cleanthes, I must allow that he has fairly represented that argument; and I shall endeavor so to state the matter to you, that you will entertain no farther scruples with regard to it.

Were a man to abstract from everything which he knows or has seen, he would be altogether incapable, merely from his own ideas, to determine what kind of scene the universe must be, or to give the preference to one state or situation of things above another. For as nothing which he clearly conceives could be esteemed[6] impossible or implying a contradiction, every chimera[7] of his fancy would be upon an equal footing; nor could he assign any just reason why he adheres to one idea or system and rejects the others, which are equally possible.

---

[4]*experiments:* experiences. [D. C. ABEL]
[5]*final causes:* the purposes of things, as reasons for their existence. [D. C. ABEL]
[6]*esteemed:* regarded. [D. C. ABEL]
[7]*chimera:* mental fabrication. [D. C. ABEL]

Again, after he opens his eyes and contemplates the world as it really is, it would be impossible for him, at first, to assign the cause of any one event—much less of the whole of things or of the universe. He might set his fancy a-rambling, and [it] might bring him in an infinite variety of reports and representations. These would all be possible; but being all equally possible, he would never, of himself, give a satisfactory account for his preferring one of them to the rest. Experience alone can point out to him the true cause of any phenomenon.

Now according to this method of reasoning, Demea, it follows (and is, indeed, tacitly allowed by Cleanthes himself) that order, arrangement, or the adjustment of final causes is not, of itself, any proof of design—but only so far as it has been experienced to proceed from that principle. For aught we can know a priori, matter may contain the source or spring of order originally, within itself, as well as mind does; and there is no more difficulty in conceiving that the several elements, from an internal unknown cause, may fall into the most exquisite arrangement, than to conceive that their ideas, in the great universal mind, from a like internal, unknown cause, fall into that arrangement. The equal possibility of both these suppositions is allowed. But by experience we find (according to Cleanthes) that there is a difference between them. Throw several pieces of steel together, without shape or form; they will never arrange themselves so as to compose a watch. Stone and mortar and wood, without an architect, never erect a house. But the ideas in a human mind, we see, by an unknown, inexplicable economy, arrange themselves so as to form the plan of a watch or house. Experience, therefore, proves that there is an original principle of order in mind, not in matter. From similar effects we infer similar causes. The adjustment of means to ends is alike in the universe, as in a machine of human contrivance. The causes therefore must be resembling.

I was from the beginning scandalized, I must own,[8] with this resemblance which is asserted between the Deity and human creatures, and must conceive it to imply such a degradation of the Supreme Being as no sound theist could endure. With your assistance therefore, Demea, I shall endeavor to defend what you justly called the adorable mysteriousness of the divine nature and shall refute this reasoning of Cleanthes, provided he allows that I have made a fair representation of it.

When Cleanthes had assented, Philo, after a short pause, proceeded in the following manner.

That all inferences, Cleanthes, concerning fact are founded on experience, and that all experimental[9] reasonings are founded on the supposition that similar causes prove similar effects, and similar effects similar causes; I shall not, at present, much dispute with you. But observe, I entreat you, with what extreme caution all just reasoners proceed in the transferring of experiments to similar cases. Unless the cases be exactly similar, they repose no perfect confidence in applying their past observation to any particular phenomenon. Every alteration of circumstances occasions a doubt concerning the event, and it requires new

---

[8]*own:* admit. [D. C. ABEL]
[9]*experimental:* based on experience. [D. C. ABEL]

experiments to prove certainly that the new circumstances are of no moment or importance. A change in bulk, situation, arrangement, age, disposition of the air, or surrounding bodies—any of these particulars may be attended with the most unexpected consequences. And unless the objects be quite familiar to us, it is the highest temerity to expect with assurance, after any of these changes, an event similar to that which before fell under our observation. The slow and deliberate steps of philosophers, here if anywhere, are distinguished from the precipitate march of the vulgar, who, hurried on by the smallest similitudes, are incapable of all discernment or consideration.

But can you think, Cleanthes, that your usual phlegm[10] and philosophy have been preserved in so wide a step as you have taken, when you compared to the universe houses, ships, furniture, machines; and from their similarity in some circumstances inferred a similarity in their causes? Thought, design, intelligence, such as we discover in men and other animals, is no more than one of the springs and principles of the universe, as well as heat or cold, attraction or repulsion, and a hundred others which fall under daily observation. It is an active cause, by which some particular parts of nature, we find, produce alterations on other parts. But can a conclusion with any propriety be transferred from parts to the whole? Does not the great disproportion bar all comparison and inference? From observing the growth of a hair, can we learn anything concerning the generation of a man? Would the manner of a leaf's blowing, even though perfectly known, afford us any instruction concerning the vegetation of a tree?

But allowing that we were to take the operations of one part of nature upon another for the foundation of our judgment concerning the origin of the whole (which never can be admitted), yet why select so minute, so weak, so bounded a principle as the reason and design of animals is found to be upon this planet? What peculiar privilege has this little agitation of the brain which we call *thought,* that we must thus make it the model of the whole universe? Our partiality in our own favor does indeed present it on all occasions, but sound philosophy ought carefully to guard against so natural an illusion.

So far from admitting, continued Philo, that the operations of a part can afford us any just conclusion concerning the origin of the whole, I will not allow any one part to form a rule for another part, if the latter be very remote from the former. Is there any reasonable ground to conclude that the inhabitants of other planets possess thought, intelligence, reason, or anything similar to these faculties in men? When Nature has so extremely diversified her manner of operation in this small globe, can we imagine that she incessantly copies herself throughout so immense a universe? And if thought, as we may well suppose, be confined merely to this narrow corner, and has even there so limited a sphere of action, with what propriety can we assign it for the original cause of all things? The narrow views of a peasant, who makes his domestic economy the rule for the government of kingdoms, is in comparison a pardonable sophism.

But were we ever so much assured that a thought and reason, resembling the human, were to be found throughout the whole universe, and were its activity elsewhere vastly greater and more commanding than it appears in this

---

[10]*phlegm:* calm self-possession. [D. C. ABEL]

globe; yet I cannot see why the operations of a world constituted, arranged, adjusted, can with any propriety be extended to a world which is in its embryo-state and is advancing towards that constitution and arrangement. By observation we know somewhat of the economy, action, and nourishment of a finished animal. But we must transfer with great caution that observation to the growth of a fetus in the womb, and still more, in the formation of an animalcule[11] in the loins of its male parent. Nature, we find, even from our limited experience, possesses an infinite number of springs and principles, which incessantly discover themselves on every change of her position and situation. And what new and unknown principles would actuate her in so new and unknown a situation as that of the formation of a universe, we cannot, without the utmost temerity, pretend to determine.

A very small part of this great system, during a very short time, is very imperfectly discovered to us. And do we then pronounce decisively concerning the origin of the whole?

Admirable conclusion! Stone, wood, brick, iron, brass, have not, at this time, in this minute globe of earth, an order or arrangement without human art and contrivance. Therefore the universe could not originally attain its order and arrangement without something similar to human art. But is a part of nature a rule for another part very wide of the former? Is it a rule for the whole? Is a very small part a rule for the universe? Is nature in one situation, a certain rule for nature in another situation, vastly different from the former?

And can you blame me, Cleanthes, if I here imitate the prudent reserve of Simonides[12] who, according to the noted story, being asked by Hiero[13] what God was, desired a day to think of it, and then two days more; and after that manner continually prolonged the term, without ever bringing in his definition or description? Could you even blame me, if I had answered at first that I did not know and was sensible[14] that this subject lay vastly beyond the reach of my faculties? You might cry out *skeptic* and *rallier* as much as you pleased; but having found in so many other subjects, much more familiar, the imperfections and even contradictions of human reason, I never should expect any success from its feeble conjectures in a subject so sublime and so remote from the sphere of our observation. When two species of objects have always been observed to be conjoined together, I can *infer,* by custom, the existence of one wherever I see the existence of the other; and this I call an argument from experience. But how this argument can have place where the objects, as in the present case, are single, individual, without parallel or specific resemblance, may be difficult to explain. And will any man tell me with a serious countenance that an orderly universe must arise from some thought and art like the human, because we have experience of it? To ascertain this reasoning, it were requisite that we had experience of the origin of worlds; and it is not sufficient, surely, that we have seen ships and cities arise from human art and contrivance. . . .

---

[11]*animalcule:* a minute organism. [D. C. ABEL]
[12]*Simonides:* a Greek poet who lived from about 556 to about 468 B.C.E. [D. C. ABEL]
[13]*Hiero:* a ruler of Syracuse, Sicily, who died about 467 B.C.E. [D. C. ABEL]
[14]*sensible:* aware. [D. C. ABEL]

PART IX

But if so many difficulties attend the argument a posteriori, said Demea, had we not better adhere to that simple and sublime argument a priori, which, by offering to us infallible demonstration, cuts off at once all doubt and difficulty? By this argument, too, we may prove the *infinity* of the divine attributes, which, I am afraid, can never be ascertained with certainty from any other topic. For how can an effect, which either is finite or, for aught we know, may be so—how can such an effect, I say, prove an infinite cause? The unity too of the divine nature it is very difficult, if not absolutely impossible, to deduce merely from contemplating the works of nature. Nor will the uniformity alone of the plan, even were it allowed, give us any assurance of that attribute. Whereas the argument a priori . . .[15]

You seem to reason, Demea, interposed Cleanthes, as if those advantages and conveniencies in the abstract argument were full proofs of its solidity. But it is first proper, in my opinion, to determine what argument of this nature you choose to insist on; and we shall afterwards, from itself, better than from its useful consequences, endeavor to determine what value we ought to put upon it.

The argument, replied Demea, which I would insist on is the common one. Whatever exists must have a cause or reason of its existence, it being absolutely impossible for anything to produce itself, or be the cause of its own existence. In mounting up, therefore, from effects to causes, we must either go on in tracing an infinite succession, without any ultimate cause at all; or must at last have recourse to some ultimate cause that is *necessarily* existent. Now, that the first supposition is absurd may be thus proved. In the infinite chain or succession of causes and effects, each single effect is determined to exist by the power and efficacy of that cause which immediately preceded. But the whole eternal chain or succession, taken together, is not determined or caused by anything; and yet it is evident that it requires a cause or reason, as much as any particular object which begins to exist in time. The question is still reasonable, why this particular succession of causes existed from eternity, and not any other succession, or no succession at all. If there be no necessarily-existent being, any supposition which can be formed is equally possible; nor is there any more absurdity in Nothing's having existed from eternity, than there is in that succession of causes which constitutes the universe. What was it, then, which determined something to exist rather than nothing, and bestowed being on a particular possibility, exclusive of the rest? External causes, there are supposed to be none. *Chance* is a word without a meaning. Was it Nothing? But that can never produce anything. We must, therefore, have recourse to a necessarily-existent Being, who carries the *reason* of his existence in himself and who cannot be supposed not to exist without an express contradiction. There is consequently such a Being—that is, there is a Deity.

I shall not leave it to Philo, said Cleanthes (though I know that starting objections is his chief delight) to point out the weakness of this metaphysical[16]

---

[15]This ellipsis is Hume's; no text has been deleted. [D. C. ABEL]

[16]*metaphysical*: relating to *metaphysics*, the study of the nature and kinds of reality. [D. C. ABEL]

reasoning. It seems to me so obviously ill-grounded and at the same time of so little consequence to the cause of true piety and religion, that I shall myself venture to show the fallacy of it.

I shall begin with observing that there is an evident absurdity in pretending to demonstrate a matter of fact or to prove it by any arguments a priori. Nothing is demonstrable unless the contrary implies a contradiction. Nothing that is distinctly conceivable implies a contradiction. Whatever we conceive as existent, we can also conceive as nonexistent. There is no being, therefore, whose nonexistence implies a contradiction. Consequently there is no being whose existence is demonstrable. I propose this argument as entirely decisive and am willing to rest the whole controversy upon it.

It is pretended[17] that the Deity is a necessarily-existent being; and this necessity of his existence is attempted to be explained by asserting that, if we knew his whole essence or nature, we should perceive it to be as impossible for him not to exist as for twice two not to be four. But it is evident that this can never happen while our faculties remain the same as at present. It will still be possible for us, at any time, to conceive the nonexistence of what we formerly conceived to exist; nor can the mind ever lie under a necessity of supposing any object to remain always in being, in the same manner as we lie under a necessity of always conceiving twice two to be four. The words, therefore, *necessary existence* have no meaning; or, which is the same thing, none that is consistent.

But farther: Why may not the material universe be the necessarily-existent Being, according to this pretended explication of necessity? We dare not affirm that we know all the qualities of matter; and for aught we can determine, it may contain some qualities which, were they known, would make its nonexistence appear as great a contradiction as that twice two is five. I find only one argument employed to prove that the material world is not the necessarily-existent Being and this argument is derived from the contingency[18] both of the matter and the form of the world. "Any particle of matter," it is said, "may be *conceived* to be annihilated, and any form may be *conceived* to be altered. Such an annihilation or alteration, therefore, is not impossible."[19] But it seems a great partiality not to perceive that the same argument extends equally to the Deity, so far as we have any conception of him; and that the mind can at least imagine him to be nonexistent, or his attributes to be altered. It must be some unknown, inconceivable qualities which can make his nonexistence appear impossible or his attributes unalterable. And no reason can be assigned why these qualities may not belong to matter. As they are altogether unknown and inconceivable, they can never be proved incompatible with it.

Add to this, that in tracing an eternal succession of objects, it seems absurd to inquire for a general cause or first author. How can anything that exists from eternity have a cause, since that relation implies a priority in time and a beginning of existence?

---

[17]*pretended:* claimed. [D. C. Abel]

[18]*contingency:* the condition of being able to exist or not to exist; contrasted with *necessary* existence. [D. C. ABEL]

[19]This quotation is from English philosopher Samuel Clarke (1675–1729). [D. C. ABEL]

In such a chain too, or succession of objects, each part is caused by that which preceded it and causes that which succeeds it. Where then is the difficulty? But the *whole,* you say, wants a cause. I answer that the uniting of these parts into a whole, like the uniting of several distinct counties into one kingdom, or several distinct members into one body, is performed merely by an arbitrary act of the mind and has no influence on the nature of things. Did I show you the particular causes of each individual in a collection of twenty particles of matter, I should think it very unreasonable, should you afterwards ask me, what was the cause of the whole twenty. This is sufficiently explained in explaining the cause of the parts.

Natural Theology

William Paley

William Paley was born in 1743 in Peterborough, England. In 1759 he entered Cambridge University, where he studied mathematics. He graduated from Cambridge in 1763 and three years later was elected a fellow there. He was ordained to the Anglican priesthood in 1767 and became a tutor at Cambridge the following year. In 1776 Paley ended his teaching career to take an ecclesiastical position, the rectorship of Musgrave. He was subsequently appointed to various offices in the Church. He became Archdeacon of Carlisle in 1782, but despite his great ability, he rose no higher in the Church—apparently because he held liberal political views. In 1785 Paley published *The Principles of Moral and Political Philosophy,* based on his lectures at Cambridge. He strongly defended the rationality of Christian belief in his two most influential works, *A View of the Evidence of Christianity* (1794) and *Natural Theology; or, Evidences of the Existence and Attributes of the Deity, Collected from the Appearances of Nature* (1802). He died in Lincoln in 1805.

Our selection is from *Natural Theology.* As Paley's subtitle indicates, "natural theology" refers to truths about God that can be known by reflecting on nature. "Revealed theology," by contrast, denotes doctrines made known through divine revelation. Paley contends that the design evident in living organisms proves that God exists. He begins his treatise by asking us to imagine that, when crossing a heath, we find a watch lying on the ground. We notice that all its parts work together for the purpose of measuring time. We would hardly conclude that the watch came to exist by chance; rather, we would infer that it was made by an intelligent artisan "who formed it for the purpose which we find it actually to answer, who comprehended its construction and designed its use." If we were to find that the watch, in addition to measuring time, could produce another watch like itself, we would admire the skill of the artisan even more; for even though the watch we encounter may have been produced by a previous watch, there must have been an intelligent agent who designed watches in such a way that they could reproduce.

The kind of design evident in artificial objects like watches, Paley argues, is also present in the works of nature, "with the difference, on the side of nature, of being greater and more, and that in a degree which exceeds all computation." For example, the design of the eye is much more complex than that of the telescope. Anticipating an objection, Paley argues that the presence of imperfections in nature no more disproves the existence of an intelligent Creator than defects in watches disprove the existence of intelligent watchmakers. Furthermore, we should judge the skill of artists by their best works, not by their least perfect ones. Imperfections in the works of accomplished artists should be attributed not to personal failings but rather to "some intractableness and imperfection in the materials, or . . . some invincible difficulty in the execution."

CHAPTER I. THE STATE OF THE ARGUMENT

In crossing a heath, suppose I pitched my foot against a stone and were asked how the stone came to be there. I might possibly answer that, for anything I knew to the contrary, it had lain there forever; nor would it perhaps be very easy to show the absurdity of this answer. But suppose I had found a *watch* upon the ground and it should be inquired how the watch happened to be in that place. I should hardly think of the answer which I had given before, that, for anything I knew, the watch might have always been there. Yet why should not this answer serve for the watch as well as for the stone? Why is it not as admissible in the second case, as in the first? For this reason, and for no other, namely, that when we come to inspect the watch, we perceive (what we could not discover in the stone) that its several parts are framed and put together for a purpose—for example, that they are so formed and adjusted as to produce motion, and that motion so regulated as to point out the hour of the day; that, if the different parts had been differently shaped from what they are, of a different size from what they are, or placed after any other manner or in any other order than that in which they are placed, either no motion at all would have been carried on in the machine, or none which would have answered the use that is now served by it. To reckon up a few of the plainest of these parts and of their offices,[1] all tending to one result: We see a cylindrical box containing a coiled elastic spring which, by its endeavor to relax itself, turns round the box. We next observe a flexible chain (artificially wrought for the sake of flexure) communicating the action of the spring from the box to the fusee.[2] We then find a series of wheels, the teeth of which catch in and apply to each other, conducting the motion from the fusee to the balance, and from the balance to the pointer; and at the same time, by the size and shape of those wheels, so regulating that motion as to terminate in causing an index,[3] by an equable and measured progression, to pass over a given space in a given time. We take notice that the wheels are made of brass in order to keep them from rust; the springs of steel, no other metal being so elastic; that over the face of the watch there is placed a glass, a material employed in no other part of the work, but in the room[4] of which, if there had been any other than a transparent substance, the hour could not be seen without opening the case. This mechanism being observed (it requires indeed an examination of the instrument, and perhaps some previous knowledge of the subject, to perceive and understand it; but being once, as we have said, observed and understood), the inference, we think, is inevitable—that the watch must have had a maker, that there must have existed, at some time and at some place or other, an artificer or artificers who formed it for the purpose which we find it actually to answer, who comprehended its construction and designed its use.

1. Nor would it, I apprehend, weaken the conclusion, that we had never seen a watch made; that we had never known an artist capable of making one; that we were altogether incapable of executing such a piece of workmanship ourselves or of understanding in what manner it was performed—all this being no more than what is true of some exquisite remains of ancient art, of some lost arts, and, to the generality of mankind, of the more curious productions of modern manufacture. Does one man in a million know how oval frames are turned?

---

[1] *offices:* functions. [D. C. ABEL]
[2] *fusee:* the cone-shaped pulley in a mechanical watch. [D. C. ABEL]
[3] *index:* indicator. [D. C. ABEL]
[4] *room:* place. [D. C. ABEL]

Ignorance of this kind exalts our opinion of the unseen and unknown artist's skill, if he be unseen and unknown, but raises no doubt in our minds of the existence and agency of such an artist at some former time and in some place or other. Nor can I perceive that it varies at all the inference, whether the question arise concerning a human agent, or concerning an agent of a different species, or an agent possessing, in some respects, a different nature.

2. Neither, secondly, would it invalidate our conclusion, that the watch sometimes went wrong or that it seldom went exactly right. The purpose of the machinery, the design, and the designer might be evident, and in the case supposed would be evident, in whatever way we accounted for the irregularity of the movement, or whether we could account for it or not. It is not necessary that a machine be perfect in order to show with what design it was made. Still less necessary, where the only question is whether it were made with any design at all.

3. Nor, thirdly, would it bring any uncertainty into the argument if there were a few parts of the watch concerning which we could not discover, or had not yet discovered, in what manner they conduced to the general effect; or even some parts concerning which we could not ascertain whether they conduced to that effect in any manner whatever. For, as to the first branch of the case: If by the loss or disorder or decay of the parts in question, the movement of the watch were found in fact to be stopped or disturbed or retarded, no doubt would remain in our minds as to the utility or intention of these parts, although we should be unable to investigate the manner according to which, or the connection by which, the ultimate effect depended upon their action or assistance. And the more complex is the machine, the more likely is this obscurity to arise. Then, as to the second thing supposed, namely, that there were parts which might be spared without prejudice[5] to the movement of the watch, and that we had proved this by experiment: These superfluous parts, even if we were completely assured that they were such, would not vacate[6] the reasoning which we had instituted concerning other parts. The indication of contrivance remained, with respect to them, nearly as it was before.

4. Nor, fourthly, would any man in his senses think the existence of the watch, with its various machinery, accounted for, by being told that it was one out of possible combinations of material forms; that whatever he had found in the place where he found the watch, must have contained some internal configuration or other; and that this configuration might be the structure now exhibited, namely, of the works of a watch, as well as a different structure.

5. Nor, fifthly, would it yield his inquiry more satisfaction to be answered that there existed in things a principle of order which had disposed the parts of the watch into their present form and situation. He never knew a watch made by the principle of order nor can he even form to himself an idea of what is meant by a principle of order distinct from the intelligence of the watchmaker.

6. Sixthly, he would be surprised to hear that the mechanism of the watch was no proof of contrivance, only a motive to induce the mind to think so—

---

[5]*prejudice:* injury. [D. C. ABEL]
[6]*vacate:* annul. [D. C. ABEL]

7. And not less surprised to be informed that the watch in his hand was nothing more than the result of the laws of metallic nature. It is a perversion of language to assign any law as the efficient, operative cause[7] of any thing. A law presupposes an agent, for it is only the mode according to which an agent proceeds. It implies a power, for it is the order according to which that power acts. Without this agent, without this power, which are both distinct from itself, the law does nothing, is nothing. The expression, "the law of metallic nature," may sound strange and harsh to a philosophic ear; but it seems quite as justifiable as some others which are more familiar to him, such as "the law of vegetable nature," "the law of animal nature," or indeed as "the law of nature" in general, when assigned as the cause of phenomena in exclusion of agency and power, or when it is substituted into the place of these.

8. Neither, lastly, would our observer be driven out of his conclusion or from his confidence in its truth by being told that he knew nothing at all about the matter. He knows enough for his argument: He knows the utility of the end;[8] he knows the subserviency and adaptation of the means to the end. These points being known, his ignorance of other points, his doubts concerning other points, affect not the certainty of his reasoning. The consciousness of knowing little need not beget a distrust of that which he does know.

CHAPTER II. THE STATE OF THE ARGUMENT CONTINUED

Suppose, in the next place, that the person who found the watch should, after some time, discover that in addition to all the properties which he had hitherto observed in it, it possessed the unexpected property of producing, in the course of its movement, another watch like itself (the thing is conceivable); that it contained within it a mechanism, a system of parts—a mold for instance, or a complex adjustment of lathes, files, and other tools—evidently and separately calculated for this purpose. Let us inquire what effect ought such a discovery to have upon his former conclusion.

1. The first effect would be to increase his admiration of the contrivance and his conviction of the consummate skill of the contriver. Whether he regarded the object of the contrivance, the distinct apparatus, the intricate yet in many parts intelligible mechanism by which it was carried on, he would perceive in this new observation nothing but an additional reason for doing what he had already done—for referring the construction of the watch to design and to supreme art. If that construction *without* this property, or which is the same thing, before this property had been noticed, proved intention and art to have been employed about it; still more strong would the proof appear, when he came to the knowledge of this further property, the crown and perfection of all the rest.

2. He would reflect that though the watch before him were *in some sense* the maker of the watch which was fabricated in the course of its movements, yet it was in a very different sense from that in which a carpenter, for instance, is the

---

[7]*efficient, operative cause:* the agent that brings something into being or imparts change. [D. C. ABEL]
[8]*end:* purpose, goal. [D. C. ABEL]

maker of a chair ([that is,] the author of its contrivance, the cause of the relation of its parts to their use). With respect to these, the first watch was no cause at all to the second: In no such sense as this was it the author of the constitution and order either of the parts which the new watch contained, or of the parts by the aid and instrumentality of which it was produced. We might possibly say, but with great latitude of expression, that a stream of water ground corn. But no latitude of expression would allow us to say, no stretch of conjecture could lead us to think, that the stream of water built the mill, though it were too ancient for us to know who the builder was. What the stream of water does in the affair, is neither more nor less than this: By the application of an unintelligent impulse to a mechanism previously arranged, arranged independently of it and arranged by intelligence, an effect is produced—namely, the corn is ground. But the effect results from the arrangement. The force of the stream cannot be said to be the cause or author of the effect, still less of the arrangement. Understanding and plan in the formation of the mill were not the less necessary, for any share which the water has in grinding the corn. Yet is this share the same as that which the watch would have contributed to the production of the new watch, upon the supposition assumed in the last section. Therefore,

3. Though it be now no longer probable that the individual watch which our observer had found was made immediately by the hand of an artificer, yet . . . this alteration [does not] in any wise affect the inference that an artificer had been originally employed and concerned in the production. The argument from design remains as it was. Marks of design and contrivance are no more accounted for now than they were before. In the same thing, we may ask for the cause of different properties. We may ask for the cause of the color of a body, of its hardness, of its head; and these causes may be all different. We are now asking for the cause of that subserviency to a use, that relation to an end, which we have remarked in the watch before us. No answer is given to this question by telling us that a preceding watch produced it. There cannot be design without a designer; contrivance without a contriver; order without choice; arrangement without anything capable of arranging; subserviency and relation to a purpose, without that which could intend a purpose; means suitable to an end and executing their office in accomplishing that end, without the end ever having been contemplated or the means accommodated to it. Arrangement, disposition of parts, subserviency of means to an end, relation of instruments to a use, imply the presence of intelligence and mind. No one therefore can rationally believe that the insensible,[9] inanimate watch from which the watch before us issued was the proper cause of the mechanism we so much admire in it—could be truly said to have constructed the instrument, disposed its parts, assigned their office, determined their order, action, and mutual dependency, combined their several motions into one result, and that also a result connected with the utilities of other beings. All these properties, therefore, are as much unaccounted for as they were before.

4. Nor is anything gained by running the difficulty farther back, that is, by supposing the watch before us to have been produced from another watch, that

---

[9]*insensible:* having no sensation. [D. C. ABEL]

from a former, and so on indefinitely. Our going back ever so far, brings us no nearer to the least degree of satisfaction upon the subject. Contrivance is still unaccounted for. We still want a contriver. A designing mind is neither supplied by this supposition nor dispensed with. If the difficulty were diminished the further we went back, by going back indefinitely we might exhaust it. And this is the only case to which this sort of reasoning applies. Where there is a tendency or, as we increase the number of terms, a continual approach towards a limit, *there,* by supposing the number of terms to be what is called infinite, we may conceive the limit to be attained. But where there is no such tendency or approach, nothing is effected by lengthening the series. There is no difference as to the point in question (whatever there may be as to many points) between one series and another, between a series which is finite and a series which is infinite. A chain composed of an infinite number of links can no more support itself than a chain composed of a finite number of links. And of this we are assured (though we never can have tried the experiment) because, by increasing the number of links, from ten for instance to a hundred, from a hundred to a thousand, and so on, we make not the smallest approach, we observe not the smallest tendency, towards self-support. There is no difference in this respect (yet there may be a great difference in several respects) between a chain of a greater or less length, between one chain and another, between one that is finite and one that is infinite. This very much resembles the case before us. The machine which we are inspecting demonstrates, by its construction, contrivance and design. Contrivance must have had a contriver; design, a designer—whether the machine immediately proceeded from another machine or not. That circumstance alters not the case. That other machine may, in like manner, have proceeded from a former machine—nor does that alter the case; contrivance must have had a contriver. That former one from one preceding it—no alteration still, a contriver is still necessary. No tendency is perceived, no approach towards a diminution of this necessity. It is the same with any and every succession of these machines; a succession of ten, of a hundred, of a thousand; with one series, as with another; a series which is finite, as with a series which is infinite. In whatever other respects they may differ, in this they do not. In all equally, contrivance and design are unaccounted for. . . .

CHAPTER III. APPLICATION OF THE ARGUMENT

. . . Every indication of contrivance, every manifestation of design which existed in the watch, exists in the works of nature—with the difference, on the side of nature, of being greater and more, and that in a degree which exceeds all computation. I mean that the contrivances of nature surpass the contrivances of art in the complexity, subtlety, and curiosity of the mechanism; and still more, if possible, do they go beyond them in number and variety; yet, in a multitude of cases, are not less evidently mechanical, not less evidently contrivances, not less evidently accommodated to their end or suited to their office, than are the most perfect productions of human ingenuity.

I know no better method of introducing so large a subject, than that of comparing a single thing with a single thing—an eye, for example, with a telescope. As far as the examination of the instrument goes, there is precisely the same proof that the eye was made for vision, as there is that the telescope was made for assisting it. They are made upon the same principles, both being adjusted to the laws by which the transmission and refraction of rays of light are regulated. I speak not of the origin of the laws themselves; but, such laws being fixed, the construction in both cases is adapted to them. For instance, these laws require, in order to produce the same effect, that the rays of light, in passing from water into the eye, should be refracted by a more convex surface than when it passes out of air into the eye. Accordingly we find that the eye of a fish, in that part of it called the crystalline lens, is much rounder than the eye of terrestrial animals. What plainer manifestation of design can there be than this difference? What could a mathematical instrument maker have done more, to show his knowledge of his principle, his application of that knowledge, his suiting of his means to his end? I will not say to display the compass or excellence of his skill and art, for in these all comparison is indecorous, but to testify counsel, choice, consideration, purpose. . . .

CHAPTER V. APPLICATION OF THE ARGUMENT CONTINUED

. . . When we are inquiring simply after the *existence* of an intelligent Creator, imperfection, inaccuracy, liability to disorder, occasional irregularities, may subsist in a considerable degree without inducing any doubt into the question— just as a watch may frequently go wrong, seldom perhaps exactly right, may be faulty in some parts, defective in some, without the smallest ground of suspicion from thence arising that it was not a watch, not made, or not made for the purpose ascribed to it. When faults are pointed out and when a question is started concerning the skill of the artist or dexterity with which the work is executed, then indeed, in order to defend these qualities from accusation, we must be able either to expose some intractableness and imperfection in the materials or point out some invincible difficulty in the execution, into which imperfection and difficulty the matter of complaint may be resolved; or if we cannot do this, we must adduce such specimens of consummate art and contrivance, proceeding from the same hand, as may convince the inquirer of the existence, in the case before him, of impediments like those which we have mentioned, although, what from the nature of the case is very likely to happen, they be unknown and unperceived by him. This we must do in order to vindicate the artist's skill, or at least the perfection of it—as we must also judge of his intention, and of the provisions employed in fulfilling that intention, not from an instance in which they fail, but from the great plurality of instances in which they succeed. But after all, these are different questions from the question of the artist's existence, or (which is the same) whether the thing before us be a work of art or not. And the questions ought always to be kept separate in the mind. So likewise it is in the works of nature. Irregularities and imperfections are of little or no weight in the consideration, when that consideration relates simply to the existence of a Creator. When the argument respects his attributes, they are of weight; but are then to be taken in conjunction (the attention is not to rest upon them, but they are to be taken in conjunction) with the unexceptionable evidences which we possess of skill, power, and benevolence displayed in other instances—which evidences may, in strength, number, and variety, be such, and may so overpower apparent blemishes, as to induce us, upon the most reasonable ground, to believe that these last ought to be referred to some cause, though we be ignorant of it, other than defect of knowledge or of benevolence in the author.

The Blind Watchmaker

Richard Dawkins

Richard Dawkins was born in 1941 in Nairobi, Kenya, where his father worked for the British Colonial Service. In 1949 his family returned to England, where he was educated at boarding schools and then at Oxford University. He chose to study zoology mainly as a way to explore the philosophical implications of evolution and the negative impact of evolutionary theory on religion. He pursued graduate studies in zoology at Oxford under Nobel Prize–winning ethologist Niko Tinbergen and received his doctorate in 1966. Dawkins then accepted a position at the University of California at Berkeley, where he taught from 1967 to 1969. The following year he returned to Oxford to become a lecturer in zoology and a fellow of New College. He was appointed a reader in zoology at Oxford in 1991, and Charles Simonyi Professor of Public Understanding of Science in 1995. He retired in 2008. Among his awards are the Royal Society of Literature Award (1987), the Los Angeles Times Literary Prize (1987), the Zoological Society of London Silver Medal (1989), the Royal Society of London's Michael Faraday Award (1990), appointment to the Royal Society of Literature (1997), and the Lewis Thomas Prize for Writing about Science (2006).

Dawkins's books include *The Selfish Gene* (1976, translated into fifteen languages), *The Extended Phenotype: The Gene as the Unit of Selection* (1982), *The Blind Watchmaker: Why the Evidence of Evolution Reveals a Universe without Design* (1986, translated into thirteen languages); *River out of Eden: A Darwinian View of Life* (1995), *Unweaving the Rainbow: Science, Delusion, and the Appetite for Wonder* (1998), *The God Delusion* (2006), and *The Greatest Show on Earth: The Evidence for Evolution* (2009).

Our selection is from *The Blind Watchmaker*. As Dawkins explains, the title alludes to a famous argument advanced by William Paley in his book *Natural Theology* (1802). Paley asks us to imagine walking across a field and finding a watch lying on the ground. The fact that all its parts work together for the purpose of measuring time would lead us to conclude that it was made by an intelligent artisan. Since living organisms are much more complex than any artificial objects, the natural world must be the product of a supremely intelligent designer—namely, God. (Paley's argument appears on pp. 55–62 of this book.) Dawkins agrees with Paley that organisms are entirely too complex to have arisen all at once by some chance occurrence, but he believes that the complexity can be fully explained by the theory of evolution. He argues that although Paley's argument was plausible in his own day, the discoveries of modern biological science have made an appeal to a conscious designer unnecessary.

Dawkins explains that the theory of evolution does not contend that any organism arose through some single chance event; each organism is the end product of a long sequence of minor transformations, each one of which was small enough to have happened by chance. Species of organisms evolve through a gradual process of "natural selection"—if an organism acquires a trait that enables it to adapt to its environment, it will survive and transmit this trait to its offspring. Natural selection is *cumulative* selection; the new traits that occur randomly in organisms are slight variations on traits already possessed by the previous generation. Cumulative selection differs from single-step selection, which does *not* build on previous variations. If natural selection were single-step selection, it admittedly would be unable to account for the complexity of organisms. Dawkins argues that the

63

cumulative nature of natural selection adequately explains the origin of species: The "designer" of species is natural selection, and natural selection is blind.

CHAPTER 1. EXPLAINING THE VERY IMPROBABLE

We animals are the most complicated things in the known universe. The universe that we know, of course, is a tiny fragment of the actual universe. There may be yet more complicated objects than us on other planets, and some of them may already know about us. But this doesn't alter the point that I want to make. Complicated things, everywhere, deserve a very special kind of explanation. We want to know how they came into existence and why they are so complicated. . . .

The process by which an airliner came into existence is not fundamentally mysterious to us, because humans built it. The systematic putting together of parts to a purposeful design is something we know and understand, for we have experienced it at first hand, even if only with our childhood Meccano or Erector set.

What about our own bodies? Each one of us is a machine, like an airliner only much more complicated. Were we designed on a drawing board too, and were our parts assembled by a skilled engineer? The answer is no. It is a surprising answer, and we have known and understood it for only a century or so. When Charles Darwin[1] first explained the matter, many people either wouldn't or couldn't grasp it. I myself flatly refused to believe Darwin's theory when I first heard about it as a child. Almost everybody throughout history, up to the second half of the nineteenth century, has firmly believed in the opposite—the conscious designer theory. Many people still do, perhaps because the true, Darwinian explanation of our own existence is still, remarkably, not a routine part of the curriculum of a general education. It is certainly very widely misunderstood.

The watchmaker of my title is borrowed from a famous treatise by the eighteenth-century theologian William Paley. His *Natural Theology; or, Evidences of the Existence and Attributes of the Deity, Collected from the Appearances of Nature*, published in 1802, is the best-known exposition of the "Argument from Design," always the most influential of the arguments for the existence of a God. It is a book that I greatly admire, for in his own time its author succeeded in doing what I am struggling to do now. He had a point to make, he passionately believed in it, and he spared no effort to ram it home clearly. He had a proper reverence for the complexity of the living world, and he saw that it demands a very special kind of explanation. The only thing he got wrong—admittedly quite a big thing!—was the explanation itself. He gave the traditional religious answer to the riddle, but he articulated it more clearly and convincingly than anybody had before. The true explanation is utterly different, and it had to wait for one of the most revolutionary thinkers of all time, Charles Darwin.

---

[1]Darwin (1809–1892) was an English naturalist. He formulated the theory of natural selection, which states that if an organism develops traits that enable it to adapt to its environment, it will survive and transmit these traits to its offspring, and that if the organism *fails* to develop adaptive traits, it will perish. [D. C. ABEL]

Paley begins *Natural Theology* with a famous passage:

> In crossing a heath, suppose I pitched my foot against a stone and were asked
> how the stone came to be there. I might possibly answer, that, for anything I knew
> to the contrary, it had lain there forever; nor would it perhaps be very easy to
> show the absurdity of this answer. But suppose I had found a *watch* upon the
> ground and it should be inquired how the watch happened to be in that place.
> I should hardly think of the answer which I had given before, that, for anything
> I knew, the watch might have always been there.[2]

Paley here appreciates the difference between natural physical objects like
stones, and designed and manufactured objects like watches. He goes on to
expound the precision with which the cogs and springs of a watch are fashioned, and the intricacy with which they are put together. If we found an object
such as a watch upon a heath, even if we didn't know how it had come into
existence, its own precision and intricacy of design would force us to conclude:

> that the watch must have had a maker that there must have existed, at some time
> and at some place or other, an artificer or artificers who formed it for the purpose
> which we find it actually to answer, who comprehended its construction and
> designed its use.

Nobody could reasonably dissent from this conclusion, Paley insists, yet that
is just what the atheist, in effect, does when he contemplates the works of
nature, for:

> every indication of contrivance, every manifestation of design, which existed in
> the watch, exists in the works of nature—with the difference, on the side of nature,
> of being greater and more, and that in a degree which exceeds all computation.

Paley drives his point home with beautiful and reverent descriptions of the dis-
sected machinery of life, beginning with the human eye, a favorite example that
Darwin was later to use. . . . Paley compares the eye with a designed instrument
such as a telescope, and concludes that "there is precisely the same proof that
the eye was made for vision, as there is that the telescope was made for
assisting it." The eye must have had a designer, just as the telescope had.

Paley's argument is made with passionate sincerity and is informed by the
best biological scholarship of his day, but it is wrong, gloriously and utterly
wrong. The analogy between telescope and eye, between watch and living
organism, is false. All appearances to the contrary, the only watchmaker in
nature is the blind forces of physics, albeit deployed in a very special way. A true
watchmaker has foresight: He designs his cogs and springs, and plans their
interconnections, with a future purpose in his mind's eye. Natural selection, the
blind, unconscious, automatic process that Darwin discovered, and that we now
know is the explanation for the existence and apparently purposeful form of all
life, has no purpose in mind. It has no mind and no mind's eye. It does not plan
for the future. It has no vision, no foresight, no sight at all. If it can be said to play
the role of watchmaker in nature, it is the *blind* watchmaker.

---

[2]This passage appears on pp. 55–56 of this book; a biography of Paley appears on p. 55. [D. C. ABEL]

I shall explain all this, and much else besides. But one thing I shall not do is belittle the wonder of the living "watches" that so inspired Paley. On the contrary, I shall try to illustrate my feeling that here Paley could have gone even further. When it comes to feeling awe over living "watches" I yield to nobody. I feel more in common with the Reverend William Paley than I do with the distinguished modern philosopher, a well-known atheist, with whom I once discussed the matter at dinner. I said that I could not imagine being an atheist at any time before 1859, when Darwin's *Origin of Species* was published. "What about Hume?"[3] replied the philosopher. "How did Hume explain the organized complexity of the living world?" I asked. "He didn't," said the philosopher. "Why does it need any special explanation?"

Paley knew that it needed a special explanation; Darwin knew it, and I suspect that in his heart of hearts my philosopher companion knew it too. In any case it will be my business to show it here. As for David Hume himself, it is sometimes said that that great Scottish philosopher disposed of the argument from design a century before Darwin. But what Hume did was criticize the logic of using apparent design in nature as *positive* evidence for the existence of a God. He did not offer any *alternative* explanation for apparent design, but left the question open. An atheist before Darwin could have said, following Hume: "I have no explanation for complex biological design. All I know is that God isn't a good explanation, so we must wait and hope that somebody comes up with a better one." I can't help feeling that such a position, though logically sound, would have left one feeling pretty unsatisfied, and that although atheism might have been *logically* tenable before Darwin, Darwin made it possible to be an intellectually fulfilled atheist. I like to think that Hume would agree, but some of his writings suggest that he underestimated the complexity and beauty of biological design. The boy naturalist Charles Darwin could have shown him a thing or two about that, but Hume had been dead 40 years when Darwin enrolled in Hume's University of Edinburgh. . . .

CHAPTER 3. ACCUMULATING SMALL CHANGE

. . . Living things are too improbable and too beautifully "designed" to have come into existence by chance. How, then, did they come into existence? The answer, Darwin's answer, is by gradual, step-by-step transformations from simple beginnings, from primordial entities sufficiently simple to have come into existence by chance. Each successive change in the gradual evolutionary process was simple enough, *relative to its predecessor,* to have arisen by chance. But the whole sequence of cumulative steps constitutes anything but a chance process, when you consider the complexity of the final end-product relative to the original starting point. The cumulative process is directed by nonrandom survival. The purpose of this chapter is to demonstrate the power of this *cumulative selection* as a fundamentally nonrandom process.

---

[3]David Hume (1711–1776) was a Scottish philosopher and historian; for a biography, see p. 46. [D. C. ABEL]

If you walk up and down a pebbly beach, you will notice that the pebbles are not arranged at random. The smaller pebbles typically tend to be found in segregated zones running along the length of the beach, the larger ones in different zones or stripes. The pebbles have been sorted, arranged, selected. A tribe living near the shore might wonder at this evidence of sorting or arrangement in the world, and might develop a myth to account for it, perhaps attributing it to a Great Spirit in the sky with a tidy mind and a sense of order. We might give a superior smile at such a superstitious notion, and explain that the arranging was really done by the blind forces of physics, in this case the action of waves. The waves have no purposes and no intentions, no tidy mind, no mind at all. They just energetically throw the pebbles around, and big pebbles and small pebbles respond differently to this treatment so they end up at different levels of the beach. A small amount of order has come out of disorder, and no mind planned it.

The waves and the pebbles together constitute a simple example of a system that automatically generates nonrandomness. The world is full of such systems. The simplest example I can think of is a hole. Only objects smaller than the hole can pass through it. This means that if you start with a random collection of objects above the hole, and some force shakes and jostles them about at random, after a while the objects above and below the hole will come to be nonrandomly sorted. The space below the hole will tend to contain objects smaller than the hole, and the space above will tend to contain objects larger than the hole. Mankind has, of course, long exploited this simple principle for generating nonrandomness, in the useful device known as the sieve.

The solar system is a stable arrangement of planets, comets, and debris orbiting the sun, and it is presumably one of many such orbiting systems in the universe. The nearer a satellite is to its sun, the faster it has to travel if it is to counter the sun's gravity and remain in stable orbit. For any given orbit, there is only one speed at which a satellite can travel and remain in that orbit. If it were travelling at any other velocity, it would either move out into deep space, or crash into the sun, or move into another orbit. And if we look at the planets of our solar system, lo and behold, every single one of them is travelling at exactly the right velocity to keep it in its stable orbit around the sun. A blessed miracle of provident design? No, just another natural "sieve." Obviously all the planets that we see orbiting the sun must be travelling at exactly the right speed to keep them in their orbits, or we wouldn't see them there because they wouldn't be there! But equally obviously this is not evidence for conscious design. It is just another kind of sieve.

Sieving of this order of simplicity is not, on its own, enough to account for the massive amounts of nonrandom order that we see in living things. Nowhere near enough. . . . The kind of nonrandomness that can be generated by simple sieving is roughly equivalent to opening a combination lock with only one dial: It is easy to open it by sheer luck. The kind of nonrandomness that we see in living systems, on the other hand, is equivalent to a gigantic combination lock with an almost uncountable number of dials. To generate a biological molecule like hemoglobin, the red pigment in blood, by simple sieving would be equiva-lent to taking all the amino-acid building blocks of hemoglobin, jumbling them up at random, and hoping that the hemoglobin molecule would reconstitute itself by sheer luck. The amount of luck that would be required for this feat is unthinkable, and has been used as a telling mind-boggler by Isaac Asimov[4] and others.

A hemoglobin molecule consists of four chains of amino acids twisted together. Let us think about just one of these four chains. It consists of 146 amino acids. There are 20 different kinds of amino acids commonly found in living things. The number of possible ways of arranging 20 kinds of thing in chains 146 links long is an inconceivably large number, which Asimov calls the "hemoglobin number." It is easy to calculate, but impossible to visualize the answer. The first link in the 146-long chain could be any one of the 20, so the number of possible 2-link chains is 20 × 20, or 400. The number of possible 3-link chains is 20 × 20 × 20, or 8000. The number of possible 146-link chains is 20 times itself 146 times. This is a staggeringly large number. A million is a 1 with 6 naughts after it. A billion (1000 million) is a 1 with 9 naughts after it. The number we seek, the "hemoglobin number," is (near enough) a 1 with 190 naughts after it! This is the chance against happening to hit upon hemoglobin by luck. And a hemoglobin molecule has only a minute fraction of the complexity of a living body. Simple sieving, on its own, is obviously nowhere near capable of generating the amount of order in a living thing. Sieving is an essential ingredient in the generation of living order, but it is very far from being the whole story. Something else is needed. To explain the point, I shall need to make a distinction between "single-step" selection and "cumulative" selection. The simple sieves we have been considering so far in this chapter are all examples of single-step selection. Living organization is the product of cumulative selection.

The essential difference between single-step selection and cumulative selection is this. In single-step selection the entities selected or sorted, pebbles or whatever they are, are sorted once and for all. In cumulative selection, on the other hand, they "reproduce"; or in some other way the results of one sieving process are fed into a subsequent sieving, which is fed into . . . , and so on. The entities are subjected to selection or sorting over many "generations" in succession. The end-product of one generation of selection is the starting point for the next generation of selection, and so on for many generations. It is natural to borrow such words as "reproduce" and "generation," which have associations with living things, because living things are the main examples we know of things that participate in cumulative selection. They may in practice be the only things that do. But for the moment I don't want to beg that question by saying so outright.

Sometimes clouds, through the random kneading and carving of the winds, come to look like familiar objects. There is a much published photograph, taken by the pilot of a small airplane, of what looks a bit like the face of Jesus, staring out of the sky. We have all seen clouds that reminded us of something—a sea horse, say, or a smiling face. These resemblances come about by single-step selection, that is to say by a single coincidence. They are, consequently, not very impressive. The resemblance of the signs of the zodiac to the animals after

---

[4]Asimov (1920–1992) was an American biochemist and author, known mainly for his science fiction novels. [D. C. ABEL]

which they are named, Scorpio, Leo, and so on, is as unimpressive as the predictions of astrologers. We don't feel overwhelmed by the resemblance, as we are by biological adaptations—the products of cumulative selection. We describe as weird, uncanny or spectacular, the resemblance of, say, a leaf insect to a leaf or a praying mantis to a cluster of pink flowers. The resemblance of a cloud to a weasel is only mildly diverting, barely worth calling to the attention of our companion. Moreover, we are quite likely to change our mind about exactly what the cloud most resembles.

Hamlet.	Do you see yonder cloud that's almost in shape of a camel?
Polonius.	By the mass, and 'tis like a camel, indeed.
Hamlet.	Methinks it is like a weasel.
Polonius.	It is backed like a weasel.
Hamlet.	Or like a whale?
Polonius.	Very like a whale.[5]

I don't know who it was first pointed out that, given enough time, a monkey bashing away at random on a typewriter could produce all the works of Shakespeare. The operative phrase is, of course, given enough time. Let us limit the task facing our monkey somewhat. Suppose that he has to produce, not the complete works of Shakespeare but just the short sentence "Methinks it is like a weasel," and we shall make it relatively easy by giving him a typewriter with a restricted keyboard, one with just the 26 (capital) letters and a space bar. How long will he take to write this one little sentence?

The sentence has 28 characters in it, so let us assume that the monkey has a series of discrete "tries," each consisting of 28 bashes at the keyboard. If he types the phrase correctly, that is the end of the experiment. If not, we allow him another "try" of 28 characters. I don't know any monkeys, but fortunately my 11-month-old daughter is an experienced randomizing device, and she proved only too eager to step into the role of monkey typist. Here is what she typed on the computer:

```
UMMK JK CDZZ F ZD DSDSKSM
S SS FMCV PU I DDRGLKDXRRDO
RDTE QDWFDVIOY UDSKZWDCCVYT
H CHVY NMGNBAYTDFCCVD D
RCDFYYYRM N DFSKD LD K WDWK
JJKAUIZMZI UXDKIDISFUMDKUDXI
```

She has other important calls on her time, so I was obliged to program the computer to simulate a randomly typing baby or monkey:

```
WDLDMNLT DTJBKWIRZREZLMQCO P
Y YVMQKZPGJXWVHGLAWFVCHQYOPY
MWR SWTNUXMLCDLEUBXTQHNZVJQF
FU OVAODVYKDGXDEKYVMOGGS VT
HZQZDSFZIHIVPHZPETPWVOVPMZGF
GEWRGZRPBCTPGQMCKHFDBGW ZCCF
```

---

[5] William Shakespeare, *Hamlet,* Act III, Scene 2, lines 384–390. [D. C. ABEL]

And so on and on. It isn't difficult to calculate how long we should reasonably expect to wait for the random computer (or baby or monkey) to type METHINKS IT IS LIKE A WEASEL. Think about the total number of *possible* phrases of the right length that the monkey or baby or random computer *could* type. It is the same kind of calculation as we did for hemoglobin, and it produces a similarly large result. There are 27 possible letters (counting "space" as one letter) in the first position. The chance of the monkey happening to get the first letter—M—right is therefore 1 in 27. The chance of it getting the first two letters—ME—right is the chance of it getting the second letter—E—right (1 in 27) *given that* it has also got the first letter—M—right, therefore $1/27 \times 1/27$, which equals 1/729. The chance of it getting the first word—METHINKS— right is 1/27 for each of the 8 letters, therefore $(1/27) \times (1/27) \times (1/27) \times (1/27) \ldots$, and so on, 8 times, or (1/27) to the power 8. The chance of it getting the entire phrase of 28 characters right is (1/27) to the power 28— that is, (1/27) multiplied by itself 28 times. These are very small odds, about 1 in 10,000 million million million million million million. To put it mildly, the phrase we seek would be a long time coming, to say nothing of the complete works of Shakespeare.

So much for single-step selection of random variation. What about cumulative selection; how much more effective should this be? Very, very much more effective, perhaps more so than we at first realize, although it is almost obvious when we reflect further. We again use our computer monkey, but with a crucial difference in its program. It again begins by choosing a random sequence of 28 letters, just as before:

WDLMNLT DTJBKWIRZREZLMQCO P

It now "breeds from" this random phrase. It duplicates it repeatedly, but with a certain chance of random error—"mutation"—in the copying. The computer examines the mutant nonsense phrases, the "progeny" of the original phrase, and chooses the one that, *however slightly,* most resembles the target phrase, METHINKS IT IS LIKE A WEASEL. In this instance the winning phrase of the next "generation" happened to be:

WDLTMNLT DTJBSWIRZREZLMQCO P

Not an obvious improvement! But the procedure is repeated, again mutant "progeny" are "bred from" the phrase, and a new "winner" is chosen. This goes on, generation after generation. After 10 generations, the phrase chosen for "breeding" was:

MDLDMNLS ITJISWHRZREZ MECS P

After 20 generations it was:

MELDINLS IT ISWPRKE Z WECSEL

By now, the eye of faith fancies that it can see a resemblance to the target phrase. By 30 generations there can be no doubt:

METHINGS IT ISWLIKE B WECSEL

Generation 40 takes us to within one letter of the target:

METHINKS IT IS LIKE I WEASEL

And the target was finally reached in generation 43. A second run of the computer began with the phrase:

Y YVMQKZPFJXWVHGLAWFVCHQXYOPY,

passed through (again reporting only every tenth generation):

Y YVMQKSPFTXWSHLIKEFV HQYSPY
YETHINKSPITXISHLIKEFA WQYSEY
METHINKS IT ISSLIKE A WEFSEY
METHINKS IT ISBLIKE A WEASES
METHINKS IT ISJLIKE A WEASEO
METHINKS IT IS LIKE A WEASEP

and reached the target phrase in generation 64. In a third run the computer started with:

GEWRGZRPBCTPGQMCKHFDBGW ZCCF

and reached METHINKS IT IS LIKE A WEASEL in 41 generations of selective "breeding."

The exact time taken by the computer to reach the target doesn't matter. If you want to know, it completed the whole exercise for me, the first time, while I was out to lunch. It took about half an hour. (Computer enthusiasts may think this unduly slow. The reason is that the program was written in BASIC, a sort of computer baby-talk. When I rewrote it in Pascal, it took 11 seconds.) Computers are a bit faster at this kind of thing than monkeys, but the difference really isn't significant. What matters is the difference between the time taken by *cumulative* selection, and the time that the same computer, working flat out at the same rate, would take to reach the target phrase if it were forced to use the other procedure of *single-step selection:* about a million million million million million years. This is more than a million million million times as long as the universe has so far existed. Actually it would be fairer just to say that, in comparison with the time it would take either a monkey or a randomly programmed computer to type our target phrase, the total age of the universe so far is a negligibly small quantity, so small as to be well within the margin of error for this sort of back-of-an-envelope calculation. Whereas the time taken for a computer working randomly but with the constraint of *cumulative selection* to perform the same task is of the same order as humans ordinarily can understand, between 11 seconds and the time it takes to have lunch.

There is a big difference, then, between cumulative selection (in which each improvement, however slight, is used as a basis for future building) and single-step selection (in which each new "try" is a fresh one). If evolutionary progress had had to rely on single-step selection, it would never have got anywhere. If, however, there was any way in which the necessary conditions for *cumulative* selection could have been set up by the blind forces of nature, strange and wonderful might have been the consequences. As a matter of fact that is exactly what happened on this planet, and we ourselves are among the most recent, if not the strangest and most wonderful, of those consequences.

It is amazing that you can still read calculations like my hemoglobin calculation, used as though they constituted arguments *against* Darwin's theory. The people who do this, often expert in their own field, astronomy or whatever it may be, seem sincerely to believe that Darwinism explains living organization in terms of chance—"single-step selection"—alone. This belief, that Darwinian evolution is "random," is not merely false. It is the exact opposite of the truth. Chance is a minor ingredient in the Darwinian recipe, but the most important ingredient is cumulative selection that is quintessentially *non*random. . . .

CHAPTER 11. DOOMED RIVALS

. . . We have dealt with all the alleged alternatives to the theory of natural selection except the oldest one. This is the theory that life was created, or its evolution master-minded, by a conscious designer. It would obviously be unfairly easy to demolish some particular version of this theory such as the one (or it may be two) spelled out in Genesis. Nearly all peoples have developed their own creation myth, and the Genesis story is just the one that happened to have been adopted by one particular tribe of Middle Eastern herders. It has no more special status than the belief of a particular West African tribe that the world was created from the excrement of ants. All these myths have in common that they depend upon the deliberate intentions of some kind of supernatural being.

At first sight there is an important distinction to be made between what might be called "instantaneous creation" and "guided evolution." Modern theologians of any sophistication have given up believing in instantaneous creation. The evidence for some sort of evolution has become too overwhelming. But many theologians who call themselves evolutionists . . . smuggle God in by the back door: They allow him some sort of supervisory role over the course that evolution has taken, either influencing key moments in evolutionary history (especially, of course, *human* evolutionary history), or even meddling more comprehensively in the day-to-day events that add up to evolutionary change.

We cannot disprove beliefs like these, especially if it is assumed that God took care that his interventions always closely mimicked what would be expected from evolution by natural selection. All that we can say about such beliefs is, firstly, that they are superfluous and, secondly, that they *assume* the existence of the main thing we want to *explain,* namely organized complexity. The one thing that makes evolution such a neat theory is that it explains how organized complexity can arise out of primeval simplicity.

If we want to postulate a deity capable of engineering all the organized complexity in the world, either instantaneously or by guiding evolution, that deity must already have been vastly complex in the first place. The creationist, whether a naive Bible-thumper or an educated bishop, simply *postulates* an already existing being of prodigious intelligence and complexity. If we are going to allow ourselves the luxury of postulating organized complexity without offering an explanation, we might as well make a job of it and simply postulate the existence of life as we know it! . . . The theory of evolution by cumulative natural selection is the only theory we know of that is in principle *capable* of explaining the existence of organized complexity. Even if the evidence did not favor it, it would *still* be the best theory available! In fact the evidence does favor it. But that is another story.

Let us hear the conclusion of the whole matter. The essence of life is statistical improbability on a colossal scale. Whatever is the explanation for life, therefore, it cannot be chance. The true explanation for the existence of life must embody the very antithesis of chance. The antithesis of chance is nonrandom survival, properly understood. Nonrandom survival, improperly understood, is not the antithesis of chance, it is chance itself. There is a continuum connecting these two extremes, and it is the continuum from single-step selection to cumulative selection. Single-step selection is just another way of saying pure chance. This is what I mean by nonrandom survival improperly understood. *Cumulative selection,* by slow and gradual degrees, is the explanation, the only workable explanation that has ever been proposed, for the existence of life's complex design.

The whole book has been dominated by the idea of chance, by the astronomically long odds against the spontaneous arising of order, complexity and apparent design. We have sought a way of taming chance, of drawing its fangs. "Untamed chance," pure, naked chance, means ordered design springing into existence from nothing, in a single leap. It would be untamed chance if once there was no eye, and then, suddenly, in the twinkling of a generation, an eye appeared, fully fashioned, perfect and whole. This is possible, but the odds against it will keep us busy writing naughts till the end of time. The same applies to the odds against the spontaneous existence of any fully fashioned, perfect and whole beings, including—I see no way of avoiding the conclusion—deities.

To "tame" chance means to break down the very improbable into less improbable small components arranged in series. No matter how improbable it is that an X could have arisen from a Y in a single step, it is always possible to conceive of a series of infinitesimally graded intermediates between them. However improbable a large-scale change may be, smaller changes are less improbable. And provided we postulate a sufficiently large series of sufficiently finely graded intermediates, we shall be able to derive anything from anything else, without invoking astronomical improbabilities. We are allowed to do this only if there has been sufficient time to fit all the intermediates in. And also only if there is a mechanism for guiding each step in some particular direction—otherwise the sequence of steps will career off in an endless random walk.

It is the contention of the Darwinian worldview that both these provisos are met, and that slow, gradual, cumulative natural selection is the ultimate explanation for our existence. If there are versions of the evolution theory that deny slow gradualism, and deny the central role of natural selection, they may be true in particular cases. But they cannot be the whole truth, for they deny the very heart of the evolution theory, which gives it the power to dissolve astronomical improbabilities and explain prodigies of apparent miracle.

B. The Problem of Evil

READING 8

On Free Choice of the Will

Augustine

Augustine was born in 354 in the town of Tagaste in northern Africa (now Souk-Ahras, Algeria). As a youth he received instruction in Christianity but was not baptized. At 17, he went to Carthage to study rhetoric, which he later taught at Tagaste, Carthage, Rome, and Milan. In 373 Augustine became a member of the Manichaean religion, which held that the equally powerful forces of Light (goodness) and Darkness (evil) govern the universe. Ten years later he abandoned Manichaeism and became attracted to skepticism, the view that it is impossible to attain truth. Augustine then became deeply influenced by the works of Plotinus, an Egyptian-born Roman philosopher who saw himself carrying forward the theories of Plato. When teaching in Milan, Augustine went to hear the sermons of the Catholic bishop Ambrose to study their rhetorical style, but he ended up paying attention to their content. After a dramatic conversion experience, he was baptized by Ambrose in 387. Augustine returned to Tagaste, where he and some friends set up a sort of monastery. In 391 he was ordained a priest at Hippo (now Annaba, Algeria) and four years later became bishop. He remained bishop until his death in 430. Augustine's works include *On Free Choice of the Will* (begun in 388, finished in 395), the *Confessions* (his autobiography, written between 397 and 401), *On the Trinity* (399–419), and *The City of God* (413–426).

Our reading is from Book I of *On Free Choice of the Will,* a work cast as a dialogue between Augustine and his friend Evodius. The topic of the conversation is stated by Evodius in the opening line: "Please tell me: Isn't God the cause of evil?" Augustine begins his answer to Evodius's question by distinguishing the evil that people *suffer* from the evil that they *do*. He argues that God causes the former kind of evil as just punishment for people's sins, but that God does not cause the latter kind. Evildoers themselves are the cause of the evil they commit because they choose evil by their own free will (hence the title of the dialogue). Augustine holds that the essence of all evildoing is inordinate desire, and that inordinate desire consists of pursuing temporal and changeable things, which can be lost against our will, at the expense of eternal and unchangeable things, which cannot be lost against our will. Because the mind is stronger than desire, if we yield to temptation and choose the temporal and changeable over the eternal and unchangeable, we do so through our own free choice. And because our evildoing is voluntary, it is just for God to punish us for it.

BOOK ONE

Chapter 1

> EVODIUS: Please tell me: Isn't God the cause of evil?
>
> AUGUSTINE: I will tell you once you have made clear what kind of evil you are asking about. For we use the word "evil" in two senses: first, when

we say that someone has *done* evil; and second, when we say that someone has *suffered* evil.

EVODIUS: I want to know about both.

AUGUSTINE: But if you know or believe that God is good—and it is not right to believe otherwise—then he does no evil. On the other hand, if we acknowledge that God is just—and it is impious to deny it—then he rewards the good and punishes the wicked. Those punishments are certainly evils for those who suffer them. Therefore, if no one is punished unjustly—and we must believe this, since we believe that this universe is governed by divine providence—it follows that God is a cause of the second kind of evil, but in no way causes the first kind.

EVODIUS: Then is there some other cause of the evil that God does not cause?

AUGUSTINE: There certainly is. Such evil could not occur unless someone caused it. But if you ask who that someone is, it is impossible to say. For there is no single cause of evil; rather, everyone who does evil is the cause of his own evildoing. If you doubt this, recall what I said earlier: Evil deeds are punished by the justice of God. They would not be punished unjustly if they had not been performed voluntarily.

EVODIUS: It seems that no one could sin unless he had first learned how to sin. And if that is the case, I must ask this: From whom did we learn to sin?

AUGUSTINE: Do you think learning is a good thing?

EVODIUS: Who would dare to say that learning is a bad thing?

AUGUSTINE: What if it is neither good nor bad?

EVODIUS: I think it is good.

AUGUSTINE: Indeed it is, since knowledge is given or awakened through learning, and no one comes to know anything except through learning. Don't you agree?

EVODIUS: I think that we come to know only good things through learning.

AUGUSTINE: Then we do not come to know evil things; for the word "learning" is correctly applied only when we come to know something.

EVODIUS: But if we do not come to know evil things, how is it that human beings perform evil acts?

AUGUSTINE: Perhaps because they turn away from learning and become strangers to it. But whether that is the correct explanation or not, one thing is certainly clear: Since learning is good, and the word "learning" is correctly applied only when we come to know something, we simply cannot come to know evil things. If we could, then they would be part of learning, and so learning would not be a good thing. But it *is* a good thing, as you said yourself. Therefore, we do not come to know evil things, and there is no point in your asking from whom we learn to do evil things. Or else we do come to know them, but only as things to be avoided, not as things to be done. It follows that doing evil is nothing but running away from learning.

EVODIUS: I rather think that there are two sorts of learning: one by means of which we learn to do right, and another by means of which we learn to do evil. But when you asked whether learning was good, the love of good itself caught my attention, and I saw only the sort of learning by which we learn to do right. That is why I answered that it is good. But now I remember that there is another sort of learning. I have no doubt that it is evil, and I would like to know its cause.

AUGUSTINE: Do you at least consider understanding good?

EVODIUS: Certainly. I consider it so good that I cannot see how any human trait could be better. And I would in no way say that any understanding can be bad.

AUGUSTINE: When someone is being taught but does not understand, would you think that he has learned?

EVODIUS: Of course not.

AUGUSTINE: Well then, if all understanding is good, and no one who does not understand learns, then everyone who learns is doing good. For everyone who learns, understands; and everyone who understands is doing good. So someone who wants to know the cause of our learning something really wants to know the cause of our doing good. So let's have no more of your wanting to hunt down this mysterious evil teacher. If he is evil, he is no teacher; and if he is a teacher, he is not evil.

Chapter 2

EVODIUS: Now that you have convinced me that we do not learn to do evil, please explain to me what *is* the source of our evildoing.

AUGUSTINE: You have hit upon the very question that worried me greatly when I was still young, a question that wore me out, drove me into the company of heretics,[1] and knocked me flat on my face. I was so hurt by this fall, buried under a mountain of silly fairy tales, that if my love of finding the truth had not secured divine help, I would not have been able to get out from under them to breathe freely and begin to seek the truth. And since such pains were taken to free me from this difficulty, I will lead you on the same path that I followed in making my escape. God will be with us, and he will make us understand what we have believed. For we are well aware that we are at the stage described by the prophet, who says, "Unless you believe, you will not understand."[2] We believe that everything that exists comes from the one God, and yet we believe that God is not the cause of sins. What is troubling is that if you admit that sins come from the souls that God created, and those souls come from God, pretty soon you'll be tracing those sins back to God.

EVODIUS: You have stated plainly what bothers me in thinking about this question. That is the problem that has compelled me and drawn me into this inquiry.

---

[1]Augustine refers to the Manichaeans, who held that the source of evil is the principle of Darkness, which is in eternal combat with the principle of Light (goodness). [D. C. ABEL]

[2]Isaiah 7:9. The text of the Hebrew Scriptures that Augustine used was a Latin translation of the Greek Septuagint version. Sometimes, as here, the Septuagint rendering of the original Hebrew is inaccurate. The Hebrew of Isaiah 7:9 means "Have faith, or you will not stand firm" (New English Bible). [D. C. ABEL]

AUGUSTINE: Be courageous and go on believing what you believe. There is no better belief, even if you do not yet see the explanation for why it is true. The truest beginning of piety is to think as highly of God as possible; and doing so means that one must believe that he is omnipotent, and not changeable in the smallest respect; that he is the creator of all good things, but is himself more excellent than all of them; that he is the supremely just ruler of everything that he created; and that he was not aided in creating by any other being, as if he were not sufficiently powerful by himself. It follows that he created all things from nothing. He did not create from himself, but generated one who is equal to himself, whom we call the only Son of God. In trying to describe the Son more clearly we call him "the power of God and the wisdom of God,"[3] through whom God made all the things that were made from nothing. On that basis let us try, with God's help, to achieve an understanding of the problem you have raised.

Chapter 3

AUGUSTINE: You want to know the source of our evildoing. So we must first discuss what evildoing *is*. State your view on the matter. If you cannot explain the whole thing at once in a few words, you can at least show me your view by naming particular evil deeds.

EVODIUS: Adultery, murder, and sacrilege, not to mention others that time and memory do not permit me to enumerate. Who could fail to recognize these as evil deeds?

AUGUSTINE: Tell me first, why do you think adultery is evil? Because the law forbids it?

EVODIUS: On the contrary. Clearly, it is not evil because the law forbids it; rather, the law forbids it because it is evil.

AUGUSTINE: But suppose someone were to make things difficult for us by extolling the pleasures of adultery and asking why we think adultery evil and deserving of condemnation. Surely you do not think that people who want to understand, and not merely to believe, would have to take refuge in an appeal to the authority of the law? Now like you I do believe, and believe most firmly, and cry out that all peoples and nations should believe, that adultery is evil. But now we are attempting to know and hold firmly by understanding what we have already accepted by faith. So think this over as carefully as you can, and tell me what reason you have by which you know that adultery is evil.

EVODIUS: I know that it is evil because I would not tolerate it if someone tried to commit adultery with my own wife. Anyone who does to another what he does not want done to himself does evil.

AUGUSTINE: What if someone's lust is so great that he offers his wife to another and willingly allows him to commit adultery with her, and is eager to enjoy the same freedom with the other man's wife? Do you think that this man has done nothing evil?

---

[3] 1 Corinthians 1:24. [T. WILLIAMS, TRANSLATOR]

EVODIUS: Far from it!

AUGUSTINE: But by your rule he does not sin, since he is not doing anything that he is unwilling to have done to himself. You must therefore look for some other argument to show that adultery is evil.

EVODIUS: The reason that I think it is evil is that I have often seen people condemned for this crime.

AUGUSTINE: But haven't people often been condemned for good deeds? Not to refer you to any other books, recall the story that is superior to all others by virtue of its divine authority. There you will find that we must think very poorly of the apostles and martyrs if we intend to make condemnation a sure sign of wrongdoing. All of them were judged worthy of condemnation because of their confession of faith. It follows that if everything that is condemned is evil, it was evil in those days to believe in Christ and to confess that faith. But if not everything that is condemned is evil, find some other way to show why adultery is evil.

EVODIUS: I can't think how to respond.

AUGUSTINE: Then perhaps what makes adultery evil is inordinate desire, whereas so long as you look for the evil in the external, visible act, you are bound to encounter difficulties. In order to understand that inordinate desire is what makes adultery evil, consider this: If a man is unable to sleep with someone else's wife, but it is somehow clear that he would like to, and would do so if he had the chance, he is no less guilty than if he were caught in the act.

EVODIUS: Nothing could be clearer. Now I see that there is no need for a long discussion to persuade me that this is the case with murder and sacrilege and every sin whatsoever. For it is clear now that inordinate desire is what drives every kind of evildoing.

Chapter 4

AUGUSTINE: Do you know that inordinate desire is also called "cupidity"?

EVODIUS: Yes.

AUGUSTINE: Do you think there is any difference between cupidity and fear? Or are they quite the same?

EVODIUS: Indeed, I think there is a huge difference between the two.

AUGUSTINE: I suppose you think so because cupidity desires its object, and fear flees from it.

EVODIUS: You're quite right.

AUGUSTINE: Then suppose a man kills someone, not out of cupidity for something that he desires to gain, but because he fears that some harm will come to himself. Would he be a murderer?

EVODIUS: Yes, he would. But even in this deed, cupidity is the driving force—for a man who kills someone out of fear surely desires to live without fear.

AUGUSTINE: Do you think that living without fear is a small good?

EVODIUS: It is a great good, but that murderer cannot achieve it by his action.

AUGUSTINE: I am not asking what he can achieve, but what he desires. Someone who desires a life free from fear certainly desires a good thing, so his desire is not blameworthy; otherwise we will have to blame everyone who loves the good. Consequently, we will have to say that there is an instance of murder in which cupidity is not the driving force; and it will be false that inordinate desire is what drives all sins, to the extent that they are evil. Either that, or there will be an instance of murder that is not sinful.

EVODIUS: If murder is just killing a human being, then there can be murder that is not sinful. When a soldier kills the enemy, when a judge or his representative puts a criminal to death, or when a weapon accidentally slips out of someone's hand without his willing or noticing it—these people do not seem to me to be sinning when they kill someone.

AUGUSTINE: I agree, but such people are not usually called murderers. So consider someone who kills his master because he fears severe torture. Do you think that he should be classed among those who kill a human being but do not deserve to be called murderers?

EVODIUS: I think this case is entirely different. In the earlier examples, those men are acting in accordance with the law, or at least not contrary to the law; but no law approves of the deed in your example.

AUGUSTINE: Again you refer me to authority. You must remember that we took up this discussion in order to understand what we believe. We believe the laws, and so we must try to understand, if we can, whether the law that punishes this deed does so unjustly.

EVODIUS: It is in no way unjust to punish someone who knowingly and willingly kills his master. None of the men in my earlier examples did that.

AUGUSTINE: But do you not remember that a little while ago you said that inordinate desire is what drives every evil deed, and that this is the very reason why the deed is evil?

EVODIUS: Of course I remember.

AUGUSTINE: And did you not also grant that someone who desires to live without fear does not have an evil desire?

EVODIUS: I remember that too.

AUGUSTINE: It follows that, since the master is killed by the slave as a result of this desire, he is not killed as a result of a blameworthy desire. And so we have not yet figured out why this deed is evil. For we are agreed that all wrongdoing is evil only because it results from inordinate desire, that is, from blameworthy cupidity.

EVODIUS: At this point it seems to me that the slave is unjustly condemned, which I would not dream of saying if I could think of some other response.

AUGUSTINE: You have let yourself be persuaded that this great crime should go unpunished, without considering whether the slave wanted to be free of the fear of his master in order to satisfy his own inordinate desires. All wicked people, just like good people, desire to live without fear. The difference is that the good, in desiring this, turn their love away from things that cannot be possessed without the fear of losing them. The wicked, on the other hand, try to get rid of anything that prevents them from enjoying such things securely. Thus they lead a wicked and criminal life, which would better be called death.

EVODIUS: Now I've come to my senses. I am glad that I understand so clearly the nature of that blameworthy cupidity that is called inordinate desire. Obviously it is the love of those things that one can lose against one's will. . . .

Chapter 10

. . . AUGUSTINE: Do you think that inordinate desire is more powerful than the mind, which we know is granted control over inordinate desires by the eternal law? I do not think so at all, for it would violate perfect order if the weaker controlled the stronger. Therefore, I think the mind must be more powerful than cupidity, precisely because it is right and just for the mind to rule over cupidity.

EVODIUS: I think so too.

AUGUSTINE: And surely we do not doubt that every virtue is superior to every vice, so that the better and more sublime the virtue, the stronger and more invincible it is.

EVODIUS: Who could doubt that?

AUGUSTINE: Then no vicious spirit defeats a spirit armed with virtue.

EVODIUS: Quite correct.

AUGUSTINE: And I don't think you will deny that any sort of spirit is better and more powerful than any material object.

EVODIUS: No one will deny it who sees (as is easy to do) that a living substance is better than a nonliving one, and one that gives life is better than one that receives life.

AUGUSTINE: Much less, then, can a material object of any sort overpower a spirit endowed with virtue.

EVODIUS: That is quite obvious.

AUGUSTINE: Can a just spirit (a mind that is preserving its proper right and authority) take another mind that is ruling with the same equity and virtue, drive it from its stronghold, and subject it to inordinate desire?

EVODIUS: Not at all, for two reasons. First, each mind possesses the same degree of excellence. And second, any mind that would attempt such a thing must have already fallen from justice and become vicious, and therefore weaker.

AUGUSTINE: Very sharp. It remains for you to say, if you can, whether you think anything is superior to a rational and wise mind.

EVODIUS: Nothing but God, I think.

AUGUSTINE: That is my view as well. But it is a difficult matter, and this is not the time to attempt to come to understand it, although we hold it most firmly by faith. We must complete our careful and deliberate investigation of the question at hand.

Chapter 11

AUGUSTINE: In the present case we can be sure that whatever nature is by right superior to a mind empowered by virtue, it cannot be an unjust one. Therefore, even if it has the power to do so, it will not force the mind to be a slave to inordinate desire.

EVODIUS: Thus far there is nothing that anyone would have the smallest hesitation about accepting.

AUGUSTINE: The conclusions that we have reached thus far indicate that a mind that is in control (one that possesses virtue) cannot be made a slave to inordinate desire by anything equal or superior to it, because such a thing would be just, or by anything inferior to it, because such a thing would be too weak. Just one possibility remains: Only its own will and free choice can make the mind a companion of cupidity.

EVODIUS: I can't see any other alternative.

AUGUSTINE: Then you must also think that the mind justly suffers punishment for so great a sin.

EVODIUS: I cannot deny it.

AUGUSTINE: Surely the very fact that inordinate desire rules the mind is itself no small punishment. Stripped by opposing forces of the splendid wealth of virtue, the mind is dragged by inordinate desire into ruin and poverty; now taking false things for true, and even defending those falsehoods repeatedly; now repudiating what it had once believed and nonetheless rushing headlong into still other falsehoods; now withholding assent and often shying away from clear arguments; now despairing completely of finding the truth and lingering in the shadows of folly; now trying to enter the light of understanding but reeling back in exhaustion.

In the meantime cupidity carries out a reign of terror, buffeting the whole human soul and life with storms coming from every direction. Fear attacks from one side and desire from the other; from one side, anxiety; from the other, an empty and deceptive happiness; from one side, the agony of losing what one loved; from the other, the passion to acquire what one did not have; from one side, the pain of an injury received; from the other, the burning desire to avenge it. Wherever you turn, avarice can pinch, extravagance squander, ambition destroy, pride swell, envy torment, apathy crush, obstinacy incite, oppression chafe, and countless other evils crowd the realm of inordinate desire and run riot. In short, can we consider this punishment trivial—a punishment that, as you realize, all who do not cleave to wisdom must suffer? . . .

Chapter 12

. . . AUGUSTINE: . . . Tell me this: Do we have a will?

EVODIUS: I don't know.

AUGUSTINE: Do you want to know?

EVODIUS: I don't know that either.

AUGUSTINE: Then don't ask me any more questions.

EVODIUS: Why not?

AUGUSTINE: First, because there's no reason for me to answer your questions unless you want to know the answer. Second, because I should not discuss these sorts of things with you unless you want to attain wisdom. And finally, because you can't be my friend unless you want things to go well for me. But surely you have already seen whether you will your own happiness.

EVODIUS: You're right; it can't be denied that we have a will. Do go on—let's see what you deduce from that fact.

AUGUSTINE: I shall. But first tell me whether you think you have a *good* will.

EVODIUS: What is a good will?

AUGUSTINE: It is a will by which we desire to live upright and honorable lives and to attain the highest wisdom. So just ask yourself: Do you desire an upright and honorable life and fervently will to be wise? And is it indisputable that when we will these things, we have a good will?

EVODIUS: My answer to both questions is yes. I now admit that I have not just a will, but a good will.

AUGUSTINE: How highly do you value this will? You surely do not think it should be compared with wealth or honors or physical pleasures, or even all of these together.

EVODIUS: God forbid such wicked madness!

AUGUSTINE: Then should we not rejoice a little that we have something in our souls—this very thing that I call a good will—in comparison with which those things we mentioned are utterly worthless, things that a great many human beings will spare no effort and shirk no danger to obtain?

EVODIUS: Indeed, we should rejoice greatly.

AUGUSTINE: Then do you think that those who do not attain such joy suffer a small loss by missing so great a good?

EVODIUS: It is a great loss.

AUGUSTINE: Then I believe you realize that it is up to our will whether we enjoy or lack such a great and true good. For what is so much in the power of the will as the will itself? To have a good will is to have something far more valuable than all earthly kingdoms and pleasures; to lack it is to lack something that only the will itself can give, something that is better than all the goods that are not in our power. Some people consider themselves utterly miserable if they do not achieve a splendid reputation, great wealth, and various goods of the body. But don't you consider them utterly miserable, even if they have all these things, when they cleave to things that they can quite easily lose, things that they do not have simply in virtue of willing them, while they lack a good will, which is incomparably better than those things and yet, even though it is such a great good, can be theirs if only they will to have it?

EVODIUS: I certainly do.

AUGUSTINE: Then fools, even if they were never wise (which is a doubtful and obscure issue), are justly and deservedly afflicted with such misery.

EVODIUS: I agree. . . .

Chapter 14

AUGUSTINE: . . . Do you think that there is anyone who does not in every way
will and desire a happy life?

EVODIUS: Clearly, every human being wills that.

AUGUSTINE: Then why doesn't everyone attain it? We have found that it is
by the will that human beings deserve—and therefore receive—either a
happy or an unhappy life. There's a sort of contradiction here; unless
we take great care to examine it, it will undermine our careful and
persuasive argument. How can anyone suffer an unhappy life by the
will, when absolutely no one wills to be unhappy? Or to put it another
way, how can we claim that it is by the will that human beings achieve
a happy life, when so many are unhappy despite the fact that everyone
wills to be happy?

Perhaps it is because it is one thing to will rightly or wrongly, and quite
another to deserve something because of a good or bad will. Those who
are happy, who must also be good, are not happy simply because they
will to be happy—even the wicked will that—but because they will it in
the right way, whereas the wicked do not. So it's no surprise that
unhappy human beings do not attain the happy life that they will. For
they do not likewise will the one thing that goes along with the happy
life, without which no one attains it or is worthy to attain it—and that
is, to live rightly. For the eternal law (to which it is time for us to return)
has established with unshakable firmness that the will is rewarded with
happiness or punished with unhappiness depending on its merit. And
so when we say that it is by the will that human beings are unhappy, we
don't mean that they will to be unhappy, but that their will is in such a
state that unhappiness must follow whether they will it or not. So it
does not contradict our earlier argument to say that everyone wills to be
happy but not everyone can be; for not everyone has the will to live
rightly, which must accompany the will to live happily. Or do you have
some objection to make?

EVODIUS: None at all. . . .

Chapter 16

AUGUSTINE: . . . We have clearly and carefully distinguished between two
sorts of things, eternal and temporal; and in turn between two sorts of
human beings, those who pursue and love eternal things and those who
pursue and love temporal things. We have determined that the choice to
follow and embrace one or the other lies with the will, and that only the
will can depose the mind from its stronghold of power and deprive it of
right order. And it has become clear that we should not blame anything
when someone uses the will wrongly; we should blame the one who uses
it wrongly. Given all of that, why don't we return to the question we
posed at the beginning of this discussion and see whether it has been
answered.

We set out to discover what evildoing is. This whole discussion was aimed at answering that question. So we are now in a position to ask whether evildoing is anything other than neglecting eternal things (which the mind perceives and enjoys by means of itself and which it cannot lose if it loves them) and instead pursuing temporal things (which are perceived by means of the body, the least valuable part of a human being, and which can never be certain) as if they were great and marvelous things. It seems to me that all evil deeds—that is, all sins— fall into this one category. But I want to know what you think about this.

EVODIUS: I agree; all sins come about when someone turns away from divine things that truly persist and toward changeable and uncertain things. These things do have their proper place, and they have a certain beauty of their own; but when a perverse and disordered soul pursues them it becomes enslaved to the very things that divine order and law command it to rule over.

And I think that we have answered another question. After we asked what evildoing is, we set out to discover the source of our evildoing. Now unless I am mistaken, our argument showed that we do evil by free choice of the will.

Evil and Omnipotence

J. L. Mackie

J. L. Mackie was born in 1917 in Sydney, Australia. He entered the University of Sydney in 1935 and received his bachelor's degree in 1938. He then went to England to study at Oxford University, where he won the Cromer Greek Essay Prize in 1941 for an essay on Heraclitus. During World War II Mackie served in the British armed forces in the Middle East and Italy, attaining the rank of captain. After the war, in 1946, he accepted a position in philosophy at the University of Sydney. He taught there until 1963, except for his four years as a faculty member at the University of Otago in New Zealand (1955–1959). In 1963 he returned to England, where he became the first holder of the Chair of Philosophy at the University of York. In 1967 he became a fellow and tutor in philosophy at Oxford University. Mackie was elected a Fellow of the British Academy in 1974. He died in Oxford in 1981.

Mackie's books include *Truth, Probability, and Paradox: Studies in Philosophical Logic* (1973), *The Cement of the Universe: A Study of Causation* (1974), *Problems from Locke* (1976), *Ethics: Inventing Right and Wrong* (1977), *Hume's Moral Theory* (1980), and *The Miracle of Theism: Arguments For and Against the Existence of God* (published posthumously, 1982).

Our reading here is Mackie's 1955 article, "Evil and Omnipotence." Mackie discusses the "problem of evil," the problem of how a theist can consistently hold all three of the following propositions: God is all-powerful, God is all-good, and evil exists. On the face of it, it seems that if there were an omnipotent and completely benevolent God, this God would not permit evil to exist.

Mackie distinguishes logically adequate and logically fallacious solutions to the problem of evil. A theist solves the problem of evil in a logically adequate way if he or she denies one or more of the initial propositions: God has limited power (and therefore cannot prevent all evil), God has limited goodness (and therefore does not want to prevent all evil), or evil does not exist (it is merely an illusion). Although these solutions are logically adequate, they require abandoning the traditional concept of God as an all-good and all-powerful being or maintaining the highly implausible view that there really is no evil.

The fallacious solutions to the problem of evil say that all three of the initial propositions are true, but in the process of explaining how they are compatible, these theories end up implicitly rejecting one or more of them. In other words, these theories *appear* to defend all three propositions but in fact do not. Mackie examines in detail four such arguments. The first two arguments are that good cannot exist without evil and that evil is a necessary means to good. Both arguments end up denying God's omnipotence. The third solution, that the universe as a whole is better with some evil in it than it would be with no evil, compromises God's benevolence. The final solution states that the possibility of evil is a necessary result of God's endowing human beings with free will, which is a good. Mackie argues that this solution denies the omnipotence and benevolence of God, because God could have made human beings in such a way that they always freely choose the good.

INTRODUCTION

The traditional arguments for the existence of God have been fairly thoroughly criticized by philosophers. But the theologian can, if he wishes, accept this criticism. He can admit that no rational proof of God's existence is possible. And he can still retain all that is essential to his position, by holding that God's existence is known in some other, nonrational way. I think, however, that a more telling criticism can be made by way of the traditional problem of evil. Here it can be shown, not that religious beliefs lack rational support, but that they are positively irrational, that the several parts of the essential theological doctrine are inconsistent with one another, so that the theologian can maintain his position as a whole only by a much more extreme rejection of reason than in the former case. He must now be prepared to believe, not merely what cannot be proved, but what can be *disproved* from other beliefs that he also holds.

The problem of evil, in the sense in which I shall be using the phrase, is a problem only for someone who believes that there is a God who is both omnipotent and wholly good. And it is a logical problem, the problem of clarifying and reconciling a number of beliefs. It is not a scientific problem that might be solved by further observations, or a practical problem that might be solved by a decision or an action. These points are obvious; I mention them only because they are sometimes ignored by theologians, who sometimes parry a statement of the problem with such remarks as "Well, can you solve the problem yourself?" or "This is a mystery that may be revealed to us later" or "Evil is something to be faced and overcome, not to be merely discussed."

In its simplest form the problem is this: God is omnipotent; God is wholly good; and yet evil exists. There seems to be some contradiction between these three propositions, so that if any two of them were true the third would be false. But at the same time all three are essential parts of most theological positions: The theologian, it seems, at once *must* adhere and *cannot consistently* adhere to all three. (The problem does not arise only for theists, but I shall discuss it in the form in which it presents itself for ordinary theism.)

However, the contradiction does not arise immediately; to show it we need some additional premises, or perhaps some quasi-logical rules connecting the terms "good," "evil," and "omnipotent." These additional principles are that good is opposed to evil, in such a way that a good thing always eliminates evil as far as it can, and that there are no limits to what an omnipotent thing can do. From these it follows that a good omnipotent thing eliminates evil completely, and then the propositions that a good omnipotent thing exists, and that evil exists, are incompatible.

A. ADEQUATE SOLUTIONS

Now once the problem is fully stated it is clear that it can be solved, in the sense that the problem will not arise if one gives up at least one of the propositions that constitute it. If you are prepared to say that God is not wholly good, or not quite omnipotent, or that evil does not exist, or that good is not opposed to the kind of evil that exists, or that there are limits to what an omnipotent thing can do, then the problem of evil will not arise for you.

There are, then, quite a number of adequate solutions of the problem of evil, and some of these have been adopted, or almost adopted, by various thinkers. For example, a few have been prepared to deny God's omnipotence, and rather more have been prepared to keep the term "omnipotence" but severely to restrict its meaning, recording quite a number of things that an omnipotent being cannot do. Some have said that evil is an illusion, perhaps because they held that the whole world of temporal, changing things is an illusion, and that what we call evil belongs only to this world, or perhaps because they held that although temporal things *are* much as we see them, those that we call evil are not really evil. Some have said that what we call evil is merely the privation of good, that evil in a positive sense, evil that would really be opposed to good, does not exist. Many have agreed with Pope that discord is harmony not understood, and that partial evil is universal good.[1] Whether any of these views is *true* is, of course, another question. But each of them gives an adequate solution of the problem of evil in the sense that if you accept it this problem does not arise for you, though you may, of course, have *other* problems to face.

But often enough these adequate solutions are only *almost* adopted. The thinkers who restrict God's power, but keep the term "omnipotence," may reasonably be suspected of thinking, in other contexts, that his power is really unlimited. Those who say that evil is an illusion may also be thinking, inconsistently, that this illusion is itself an evil. Those who say that "evil" is merely privation of good may also be thinking, inconsistently, that privation of good is an evil. (The fallacy here is akin to some forms of the "naturalistic fallacy"[2] in ethics, where some think, for example, that "good" is just what contributes to evolutionary progress, and that evolutionary progress is itself good.) If Pope meant what he said in the first line of his couplet, that "discord" is only harmony not understood, the "partial evil" of the second line must, for consistency, mean "that which, taken in isolation, falsely appears to be evil," but it would more naturally mean "that which, in isolation, really is evil." The second line, in fact, hesitates between two views, that "partial evil" isn't really evil, since only the universal quality is real, and that "partial evil" is really an evil, but only a little one.

In addition, therefore, to adequate solutions, we must recognize unsatisfactory inconsistent solutions, in which there is only a half-hearted or temporary rejection of one of the propositions that together constitute the problem. In these, one of the constituent propositions is explicitly rejected, but it is covertly reasserted or assumed elsewhere in the system.

---

[1]Alexander Pope (1688–1744), an English poet, writes in *An Essay on Man* (Epistle 1, lines 290–91): "All Discord, Harmony, not understood; / All partial Evil, universal Good." [D. C. ABEL]

[2]*"naturalistic fallacy"*: the alleged mistake of identifying ethical goodness with a "natural" object. [D. C. ABEL]

B. FALLACIOUS SOLUTIONS

Besides these half-hearted solutions, which explicitly reject but implicitly assert one of the constituent propositions, there are definitely fallacious solutions that explicitly maintain all the constituent propositions, but implicitly reject at least one of them in the course of the argument that explains away the problem of evil.

There are, in fact, many so-called solutions that purport to remove the contradiction without abandoning any of its constituent propositions. These must be fallacious, as we can see from the very statement of the problem, but it is not so easy to see in each case precisely where the fallacy lies. I suggest that in all cases the fallacy has the general form suggested above: In order to solve the problem one (or perhaps more) of its constituent propositions is given up, but in such a way that it appears to have been retained, and can therefore be asserted without qualification in other contexts. Sometimes there is a further complication: The supposed solution moves to and fro between, say, two of the constituent propositions, at one point asserting the first of these but covertly abandoning the second, at another point asserting the second but covertly abandoning the first. These fallacious solutions often turn upon some equivocation[3] with the words "good" and "evil," or upon some vagueness about the way in which good and evil are opposed to one another, or about how much is meant by "omnipotence." I propose to examine some of these so-called solutions, and to exhibit their fallacies in detail. Incidentally, I shall also be considering whether an adequate solution could be reached by a minor modification of one or more of the constituent propositions, which would, however, still satisfy all the essential requirements of ordinary theism.

1. "Good cannot exist without evil" or "Evil is necessary as a counterpart to good."

It is sometimes suggested that evil is necessary as a counterpart to good, that if there were no evil there could be no good either, and that this solves the problem of evil. It is true that it points to an answer to the question "Why should there be evil?" But it does so only by qualifying some of the propositions that constitute the problem.

First, it sets a limit to what God can do, saying that God *cannot* create good without simultaneously creating evil, and this means either that God is not omnipotent or that there are *some* limits to what an omnipotent thing can do. It may be replied that these limits are always presupposed, that omnipotence has never meant the power to do what is logically impossible, and on the present view the existence of good without evil would be a logical impossibility. This interpretation of omnipotence may, indeed, be accepted as a modification of our original account that does not reject anything that is essential to theism, and I shall in general assume it in the subsequent

---

[3] *equivocation:* the use of a word or phrase in different senses, which makes an apparently correct argument actually incorrect. [D. C. ABEL]

discussion. It is, perhaps, the most common theistic view, but I think that some theists at least have maintained that God can do what is logically impossible. Many theists, at any rate, have held that logic itself is created or laid down by God, that logic is the way in which God arbitrarily chooses to think. (This is, of course, parallel to the ethical view that morally right actions are those that God arbitrarily chooses to command, and the two views encounter similar difficulties.) And *this* account of logic is clearly inconsistent with the view that God is bound by logical necessities—unless it is possible for an omnipotent being to bind himself, an issue that we shall consider later, when we come to the paradox of omnipotence. This solution of the problem of evil cannot, therefore, be consistently adopted along with the view that logic is itself created by God.

But, secondly, this solution denies that evil is opposed to good in our original sense. If good and evil are counterparts, a good thing will not "eliminate evil as far as it can." Indeed, this view suggests that good and evil are not strictly qualities of things at all. Perhaps the suggestion is that good and evil are related in much the same way as great and small. Certainly, when the term "great" is used relatively as a condensation of "greater than so-and-so," and "small" is used correspondingly, greatness and smallness are counterparts and cannot exist without each other. But in this sense greatness is not a quality, not an intrinsic feature of anything; and it would be absurd to think of a movement in favor of greatness and against smallness in this sense. Such a movement would be self-defeating, since relative greatness can be promoted only by a simultaneous promotion of relative smallness. I feel sure that no theists would be content to regard God's goodness as analogous to this—as if what he supports were not the *good* but the *better,* and as if he had the paradoxical aim that all things should be better than other things.

This point is obscured by the fact that "great" and "small" seem to have an absolute as well as a relative sense. I cannot discuss here whether there is absolute magnitude or not, but if there is, there could be an absolute sense for "great," it could mean of at least a certain size, and it would make sense to speak of all things getting bigger, of a universe that was expanding all over, and therefore it would make sense to speak of promoting greatness. But in *this* sense great and small are not logically necessary counterparts: Either quality could exist without the other. There would be no logical impossibility in everything's being small or in everything's being great.

Neither in the absolute nor in the relative sense, then, of "great" and "small" do these terms provide an analogy of the sort that would be needed to support this solution of the problem of evil. In neither case are greatness and smallness *both* necessary counterparts *and* mutually opposed forces or possible objects for support and attack.

It may be replied that good and evil are necessary counterparts in the same way as any quality and its logical opposite. Redness can occur, it is suggested, only if nonredness also occurs. But unless evil is merely the privation of good, they are not logical opposites, and some further argument would be needed to show that they are counterparts in the same way as genuine logical opposites. Let us assume that this could be given. There is still doubt of the correctness of the metaphysical[4] principle that a quality must have a real opposite: I suggest that it is not really impossible that everything should be, say, red, that the truth is merely that if everything were red we should not notice redness, and so we should have no word "red"; we observe and give names to qualities only if they have real opposites. If so, the principle that a term must have an opposite would belong only to our language or to our thought, and would not be an ontological[5] principle, and, correspondingly, the rule that good cannot exist without evil would not state a logical necessity of a sort that God would just have to put up with. God might have made everything good, though *we* should not have noticed it if he had.

But, finally, even if we concede that this *is* an ontological principle, it will provide a solution for the problem of evil only if one is prepared to say, "Evil exists, but only just enough evil to serve as the counterpart of good." I doubt whether any theist will accept this. After all, the *ontological* requirement that nonredness should occur would be satisfied even if all the universe, except for a minute speck, were red, and, if there were a corresponding requirement for evil as a counterpart to good, a minute dose of evil would presumably do. But theists are not usually willing to say, in all contexts, that all the evil that occurs is a minute and necessary dose.

2. "Evil is necessary as a means to good."

It is sometimes suggested that evil is necessary for good not as a counterpart but as a means. In its simple form this has little plausibility as a solution of the problem of evil, since it obviously implies a severe restriction of God's power. It would be a *causal* law that you cannot have a certain end without a certain means, so that if God has to introduce evil as a means to good, he must be subject to at least some causal laws. This certainly conflicts with what a theist normally means by omnipotence. This view of God as limited by causal laws also conflicts with the view that causal laws are themselves made by God, which is more widely held than the corresponding view about the laws of logic. This conflict would, indeed, be resolved if it were possible for an omnipotent being to bind himself, and this possibility has still to be considered. Unless a favorable answer can be given to this question, the suggestion that evil is necessary as a means to good solves the problem of evil only by denying one of its constituent propositions, either that God is omnipotent or that "omnipotent" means what it says.

3. "The universe is better with some evil in it than it could be if there were no evil."

Much more important is a solution that at first seems to be a mere variant of the previous one, that evil may contribute to the goodness of a whole in which it is found, so that the universe as a whole is better as it is, with some evil in it, than it would be if there were no evil. This solution may be developed in either of two ways. It may be supported by an aesthetic analogy, by the fact that contrasts heighten beauty, that in a musical work, for example, there may occur discords

---

[4]*metaphysical:* relating to *metaphysics,* the study of the nature and kinds of reality. [D. C. ABEL]
[5]*ontological:* relating to *ontology,* a synonym for *metaphysics* (see footnote 4). [D. C. ABEL]

that somehow add to the beauty of the work as a whole. Alternatively, it may be worked out in connection with the notion of progress, that the best possible organization of the universe will not be static, but progressive, that the gradual overcoming of evil by good is really a finer thing than would be the eternal unchallenged supremacy of good.

In either case, this solution usually starts from the assumption that the evil whose existence gives rise to the problem of evil is primarily what is called physical evil, that is to say, pain. In Hume's[6] rather half-hearted presentation of the problem of evil, the evils that he stresses are pain and disease, and those who reply to him argue that the existence of pain and disease makes possible the existence of sympathy, benevolence, heroism, and the gradually success-ful struggle of doctors and reformers to overcome these evils. In fact, theists often seize the opportunity to accuse those who stress the problem of evil of taking a low, materialistic view of good and evil, equating these with pleasure and pain, and of ignoring the more spiritual goods that can arise in the struggle against evils.

But let us see exactly what is being done here. Let us call pain and misery "first-order evil" or "evil (1)." What contrasts with this, namely pleasure and happiness, will be called "first-order good" or "good (1)." Distinct from this is "second-order good" or "good (2)," which somehow emerges in a complex sit-uation in which evil (1) is a necessary component—logically, not merely causally, necessary. (Exactly *how* it emerges does not matter: In the crudest ver-sion of this solution, good (2) is simply the heightening of happiness by the con-trast with misery; in other versions it includes sympathy with suffering, heroism in facing danger, and the gradual decrease of first-order evil and increase of first-order good.) It is also being assumed that second-order good is more important than first-order good or evil, in particular that it more than outweighs the first-order evil it involves.

Now this is a particularly subtle attempt to solve the problem of evil. It defends God's goodness and omnipotence on the ground that (on a sufficiently long view) this is the best of all logically possible worlds, because it includes the important second-order goods, and yet it admits that real evils—namely first-order evils—exist. But does it still hold that good and evil are opposed? Not, clearly, in the sense that we set out originally. Good does not tend to elim-inate evil in general. Instead, we have a modified, a more complex pattern. First-order good (for example, happiness) *contrasts with* first-order evil (for example, misery): These two are opposed in a fairly mechanical way; some second-order goods (for example, benevolence) try to maximize first-order good and minimize first-order evil; but God's goodness is not this, it is rather the will to maximize *second*-order good. We might, therefore, call God's good-ness an example of a third-order goodness, or good (3). While this account is different from our original one, it might well be held to be an improvement on it, to give a more accurate description of the way in which good is opposed to evil, and to be consistent with the essential theist position.

---

[6]David Hume (1711–1776) was a Scottish philosopher and historian; for a biography, see p. 46. [D. C. Abel]

There might, however, be several objections to this solution.

First, some might argue that such qualities as benevolence—and a fortiori[7] the third-order goodness that promotes benevolence—have a merely derivative value, that they are not higher sorts of good, but merely means to good (1), that is, to happiness, so that it would be absurd for God to keep misery in existence in order to make possible the virtues of benevolence, heroism, and so on. The theist who adopts the present solution must, of course, deny this, but he can do so with some plausibility, so I should not press this objection.

Secondly, it follows from this solution that God is not in our sense benevolent or sympathetic: He is not concerned to minimize evil (1), but only to promote good (2); and this might be a disturbing conclusion for some theists.

But, thirdly, the fatal objection is this. Our analysis shows clearly the possibility of the existence of a *second*-order evil, an evil (2) contrasting with good (2) as evil (1) contrasts with good (1). This would include malevolence, cruelty, callousness, cowardice, and states in which good (1) is decreasing and evil (1) increasing. And just as good (2) is held to be the important kind of good, the kind that God is concerned to promote, so evil (2) will, by analogy, be the important kind of evil, the kind that God, if he were wholly good and omnipotent, would eliminate. And yet evil (2) plainly exists, and indeed most theists (in other contexts) stress its existence more than that of evil (1). We should, therefore, state the problem of evil in terms of second-order evil, and against this form of the problem the present solution is useless.

An attempt might be made to use this solution again, at a higher level, to explain the occurrence of evil (2). Indeed, the next main solution that we shall examine does just this, with the help of some new notions. Without any fresh notions, such a solution would have little plausibility. For example, we could hardly say that the really important good was a good (3), such as the increase of benevolence in proportion to cruelty, which logically required for its occurrence the occurrence of some second-order evil. But even if evil (2) could be explained in this way, it is fairly clear that there would be third-order evils contrasting with this third-order good—and we should be well on the way to an infinite regress, where the solution of a problem of evil, stated in terms of evil (n), indicated the existence of an evil ($n + 1$), and a further problem to be solved.

4. "Evil is due to human free will."

Perhaps the most important proposed solution of the problem of evil is that evil is not to be ascribed to God at all, but to the independent actions of human beings, supposed to have been endowed by God with freedom of the will. This solution may be combined with the preceding one: First-order evil (for example, pain) may be justified as a logically necessary component in second-order good (for example, sympathy), while second-order evil (for example, cruelty) is not *justified*, but is so ascribed to human beings that God cannot be held responsible for it. This combination evades my third criticism of the preceding solution.

The free will solution also involves the preceding solution at a higher level. To explain why a wholly good God gave men free will although it would lead to

---

[7]*a fortiori*: (Latin, "from the stronger [argument]") with all the more reason. [D. C. ABEL]

some important evils, it must be argued that it is better on the whole that men should act freely, and sometimes err, than that they should be innocent automata, acting rightly in a wholly determined way. Freedom, that is to say, is now treated as a third-order good, and as being more valuable than second-order goods (such as sympathy and heroism) would be if they were deterministically[8] produced, and it is being assumed that second-order evils, such as cruelty, are logically necessary accompaniments of freedom, just as pain is a logically necessary precondition of sympathy.

I think that this solution is unsatisfactory primarily because of the incoherence of the notion of freedom of the will. But I cannot discuss this topic adequately here, although some of my criticisms will touch upon it.

First, I should query the assumption that second-order evils are logically necessary accompaniments of freedom. I should ask this: If God has made men such that in their free choices they sometimes prefer what is good and sometimes what is evil, why could he not have made men such that they always freely choose the good? If there is no logical impossibility in a man's freely choosing the good on one, or on several occasions, there cannot be a logical impossibility in his freely choosing the good on every occasion. God was not, then, faced with a choice between making innocent automata and making beings who, in acting freely, would sometimes go wrong; there was open to him the obviously better possibility of making beings who would act freely but always go right. Clearly, his failure to avail himself of this possibility is inconsistent with his being both omnipotent and wholly good.

If it is replied that this objection is absurd, that the making of some wrong choices is logically necessary for freedom, it would seem that "freedom" must here mean complete randomness or indeterminacy, including randomness with regard to the alternatives good and evil—in other words, that men's choices and consequent actions can be "free" only if they are not determined by their characters. Only on this assumption can God escape the responsibility for men's actions; for if he made them as they are, but did not determine their wrong choices, this can only be because the wrong choices are not determined by men as they are. But then if freedom is randomness, how can it be a characteristic of *will?* And, still more, how can it be the most important good? What value or merit would there be in free choices if these were random actions that were not determined by the nature of the agent?

I conclude that to make this solution plausible two different senses of "freedom" must be confused, one sense that will justify the view that freedom is a third-order good, more valuable than other goods would be without it, and another sense, sheer randomness, to prevent us from ascribing to God a decision to make men such that they sometimes go wrong when he might have made them such that they would always freely go right.

This criticism is sufficient to dispose of this solution. But besides this there is a fundamental difficulty in the notion of an omnipotent God creating men

---

[8]*deterministically:* in accordance with *determinism,* the doctrine that all events are determined by preceding causes and that we can never act otherwise than we do. [D. C. ABEL]

with free will, for if men's wills are really free this must mean that even God cannot control them—that is, that God is no longer omnipotent. It may be objected that God's gift of freedom to men does not mean that he *cannot* control their wills, but that he always *refrains* from controlling their wills. But why, we may ask, should God refrain from controlling evil wills? Why should he not leave men free to will rightly, but intervene when he sees them beginning to will wrongly? If God could do this, but does not, and if he is wholly good, the only explanation could be that even a wrong free act of will is not really evil, that its freedom is a value that outweighs its wrongness, so that there would be a loss of value if God took away the wrongness and the freedom together. But this is utterly opposed to what theists say about sin in other contexts. The present solution of the problem of evil, then, can be maintained only in the form that God has made men so free that he *cannot* control their wills.

This leads us to what I call the paradox of omnipotence: Can an omnipotent being make things that he cannot subsequently control? Or, what is practically equivalent to this, can an omnipotent being make rules that then bind himself? (These are practically equivalent because any such rules could be regarded as setting certain things beyond his control, and vice versa.) The second of these formulations is relevant to the suggestions that we have already met, that an omnipotent God creates the rules of logic or causal laws, and is then bound by them.

It is clear that this is a paradox: The questions cannot be answered satisfactorily either in the affirmative or in the negative. If we answer "Yes," it follows that if God actually makes things that he cannot control, or makes rules that bind himself, he is not omnipotent once he has made them; there are *then* things that he cannot do. But if we answer "No," we are immediately asserting that there are things that he cannot do—that is to say, that he is already not omnipotent.

It cannot be replied that the question that sets this paradox is not a proper question. It would make perfectly good sense to say that a human mechanic has made a machine that he cannot control. If there is any difficulty about the question, it lies in the notion of omnipotence itself.

This, incidentally, shows that although we have approached this paradox from the free will theory, it is equally a problem for a theological determinist. No one thinks that machines have free will, yet they may well be beyond the control of their makers. The determinist might reply that anyone who makes anything determines its ways of acting, and so determines its subsequent behavior. Even the human mechanic does this by his *choice* of materials and structure for his machine, though he does not know all about either of these: The Mechanic determines, though he may not foresee, his machine's actions. And since God is omniscient, and since his creation of things is total, he both determines and foresees the ways in which his creatures will act. We may grant this, but it is beside the point. The question is not whether God *originally* determined the future actions of his creatures, but whether he can *subsequently* control their actions, or whether he was able in his original creation to put things beyond his subsequent control. Even on determinist principles the answers "Yes" and "No" are equally irreconcilable with God's omnipotence.

Before suggesting a solution of this paradox, I would point out that there is a parallel paradox of sovereignty. Can a legal sovereign make a law restricting its own future legislative power? For example, could the British parliament make a law forbidding any future parliament to socialize banking, and also forbidding the future repeal of this law itself? Or could the British parliament, which was legally sovereign in Australia in, say, 1899, pass a valid law, or series of laws, which made it no longer sovereign in 1933? Again, neither the affirmative nor the negative answer is really satisfactory. If we were to answer "Yes," we should be admitting the validity of a law that, if it were actually made, would mean that parliament was no longer sovereign. If we were to answer "No," we should be admitting that there is a law, not logically absurd, which parliament cannot validly make—that is, that parliament is not now a legal sovereign. This paradox can be solved in the following way. We should distinguish between first-order laws, that is, laws governing the actions of individuals and bodies other than the legislature; and second-order laws, that is, laws about laws, laws governing the actions of the legislature itself. Correspondingly, we should distinguish two orders of sovereignty, first-order sovereignty (sovereignty (1)), which is unlimited authority to make first-order laws; and second-order sovereignty (sovereignty (2)), which is unlimited authority to make second-order laws. If we say that parliament is sovereign we might mean that any parliament at any time has sovereignty (1), or we might mean that parliament has both sovereignty (1) and sovereignty (2) at present, but we cannot without contradiction mean both that the present parliament has sovereignty (2) and that every parliament at every time has sovereignty (1), for if the present parliament has sovereignty (2) it may use it to take away the sovereignty (1) of later parliaments. What the paradox shows is that we cannot ascribe to any continuing institution legal sovereignty in an inclusive sense.

The analogy between omnipotence and sovereignty shows that the paradox of omnipotence can be solved in a similar way. We must distinguish between first-order omnipotence (omnipotence (1)), that is, unlimited power to act; and second-order omnipotence (omnipotence (2)), that is, unlimited power to determine what powers to act things shall have. Then we could consistently say that God all the time has omnipotence (1), but if so no beings at any time have powers to act independently of God. Or we could say that God at once time had omnipotence (2), and used it to assign independent powers to act to certain things, so that God thereafter did not have omnipotence (1). But what the paradox shows is that we cannot consistently ascribe to any continuing being omnipotence in an inclusive sense.

An alternative solution of this paradox would be simply to deny that God is a continuing being, that any times can be assigned to his actions at all. But on this assumption (which also has difficulties of its own) no meaning can be given to the assertion that God made men with wills so free that he could not control them. The paradox of omnipotence can be avoided by putting God outside time, but the free will solution of the problem of evil cannot be saved in this way, and equally it remains impossible to hold that an omnipotent God *binds himself* by causal or logical laws.

CONCLUSION

Of the proposed solutions of the problem of evil that we have examined, none has stood up to criticism. There may be other solutions that require examination, but this study strongly suggests that there is no valid solution of the problem that does not modify at least one of the constituent propositions in a way that would seriously affect the essential core of the theistic position.

Quite apart from the problem of evil, the paradox of omnipotence has shown that God's omnipotence must in any case be restricted in one way or another, that unqualified omnipotence cannot be ascribed to any being that continues through time. And if God and his actions are not in time, can omnipotence, or power of any sort, be meaningfully ascribed to him?

An Irenaean Theodicy

John Hick

John Hick was born in 1922 in Scarborough, England. He received his master's degree from the University of Edinburgh in Scotland in 1948 and his doctorate from Oxford University in 1950. He spent the next three years studying theology at Westminster Theological College in Cambridge, England. Hick then served as a Presbyterian minister in Northumberland, England. In 1956 he came to the United States, where he taught at Cornell University for three years and at Princeton Theological Seminary for five years. Returning to England in 1964, he taught at Cambridge University for three years and then was named H. G. Wood Professor of Theology at the University of Birmingham. From 1982 until his retirement in 1992, Hick was Danforth Professor of the Philosophy of Religion and director of the Blaisdell Programs in World Religions and Cultures at the Claremont Graduate School in California. He currently lives in Birmingham, England, where he is a Fellow of the Institute for Advanced Research in the Humanities at the University of Birmingham.

Hick's publications include *Philosophy of Religion* (1963; 4th ed., 1990); *Evil and the God of Love* (1966; 2d ed., 1977); *Arguments for the Existence of God* (1971); *An Interpretation of Religion: Human Responses to the Transcendent* (1989; 2d ed., 2004); *The Metaphor of God Incarnate* (1993; 2d ed., 2006); *The Fifth Dimension: An Exploration of the Spiritual Realm* (1999); and *The New Frontier of Religion and Science: Religious Experience, Neuroscience, and the Transcendent* (2006).

Our reading is from Hick's 1981 article "An Irenaean Theodicy." *Theodicy* is an attempt to "justify God" in the sense of showing that the existence of evil in the world is compatible with belief in an all-good and all-powerful God who created and governs the world. (The word "theodicy" is formed from the Greek nouns *theos* ["God"] and *dikē* ["law, right"].) Hick develops a theodicy based on the views of Irenaeus, as 2nd-century Christian theologian. A tenable theodicy, Hick explains, must be internally coherent and must be consistent with both the religious tradition on which it is based (in this case, the Christian tradition) and the data of science. Hick argues that most widely accepted Christian theodicy, which is based on the thought of the theologian Augustine (354–430), is untenable because it is inconsistent with the contemporary scientific account of the origin of the human species. Hick proposes that we replace Augustinian theodicy with an Irenaean one. Although Irenaeus himself did not develop a theodicy, his theological view that humankind was created in two stages (the "image" of God and the "likeness" of God) can be developed into a theodicy that integrates Christian belief with modern evolution theory. Hick argues the existence of evil is necessary if human beings, at the present state of their growth toward spiritual maturity, are to fulfill their potential to love God freely and to achieve the most valuable kind of moral goodness. Hick concludes by noting that the ultimate plausibility of his Irenaean theodicy requires belief in "a continuation of our lives in another sphere of existence after bodily death."

[I. INTRODUCTION]

Can a world in which sadistic cruelty often has its way, in which selfish love-lessness is so rife, in which there are debilitating diseases, crippling accidents, bodily and mental decay, insanity, and all manner of natural disasters be regarded as the expression of infinite creative goodness? Certainly all this could never by itself lead anyone to believe in the existence of a limitlessly powerful God. And yet even in a world that contains these things, innumerable men and women have believed and do believe in the reality of an infinite creative good-ness, which they call God. The theodicy project starts at this point, with an already operating belief in God, embodied in human living, and attempts to show that this belief is not rendered irrational by the fact of evil. It attempts to explain how it is that the universe, assumed to be created and ultimately ruled by a limitlessly good and limitlessly powerful Being, is as it is, including all the pain and suffering and all the wickedness and folly that we find around us and within us. The theodicy project is thus an exercise in metaphysical construction, in the sense that it consists in the formation and criticism of large-scale hypotheses concerning the nature and process of the universe.

Since a theodicy both starts from and tests belief in the reality of God, it nat-urally takes different forms in relation to different concepts of God. In this paper I shall be discussing the project of a specifically Christian theodicy; I shall not be attempting the further and even more difficult work of comparative theodicy, leading in turn to the question of a global theodicy.

The two main demands upon a theodicy hypothesis are (1) that it be inter-nally coherent, and (2) that it be consistent with the data both of the religious tradition on which it is based, and of the world, in respect both of the latter's general character as revealed by scientific inquiry and of the specific facts of moral and natural evil. These two criteria demand, respectively, possibility and plausibility.

Traditionally, Christian theology has centered upon the concept of God as both limitlessly powerful and limitlessly good and loving; and it is this concept of deity that gives rise to the problem of evil as a threat to theistic faith. The threat was definitively expressed in Stendhal's bombshell, "The only excuse for God is that he does not exist!"[1] The theodicy project is the attempt to offer a dif-ferent view of the universe that is both possible and plausible and that does not ignite Stendhal's bombshell.

Christian thought has always included a certain range of variety, and in the area of theodicy it offers two broad types of approach. The Augustinian approach, representing until fairly recently the majority report of the Christian mind, hinges upon the idea of the Fall [of the human race through the sin of Adam and Eve], which has in turn brought about the disharmony of nature. This type of theodicy is developed today as "the free will defense." The Irenaean approach, representing in the past a minority report, hinges upon the creation

---

[1]Stendhal (1783–1842) was the pen name of Marie-Henri Beyle, a French writer. [D. C. ABEL, EDITOR]

of humankind through the evolutionary process as an immature creature living in a challenging and therefore person-making world. I shall indicate very briefly why I do not find the first type of theodicy satisfactory, and then spend the remainder of this paper in exploring the second type.

[II. AUGUSTINIAN THEODICY]

In recent years the philosophical discussion of the problem of evil has been dominated by the free will defense. A major effort has been made by Alvin Plantinga and a number of other Christian philosophers to show that it is logically possible that a limitlessly powerful and limitlessly good God is responsible for the existence of this world. For all evil may ultimately be due to misuses of creaturely freedom. But it may nevertheless be better for God to have created free than unfree beings; and it is logically possible that any and all free beings whom God might create would, as a matter of contingent fact, misuse their freedom by falling into sin. In that case it would be logically impossible for God to have created a world containing free beings and yet not containing sin and the suffering that sin brings with it. Thus it is logically possible, despite the fact of evil, that the existing universe is the work of a limitlessly good Creator.

These writers are in effect arguing that the traditional Augustinian type of theodicy, based upon the Fall from grace of free finite creatures—first angels and then human beings—and a consequent going wrong of the physical world, is not logically impossible. I am in fact doubtful whether their argument is sound, and will return to the question later. But even if it should be sound, I suggest that their argument wins only a Pyrrhic victory,[2] since the logical possibility that it would establish is one that, for very many people today, is fatally lacking in plausibility. For most educated inhabitants of the modern world regard the biblical story of Adam and Eve, and their temptation by the devil, as myth rather than as history; and they believe that so far from having been created finitely perfect and then falling, humanity evolved out of lower forms of life, emerging in a morally, spiritually, and culturally primitive state. Further, they reject as incredible the idea that earthquake and flood, disease, decay, and death are consequences either of a human fall, or of a prior fall of angelic beings who are now exerting an evil influence upon the Earth. They see all this as part of a prescientific world view, along with the stories of the world having been created in six days and of the sun standing still for twenty-four hours at Joshua's command.[3] One cannot, strictly speaking, disprove any of these ancient biblical myths and sagas, or refute their confident elaboration in the medieval Christian picture of the universe. But those of us for whom the resulting theodicy, even if logically possible, is radically implausible, must look elsewhere for light on the problem of evil.

---

[2]*Pyrrhic victory:* a victory gained at excessive cost. [D. C. ABEL]
[3]Joshua 10:12–13. [D. C. ABEL]

[III. AN IRENAEAN THEODICY]

I believe that we find the light that we need in the main alternative strand of Christian thinking, which goes back to important constructive suggestions by the early Hellenistic Fathers of the Church, particularly St. Irenaeus (120–202 B.C.E.). Irenaeus himself did not develop a theodicy, but he did—together with other Greek-speaking Christian writers of that period, such as Clement of Alexandria—build a framework of thought within which a theodicy became possible that does not depend upon the idea of the Fall, and that is consonant with modern knowledge concerning the origins of the human race. . . .

The central theme out of which this Irenaean type of theodicy has arisen is the two-stage conception of the creation of humankind, first in the "image" and then in the "likeness" of God.[4] Re-expressing this in modern terms, the first stage was the gradual production of Homo sapiens, through the long evolutionary process, as intelligent ethical and religious animals. The human being is an animal, one of the varied forms of earthly life and continuous as such with the whole realm of animal existence. But the human being is uniquely intelligent, having evolved a large and immensely complex brain. Further, the human being is ethical—that is, a gregarious as well as an intelligent animal, able to realize and respond to the complex demands of social life. And the human being is a religious animal, with an innate tendency to experience the world in terms of the presence and activity of supernatural beings and powers. This then is early Homo sapiens, the intelligent social animal capable of awareness of the divine. But early Homo sapiens is not the Adam and Eve of Augustinian theology, living in perfect harmony with self, with nature, and with God. On the contrary, the life of this being must have been a constant struggle against a hostile environment, and capable of savage violence against one's fellow human beings, particularly outside one's own immediate group; and this being's concepts of the divine were primitive and often bloodthirsty. Thus existence "in the image of God" was a potentiality for knowledge of and relationship with one's Maker rather than such knowledge and relationship as a fully realized state. In other words, people were created as spiritually and morally immature creatures, at the beginning of a long process of further growth and development, which constitutes the second stage of God's creative work. In this second stage, of which we are a part, the intelligent, ethical, and religious animal is being brought through one's own free responses into what Irenaeus called the divine "likeness." . . . His conception of a two-stage creation of the human, with perfection lying in the future rather than in the past, is of fundamental importance. The notion of the Fall was not basic to this picture. . . . Irenaeus himself however could not, in the historical knowledge of his time, question the fact of the Fall; though he treated it as a relatively minor lapse, a youthful error, rather than as the infinite crime and cosmic disaster that has ruined the whole creation. But today we can acknowledge that there is no evidence at all of a period in the distant past when humankind was in the ideal state of a fully realized "child of God." . . .

---

[4]Genesis 1:26 states that God created human beings in God's "image and likeness." [D. C. ABEL]

Let us now try to formulate a contemporary version of the Irenaean type of theodicy, based on this suggestion of the initial creation of humankind, not as a finitely perfect, but as an immature creature at the beginning of a long process of further growth and development. We may begin by asking why one should have been created as an imperfect and developing creature rather than as the perfect being whom God is presumably intending to create. The answer, I think, consists in two considerations that converge in their practical implications—one concerned with the human's relationship to God and the other with the relationship to other human beings. As to the first, we could have the picture of God creating finite beings, whether angels or persons, directly in his own presence, so that in being conscious of that which is other than one's self the creature is automatically conscious of God, the limitless divine reality and power, goodness and love, knowledge and wisdom, towering above one's self. In such a situation the disproportion between Creator and creatures would be so great that the latter would have no freedom in relation to God; they would indeed not exist as independent autonomous persons. For what freedom could finite beings have in an immediate consciousness of the presence of the one who has created them, who knows them through and through, who is limitlessly powerful as well as limitlessly loving and good, and who claims their total obedience? In order to be a person, exercising some measure of genuine freedom, the creature must be brought into existence, not in the immediate divine presence, but at a "distance" from God. This "distance" cannot of course be spatial; for God is omnipresent. It must be an epistemic[5] distance, a distance in the cognitive dimension. And the Irenaean hypothesis is that this "distance" consists, in the case of humans, in their existence within and as part of a world that functions as an autonomous system and from within which God is not overwhelmingly evident. . . . In such a world one can exist as a person over against the Creator. One has space to exist as a finite being, a space created by the epistemic distance from God and protected by one's basic cognitive freedom, one's freedom to open or close oneself to the dawning awareness of God that is experienced naturally by a religious animal.

This Irenaean picture corresponds, I suggest, to our actual human situation. Emerging within the evolutionary process as part of the continuum of animal life, in a universe that functions in accordance with its own laws and whose workings can be investigated and described without reference to a Creator, the human being has a genuine, even awesome, freedom in relation to one's Maker. The human being is free to acknowledge and worship God; and is free—particularly since the emergence of human individuality and the beginnings of critical consciousness during the first millennium B.C.E.—to doubt the reality of God.

Within such a situation there is the possibility of the human being coming freely to know and love one's Maker. Indeed, if the end-state that God is seeking to bring about is one in which finite persons have come in their own freedom to know and love him, this requires creating them initially in a state that is not that of their already knowing and loving him. For it is logically impossible to create beings already in a state of having come into that state by their own free choices.

---

[5]*epistemic:* relating to knowledge. [D. C. ABEL]

The other consideration, which converges with this in pointing to something like the human situation as we experience it, concerns our human moral nature. We can approach it by asking why humans should not have been created at this epistemic distance from God, and yet at the same time as morally perfect beings. . . .

Why was humanity not initially created in possession of all the virtues, instead of having to acquire them through the long hard struggle of life as we know it? The answer, I suggest, appeals to the principle that virtues that have been formed within the agent as a hard-won deposit of his own right decisions in situations of challenge and temptation, are intrinsically more valuable than virtues created within him ready-made and without any effort on his own part. This principle expresses a basic value judgment that cannot be established by argument, but that one can only present, in the hope that it will be as morally plausible, and indeed compelling, to others as to oneself. It is, to repeat, the judgment that a moral goodness which exists as the agent's initial given nature, without ever having been chosen by him in the face of temptations to the contrary, is intrinsically less valuable than a moral goodness that has been built up through the agent's own responsible choices through time in the face of alternative possibilities.

If, then, God's purpose was to create finite persons embodying the most valuable kind of moral goodness, he would have to create them, not as already perfect beings but rather as imperfect creatures who can then attain to the more valuable kind of goodness through their own free choices as, in the course of their personal and social history, new responses prompt new insights—opening up new moral possibilities and providing a milieu in which the most valuable kind of moral nature can be developed.

We have thus far, then, the hypothesis that one is created at an epistemic distance from God in order to come freely to know and love the Maker; and that one is at the same time created as a morally immature and imperfect being in order to attain through freedom the most valuable quality of goodness. The end sought, according to this hypothesis, is the full realization of the human potentialities in a unitary spiritual and moral perfection in the divine kingdom. And the question we have to ask is whether humans as we know them, and the world as we know it, are compatible with this hypothesis. . . .

As animal organisms integral to the whole ecology of life, we are programmed for survival. In pursuit of survival, primitives not only killed other animals for food but fought other human beings when their vital interests conflicted. The life of prehistoric persons must indeed have been a constant struggle to stay alive, prolonging an existence that was, in Hobbes's phrase, "poor, nasty, brutish and short."[6] And in his basic animal self-regardingness humankind was, and is, morally imperfect. In saying this I am assuming that the essence of moral evil is selfishness, the sacrificing of others to one's own interests. It consists, in Kantian[7] terminology, in treating others, not as ends in themselves, but as means to one's own ends. This is what the survival instinct demands. And yet we are

---

[6]Thomas Hobbes, *Leviathan*, Part I, Chapter XIII. Hobbes (1588–1679) was an English philosopher. [D. C. ABEL]

[7]*Kantian:* based on the thought of the German philosopher Immanuel Kant (1724–1804). [D. C. ABEL]

also capable of love, of self-giving in a common cause, of a conscience that responds to others in their needs and dangers. And with the development of civilization we see the growth of moral insight, the glimpsing and gradual assimilation of higher ideals, and tension between our animality and our ethical values. But that the human being has a lower as well as a higher nature, that one is an animal as well as a potential child of God, and that one's moral goodness is won from a struggle with one's own innate selfishness, is inevitable given one's continuity with the other forms of animal life. Further, the human animal is not responsible for having come into existence as an animal. The ultimate responsibility for humankind's existence, as a morally imperfect creature, can only rest with the Creator. The human does not, in one's own degree of freedom and responsibility, choose one's origin, but rather one's destiny.

This then, in brief outline, is the answer of the Irenaean type of theodicy to the question of the origin of moral evil: The general fact of humankind's basic self-regarding animality is an aspect of creation as part of the realm of organic life; and this basic self-regardingness has been expressed over the centuries both in sins of individual selfishness and in the much more massive sins of corporate selfishness, institutionalized in slavery and exploitation, and all the many and complex forms of social injustice.

But nevertheless our sinful nature in a sinful world is the matrix within which God is gradually creating children for himself out of human animals. For it is as men and women freely respond to the claim of God upon their lives, transmuting their animality into the structure of divine worship, that the creation of humanity is taking place. And in its concrete character this response consists in every form of moral goodness, from unselfish love in individual personal relationships to the dedicated and selfless striving to end exploitation and to create justice within and between societies.

But one cannot discuss moral evil without at the same time discussing the nonmoral evil of pain and suffering. (I propose to mean by "pain" physical pain, including the pains of hunger and thirst; and by "suffering" the mental and emotional pain of loneliness, anxiety, remorse, lack of love, fear, grief, envy, and so on.) For what constitutes moral evil as evil is the fact that it causes pain and suffering. It is impossible to conceive of an instance of moral evil, or sin, that is not productive of pain or suffering to anyone at any time. But in addition to moral evil there is another source of pain and suffering in the structure of the physical world, which produces storms, earthquakes, and floods and which afflicts the human body with diseases—cholera, epilepsy, cancer, malaria, arthritis, rickets, meningitis, and so on—as well as with broken bones and other outcomes of physical accidents. It is true that a great deal both of pain and of suffering is humanly caused, not only by the inhumanity of man to man but also by the stresses of our individual and corporate lifestyles, causing many disorders—not only lung cancer and cirrhosis of the liver but many cases of heart disease, stomach and other ulcers, strokes, and so on—as well as accidents. But there remain nevertheless, in the natural world itself, permanent causes of human pain and suffering. And we have to ask why an unlimitedly good and unlimitedly powerful God should have created so dangerous a world, both as regards its purely natural hazards of earthquake and flood and so on, and as regards the liability of the human body to so many ills, both psychosomatic and purely somatic.

The answer offered by the Irenaean type of theodicy follows from and is indeed integrally bound up with its account of the origin of moral evil. We have the hypothesis of humankind being brought into being within the evolutionary process as a spiritually and morally immature creature, and then growing and developing through the exercise of freedom in this religiously ambiguous world. We can now ask what sort of a world would constitute an appropriate environment for this second stage of creation. The development of human personality— moral, spiritual, and intellectual—is a product of challenge and response. It does not occur in a static situation demanding no exertion and no choices. . . . The intellectual development of humanity has been due to interaction with an objective environment functioning in accordance with its own laws, an environment that we have had actively to explore and to cooperate with in order to escape its perils and exploit its benefits. In a world devoid both of dangers to be avoided and rewards to be won we may assume that there would have been virtually no development of the human intellect and imagination, and hence of either the sciences or the arts, and hence of human civilization or culture.

The fact of an objective world within which one has to learn to live, on penalty of pain or death, is also basic to the development of one's moral nature. For it is because the world is one in which men and women can suffer harm—by violence, disease, accident, starvation, and so on—that our actions affecting one another have moral significance. A morally wrong act is, basically, one that harms some part of the human community; while a morally right action is, on the contrary, one that prevents or neutralizes harm or that preserves or increases human well being. Now we can imagine a paradise in which no one can ever come to any harm. It could be a world which, instead of having its own fixed structure, would be plastic to human wishes. Or it could be a world with a fixed structure, and hence the possibility of damage and pain, but whose structure is suspended or adjusted by special divine action whenever necessary to avoid human pain. Thus, for example, in such a miraculously pain-free world one who falls accidentally off a high building would presumably float unharmed to the ground; bullets would become insubstantial when fired at a human body; poisons would cease to poison, water to drown; and so on. . . . But a world in which there can be no pain or suffering would also be one in which there can be no moral choices and hence no possibility of moral growth and development. For in a situation in which no one can ever suffer injury or be liable to pain or suffering there would be no distinction between right and wrong action. No action would be morally wrong, because no action could have harmful consequences; and likewise no action would be morally right in contrast to wrong. Whatever the values of such a world, it clearly could not serve a purpose of the development of its inhabitants from self-regarding animality to self-giving love.

Thus the hypothesis of a divine purpose in which finite persons are created at an epistemic distance from God, in order that they may gradually become children of God through their own moral and spiritual choices, requires that their environment, instead of being a pain free and stress-free paradise, be broadly the kind of world of which we find ourselves to be a part. It requires that it be such as to provoke the theological problem of evil. For it requires that it be an environment that offers challenges to be met, problems to be solved, dangers to be faced, and that accordingly involves real possibilities of hardship, disaster, failure, defeat, and misery as well as of delight and happiness, success, triumph, and achievement. For it is by grappling with the real problems of a real environment, in which a person is one form of life among many, and which is not designed to minister exclusively to one's well-being, that one can develop in intelligence and in such qualities as courage and determination. And it is in the relationships of human beings with one another, in the context of this struggle to survive and flourish, that they can develop the higher values of mutual love and care, of self-sacrifice for others, and of commitment to a common good. . . .

In terms of this hypothesis, as we have developed it thus far, then, both the basic moral evil in the human heart and the natural evils of the world are compatible with the existence of a Creator who is unlimited in both goodness and power. But is the hypothesis plausible as well as possible? The principal threat to its plausibility comes, I think, from the sheer amount and intensity of both moral and natural evil. One can accept the principle that in order to arrive at a freely chosen goodness one must start out in a state of moral immaturity and imperfection. But is it necessary that there should be the depths of demonic malice and cruelty that each generation has experienced, and that we have seen above all in recent history in the Nazi attempt to exterminate the Jewish population of Europe? Can any future fulfillment be worth such horrors? . . . .

Concerning the intensity of natural evil, the truth is probably that our judgments of intensity are relative. We might identify some form of natural evil as the worst that there is—say the agony that can be caused by death from cancer—and claim that a loving God would not have allowed this to exist. But in a world in which there was no cancer, something else would then rank as the worst form of natural evil. If we then eliminate this, something else; and so on. And the process would continue until the world was free of all natural evil. For whatever form of evil for the time being remained would be intolerable to the inhabitants of that world. But in removing all occasions of pain and suffering, and hence all challenge and all need for mutual care, we should have converted the world from a person-making into a static environment, which could not elicit moral growth. In short, having accepted that a person-making world must have its dangers and therefore also its tragedies, we must accept that whatever form these take will be intolerable to the inhabitants of that world. There could not be a person-making world devoid of what we call evil; and evils are never tolerable—except for the sake of greater goods that may come out of them.

But accepting that a person-making environment must contain causes of pain and suffering, and that no pain or suffering is going to be acceptable, one of the most daunting and even terrifying features of the world is that calamity strikes indiscriminately. There is no justice in the incidence of disease, accident, disaster, and tragedy. The righteous as well as the unrighteous are struck down by illness and afflicted by misfortune. There is no security in goodness, but the good are as likely as the wicked to suffer "the slings and arrows of outrageous fortune."[8]

---

[8]William Shakespeare, *Hamlet*, Act III, Scene 1, line 58. [D. C. ABEL]

From the time of Job this fact has set a glaring question mark against the goodness of God. But let us suppose that things were otherwise. Let us suppose that misfortune came upon humankind, not haphazardly and therefore unjustly, but justly and therefore not haphazardly. Let us suppose that instead of coming without regard to moral considerations, it was proportioned to desert, so that the sinner was punished and the virtuous rewarded. Would such a dispensation serve a person-making purpose? Surely not. For it would be evident that wrong deeds bring disaster upon the agent whilst good deeds bring health and prosperity; and in such a world truly moral action, action done because it is right, would be impossible. The fact that natural evil is not morally directed, but is a hazard that comes by chance, is thus an intrinsic feature of a person-making world.

In other words, the very mystery of natural evil, the very fact that disasters afflict human beings in contingent, undirected, and haphazard ways, is itself a necessary feature of a world that calls forth mutual aid and builds up mutual caring and love. Thus, on the one hand, it would be completely wrong to say that God sends misfortune upon individuals, so that their death, maiming, starvation, or ruin is God's will for them. But, on the other hand, God has set us in a world containing unpredictable contingencies and dangers, in which unexpected and undeserved calamities may occur to anyone; because only in such a world can mutual caring and love be elicited. As an abstract philosophical hypothesis, this may offer little comfort. But translated into religious language it tells us that God's good purpose enfolds the entire process of this world, with all its good and bad contingencies, and that even amidst tragic calamity and suffering we are still within the sphere of his love and are moving towards his kingdom.

But there is one further all-important aspect of the Irenaean type of theodicy, without which all the foregoing would lose its plausibility. This is the eschatological[9] aspect. Our hypothesis depicts persons as still in course of creation towards an end-state of perfected personal community in the divine kingdom. This end-state is conceived of as one in which individual egoity[10] has been transcended in communal unity before God. And in the present phase of that creative process, the naturally self-centered human animal has the opportunity freely to respond to God's noncoercive self-disclosures, through the work of prophets and saints, through the resulting religious traditions, and through the individual's religious experience. Such response always has an ethical aspect; for the growing awareness of God is at the same time a growing awareness of the moral claim that God's presence makes upon the way in which we live.

But it is very evident that this person-making process, leading eventually to perfect human community, is not completed on this Earth. It is not completed in the life of the individual—or at best only in the few who have attained

---

[9]*eschatological:* relating to *eschatology,* the branch of theology that concerns the end of the world, divine judgment, and the afterlife. [D. C. ABEL]

[10]*egoity:* selfhood. [D. C. ABEL]

to sanctification, or *moksha*,[11] or nirvana[12] on this Earth. Clearly the enormous majority of men and women die without having attained to this. As Eric Fromm has said, "The tragedy in the life of most of us is that we die before we are fully born."[13] And therefore if we are ever to reach the full realization of the potentialities of our human nature, this can only be in a continuation of our lives in another sphere of existence after bodily death. And it is equally evident that the perfect all-embracing human community, in which self-regarding concern has been transcended in mutual love, not only has not been realized in this world, but never can be, since hundreds of generations of human beings have already lived and died and accordingly could not be part of any ideal community established at some future moment of earthly history. Thus if the unity of humankind in God's presence is ever to be realized it will have to be in some sphere of existence other than our Earth. In short, the fulfillment of the divine purpose, as it is postulated in the Irenaean type of theodicy, presupposes each person's survival, in some form of bodily death, and further living and growing towards that end-state. Without such an eschatological fulfillment, this theodicy would collapse. . . .

On this view the human, endowed with a real though limited freedom, is basically formed for relationship with God and destined ultimately to find the fulfillment of his or her nature in that relationship. This does not seem to me excessively paradoxical. On the contrary, given the theistic postulate, it seems to me to offer a very probable account of our human situation.

---

[11]*moksha:* in Hindu doctrine, liberation, emancipation. [D. C. ABEL]

[12]*nirvana:* in Buddhist doctrine, the extinction of desire, which brings complete liberation from suffering. [D. C. ABEL]

[13]Erich Fromm, "Values, Psychology and Human Existence," in *New Knowledge in Human Values,* ed. Abraham H. Maslow (New York: Harper, 1959), p. 156. [J. HICK]

C. Faith and Reason

READING 11

Euthyphro

Plato

Plato was born in Athens in about 428 B.C.E. As a youth he associated with Socrates, a philosopher who constantly challenged fellow Athenians to think about virtue and to improve their souls. Plato's initial interest was in politics, but he soon became disillusioned, especially when, under the democracy that was restored after the rule of the "Thirty Tyrants," Socrates was arrested on false charges of impiety and the corruption of youth, convicted, and condemned to die. After the execution of Socrates, Plato moved to nearby Megara for a time and may have traveled to Egypt. In 388 he visited Italy and the city of Syracuse in Sicily. Returning to Athens, he founded the Academy, a school devoted both to philosophical inquiry and to the philosophically based education of politicians. Plato spent most of his life teaching at the Academy (Aristotle was his most famous student) and writing philosophical works. He made two more trips to Syracuse, in 368 and 361, apparently with the intention of turning the city's ruler, Dionysius the Younger, into a "philosopher-king." (If this was indeed his purpose, he failed.) Plato died in Athens in 347 at the age of 81.

Most of Plato's works are written as conversations between Socrates and one or more interlocutors on some topic concerning morality. His best-known "dialogues" (the name by which his surviving works are known) are the *Euthyphro, Apology, Crito, Phaedo, Meno, Symposium,* and *Republic.*

Our reading here is the *Euthyphro,* in which Socrates engages a priest named Euthyphro in a conversation about piety. Socrates uses his dialectical ("Socratic") method of inquiry to elicit Euthyphro's thoughts about piety, to point out inconsistencies in his views, and to lead him to think more coherently and deeply about the nature of piety. The dialogue begins when Socrates meets Euthyphro at the court of the magistrate in charge of cases involving the state religion. Socrates has come there to deal with preliminary matters concerning the charges of impiety and corruption of youth that a man named Meletus has filed against him; Euthyphro is at the court to charge his father with murder. Since it was generally considered highly impious to bring legal action against one's father, Socrates tells Euthyphro that he must be very knowledgeable about piety, or else he would never have initiated such an action. Euthyphro quickly agrees that he is "far advanced in wisdom." At Socrates' request, he agrees to explain the nature of piety. Socrates expresses his gratitude, since a knowledge of piety will enable him to defend himself in court against the charge of impiety.

Euthyphro first says that piety (holiness, godliness) is doing what he is doing: prosecuting the wrongdoer. Socrates points out that while prosecuting wrongdoers may be an *example* of piety, it is not a *definition* because it does not specify the form (characteristic) of piety—the element that is common to all instances of piety and makes them be instances of piety. Euthyphro proceeds to define piety as "what is dear to the gods." Socrates' questioning shows Euthyphro the inadequacy of this definition. Euthyphro then proposes other definitions, but each time Socrates points out inconsistencies in Euthyphro's thought. The dialogue ends with Euthyphro telling Socrates that he is in a hurry and has to go.

[INTRODUCTION]

EUTHYPHRO: What's new, Socrates, to make you leave your usual haunts in the Lyceum[1] and spend your time here by the king-archon's[2] court? Surely you are not prosecuting anyone before the king-archon as I am?

SOCRATES: The Athenians do not call this a prosecution but an indictment, Euthyphro.

EUTHYPHRO: What is this you say? Someone must have indicted you, for you are not going to tell me that you have indicted someone else.

SOCRATES: No indeed.

EUTHYPHRO: But someone else has indicted you?

SOCRATES: Quite so.

EUTHYPHRO: Who is he?

SOCRATES: I do not really know him myself, Euthyphro. He is apparently young and unknown. They call him Meletus, I believe. He belongs to the Pitthean deme,[3] if you know anyone from that deme called Meletus, with long hair, not much of a beard, and a rather aquiline nose.

EUTHYPHRO: I don't know him, Socrates. What charge does he bring against you?

SOCRATES: What charge? A not ignoble one I think, for it is no small thing for a young man to have knowledge of such an important subject. He says he knows how our young men are corrupted and who corrupts them. He is likely to be wise, and when he sees my ignorance corrupting his contemporaries, he proceeds to accuse me to the city as to their mother. I think he is the only one of our public men to start out the right way, for it is right to care first that the young should be as good as possible, just as a good farmer is likely to take care of the young plants first, and of the others later. So, too, Meletus first gets rid of us who corrupt the young shoots, as he says, and then afterwards he will obviously take care of the older ones and become a source of great blessings for the city, as seems likely to happen to one who started out this way.

EUTHYPHRO: I could wish this were true, Socrates, but I fear the opposite may happen. He seems to me to start out by harming the very heart of the city by attempting to wrong you. Tell me, what does he say you do to corrupt the young?

SOCRATES: Strange things, to hear him tell it, for he says that I am a maker of gods, and on the ground that I create new gods while not believing in the old gods, he has indicted me for their sake, as he puts it.

EUTHYPHRO: I understand, Socrates. This is because you say that the divine sign[4] keeps coming to you. So he has written this indictment against

---

[1]*Lyceum:* a public facility for gymnastic exercise, named for the god Apollo Lyceios. [D. C. ABEL]
[2]*king-archon:* the magistrate with jurisdiction of cases involving the state religion. [D. C. ABEL]
[3]*deme:* a unit of local government. [D. C. ABEL]
[4]*divine sign:* In the defense speech he gave at his trial, Socrates explained that he hears a divine voice that sometimes turns him away from something he is about to do. [D. C. ABEL].

you as one who makes innovations in religious matters, and he comes to court to slander you, knowing that such things are easily misrepresented to the crowd. The same is true in my case. Whenever I speak of divine matters in the assembly and foretell the future, they laugh me down as if I were crazy; and yet I have foretold nothing that did not happen. Nevertheless, they envy all of us who do this. One need not worry about them, but meet them head-on.

SOCRATES: My dear Euthyphro, to be laughed at does not matter perhaps, for the Athenians do not mind anyone they think clever, as long as he does not teach his own wisdom. But if they think that he makes others to be like himself they get angry, whether through envy, as you say, or for some other reason.

EUTHYPHRO: I have certainly no desire to test their feelings towards me in this matter.

SOCRATES: Perhaps you seem to make yourself but rarely available, and not be willing to teach your own wisdom, but I'm afraid that my liking for people makes them think that I pour out to anybody anything I have to say, not only without charging a fee but even glad to reward anyone who is willing to listen. If then they were intending to laugh at me, as you say they laugh at you, there would be nothing unpleasant in their spending their time in court laughing and jesting, but if they are going to be serious, the outcome is not clear except to you prophets.

EUTHYPHRO: Perhaps it will come to nothing, Socrates, and you will fight your case as you think best, as I think I will mine.

SOCRATES: What is your case, Euthyphro? Are you the defendant or the prosecutor?

EUTHYPHRO: The prosecutor.

SOCRATES: Whom do you prosecute?

EUTHYPHRO: One whom I am thought crazy to prosecute.

SOCRATES: Are you pursuing someone who will easily escape you?

EUTHYPHRO: Far from it, for he is quite old.

SOCRATES: Who is it?

EUTHYPHRO: My father.

SOCRATES: My dear sir! Your own father?

EUTHYPHRO: Certainly.

SOCRATES: What is the charge? What is the case about?

EUTHYPHRO: Murder, Socrates.

SOCRATES: Good heavens! Certainly, Euthyphro, most men would not know how they could do this and be right. It is not the part of anyone to do this, but of one who is far advanced in wisdom.

EUTHYPHRO: Yes, by Zeus, Socrates, that is so.

SOCRATES: Is then the man your father killed one of your relatives? Or is that obvious—for you would not prosecute your father for the murder of a stranger.

EUTHYPHRO: It is ridiculous, Socrates, for you to think that it makes any difference whether the victim is a stranger or a relative. One should only watch whether the killer acted justly or not; if he acted justly, let him go, but if not, one should prosecute, if, that is to say, the killer shares your hearth and table. The pollution is the same if you knowingly keep company with such a man and do not cleanse yourself and him by bringing him to justice. The victim was a dependent of mine, and when we were farming in Naxos[5] he was a servant of ours. He killed one of our household slaves in drunken anger, so my father bound him hand and foot and threw him in a ditch, then sent a man here to inquire from the priest what should be done. During that time he gave no thought or care to the bound man, as being a killer, and it was no matter if he died, which he did. Hunger and cold and his bonds caused his death before the messenger came back from the seer. Both my father and my other relatives are angry that I am prosecuting my father for murder on behalf of a murderer when he hadn't even killed him, they say, and even if he had, the dead man does not deserve a thought, since he was a killer. For, they say, it is impious for a son to prosecute his father for murder. But their ideas of the divine attitude to piety and impiety are wrong, Socrates.

SOCRATES: Whereas, by Zeus, Euthyphro, you think that your knowledge of the divine, and of piety and impiety, is so accurate that, when those things happened as you say, you have no fear of having acted impiously in bringing your father to trial?

EUTHYPHRO: I should be of no use, Socrates, and Euthyphro would not be superior to the majority of men, if I did not have accurate knowledge of all such things.

SOCRATES: It is indeed most important, my admirable Euthyphro, that I should become your pupil and, as regards this indictment, challenge Meletus about these very things and say to him that in the past too I considered knowledge about the divine to be most important, and that now that he says that I am guilty of improvising and innovating about the gods, I have become your pupil. I would say to him: "If, Meletus, you agree that Euthyphro is wise in these matters, consider me, too, to have the right beliefs and do not bring me to trial. If you do not think so, then prosecute that teacher of mine, not me, for corrupting the older men—me and his own father—by teaching me and by exhorting and punishing him." If he is not convinced, and does not discharge me or indict you instead of me, I shall repeat the same challenge in court.

EUTHYPHRO: Yes, by Zeus, Socrates, and, if he should try to indict me, I think I would find his weak spots and the talk in court would be about him rather than about me.

SOCRATES: It is because I realize this that I am eager to become your pupil, my dear friend. I know that other people as well as this Meletus do not even seem to notice you, whereas he sees me so sharply and clearly that he indicts me for ungodliness. So tell me now, by Zeus, what you just now maintained you clearly knew. What kind of thing do you say that godliness and ungodliness are, both as regards murder and other

---

[5]*Naxos:* a large island in the Aegean Sea, southeast of Athens. [G. M. A. GRUBE, TRANSLATOR]

things? Or is the pious not the same and alike in every action, and the impious the opposite of all that is pious and like itself, and everything that is to be impious presents us with one form or appearance insofar as it is impious?

EUTHYPHRO: Most certainly, Socrates.

SOCRATES: Tell me then, what is the pious, and what the impious—what do you say?

[EUTHYPHRO'S DEFINITIONS OF PIETY]

[1. Prosecuting the Wrongdoer]

EUTHYPHRO: I say that the pious is to do what I am doing now, to prosecute the wrongdoer, be it about murder or temple robbery or anything else, whether the wrongdoer is your father or your mother or anyone else; not to prosecute is impious. And observe, Socrates, that I can cite powerful evidence that the law is so. I have already said to others that such actions are right, not to favor the ungodly, whoever they are. These people themselves believe that Zeus is the best and most just of the gods, yet they agree that he bound his father because he unjustly swallowed his sons, and that he in turn castrated his father for similar reasons. But they are angry with me because I am prosecuting my father for his wrongdoing. They contradict themselves in what they say about the gods and about me.

SOCRATES: Indeed, Euthyphro, this is the reason why I am a defendant in the case, because I find it hard to accept things like that being said about the gods, and it is likely to be the reason why I shall be told I do wrong. Now, however, if you, who have full knowledge of such things, share their opinions, then we must agree with them, too, it would seem. For what are we to say, we who agree that we ourselves have no knowledge of them? Tell me, by the god of friendship, do you really believe these things are true?

EUTHYPHRO: Yes, Socrates, and so are even more surprising things, of which the majority has no knowledge.

SOCRATES: And do you believe that there really is war among the gods, and terrible enmities and battles, and other such things as are told by the poets, and other sacred stories such as are embroidered by good writers and by representations of which the robe of the goddess is adorned when it is carried up to the Acropolis?[6] Are we to say these things are true, Euthyphro?

EUTHYPHRO: Not only these, Socrates, but, as I was saying just now, I will, if you wish, relate many other things about the gods which I know will amaze you.

---

[6]*Acropolis:* the fortified section of Athens, where the Parthenon, a temple of Athena, the patron goddess of Athens, was located. The robe of Athena was carried to the Parthenon during certain religious festivals. [D. C. ABEL]

SOCRATES: I should not be surprised, but you will tell me these at leisure some other time. For now, try to tell me more clearly what I was asking just now; for, my friend, you did not teach me adequately when I asked you what the pious was, but you told me that what you are doing now, in prosecuting your father for murder, is pious.

EUTHYPHRO: And I told the truth, Socrates.

SOCRATES: Perhaps. You agree, however, that there are many other pious actions.

EUTHYPHRO: There are.

SOCRATES: Bear in mind then that I did not bid you tell me one or two of the many pious actions but that form itself that makes all pious actions pious, for you agreed that all impious actions are impious and all pious actions pious through one form, or don't you remember?

EUTHYPHRO: I do.

SOCRATES: Tell me then what this form itself is, so that I may look upon it, and using it as a model, say that any action of yours or another's that is of that kind is pious, and if it is not that it is not.

EUTHYPHRO: If that is how you want it, Socrates, that is how I will tell you.

SOCRATES: That is what I want.

[2. What Is Dear to the Gods]

EUTHYPHRO: Well then, what is dear to the gods is pious, what is not is impious.

SOCRATES: Splendid, Euthyphro! You have now answered in the way I wanted. Whether your answer is true I do not know yet, but you will obviously show me that what you say is true.

EUTHYPHRO: Certainly.

SOCRATES: Come then, let us examine what we mean. An action or a man dear to the gods is pious, but an action or a man hated by the gods is impious. They are not the same, but quite opposite, the pious and the impious. Is that not so?

EUTHYPHRO: It is indeed.

SOCRATES: And that seems to be a good statement?

EUTHYPHRO: I think so, Socrates.

SOCRATES: We have also stated that the gods are in a state of discord, that they are at odds with each other, Euthyphro, and that they are at enmity with each other. Has that, too, been said?

EUTHYPHRO: It has.

SOCRATES: What are the subjects of difference that cause hatred and anger? Let us look at it this way. If you and I were to differ about numbers as to which is the greater, would this difference make us enemies and angry with each other, or would we proceed to count and soon resolve our difference about this?

EUTHYPHRO: We would certainly do so.

SOCRATES: Again, if we differed about the larger and the smaller, we would turn to measurement and soon cease to differ.

EUTHYPHRO: That is so.

SOCRATES: And about the heavier and the lighter, we would resort to weighing and be reconciled.

EUTHYPHRO: Of course.

SOCRATES: What subject of difference would make us angry and hostile to each other if we were unable to come to a decision? Perhaps you do not have an answer ready, but examine as I tell you whether these subjects are the just and the unjust, the beautiful and the ugly, the good and the bad. Are these not the subjects of difference about which, when we are unable to come to a satisfactory decision, you and I and other men become hostile to each other whenever we do?

EUTHYPHRO: That is the difference, Socrates, about those subjects.

SOCRATES: What about the gods, Euthyphro? If indeed they have differences, will it not be about these same subjects?

EUTHYPHRO: It certainly must be so.

SOCRATES: Then according to your argument, my good Euthyphro, different gods consider different things to be just, beautiful, ugly, good, and bad, for they would not be at odds with one another unless they differed about these subjects, would they?

EUTHYPHRO: You are right.

SOCRATES: And they like what each of them considers beautiful, good, and just, and hate the opposites of these?

EUTHYPHRO: Certainly.

SOCRATES: But you say that the same things are considered just by some gods and unjust by others, and as they dispute about these things they are at odds and at war with each other. Is that not so?

EUTHYPHRO: It is.

SOCRATES: The same things then are loved by the gods and hated by the gods, and would be both god-loved and god-hated.

EUTHYPHRO: It seems likely.

SOCRATES: And the same things would be both pious and impious, according to this argument?

EUTHYPHRO: I'm afraid so.

SOCRATES: So you did not answer my question, you surprising man. I did not ask you what same thing is both pious and impious, and it appears that what is loved by the gods is also hated by them. So it is in no way surprising if your present action, namely punishing your father, may be pleasing to Zeus but displeasing to Cronus and Uranus, pleasing to Hephaestus but displeasing to Hera, and so with any other gods who differ from each other on this subject.

EUTHYPHRO: I think, Socrates, that on this subject no gods would differ from one another, that whoever has killed anyone unjustly should pay the penalty.

SOCRATES: Well now, Euthyphro, have you ever heard any man maintaining that one who has killed or done anything else unjustly should not pay the penalty?

EUTHYPHRO: They never cease to dispute on this subject, both elsewhere and in the courts, for when they have committed many wrongs they do and say anything to avoid the penalty.

SOCRATES: Do they agree they have done wrong, Euthyphro, and in spite of so agreeing do they nevertheless say they should not be punished?

EUTHYPHRO: No, they do not agree on that point.

SOCRATES: So they do not say or do just anything. For they do not venture to say this, or dispute that they must not pay the penalty if they have done wrong, but I think they deny doing wrong. Is that not so?

EUTHYPHRO: That is true.

SOCRATES: Then they do not dispute that the wrongdoer must be punished, but they may disagree as to who the wrongdoer is, what he did and when.

EUTHYPHRO: You are right.

SOCRATES: Do not the gods have the same experience, if indeed they are at odds with each other about the just and the unjust, as your argument maintains? Some assert that they wrong one another, while others deny it, but no one among gods or men ventures to say that the wrongdoer must not be punished.

EUTHYPHRO: Yes, that is true, Socrates, as to the main point.

SOCRATES: And those who disagree, whether men or gods, dispute about each action, if indeed the gods disagree. Some say it is done justly, others unjustly. Is that not so?

EUTHYPHRO: Yes, indeed.

SOCRATES: Come now, my dear Euthyphro, tell me, too, that I may become wiser, what proof you have that all the gods consider that man to have been killed unjustly who became a murderer while in your service, was bound by the master of his victim, and died in his bonds before the one who bound him found out from the seers what was to be done with him, and that it is right for a son to denounce and to prosecute his father on behalf of such a man. Come, try to show me a clear sign that all the gods definitely believe this action to be right. If you can give me adequate proof of this, I shall never cease to extol your wisdom.

EUTHYPHRO: This is perhaps no light task, Socrates, though I could show you very clearly.

SOCRATES: I understand that you think me more dull-witted than the jury, as you will obviously show them that these actions were unjust and that all the gods hate such actions.

EUTHYPHRO: I will show it to them clearly, Socrates, if only they will listen to me.

[3. What Is Loved by All the Gods]

SOCRATES: They will listen if they think you show them well. But this thought came to me as you were speaking, and I am examining it, saying to myself: "If Euthyphro shows me conclusively that all the gods consider such a death unjust, to what greater extent have I learned from him the nature of piety and impiety? This action would then, it seems, be hated by the gods, but the pious and the impious were not thereby now defined, for what is hated by the gods has also been shown to be loved by them." So I will not insist on this point; let us assume, if you wish, that all the gods consider this unjust and that they all hate it. However, is this the correction we are making in our discussion, that what all the gods hate is impious, and what they all love is pious, and that what some gods love and others hate is neither or both? Is that how you now wish us to define piety and impiety?

EUTHYPHRO: What prevents us from doing so, Socrates?

SOCRATES: For my part nothing, Euthyphro. But you look whether on your part this proposal will enable you to teach me most easily what you promised.

EUTHYPHRO: I would certainly say that the pious is what all the gods love, and the opposite, what all the gods hate, is the impious.

SOCRATES: Then let us again examine whether that is a sound statement, or do we let it pass, and if one of us, or someone else, merely says that something is so, do we accept that it is so? Or should we examine what the speaker means?

EUTHYPHRO: We must examine it, but I certainly think that this is now a fine statement.

SOCRATES: We shall soon know better whether it is. Consider this: Is the pious being loved by the gods because it is pious, or is it pious because it is being loved by the gods?

EUTHYPHRO: I don't know what you mean, Socrates.

SOCRATES: I shall try to explain more clearly. We speak of something carried and something carrying, of something led and something leading, of something seen and something seeing, and you understand that these things are all different from one another and how they differ?

EUTHYPHRO: I think I do.

SOCRATES: So there is also something loved and—a different thing—something loving.

EUTHYPHRO: Of course.

SOCRATES: Tell me then whether the thing carried is a carried thing because it is being carried, or for some other reason?

EUTHYPHRO: No, that is the reason.

SOCRATES: And the thing led is so because it is being led, and the thing seen because it is being seen?

EUTHYPHRO: Certainly.

SOCRATES: It is not being seen because it is a thing seen, but on the contrary it is a thing seen because it is *being* seen;[7] nor is it because it is something led that it is being led, but because it is *being* led that it is something led; nor is something being carried because it is something carried, but it is something carried because it is *being* carried. Is what I want to say

---

[7]The reason that something is seen is because of its *"being seen,"* that is, because of the act of the other entity that sees it; it is not seen because of its own state of being seen. [D. C. ABEL]

clear, Euthyphro? I want to say this, namely, that if anything is being changed or is being affected in any way, it is not being changed because it is something changed, but rather it is something changed because it is *being* changed; nor is it being affected because it is something affected, but it is something affected because it is *being* affected. Or do you not agree?

EUTHYPHRO: I do.

SOCRATES: Is something loved either something changed or something affected by something?

EUTHYPHRO: Certainly.

SOCRATES: So it is in the same case as the things just mentioned: It is not being loved by those who love it because it is something loved, but it is something loved because it is *being* loved by them.

EUTHYPHRO: Necessarily.

SOCRATES: What then do we say about the pious, Euthyphro? Surely that it is *being* loved by all the gods, according to what you say?

EUTHYPHRO: Yes.

SOCRATES: Is it being loved because it is pious, or for some other reason?

EUTHYPHRO: For no other reason.

SOCRATES: It is being loved then because it is pious, but it is not pious because it is being loved?

EUTHYPHRO: Apparently.

SOCRATES: And yet it is something loved and god-loved because it is being loved by the gods?

EUTHYPHRO: Of course.

SOCRATES: Then the god-loved is not the same as the pious, Euthyphro, nor the pious the same as the god-loved, as you say it is, but one differs from the other.

EUTHYPHRO: How so, Socrates?

SOCRATES: Because we agree that the pious is being loved for this reason, that it is pious, but it is not pious because it is being loved. Is that not so?

EUTHYPHRO: Yes.

SOCRATES: And that the god-loved, on the other hand, is so because it is being loved by the gods, by the very fact of being loved, but it is not being loved because it is god-loved.

EUTHYPHRO: True.

SOCRATES: But if the god-loved and the pious were the same, my dear Euthyphro, then if the pious was being loved because it was pious, the god-loved would also be being loved because it was god-loved; and if the god-loved was god-loved because it was being loved by the gods, then the pious would also be pious because it was being loved by the gods. But now you see that they are in opposite cases as being altogether different from each other: The one is such as to be loved because it is being loved, the other is being loved because it is such as to be loved. I'm afraid, Euthyphro, that when you were asked what piety is, you did not wish to make its nature clear to me, but you told me an affect or quality of it, that the pious has the quality of being loved by all the gods, but you have not yet told me what the pious is. Now, if you will, do not hide things from me but tell me again from the beginning what piety is, whether being loved by the gods or having some other quality—we shall not quarrel about that—but be keen to tell me what the pious and the impious are.

EUTHYPHRO: But Socrates, I have no way of telling you what I have in mind, for whatever proposition we put forward goes around and refuses to stay put where we establish it.

SOCRATES: Your statements, Euthyphro, seem to belong to my ancestor, Daedalus.[8] If I were stating them and putting them forward, you would perhaps be making fun of me and say that because of my kinship with him my conclusions in discussion run away and will not stay where one puts them. As these propositions are yours, however, we need some other jest, for they will not stay put for you, as you say yourself.

EUTHYPHRO: I think the same jest will do for our discussion, Socrates, for I am not the one who makes them go around and not remain in the same place. It is you who are the Daedalus, for as far as I am concerned they would remain as they were.

SOCRATES: It looks as if I was cleverer than Daedalus in using my skill, my friend, insofar as he could only cause to move the things he made himself, but I can make other people's move as well as my own. And the smartest part of my skill is that I am clever without wanting to be, for I would rather have your statements to me remain unmoved than possess the wealth of Tantalus[9] as well as the cleverness of Daedalus. But enough of this. Since I think you are making unnecessary difficulties, I am as eager as you are to find a way to teach me about piety, and do not give up before you do.

[4. The Part of Justice Concerned with Care of the Gods]

[SOCRATES:] See whether you think all that is pious is of necessity just.

EUTHYPHRO: I think so.

SOCRATES: And is then all that is just pious? Or is all that is pious just, but not all that is just pious, but some of it is and some is not?

EUTHYPHRO: I do not follow what you are saying, Socrates.

SOCRATES: Yet you are younger than I by as much as you are wiser. As I say, you are making difficulties because of your wealth of wisdom. Pull yourself together, my dear sir; what I am saying is not difficult to grasp. I am saying the opposite of what the poet said who wrote:

You do not wish to name Zeus, who had done it, and who made
All things grow, for where there is fear there is also shame.[10]

I disagree with the poet. Shall I tell you why?

---

[8]*Daedalus:* a legendary artist, inventor, and artisan. His statues were said to be so lifelike that they moved. [D. C. ABEL]

[9]*Tantalus:* a legendary king of Lydia. [D. C. ABEL]

[10]Author unknown. [G. M. A. GRUBE]

EUTHYPHRO: Please do.

SOCRATES: I do not think that "where there is fear there is also shame," for I think that many people who fear disease and poverty and many other such things feel fear, but are not ashamed of the things they fear. Do you not think so?

EUTHYPHRO: I do indeed.

SOCRATES: But where there is shame there is also fear. For is there anyone who, in feeling shame and embarrassment at anything, does not also at the same time fear and dread a reputation for wickedness?

EUTHYPHRO: He is certainly afraid.

SOCRATES: It is then not right to say "where there is fear there is also shame," but that where there is shame there is also fear, for fear covers a larger area than shame. Shame is a part of fear just as odd is a part of number, with the result that it is not true that where there is number there is also oddness, but that where there is oddness there is also number. Do you follow me now?

EUTHYPHRO: Surely.

SOCRATES: This is the kind of thing I was asking before, whether where there is piety there is also justice, but where there is justice there is not always piety, for the pious is a part of justice. Shall we say that, or do you think. otherwise?

EUTHYPHRO: No, but like that, for what you say appears to be right.

SOCRATES: See what comes next: If the pious is a part of the just, we must, it seems, find out what part of the just it is. Now if you asked me something of what we mentioned just now, such as what part of number is the even, and what number that is, I would say it is the number that is divisible into two equal, not unequal, parts. Or do you not think so?

EUTHYPHRO: I do.

SOCRATES: Try in this way to tell me what part of the just the pious is, in order to tell Meletus not to wrong us any more and not to indict me for ungodliness, since I have learned from you sufficiently what is godly and pious and what is not.

EUTHYPHRO: I think, Socrates, that the godly and pious is the part of the just that is concerned with the care of the gods, while that concerned with the care of men is the remaining part of justice.

SOCRATES: You seem to me to put that very well, but I still need a bit of information. I do not know yet what you mean by care, for you do not mean the care of the gods in the same sense as the care of other things—as, for example, we say, don't we, that not everyone knows how to care for horses, but the horse breeder does.

EUTHYPHRO: Yes, I do mean it that way.

SOCRATES: So horse breeding is the care of horses.

EUTHYPHRO: Yes.

SOCRATES: Nor does everyone know how to care for dogs, but the hunter does.

EUTHYPHRO: That is so.

SOCRATES: So hunting is the care of dogs.

EUTHYPHRO: Yes.

SOCRATES: And cattle raising is the care of cattle.

EUTHYPHRO: Quite so.

SOCRATES: While piety and godliness is the care of the gods, Euthyphro. Is that what you mean?

EUTHYPHRO: It is.

SOCRATES: Now care in each case has the same effect; it aims at the good and the benefit of the object cared for, as you can see that horses cared for by horse breeders are benefited and become better. Or do you not think so?

EUTHYPHRO: I do.

SOCRATES: So dogs are benefited by dog breeding, cattle by cattle raising, and so with all the others. Or do you think that care aims to harm the object of its care?

EUTHYPHRO: By Zeus, no.

SOCRATES: It aims to benefit the object of its care?

EUTHYPHRO: Of course.

SOCRATES: Is piety then, which is the care of the gods, also to benefit the gods and make them better? Would you agree that when you do something pious you make some one of the gods better?

EUTHYPHRO: By Zeus, no.

SOCRATES: Nor do I think that this is what you mean—far from it—but that is why I asked you what you meant by the care of gods, because I did not believe you meant this kind of care.

EUTHYPHRO: Quite right, Socrates, that is not the kind of care I mean.

SOCRATES: Very well, but what kind of care of the gods would piety be?

EUTHYPHRO: The kind of care, Socrates, that slaves take of their masters.

SOCRATES: I understand. It is likely to be a kind of service of the gods.

EUTHYPHRO: Quite so.

SOCRATES: Could you tell me to the achievement of what goal service to doctors tends? Is it not, do you think, to achieving health?

EUTHYPHRO: I think so.

SOCRATES: What about service to shipbuilders? To what achievement is it directed?

EUTHYPHRO: Clearly, Socrates, to the building of a ship.

SOCRATES: And service to housebuilders to the building of a house?

EUTHYPHRO: Yes.

SOCRATES: Tell me then, my good sir, to the achievement of what aim does service to the gods tend? You obviously know since you say that you, of all men, have the best knowledge of the divine.

EUTHYPHRO: And I am telling the truth, Socrates.

SOCRATES: Tell me then, by Zeus, what is that excellent aim that the gods achieve, using us as their servants?

EUTHYPHRO: Many fine things, Socrates.

SOCRATES: So do generals, my friend. Nevertheless you could easily tell me their main concern, which is to achieve victory in war, is it not?

EUTHYPHRO: Of course.

SOCRATES: The farmers, too, I think, achieve many fine things, but the main point of their efforts is to produce food from the earth.

EUTHYPHRO: Quite so.

SOCRATES: Well then, how would you sum up the many fine things that the gods achieve?

[5. Giving to and Begging from the Gods]

EUTHYPHRO: I told you a short while ago, Socrates, that it is a considerable task to acquire any precise knowledge of these things, but, to put it simply, I say that if a man knows how to say and do what is pleasing to the gods at prayer and sacrifice, those are pious actions such as preserve both private houses and public affairs of state. The opposite of these pleasing actions are impious and overturn and destroy everything.

SOCRATES: You could tell me in far fewer words, if you were willing, the sum of what I asked, Euthyphro, but you are not keen to teach me, that is clear. You were on the point of doing so, but you turned away. If you had given that answer, I should now have acquired from you sufficient knowledge of the nature of piety. As it is, the lover of inquiry must follow his beloved wherever it may lead him. Once more then, what do you say that piety and the pious are? Are they a knowledge of how to sacrifice and pray?

EUTHYPHRO: They are.

SOCRATES: To sacrifice is to make a gift to the gods, whereas to pray is to beg from the gods?

EUTHYPHRO: Definitely, Socrates.

SOCRATES: It would follow from this statement that piety would be a knowledge of how to give to and beg from the gods.

EUTHYPHRO: You understood what I said very well, Socrates.

SOCRATES: That is because I am so desirous of your wisdom, and I concentrate my mind on it, so that no word of yours may fall to the ground. But tell me, what is this service to the gods? You say it is to beg from them and to give to them?

EUTHYPHRO: I do.

SOCRATES: And to beg correctly would be to ask from them things that we need?

EUTHYPHRO: What else?

SOCRATES: And to give correctly is to give them what they need from us, for it would not be skillful to bring gifts to anyone that are in no way needed.

EUTHYPHRO: True, Socrates.

SOCRATES: Piety would then be a sort of trading skill between gods and men?

EUTHYPHRO: Trading yes, if you prefer to call it that.

SOCRATES: I prefer nothing, unless it is true. But tell me, what benefit do the gods derive from the gifts they receive from us? What they give us is obvious to all. There is for us no good that we do not receive from them. But how are they benefited by what they receive from us? Or do we have such an advantage over them in the trade that we receive all our blessings from them and they receive nothing from us?

EUTHYPHRO: Do you suppose, Socrates, that the gods are benefited by what they receive from us?

SOCRATES: What could those gifts from us to the gods be, Euthyphro?

EUTHYPHRO: What else, do you think, than honor, reverence, and what I mentioned just now, gratitude?

SOCRATES: The pious is then, Euthyphro, pleasing to the gods, but not beneficial or dear to them?

EUTHYPHRO: I think it is of all things most dear to them.

SOCRATES: So the pious is once again what is dear to the gods.

EUTHYPHRO: Most certainly.

SOCRATES: When you say this, will you be surprised if your arguments seem to move about instead of staying put? And will you accuse me of being Daedalus who makes them move, though you are yourself much more skillful than Daedalus and make them go around in a circle? Or do you not realize that our argument has moved around and come again to the same place? You surely remember that earlier the pious and the god-loved were shown not to be the same but different from each other. Or do you not remember?

EUTHYPHRO: I do.

SOCRATES: Do you then not realize now that you are saying that what is dear to the gods is the pious? Is this not the same as the god-loved? Or is it not?

EUTHYPHRO: It certainly is.

SOCRATES: Either we were wrong when we agreed before, or, if we were right then, we are wrong now.

EUTHYPHRO: That seems to be so.

[CONCLUSION]

SOCRATES: So we must investigate again from the beginning what piety is, as I shall not willingly give up before I learn this. Do not think me unworthy, but concentrate your attention and tell the truth. For you know it, if any man does, and I must not let you go, like Proteus,[11] before you tell me. If you had no clear knowledge of piety and impiety you would never have ventured to prosecute your old father for murder on behalf of a servant. For fear of the gods you would have been afraid to take the risk lest you should not be acting rightly, and would have been ashamed before men, but now I know well that you believe you have clear knowledge of piety and impiety. So tell me, my good Euthyphro, and do not hide what you think it is.

EUTHYPHRO: Some other time, Socrates, for I am in a hurry now, and it is time for me to go.

---

[11]*Proteus:* a sea god able to assume different shapes. If held until he takes his true shape, he will answer questions. [D. C. ABEL]

SOCRATES: What a thing to do, my friend! By going you have cast me down from a great hope I had, that I would learn from you the nature of the pious and the impious and so escape Meletus' indictment by showing him that I had acquired wisdom in divine matters from Euthyphro, and my ignorance would no longer cause me to be careless and inventive about such things, and that I would be better for the rest of my life.

Pensées

Blaise Pascal

Blaise Pascal was born in 1623 in Clermont (now Clermont-Ferrand), France. His mother died when he was three, and in 1631 his father moved the family to Paris. Pascal had no formal schooling; he was educated by his father. He proved to be a precocious mathematician, publishing a paper on conic sections at the age of 16 and inventing a calculating machine when he was 19. Pascal then turned his attention to physics. He made important discoveries—and published his findings—on such topics as atmospheric pressure, the equilibrium of fluids, and the problem of the vacuum. His later work on the mathematics of chance laid the foundations of modern probability theory. In 1646 Pascal's entire family converted to Jansenism (a highly rigorous form of Roman Catholicism, later condemned as heretical). One night in November 1654 Pascal had a powerful religious experience, and from that time on he devoted his intellectual energies primarily to religious matters. He defended Jansenism in a series of satirical letters known as the *Provincial Letters,* written in 1656 and 1657 under an assumed name. In 1659 he began (but never finished) a general defense of Christianity entitled *Apologie de la religion chrétienne* ("Apology for the Christian Religion"). Pascal died in Paris in 1662, at the age of 39, apparently from meningitis following a stomach ulcer.

In 1670 Pascal's fragmentary notes for the *Apologie* were published in a rearranged and abridged form. The editor called the work *Pensées sur la religion* ("Thoughts on Religion"), and they have been known by the shortened French title *Pensées* ever since. Our reading is from sections of the *Pensées* in which Pascal presents an argument (now known as "Pascal's wager") for believing in God and discusses the immortality of the soul.

Pascal explains that, in this life, we will never be able to know whether God exists, because our minds are finite and God (if God exists) is infinite and "infinitely beyond our comprehension." Despite our inability to know whether God exists, we must make a "wager" and either believe or not believe in God—there is no way to avoid the choice. If we bet that God exists and are right (assuming that we live morally and that there is an afterlife), we gain an eternity of happiness; if we are wrong, we lose nothing except the finite benefits we might have gained from immoral behavior. We may either win or lose our bet, but because we stand to make an infinite gain from a finite amount wagered, we would be foolish not to believe in God. Those who find themselves unable to believe despite their acceptance of the logic of this argument must learn to control their passions and love of pleasure, and begin to behave as if they did believe. Pascal goes on to stress the importance of trying to find out whether the soul is immortal and whether anything lies beyond the unhappiness of this life, and he castigates those who ignore these vital questions.

387

Order. I should be much more afraid of being mistaken and then finding out that Christianity is true, than of being mistaken in believing it to be true. . . .

418

Infinity—nothing. . . . If there is a God, he is infinitely beyond our comprehension, since, being indivisible and without limits, he bears no relation to us. We are therefore incapable of knowing either *what* he is or *whether* he is. That being so, who would dare to attempt an answer to the question? Certainly not we, who bear no relation to him.

Who then will condemn Christians for being unable to give rational grounds for their belief, professing as they do a religion for which they cannot give rational grounds? They declare that it is a folly, *stultitia*,[1] in expounding it to the world, and then you complain that they do not prove it. If they did prove it they would not be keeping their word. It is by being without proof that they show they are not without sense. "Yes, but although that excuses those who offer their religion as such, and absolves them from the criticism of producing it without rational grounds, it does not absolve those who accept it." Let us then examine this point, and let us say: "Either God is or he is not." But to which view shall we be inclined? Reason cannot decide this question. Infinite chaos separates us. At the far end of this infinite distance a coin is being spun that will come down heads or tails. How will you wager? Reason cannot make you choose either; reason cannot prove either wrong.

Do not then condemn as wrong those who have made a choice, for you know nothing about it. "No, but I will condemn them not for having made this particular choice, but any choice, for, although the one who calls heads and the other one are equally at fault, the fact is that they are both at fault: The right thing is not to wager at all."

Yes, but you must wager. There is no choice, you are already committed. Which will you choose then? Let us see: Since a choice must be made, let us see which offers you the least interest. You have two things to lose: the true and the good; and two things to stake: your reason and your will (your knowledge and your happiness). And your nature has two things to avoid: error and wretchedness. Since you must necessarily choose, your reason is no more affronted by choosing one rather than the other. That is one point cleared up. But your happiness? Let us weigh up the gain and the loss involved in calling heads that God exists. Let us assess the two cases: If you win you win everything, if you lose you lose nothing. Do not hesitate then; wager that he does exist. "That is wonderful. Yes, I must wager, but perhaps I am wagering too much." Let us see: Since there is an equal chance of gain and loss, if you stood to win only two lives for one you could still wager, but supposing you stood to win three?

You would have to play (since you must necessarily play) and it would be unwise of you, once you are obliged to play, not to risk your life in order to win three lives at a game in which there is an equal chance of losing and winning. But there is an eternity of life and happiness. That being so, even though there were an infinite number of chances, of which only one were in your favor, you

---

[1]*stultitia:* the Latin equivalent of the Greek noun *mōria* ("folly"), a term Paul uses in 1 Corinthians 1:18 and 21. [D. C. Abel]

would still be right to wager one in order to win two; and you would be acting wrongly, being obliged to play, in refusing to stake one life against three in a game where out of an infinite number of chances there is one in your favor, if there were an infinity of infinitely happy life to be won. But here there is an infinity of infinitely happy life to be won, one chance of winning against a finite number of chances of losing, and what you are staking is finite. That leaves no choice; wherever there is infinity, and where there are not infinite chances of losing against that of winning, there is no room for hesitation—you must give everything. And thus, since you are obliged to play, you must be renouncing reason if you hoard your life rather than risk it for an infinite gain, just as likely to occur as a loss amounting to nothing.

For it is no good saying that it is uncertain whether you will win, that it is certain that you are taking a risk, and that the infinite distance between the certainty of what you are risking and the uncertainty of what you may gain makes the finite good you are certainly risking equal to the infinite good that you are not certain to gain. This is not the case. Every gambler takes a certain risk for an uncertain gain, and yet he is taking a certain finite risk for an uncertain finite gain without sinning against reason. Here there is no infinite distance between the certain risk and the uncertain gain—that is not true. There is, indeed, an infinite distance between the certainty of winning and the certainty of losing, but the proportion between the uncertainty of winning and the certainty of what is being risked is in proportion to the chances of winning or losing. And hence, if there are as many chances on one side as on the other, you are playing for even odds. And in that case the certainty of what you are risking is equal to the uncertainty of what you may win; it is by no means infinitely distant from it. Thus our argument carries infinite weight, when the stakes are finite in a game where there are even chances of winning and losing and an infinite prize to be won.

This is conclusive; and if men are capable of any truth, this is it.

"I confess, I admit it, but is there really no way of seeing what the cards are?"—"Yes. Scripture and the rest, and so on."—"Yes, but my hands are tied and my lips are sealed; I am being forced to wager and I am not free; I am being held fast and I am so made that I cannot believe. What do you want me to do then?"—"That is true, but at least get it into your head that, if you are unable to believe, it is because of your passions, since reason impels you to believe and yet you cannot do so. Concentrate then not on convincing yourself by multiplying proofs of God's existence but by diminishing your passions. You want to find faith and you do not know the road. You want to be cured of unbelief and you ask for the remedy. Learn from those who were once bound like you and who now wager all they have. These are people who know the road you wish to follow, who have been cured of the affliction of which you wish to be cured: Follow the way by which they began. They behaved just as if they did believe, taking holy water, having Masses said, and so on. That will make you believe quite naturally, and will make you more docile."—"But that is what I am afraid of."—"But why? What have you to lose? But to show you that this is the way, the fact is that this diminishes the passions, which are your great obstacles. . . ."

End of this address. "Now what harm will come to you from choosing this course? You will be faithful, honest, humble, grateful, full of good works, a sincere, true friend. . . . It is true you will not enjoy noxious pleasures, glory, and good living; but will you not have others? I tell you that you will gain even in this life, and that at every step you take along this road you will see that your gain is so certain and your risk so negligible that in the end you will realize that you have wagered on something certain and infinite for which you have paid nothing."

"How these words fill me with rapture and delight!"

"If my words please you and seem cogent, you must know that they come from a man who went down upon his knees before and after to pray this infinite and indivisible being, to whom he submits his own, that he might bring your being also to submit to him for your own good and for his glory, and that strength might thus be reconciled with lowliness." . . .

427

. . . The immortality of the soul is something of such vital importance to us, affecting us so deeply, that one must have lost all feeling not to care about knowing the facts of the matter. All our actions and thoughts must follow such different paths, according to whether there is hope of eternal blessings or not, that the only possible way of acting with sense and judgment is to decide our course in the light of this point, which ought to be our ultimate objective.

Thus our chief interest and chief duty is to seek enlightenment on this subject, on which all our conduct depends. And that is why, amongst those who are not convinced, I make an absolute distinction between those who strive with all their might to learn and those who live without troubling themselves or thinking about it.

I can feel nothing but compassion for those who sincerely lament their doubt, who regard it as the ultimate misfortune, and who, sparing no effort to escape from it, make their search their principal and most serious business.

But as for those who spend their lives without a thought for this final end of life and who, solely because they do not find within themselves the light of conviction, neglect to look elsewhere and to examine thoroughly whether this opinion is one of those that people accept out of credulous simplicity or one of those that, though obscure in themselves, nonetheless have a most solid and unshakeable foundation—as for them, I view them very differently.

This negligence in a matter where they themselves, their eternity, their all are at stake, fills me more with irritation than pity; it astounds and appalls me; it seems quite monstrous to me. I do not say this prompted by the pious zeal of spiritual devotion. I mean on the contrary that we ought to have this feeling from principles of human interest and self-esteem. For that we need only see what the least enlightened see.

One needs no great sublimity of soul to realize that in this life there is no true and solid satisfaction, that all our pleasures are mere vanity, that our afflictions are infinite, and finally that death, which threatens us at every moment, must in a few years infallibly face us with the inescapable and appalling alternative of being annihilated or wretched throughout eternity.

Nothing could be more real or more dreadful than that. Let us put on as bold a face as we like—that is the end awaiting the world's most illustrious life.

Let us ponder these things, and then say whether it is not beyond doubt that the only good thing in this life is the hope of another life, that we become happy only as we come nearer to it, and that, just as no more unhappiness awaits those who have been quite certain of eternity, so there is no happiness for those who have no inkling of it.

It is therefore quite certainly a great evil to have such doubts, but it is at least an indispensable obligation to seek when one does thus doubt; so the doubter who does not seek is at the same time very unhappy and very wrong. If in addition he feels a calm satisfaction that he openly professes, and even regards as a reason for joy and vanity, I can find no terms to describe so extravagant a creature. . . .

428

. . . It is indubitable that this life is but an instant of time, that the state of death is eternal, whatever its nature may be, and thus that all our actions and thoughts must follow such different paths according to the state of this eternity, that the only possible way of acting with sense and judgment is to decide our course in the light of this point, which ought to be our ultimate objective.

There is nothing more obvious than this, and it follows, according to rational principles, that men are behaving quite reasonably if they do not choose another path. Let us then judge on that score those who live without a thought for the final end of life, drifting wherever their inclinations and pleasures may take them, without reflection or anxiety, as if they could annihilate eternity by keeping their minds off it, concerned solely with attaining instant happiness.

However, eternity exists, and death, which must begin it and which threatens at every moment, must infallibly face them with the inescapable and appalling alternative of being either eternally annihilated or wretched, without their knowing which of these two forms of eternity stands ready to meet them forever.

The consequences are undeniably terrible. They risk an eternity of wretchedness; whereupon, as if the matter were not worth their trouble, they omit to consider whether this is one of those opinions that are accepted by the people with too ready credulity or one of those that, though obscure in themselves, have a very solid, though concealed, foundation. Thus they do not know whether the fact is true or false, nor whether the proofs are strong or weak. The proofs lie before their eyes, but they refuse to look, and in this state of ignorance they choose to do everything necessary to fall into this calamity, if it exists, to wait for death before testing the proofs, while yet remaining highly satisfied in that state, professing it openly, and indeed with pride. Can we seriously think how important this matter is without being horrified at such extravagant behavior?

To settle down in such ignorance is a monstrous thing, and those who spend their lives thus must be made to feel how extravagant and stupid it is by having it pointed out to them so that they are confounded by the sight of their own folly. For this is how men argue when they choose to live without knowing what they are and without seeking enlightenment. "I do not know," they say. . . .

577

If we must never take any chances, we ought not to do anything for religion, for it is not certain. But how many chances we do take—sea voyages, battles. Therefore, I say, we should have to do nothing at all, for nothing is certain. And there is more certainty in religion than that we shall live to see tomorrow.

For it is not certain that we shall see tomorrow, but it is certainly possible that we shall not. We cannot say the same of religion. It is not certain that it is true, but who would dare to say that it is certainly possible that it is not?

Now when we work for tomorrow and take chances we are behaving reasonably, for we ought to take chances, according to the rule of probability already demonstrated. . . .

748

Objection. Those who hope for salvation are happy in that respect, but this is counterbalanced by their fear of hell.

Reply. Who has more cause to fear hell, someone who does not know whether there is a hell, but is certain to be damned if there is, or someone who is completely convinced that there is a hell, and hopes to be saved if there is?

816

"I would soon have given up a life of pleasure," they say, "if I had faith." But I tell you: "You would soon have faith if you gave up a life of pleasure. Now it is up to you to begin. If I could give you faith, I would. But I cannot, nor can I test the truth of what you say, but you can easily give up your pleasure and test whether I am telling the truth."

CHAPTER 3

Theories of Knowledge

Nome of us would be so presumptuous as to claim that we know everything, but we all are quite sure that we know *some* things. But what do we mean when we say that we know something? Does knowing something imply that we have verified it for ourselves? If we have not verified it, do we have *belief* rather than knowledge? If I have never been to India, can I legitimately say that I *know* India exists? Is it more accurate to say that I *believe* that it exists because I trust publishers who sell atlases that label a certain region "India," newspapers that print stories about India, teachers who lecture about India, and friends who tell me about their travels there and show me photographs? Perhaps one kind of verification is *sight*: If I see it, I know it is true. If so, do I know that the print on this page is black because I am looking at it and it appears black? Is it possible that even though the print *appears* black, it is really some other color? But how can print have any color *at all* if it is made up of colorless atoms? Is it more accurate to say that the print causes me to *experience* a color, but that the print itself is colorless? To carry this questioning even further, how can I even be sure that I am looking at a printed page right now? Could I really be home sleeping and simply *dreaming* that I am reading a book? Can I be absolutely certain of anything at all? Is absolute certainty necessary for knowledge? Assuming that I can attain knowledge, is the ultimate source of my knowledge sensation, reason, intuition, or some combination of these and/or other factors?

These are some of the questions addressed by *epistemology,* the study of the nature and grounds of knowledge. This section presents eight readings that address these and related epistemological issues.

Plato in the *Republic* contrasts knowledge and opinion. The objects of knowledge are the forms—immaterial and unchanging realities, such as the beautiful itself. The objects of opinion are the Many—material and changing things, such as beautiful trees and horses. The forms are fully real and grasped by the mind, whereas the Many are partly real and partly unreal and are grasped by the senses.

René Descartes argues that genuine knowledge requires absolute certainty. Trying to achieve certainty by using a "method of doubt," he refuses to accept as true anything about which he could possibly be deceived. Descartes discovers that he can be sure that he exists, because he could not even be deceived if he did not exist. This discovery leads him to claim that anything that he perceives very clearly and distinctly is true. He also holds that the mind contains innate ideas, including the idea of God.

Descartes' theory of knowledge is considered a form of *rationalism* (derived from *ratio,* Latin for "reason") because it emphasizes knowledge attained through the mind (innate ideas, intuition, relations among ideas, logical inference, and so on). The next two theories, by contrast, are forms of *empiricism* (derived from *empeiria,* Greek for "experience") because they emphasize knowledge attained through sense experience.

John Locke rejects Descartes' rationalist doctrine that the mind is furnished with innate ideas. Locke claims that the mind is originally blank, like a sheet of white paper; all of our ideas come either from experiencing external objects or from experiencing the operations of our mind. He distinguishes two kinds of qualities that objects cause us to experience: *primary qualities,* which really exist in things (three-dimensionality and shape, for example), and *secondary qualities,* which do not exist in things but are only in our mind (color and taste, for example). The second empiricist theory is that of David Hume. Hume holds that all knowledge begins with "impressions" (direct sense experiences) and that impressions give rise to "ideas" (copies of impressions). When we attempt to extend our knowledge beyond that provided by impressions and ideas, we rely on the notion of cause and effect. But we cannot *know* that causality exists because we have no impression of a "cause" linking two events: All we experience is the temporal succession of the two events.

Immanuel Kant proposes a theory of knowledge that combines elements of rationalism and empiricism. He accepts the empiricist claim that our knowledge begins with experience, but also accepts the rationalist contention that part of the content of knowledge comes from our mind. Both points are correct, Kant argues, because our mind is constructed in such a way that we necessarily experience objects in certain ways (for example, as being caused and as existing in space and time). Therefore, although we know that objects will invariably *appear to us* to possess certain attributes, we do not experience objects as they are *in themselves.* It would be an error, for example, to say that things themselves are caused, spatial, or temporal.

Our final reading is from Alison M. Jaggar, who points out that most theories of knowledge exalt dispassionate reason as the sole path to knowledge and see emotion as subverting the knowing process. Jaggar argues that emotion in fact plays a helpful and necessary role in attaining knowledge. She contends that an important avenue to knowledge is the exploration of the emotional responses of members of subordinate groups in society.

Republic

Plato

A biography of Plato appears on p. 5.

Our reading is from the *Republic,* a work cast as a report by Socrates of a conversation he had the previous day with several people, including Glaucon and Adeimantus (Plato's older brothers). In the dialogue, Socrates presents his views on a number of topics, but scholars agree these views are Plato's own, not those of the historical Socrates. Our readings are taken from exchanges between Socrates and Glaucon in Books V, VI, and VII.

In Book V, Glaucon asks Socrates who the true philosophers are. Socrates, alluding to the etymology of the word ("lovers of wisdom"), says that they are "lovers of seeing the truth." Expanding on this notion, Socrates explains that philosophers are those who love the One rather than the Many. For example, a philosopher goes beyond the love of individual beautiful things to love the beautiful itself (the *form* of beauty—that which all beautiful things have in common, and makes them beautiful). The forms are fully real and are the objects of genuine knowledge, whereas the Many lie between being and not-being and are the objects of mere opinion.

In Book VI, Socrates explains that the Many belong to the visible world, which is seen by the eye, whereas the forms reside in the intelligible world, which is grasped by the mind. He illustrates the two worlds by describing a line divided into two main parts, with each of these parts subdivided into two parts. Each of the resulting four segments of the line represents a type of object of cognition. Corresponding to each of the four types of object of cognition is a distinct condition of the soul. (See the diagram of the divided line on p. 137.)

Socrates further illustrates this theory of knowledge in Book VII through the famous allegory of the cave. We are like prisoners who live their entire lives inside a cave. Just as such prisoners would think that shadows on the cave wall were real and would be unaware of the real world outside the cave, so we think that the visible world of the Many is real, ignorant of the intelligible world of forms. (See the diagram of the cave on p. 139.)

BOOK V

... GLAUCON: Who do you think . . . are the true philosophers?

SOCRATES: The lovers of seeing the truth.

GLAUCON: That . . . is no doubt correct, but what exactly do you mean by it?

SOCRATES: It would not be easy to explain to someone else. But you, I imagine, will agree to the following.

SOCRATES: What?

SOCRATES: That since beautiful is the opposite of ugly, they are two things.

GLAUCON: Of course.

SOCRATES: And since they are two things, each of them is also one?

GLAUCON: That's true too.

SOCRATES: And the same argument applies, then, to just and unjust, good and bad, and all the forms:[1] Each of them is itself one thing, but because they appear all over the place in partnership with actions and bodies, and with one another, each of them appears to be many things.

GLAUCON: That's right.

SOCRATES: Well, then, that is the basis of the distinction I draw: On one side are the lovers of seeing, the lovers of crafts . . . ; on the other, the only ones it is correct to call philosophers.

GLAUCON: How do you mean?

SOCRATES: The lovers of listening and seeing are passionately devoted to beautiful sounds, colors, shapes, and everything fashioned out of such things. But their thought is unable to see the nature of the beautiful itself or to be passionately devoted to it.

GLAUCON: That's certainly true.

SOCRATES: On the other hand, won't those who *are* able to approach the beautiful itself, and see it by itself, be rare?

GLAUCON: Very.

SOCRATES: What about someone who believes in beautiful things but does not believe in the beautiful itself, and would not be able to follow anyone who tried to lead him to the knowledge of it? Do you think he is living in a dream, or is he awake? Just consider: Isn't it dreaming to think—whether asleep or awake—that a likeness is not a likeness, but rather the thing itself that it is like?

GLAUCON: I certainly think that someone who does that is dreaming.

SOCRATES: But what about someone who, to take the opposite case, does believe in the beautiful itself, is able to observe both it and the things that participate[2] in it, and does not think that the participants are it, or that it is the participants—do you think he is living in a dream or is awake?

GLAUCON: He is very much awake.

SOCRATES: So, because this person knows these things, we would be right to describe his thought as knowledge; but the other's we would be right to describe as opinion, because he opines?

GLAUCON: Certainly. . . .

SOCRATES: Now that all that has been established, I want him to tell me this—the excellent fellow who believes that there is no beautiful itself, no form of beauty itself that remains always the same in all respects, but who does believe that there are many beautiful

---

[1]*forms:* A *form* is that which all things included under the same concept have in common, and makes them fall under that concept. For example, two just actions are just because they have the just itself (the form of justice) in common. [D. C. ABEL]

[2]*participate:* Particular instantiations of a form (see footnote 1) are said to participate ("take part") in that form. For example, a beautiful tree participates in the beautiful itself (the form of beauty). [D. C. ABEL]

things—I mean, that lover of seeing who cannot bear to hear anyone say that the beautiful is one thing, or the just, or any of the rest—I want him to answer this question: "My very good fellow," we will say, "of all the many beautiful things, is there one that won't also seem ugly? Or any just one that won't seem unjust? Or any pious one that won't seem impious?"

GLAUCON: There is not. On the contrary, it is inevitable that they would somehow seem both beautiful and ugly; and the same with the other things you asked about.

SOCRATES: What about the many things that are doubles? Do they seem to be any the less halves than doubles?

GLAUCON: No.

SOCRATES: And again, will things that we say are big, small, light, or heavy be any more what we say they are than they will be the opposite?

GLAUCON: No, each of them is always both.

SOCRATES: Then is each of the many things any more what one says it is than it is *not* what one says it is?

GLAUCON: No, they are like those puzzles one hears at parties, or the children's riddle about the eunuch who threw something at a bat—the one about what he threw at it and what it was in.[3] For these things, too, are ambiguous, and one cannot understand them as fixedly being or fixedly not-being, or as both, or as neither.

SOCRATES: Do you know what to do with them, then, or anywhere better to put them than in between being and not-being? Surely they cannot be more opaque than what is not, by not-being more than it; nor clearer than what is, by being more than it.

GLAUCON: That's absolutely true.

SOCRATES: So, we have now discovered, it seems, that the majority of people's many conventional views about beauty and the rest are somehow rolling around between what is not and what purely is.

GLAUCON: We have.

SOCRATES: And we agreed earlier that if anything turned out to be of that sort, it would have to be called an object of opinion, not an object of knowledge—a wandering, in-between object grasped by the in-between power.

GLAUCON: We did.

SOCRATES: As for those, then, who look at many beautiful things but do not see the beautiful itself and are incapable of following another who would lead them to it; or many just things but not the just itself; and similarly with all the rest—these people, we will say, have opinions about all these things but have no knowledge of what their opinions are about.

---

[3]The children's riddle illustrates Socrates's point about the same thing having opposite qualities. A eunuch is a man and not a man, a bat is a bird and not a bird, the pumice stone thrown by the eunuch is a stone and not a stone, and the tree that the poor-sighted eunuch thought the bat was in is not a tree but a piece of timber. [D. C. ABEL]

GLAUCON: That is what we would have to say.

SOCRATES: On the other hand, what about those who in each case look at the things themselves that are always the same in every respect? Won't we say that they have knowledge, not mere opinion?

GLAUCON: Once again, we would have to.

SOCRATES: Shall we say, then, that these people are passionately devoted to and love the things with which knowledge deals, as the others are devoted to and love the things with which opinion deals? We have not forgotten, have we, that the latter love and look at beautiful sounds, colors, and things of that sort, but cannot even bear the idea that the beautiful itself is a thing that is?

GLAUCON: No, we have not.

SOCRATES: Will we be striking a false note, then, if we call such people "philodoxers" (lovers of opinion) rather than "philosophers" (lovers of wisdom or knowledge)? Will they be very angry with us if we call them that?

GLAUCON: Not if they take my advice. It is not in accord with divine law to be angry with the truth.

SOCRATES: So, those who in each case are passionately devoted to the thing itself are the ones we must call, not "philodoxers," but "philosophers"?

GLAUCON: Absolutely.

BOOK VI

SOCRATES: We say that there are many beautiful, many good, and many other such things, thereby distinguishing them in words.

GLAUCON: We do.

SOCRATES: We also say there is a beautiful itself and a good itself. And so, in the case of all the things that we then posited as many, we reverse ourselves and posit a single form belonging to each, since we suppose there is a single one, and call it what each is.

GLAUCON: That's true.

SOCRATES: And we say that the one class of things is visible but not intelligible, while the forms are intelligible but not visible.

GLAUCON: Absolutely. . . .

SOCRATES: Do you understand these two kinds, visible and intelligible?

GLAUCON: I do.

SOCRATES: Represent them, then, by a line divided into two unequal sections. Then divide each section—that of the visible kind and that of the intelligible—in the same proportion as the line. In terms now of relative clarity and opacity, you will have as one subsection of the visible, images. By images I mean, first, shadows, then reflections in bodies of water and in all close-packed, smooth, and shiny materials, and everything of that sort. Do you understand?

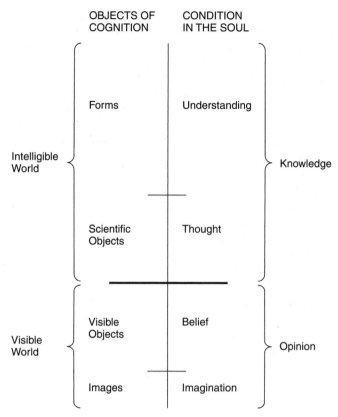

OBJECTS OF COGNITION — CONDITION IN THE SOUL

Forms — Understanding

Intelligible World

Scientific Objects — Thought

Knowledge

Visible Objects — Belief

Visible World

Images — Imagination

Opinion

The Divided Line

GLAUCON: I do understand.

SOCRATES: Then, in the other subsection of the visible, put the originals of these images—that is, the animals around us, every plant, and the whole class of manufactured things.

GLAUCON: I will.

SOCRATES: Would you also be willing to say, then, that, as regards truth and untruth, the division is in this ratio: As what is opined is to what is known, so the likeness is to the thing it is like?

GLAUCON: Certainly.

SOCRATES: Next, consider how the section of the intelligible is to be divided.

GLAUCON: How?

SOCRATES: As follows: In one subsection, the soul, using as images the things that were imitated before, is forced to base its inquiry on hypotheses, proceeding not to a first principle but to a conclusion. In the other subsection, by contrast, it makes its way to an unhypothetical first principle, proceeding from a hypothesis but without the images used in the previous subsection, using forms themselves and making its investigation through them.

GLAUCON: I do not fully understand what you are saying.

SOCRATES: Let's try again. You see, you will understand it more easily after this explanation. I think you know that students of geometry, calculation, and the like hypothesize the odd and the even, the various figures, the three kinds of angles, and other things akin to these in each of their investigations, regarding them as known. These they treat as hypotheses and do not think it necessary to give any argument for them, either to themselves or to others, as if they were evident to everyone. And going from these first principles through the remaining steps, they arrive in full agreement at the point they set out to reach in their investigation.

GLAUCON: I certainly know that much.

SOCRATES: Then don't you also know that they use visible forms and make their arguments about them, although they are not thinking about them, but about those other things that they are like? They make their arguments with a view to the square itself and the diagonal itself, not the diagonal they draw, and similarly with the others. The very things they make and draw, of which shadows and reflections in water are images, they now in turn use as images in seeking to see those other things themselves that one cannot see except by means of thought.

GLAUCON: That's true.

SOCRATES: This, then, is the kind of thing that I said was intelligible. The soul forced to use hypotheses in the investigation of it, not traveling up to a first principle, since it cannot escape or get above its hypotheses, but using as images those very things of which images were made by the things below them, and that, by comparison to their images, were thought to be clear and to be honored as such.

GLAUCON: I understand that you mean what is dealt with in geometry and related crafts.

SOCRATES: Also understand, then, that by the other subsection of the intelligible I mean what reason itself grasps by the power of dialectical discussion,[4] treating its hypotheses, not as first principles, but as genuine hypotheses (that is, stepping stones and links in a chain), in order to arrive at what is unhypothetical and the first principle of everything. Having grasped this principle, it reverses itself and, keeping hold of what follows from it, comes down to a conclusion, making no use of anything visible at all, but only of forms themselves, moving on through forms to forms, and ending in forms.

GLAUCON: I understand, though not adequately—you see, in my opinion you are speaking of an enormous task. You want to distinguish the part of what is and is intelligible, the part looked at by the science of dialectical discussion, as clearer than the part looked at by the so-called sciences—those for which hypotheses are first principles. And although those who look at the latter part are forced to do so by

---

[4]*dialectical discussion:* a process of inquiry in which one person, by asking a series of probing questions on a topic, leads the other person to reflect more deeply on the topic and understand it more fully. This process is illustrated clearly in Plato's *Euthyphro,* Reading 11 in this book. [D. C. ABEL]

means of thought rather than sense perception, still, because they do not go back to a genuine first principle in considering it, but proceed from hypotheses, you do not think that they have true understanding of them, even though—given such a first principle—they are intelligible. And you seem to me to call the state of mind of the geometers—and the others of that sort—*thought* but not *understanding;* thought being intermediate between belief and understanding.

SOCRATES: You have grasped my meaning most adequately. Join me, then, in taking these four conditions in the soul as corresponding to the four subsections of the line: understanding dealing with the highest, thought dealing with the second; assign belief to the third, and imagination to the last. Arrange them in a proportion and consider that each shares in clarity to the degree that the subsection it deals with shares in truth.

GLAUCON: I understand, agree, and arrange them as you say.

BOOK VII

SOCRATES: Next, then. compare the effect of education and that of the lack of it on our nature to an experience like this. Imagine human beings living in an underground. cavelike dwelling, with an entrance a long way up that is open to the light and as wide as the cave itself. They have been there since childhood, with their necks and legs fettered, so that they are fixed in the same place, able to see only in front of them, because their fetter prevents them from turning their heads around. Light is provided by a fire burning far above and behind them. Between the prisoners and the fire, there is an elevated road stretching. Imagine that along this road a low wall has been built—like the screen in front of people that is provided by puppeteers, and above which they show their puppets.

The Cave

GLAUCON: I am imagining it.

SOCRATES: Also imagine, then, that there are people alongside the wall carrying multifarious artifacts that project above it—statues of people and other animals, made of stone, wood, and every material. And as you would expect, some of the carriers are talking and some are silent.

GLAUCON: It is a strange image you are describing, and strange prisoners.

SOCRATES: They are like us. I mean, in the first place, do you think these prisoners have ever seen anything of themselves and one another besides the shadows that the fire casts on the wall of the cave in front of them?

GLAUCON: How could they, if they have to keep their heads motionless throughout life?

SOCRATES: What about the things carried along the wall? Isn't the same true where they are concerned?

GLAUCON: Of course.

SOCRATES: And if they could engage in discussion with one another, don't you think they would assume that the words they used applied to the things they see passing in front of them?

GLAUCON: They would have to.

SOCRATES: What if their prison also had an echo from the wall facing them? When one of the carriers passing along the wall spoke, do you think they would believe that anything other than the shadow passing in front of them was speaking?

GLAUCON: I do not, by Zeus.

SOCRATES: All in all, then, what the prisoners would take for true reality is nothing other than the shadows of those artifacts.

GLAUCON: That's entirely inevitable.

SOCRATES: Consider, then, what being released from their bonds and cured of their foolishness would naturally be like, if something like this should happen to them. When one was freed and suddenly compelled to stand up, turn his neck around, walk, and look up toward the light, he would be pained by doing all these things and be unable to see the things whose shadows he had seen before, because of the flashing lights. What do you think he would say if we told him that what he had seen before was silly nonsense, but that now—because he is a bit closer to what is, and is turned toward things that *are* more—he sees more correctly? And in particular, if we pointed to each of the things passing by and compelled him to answer what each of them is, don't you think he would be puzzled and believe that the things he saw earlier were more truly real than the ones he was being shown?

GLAUCON: Much more so.

SOCRATES: And if he were compelled to look at the light itself, wouldn't his eyes be pained and wouldn't he turn around and flee toward the things he is able to see, and believe that they are really clearer than the ones he is being shown?

GLAUCON: He would.

SOCRATES: And if someone dragged him by force away from there, along the rough, steep, upward path, and did not let him go until he had dragged him into the light of the sun, wouldn't he be pained and angry at being treated that way? And when he came into the light, wouldn't he have his eyes filled with sunlight and be unable to see a single one of the things now said to be truly real?

GLAUCON: No, he would not be able to—at least not right away.

SOCRATES: He would need time to get adjusted, I suppose, if he is going to see the things in the world above. At first, he would see shadows most easily, then images of men and other things in water, then the things themselves. From these, it would be easier for him to go on to look at the things in the sky and the sky itself at night, gazing at the light of the stars and the moon, than during the day, gazing at the sun and the light of the sun.

GLAUCON: Of course.

SOCRATES: Finally, I suppose, he would be able to see the sun—not reflections of it in water or some alien place, but the sun just by itself in its own place—and be able to look at it and see what it is like.

GLAUCON: He would have to.

SOCRATES: After that, he would already be able to conclude about it that it provides the seasons and the years, governs everything in the visible world, and is in some way the cause of all the things that he and his fellows used to see.

GLAUCON: That would clearly be his next step.

SOCRATES: What about when he reminds himself of his first dwelling place, what passed for wisdom there, and his fellow prisoners? Don't you think he would count himself happy for the change and pity the others?

GLAUCON: Certainly.

SOCRATES: And if there had been honors, praises, or prizes among them for the one who was sharpest at identifying the shadows as they passed by; and was best able to remember which usually came earlier, which later, and which simultaneously; and who was thus best able to prophesy the future—do you think that our man would desire these rewards or envy those among the prisoners who were honored and held power? Or do you think he would feel with Homer that he would much prefer to "work the earth as a serf for another man, a man without possessions of his own"[5] and go through any sufferings rather than share their beliefs and live as they do?

GLAUCON: Yes, I think he would rather suffer anything than live like that.

SOCRATES: Consider this too, then. If this man went back down into the cave and sat down in his same seat, wouldn't his eyes be filled with darkness, coming suddenly out of the sun like that?

GLAUCON: Certainly.

---

[5]Homer, *Odyssey*, Book XI, lines 489–90. [C. D. C. REEVE, TRANSLATOR] The words are spoken by the ghost of Achilles, the greatest Greek warrior of the Trojan War. Homer (8th century B.C.E.) was a Greek epic poet. [D. C. ABEL]

SOCRATES: Now, if he had to compete once again with the perpetual prisoners in recognizing the shadows, while his sight was still dim and before his eyes had recovered, and if the time required for readjustment was not short, wouldn't he provoke ridicule? Wouldn't it be said of him that he had returned from his upward journey with his eyes ruined, and that it is not worthwhile even to try to travel upward? And as for anyone who tried to free the prisoners and lead them upward, if they could somehow get their hands on him, wouldn't they kill him?[6]

GLAUCON: They certainly would.

SOCRATES: This image, my dear Glaucon, must be fitted together as a whole with what we said before. The realm revealed through sight should be likened to the prison dwelling, and the light of the fire inside it to the sun's power. And if you think of the upward journey and the seeing of things above as the upward journey of the soul to the intelligible realm, you won't mistake my intention—since it is what you wanted to hear about. Only the god knows whether it is true. But this is how these phenomena seem to me: In the knowable realm, the last thing to be seen is the form of the good, and it is seen only with toil and trouble. Once one has seen it, however, one must infer that it is the cause of all that is correct and beautiful in anything, that in the visible realm it produces both light and its source, and that in the intelligible realm it controls and provides truth and understanding; and that anyone who is to act sensibly in private or public must see it.

GLAUCON: I agree, so far as I am able.

SOCRATES: Come on, then, and join me in this further thought: You should not be surprised that the ones who get to this point are not willing to occupy themselves with human affairs, but that, on the contrary, their souls are always eager to spend their time above. I mean, that is surely what we would expect, if indeed the image I described before is also accurate here.

GLAUCON: It is what we would expect.

SOCRATES: What about when someone, coming from looking at divine things, looks to the evils of human life? Do you think it is surprising that he behaves awkwardly and appears completely ridiculous, if—while his sight is still dim and he has not yet become accustomed to the darkness around him—he is compelled, either in the courts or elsewhere, to compete about the shadows of justice,[7] or about the statues of which they are the shadows; and to dispute the way these things are understood by people who have never seen justice itself?

GLAUCON: It is not surprising at all.

SOCRATES: On the contrary, anyone with any sense, at any rate, would remember that eyes may be confused in two ways and from two

---

[6]Plato alludes to the fate of Socrates, whom the Athenians convicted of impiety and the corruption of youth, and executed. [D. C. ABEL]

[7]Plato alludes to the trial of Socrates, which he recounts in *The Apology* (Reading 1 in this book). [D. C. ABEL]

causes: when they change from the light into the darkness, or from the darkness into the light. If he kept in mind that the same applies to the soul, then when he saw a soul disturbed and unable to see something, he would not laugh absurdly. Instead, he would see whether it had come from a brighter life and was dimmed through not having yet become accustomed to the dark, or from greater ignorance into greater light and was dazzled by the increased brilliance. Then he would consider the first soul happy in its experience and life, and pity the latter. But even if he wanted to ridicule it, at least his ridiculing it would make him less ridiculous than ridiculing a soul that had come from the light above.

GLAUCON: That's an entirely reasonable claim.

SOCRATES: Then here is how we must think about these matters, if that is true: Education is not what some people boastfully declare it to be. They presumably say they can put knowledge into souls that lack it, as if they could put sight into blind eyes.

GLAUCON: Yes, they do say that.

SOCRATES: But here is what our present account shows about this power to learn that is present in everyone's soul, and the instrument with which each of us learns: Just as an eye cannot be turned around from darkness to light except by turning the whole body, so this instrument must be turned around from what-comes-to-be together with the whole soul, until it is able to bear to look at what is and at the brightest thing that is—the one we call the good: Isn't that right?

GLAUCON: Yes.

READING 14　　　　　# Meditations on First Philosophy
René Descartes

René Descartes was born in La Haye (now called Descartes), France, in 1596. As a youth he was educated by the Jesuits at their college in La Flèche. Around 1614 he began study-ing at the University of Poitiers, receiving his law degree in 1616. Deciding to travel rather than practice law, he went to Holland in 1618 to serve in the army of the Dutch Prince Mau-rice of Nassau as a gentleman volunteer. One day in November 1619, while on a military tour of Germany, Descartes sat alone in a room reflecting on a new philosophical system that would unify all branches of knowledge and give them the certainty of mathematics. That night he had three dreams, which he interpreted as a divine commission to construct this new system of knowledge. He left the army shortly afterwards and traveled for several years. In 1628 he settled in Holland, where he lived for more than 20 years. There he did research in science and in mathematics (laying the foundations for analytic geometry) and developed his philosophy. In 1649, after much hesitation, Descartes acceded to the request of Queen Christina of Sweden to come to Stockholm to tutor her in philosophy. The harsh winter and the rigorous schedule imposed on him by the queen (philosophy lessons at five o'clock in the morning, for example) took their toll on his health: He died of pneumonia in 1650.

Descartes' major works are *Rules for the Direction of the Mind* (written in 1628, published posthumously), *Discourse on Method* (1637), *Meditations on First Philosophy* (1641), *Principles of Philosophy* (1644), and *The Passions of the Soul* (1649).

Our reading is from *Meditations on First Philosophy*. (By "first philosophy" Descartes means truths about the basic topics of philosophy, which for him are God, the soul [mind], and the external world.) In the First Meditation, Descartes explains his "method of doubt": He will not accept as true anything of which he cannot be absolutely certain. But practi-cally everything seems open to doubt; Descartes reflects that he might even be deceived in his belief that there is an external world. For how can he be sure that there is not some pow-erful "malicious demon" who tricks him into thinking there is an external world by placing images directly in his mind?

In the Second Meditation, Descartes realizes that he can be absolutely certain of at least one thing—that he exists. For even if he is deceived about the existence of the external world, he could not be deceived unless he existed. As he formulates this argument elsewhere, "I think, therefore I am." This "I" that exists is "a thing that thinks." Descartes goes on to argue that if there are material things, their essential nature would be extension (three-dimensionality), and that extension is grasped by the mind, not by the senses.

In our selection from the Third Meditation, Descartes reflects on the certitude of his own existence and formulates a general criterion for truth: "Whatever I perceive very clearly and distinctly is true." He then presents a proof for the existence of God. He finds that his mind contains an idea of an infinite being, and reasons that he himself—who is merely a *finite* being—could not have invented such an idea. Descartes concludes that the idea of an infinite being must have been placed in his mind by the infinite being itself. Therefore this infinite being (God) exists.

FIRST MEDITATION. WHAT CAN BE CALLED INTO DOUBT

Some years ago I was struck by the large number of falsehoods that I had accepted as true in my childhood, and by the highly doubtful nature of the whole edifice that I had subsequently based on them. I realized that it was necessary, once in the course of my life, to demolish everything completely and start again right from the foundations if I wanted to establish anything at all in the sciences that was stable and likely to last. But the task looked an enormous one, and I began to wait until I should reach a mature enough age to ensure that no subsequent time of life would be more suitable for tackling such inquiries. This led me to put the project off for so long that I would now be to blame if by pondering over it any further I wasted the time still left for carrying it out. So today I have expressly rid my mind of all worries and arranged for myself a clear stretch of free time. I am here quite alone, and at last I will devote myself sincerely and without reservation to the general demolition of my opinions.

But to accomplish this, it will not be necessary for me to show that all my opinions are false, which is something I could perhaps never manage. Reason now leads me to think that I should hold back my assent from opinions that are not completely certain and indubitable just as carefully as I do from those that are patently false. So, for the purpose of rejecting all my opinions, it will be enough if I find in each of them at least some reason for doubt. And to do this I will not need to run through them all individually, which would be an endless task. Once the foundations of a building are undermined, anything built on them collapses of its own accord; so I will go straight for the basic principles on which all my former beliefs rested.

Whatever I have up till now accepted as most true I have acquired either from the senses or through the senses. But from time to time I have found that the senses deceive, and it is prudent never to trust completely those who have deceived us even once.

Yet although the senses occasionally deceive us with respect to objects that are very small or in the distance, there are many other beliefs about which doubt is quite impossible, even though they are derived from the senses—for example, that I am here, sitting by the fire, wearing a winter dressing-gown, holding this piece of paper in my hands, and so on. Again, how could it be denied that these hands or this whole body are mine? Unless perhaps I were to liken myself to madmen, whose brains are so damaged by the persistent vapors of melancholia that they firmly maintain they are kings when they are paupers, or say they are dressed in purple when they are naked, or that their heads are made of earthenware, or that they are pumpkins, or made of glass. But such people are insane, and I would be thought equally mad if I took anything from them as a model for myself.

A brilliant piece of reasoning! As if I were not a man who sleeps at night, and regularly has all the same experiences while asleep as madmen do when awake—indeed sometimes even more improbable ones. How often, asleep at night, am I convinced of just such familiar events—that I am here in my dressing-gown, sitting by the fire—when in fact I am lying undressed in bed!

Yet at the moment my eyes are certainly wide awake when I look at this piece of paper; I shake my head and it is not asleep; as I stretch out and feel my hand I do so deliberately, and I know what I am doing. All this would not happen with such distinctness to someone asleep. Indeed! As if I did not remember other occasions when I have been tricked by exactly similar thoughts while asleep! As I think about this more carefully, I see plainly that there are never any sure signs by means of which being awake can be distinguished from being asleep. The result is that I begin to feel dazed, and this very feeling only reinforces the notion that I may be asleep.

Suppose then that I am dreaming, and that these particulars—that my eyes are open, that I am moving my head and stretching out my hands—are not true. Perhaps, indeed, I do not even have such hands or such a body at all. Nonetheless, it must surely be admitted that the visions that come in sleep are like paintings, which must have been fashioned in the likeness of things that are real, and hence that at least these general kinds of things—eyes, head, hands, and the body as a whole—are things that are not imaginary but are real and exist. For even when painters try to create sirens and satyrs[1] with the most extraordinary bodies, they cannot give them natures that are new in all respects; they simply jumble up the limbs of different animals. Or if perhaps they manage to think up something so new that nothing remotely similar has ever been seen before—something that is therefore completely fictitious and unreal—at least the colors used in the composition must be real. By similar reasoning, although these general kinds of things—eyes, head, hands, and so on—could be imaginary, it must at least be admitted that certain other even simpler and more universal things are real. These are as it were the real colors from which we form all the images of things, whether true or false, that occur in our thought.

This class appears to include corporeal nature in general, and its extension; the shape of extended things; the quantity, or size and number of these things; the place in which they may exist, the time through which they may endure, and so on.

So a reasonable conclusion from this might be that physics, astronomy, medicine, and all other disciplines that depend on the study of composite things, are doubtful; while arithmetic, geometry, and other subjects of this kind, which deal only with the simplest and most general things, regardless of whether they really exist in nature or not, contain something certain and indubitable. For whether I am awake or asleep, two and three added together are five, and a square has no more than four sides. It seems impossible that such transparent truths should incur any suspicion of being false.

And yet firmly rooted in my mind is the long-standing opinion that there is an omnipotent God who made me the kind of creature that I am. How do I know that he has not brought it about that there is no earth, no sky, no extended thing, no shape, no size, no place, while at the same time ensuring that all these things appear to me to exist just as they do now? What is more, just as I consider that

---

[1]In Greek mythology, *sirens* are female, partly human creatures who lure sailors to their destruction with their beautiful singing; *satyrs* are woodland creatures with features of both a horse and a goat, fond of unrestrained revelry. [D. C. ABEL]

others sometimes go astray in cases where they think they have the most perfect knowledge, how do I know that God has not brought it about that I too go wrong every time I add two and three or count the sides of a square, or in some even simpler matter, if that is imaginable? But perhaps God would not have allowed me to be deceived in this way, since he is said to be supremely good. But if it were inconsistent with his goodness to have created me such that I am deceived all the time, it would seem equally foreign to his goodness to allow me to be deceived even occasionally; yet this last assertion cannot be made.

Perhaps there may be some who would prefer to deny the existence of so powerful a God rather than believe that everything else is uncertain. Let us not argue with them, but grant them that everything said about God is a fiction. According to their supposition, then, I have arrived at my present state by fate or chance or a continuous chain of events, or by some other means; yet since deception and error seem to be imperfections, the less powerful they make my original cause, the more likely it is that I am so imperfect as to be deceived all the time. I have no answer to these arguments, but am finally compelled to admit that there is not one of my former beliefs about which a doubt may not properly be raised; and this is not a flippant or ill-considered conclusion, but is based on powerful and well-thought-out reasons. So in the future I must withhold my assent from these former beliefs just as carefully as I would from obvious falsehoods, if I want to discover any certainty.

But it is not enough merely to have noticed this; I must make an effort to remember it. My habitual opinions keep coming back, and, despite my wishes, they capture my belief, which is as it were bound over to them as a result of long occupation and the law of custom. I shall never get out of the habit of confidently assenting to these opinions, so long as I suppose them to be what in fact they are, namely highly probable opinions—opinions that, despite the fact that they are in a sense doubtful, as has just been shown, it is still much more reasonable to believe than to deny. In view of this, I think it will be a good plan to turn my will in completely the opposite direction and deceive myself, by pretending for a time that these former opinions are utterly false and imaginary. I shall do this until the weight of preconceived opinion is counterbalanced and the distorting influence of habit no longer prevents my judgment from perceiving things correctly. In the meantime, I know that no danger or error will result from my plan, and that I cannot possibly go too far in my distrustful attitude. This is because the task now in hand does not involve action but merely the acquisition of knowledge.

I will suppose therefore that not God, who is supremely good and the source of truth, but rather some malicious demon of the utmost power and cunning has employed all his energies in order to deceive me. I shall think that the sky, the air, the earth, colors, shapes, sounds, and all external things are merely the delusions of dreams that he has devised to ensnare my judgment. I shall consider myself as not having hands or eyes, or flesh, or blood or senses, but as falsely believing that I have all these things. I shall stubbornly and firmly persist in this meditation; and, even if it is not in my power to know any truth, I shall at least do what is in my power, that is, resolutely guard against assenting to any falsehoods, so that the deceiver, however powerful and cunning he may be, will be unable to impose on me in the slightest degree. But this is an arduous undertaking, and a kind of laziness brings me back to normal life. I am like a prisoner who is enjoying an imaginary freedom while asleep; as he begins to suspect that he is asleep, he dreads being woken up, and goes along with the pleasant illusion as long as he can. In the same way, I happily slide back into my old opinions and dread being shaken out of them, for fear that my peaceful sleep may be followed by hard labor when I wake, and that I shall have to toil not in the light, but amid the inextricable darkness of the problems I have now raised.

SECOND MEDITATION. THE NATURE OF THE HUMAN MIND, AND HOW IT IS BETTER KNOWN THAN THE BODY

So serious are the doubts into which I have been thrown as a result of yesterday's meditation that I can neither put them out of my mind nor see any way of resolving them. It feels as if I have fallen unexpectedly into a deep whirlpool that tumbles me around so that I can neither stand on the bottom nor swim up to the top. Nevertheless I will make an effort and once more attempt the same path that I started on yesterday. Anything that admits of the slightest doubt I will set aside just as if I had found it to be wholly false; and I will proceed in this way until I recognize something certain, or, if nothing else, until I at least recognize for certain that there is no certainty. Archimedes[2] used to demand just one firm and immovable point in order to shift the entire earth; so I too can hope for great things if I manage to find just one thing, however slight, that is certain and unshakable.

I will suppose then, that everything I see is spurious. I will believe that my memory tells me lies, and that none of the things that it reports ever happened. I have no senses. Body, shape, extension, movement, and place are chimeras.[3] So what remains true? Perhaps just the one fact that nothing is certain.

Yet apart from everything I have just listed, how do I know that there is not something else that does not allow even the slightest occasion for doubt? Is there not a God, or whatever I may call him, who puts into me the thoughts I am now having? But why do I think this, since I myself may perhaps be the author of these thoughts? In that case am not I, at least, something? But I have just said that I have no senses and no body. This is the sticking point: What follows from this? Am I not so bound up with a body and with senses that I cannot exist without them? But I have convinced myself that there is absolutely nothing in the world, no sky, no earth, no minds, no bodies. Does it now follow that I too do not exist? No: If I convinced myself of something, then I certainly existed. But there is a deceiver of supreme power and cunning who is deliberately and constantly deceiving me. In that case I too undoubtedly exist, if he is deceiving me; and let him deceive me as much as he can, he will never bring it about that I am nothing so long as I think that I am something. So after considering everything

---

[2]Archimedes (about 287–212 B.C.E.) was a Greek mathematician and inventor. [D. C. ABEL]
[3]*chimeras:* mental fabrications. [D. C. ABEL]

very thoroughly, I must finally conclude that this proposition "I am, I exist" is necessarily true whenever it is put forward by me or conceived in my mind.

But I do not yet have a sufficient understanding of what this "I" is, that now necessarily exists. So I must be on my guard against carelessly taking something else to be this "I," and so making a mistake in the very item of knowledge that I maintain is the most certain and evident of all. I will therefore go back and meditate on what I originally believed myself to be, before I embarked on this present train of thought. I will then subtract anything capable of being weakened, even minimally, by the arguments now introduced, so that what is left at the end may be exactly and only what is certain and unshakable.

What then did I formerly think I was? A man. But what is a man? Shall I say "a rational animal"? No; for then I should have to inquire what an animal is, what rationality is, and in this way one question would lead me down the slope to other harder ones, and I do not now have the time to waste on subtleties of this kind. Instead I propose to concentrate on what came into my thoughts spontaneously and quite naturally whenever I used to consider what I was. Well, the first thought to come to mind was that I had a face, hands, arms, and the whole mechanical structure of limbs that can be seen in a corpse, and which I called the body. The next thought was that I was nourished, that I moved about, and that I engaged in sense-perception and thinking; and these actions I attributed to the soul. But as to the nature of this soul, either I did not think about this or else I imagined it to be something tenuous, like a wind or fire or ether, that permeated my more solid parts. As to the body, however, I had no doubts about it, but thought I knew its nature distinctly. If I had tried to describe the mental conception I had of it, I would have expressed it as follows: By a body I understand whatever has a determinable shape and a definable location and can occupy a space in such a way as to exclude any other body; it can be perceived by touch, sight, hearing, taste, or smell, and can be moved in various ways, not by itself but by whatever else comes into contact with it. For, according to my judgment, the power of self-movement, like the power of sensation or of thought, was quite foreign to the nature of a body; indeed, it was a source of wonder to me that certain bodies were found to contain faculties of this kind.

But what shall I now say that I am, when I am supposing that there is some supremely powerful and, if it is permissible to say so, malicious deceiver, who is deliberately trying to trick me in every way he can? Can I now assert that I possess even the most insignificant of all the attributes that I have just said belong to the nature of a body? I scrutinize them, think about them, go over them again, but nothing suggests itself; it is tiresome and pointless to go through the list once more. But what about the attributes I assigned to the soul? Nutrition or movement? Since now I do not have a body, these are mere fabrications. Sense-perception? This surely does not occur without a body, and besides, when asleep I have appeared to perceive through the senses many things that I afterwards realized I did not perceive through the senses at all. Thinking? At last I have discovered it: thought—this alone is inseparable from me. I am, I exist—that is certain. But for how long? For as long as I am thinking. For it could be that were I totally to cease from thinking, I should totally cease to exist. At present I am not admitting anything except what is necessarily true.

I am, then, in the strict sense, only a thing that thinks; that is, I am a mind, or intelligence, or intellect, or reason—words whose meaning I have been ignorant of until now. But for all that, I am a thing that is real and that truly exists. But what kind of a thing? As I have just said—a thinking thing.

What else am I? I will use my imagination. I am not that structure of limbs that is called a human body. I am not even some thin vapor that permeates the limbs—a wind, fire, air, breath, or whatever I depict in my imagination; for these are things that I have supposed to be nothing. Let this supposition stand; for all that, I am still something. And yet may it not perhaps be the case that these very things that I am supposing to be nothing, because they are unknown to me, are in reality identical with the "I" of which I am aware? I do not know, and for the moment I shall not argue the point, since I can make judgments only about things that are known to me. I know that I exist; the question is, what is this "I" that I know? If the "I" is understood strictly as we have been taking it, then it is quite certain that knowledge of it does not depend on things of whose existence I am as yet unaware; so it cannot depend on any of the things that I invent in my imagination. And this very word "invent" shows me my mistake. It would indeed be a case of fictitious invention if I used my imagination to establish that I was something or other; for imagining is simply contemplating the shape or image of a corporeal thing. Yet now I know for certain both that I exist and at the same time that all such images and, in general, everything relating to the nature of body, could be mere dreams <and chimeras>.[4] Once this point has been grasped, to say "I will use my imagination to get to know more distinctly what I am" would seem to be as silly as saying "I am now awake, and see some truth; but since my vision is not yet clear enough, I will deliberately fall asleep so that my dreams may provide a truer and clearer representation." I thus realize that none of the things that the imagination enables me to grasp is at all relevant to this knowledge of myself that I possess, and that the mind must therefore be most carefully diverted from such things if it is to perceive its own nature as distinctly as possible.

But what then am I? A thing that thinks. What is that? A thing that doubts, understands, affirms, denies, is willing, is unwilling, and also imagines and has sensory perceptions. . . .

Let us consider the things that people commonly think they understand most distinctly of all; that is, the bodies that we touch and see. I do not mean bodies in general—for general perceptions are apt to be somewhat more confused—but one particular body. Let us take, for example, this piece of wax. It has just been taken from the honeycomb; it has not yet quite lost the taste of the honey; it retains some of the scent of the flowers from which it was gathered; its color, shape, and size are plain to see; it is hard, cold, and can be handled without difficulty; if you rap it with your knuckles it makes a sound. In short, it has everything that appears necessary to enable a body to be known as

---

[4]Words placed in angle brackets appear in the French version of *Meditations on First Philosophy* but not in the original Latin version. Louis-Charles d'Albert, Duc de Luyens (1620–1690), published a French translation that included some alterations from the original text. Descartes approved the translation, but scholars do not consider it as authoritative as the original Latin text. [D. C. ABEL]

distinctly as possible. But even as I speak, I put the wax by the fire, and look: The residual taste is eliminated, the smell goes away, the color changes, the shape is lost, the size increases; it becomes liquid and hot; you can hardly touch it, and if you strike it, it no longer makes a sound. But does the same wax remain? It must be admitted that it does; no one denies it, no one thinks otherwise. So what was it in the wax that I understood with such distinctness? Evidently none of the features that I arrived at by means of the senses; for whatever came under taste, smell, sight, touch, or hearing has now altered—yet the wax remains.

Perhaps the answer lies in the thought that now comes to my mind—namely, the wax was not after all the sweetness of the honey, or the fragrance of the flowers, or the whiteness, or the shape, or the sound, but was rather a body that presented itself to me in these various forms a little while ago, but that now exhibits different ones. But what exactly is it that I am now imagining? Let us concentrate, take away everything that does not belong to the wax, and see what is left: merely something extended, flexible, and changeable. But what is meant here by "flexible" and "changeable"? Is it what I picture in my imagination: that this piece of wax is capable of changing from a round shape to a square shape, or from a square shape to a triangular shape? Not at all; for I can grasp that the wax is capable of countless changes of this kind, yet I am unable to run through this immeasurable number of changes in my imagination, from which it follows that it is not the faculty of imagination that gives me my grasp of the wax as flexible and changeable. And what is meant by "extended"? Is the extension of the wax also unknown? For it increases if the wax melts, increases again if it boils, and is greater still if the heat is increased. I would not be making a correct judgment about the nature of wax unless I believed it capable of being extended in many more different ways than I will ever encompass in my imagination. I must therefore admit that the nature of this piece of wax is in no way revealed by my imagination, but is perceived by the mind alone. (I am speaking of this particular piece of wax; the point is even clearer with regard to wax in general.) But what is this wax that is perceived by the mind alone? It is of course the same wax that I see, that I touch, that I picture in my imagination, in short the same wax that I thought it to be from the start. And yet, and here is the point, the perception I have of it is a case not of vision or touch or imagination—nor has it ever been, despite previous appearances—but of purely mental scrutiny; and this can be imperfect and confused, as it was before, or clear and distinct as it is now, depending on how carefully I concentrate on what the wax consists in.

But as I reach this conclusion I am amazed at how <weak and> prone to error my mind is. For although I am thinking about these matters within myself, silently and without speaking, nonetheless the actual words bring me up short, and I am almost tricked by ordinary ways of talking. We say that we see the wax itself, if it is there before us, not that we judge it to be there from its color or shape; and this might lead me to conclude without more ado that knowledge of the wax comes from what the eye sees, and not from the scrutiny of the mind alone. But then if I look out of the window and see men crossing the square, as I just happen to have done, I normally say that I see the men themselves, just as I say that I see the wax. Yet do I see any more than hats and coats that could conceal automatons? I *judge* that they are men. And so something that I thought

I was seeing with my eyes is in fact grasped solely by the faculty of judgment that is in my mind. . . .

THIRD MEDITATION. THE EXISTENCE OF GOD

I will now shut my eyes, stop my ears, and withdraw all my senses. I will eliminate from my thoughts all images of bodily things, or rather, since this is hardly possible, I will regard all such images as vacuous, false, and worthless. I will converse with myself and scrutinize myself more deeply; and in this way I will attempt to achieve, little by little, a more intimate knowledge of myself. I am a thing that thinks—that is, a thing that doubts, affirms, denies, understands a few things, is ignorant of many things, is willing, is unwilling, and also that imagines and has sensory perceptions. For, as I have noted before, even though the objects of my sensory experience and imagination may have no existence outside me, nonetheless the modes of thinking that I refer to as cases of sensory perception and imagination, insofar as they are simply modes of thinking, do exist within me—of that I am certain.

In this brief list I have gone through everything I truly know, or at least everything I have so far discovered that I know. Now I will cast around more carefully to see whether there may be other things within me that I have not yet noticed. I am certain that I am a thinking thing. Do I not therefore also know what is required for my being certain about anything? In this first item of knowledge there is simply a clear and distinct perception of what I am asserting; this would not be enough to make me certain of the truth of the matter if it could ever turn out that something that I perceived with such clarity and distinctness was false. So I now seem to be able to lay it down as a general rule that whatever I perceive very clearly and distinctly is true. . . .

Among my ideas, some appear to be innate, some to be adventitious,[5] and others to have been invented by me. My understanding of what a thing is, what truth is, and what thought is, seems to derive simply from my own nature. But my hearing a noise, as I do now, or seeing the sun or feeling the fire, comes from things that are located outside me, or so I have hitherto judged. Lastly, sirens, hippogriffs,[6] and the like are my own invention. But perhaps all my ideas may be thought of as adventitious, or they may all be innate, or all made up; for as yet I have not clearly perceived their true origin.

But the chief question at this point concerns the ideas that I take to be derived from things existing outside me: What is my reason for thinking that they resemble these things? Nature has apparently taught me to think this. But in addition I know by experience that these ideas do not depend on my will, and hence that they do not depend simply on me. Frequently I notice them even when I do not want to. Now, for example, I feel the heat whether I want to or not, and this is why I think that this sensation or idea of heat comes to me from

---

[5]*adventitious:* coming from an external source. [D. C. ABEL]
[6]*hippogriffs:* mythical animals that are part horse and part griffin (a griffin itself is a mythological animal that is part eagle and part lion). [D. C. ABEL]

something other than myself, namely the heat of the fire by which I am sitting. And the most obvious judgment for me to make is that the thing in question transmits to me its own likeness rather than something else.

I will now see if these arguments are strong enough. When I say "Nature taught me to think this," all I mean is that a spontaneous impulse leads me to believe it, not that its truth has been revealed to me by some natural light. There is a big difference here. Whatever is revealed to me by the natural light—for example that from the fact that I am doubting it follows that I exist, and so on—cannot in any way be open to doubt. This is because there cannot be another faculty both as trustworthy as the natural light and also capable of showing me that such things are not true. But as for my natural impulses, I have often judged in the past that they were pushing me in the wrong direction when it was a question of choosing the good, and I do not see why I should place any greater confidence in them in other matters.

Then again, although these ideas do not depend on my will, it does not follow that they must come from things located outside me. Just as the impulses that I was speaking of a moment ago seem opposed to my will even though they are within me, so there may be some other faculty, not yet fully known to me, that produces these ideas without any assistance from external things; this is, after all, just how I have always thought ideas are produced in me when I am dreaming.

And finally, even if these ideas did come from things other than myself, it would not follow that they must resemble those things. Indeed, I think I have often discovered a great disparity <between an object and its idea> in many cases. For example, there are two different ideas of the sun that I find within me. One of them, which is acquired as it were from the senses and which is a prime example of an idea that I reckon to come from an external source, makes the sun appear very small. The other idea is based on astronomical reasoning, that is, it is derived from certain notions that are innate in me (or else it is constructed by me in some other way), and this idea shows the sun to be several times larger than the earth. Obviously both these ideas cannot resemble the sun that exists outside me; and reason persuades me that the idea that seems to have emanated most directly from the sun itself has in fact no resemblance to it at all.

All these considerations are enough to establish that it is not reliable judgment but merely some blind impulse that has made me believe up till now that there exist things distinct from myself that transmit to me ideas or images of themselves through the sense organs or in some other way. . . .

Among my ideas, apart from the idea that gives me a representation of myself, which cannot present any difficulty in this context, there are ideas that variously represent God, corporeal and inanimate things, angels, animals, and finally other men like myself.

As far as concerns the ideas that represent other men, or animals, or angels, I have no difficulty in understanding that they could be put together from the ideas I have of myself, of corporeal things and of God, even if the world contained no men besides me, no animals and no angels.

As to my ideas of corporeal things, I can see nothing in them that is so great <or excellent> as to make it seem impossible that it originated in myself. . . .

So there remains only the idea of God; and I must consider whether there is anything in the idea that could not have originated in myself. By the word "God" I understand a substance that is infinite, <eternal, immutable,> independent, supremely intelligent, supremely powerful, and that created both myself and everything else (if anything else there be) that exists. All these attributes are such that, the more carefully I concentrate on them, the less possible it seems that they could have originated from me alone. So from what has been said it must be concluded that God necessarily exists.

It is true that I have the idea of substance in me in virtue of the fact that I am a substance. But this would not account for my having the idea of an infinite substance, when I am finite, unless this idea proceeded from some substance that really was infinite.

And I must not think that, just as my conceptions of rest and darkness are arrived at by negating movement and light, so my perception of the infinite is arrived at not by means of a true idea but merely by negating the finite. On the contrary, I clearly understand that there is more reality in an infinite substance than in a finite one, and hence that my perception of the infinite—that is, God— is in some way prior to my perception of the finite—that is, myself. For how could I understand that I doubted or desired (that is, lacked something) and that I was not wholly perfect, unless there were in me some idea of a more perfect being that enabled me to recognize my own defects by comparison? . . .

It only remains for me to examine how I received this idea from God. For I did not acquire it from the senses; it has never come to me unexpectedly, as usually happens with the ideas of things that are perceivable by the senses, when these things present themselves to the external sense organs—or seem to do so. And it was not invented by me either; for I am plainly unable either to take away anything from it or to add anything to it. The only remaining alternative is that it is innate in me, just as the idea of myself is innate in me.[7]

---

[7]In his Fifth Meditation, Descartes gives an additional proof for the existence of God. The argument appears on pp. 206–207 of this book. [D. C. ABEL]

An Essay Concerning Human Understanding

John Locke

John Locke was born in Wrington, England, in 1632. After attending Westminster School, he enrolled in Oxford University, receiving his bachelor's degree in 1656 and his master's degree two years later. He then taught Latin and Greek at Oxford. In 1661 he began the study of medicine. He was appointed censor of moral philosophy in 1664, but two years later he left Oxford to become the personal physician of influential politician Anthony Ashley Cooper, Earl of Shaftesbury. He completed his medical degree in 1674. Locke then spent four years in France (1675–1679), where he explored the philosophical ideas of René Descartes, Pierre Gassendi, and others. The England to which Locke returned was in political turmoil, and Shaftesbury fled to Holland in 1682. The next year, Locke, who was under suspicion because of his close association with Shaftesbury, also fled to Holland. He returned to England in 1689, and the next year published two major philosophical works that were the fruit of many years of thought: *An Essay Concerning Human Understanding* and *Two Treatises of Government.* Locke continued to write and publish, his final project (published posthumously) being a series of commentaries on the epistles of Paul. He died in Oates in 1704 at the age of 72.

Locke's main works, in addition to the *Essay* and the *Two Treatises,* are *A Letter Concerning Toleration* (1689), *Some Thoughts Concerning Education* (1693), and *The Reasonableness of Christianity* (1695).

Our selection is from the *Essay Concerning Human Understanding.* Locke begins by rejecting the view, popular in his day, that the mind is endowed with innate principles—the view that the mind by its very nature, prior to any experience, knows such truths as "it is impossible for the same thing to be and not to be." He argues that such principles cannot be innate because some people ("children and idiots") have no knowledge of them. Locke then proceeds to present his own theory of how ideas enter the mind. The mind is originally blank, like a sheet of white paper; ideas are imprinted through experience. All ideas arise either through sensation (experience of external objects) or reflection (experience of the operations of our mind). According to Locke, "we have nothing in our minds which did not come about in one of these two ways." After experience has furnished the mind with simple ideas, the mind can go on to combine them into complex ideas that are not the direct objects of experience.

Locke then explains how ideas are related to qualities. By "quality" he means the power by which an object can produce an idea in our mind. For example, to say that a snowball has the qualities of being round and white means that it can create these ideas in us. Locke proceeds to distinguish two kinds of qualities. *Primary qualities* (which Locke also calls *original qualities*) are those that can produce ideas that resemble the object and really exist in it; examples of these qualities are figure, extension, and motion or rest. Secondary qualities, by contrast, can produce ideas that do *not* resemble the object and do *not* exist in it; examples of such qualities are color, sound, and taste. So although we experience a snowball as both round and white, it really is round but really is not white. Locke goes on to explain *how* qualities produce ideas in us.

BOOK I

Chapter II. No Innate Speculative Principles[1]

1. It is an established opinion among some men that there are in the under-standing certain innate principles—some primary notions, *koinai ennoiai*,[2] char-acters, as it were, stamped upon the mind of man, which the soul receives in its very first being and brings into the world with it. It would be sufficient to con-vince unprejudiced readers of the falseness of this supposition, if I should only show (as I hope I shall in the following parts of this discourse) how men, barely[3] by the use of their natural faculties, may attain to all the knowledge they have without the help of any innate impressions, and may arrive at certainty without any such original notions or principles. For I imagine anyone will easily grant that it would be impertinent to suppose the ideas of colors innate in a creature to whom God has given sight and a power to receive them by the eyes from external objects. And no less unreasonable would it be to attribute several truths to the impressions of nature and innate characters, when we may observe in ourselves faculties fit to attain as easy and certain knowledge of them as if they were originally imprinted on the mind.

But because a man is not permitted without censure to follow his own thoughts in the search of truth when they lead him ever so little out of the common road, I shall set down the reasons that made me doubt of the truth of that opinion, as an excuse for my mistake, if I be in one—which I leave to be considered by those who, with me, dispose themselves to embrace truth wherever they find it.

2. There is nothing more commonly taken for granted than that there are certain principles, both speculative and practical (for they speak of both), uni-versally agreed upon by all mankind; which therefore, they argue, must needs[4] be the constant impressions which the souls of men receive in their first beings, and which they bring into the world with them, as necessarily and really as they do any of their inherent faculties.

3. This argument, drawn from universal consent, has this misfortune in it, that if it were true in matter of fact, that there were certain truths wherein all mankind agreed, it would not prove them innate, if there can be any other way shown how men may come to that universal agreement in the things they do consent in, which I presume may be done.

4. But, which is worse, this argument of universal consent, which is made use of to prove innate principles, seems to me a demonstration that there are none such, because there are none to which all mankind give an universal assent. I shall begin with the speculative, and instance in those magnified prin-ciples of demonstration, "Whatsoever is, is" and "It is impossible for the same thing to be and not to be"—which, of all others, I think have the most allowed title to innate. These have so settled a reputation of maxims universally received

---

[1]The chapter numbers vary from edition to edition. The numbering here follows the edition of Peter H. Nidditch (New York: Oxford University Press, 1975, 2nd ed., 1979). [D. C. ABEL]
[2]*koinai ennoiai*: (Greek) "common conceptions." [D. C. ABEL]
[3]*barely*: merely. [D. C. ABEL]
[4]*needs*: necessarily. [D. C. ABEL]

that it will no doubt be thought strange if anyone should seem to question it. But yet I take liberty to say that these propositions are so far from having an universal assent, that there are a great part of mankind to whom they are not so much as known.

5. For first it is evident that all children and idiots have not the least apprehension or thought of them. And the want[5] of that is enough to destroy that universal assent which must needs be the necessary concomitant of all innate truths—it seeming to me near a contradiction to say that there are truths imprinted on the soul, which it perceives or understands not; imprinting, if it signify anything, being nothing else but the making certain truths to be perceived. For to imprint anything on the mind without the mind's perceiving it seems to me hardly intelligible. If therefore children and idiots have souls, have minds, with those impressions upon them, they must unavoidably perceive them and necessarily know and assent to these truths; which since they do not, it is evident that there are no such impressions. For if they are not notions naturally imprinted, how can they be innate? And if they are notions imprinted, how can they be unknown? To say a notion is imprinted on the mind, and yet at the same time to say that the mind is ignorant of it and never yet took notice of it, is to make this impression nothing. No proposition can be said to be in the mind which it never yet knew, which it was never yet conscious of. For if any *one* [proposition] may, then, by the same reason, *all* propositions that are true and the mind is capable ever of assenting to, may be said to be in the mind, and to be imprinted: Since, if any one can be said to be in the mind, which it never yet knew, it must be only because it is capable of knowing it; and so the mind is of all truths it ever shall know. Nay, thus truths may be imprinted on the mind which it never did nor ever shall know; for a man may live long, and die at last in ignorance of many truths which his mind was capable of knowing, and that with certainty. So that if the capacity of knowing be the natural impression contended for, all the truths a man ever comes to know will, by this account, be every one of them innate; and this great point will amount to no more, but only to a very improper way of speaking—which, while it pretends to assert the contrary, says nothing different from those who deny innate principles. For nobody, I think, ever denied that the mind was capable of knowing several truths. The capacity, they say, is innate; the knowledge acquired. But then to what end such contest for certain innate maxims? If truths can be imprinted on the understanding without being perceived, I can see no difference there can be between any truths the mind is capable of knowing in respect of their original:[6] They must all be innate or all adventitious;[7] in vain shall a man go about to distinguish them. He therefore that talks of innate notions in the understanding cannot (if he intend thereby any distinct sort of truths) mean such truths to be in the understanding as it never perceived, and is yet wholly ignorant of. For if these words "to be in the understanding" have any propriety, they signify to be understood. So that to be in the understanding and not to be understood, to be

---

[5]*want:* lack. [D. C. ABEL]
[6]*original:* origin. [D. C. ABEL]
[7]*adventitious:* coming from an external source. [D. C. ABEL]

in the mind and never to be perceived, is all one as to say anything is and is not in the mind or understanding. If therefore these two propositions, "Whatsoever is, is" and "It is impossible for the same thing to be and not to be," are by nature imprinted, children cannot be ignorant of them: Infants and all that have souls must necessarily have them in their understandings, know the truth of them, and assent to [them] . . . .

BOOK II

Chapter I. Of Ideas in General, and Their Original

1. Every man being conscious to himself that he thinks, and that which his mind is applied about while thinking being the ideas that are there, it is past doubt that men have in their minds several ideas—such as are those expressed by the words whiteness, hardness, sweetness, thinking, motion, man, elephant, army, drunkenness, and others. It is in the first place then to be inquired, how he comes by them. I know it is a received doctrine that men have native ideas and original characters stamped upon their minds in their very first being. This opinion I have at large examined already; and I suppose what I have said in the foregoing Book will be much more easily admitted when I have shown whence the understanding may get all the ideas it has, and by what ways and degrees they may come into the mind—for which I shall appeal to everyone's own observation and experience.

2. Let us then suppose the mind to be, as we say, white paper, void of all characters, without any ideas. How comes it to be furnished? Whence comes it by that vast store which the busy and boundless fancy of man has painted on it with an almost endless variety? Whence has it all the materials of reason and knowledge? To this I answer, in one word, from *experience.* In that all our knowledge is founded; and from that it ultimately derives itself. Our observation, employed either about external sensible[8] objects or about the internal operations of our minds perceived and reflected on by ourselves, is that which supplies our understandings with all the materials of thinking. These two are the fountains of knowledge from whence all the ideas we have, or can naturally have, do spring.

3. First, our senses, conversant about particular sensible objects, do convey into the mind several distinct perceptions of things, according to those various ways wherein those objects do affect them. And thus we come by those ideas we have of yellow, white, heat, cold, soft, hard, bitter, sweet, and all those which we call sensible qualities; which when I say the senses convey into the mind, I mean, they from external objects convey into the mind what produces there those perceptions. This great source of most of the ideas we have, depending wholly upon our senses, and derived by them to the understanding, I call *sensation.*

4. Secondly, the other fountain from which experience furnishes the understanding with ideas is the perception of the operations of our own mind within us, as it is employed about the ideas it has got—which operations, when the soul

---

[8]*sensible:* able to be sensed. [D. C. ABEL]

comes to reflect on and consider, do furnish the understanding with another set of ideas, which could not be had from things without.[9] And such are perception, thinking, doubting, believing, reasoning, knowing, willing, and all the different actings of our own minds—which we being conscious of, and observing in ourselves, do from these receive into our understandings,as distinct ideas as we do from bodies affecting our senses. This source of ideas every man has wholly in himself; and though it be not sense, as having nothing to do with external objects, yet it is very like it, and might properly enough be called internal sense. But as I call the other sensation, so I call this reflection, the ideas it affords being such only as the mind gets by reflecting on its own operations within itself. By reflection, then, in the following part of this discourse, I would be understood to mean, that notice which the mind takes of its own operations, and the manner of them, by reason whereof there come to be ideas of these operations in the understanding. These two, I say—namely, external material things, as the objects of sensation, and the operations of our own minds within, as the objects of reflection—are to me the only originals from whence all our ideas take their beginnings. The term operations here I use in a large sense, as comprehending not barely the actions of the mind about its ideas, but some sort of passions[10] arising sometimes from them, such as is the satisfaction or uneasiness arising from any thought.

5. The understanding seems to me not to have the least glimmering of any ideas which it does not receive from one of these two. External objects furnish the mind with the ideas of sensible qualities, which are all those different perceptions they produce in us; and the mind furnishes the understanding with ideas of its own operations.

These, when we have taken a full survey of them and their several modes, combinations, and relations, we shall find to contain all our whole stock of ideas; and that we have nothing in our minds which did not come in one of these two ways. Let anyone examine his own thoughts and thoroughly search into his understanding; and then let him tell me, whether all the original ideas he has there, are any other than of the objects of his senses, or of the operations of his mind, considered as objects of his reflection. And how great a mass of knowledge soever he imagines to be lodged there, he will, upon taking a strict view, see that he has not any idea in his mind but what one of these two have imprinted—though perhaps, with infinite variety compounded and enlarged by the understanding, as we shall see hereafter.

6. He that attentively considers the state of a child at his first coming into the world, will have little reason to think him stored with plenty of ideas that are to be the matter of his future knowledge. It is by degrees he comes to be furnished with them. And though the ideas of obvious and familiar qualities imprint themselves before the memory begins to keep a register of time or order, yet it is often so late before some unusual qualities come in the way, that there are few men that cannot recollect the beginning of their acquaintance with them. And if it were worthwhile, no doubt a child might be so ordered as to have but

---

[9]*without:* outside. [D. C. ABEL]

[10]*passions:* states of being acted upon (being "passive"); contrasted with *actions.* [D. C. ABEL]

what we are after (handwritten note in left margin)

a very few, even of the ordinary ideas, till he were grown up to a man. But all that are born into the world, being surrounded with bodies that perpetually and diversely affect them—[a] variety of ideas, whether care be taken of it or not, are imprinted on the minds of children. Light and colors are busy at hand everywhere, when the eye is but open; sounds and some tangible qualities fail not to solicit their proper senses and force an entrance to the mind—but yet, I think, it will be granted easily that if a child were kept in a place where he never saw any other but black and white till he were a man, he would have no more ideas of scarlet or green, than he that from his childhood never tasted an oyster or a pineapple has of those particular relishes.

7. Men then come to be furnished with fewer or more simple ideas from without, according as the objects they converse with afford greater or less variety; and from the operations of their minds within, according as they more or less reflect on them. For, though he that contemplates the operations of his mind cannot but have plain and clear ideas of them, yet, unless he turn his thoughts that way and considers them attentively, he will no more have clear and distinct ideas of all the operations of his mind and all that may be observed therein, than he will have all the particular ideas of any landscape, or of the parts and motions of a clock, who will not turn his eyes to it and with attention heed all the parts of it. The picture or clock may be so placed that they may come in his way every day, but yet he will have but a confused idea of all the parts they are made up of, till he applies himself with attention to consider them each in particular.

8. And hence we see the reason why it is pretty late before most children get ideas of the operations of their own minds, and [why] some have not any very clear or perfect ideas of the greatest part of them all their lives. Because, though they pass there continually, yet, like floating visions, they make not deep impressions enough to leave in their mind clear, distinct, lasting ideas, till the understanding turns inward upon itself, reflects on its own operations, and makes them the objects of its own contemplation. Children, when they come first into it, are surrounded with a world of new things which, by a constant solicitation of their senses, draw the mind constantly to them, forward to take notice of new—and [they are] apt to be delighted with the variety of changing objects. Thus the first years are usually employed and diverted in looking abroad.[11] Men's business in them is to acquaint themselves with what is to be found without, and so, growing up in a constant attention to outward sensations, seldom make any considerable reflection on what passes within them, till they come to be of riper years—and some scarce ever at all. . . .

Chapter II. Of Simple Ideas

1. The better to understand the nature, manner, and extent of our knowledge, one thing is carefully to be observed concerning the ideas we have; and that is, that some of them are *simple* and some *complex.*

Though the qualities that affect our senses are, in the things themselves, so united and blended that there is no separation, no distance between them; yet it

---

[11]*abroad:* about. [D. C. ABEL]

is plain, the ideas they produce in the mind enter by the senses simple and unmixed. For, though the sight and touch often take in from the same object, at the same time, different ideas—as a man sees at once motion and color, the hand feels softness and warmth in the same piece of wax—yet the simple ideas thus united in the same subject are as perfectly distinct as those that come in by different senses. The coldness and hardness which a man feels in a piece of ice [are] as distinct ideas in the mind as the smell and whiteness of a lily, or as the taste of sugar and smell of a rose. And there is nothing can be plainer to a man than the clear and distinct perception he has of those simple ideas; which, being each in itself uncompounded, contains in it nothing but one uniform appearance, or conception in the mind, and is not distinguishable into different ideas.

2. These simple ideas, the materials of all our knowledge, are suggested and furnished to the mind only by those two ways above mentioned, namely sensation and reflection. When the understanding is once stored with these simple ideas, it has the power to repeat, compare, and unite them, even to an almost infinite variety, and so can make at pleasure new complex ideas. But it is not in the power of the most exalted wit or enlarged understanding, by any quickness or variety of thought, to invent or frame one new simple idea in the mind, not taken in by the ways before mentioned; nor can any force of the understanding destroy those that are there. The dominion of man in this little world of his own understanding [is] much the same as it is in the great world of visible things; wherein his power, however managed by art and skill, reaches no farther than to compound and divide the materials that are made to his hand, but can do nothing towards the making the least particle of new matter or destroying one atom of what is already in being. The same inability will everyone find in himself, who shall go about to fashion in his understanding one simple idea not received in by his senses from external objects or by reflection from the operations of his own mind about them. I would have anyone try to fancy any taste which had never affected his palate, or frame the idea of a scent he had never smelled, and when he can do this, I will also conclude that a blind man has ideas of colors, and a deaf man true distinct notions of sounds. . . .

Chapter VIII. Some Further Considerations Concerning Our Simple Ideas

1. Concerning the simple ideas of sensation, it is to be considered that whatsoever is so constituted in nature as to be able, by affecting our senses, to cause any perception in the mind, does thereby produce in the understanding a simple idea; which, whatever be the external cause of it, when it comes to be taken notice of by our discerning faculty, it is by the mind looked on and considered there to be a real positive idea in the understanding, as much as any other whatsoever; though, perhaps, the cause of it be but a privation of the subject.

2. Thus the ideas of heat and cold, light and darkness, white and black, motion and rest, are equally clear and positive ideas in the mind; though, perhaps, some of the causes which produce them are barely privations in those subjects from whence our senses derive those ideas. These the understanding, in its view of them, considers all as distinct positive ideas, without taking notice of the causes

that produce them—which is an inquiry not belonging to the idea, as it is in the understanding, but to the nature of the things existing without us. These are two very different things and carefully to be distinguished, it being one thing to perceive and know the idea of white or black, and quite another to examine what kind of particles they must be, and how ranged in the superficies,[12] to make any object appear white or black . . . .

7. To discover the nature of our ideas the better, and to discourse of them intelligibly, it will be convenient to distinguish them as they are ideas or perceptions in our minds, and as they are modifications of matter in the bodies that cause such perceptions in us, that so we may not think (as perhaps usually is done) that they are exactly the images and resemblances of something inherent in the subject—most of those of sensation being in the mind no more the likeness of something existing without us, than the names that stand for them are the likeness of our ideas, which yet upon hearing they are apt to excite in us.

8. Whatsoever the mind perceives in itself, or is the immediate object of perception, thought, or understanding, that I call *idea;* and the power to produce any idea in our mind, I call *quality* of the subject wherein that power is. Thus a snowball having the power to produce in us the ideas of white, cold, and round, the power to produce those ideas in us as they are in the snowball, I call qualities; and as they are sensations or perceptions in our understandings, I call them ideas; which ideas, if I speak of sometimes as in the things themselves, I would be understood to mean those qualities in the objects which produce them in us.

9. Qualities thus considered in bodies are: First, such as are utterly inseparable from the body, in what state soever it be; and such as in all the alterations and changes it suffers, all the force can be used upon it, it constantly keeps; and such as sense constantly finds in every particle of matter which has bulk enough to be perceived; and the mind finds inseparable from every particle of matter, though less than to make itself singly be perceived by our senses. For example, take a grain of wheat, divide it into two parts. Each part has still solidity, extension, figure, and mobility. Divide it again, and it retains still the same qualities; and so divide it on, till the parts become insensible;[13] they must retain still each of them all those qualities. For division (which is all that a mill, or pestle, or any other body, does upon another, in reducing it to insensible parts) can never take away either solidity, extension, figure, or mobility from any body, but only makes two or more distinct separate masses of matter, of that which was but one before; all which distinct masses, reckoned as so many distinct bodies, after division, make a certain number. These I call *original* or *primary qualities* of body, which I think we may observe to produce simple ideas in us, namely solidity, extension, figure, motion or rest, and number.

10. Secondly, such qualities which in truth are nothing in the objects themselves but powers to produce various sensations in us by their primary qualities, that is, by the bulk, figure, texture, and motion of their insensible parts, as colors, sounds, tastes, and so on. These I call *secondary qualities.* To these might

---

[12]*superficies:* surface. [D. C. ABEL]
[13]*insensible:* not able to be sensed. [D. C. ABEL]

be added a *third* sort, which are allowed to be barely powers; though they are as much real qualities in the subject as those which I, to comply with the common way of speaking, call qualities—but for distinction [call] *secondary* qualities. For the power in fire to produce a new color or consistency *in wax or clay* by its primary qualities, is as much a quality in fire as the power it has to produce *in me* a new idea or sensation of warmth or burning which I felt not before, by the same primary qualities (namely the bulk, texture, and motion of its insensible parts).

11. The next thing to be considered is how bodies produce ideas in us; and that is manifestly by impulse, the only way which we can conceive bodies to operate in.

12. If then external objects be not united to our minds when they produce ideas therein; and yet we perceive these original qualities in such of them as singly fall under our senses, it is evident that some motion must be thence continued by our nerves or animal spirits, by some parts of our bodies, to the brains or the seat of sensation, there to produce in our minds the particular ideas we have of them. And since the extension, figure, number, and motion of bodies of an observable bigness may be perceived at a distance by the sight, it is evident some singly imperceptible bodies must come from them to the eyes, and thereby convey to the brain some motion; which produces these ideas which we have of them in us.

13. After the same manner that the ideas of these original qualities are produced in us, we may conceive that the ideas of secondary qualities are also produced, namely by the operation of insensible particles on our senses. For, it being manifest that there are bodies and good store of bodies, each [of which] are so small that we cannot by any of our senses discover either their bulk, figure, or motion—as is evident in the particles of the air and water, and others extremely smaller than those; perhaps as much smaller than the particles of air and water, as the particles of air and water are smaller than peas or hailstones—let us suppose at present that the different motions and figures, bulk and number, of such particles, affecting the several organs of our senses, produce in us those different sensations which we have from the colors and smells of bodies; for example, that a violet, by the impulse of such insensible particles of matter, of peculiar figures and bulks, and in different degrees and modifications of their motions, causes the ideas of the blue color and sweet scent of that flower to be produced in our minds. It [is] no more impossible to conceive that God should annex such ideas to such motions, with which they have no similitude, than that he should annex the idea of pain to the motion of a piece of steel dividing our flesh, with which that idea has no resemblance.

14. What I have said concerning colors and smells may be understood also of tastes and sounds, and other the like sensible qualities; which, whatever reality we by mistake attribute to them, are in truth nothing in the objects themselves, but powers to produce various sensations in us; and depend on those primary qualities, namely bulk, figure, texture, and motion of parts, as I have said.

15. From whence I think it easy to draw this observation—that the ideas of primary qualities of bodies are resemblances of them, and their patterns do really exist in the bodies themselves, but the ideas produced in us by these secondary qualities have no resemblance of them at all. There is nothing like our ideas, existing in the bodies themselves. They are, in the bodies we denominate

from them, only a power to produce those sensations in us; and what is sweet, blue, or warm in idea, is but the certain bulk, figure, and motion of the insensible parts in the bodies themselves, which we call so.

16. Flame is denominated hot and light; snow, white and cold; and manna, white and sweet, from the ideas they produce in us—which qualities are commonly thought to be the same in those bodies [as] those ideas are in us, the one the perfect resemblance of the other, as they are in a mirror, and it would by most men be judged very extravagant if one should say otherwise. And yet he that will consider that the same fire that at one distance produces in us the sensation of warmth, does, at a nearer approach, produce in us the far different sensation of pain, ought to bethink himself what reason he has to say that this idea of warmth, which was produced in him by the fire, is *actually in the fire;* and his idea of pain, which the same fire produced in him the same way, is *not* in the fire. Why are whiteness and coldness in snow, and pain not, when it produces the one and the other idea in us; and can do neither, but by the bulk, figure, number, and motion of its solid parts?

17. The particular bulk, number, figure, and motion of the parts of fire or snow are really in them—whether anyone's senses perceive them or no. And therefore they may be called *real* qualities, because they really exist in those bodies. But light, heat, whiteness, or coldness are no more really in them than sickness or pain is in manna. Take away the sensation of them; let not the eyes see light or colors, nor the ears hear sounds; let the palate not taste, nor the nose smell—and [then] all colors, tastes, odors, and sounds, as they are such particular ideas, vanish and cease and are reduced to their causes, that is, bulk, figure, and motion of parts. . . .

26. To conclude: Beside those before-mentioned primary qualities in bodies— namely bulk, figure, extension, number, and motion of their solid parts—all the rest, whereby we take notice of bodies and distinguish them one from another, are nothing else but several powers in them, depending on those primary qualities; whereby they are fitted, either by immediately operating on our bodies to produce several different ideas in us; or else, by operating on other bodies, so to change their primary qualities as to render them capable of producing ideas in us different from what before they did. The former of these, I think, may be called secondary qualities *immediately perceivable;* the latter, secondary qualities *mediately perceivable.*

An Enquiry Concerning Human Understanding

David Hume

A biography of David Hume appears on p. 46.

This reading is from Hume's *Enquiry Concerning Human Understanding*. Hume begins by distinguishing two kinds of perceptions of the mind: impressions and ideas. *Impressions* consist of direct sense experiences of things outside us (sensations) or inside us (passions and emotions); *ideas* are copies of such impressions. Impressions are distinguished from ideas by their greater "force and vivacity"; hearing a sound is an impression, whereas recalling the sound is an idea. Some ideas (for example, a gold mountain) are not direct copies of a particular impression, but modifications or combinations of impressions (gold and a mountain). To clarify an idea, we need simply go back to the impression(s) from which it derives.

Hume next inquires about our knowledge of "matters of fact" (things that could be otherwise than they are). He observes that we rely on the notion of cause and effect when we go beyond the matters of fact provided by impressions and memories of impressions. But how do we *know* that one thing is caused by another? Judgments of causality are based on experience; when we see that event A is followed regularly by event B, we infer that A causes B and that if A occurs in the future, it will be followed by B. But what justifies this inference? It is not based on impressions—for although we do have impressions of A and B as successive events, we have no impression of a third entity, a "cause," that links A and B. Consequently, we can *never know* that there is such a thing as causality. Hume argues that our belief in causality results not from a reasoning process, but from the unavoidable human tendency to believe that two events we experience as constantly conjoined are related as cause and effect.

SECTION II. OF THE ORIGIN OF IDEAS

Everyone will readily allow that there is a considerable difference between the perceptions of the mind when a man feels the pain of excessive heat or the pleasure of moderate warmth, and when he afterwards recalls to his memory this sensation or anticipates it by his imagination. These faculties may mimic or copy the perceptions of the senses, but they never can entirely reach the force and vivacity of the original sentiment.[1] The utmost we say of them, even when they operate with greatest vigor, is that they represent their object in so lively a manner that we could *almost* say we feel or see it. But, except the mind be disordered by disease or madness, they never can arrive at such a pitch of vivacity as to render these perceptions altogether undistinguishable. All the colors of poetry, however splendid, can never paint natural objects in such a manner as to make the description be taken for a real landscape. The most lively thought is still inferior to the dullest sensation.

------

[1] *sentiment:* perception. [D. C. ABEL]

165

We may observe a like distinction to run through all the other perceptions of the mind. A man in a fit of anger is actuated in a very different manner from one who only thinks of that emotion. If you tell me that any person is in love, I easily understand your meaning and form a just[2] conception of his situation, but never can mistake that conception for the real disorders and agitations of the passion. When we reflect on our past sentiments and affections, our thought is a faithful mirror and copies its objects truly, but the colors which it employs are faint and dull in comparison of those in which our original perceptions were clothed. It requires no nice discernment or metaphysical[3] head to mark the distinction between them.

Here therefore we may divide all the perceptions of the mind into two classes or species, which are distinguished by their different degrees of force and vivacity. The less forcible and lively are commonly denominated *thoughts* or *ideas.* The other species want[4] a name in our language, and in most others—I suppose because it was not requisite for any but philosophical purposes to rank them under a general term or appellation. Let us, therefore, use a little freedom and call them *impressions,* employing that word in a sense somewhat different from the usual. By the term *impression,* then, I mean all our more lively perceptions, when we hear or see or feel or love or hate or desire or will. And impressions are distinguished from ideas, which are the less lively perceptions, of which we are conscious when we reflect on any of those sensations or movements above mentioned.

Nothing at first view may seem more unbounded than the thought of man, which not only escapes all human power and authority, but is not even restrained within the limits of nature and reality. To form monsters and join incongruous shapes and appearances costs the imagination no more trouble than to conceive the most natural and familiar objects. And while the body is confined to one planet, along which it creeps with pain and difficulty, the thought can in an instant transport us into the most distant regions of the universe—or even beyond the universe into the unbounded chaos, where nature is supposed to lie in total confusion. What never was seen or heard of may yet be conceived; nor is anything beyond the power of thought, except what implies an absolute contradiction.

But though our thought seems to possess this unbounded liberty, we shall find, upon a nearer examination, that it is really confined within very narrow limits and that all this creative power of the mind amounts to no more than the faculty of compounding, transposing, augmenting, or diminishing the materials afforded us by the senses and experience. When we think of a golden mountain, we only join two consistent ideas, *gold* and *mountain,* with which we were formerly acquainted. A virtuous horse we can conceive because, from our own feeling, we can conceive virtue; and this we may unite to the figure and shape of a horse, which is an animal familiar to us. In short, all the materials of thinking are derived either from our outward or inward sentiment: The mixture and

---

[2]*just:* correct. [D. C. ABEL]
[3]*metaphysical:* relating to *metaphysics,* the study of the nature and kinds of reality. [D. C. ABEL]
[4]*want:* lack. [D. C. ABEL]

composition of these belongs alone to the mind and will. Or, to express myself in philosophical language, all our ideas or more feeble perceptions are copies of our impressions or more lively ones.

To prove this, the two following arguments will, I hope, be sufficient. First, when we analyze our thoughts or ideas, however compounded or sublime, we always find that they resolve themselves into such simple ideas as were copied from a precedent[5] feeling or sentiment. Even those ideas which at first view seem the most wide of this origin are found, upon a nearer scrutiny, to be derived from it. The idea of God, as meaning an infinitely intelligent, wise, and good Being, arises from reflecting on the operations of our own mind and augmenting, without limit, those qualities of goodness and wisdom. We may prosecute[6] this inquiry to what length we please, where we shall always find that every idea which we examine is copied from a similar impression. Those who would assert that this position is not universally true nor without exception have only one, and that an easy method of refuting it—by producing that idea which, in their opinion, is not derived from this source. It will then be incumbent on us, if we would maintain our doctrine, to produce the impression, or lively perception, which corresponds to it.

Secondly, if it happen from a defect of the organ that a man is not susceptible of any species of sensation, we always find that he is as little susceptible of the correspondent ideas. A blind man can form no notion of colors; a deaf man of sounds. Restore either of them that sense in which he is deficient. By opening this new inlet for his sensations, you also open an inlet for the ideas, and he finds no difficulty in conceiving these objects. . . .

When we entertain, therefore, any suspicion that a philosophical term is employed without any meaning or idea (as is but too frequent), we need but inquire, *from what impression is that supposed idea derived?* And if it be impossible to assign any, this will serve to confirm our suspicion. By bringing ideas into so clear a light we may reasonably hope to remove all dispute which may arise concerning their nature and reality. . . .

SECTION IV. SKEPTICAL[7] DOUBTS CONCERNING THE OPERATIONS OF THE UNDERSTANDING

Part I

All the objects of human reason or inquiry may naturally be divided into two kinds, to wit, *relations of ideas* and *matters of fact.* Of the first kind are the sciences of geometry, algebra, and arithmetic; and in short, every affirmation which is either intuitively or demonstratively certain. *That the square of the hypotenuse is equal to the square of the two sides* is a proposition which expresses a relation

---

[5]*precedent:* prior. [D. C. ABEL]
[6]*prosecute:* pursue. [D. C. ABEL]
[7]*skeptical:* relating to *skepticism,* the doctrine that we cannot attain certainty in knowledge. [D. C. ABEL]

between these figures. *That three times five is equal to the half of thirty* expresses a relation between these numbers. Propositions of this kind are discoverable by the mere operation of thought, without dependence on what is anywhere existent in the universe. Though there never were a circle or triangle in nature, the truths demonstrated by Euclid[8] would forever retain their certainty and evidence.

Matters of fact, which are the second objects of human reason, are not ascertained in the same manner; nor is our evidence of their truth, however great, of a like nature with the foregoing. The contrary of every matter of fact is still possible because it can never imply a contradiction and is conceived by the mind with the same facility and distinctness, as if ever so conformable to reality. *That the sun will not rise tomorrow* is no less intelligible a proposition and implies no more contradiction than the affirmation *that it will rise*. We should in vain, therefore, attempt to demonstrate its falsehood. Were it demonstratively false, it would imply a contradiction and could never be distinctly conceived by the mind.

It may, therefore, be a subject worthy of curiosity to inquire what is the nature of that evidence which assures us of any real existence and matter of fact, beyond the present testimony of our senses or the records of our memory. This part of philosophy, it is observable, has been little cultivated either by the ancients or moderns, and therefore our doubts and errors in the prosecution of so important an inquiry may be the more excusable, while we march through such difficult paths without any guide or direction. They may even prove useful, by exciting curiosity and destroying that implicit faith and security which is the bane of all reasoning and free inquiry. The discovery of defects in the common philosophy, if any such there be, will not, I presume, be a discouragement but rather an incitement, as is usual, to attempt something more full and satisfactory than has yet been proposed to the public.

All reasonings concerning matter of fact seem to be founded on the relation of *cause and effect*. By means of that relation alone we can go beyond the evidence of our memory and senses. If you were to ask a man why he believes any matter of fact which is absent—for instance, that his friend is in the country, or in France—he would give you a reason; and this reason would be some other fact, as a letter received from him or the knowledge of his former resolutions and promises. A man finding a watch or any other machine in a desert[9] island would conclude that there had once been men in that island. All our reasonings concerning fact are of the same nature. And here it is constantly supposed that there is a connection between the present fact and that which is inferred from it. Were there nothing to bind them together, the inference would be entirely precarious. The hearing of an articulate voice and rational discourse in the dark assures us of the presence of some person. Why? Because these are the effects of the human make and fabric, and closely connected with it. If we anatomize all the other reasonings of this nature, we shall find that they are founded on the relation of cause and effect, and that this relation is either near or remote, direct or collateral. Heat and light are collateral effects of fire, and the one effect may justly be inferred from the other.

---

[8]Euclid (flourished around 300 B.C.E.) was a Greek geometer. [D. C. ABEL]
[9]*desert:* desolate. [D. C. ABEL]

If we would satisfy ourselves, therefore, concerning the nature of that evidence which assures us of matters of fact, we must inquire how we arrive at the knowledge of cause and effect.

I shall venture to affirm, as a general proposition which admits of no exception, that the knowledge of this relation is not, in any instance, attained by reasonings a priori[10] but arises entirely from experience, when we find that any particular objects are constantly conjoined with each other. Let an object be presented to a man of ever so strong natural reason and abilities; if that object be entirely new to him, he will not be able, by the most accurate examination of its sensible[11] qualities, to discover any of its causes or effects. Adam, though his rational faculties be supposed, at the very first, entirely perfect, could not have inferred from the fluidity and transparency of water that it would suffocate him, or from the light and warmth of fire that it would consume him. No object ever discovers, by the qualities which appear to the senses, either the causes which produced it or the effects which will arise from it; nor can our reason, unassisted by experience, ever draw any inference concerning real existence and matter of fact.

This proposition *that causes and effects are discoverable, not by reason but by experience* will readily be admitted with regard to such objects as we remember to have once been altogether unknown to us, since we must be conscious of the utter inability, which we then lay under, of foretelling what would arise from them. Present two smooth pieces of marble to a man who has no tincture of natural philosophy[12]—he will never discover that they will adhere together in such a manner as to require great force to separate them in a direct line, while they make so small a resistance to a lateral pressure. Such events as bear little analogy to the common course of nature are also readily confessed to be known only by experience; nor does any man imagine that the explosion of gunpowder or the attraction of a lodestone could ever be discovered by arguments a priori. In like manner, when an effect is supposed to depend upon an intricate machinery or secret[13] structure of parts, we make no difficulty in attributing all our knowledge of it to experience. Who will assert that he can give the ultimate reason why milk or bread is proper nourishment for a man, not for a lion or a tiger?

But the same truth may not appear, at first sight, to have the same evidence with regard to events which have become familiar to us from our first appearance in the world, which bear a close analogy to the whole course of nature and which are supposed to depend on the simple qualities of objects, without any secret structure of parts. We are apt to imagine that we could discover these effects by the mere operation of our reason, without experience. We fancy that were we brought on a sudden into this world, we could at first have inferred that one billiard ball would communicate motion to another upon impulse, and that we needed not to have waited for the event in order to pronounce with certainty concerning it. Such is the influence of custom, that, where it is strongest, it not only

---

[10]*a priori:* based on abstract reasoning, independent of experience (literally, in Latin, "from what comes earlier"). [D. C. ABEL]

[11]*sensible:* able to be sensed. [D. C. ABEL]

[12]*natural philosophy:* the philosophy of nature; natural science. [D. C. ABEL]

[13]*secret:* unseen. [D. C. ABEL]

covers our natural ignorance but even conceals itself and seems not to take place, merely because it is found in the highest degree.

But to convince us that all the laws of nature and all the operations of bodies, without exception, are known only by experience, the following reflections may perhaps suffice. Were any object presented to us and were we required to pronounce concerning the effect which will result from it, without consulting past observation; after what manner, I beseech you, must the mind proceed in this operation? It must invent or imagine some event which it ascribes to the object as its effect, and it is plain that this invention must be entirely arbitrary. The mind can never possibly find the effect in the supposed cause by the most accurate scrutiny and examination. For the effect is totally different from the cause and consequently can never be discovered in it. Motion in the second billiard ball is a quite distinct event from motion in the first; nor is there anything in the one to suggest the smallest hint of the other. A stone or piece of metal raised into the air and left without any support immediately falls. But to consider the matter a priori, is there anything we discover in this situation which can beget the idea of a downward, rather than an upward or any other motion in the stone or metal?

And as the first imagination or invention of a particular effect in all natural operations is arbitrary, where we consult not experience; so must we also esteem[14] the supposed tie or connection between the cause and effect, which binds them together and renders it impossible that any other effect could result from the operation of that cause. When I see, for instance, a billiard ball moving in a straight line towards another; even suppose motion in the second ball should by accident be suggested to me, as the result of their contact or impulse; may I not conceive that a hundred different events might as well follow from that cause? May not both these balls remain at absolute rest? May not the first ball return in a straight line or leap off from the second in any line or direction? All these suppositions are consistent and conceivable. Why then should we give the preference to one, which is no more consistent or conceivable than the rest? All our reasonings a priori will never be able to show us any foundation for this preference.

In a word, then, every effect is a distinct event from its cause. It could not, therefore, be discovered in the cause, and the first invention or conception of it a priori must be entirely arbitrary. And even after it is suggested, the conjunction of it with the cause must appear equally arbitrary, since there are always many other effects which to reason must seem fully as consistent and natural. In vain, therefore, should we pretend[15] to determine any single event, or infer any cause or effect, without the assistance of observation and experience. . . .

Part II

But we have not yet attained any tolerable satisfaction with regard to the question first proposed. Each solution still gives rise to a new question as difficult as the foregoing and leads us on to farther inquiries. When it is asked, "What is the

---

[14]*esteem:* regard. [D. C. ABEL]
[15]*pretend:* undertake. [D. C. ABEL]

nature of all our reasonings concerning matter of fact?," the proper answer seems to be that they are founded on the relation of cause and effect. When again it is asked, "What is the foundation of all our reasonings and conclusions concerning that relation?," it may be replied in one word, experience. But if we still carry on our sifting humor[16] and ask, "What is the foundation of all conclusions from experience?," this implies a new question, which may be of more difficult solution and explication. Philosophers that give themselves airs of superior wisdom and sufficiency have a hard task when they encounter persons of inquisitive dispositions who push them from every corner to which they retreat, and who are sure at last to bring them to some dangerous dilemma. The best expedient to prevent this confusion is to be modest in our pretensions and even to discover the difficulty ourselves before it is objected to us. By this means, we may make a kind of merit of our very ignorance.

I shall content myself, in this section, with an easy task and shall pretend only to give a negative answer to the question here proposed. I say then, that even after we have experience of the operations of cause and effect, our conclusions from that experience are *not* founded on reasoning or any process of the understanding. This answer we must endeavor both to explain and to defend.

It must certainly be allowed that nature has kept us at a great distance from all her secrets and has afforded us only the knowledge of a few superficial qualities of objects, while she conceals from us those powers and principles on which the influence of those objects entirely depends. . . . If a body of like color and consistence with that bread which we have formerly eaten be presented to us, we make no scruple of repeating the experiment[17] and foresee, with certainty, like nourishment and support. Now this is a process of the mind or thought, of which I would willingly know the foundation. It is allowed on all hands that there is no known connection between the sensible qualities and the secret powers, and consequently that the mind is not led to form such a conclusion concerning their constant and regular conjunction, by anything which it knows of their nature. As to past *experience,* it can be allowed to give *direct* and *certain* information of those precise objects only, and that precise period of time, which fell under its cognizance. But why this experience should be extended to future times and to other objects which, for aught we know, may be only in appearance similar—this is the main question on which I would insist. The bread which I formerly ate nourished me; that is, a body of such sensible qualities was, at that time, endued with such secret powers. But does it follow that other bread must also nourish me at another time, and that like sensible qualities must always be attended with like secret powers? The consequence seems nowise necessary. At least it must be acknowledged that there is here a consequence drawn by the mind; that there is a certain step taken—a process of thought and an inference which wants to be explained. These two propositions are far from being the same: "I have found that such an object has always been attended with such an effect" and "I foresee that other objects which are in appearance similar

---

[16]*sifting humor:* questioning frame of mind. [D. C. ABEL]
[17]*experiment:* experience. [D. C. ABEL]

will be attended with similar effects." I shall allow, if you please, that the one proposition may justly be inferred from the other; I know, in fact, that it always is inferred. But if you insist that the inference is made by a chain of reasoning, I desire you to produce that reasoning. The connection between these propositions is not intuitive. There is required a medium[18] which may enable the mind to draw such an inference, if indeed it be drawn by reasoning and argument. What that medium is, I must confess, passes my comprehension—and it is incumbent on those to produce it, who assert that it really exists and is the origin of all our conclusions concerning matter of fact. . . .

When a new object endowed with similar sensible qualities is produced, we expect similar powers and forces and look for a like effect. From a body of like color and consistence with bread we expect like nourishment and support. But this surely is a step or progress of the mind, which wants to be explained. When a man says, "I have found, in all past instances, such sensible qualities conjoined with such secret powers," and when he says, "Similar sensible qualities will always be conjoined with similar secret powers," he is not guilty of a tautology, nor are these propositions in any respect the same. You say that the one proposition is an inference from the other. But you must confess that the inference is not intuitive; neither is it demonstrative. Of what nature is it, then? To say it is experimental[19] is begging the question. For all inferences from experience suppose, as their foundation, that the future will resemble the past and that similar powers will be conjoined with similar sensible qualities. If there be any suspicion that the course of nature may change and that the past may be no rule for the future, all experience becomes useless and can give rise to no inference or conclusion. It is impossible, therefore, that any arguments from experience can prove this resemblance of the past to the future, since all these arguments are founded on the supposition of that resemblance. Let the course of things be allowed hitherto ever so regular—that alone, without some new argument or inference, proves not that, for the future, it will continue so. In vain do you pretend to have learned the nature of bodies from your past experience. Their secret nature, and consequently all their effects and influence, may change without any change in their sensible qualities. This happens sometimes and with regard to some objects—why may it not happen always and with regard to all objects? What logic, what process of argument secures you against this supposition? My practice, you say, refutes my doubts. But you mistake the purport of my question. As an agent, I am quite satisfied in the point; but as a philosopher who has some share of curiosity (I will not say skepticism), I want to learn the foundation of this inference. No reading, no inquiry has yet been able to remove my difficulty or give me satisfaction in a matter of such importance. Can I do better than propose the difficulty to the public, even though, perhaps, I have small hopes of obtaining a solution? We shall at least, by this means, be sensible[20] of our ignorance, if we do not augment our knowledge. . . .

---

[18]*medium:* basis for an inference. [D. C. ABEL]
[19]*experimental:* based on experience. [D. C. ABEL]
[20]*sensible:* aware. [D. C. ABEL]

SECTION V. SKEPTICAL SOLUTION OF THESE DOUBTS

Part I

. . . Suppose a person, though endowed with the strongest faculties of reason and reflection, to be brought on a sudden into this world. He would, indeed, immediately observe a continual succession of objects, and one event following another; but he would not be able to discover anything farther. He would not at first, by any reasoning, be able to reach the idea of cause and effect, since the particular powers by which all natural operations are performed never appear to the senses. Nor is it reasonable to conclude, merely because one event, in one instance, precedes another, that therefore the one is the cause, the other the effect. Their conjunction may be arbitrary and casual. There may be no reason to infer the existence of one from the appearance of the other. And in a word, such a person, without more experience, could never employ his conjecture or reasoning concerning any matter of fact, or be assured of anything beyond what was immediately present to his memory and senses.

Suppose, again, that he has acquired more experience and has lived so long in the world as to have observed familiar objects or events to be constantly conjoined together. What is the consequence of this experience? He immediately infers the existence of one object from the appearance of the other. Yet he has not, by all his experience, acquired any idea or knowledge of the secret power by which the one object produces the other; nor is it by any process of reasoning [that] he is engaged to draw this inference. But still he finds himself determined to draw it. And though he should be convinced that his understanding has no part in the operation, he would nevertheless continue in the same course of thinking. There is some other principle which determines him to form such a conclusion.

This principle is custom or habit. For wherever the repetition of any particular act or operation produces a propensity to renew the same act or operation, without being impelled by any reasoning or process of the understanding, we always say that this propensity is the effect of *custom.* By employing that word, we pretend not to have given the ultimate reason of such a propensity. We only point out a principle of human nature which is universally acknowledged and which is well known by its effects. Perhaps we can push our inquiries no farther or pretend to give the cause of this cause, but must rest contented with it as the ultimate principle which we can assign of all our conclusions from experience. It is sufficient satisfaction that we can go so far, without repining at the narrowness of our faculties because they will carry us no farther. And it is certain we here advance a very intelligible proposition at least, if not a true one, when we assert that after the constant conjunction of two objects—heat and flame, for instance, weight and solidity—we are determined by custom alone to expect the one from the appearance of the other. This hypothesis seems even the only one which explains the difficulty why we draw from a thousand instances an inference which we are not able to draw from one instance that is in no respect different from them. Reason is incapable of any such variation. The conclusions which it draws from considering one circle are the same which it would form upon surveying all the circles in the universe. But no man, having seen only one body move after being impelled by another, could infer that every other body will move after a like impulse. All inferences from experience, therefore, are effects of custom, not of reasoning.

Custom, then, is the great guide of human life. It is that principle alone which renders our experience useful to us and makes us expect for the future a similar train of events with those which have appeared in the past. Without the influence of custom, we should be entirely ignorant of every matter of fact beyond what is immediately present to the memory and senses. We should never know how to adjust means to ends, or to employ our natural powers in the production of any effect. There would be an end at once of all action as well as of the chief part of speculation.

But here it may be proper to remark that though our conclusions from experience carry us beyond our memory and senses and assure us of matters of fact which happened in the most distant places and most remote ages, yet some fact must always be present to the senses or memory, from which we may first proceed in drawing these conclusions. A man who should find in a desert country the remains of pompous[21] buildings would conclude that the country had, in ancient times, been cultivated by civilized inhabitants. But did nothing of this nature occur to him, he could never form such an inference. We learn the events of former ages from history; but then we must peruse the volumes in which this instruction is contained, and thence carry up our inferences from one testimony to another till we arrive at the eyewitnesses and spectators of these distant events. In a word, if we proceed not upon some fact present to the memory or senses, our reasonings would be merely hypothetical; and however the particular links might be connected with each other, the whole chain of inferences would have nothing to support it, nor could we ever by its means arrive at the knowledge of any real existence. If I ask why you believe any particular matter of fact which you relate, you must tell me some reason; and this reason will be some other fact connected with it. But as you cannot proceed after this manner *in infinitum*,[22] you must at last terminate in some fact which is present to your memory or senses, or must allow that your belief is entirely without foundation.

What, then, is the conclusion of the whole matter? A simple one—though, it must be confessed, pretty remote from the common theories of philosophy. All belief of matter of fact or real existence is derived merely from some object present to the memory or senses and a customary conjunction between that and some other object. Or in other words, having found in many instances that any two kinds of objects—flame and heat, snow and cold—have always been conjoined together; if flame or snow be presented anew to the senses, the mind is carried by custom to expect heat or cold and to *believe* that such a quality does exist and will discover itself upon a nearer approach. This belief is the necessary result of placing the mind in such circumstances. It is an operation of the soul when we are so situated, as unavoidable as to feel the passion of love when we receive benefits, or hatred when we meet with injuries. All these operations are a species of natural instincts, which no reasoning or process of the thought and understanding is able either to produce or to prevent.

---

[21]*pompous:* magnificent. [D. C. ABEL]
[22]*in infinitum:* (Latin) "to infinity." [D. C. ABEL]

Critique of Pure Reason

Immanuel Kant

Immanuel Kant was born in 1724 in Königsberg, Prussia, where he spent his entire life. As a boy he attended the Collegium Fridericanum, a school run by the Pietists (the Lutheran sect to which his family belonged). In 1740 he enrolled in the University of Königsberg, where he studied a wide variety of subjects, including theology, philosophy, mathematics, physics, and medicine. He withdrew from the university in 1747 to support himself by working as a private tutor for various families in eastern Prussia. He resumed his studies in 1754 and completed his degree the following year. He then became a lecturer at the University of Königsberg, teaching such diverse subjects as mathematics, geography, mineralogy, and philosophy. Fifteen years later he was appointed professor of logic and metaphysics. His writings—especially his monumental *Critique of Pure Reason* (1781)—brought him increasing fame, and students came from afar to hear him lecture. In 1797 he stopped lecturing, but he continued to write. He died in Königsberg in 1804 at the age of 79.

Kant's principal works, in addition to *Critique of Pure Reason,* are *Prolegomena to Any Future Metaphysics* (1783), *Groundwork of the Metaphysics of Morals* (1785), *Critique of Practical Reason* (1788), and *Critique of Judgment* (1790).

Our reading is taken from Kant's second edition of *Critique of Pure Reason,* published in 1787. Kant's project in this book is to investigate how much we can know by "pure reason" (reason itself, apart from any experience). In his preface, Kant observes that we typically assume that our knowledge (cognition) must conform to objects—that when we know something, our mind must match the way the objects are. If this assumption is correct, it would be impossible to have any knowledge of objects a priori (prior to our experience of them). Kant rejects this assumption; he holds the converse, that *objects* must conform to our *knowledge*—that when we know something, objects must match the way our minds are. Objects conform to our way of receiving sense experience (intuition) and to our way of intellectually synthesizing this sense experience (thought). That is to say, our minds are constructed in such a way that we necessarily *sense* objects through the forms of "sensibility" (namely, space and time) and we necessarily *think* objects through certain "categories" (also called "concepts") of the understanding, such as causality and unity. This means that we can know certain things about objects a priori. For example, we know that we will experience them as existing in space and as being caused. But according to Kant, even though we know that objects will invariably *appear to us* in certain ways, we can never know how things are *in themselves.*

In his introduction, Kant explains that a priori knowledge is characterized by necessity and universality. He then explains that some of our judgments (those in mathematics and metaphysics, for example) are not only a priori but synthetic. (A *synthetic* statement adds something to a concept; an *analytic* one does not.) Kant's doctrine about the structure of the mind is designed to explain how such synthetic a priori judgments are possible.

In the final two sections of our reading, Kant gives arguments to show that space and time (the forms of sensibility) are a priori, and explains that there are 12 categories of the understanding, corresponding to the 12 kinds of judgment.

PREFACE TO THE SECOND EDITION

Whether or not the treatment of the cognitions belonging to the concern of reason travels the secure course of a science is something which can soon be judged by its success. If after many preliminaries and preparations are made, a science gets stuck as soon as it approaches its end, or if in order to reach this end it must often go back and set out on a new path; or likewise if it proves impossible for the different coworkers to achieve unanimity as to the way in which they should pursue their common aim; then we may be sure that such a study is merely groping about, that it is still far from having entered upon the secure course of a science. And it is already a service to reason if we can possibly find that path for it, even if we have to give up as futile much of what was included in the end previously formed without deliberation. . . .

Up to now it has been assumed that all our cognition must conform to the objects; but all attempts to find out something about them a priori[1] through concepts that would extend our cognition have, on this presupposition, come to nothing. Hence let us once try whether we do not get farther with the problems of metaphysics[2] by assuming that the objects must conform to our cognition, which would agree better with the requested possibility of an a priori cognition of them, which is to establish something about objects before they are given to us. This would be just like the first thoughts of Copernicus,[3] who, when he did not make good progress in the explanation of the celestial motions if he assumed that the entire celestial host revolves around the observer, tried to see if he might not have greater success if he made the observer revolve and left the stars at rest. Now in metaphysics we can try in a similar way regarding the *intuition*[4] of objects. If intuition has to conform to the constitution of the objects, then I do not see how we can know anything of them a priori; but if the object (as an object of the senses) conforms to the constitution of our faculty of intuition, then I can very well represent this possibility to myself. Yet because I cannot stop with these intuitions, if they are to become cognitions, but must refer them as representations to something as their object and determine this object through them, I can assume *either* that the concepts through which I bring about this determination also conform to the objects, and then I am once again in the same difficulty about how I could know anything about them a priori, *or else* I assume that the objects, or what is the same thing, the *experience* in which alone they can be cognized (as given objects), conforms to those concepts—in which case I immediately see an easier way out of the difficulty, since experience itself is a kind of cognition requiring the understanding, whose rule I have to presuppose in myself before any object is given to me, hence a priori, which rule is expressed in

---

[1] *a priori:* independent of experience (literally, in Latin, "from what comes earlier"); contrasted with *a posteriori,* dependent on experience ("from what comes later"). [D. C. ABEL]
[2] *metaphysics:* the study of the nature and kinds of reality. [D. C. ABEL]
[3] Nicolaus Copernicus (1473–1543) was a Polish astronomer. [D. C. ABEL]
[4] *intuition:* sense experience. [D. C. ABEL]

concepts a priori, to which all objects of experience must therefore necessarily conform, and with which they must agree. . . .

INTRODUCTION TO THE SECOND EDITION

I. On the Difference Between Pure and Empirical Cognition

There is no doubt whatever that all our cognition begins with experience; for how else should the cognitive faculty be awakened into exercise if not through objects that stimulate our senses and in part themselves produce representations, in part bring the activity of our understanding into motion to compare these, to connect or separate them, and thus to work up the raw material of sensible impressions into a cognition of objects that is called experience? *As far as time is concerned,* then, no cognition in us precedes experience, and with experience every cognition begins.

But although all our cognition commences *with* experience, yet it does not on that account all arise *from* experience. For it could well be that even our experiential cognition is a composite of that which we receive through impressions and that which our own cognitive faculty (merely prompted by sensible impressions) provides out of itself, which addition we cannot distinguish from that fundamental material until long practice has made us attentive to it and skilled in separating it out.

It is therefore at least a question requiring closer investigation, and one not to be dismissed at first glance, whether there is any such cognition independent of all experience and even of all impressions of the senses. One calls such cognitions a priori, and distinguishes them from *empirical* ones, which have their sources a posteriori, namely in experience.

The former expression is nevertheless not yet sufficiently determinate to designate the whole sense of the question before us. For it is customary to say of many a cognition derived from experiential sources that we are capable of it or partake in it a priori, because we do not derive it immediately from experience, but rather from a general rule that we have nevertheless itself borrowed from experience. So one says of someone who undermined the foundation of his house that he could have known a priori that it would collapse—he need not have waited for the experience of it actually collapsing. Yet he could not have known this entirely a priori. For that bodies are heavy and hence fall if their support is taken away must first have become known to him through experience.

In the sequel therefore we will understand by a priori cognitions not those that occur independently of this or that experience, but rather those that occur *absolutely* independently of all experience. Opposed to them are empirical cognitions, or those that are possible only a posteriori, that is, through experience. Among a priori cognitions, however, those are called *pure* with which nothing empirical is intermixed. Thus, for example, the proposition "Every alteration has its cause" is an a priori proposition, only not pure, since alteration is a concept that can be drawn only from experience.

II. We Are in Possession of Certain A Priori Cognitions, and Even the Common Understanding Is Never Without Them

At issue here is a mark by means of which we can securely distinguish a pure cognition from an empirical one. Experience teaches us, to be sure, that something is constituted thus and so, but not that it could not be otherwise. *First*, then, if a proposition is thought along with its *necessity*, it is an a priori judgment. If it is, moreover, also not derived from any proposition except one that in turn is valid as a necessary proposition, then it is absolutely a priori. *Second*, experience never gives its judgments true or strict but only assumed and comparative *universality* (through induction), so properly it must be said: As far as we have yet perceived, there is no exception to this or that rule. Thus if a judgment is thought in strict universality—that is, in such a way that no exception at all is allowed to be possible—then it is not derived from experience, but is rather valid absolutely a priori. Empirical universality is therefore only an arbitrary increase in validity from that which holds in *most* cases to that which holds in *all* (as in, for example, the proposition "All bodies are heavy"), whereas strict universality belongs to a judgment essentially; this points to a special source of cognition for it, namely a faculty of a priori cognition. Necessity and strict universality are therefore secure indications of an a priori cognition, and also belong together inseparably. But since in their use it is sometimes easier to show the empirical limitation in judgments than the contingency[5] in them, or is often more plausible to show the unrestricted universality that we ascribe to a judgment than its necessity, it is advisable to employ separately these two criteria, each of which is in itself infallible.

Now it is easy to show that in human cognition there actually are such necessary and in the strictest sense universal, thus pure a priori judgments. If one wants an example from the sciences, one need only look at all the propositions of mathematics; if one would have one from the commonest use of the understanding, the proposition that every alteration must have a cause will do;[6] indeed in the latter the very concept of a cause so obviously contains the concept of a necessity of connection with an effect and a strict universality of rule that it would be entirely lost if one sought, as Hume[7] did, to derive it from a frequent association of that which happens with that which precedes and a habit (thus a merely subjective necessity) of connecting representations arising from

---

[5]*contingency:* the state of being able to be or not to be; contrasted with *necessity.* [D. C. ABEL]

[6]At the end of the previous section, Kant stated that the proposition "Every alteration has a cause" is absolutely a priori *but not pure;* but here he states that this proposition is absolutely a priori *and also pure.* Kant evidently means to distinguish a strict and a loose sense in which an absolutely a priori proposition can be pure. In the *strict* sense, an absolutely a priori proposition is pure if it contains no empirical element at all; and since alteration is a concept drawn from experience, "Every alteration has a cause" is *not* purely a priori in the strict sense. In the *loose* sense, an absolutely a priori proposition is pure if the concept of the predicate is contained in the concept of the subject, even if the concepts themselves are derived from experience; and therefore "Every alteration has a cause" is purely a priori in this loose sense. [D. C. ABEL]

[7]David Hume (1711–1776) was a Scottish philosopher and historian; for a biography, see p. 46. [D. C. ABEL]

that association. Even without requiring such examples for the proof of the reality of pure a priori principles in our cognition, one could establish their indispensability for the possibility of experience itself, thus establish it a priori. For where would experience itself get its certainty if all rules in accordance with which it proceeds were themselves in turn always empirical, thus contingent? Hence one could hardly allow these to count as first principles. Yet here we can content ourselves with having displayed the pure use of our cognitive faculty as a fact together with its indication. Not merely in judgments, however, but even in concepts is an origin of some of them revealed a priori. Gradually remove from your experiential concept of a *body* everything that is empirical in it—the color, the hardness or softness, the weight, even the impenetrability—there still remains the *space* that was occupied by the body (which has now entirely disappeared), and you cannot leave that out. Likewise, if you remove from your empirical concept of every object, whether corporeal or incorporeal, all those properties of which experience teaches you, you could still not take from it that by means of which you think of it as a *substance* or as *dependent* on a substance (even though this concept contains more determination than that of an object in general). Thus, convinced by the necessity with which this concept presses itself on you, you must concede that it has its seat in your faculty of cognition a priori. . . .

IV. On the Difference Between Analytic and Synthetic Judgments

In all judgments in which the relation of a subject to the predicate is thought (if I consider only affirmative judgments, since the application to negative ones is easy), this relation is possible in two different ways. Either the predicate *B* belongs to the subject *A* as something that is (covertly) contained in this concept *A*; or *B* lies entirely outside the concept *A*, though to be sure it stands in connection with it. In the first case I call the judgment *analytic,* in the second *synthetic.* Analytic judgments (affirmative ones) are thus those in which the connection of the predicate is thought through identity, but those in which this connection is thought without identity are to be called synthetic judgments. One could also call the former *judgments of clarification,* and the latter *judgments of amplification,* since through the predicate the former do not add anything to the concept of the subject, but only break it up by means of analysis into its component concepts, which were already thought in it (though confusedly); while the latter, on the contrary, add to the concept of the subject a predicate that was not thought in it at all, and could not have been extracted from it through any analysis. For example, if I say "All bodies are extended," then this is an analytic judgment. For I do not need to go beyond the concept that I combine with the body in order to find that extension is connected with it, but rather I need only to analyze that concept—that is, become conscious of the manifold that I always think in it—in order to encounter this predicate therein. It is therefore an analytic judgment. On the contrary, if I say "All bodies are heavy," then the predicate is something entirely different from that which I think in the mere concept of a body in general. The addition of such a predicate thus yields a synthetic judgment.

Judgments of experience, as such, are all synthetic. For it would be absurd to ground an analytic judgment on experience, since I do not need to go beyond my concept at all in order to formulate the judgment, and therefore need no testimony from experience for that. That a body is extended is a proposition that is established a priori, and is not a judgment of experience. For before I go to experience, I already have all the conditions for my judgment in the concept, from which I merely draw out the predicate in accordance with the principle of contradiction, and can thereby at the same time become conscious of the necessity of the judgment, which experience could never teach me. On the contrary, although I do not at all include the predicate of weight in the concept of a body in general, the concept nevertheless designates an object of experience through a part of it, to which I can therefore add still other parts of the same experience as belonging with the former. I can first cognize the concept of body analytically through the marks of extension, of impenetrability, of shape, and so on, which are all thought in this concept. But now I amplify my cognition and, looking back to the experience from which I had extracted this concept of body, I find that weight is also always connected with the previous marks, and I therefore add this synthetically as predicate to that concept. It is thus experience on which the possibility of the synthesis of the predicate of weight with the concept of body is grounded, since both concepts, though the one is not contained in the other, nevertheless belong together, though only contingently, as parts of a whole, namely experience, which is itself a synthetic combination of intuitions.

But in synthetic a priori judgments this means of help is entirely lacking. If I am to go beyond the concept *A* in order to cognize another *B* as combined with it, what is it on which I depend and by means of which the synthesis becomes possible, since I here do not have the advantage of looking around for it in the field of experience? Take the proposition "Everything that happens has its cause." In the concept of something that happens, I think, to be sure, of an existence that was preceded by a time, and so on, and from that analytic judgments can be drawn. But the concept of a cause lies entirely outside that concept, and indicates something different from the concept of what happens in general, and is therefore not contained in the latter representation at all. How then do I come to say something quite different about that which happens in general, and to cognize the concept of cause as belonging to it, indeed necessarily, even though not contained in it? What is the unknown = *X* here on which the understanding depends when it believes itself to discover beyond the concept of *A* a predicate that is foreign to it yet that it nevertheless believes to be connected with it? It cannot be experience, for the principle that has been adduced adds the latter representations to the former not only with greater generality than experience can provide, but also with the expression of necessity, hence entirely a priori and from mere concepts. Now the entire final aim of our speculative a priori cognition rests on such synthetic, that is, ampliative principles; for the analytic ones are, to be sure, most important and necessary, but only for attaining that distinctness of concepts that is requisite for a secure and extended synthesis as a really new acquisition.

V. Synthetic A Priori Judgments Are Contained as Principles in All Theoretical Sciences of Reason

1. *Mathematical judgments are all synthetic.* This proposition seems to have escaped the notice of the analysts of human reason until now, indeed to be diametrically opposed to all of their conjectures, although it is incontrovertibly certain and is very important in the sequel. For since one found that the inferences of the mathematicians all proceed in accordance with the principle of contradiction (which is required by the nature of any apodictic[8] certainty), one was persuaded that the principles could also be cognized from the principle of contradiction, in which, however, they erred; for a synthetic proposition can of course be comprehended in accordance with the principle of contradiction, but only insofar as another synthetic proposition is presupposed from which it can be deduced, never in itself.

It must first be remarked that properly mathematical propositions are always a priori judgments and are never empirical, because they carry necessity with them, which cannot be derived from experience. But if one does not want to concede this, well then, I will restrict my proposition to *pure mathematics*, the concept of which already implies that it does not contain empirical but merely pure a priori cognition.

To be sure, one might initially think that the proposition "7 + 5 = 12" is a merely analytic proposition that follows from the concept of a sum of 7 and 5 in accordance with the principle of contradiction. Yet if one considers it more closely, one finds that the concept of the sum of 7 and 5 contains nothing more than the unification of both numbers in a single one, through which it is not at all thought what this single number is that comprehends the two of them. The concept of 12 is by no means already thought merely by my thinking of that unification of 7 and 5, and no matter how long I analyze my concept of such a possible sum I will still not find 12 in it. One must go beyond these concepts, seeking assistance in the intuition that corresponds to one of the two—one's 5 fingers, say, or (as in Segner's arithmetic)[9] 5 points—and one after another add the units of the 5 given in the intuition to the concept of 7. For I take first the number 7, and, as I take the fingers of my hand as an intuition for assistance with the concept of 5, to that image of mine I now add the units that I have previously taken together in order to constitute the number 5 one after another to the number 7, and thus see the number 12 arise. That 7 *should* be added to 5 I have, to be sure, thought in the concept of a sum = 7 + 5, but not that this sum is equal to the number 12. The arithmetical proposition is therefore always synthetic; one becomes all the more distinctly aware of that if one takes somewhat larger numbers, for it is then clear that, twist and turn our concepts as we will, without getting help from intuition we could never find the sum by means of the mere analysis of our concepts.

---

[8]*apodictic:* absolute. [D. C. ABEL]

[9]Johann Andreas von Segner, *Anfangsgründe der Arithmetic, Geometrie and der Geometrischen Berechnungen* ("Elements of Arithmetic, Geometry, and Geometric Calculations"), published in 1756. Segner (1704–1777) was a German mathematician and naturalist. [D. C. ABEL]

Just as little is any principle of pure geometry analytic. That the straight line between two points is the shortest is a synthetic proposition. For my concept of *the straight* contains nothing of quantity, but only a quality. The concept of the shortest is therefore entirely additional to it, and cannot be extracted out of the concept of the straight line by any analysis. Help must here be gotten from intuition, by means of which alone the synthesis is possible. . . .

2. *Natural science* (physica)[10] *contains within itself synthetic a priori judgments as principles.* I will adduce only a couple of propositions as examples, such as the proposition that in all alterations of the corporeal world the quantity of matter remains unaltered; or that in all communication of motion, effect and counter-effect must always be equal. In both of these not only the necessity, thus their a priori origin, but also that they are synthetic propositions is clear. For in the concept of matter I do not think persistence, but only its presence in space through the filling of space. Thus I actually go beyond the concept of matter in order to add something to it a priori that I did not think *in it.* The proposition is thus not analytic, but synthetic, and nevertheless thought a priori, and likewise with the other propositions of the pure part of natural science.

3. *In metaphysics,* even if one regards it as a science that has thus far merely been sought but is nevertheless indispensable because of the nature of human reason, synthetic a priori cognitions are supposed to be contained, and it is not concerned merely with analyzing concepts that we make of things a priori and thereby clarifying them analytically, but we want to amplify our cognition a priori. To this end we must make use of such principles that add something to the given concepts that was not contained in them, and through synthetic a priori judgments go so far beyond that experience itself cannot follow us that far—for example, in the proposition "The world must have a first beginning" and others besides—and thus metaphysics, at least as far as its end is concerned, consists of purely synthetic a priori propositions.

VI. THE GENERAL PROBLEM OF PURE REASON

One has already gained a great deal if one can bring a multitude of investigations under the formula of a single problem. For one thereby not only lightens one's own task, by determining it precisely, but also the judgment of anyone else who wants to examine whether we have satisfied our plan or not. The real problem of pure reason is now contained in the question: *How are synthetic judgments a priori possible?*

That metaphysics has until now remained in such a vacillating state of uncertainty and contradictions is to be ascribed solely to the cause that no one has previously thought of this problem and perhaps even of the distinction between analytic and synthetic judgments. On the solution of this problem, or on a satisfactory proof that the possibility that it demands to have explained

---

[10]*physica:* the Greek term for (the study of) "natural things," rendered in English as "physics." [D. C. ABEL]

does not in fact exist at all, metaphysics now stands or falls. David Hume, who among all philosophers came closest to this problem, still did not conceive of it anywhere near determinately enough and in its universality, but rather stopped with the synthetic proposition of the connection of the effect with its cause (*principium causalitatis*),[11] believing himself to have brought out that such an a priori proposition is entirely impossible. And according to his inferences everything that we call metaphysics would come down to a mere delusion of an alleged insight of reason into that which has in fact merely been borrowed from experience and from habit has taken on the appearance of necessity—an assertion, destructive of all pure philosophy, on which he would never have fallen if he had had our problem in its generality before his eyes, since then he would have comprehended that according to his argument there could also be no pure mathematics, since this certainly contains synthetic a priori propositions, an assertion from which his sound understanding would surely have protected him.

In the solution of the above problem there is at the same time contained the possibility of the pure use of reason in the grounding and execution of all sciences that contain a theoretical a priori cognition of objects—that is, the answer to the questions:

How is pure mathematics possible?

How is pure natural science possible?

About these sciences, since they are actually given, it can appropriately be asked *how* they are possible; for that they must be possible is proved through their actuality. As far as *metaphysics* is concerned, however, its poor progress up to now, and the fact that of no metaphysics thus far expounded can it even be said that, as far as its essential end is concerned, it even really exists, leaves everyone with ground to doubt its possibility.

But now this kind of cognition is in a certain sense also to be regarded as given, and metaphysics is actual, if not as a science yet as a natural predisposition (*metaphysica naturalis*).[12] For human reason, without being moved by the mere vanity of knowing it all, inexorably pushes on, driven by its own need, to such questions that cannot be answered by any experiential use of reason and of principles borrowed from such a use; and thus a certain sort of metaphysics has actually been present in all human beings as soon as reason has extended itself to speculation in them, and it will also always remain there. And now about this too the question is *How is metaphysics as a natural predisposition possible?*—that is, how do the questions that pure reason raises, and which it is driven by its own need to answer as well as it can, arise from the nature of universal human reason?

But since unavoidable contradictions have always been found in all previous attempts to answer these natural questions—for example, whether the world has a beginning or exists from eternity, and so on—one cannot leave it up to the mere natural predisposition to metaphysics, that is, to the pure faculty of

---

[11]*principium causalitatis:* (Latin) "the principle of causality." [D. C. ABEL]
[12]*metaphysica naturalis:* (Latin) "natural metaphysics." [D. C. ABEL]

reason itself, from which, to be sure, some sort of metaphysics (whatever it might be) always grows, but it must be possible to bring it to certainty regarding either the knowledge or ignorance of objects, that is, to come to a decision either about the objects of its questions or about the capacity and incapacity of reason for judging something about them, thus either reliably to extend our pure reason or else to set determinate and secure limits for it. This last question, which flows from the general problem above, would rightly be this: *How is metaphysics possible as science?*

The critique of reason thus finally leads necessarily to science; the dogmatic use of it without critique, on the contrary, leads to groundless assertions, to which one can oppose equally plausible ones, and thus leads to skepticism.

Further, this science cannot be terribly extensive, for it does not deal with objects of reason, whose multiplicity is infinite, but merely with itself, with problems that spring entirely from its own womb, and that are not set before it by the nature of things that are distinct from it but through its own nature; so that, once it has become completely familiar with its own capacity in regard to the objects that may come before it in experience, then it must become easy to determine, completely and securely, the domain and the bounds of its attempted use beyond all bounds of experience. . . .

THE TRANSCENDENTAL DOCTRINE OF ELEMENTS.[13]
FIRST PART: THE TRANSCENDENTAL AESTHETIC[14]

In whatever way and through whatever means a cognition may relate to objects, that through which it relates immediately to them, and at which all thought as a means is directed as an end, is *intuition*. This, however, takes place only insofar as the object is given to us; but this in turn, <at least for us humans,>[15] is possible only if it affects the mind in a certain way. The capacity (receptivity) to acquire representations through the way in which we are affected by objects is called *sensibility*. Objects are therefore *given* to us by means of sensibility, and it alone affords us *intuitions*; but they are *thought* through the understanding, and from it arise *concepts*. But all thought, whether straightaway (*directe*) or through a detour (*indirecte*),[16] must, <by means of certain marks,> ultimately be related to intuitions, thus, in our case, to sensibility, since there is no other way in which objects can be given to us. . . .

I call a science of all principles of a priori sensibility the *transcendental aesthetic*. There must therefore be such a science, which constitutes the first part

---

[13]*transcendental doctrine of elements: Elements* are the forms that our minds impose on objects; the doctrine Kant proposes is *transcendental* because the forms that our minds impose are a priori and thus transcend the objects themselves. [D. C. ABEL]

[14]*aesthetic*: something pertaining to sensation (*aisthēsis* in Greek). [D. C. ABEL]

[15]Words placed in angle brackets were added by Kant to the second edition of his book. [D. C. ABEL]

[16]*Directe* and *indirecte* are Latin terms meaning, respectively, "directly" and "indirectly." [D. C. ABEL]

of the transcendental doctrine of elements, in opposition to that which contains the principles of pure thinking, and which is named *transcendental logic*.

First Section. On Space

By means of outer sense (a property of our mind) we represent to ourselves objects as outside us, and all as in space. In space their shape, magnitude, and relation to one another is determined, or determinable. Inner sense, by means of which the mind intuits itself, or its inner state, gives, to be sure, no intuition of the soul itself, as an object; yet it is still a determinate form, under which the intuition of its inner state is alone possible, so that everything that belongs to the inner determinations is represented in relations of time. Time can no more be intuited externally than space can be intuited as something in us. Now what are space and time? Are they actual entities? Are they only determinations or relations of things, yet ones that would pertain to them even if they were not intuited, or are they relations that only attach to the form of intuition alone, and thus to the subjective constitution of our mind, without which these predicates could not be ascribed to any thing at all? In order to instruct ourselves about this, we will <expound the concept of space> first. . . .

1. Space is not an empirical concept that has been drawn from outer experiences. For in order for certain sensations to be related to something outside me (that is, to something in another place in space from that in which I find myself), thus in order for me to represent them as outside <and next to> one another, thus not merely as different but as in different places, the representation of space must already be their ground. Thus the representation of space cannot be obtained from the relations of outer appearance through experience, but this outer experience is itself first possible only through this representation.

2. Space is a necessary representation, a priori, that is the ground of all outer intuitions. One can never represent that there is no space, though one can very well think that there are no objects to be encountered in it. It is therefore to be regarded as the condition of the possibility of appearances, not as a determination dependent on them, and is an a priori representation that necessarily grounds outer appearances. . . .

Second Section: On Time

1. Time is not an empirical concept that is somehow drawn from an experience. For simultaneity or succession would not themselves come into perception if the representation of time did not ground them a priori. Only under its presupposition can one represent that several things exist at one and the same time (simultaneously) or in different times (successively).

2. Time is a necessary representation that grounds all intuitions. In regard to appearances in general one cannot remove time, though one can very well take the appearances away from time. Time is therefore given a priori. In it

alone is all actuality of appearances possible. The latter could all disappear, but time itself (as the universal condition of their possibility) cannot be removed. . . .

THE ANALYTIC OF CONCEPTS.[17] FIRST CHAPTER: ON THE CLUE TO THE DISCOVERY OF ALL PURE CONCEPTS OF UNDERSTANDING

Second Section. On the Logical Function of Understanding in Judgments

If we abstract from all content of a judgment in general, and attend only to the mere form of the understanding in it, we find that the function of thinking in that can be brought under four titles, each of which contains under itself three moments. They can suitably be represented in the following table.

1.
Quantity of Judgments
Universal
Particular
Singular

2.	3.
Quality	*Relation*
Affirmative	Categorical
Negative	Hypothetical
Infinite	Disjunctive

4.
Modality
Problematic
Assertoric
Apodictic . . .

Third Section. On the Pure Concepts of the Understanding, or Categories

. . . There arise exactly as many pure concepts of the understanding, which apply to objects of intuition in general a priori, as there were logical functions of all possible judgments in the table; for the understanding is completely exhausted and its capacity entirely measured by these functions. Following Aristotle we will call these concepts *categories*,[18] for our aim is basically identical with his although very distant from it in execution.

---

[17]*analytic of concepts:* the study of the a priori forms of understanding (categories of the understanding), which synthesize what we perceive through sensation. The analytic of concepts is a part of *transcendental logic,* the study of the principles of pure thinking. [D. C. ABEL]

[18]Aristotle wrote a treatise called *Categories* (*Katēgoriai,* "predicates"), which postulates 10 ways in which we think about things and in which things exist. For a biography of Aristotle, see p. 331. [D. C. ABEL]

TABLE OF CATEGORIES

1.
Of Quantity
Unity
Plurality
Totality

2.	3.
Of Quality	*Of Relation*
Reality	Of Inherence and Subsistence
Negation	*(substantia et accidens)*[19]
Limitation	Of Causality and Dependence
	(cause and effect)
	Of Community (reciprocity
	between agent and patient)[20]

4.
Of Modality
Possibility—Impossibility
Existence—Nonexistence
Necessity—Contingency

Now this is the listing of all original pure concepts of synthesis that the understanding contains in itself a priori, and on account of which it is only a pure understanding; for by these concepts alone can it understand something in the manifold of intuition—that is, think an object for it. This division is systematically generated from a common principle, namely the faculty for judging (which is the same as the faculty for thinking), and has not arisen rhapsodically from a haphazard search for pure concepts, of the completeness of which one could never be certain, since one would only infer it through induction, without reflecting that in this way one would never see why just these and not other concepts should inhabit the pure understanding.

---

[19]*substantia et accidens:* (Latin) substance [what subsists in itself] and accident [what inheres in a substance]. [D. C. ABEL]

[20]*agent and patient:* that which acts and that which is acted upon. [D. C. ABEL]

Love and Knowledge: Emotion in Feminist Epistemology

Alison M. Jaggar

Alison M. Jaggar was born in Sheffield, England, in 1942. She received her bachelor's degree in philosophy from the University of London in 1964 and her master's degree from the University of Edinburgh in Scotland three years later. She then came to the United States to pursue doctoral studies in philosophy at the State University of New York at Buffalo. Upon completing her doctorate in 1970, Jaggar began teaching at Miami University in Ohio. Two years later she went to the University of Cincinnati, where she later was appointed Obed J. Wilson Professor of Ethics. In 1990 Jaggar accepted her current position, professor of philosophy and women's studies at the University of Colorado at Boulder. She has also held visiting professorships at the University of Illinois at Chicago, the University of California at Los Angeles, Rutgers University (where she was the first occupant of the Laurie New Jersey Chair in Women's Studies), Victoria University of Wellington, New Zealand, and the University of Oslo, Norway. Jaggar was a founding member of the Society for Women in Philosophy and has received fellowships from the American Association of University Women (1976), the National Endowment for the Humanities (1980, 1998), and the Rockefeller Foundation (1990).

Jaggar's books include *Feminist Frameworks: Alternative Theoretical Accounts of the Relations Between Women and Men* (coeditor with Paula S. Rothenberg, 1978; 3d ed., 1993), *Feminist Politics and Human Nature* (1983), *Gender/Body/Knowledge: Feminist Reconstructions of Being and Knowing* (coeditor with Susan R. Bordo, 1989), *A Companion to Feminist Philosophy* (coeditor with Iris M. Young, 1998), and *Just Methodologies: An Interdisciplinary Feminist Reader* (editor, 2006).

Our selection is taken from Jaggar's 1989 article "Love and Knowledge: Emotion in Feminist Epistemology." Jaggar rejects the traditional Western philosophical doctrines that reason and emotion are completely separate faculties, that reason is the sole path to knowledge, and that emotion subverts knowledge. She argues that reason and emotion must be seen as interrelated and interdependent and that feelings play an essential role in attaining knowledge. Modern science has created the "myth of dispassionate investigation"—the notion that scientific inquiry is completely severed from values and feelings. Jaggar contends that this notion is false and that it is in fact an ideology that helps preserve the political power of the dominant group in a society. It does this by exalting reason and associating it with the dominant group, while devaluing emotion and associating it with subordinate groups. This ideology gives more credibility to the observations of members of the dominant group (in our society, mainly white males) than to the observations of members of subordinate groups (mainly people of color and women), thereby justifying the dominant group's claim to political authority.

The ideologies of a society greatly influence the emotional responses of all the members of the society; certain kinds of responses to certain kinds of situations become conventional and expected. But significant numbers of people in subordinate groups may not experience these expected emotions. For example, people on welfare may feel resentment rather than gratitude for what they receive. Jaggar calls these unconventional feelings of subordinate groups "outlaw emotions" and contends that by exploring them we can often come to see things differently and more accurately than we presently do. The reason is that outlaw emotions of people in subordinate groups (especially of women) are usually more appropriate to the situation than conventional emotions. Jaggar concludes that because outlaw emotions are more appropriate responses, they are more reliable guides to the way things are, and therefore important elements in an adequate theory of knowledge.

INTRODUCTION

Within the Western philosophical tradition, emotions have usually been considered potentially or actually subversive of knowledge. From Plato until the present, with a few notable exceptions, reason rather than emotion has been regarded as the indispensable faculty for acquiring knowledge.

Typically, although again not invariably, the rational has been contrasted with the emotional, and this contrasted pair then often linked with other dichotomies. Not only has reason been contrasted with emotion, but it has also been associated with the mental, the cultural, the universal, the public, and the male, whereas emotion has been associated with the irrational, the physical, the natural, the particular, the private, and, of course, the female.

Although Western epistemology[1] has tended to give pride of place to reason rather than emotion, it has not always excluded emotion completely from the realm of reason. In the *Phaedrus,* Plato portrayed emotions, such as anger or curiosity, as irrational urges (horses) that must always be controlled by reason (the charioteer). On this model, the emotions were not seen as needing to be totally suppressed, but rather as needing direction by reason. For example, in a genuinely threatening situation, it was thought not only irrational but foolhardy not to be afraid. The split between reason and emotion was not absolute, therefore, for the Greeks. Instead, the emotions were thought of as providing indispensable motive power that needed to be channeled appropriately. Without horses, after all, the skill of the charioteer would be worthless.

The contrast between reason and emotion was sharpened in the seventeenth century by redefining reason as a purely instrumental faculty. For both the Greeks and the medieval philosophers, reason had been linked with value insofar as reason provided access to the objective structure or order of reality, seen as simultaneously natural and morally justified. With the rise of modern science, however, the realms of nature and value were separated: Nature was stripped of value and reconceptualized as an inanimate mechanism of no intrinsic worth. Values were relocated in human beings, rooted in their preferences and emotional responses. The separation of supposedly natural fact from human value meant that reason, if it were to provide trustworthy insight into reality, had to be uncontaminated by or abstracted from value. Increasingly, therefore, though never universally, reason was reconceptualized as the ability to make valid inferences from premises established elsewhere, the ability to

---

[1]*epistemology:* the study of the nature and grounds of knowledge. [D. C. ABEL]

calculate means but not to determine ends. The validity of logical inferences was thought independent of human attitudes and preferences; this was now the sense in which reason was taken to be objective and universal.

The modern redefinition of rationality required a corresponding reconceptualization of emotion. This was achieved by portraying emotions as nonrational and often irrational urges that regularly swept the body, rather as a storm sweeps over the land. The common way of referring to the emotions as the "passions" emphasized that emotions happened to or were imposed upon an individual, something she suffered rather than something she did.[2]

The epistemology associated with this new ontology[3] rehabilitated sensory perception, which like emotion, typically had been suspected or even discounted by the Western tradition as a reliable source of knowledge. British empiricism,[4] succeeded in the nineteenth century by positivism,[5] took its epistemological task to be the formulation of rules of inference that would guarantee the derivation of certain knowledge from the "raw data" supposedly given directly to the senses. Empirical testability became accepted as the hallmark of natural science; this, in turn, was viewed as the paradigm of genuine knowledge. Often epistemology was equated with the philosophy of science, and the dominant methodology of positivism prescribed that truly scientific knowledge must be capable of inter-subjective verification. Because values and emotions had been defined as variable and idiosyncratic, positivism stipulated that trustworthy knowledge could be established only by methods that neutralized the values and emotions of individual scientists.

Recent approaches to epistemology have challenged some fundamental assumptions of the positivist epistemological model. . . . However, few challenges have been raised thus far to the purported gap between emotion and knowledge. In this paper, I wish to begin bridging this gap through the suggestion that emotions may be helpful and even necessary rather than inimical to the construction of knowledge. . . .

THE MYTH OF DISPASSIONATE INVESTIGATION

. . . [The] derogatory Western attitude toward emotion, like the earlier Western contempt for sensory observation, fails to recognize that emotion, like sensory perception, is necessary to human survival. Emotions prompt us to act appropriately, to approach some people and situations and to avoid others, to caress or cuddle, fight or flee. Without emotion, human life would be unthinkable. Moreover, emotions have an intrinsic as well as an instrumental value.[6]

---

[2]The noun "passion" derives from the Latin verb *pati*, "to undergo, to be acted upon." The adjective "passive" also derives from *pati*. [D. C. ABEL]
[3]*ontology:* the study of the nature and kinds of reality. [D. C. ABEL]
[4]*empiricism:* the doctrine that knowledge is attained primarily through sense experience. [D. C. ABEL]
[5]*positivism:* the doctrine that the only source of genuine knowledge is empirical science. [D. C. ABEL]
[6]Something *intrinsically valuable* is valuable for its own sake; something *instrumentally valuable* is valuable as a means (an instrument a tool) to something else. [D. C. ABEL]

Although not all emotions are enjoyable or even justifiable, as we shall see, life without any emotion would be life without any meaning.

Within the context of Western culture, however, people have often been encouraged to control or even suppress their emotions. Consequently, it is not unusual for people to be unaware of their emotional state or to deny it to themselves and others. This lack of awareness, especially combined with a neopositivist[7] understanding of emotion that construes it as just a feeling of which one is aware, lends plausibility to the myth of dispassionate investigation. But lack of awareness of emotions certainly does not mean that emotions are not present subconsciously or unconsciously, or that subterranean emotions do not exert a continuing influence on people's articulated values and observations, thoughts, and actions.

Within the positivist tradition, the influence of emotion is usually seen only as distorting or impeding observation or knowledge. Certainly it is true that contempt, disgust, shame, revulsion, or fear may inhibit investigation of certain situations or phenomena. Furiously angry or extremely sad people often seem quite unaware of their surroundings or even of their own conditions; they may fail to hear or may systematically misinterpret what other people say. People in love are notoriously oblivious to many aspects of the situation around them.

In spite of these examples, however, positivist epistemology recognizes that the role of emotion in the construction of knowledge is not invariably deleterious and that emotions may make a valuable contribution to knowledge. But the positivist tradition will allow emotion to play only the role of suggesting hypotheses for investigation. Emotions are allowed this because the so-called logic of discovery sets no limits on the idiosyncratic methods that investigators may use for generating hypotheses.

When hypotheses are to be tested, however, positivist epistemology imposes the much stricter logic of justification. The core of this logic is replicability, a criterion believed capable of eliminating or canceling out what are conceptualized as emotional as well as evaluative biases on the part of individual investigators. The conclusions of Western science thus are presumed "objective," precisely in the sense that they are uncontaminated by the supposedly "subjective" values and emotions that might bias individual investigators.

But if . . . the positivist distinction between discovery and justification is not viable, then such a distinction is incapable of filtering out values in science. For example, although such a split, when built into the Western scientific method, is generally successful in neutralizing the idiosyncratic or unconventional values of individual investigators, it has been argued that it does not, indeed, cannot, eliminate generally accepted social values. These values are implicit in the identification of the problems that are considered worthy of investigation, in the selection of the hypotheses that are considered worthy of testing, and in the solutions to the problems that are considered worthy of acceptance. The science of past centuries provides ample evidence of the influence of prevailing social

---

[7]*neopositivist:* relating to a revised, twentieth-century version of positivism (see footnote 5). [D. C. ABEL]

values, whether seventeenth-century atomistic physics or nineteenth-century competitive interpretations of natural selection. . . .

Positivism views values and emotions as alien invaders that must be repelled by a stricter application of the scientific method. If the foregoing claims are correct, however, the scientific method and even its positivist construals themselves incorporate values and emotions. Moreover, such an incorporation seems a necessary feature of all knowledge and conceptions of knowledge. Therefore, rather than repressing emotion in epistemology it is necessary to rethink the relation between knowledge and emotion and construct conceptual models that demonstrate the mutually constitutive rather than oppositional relation between reason and emotion. Far from precluding the possibility of reliable knowledge, emotion as well as value must be shown as necessary to such knowledge. Despite its classical antecedents and as in the ideal of disinterested inquiry, the ideal of dispassionate inquiry is an impossible dream, but a dream nonetheless or perhaps a myth that has exerted enormous influence on Western epistemology. Like all myths, it is a form of ideology that fulfills certain social and political functions.

THE IDEOLOGICAL FUNCTION OF THE MYTH

So far, I have spoken very generally of people and their emotions, as though everyone experienced similar emotions and dealt with them in similar ways. It is an axiom of feminist theory, however, that all generalizations about "people" are suspect. The divisions in our society are so deep, particularly the divisions of race, class, and gender, that many feminist theorists would claim that talk about people in general is ideologically dangerous because such talk obscures the fact that no one is simply a person but instead is constituted fundamentally by race, class, and gender. Race, class, and gender shape every aspect of our lives, and our emotional constitution is not excluded. Recognizing this helps us to see more clearly the political functions of the myth of the dispassionate investigator.

Feminist theorists have pointed out that the Western tradition has not seen everyone as equally emotional. Instead, reason has been associated with members of dominant political, social, and cultural groups and emotion with members of subordinate groups. Prominent among those subordinate groups in our society are people of color, except for supposedly "inscrutable Orientals," and women.

Although the emotionality of women is a familiar cultural stereotype, its grounding is quite shaky. Women appear to be more emotional than men because they, along with some groups of people of color, are permitted and even required to express emotion more openly. In contemporary Western culture, emotionally inexpressive women are suspect as not being real women, whereas men who express their emotions freely are suspected of being homosexual or in some other way deviant from the masculine ideal. Modern Western men, in contrast with Shakespeare's heroes, for instance, are required to present a facade of coolness, lack of excitement, even boredom, to express emotion only rarely and then for relatively trivial events, such as sporting occasions, where the emotions expressed are acknowledged to be dramatized and so are not taken entirely seriously. Thus, women in our society form the main group allowed or even expected to express emotion. A woman may cry in the face of disaster, and a man of color may gesticulate, but a white man merely sets his jaw.

White men's control of their emotional expression may go to the extremes of repressing their emotions, failing to develop emotionally, or even losing the capacity to experience many emotions. Not uncommonly, these men are unable to identify what they are feeling, and even they may be surprised, on occasion, by their own apparent lack of emotional response to a situation, such as a death, where emotional reaction is perceived to be appropriate. . . . Paradoxically, men's lacking awareness of their own emotional responses frequently results in their being more influenced by emotion rather than less.

Although there is no reason to suppose that the thoughts and actions of women are any more influenced by emotion than the thoughts and actions of men, the stereotypes of cool men and emotional women continue to flourish because they are confirmed by an uncritical daily experience. In these circumstances, where there is a differential assignment of reason and emotion, it is easy to see the ideological function of the myth of the dispassionate investigator. It functions, obviously, to bolster the epistemic[8] authority of the currently dominant groups, composed largely of white men, and to discredit the observations and claims of the currently subordinate groups including, of course, the observations and claims of many people of color and women. The more forcefully and vehemently the latter groups express their observations and claims, the more emotional they appear and so the more easily they are discredited. The alleged epistemic authority of the dominant groups then justifies their political authority.

The previous section of this paper argued that dispassionate inquiry was a myth. This section has shown that the myth promotes a conception of epistemological justification vindicating the silencing of those, especially women, who are defined culturally as the bearers of emotion and so are perceived as more "subjective," biased, and irrational. In our present social context, therefore, the ideal of the dispassionate investigator is a classist, racist, and especially masculinist myth.

EMOTIONAL HEGEMONY AND EMOTIONAL SUBVERSION

. . . Within a hierarchical society, the norms and values that predominate tend to serve the interests of the dominant groups. Within a capitalist, white supremacist, and male-dominant society, the predominant values will tend to be those that serve the interests of rich white men. Consequently, we are all likely to develop an emotional constitution that is quite inappropriate for feminism. Whatever our color, we are likely to feel what Irving Thalberg[9] has called "visceral racism"; whatever our sexual orientation, we are likely to be homophobic; whatever our class, we are likely to be at least somewhat ambitious and competitive; whatever our sex, we are likely to feel contempt for women. Such emotional responses may be rooted in us so deeply that they are relatively

---

[8]*epistemic:* relating to knowledge. [D. C. ABEL]
[9]Irving Thalberg, Jr. (1930–1987), was an American philosopher. [D. C. ABEL]

impervious to intellectual argument and may recur even when we pay lip service to changed intellectual convictions.

By forming our emotional constitution in particular ways, our society helps to ensure its own perpetuation. The dominant values are implicit in responses taken to be precultural or acultural, our so-called gut responses. Not only do these conservative responses hamper and disrupt our attempts to live in or prefigure alternative social forms but also, and insofar as we take them to be natural responses, they blinker us theoretically. For instance, they limit our capacity for outrage; they either prevent us from despising or encourage us to despise; they lend plausibility to the belief that greed and domination are inevitable human motivations; in sum, they blind us to the possibility of alternative ways of living.

This picture may seem at first to support the positivist claim that the intrusion of emotion only disrupts the process of seeking knowledge and distorts the results of that process. The picture, however, is not complete; it ignores the fact that people do not always experience the conventionally acceptable emotions. They may feel satisfaction rather than embarrassment when their leaders make fools of themselves. They may feel resentment rather than gratitude for welfare payments and hand-me-downs. They may be attracted to forbidden modes of sexual expression. They may feel revulsion for socially sanctioned ways of treating children or animals. In other words, the hegemony that our society exercises over people's emotional constitution is not total.

People who experience conventionally unacceptable, or what I call "outlaw" emotions often are subordinated individuals who pay a disproportionately high price for maintaining the status quo. The social situation of such people makes them unable to experience the conventionally prescribed emotions. For instance, people of color are more likely to experience anger than amusement when a racist joke is recounted, and women subjected to male sexual banter are less likely to be flattered than uncomfortable or even afraid.

When unconventional emotional responses are experienced by isolated individuals, those concerned may be confused, unable to name their experience; they may even doubt their own sanity. Women may come to believe that they are "emotionally disturbed" and that the embarrassment or fear aroused in them by male sexual innuendo is prudery or paranoia. When certain emotions are shared or validated by others, however, the basis exists for forming a subculture defined by perceptions, norms, and values that systematically oppose the prevailing perceptions, norms, and values. By constituting the basis for such a subculture, outlaw emotions may be politically (because epistemologically) subversive.

Outlaw emotions are distinguished by their incompatibility with the dominant perceptions and values; and some, though certainly not all, of these outlaw emotions are potentially or actually feminist emotions. Emotions become feminist when they incorporate feminist perceptions and values, just as emotions are sexist or racist when they incorporate sexist or racist perceptions and values. For example, anger becomes feminist anger when it involves the perception that the persistent importuning endured by one woman is a single instance of a widespread pattern of sexual harassment, and pride becomes feminist pride when it is evoked by realizing that a certain person's achievement was possible only because that individual overcame specifically gendered obstacles to success. . . .

OUTLAW EMOTIONS AND FEMINIST THEORY

. . . Outlaw emotions may . . . enable us to perceive the world differently from its portrayal in conventional descriptions. They may provide the first indications that something is wrong with the way alleged facts have been constructed, with accepted understandings of how things are. Conventionally unexpected or inappropriate emotions may precede our conscious recognition that accepted descriptions and justifications often conceal as much as reveal the prevailing state of affairs. Only when we reflect on our initially puzzling irritability, revulsion, anger, or fear may we bring to consciousness our "gut-level" awareness that we are in a situation of coercion, cruelty, injustice, or danger. Thus, conventionally inexplicable emotions, particularly though not exclusively those experienced by women, may lead us to make subversive observations that challenge dominant conceptions of the status quo. They may help us to realize that what are taken generally to be facts have been constructed in a way that obscures the reality of subordinated people, especially women's reality.

But why should we trust the emotional responses of women and other subordinated groups? How can we determine which outlaw emotions are to be endorsed or encouraged and which rejected? In what sense can we say that some emotional responses are more appropriate than others? What reason is there for supposing that certain alternative perceptions of the world, perceptions informed by outlaw emotions, are to be preferred to perceptions informed by conventional emotions? Here I can indicate only the general direction of an answer, whose full elaboration must await another occasion.

I suggest that emotions are appropriate if they are characteristic of a society in which all humans (and perhaps some nonhuman life too) thrive, or if they are conducive to establishing such a society. For instance, it is appropriate to feel joy when we are developing or exercising our creative powers, and it is appropriate to feel anger and perhaps disgust in those situations where humans are denied their full creativity or freedom. Similarly, it is appropriate to feel fear if those capacities are threatened in us.

This suggestion, obviously, is extremely vague and may even verge on the tautologous. How can we apply it in situations where there is disagreement over what is or is not disgusting or exhilarating or unjust? Here I appeal to a claim for which I have argued elsewhere: The perspective on reality that is available from the standpoint of the subordinated, which in part at least is the standpoint of women, is a perspective that offers a less partial and distorted and therefore more reliable view.[10] Subordinated people have a kind of epistemological privilege insofar as they have easier access to this standpoint and therefore a better chance of ascertaining the possible beginnings of a society in which all could thrive. For this reason, I would claim that the emotional responses of subordinated people in general, and often of women in particular, are more likely to be appropriate than the emotional responses of the dominant class. That is, they are more likely to incorporate reliable appraisals of situations.

---

[10]Alison M. Jaggar, *Feminist Politics and Human Nature* (Totowa, NJ: Rowman & Allanheld, 1983), Chapter 11. [A. M. JAGGAR]

Even in contemporary science, where the ideology of dispassionate inquiry is almost overwhelming, it is possible to discover a few examples that seem to support the claim that certain emotions are more appropriate than others in both a moral and epistemological sense. For instance, Hilary Rose claims that women's practice of caring, even though warped by its containment in the alienated context of a coercive sexual division of labor, has nevertheless generated more accurate and less oppressive understandings of women's bodily functions, such as menstruation.[11] Certain emotions may be both morally appropriate and epistemologically advantageous in approaching the nonhuman and even the inanimate world. Jane Goodall's scientific contribution to our understanding of chimpanzee behavior seems to have been made possible only by her amazing empathy with or even love for these animals.[12] In her study of Barbara McClintock, Evelyn Fox Keller describes McClintock's relation to the objects of her research—grains of maize and their genetic properties—as a relation of affection, empathy, and "the highest form of love: love that allows for intimacy without the annihilation of difference." She notes that McClintock's "vocabulary is consistently a vocabulary of affection, of kinship, of empathy."[13] Examples like these prompt Hilary Rose to assert that a feminist science of nature needs to draw on heart as well as hand and brain.

SOME IMPLICATIONS OF RECOGNIZING THE EPISTEMIC POTENTIAL OF EMOTION

Accepting that appropriate emotions are indispensable to reliable knowledge does not mean, of course, that uncritical feeling may be substituted for supposedly dispassionate investigation. Nor does it mean that the emotional responses of women and other members of the underclass are to be trusted without question. Although our emotions are epistemologically indispensable, they are not epistemologically indisputable. Like all our faculties, they may be misleading, and their data, like all data, are always subject to reinterpretation and revision. Because emotions are not presocial, physiological responses to unequivocal situations, they are open to challenge on various grounds. They may be dishonest or self-deceptive, they may incorporate inaccurate or partial perceptions, or they may be constituted by oppressive values. Accepting the indispensability of appropriate emotions to knowledge means no more (and no less) than that discordant emotions should be attended to seriously and respectfully rather than condemned, ignored, discounted, or suppressed.

Just as appropriate emotions may contribute to the development of knowledge, so the growth of knowledge may contribute to the development of appropriate emotions. For instance, the powerful insights of feminist theory often

---

[11]Hilary Rose, "Hand, Brain, and Heart: A Feminist Epistemology for the Natural Sciences," *Signs: Journal of Women in Culture and Society* 9 (Autumn 1983): 73–90. [A. M. JAGGAR]

[12]Jane Goodall, *The Chimpanzees of Gombe: Patterns of Behavior* (Cambridge, MA: Harvard University Press, 1986). [A. M. JAGGAR]

[13]Evelyn Fox Keller, *Gender and Science* (New Haven, CT: Yale University Press, 1984), p. 184. [A. M. JAGGAR]

stimulate new emotional responses to past and present situations. Inevitably, our emotions are affected by the knowledge that the women on our faculty are paid systematically less than the men, that one girl in four is subjected to sexual abuse from heterosexual men in her own family, and that few women reach orgasm in heterosexual intercourse. We are likely to feel different emotions toward older women or people of color as we reevaluate our standards of sexual attractiveness or acknowledge that black is beautiful. The new emotions evoked by feminist insights are likely in turn to stimulate further feminist observations and insights, and these may generate new directions in both theory and political practice. There is a continuous feedback loop between our emotional constitution and our theorizing such that each continually modifies the other and is in principle inseparable from it.

The ease and speed with which we can reeducate our emotions is unfortunately not great. Emotions are only partially within our control as individuals. Although affected by new information, they are habitual responses not quickly unlearned. Even when we come to believe consciously that our fear or shame or revulsion is unwarranted, we may still continue to experience emotions inconsistent with our conscious politics. We may still continue to be anxious for male approval, competitive with our comrades and sisters, and possessive with our lovers. These unwelcome, because apparently inappropriate emotions, should not be suppressed or denied; instead, they should be acknowledged and subjected to critical scrutiny. The persistence of such recalcitrant emotions probably demonstrates how fundamentally we have been constituted by the dominant worldview, but it may also indicate superficiality or other inadequacy in our emerging theory and politics. We can only start from where we are—beings who have been created in a cruelly racist, capitalist, and male-dominated society that has shaped our bodies and our minds, our perceptions, our values and our emotions, our language, and our systems of knowledge.

The alternative epistemological models that I suggest would display the continuous interaction between how we understand the world and who we are as people. They would show how our emotional responses to the world change as we conceptualize it differently and how our changing emotional responses then stimulate us to new insights. They would demonstrate the need for theory to be self-reflexive, to focus not only on the outer world but also on ourselves and our relation to that world, to examine critically our social location, our actions, our values, our perceptions, and our emotions. The models would also show how feminist and other critical social theories are indispensable psychotherapeutic tools because they provide some insights necessary to a full understanding of our emotional constitution. Thus, the models would explain how the reconstruction of knowledge is inseparable from the reconstruction of ourselves. . . .

We can now see that women's subversive insights owe much to women's outlaw emotions, themselves appropriate responses to the situations of women's subordination. In addition to their propensity to experience outlaw emotions, at least on some level, women are relatively adept at identifying such emotions, in themselves and others, in part because of their social responsibility for caretaking, including emotional nurturance. It is true that women, like all subordinated peoples, especially those who must live in close proximity with their masters, often engage in emotional deception and even self-deception as the price of their survival. Even so, women may be less likely than other subordinated groups to engage in denial or suppression of outlaw emotions. Women's work of emotional nurturance has required them to develop a special acuity in recognizing hidden emotions and in understanding the genesis of those emotions. This emotional acumen can now be recognized as a skill in political analysis and validated as giving women a special advantage both in understanding the mechanisms of domination and in envisioning freer ways to live.

CONCLUSION

The claim that emotion is vital to systematic knowledge is only the most obvious contrast between the conception of theoretical investigation that I have sketched here and the conception provided by positivism. For instance, the alternative approach emphasizes that what we identify as emotion is a conceptual abstraction from a complex process of human activity that also involves acting, sensing, and evaluating. This proposed account of theoretical construction demonstrates the simultaneous necessity for and interdependence of faculties that our culture has abstracted and separated from each other: emotion and reason, evaluation and perception, observation and action. The model of knowing suggested here is nonhierarchical and antifoundationalist;[14] instead, it is appropriately symbolized by the radical feminist metaphor of the upward spiral.[15] Emotions are neither more basic than observation, reason, or action in building theory, nor secondary to them. Each of these human faculties reflects an aspect of human knowing inseparable from the other aspects. Thus, to borrow a famous phrase from a Marxian context,[16] the development of each of these faculties is a necessary condition for the development of all.

In conclusion, it is interesting to note that acknowledging the importance of emotion for knowledge is not an entirely novel suggestion within the Western epistemological tradition. That archrationalist, Plato himself, came to accept in the end that knowledge required a (very purified form of) love. It may be no accident that in the *Symposium* Socrates learns this lesson from Diotima, the wise woman!

---

[14]*antifoundationalist:* opposed to "foundationalist" theories of knowledge, which claim that all knowledge is founded ultimately on one basic class of things known. [D. C. ABEL]

[15]The metaphor of knowledge as an upward spiral emphasizes the interaction among the various human faculties involved in the knowing process; it is intended as an alternative to the linear conception of knowledge implied by foundationalism. [D. C. ABEL]

[16]The reference is to the statement by Karl Marx and Friedrich Engels that, in a communist society, "the free development of each is the condition for the free development of all" (*Manifesto of the Communist Party,* end of Section II). The passage appears on p. 475 of this book; biographies of Marx and Engels are on p. 466. [D. C. ABEL]

CHAPTER 4

Philosophy of Mind

The mind is perhaps the most elusive aspect of human nature. Although it is clear that we have a mind (how could we inquire about the mind if we didn't have one?), it is not at all clear what the mind is. Is it something located inside the brain? Is it *identical* with the brain, or perhaps an *activity* of the brain? Or is the mind a nonphysical entity, not located in space? Is the mind what accounts for me being the same person throughout my life? Or is the notion of a continuing "self" an illusion? These kinds of questions constitute the branch of philosophy known as the philosophy of mind.

The readings in this chapter are divided into two sections, "The Mind-Body Problem" and "Personal Identity." The mind-body problem is the problem of explaining how the mind and body (or, more specifically, the mind and brain) are related. Is the mind a nonphysical entity, distinct from the body? If so, how does it interact with the body, which is physical? For example, if we assume that fear is a state of a nonphysical mind, how can it *cause* my heart to beat faster? And if pleasure is a nonphysical state, how can it *be caused* by the eating of ice cream? Our readings on the mind-body problem are from René Descartes, David Carruthers, and Thomas Nagel. Descartes holds that the mind is a nonphysical substance (thing), but that the mind is somehow connected to the body. The mind is a *nonextended* (non-three-dimensional) and *thinking* substance, whereas the body is an *extended* and *nonthinking* substance. Descartes finds it difficult to explain how these two different substances are joined together and how they can interact. Carruthers rejects Descartes' *dualism* (two-substance theory of human nature). Basing his argument

199

on principles of science, he contends that mental states and processes are simply brain states and processes, and that human beings therefore are entirely physical creatures. Nagel claims that theorists like Carruthers have not been able to explain the mental state of consciousness in wholly physical terms. Nagel asks how it could be possible to provide an *objective* account of conscious experience, which by its very nature is *subjective.* How could objective, scientific analysis, which strives not to depend on any particular point of view, give an account of consciousness, which by its nature involves the subject's point of view?

The second section, "Personal Identity," addresses the question of what, if anything, makes us the same person throughout our life. The readings are from John Locke, Marya Schechtman, James Giles, and Daniel C. Dennett. Locke draws a distinction between being the same *human being* and the being same *person:* Being the same human being depends on having the same physical organization, whereas being the same person depends on having the same consciousness—and personal identity extends as far back as one's consciousness (memory) of past experiences. Schechtman modifies Locke's theory by claiming the personal identity depends on unconscious memories as well as conscious ones, and on understanding of how these conscious and unconscious memories form a trajectory from the past, to the present, and into the future. Giles presents David Hume's theory that what we call the self is simply a bundle of rapidly changing perceptions, develops it in terms of the Buddhist no-self doctrine, and then expands this compound theory by explaining how self-image and self-awareness arise. In the last reading, Daniel C. Dennett holds that there *is* a self, and that we can understand its nature by seeing how selves arose in the course of evolution. He contends that selves originated when organisms began to distinguish themselves from their environment, and that the distinctively *human* self, which produces personal identity, results from the narrative that one creates about oneself.

A. The Mind-Body Problem

READING 19 # Meditations on First Philosophy

René Descartes

A biography of René Descartes appears on p. 144.

This selection is from Descartes' *Meditations on First Philosophy.* (By "first philosophy" Descartes means truths about the basic topics of philosophy, which for him are God, the soul [mind], and the external world.) Our reading begins with the Second Meditation, in which Descartes tries to find something of which he can be absolutely certain—something about which not even a powerful "malicious demon" (a term he used in the First Meditation, p. 145 of this book) could deceive him. Descartes points out that he might be deceived even about such seemingly obvious things as the existence of the external world. But there is one thing he can be certain of—that he exists. For it would not even be possible for him to be deceived, if he did not exist. As he formulates this argument elsewhere, "I think, therefore I am." But what is this "I" that exists? Descartes argues that because he could be deceived about having a body, he is simply "a thing that thinks." He goes on to point out that if material things do exist, their essential nature would be extension (three-dimensionality).

In the Fifth Meditation, Descartes presents a proof for God's existence. Descartes has an idea of a supremely perfect being, and because existence is a necessary attribute of such a being, his idea would be self-contradictory if God did not exist. In the Sixth Meditation, Descartes uses his knowledge that God exists to prove that the external world exists: Because God is good and not a deceiver, it would be contrary to God's nature to give someone the inclination to believe that material things (including one's body) exist, if they didn't actually exist. Descartes has a body, then, but how is he (a thinking, nonextended thing) related to it (an extended, nonthinking thing)? Descartes states (with little further explanation) that he is "very closely joined and, as it were, intermingled with it."

SECOND MEDITATION. THE NATURE OF THE HUMAN MIND, AND HOW IT IS BETTER KNOWN THAN THE BODY

. . . Anything that admits of the slightest doubt I will set aside just as if I had found it to be wholly false; and I will proceed in this way until I recognize something certain, or, if nothing else, until I at least recognize for certain that there is no certainty. Archimedes[1] used to demand just one firm and immovable point in order to shift the entire earth; so I too can hope for great things if I manage to find just one thing, however slight, that is certain and unshakable.

I will suppose then, that everything I see is spurious. I will believe that my memory tells me lies, and that none of the things that it reports ever happened.

---

[1]Archimedes (about 287–212 B.C.E.) was a Greek mathematician and inventor. [D. C. ABEL]

I have no senses. Body, shape, extension, movement, and place are chimeras.[2] So what remains true? Perhaps just the one fact that nothing is certain.

Yet apart from everything I have just listed, how do I know that there is not something else that does not allow even the slightest occasion for doubt? Is there not a God, or whatever I may call him, who puts into me the thoughts I am now having? But why do I think this, since I myself may perhaps be the author of these thoughts? In that case am not I, at least, something? But I have just said that I have no senses and no body. This is the sticking point: What follows from this? Am I not so bound up with a body and with senses that I cannot exist without them? But I have convinced myself that there is absolutely nothing in the world, no sky, no earth, no minds, no bodies. Does it now follow that I too do not exist? No: If I convinced myself of something, then I certainly existed. But there is a deceiver of supreme power and cunning who is deliberately and constantly deceiving me. In that case I too undoubtedly exist, if he is deceiving me; and let him deceive me as much as he can, he will never bring it about that I am nothing so long as I think that I am something. So after considering everything very thoroughly, I must finally conclude that this proposition, "I am, I exist" is necessarily true whenever it is put forward by me or conceived in my mind.

But I do not yet have a sufficient understanding of what this "I" is, that now necessarily exists. So I must be on my guard against carelessly taking something else to be this "I," and so making a mistake in the very item of knowledge that I maintain is the most certain and evident of all. I will therefore go back and meditate on what I originally believed myself to be, before I embarked on this present train of thought. I will then subtract anything capable of being weakened, even minimally, by the arguments now introduced, so that what is left at the end may be exactly and only what is certain and unshakable.

What then did I formerly think I was? A man. But what is a man? Shall I say "a rational animal"? No; for then I should have to inquire what an animal is, what rationality is, and in this way one question would lead me down the slope to other harder ones, and I do not now have the time to waste on subtleties of this kind. Instead I propose to concentrate on what came into my thoughts spontaneously and quite naturally whenever I used to consider what I was. Well, the first thought to come to mind was that I had a face, hands, arms, and the whole mechanical structure of limbs that can be seen in a corpse, and that I called the body. The next thought was that I was nourished, that I moved about, and that I engaged in sense-perception and thinking; and these actions I attributed to the soul. But as to the nature of this soul, either I did not think about this or else I imagined it to be something tenuous, like a wind or fire or ether, that permeated my more solid parts. As to the body, however, I had no doubts about it, but thought I knew its nature distinctly. If I had tried to describe the mental conception I had of it, I would have expressed it as follows: By a body I understand whatever has a determinable shape and a definable location and can occupy a space in such a way as to exclude any other body; it can be perceived by touch, sight, hearing, taste, or smell, and can be moved in

---

[2]*chimeras:* mental fabrications. [D. C. Abel]

various ways, not by itself but by whatever else comes into contact with it. For, according to my judgment, the power of self-movement, like the power of sensation or of thought, was quite foreign to the nature of a body; indeed, it was a source of wonder to me that certain bodies were found to contain faculties of this kind.

But what shall I now say that I am, when I am supposing that there is some supremely powerful and, if it is permissible to say so, malicious deceiver, who is deliberately trying to trick me in every way he can? Can I now assert that I possess even the most insignificant of all the attributes that I have just said belong to the nature of a body? I scrutinize them, think about them, go over them again, but nothing suggests itself; it is tiresome and pointless to go through the list once more. But what about the attributes I assigned to the soul? Nutrition or movement? Since now I do not have a body, these are mere fabrications. Sense-perception? This surely does not occur without a body, and besides, when asleep I have appeared to perceive through the senses many things that I afterwards realized I did not perceive through the senses at all. Thinking? At last I have discovered it: thought—this alone is inseparable from me. I am, I exist—that is certain. But for how long? For as long as I am thinking. For it could be that were I totally to cease from thinking, I should totally cease to exist. At present I am not admitting anything except what is necessarily true. I am, then, in the strict sense, only a thing that thinks; that is, I am a mind, or intelligence, or intellect, or reason—words whose meaning I have been ignorant of until now. But for all that, I am a thing that is real and that truly exists. But what kind of a thing? As I have just said—a thinking thing.

What else am I? I will use my imagination. I am not that structure of limbs that is called a human body. I am not even some thin vapor that permeates the limbs—a wind, fire, air, breath, or whatever I depict in my imagination; for these are things that I have supposed to be nothing. Let this supposition stand; for all that, I am still something. And yet may it not perhaps be the case that these very things that I am supposing to be nothing, because they are unknown to me, are in reality identical with the "I" of which I am aware? I do not know, and for the moment I shall not argue the point, since I can make judgments only about things that are known to me. I know that I exist; the question is, what is this "I" that I know? If the "I" is understood strictly as we have been taking it, then it is quite certain that knowledge of it does not depend on things of whose existence I am as yet unaware; so it cannot depend on any of the things that I invent in my imagination. And this very word "invent" shows me my mistake. It would indeed be a case of fictitious invention if I used my imagination to establish that I was something or other; for imagining is simply contemplating the shape or image of a corporeal thing. Yet now I know for certain both that I exist and at the same time that all such images and, in general, everything relating to the nature of body, could be mere dreams <and chimeras>.[3] Once

---

[3]Words placed in angle brackets appear in the French version of *Meditations on First Philosophy* but not in the original Latin version. Louis-Charles d'Albert, Duc de Luyens (1620–1690), published a French translation that included some alterations from the original text. Descartes approved the translation, but scholars do not consider it as authoritative as the original Latin text. [D. C. ABEL]

this point has been grasped, to say "I will use my imagination to get to know more distinctly what I am" would seem to be as silly as saying "I am now awake, and see some truth; but since my vision is not yet clear enough, I will deliberately fall asleep so that my dreams may provide a truer and clearer representation." I thus realize that none of the things that the imagination enables me to grasp is at all relevant to this knowledge of myself that I possess, and that the mind must therefore be most carefully diverted from such things if it is to perceive its own nature as distinctly as possible.

But what then am I? A thing that thinks. What is that? A thing that doubts, understands, affirms, denies, is willing, is unwilling, and also imagines and has sensory perceptions.

This is a considerable list, if everything on it belongs to me. But does it? Is it not one and the same "I" who is now doubting almost everything, who nonetheless understands some things, who affirms that this one thing is true, denies everything else, desires to know more, is unwilling to be deceived, imagines many things even involuntarily, and is aware of many things that apparently come from the senses? Are not all these things just as true as the fact that I exist, even if I am asleep all the time, and even if he who created me is doing all he can to deceive me? Which of all these activities is distinct from my thinking? Which of them can be said to be separate from myself? The fact that it is I who am doubting and understanding and willing is so evident that I see no way of making it any clearer. But it is also the case that the "I" who imagines is the same "I." For even if, as I have supposed, none of the objects of imagination are real, the power of imagination is something that really exists and is part of my thinking. Lastly, it is also the same "I" who has sensory perceptions, or is aware of bodily things as it were through the senses. For example, I am now seeing light, hearing a noise, feeling heat. But I am asleep, so all this is false. Yet I certainly *seem* to see, to hear, and to be warmed. This cannot be false; what is called "having a sensory perception" is strictly just this, and in this restricted sense of the term it is simply thinking.

From all this I am beginning to have a rather better understanding of what I am. But it still appears—and I cannot stop thinking this—that the corporeal things of which images are formed in my thought, and that the senses investigate, are known with much more distinctness than this puzzling "I" that cannot be pictured in the imagination. And yet it is surely surprising that I should have a more distinct grasp of things that I realize are doubtful, unknown, and foreign to me, than I have of that which is true and known—my own self. But I see what it is: My mind enjoys wandering off and will not yet submit to being restrained within the bounds of truth. Very well then; just this once let us give it a completely free rein, so that after a while, when it is time to tighten the reins, it may more readily submit to being curbed.

Let us consider the things that people commonly think they understand most distinctly of all; that is, the bodies that we touch and see. I do not mean bodies in general—for general perceptions are apt to be somewhat more confused—but one particular body. Let us take, for example, this piece of wax. It has just been taken from the honeycomb; it has not yet quite lost the taste of the honey; it retains some of the scent of the flowers from which it was gathered;

its color, shape, and size are plain to see; it is hard, cold, and can be handled without difficulty; if you rap it with your knuckles it makes a sound. In short, it has everything that appears necessary to enable a body to be known as distinctly as possible. But even as I speak, I put the wax by the fire, and look: The residual taste is eliminated, the smell goes away, the color changes, the shape is lost, the size increases; it becomes liquid and hot; you can hardly touch it, and if you strike it, it no longer makes a sound. But does the same wax remain? It must be admitted that it does; no one denies it, no one thinks otherwise. So what was it in the wax that I understood with such distinctness? Evidently none of the features that I arrived at by means of the senses; for whatever came under taste, smell, sight, touch, or hearing has now altered—yet the wax remains.

Perhaps the answer lies in the thought that now comes to my mind—namely, the wax was not after all the sweetness of the honey, or the fragrance of the flowers, or the whiteness, or the shape, or the sound, but was rather a body that presented itself to me in these various forms a little while ago, but that now exhibits different ones. But what exactly is it that I am now imagining? Let us concentrate, take away everything that does not belong to the wax, and see what is left: merely something extended, flexible and changeable. But what is meant here by "flexible" and "changeable"? Is it what I picture in my imagination: that this piece of wax is capable of changing from a round shape to a square shape, or from a square shape to a triangular shape? Not at all; for I can grasp that the wax is capable of countless changes of this kind, yet I am unable to run through this immeasurable number of changes in my imagination, from which it follows that it is not the faculty of imagination that gives me my grasp of the wax as flexible and changeable. And what is meant by "extended"? Is the extension of the wax also unknown? For it increases if the wax melts, increases again if it boils, and is greater still if the heat is increased. I would not be making a correct judgment about the nature of wax unless I believed it capable of being extended in many more different ways than I will ever encompass in my imagination. I must therefore admit that the nature of this piece of wax is in no way revealed by my imagination, but is perceived by the mind alone. (I am speaking of this particular piece of wax; the point is even clearer with regard to wax in general.) But what is this wax that is perceived by the mind alone? It is of course the same wax that I see, that I touch, that I picture in my imagination, in short the same wax that I thought it to be from the start. And yet, and here is the point, the perception I have of it is a case not of vision or touch or imagination—nor has it ever been, despite previous appearances—but of purely mental scrutiny; and this can be imperfect and confused, as it was before, or clear and distinct as it is now, depending on how carefully I concentrate on what the wax consists in. . . .

But what am I to say about this mind, or about myself? (So far, remember, I am not admitting that there is anything else in me except a mind.) What, I ask, is this "I" that seems to perceive the wax so distinctly? Surely my awareness of my own self is not merely much truer and more certain than my awareness of the wax, but also much more distinct and evident. For if I judge that the wax exists from the fact that I see it, clearly this same fact entails much more evidently that I myself also exist. It is possible that what I see is not really the wax; it is possible that I do not even have eyes with which to see anything. But when I see, or think

I see (I am not here distinguishing the two), it is simply not possible that I who am now thinking am not something. By the same token, if I judge that the wax exists from the fact that I touch it, the same result follows, namely that I exist. If I judge that it exists from the fact that I imagine it, or for any other reason, exactly the same thing follows. And the result that I have grasped in the case of the wax may be applied to everything else located outside me. Moreover, if my perception of the wax seemed more distinct after it was established not just by sight or touch but by many other considerations, it must be admitted that I now know myself even more distinctly. This is because every consideration what-soever that contributes to my perception of the wax, or of any other body, cannot but establish even more effectively the nature of my own mind. . . .

FIFTH MEDITATION. THE ESSENCE OF MATERIAL THINGS, AND THE EXISTENCE OF GOD CONSIDERED A SECOND TIME

. . . The idea of God, or a supremely perfect being, is one that I find within me just as surely as the idea of any shape or number. And my understanding that it belongs to his nature that he always exists is no less clear and distinct than is the case when I prove of any shape or number that some property belongs to its nature. Hence, even if it turned out that not everything on which I have medi-tated in these past days is true, I ought still to regard the existence of God as having at least the same level of certainty as I have hitherto attributed to the truths of mathematics.

At first sight, however, this is not transparently clear, but has some appear-ance of being a sophism.[4] Since I have been accustomed to distinguish between existence and essence in everything else, I find it easy to persuade myself that existence can also be separated from the essence of God, and hence that God can be thought of as not existing. But when I concentrate more carefully, it is quite evident that existence can no more be separated from the essence of God than the fact that its three angles equal two right angles can be separated from the essence of a triangle, or than the idea of a mountain can be separated from the idea of a valley. Hence it is just as much of a contradiction to think of God (that is, a supremely perfect being) lacking existence (that is, lacking a perfection), as it is to think of a mountain without a valley.

However, even granted that I cannot think of God except as existing, just as I cannot think of a mountain without a valley, it certainly does not follow from the fact that I think of a mountain with a valley that there is any mountain in the world; and similarly, it does not seem to follow from the fact that I think of God as existing that he does exist. For my thought does not impose any necessity on things; and just as I may imagine a winged horse even though no horse has wings, so I may be able to attach existence to God even though no God exists.

But there is a sophism concealed here. From the fact that I cannot think of a mountain without a valley, it does not follow that a mountain and valley exist anywhere, but simply that a mountain and a valley, whether they exist or not,

---

[4]*sophism:* a plausible but incorrect argument, intended to deceive. [D. C. ABEL]

are mutually inseparable. But from the fact that I cannot think of God except as existing, it follows that existence is inseparable from God, and hence that he really exists. It is not that my thought makes it so, or imposes any necessity on any thing; on the contrary, it is the necessity of the thing itself, namely the existence of God, that determines my thinking in this respect. For I am not free to think of God without existence (that is, a supremely perfect being without a supreme perfection) as I am free to imagine a horse with or without wings. . . .[5]

SIXTH MEDITATION. THE EXISTENCE OF MATERIAL THINGS, AND THE REAL DISTINCTION BETWEEN MIND AND BODY

. . . Now, when I am beginning to achieve a better knowledge of myself and the author of my being, although I do not think I should heedlessly accept everything I seem to have acquired from the senses, neither do I think that everything should be called into doubt.

First, I know that everything that I clearly and distinctly understand is capable of being created by God so as to correspond exactly with my understanding of it. Hence the fact that I can clearly and distinctly understand one thing apart from another is enough to make me certain that the two things are distinct, since they are capable of being separated, at least by God. The question of what kind of power is required to bring about such a separation does not affect the judgment that the two things are distinct. Thus, simply by knowing that I exist and seeing at the same time that absolutely nothing else belongs to my nature or essence except that I am a thinking thing, I can infer correctly that my essence consists solely in the fact that I am a thinking thing. It is true that I may have (or, to anticipate, that I certainly have) a body that is very closely joined to me. But nevertheless, on the one hand I have a clear and distinct idea of myself, insofar as I am simply a thinking, nonextended thing; and on the other hand I have a distinct idea of body, insofar as this is simply an extended, nonthinking thing. And accordingly, it is certain that I am really distinct from my body and can exist without it.

Besides this, I find in myself faculties for certain special modes of thinking, namely imagination and sensory perception. Now I can clearly and distinctly understand myself as a whole without these faculties; but I cannot, conversely, understand these faculties without me, that is, without an intellectual substance to inhere in. This is because there is an intellectual act included in their essential definition; and hence I perceive that the distinction between them and myself corresponds to the distinction between the modes of a thing and the thing itself. Of course I also recognize that there are other faculties (like those of changing position, of taking on various shapes, and so on) that, like sensory perception and imagination, cannot be understood apart from some substance for them to inhere in, and hence cannot exist without it. But it is clear that these other faculties, if they exist, must be in a corporeal or extended substance and not an intellectual one; for the clear and distinct conception of them includes extension, but does not include

---

[5]Earlier, in his Third Meditation, Descartes gave an additional proof for the existence of God (alluded to in the title of this Fifth Mediation). The argument appears on pp. 152–154 of this book. [D. C. ABEL]

any intellectual act whatsoever. Now there is in me a passive faculty of sensory perception, that is, a faculty for receiving and recognizing the ideas of sensible[6] objects; but I could not make use of it unless there was also an active faculty, either in me or in something else, that produced or brought about these ideas. But this faculty cannot be in me, since clearly it presupposes no intellectual act on my part, and the ideas in question are produced without my cooperation and often even against my will. So the only alternative is that it is in another substance distinct from me—a substance that contains either formally or eminently[7] all the reality that exists objectively in the ideas[8] produced by this faculty. . . . This substance is either a body, that is, a corporeal nature, in which case it will contain formally <and in fact> everything that is to be found objectively <or representatively> in the ideas; or else it is God, or some creature more noble than a body, in which case it will contain eminently whatever is to be found in the ideas. But since God is not a deceiver, it is quite clear that he does not transmit the ideas to me either directly from himself, or indirectly via some creature that contains the objective reality of the ideas not formally but only eminently. For God has given me no faculty at all for recognizing any such source for these ideas; on the contrary, he has given me a great propensity to believe that they are produced by corporeal things. So I do not see how God could be understood to be anything but a deceiver if the ideas were transmitted from a source other than corporeal things. It follows that corporeal things exist. They may not all exist in a way that exactly corresponds with my sensory grasp of them, for in many cases the grasp of the senses is very obscure and confused. But at least they possess all the properties that I clearly and distinctly understand—that is, all those that, viewed in general terms, are comprised within the subject matter of pure mathematics. . . .

There is nothing that my own nature teaches me more vividly than that I have a body, and that when I feel pain there is something wrong with the body, and that when I am hungry or thirsty the body needs food and drink, and so on. So I should not doubt that there is some truth in this.

Nature also teaches me, by these sensations of pain, hunger, thirst, and so on, that I am not merely present in my body as a sailor is present in a ship, but that I am very closely joined and, as it were, intermingled with it, so that I and the body form a unit. If this were not so, I, who am nothing but a thinking thing, would not feel pain when the body was hurt, but would perceive the damage purely by the intellect, just as a sailor perceives by sight if anything in his ship is broken. Similarly, when the body needed food or drink, I should have an explicit understanding of the fact, instead of having confused sensations of hunger and thirst. For these sensations of hunger, thirst, pain, and so on are nothing but confused modes of thinking that arise from the union and, as it were, intermingling of the mind with the body.

---

[6]*sensible*: able to be sensed. [D. C. ABEL]

[7]A substance contains something *formally* if it possesses that thing in the *same form* as in the effect it produces; it contains something *eminently* if it possesses that thing in a form *higher* than the one it produces in the effect. For example, a tree as a cause of another tree contains "treeness" formally, but God as the cause of a tree contains "treeness" eminently. [D. C. ABEL]

[8]*objectively in the ideas*: in the ideas as representing the object (subject matter) of the ideas. [D. C. ABEL]

The Case for Physicalism

Peter Carruthers

Peter Carruthers was born 1952 in Manila, Republic of the Philippines. He attended the University of Leeds, England, where he completed his bachelor's degree in philosophy in 1975 and his master's degree in 1977. He pursued further studies at Balliol College, Oxford University, finishing his doctorate in philosophy in 1980. The following year Carruthers accepted a position as Lecturer in Philosophy Queens University of Belfast, Ireland. In 1985 he transferred to the University of Essex, England. Six years later he was appointed senior lecturer at the University of Sheffield, England, and was made professor the next year. At Sheffield he founded and directed the Hang Seng Centre for Cognitive Studies. Carruthers moved to the United States in 2001, becoming professor of philosophy at the University of Maryland and associate member of the Neuroscience and Cognitive Science Program. He chaired the Philosophy Department at Maryland from 2001 to 2008. In 2007 he was visiting research scientist at the Center for Adaptive Behavior and Cognition at the Max Planck Institute for Human Development in Berlin, Germany. In 2009 he received a National Science Foundation Scholar's Award to do research on the cognitive science of self-knowledge.

Carruthers has published numerous journal articles and a dozen books, including *Introducing Persons: Theories and Arguments in the Philosophy of Mind* (1986); *Language, Thought, and Consciousness: An Essay in Philosophical Psychology* (1996); *Phenomenal Consciousness: A Naturalistic Theory* (2002); *The Nature of the Mind: An Introduction* (2004); and *The Architecture of the Mind: Massive Modularity and the Flexibility of Thought* (2007).

Our reading is from Chapter 5 of *The Nature of the Mind*, "The Case for Physicalism." *Physicalism* is the view that all the states and processes involved in the human mind are ultimately physical states and processes. Carruthers argues for the "mind-brain identity" version of physicalism—that all mental states and processes are in fact brain states and processes. He bases his argument on two generally accepted scientific principles. The first one, the *closure of physics* states that all atomic and subatomic events happen in accordance with the laws of physics, that events at higher levels of description (for example, chemistry, biology, neurology, psychology) are *realized in* or *constituted by* atomic and subatomic events, and that therefore no nonphysical mental events could affect bodily behavior. The second principle, the *unity of nature,* states that nature is a system of layers of causal organization, that the bottom layer is physics, that all the ascending, higher layers (chemistry, biochemistry, biology, and so on) can be explained in terms of lower levels, and that therefore all events in nature can be explained ultimately in terms of physics. Carruthers argues that we should accept these principles because they have been successful methodological assumptions of scientific inquiry. Applying these principles to the explanation mental events, we can reasonably conclude that mental events are realized in the brain.

Carruthers discusses and rejects two theories that deny that mental events are brain events: *causal overdetermination,* which holds that mental events have *both* physical *and* nonphysical causes, with each type of cause being sufficient to produce mental events; and *epiphenomenalism,* which holds that mental events are secondary, nonphysical phenomena that are caused by physical events but have no causal power themselves. Carruthers concludes by pointing out that his mind-brain identity theory does not *reduce* mental events to brain events, but simply gives a *reductive explanation* of them. His theory does not say that mental events are *nothing but* brain events (reductionism); it simply says that a particular mental event is *constituted by* a particular brain event (a reductive explanation of that mental event), without making the further claim that a certain type of brain event *always* constitutes a certain type mental event, or that we can *deduce* a particular mental event from a particular brain event.

1. ARGUMENTS FOR MIND-BRAIN IDENTITY

[Introduction]

What the thesis of mind-brain identity affirms is that descriptions of our mental states, on the one hand, and some descriptions of our brain states, on the other, are in fact descriptions of the very same things. It holds that just as a particular cloud is, as a matter of fact, a great many water droplets suspended close together in the atmosphere; and just as a flash of lightning is, as a matter of fact, a certain sort of discharge of electrical energy; so a pain or a thought is (is identical with) some state of the brain or central nervous system.

The identity-thesis is a version of physicalism: It holds that all mental states and events are in fact physical states and events. But it is not, of course, a thesis about meaning: It does not claim that words such as "pain" and "after-image" may be *analyzed* or *defined* in terms of descriptions of brain processes. (That would be absurd.) Rather, it is an empirical thesis about the things in the world to which our words refer: It holds that the ways of thinking represented by our terms for conscious states, and the ways of thinking represented by some of our terms for brain states, are in fact different ways of thinking of the very same (physical) states and events. So "pain" doesn't *mean* "such-and-such a stimulation of the neural fibers" (just as "lightning" doesn't *mean* "such-and-such a discharge of electricity"); yet, for all that, the two terms in fact refer to the very same thing.

In this section a number of arguments in support of mind-brain identity will be set out and discussed. All of these arguments are broadly empirical ones, drawing on our beliefs about the causal order of the world, and our place within it.

1.1. The Closure of Physics and the Unity of Nature

Almost everyone believes that mind and matter interact causally with one another. For example, stimulation of our sense organs causes conscious experiences, and decisions cause bodily movements. . . .

One of the main objections to dualism has always been the difficulty of making sense of causal connections between mind and brain. . . . Now, there isn't any problem of *principle* in understanding causal connections between physical and nonphysical realms. For there is nothing in the concept of causation, as such, that requires all that causes be mediated by physical mechanisms. The real problem is to understand *how* such causation can occur, given what we already know or believe about the physical world, and about causation in the brain.

Consider, first, the physical world in general. Most scientists now believe that *physics is closed,* in the sense of permitting no interference from, or causation by, events at higher levels of description (for example, chemical or biological). On this view, all atomic and subatomic events happen in accordance with physical laws (albeit probabilistic ones), and all events at higher, more abstract, levels of description must be *realized* in, or *constituted* by, those physical processes in such a way as to allow no independent point of causal leverage. So while there may be chemical and biological laws, the events that figure in these laws must always, at the same time fall under the laws of physics.

On this conception, there is simply *no room* for a distinct and independent psychological level of nature, whose events are not physically constituted, but that can have an impact upon the physical behavior of the body. For in order for such a thing to be possible, it would have to be the case that nonphysical mental events could have an impact on causal sequences at the physical level. But this would conflict with the causal closure of physics—it would mean that some physical events would be caused, not by other physical events or processes, but rather by nonphysical mental events.

What reason do we have for believing in the causal closure of physics? This is not something that can be proved (least of all by thought alone, of course). But for some centuries it has been a successful methodological assumption of scientific inquiry. Scientists work under the assumption that processes in physics brook no interference from higher levels of causation. Whenever they come across physical phenomena that cannot presently be explained in physical terms, instead of postulating causation by *élan vital* (a supposed independent biological life-force), or causation by *ectoplasm* (a supposed independent psychic force), or whatever, they look deeper into the physical mechanisms. In many such cases this deeper look has proved successful; and in all such cases physicalistic scientific inquiries continue to make progress. This gives us good reason to think that the scientific methodology is correct, and that physics is indeed closed.

Closely related to the principle of the causal closure of physics is the principle of the *unity of nature.* On this conception, nature is *layered* into a unitary system of laws and patterns of causal organization, with the processes in any given layer being realized in the one below it. The bottom layer is fundamental physics, which *realizes* (or *constitutes*) all the rest. Chemical laws and processes are realized in those of atomic physics, biochemical processes are constituted by those of molecular chemistry, biological and neurological processes are realized in those of biochemistry, and so on. In accordance with this layered picture of nature, we should expect the principles and processes of human psychology—or the "laws" of operation of the human mind—to be realized in those of neurology. That is to say, we should expect mental events to be constituted by physical events in the brain.

The basic reason for believing in the unity of nature (like our reason for believing in the closure of physics) is that it is a highly successful working methodological assumption of much scientific inquiry. Although scientists are concerned to discover the laws and principles that operate at any given level of organization in nature—biological, say—it is also an important goal of science to try to understand how those same laws might be *constituted* or *realized* by patternings of events at lower levels. They seek to understand how the right sequences of events at the lower level—that of biochemistry, say—would give rise to the patterns observed at the higher one. (When successful, the result is a *reductive explanation* of the higher-level phenomenon. The difference between *reduction* and *reductive explanation* is discussed in Section 2.2.) This methodological assumption, too, has proved immensely successful, giving us reason to believe that mental processes will somehow be constituted by processes in the brain.

These arguments may be summarized as follows:

(1) It is a successful methodological assumption of science that nonphysical events cannot cause physical ones. *(The closure of physics.)*

(2) It is a successful methodological assumption of science that higher-level events and processes in nature must be realized in lower-level (ultimately physical) ones. *(The unity of nature.)*

(3) So we have reason to think that mental events must be realized in physical ones, probably in physical events in the brain.

The argument is broadly inductive[1] in form, since it projects forward from the success of assumptions made by scientists in the past to a new case. But it seems none the worse for that. . . .

1.2. The Argument from Causation in the Brain

Now consider, more particularly, what we believe about the nature of the causal processes that take place in the human brain. There is still much to learn about the brain—about the functions and interactions of its parts, for example. But much is already known. It is known that the brain consists of nerve cells, of various known types. Much is known about how such cells function and the physical causes that lead to their activity. Certainly there appear to be no "inverse causal black holes" in the brain, such as would seem to be required by the interactionist[2] picture. (That is, there are no places in the brain where brain activity begins to occur *for no physical reason*.) Indeed, I claim that enough is already known about the brain to justify the following principle: *Each event in the brain has a sufficient physical cause.* . . .

[Most of us] believe very firmly that some mental states and events are causally necessary for the occurrence of some physical ones. For example, I believe that if I had not been conscious of a pain in my foot (mental event), I would not have gone to the doctor (physical event). My awareness of the pain was, I believe, a causally necessary condition of my later visit to the doctor. But as we noted above, it seems most unlikely that we shall ever need to advert

---

[1]An *inductive argument* is one that claims to lead from the premises (the statements used to establish the conclusion) to the conclusion in a *probable* way (contrasted with a *deductive argument*, which claims to lead from the premises to the conclusion in a *necessary* way). [D. C. ABEL]

[2]*interactionist*: relating to *interactionism*, the doctrine that the mind and body causally interact; also called *interactive dualism*. [D. C. ABEL]

to anything other than physical-to-physical causality when we investigate the detailed causal nexus behind any given bodily movement. On the contrary, it seems likely that there will always be physical events providing us with a sufficient causal explanation of the brain events giving rise to any particular bodily movement. For example, as we trace the causes of my legs moving me in the direction of the doctor's surgery,[3] through events in the muscles of my legs and feet, through events in the nerves of my spinal column, into events in the cells of my brain, it seems most unlikely that the chain of physical causation will eventually run out. Indeed, according to the principle set out above, we already know enough about causation in the brain to know that it won't. So we shall never be forced to appeal to any nonphysical event in order to provide a satisfactory causal explanation of the movements leading to my visit to the surgery.

Now the only way in which we can hold onto both beliefs—the belief that some mental events are causally necessary for the occurrence of some physical ones, and the belief that it is unnecessary to appeal to anything other than physical events in providing causal explanations of brain events—is by believing that some mental events *are* physical ones. Then somewhere in the chain of physical causes of my visit to the doctor there will be a brain event that is (is identical with) my awareness of a sensation of pain.

This argument for the general truth of the mind-brain identity thesis may be summarized as follows:

(1) Some mental states and events are causally necessary for the occurrence of some physical ones.
(2) In a completed neurophysiological science there will be no need to advert to anything other than physical-to-physical causality in the brain.
(3) So some mental states and events are (are identical with) physical (brain) states and events.

The argument is valid.[4] Although its conclusion only claims that *some* mental states are physical, it can easily be developed in such a way as to entail the stronger conclusion that *all* are. For almost every kind of mental state can sometimes be causally necessary for a physical one, we think. Sometimes a particular bodily movement would not have taken place if I had not made a particular decision; or if I had not entertained a particular thought; or if I had not been aware of a particular sensation; or if I had not had a particular afterimage; and so on. Then since it seems extremely unlikely that some mental states are physical while some are not, it follows that all are.

1.3. Causal Overdetermination

An interactive dualist[5] may try to get around the difficulty by appealing to the notion of "causal overdetermination." Very roughly, this is the idea that an event may have more causes than are necessary. For example, imagine someone being

---

[3] *surgery:* the room in a medical facility where patients are seen. [D. C. Abel]
[4] *valid:* A deductive argument (see footnote 1) is *valid* when the conclusion follows necessarily from the premises, whether or not the premises are true. [D. C. Abel]
[5] *interactive dualist:* See footnote 2. [D. C. Abel]

shot by a firing squad, each member of which has a loaded gun (contrary to normal practice). Suppose that every soldier's aim is true, that all fire at the same time, and that every bullet strikes the heart. Then it is true of every soldier, that even if the others had not fired, his action would still have caused the prisoner's death. (Each shot individually is causally sufficient for death.) But it is also true of every soldier, that even if he himself had *not* fired, the prisoner's death would still have been caused by the others. (No shot individually is causally necessary for death.) Similarly then, the dualist may propose that brain events are caused *both* by prior brain events (so the chain of physical causes is unbroken) *and* by prior mental events—where either type of event on its own is sufficient to produce the effect, but neither type of event on its own is necessary.

So we have: Each shot is *causally sufficient* for death, in that death will follow from it in the circumstances, even if the other shots aren't fired; but no shot is (individually) *causally necessary*, since even if it isn't fired, death will still be caused by the other shots. Perhaps, similarly, the events in the brain that cause bodily movements are caused *both* by earlier brain events *and* by certain mental events, such as a decision. . . .

By deploying the thesis of causal overdetermination, a dualist can hold onto one aspect of our commonsense beliefs in face of the likely discovery of unbroken causal chains of brain events—namely, the belief that our decisions are sometimes, in the circumstances, *sufficient* to bring about a bodily movement. Yet one aspect of common sense would still have to be given up—namely, the belief that a decision is sometimes causally *necessary* for a bodily movement to occur.

People who take the overdetermination view can believe the following: Given that a subject is sitting at a keyboard and decides to start typing, then this is, in the circumstances, sufficient for typing to begin. But they can no longer claim that had the subject *not* decided in that way, then the bodily movement wouldn't have taken place. On the contrary, it would still have occurred, brought about by its other cause: a particular brain event. But are we really prepared to give up this belief? Don't I believe, almost as firmly as I believe anything, that if I had not decided to write this book (mental event) I would not now be typing at this keyboard (physical event)?

How, then, can a dualist explain the fact that decisions are causally necessary *and* sufficient for bodily movements, consistent with our beliefs about the brain?

1.4. Epiphenomenalism

One suggestion is that we should give up believing that our decisions make any real causal difference. Rather, those decisions are mere *epiphenomena*,[6] produced as a by-product by the brain events that are the true causes of our actions.

An attractive feature of this account is that it can explain how we come to be under the *illusion* of agency, falsely believing that our decisions are *causally* necessary and sufficient for some of our movements. For a given mental event will,

------

[6]*epiphenomena:* secondary phenomena (in this case, mental events) that are caused by and accompany primary phenomena (in this case, brain events) but have no causal power themselves. [D. C ABEL]

on this account, be *noncausally* necessary and sufficient for a given movement, since each of them has a common cause. In fact the epiphenomenalist-dualist can claim that each mental event will be correlated with a particular brain event as a matter of causal necessity, in which case it will be causally impossible for the mental event to occur without the corresponding brain event occurring.

So, given that the mental event occurs, then so too must the action occur that is caused by the underlying brain event. (That is to say, the mental event is noncausally sufficient for the occurrence of the action.) And if the mental event *hadn't* occurred, then that would mean that the brain event hadn't occurred either, and so nor would the movement happen. (That is to say, the mental event is noncausally necessary for the occurrence of the action.) On this account, then, it will be *true* that if I hadn't decided to write this book, I wouldn't now be typing. For the only way in which I could have failed to take that decision would have been if the corresponding brain event had failed to occur; and if that had failed to occur, then the bodily movement wouldn't have been caused.

Compare the froth on the wave that breaks a sand castle on the beach. Supposing that it is a law of nature that breaking waves produce froth on their leading edge, then we can say this: If the froth had not been there, the sand castle wouldn't have been broken; and given that the froth is there, the sand castle must be broken shortly thereafter. But it isn't really the froth that causes the sand castle to break; rather, it is the wave that causes *both* the frothing *and* the breaking.

Similarly we can say: If I hadn't decided to type, then I wouldn't now be typing. (This is because, if the event of my deciding hadn't occurred, then that would have been because the brain event that caused my movement hadn't occurred.) And we can say: Given that I decide to type, in the circumstances, then typing occurs. (This is because, if the decision to type occurs, then that will have been caused by the brain event that causes the relevant movements.) But my decision won't be the true cause of my typing, any more than the froth on the wave is the true cause of the sand castle breaking.

Although a theory of this sort can save our belief that certain of our bodily movements wouldn't have occurred if certain decisions hadn't been taken, it does so at the cost of explanatory redundancy. For the decision is no longer part of the true causal explanation of why the bodily movement took place. To say that our decisions are causally correlated with the events that cause our bodily movements, isn't the same as saying (what we intuitively believe) that our decisions themselves constitute the true causal explanations of our actions.

It seems that epiphenomenalism must conflict with our commonsense belief in the reality of agency—it conflicts with our belief that our decisions can make a causal difference to what we do. But another reason why epiphenomenalism is unacceptable is that, if it were true, it would remain a complete mystery why our decisions should march so neatly in step with our actions. Why is it that the brain event that causes me to sit down to type *also* causes me to think "Now I will begin typing"? For, by hypothesis, it wouldn't have made the slightest bit of difference if that brain event had caused me to think instead "Now I'll go swimming."

How would the underlying causal properties of the brain ever have evolved, for example? What would be the [evolutionary] advantage if the brain event that causes my arm to go up also causes me to decide "Now I shall raise my arm"? For, by hypothesis, the latter has no causal effects in its own right. What difference would it have made if the brain event had caused me to decide "Now I shall open my mouth" or "Now I shall sit down" instead? It would seem to be a quite remarkable cosmic coincidence that the evolutionary processes that caused our brains to have their causal powers in respect of bodily movement, *also* led them to cause content-relevant mental events. Then since it is good explanatory practice to minimize miracles, we have good reason to reject epiphenomenalism and to endorse the thesis of mind-brain identity instead.

1.5. Mind-Brain Identity

In fact our belief in the reality of agency (that is, our belief that our decisions are often part of the true causal explanation of our actions) is very deeply held. If we are to give it up, then there had better be some powerful arguments for dualism to force us to do so. But in fact . . . there are none. The only remaining picture of the relation between mind and brain, then, is one of *identity*. . . . On this account, decisions are part of the true causal explanations of actions, because they are none other than (they are strictly identical to) the brain events that cause those actions.

The main argument for the thesis of mind-brain identity, then, can be represented as follows:

(1) Our bodily movements are caused by brain events.
(2) Each event in the brain has a sufficient physical cause.
(3) Our decisions are sometimes necessary conditions for some of our movements.
(4) Our decisions sometimes form part of the true causal explanation of some of our movements.
(5) So decisions *are* brain events.

Premises (1) and (2) are intended to rule out classic interactive dualism, premise (3) rejects causal overdetermination, and premise (4) rules out epiphenomenalism—thus leaving physicalism as the only remaining possibility.

Premise (1) seems undeniable in the light of modern scientific knowledge. Premise (2) also seems sufficiently well-supported, given what is known about causal processes in the brain. Premises (3) and (4) form an important part of our commonsense view of ourselves and the world. We believe that mental processes can make a difference to the world. Then the only way in which we can hold on to this belief, together with the other premises, is to endorse the conclusion, which is the identity thesis (or at least a limited version of it; see below). The argument as a whole seems rationally convincing in the absence of evidence to the contrary.

Here, as previously, it should be easy to extend the argument to justify the physical nature of *all* mental states, and not just decisions. This is because any mental state can play a part in causing a decision. I sometimes take a decision because of what I see, or what I feel, or what I want, or what I think—in which case these states, too, will form part of the true causal explanation of my action, and the same argument will lead to the conclusion that they, too, are physical. . . .

2. RAMIFICATIONS: TYPES, TOKENS . . .

In this section we will first clarify the thesis of mind-brain identity, distinguishing between two different versions of it, and relating it to different varieties of reductionism in general. . . .

2.1. Type- versus Token-Identity

There is an important distinction to be drawn between *type-identity* and *token-identity*. The thesis of mind-brain *type*-identity holds that each general type of mental state—for instance, sensations of red, or pains in general—is identical with some general type of brain state. So whenever a pain is felt it will be identical with a particular instance of some general type of brain state, the same type of brain state in each case. The thesis of mind-brain *token*-identity is much weaker. It holds only that each particular instance of pain is identical with some particular brain state, those brain states perhaps belonging to distinct kinds. It holds that each particular occurrence of a mental state will be identical with some particular occurrence of a brain state, but that there may be no general identities between types of mental state and types of brain state. Note that the arguments for the identity-thesis that we sketched above are indifferent between these two versions of it.

There is some reason to think that the thesis of mind-brain token-identity is the better theory. One argument would be this: We know that there is a considerable degree of plasticity in the human brain. For instance, although speech is normally controlled from a particular region in the left hemisphere, someone who has had that region damaged (especially when young) can sometimes recover the ability to speak, with practice. So a particular decision to speak may sometimes be identical with an event in one part of the brain, while sometimes it may be identical with an event in quite a different part. Now it doesn't immediately follow from this that the brain events are of different types; this will depend upon what counts as a "type" of brain event. But there seems at least no particular reason to *assume* that the events will all be of the same type.

The case can be made even stronger if we recall that many creatures besides human beings can possess mental states. If not only mammals, birds, and reptiles, but perhaps also nonbiological systems such as robot-computers can possess mental states, then it is obviously false that there will always be the same one type of physical state in existence whenever there exists an instance of a given type of mental state. For the physical control-structures of these creatures will be very different from one another, and from the structure of the human brain. . . .

2.2. Reduction versus Reductive Explanation

Does the thesis of mind-brain identity commit us to *reducing* the mind to the brain? Are we required to say that the human mind is *nothing but* the activity of neurons and groups of neurons? The answer to these questions is negative, in fact. For a distinction closely related to the one just drawn between type and token identity is the distinction between *reduction* (of properties), on the one hand, and *reductive explanation* (of tokens), on the other. We need only be committed to the latter. Let me explain.

Most philosophers and scientists today are physicalists. They believe that all things, events, and processes in the natural world are, at bottom, physical things, events, and processes. But few are *type*-physicalists, in the sense explained in Section 2.1 above. Few believe that higher-level properties in chemistry, biology, and psychology, for example, will line up type-for-type with properties in fundamental physics. On the contrary, most believe that the special sciences (chemistry, biology, and the rest) are, in a sense, *autonomous*—dealing with laws and properties that cannot be reduced directly to those of physics (or indeed to any other science).[7] . . .

What we do regularly find in science . . . is reductive *explanation*. A given higher-level process—in biology, say—is reductively explained when we can show that suitable lower-level event-sequences, happening in accordance with lower-level laws, are sufficient to *realize,* or *constitute,* the higher-level process in question. To put the same point rather differently: A successful reductive explanation shows how a particular instantiation (or type of instantiation) of a higher-level property is constituted by some lower-level property or process. But it does so without reducing the higher-level property as such, since there may be no lower-level process-type that is *always* instantiated whenever the higher-level property is instantiated.

Most physicalists believe in the unity of science, in the sense that they expect all higher-level properties and processes to be reductively explicable in principle. They think that it must be possible, in the end, to show how any higher-level property or process (of biology, psychology, or whatever) is realized in—or constituted by—some lower-level property or process (and ultimately by processes in fundamental physics). It must be possible to take a particular occurrence of a higher-level property and show how, on at least that occasion, it was constituted by some lower-level physical property or process. But physicalists don't have to say that biology is *nothing but* chemistry, or that chemistry is *nothing but* quantum mechanics.

It is thus possible to be a physicalist about the mind, while at the same time believing in the reality and irreducibility of mental properties. . . . While in one sense the mind is *nothing but* the operation of the brain, for a physicalist—since each token mental state will be none other than some token brain state—it may still be the case that if we want to understand the operations of minds in general, we shall unavoidably have to couch our explanations in terms of mental properties; just as if we want to understand the operations of wings in general, we cannot appeal to the specific physical structures of specific wings.

---

[7]In other words, few philosophers and scientists believe that any particular type of lower-level property (for example, a property studied by physics, the lowest-level science) will necessarily always produce a particular type of higher-level property (for example, a property studied by psychology). Most philosophers (including Carruthers) and scientists believe that a higher-level science is *autonomous* in the sense that its laws cannot be *deduced* from the laws of a lower-level science. In this sense, it is false that mental events (studied by psychology) can be reduced to (are *nothing but*) brain events (studied by neurology, and ultimately by physics). [D. C. ABEL]

What Is It Like to Be a Bat?
Thomas Nagel

Thomas Nagel was born in Belgrade, Yugoslavia, in 1937. He came to the United States in 1939 and became a naturalized citizen five years later. After completing his undergraduate degree from Cornell University in 1958, he studied at Oxford University, where he earned a bachelor of philosophy degree in 1960. Nagel then enrolled in the graduate program in philosophy at Harvard University, receiving his doctorate in 1963. He taught at the University of California at Berkeley until 1966 and at Princeton University for the next 14 years. In 1980 he accepted an appointment as professor of philosophy at New York University. He was named professor of philosophy and law in 1986, Fiorello LaGuardia Professor of Law in 2001, and university professor in 2002. Nagel has held visiting appointments at Rockefeller University, the University of Pittsburgh, the University of Mexico, the University of Witwatersrand (Republic of South Africa), the University of California at Los Angeles, and All Souls College at Oxford University. He is a Fellow of the American Academy of Arts and Sciences, a Corresponding Fellow of the British Academy, and an Honorary Fellow of Corpus Christi College at Oxford University.

Nagel's publications include *The Possibility of Altruism* (1970), *Mortal Questions* (1979; translated into 10 languages), *The View from Nowhere* (1986), *What Does It All Mean? A Very Short Introduction to Philosophy* (1987; translated into 20 languages), *The Last Word* (1997), *Concealment and Exposure and Other Essays* (2002), and *Secular Philosophy and the Religious Temperament: Essays 2002–2008* (2010).

Our reading is Nagel's 1974 article, "What Is It Like to Be a Bat?" Nagel examines the *reductionist* theory that some contemporary philosophers propose as a solution to the problem of how the mind and body are related. Reductionism is the view that one kind of thing can be "reduced to" (explained fully in terms of) another kind of thing. In the philosophy of mind, reductionism holds that the mind and mental phenomena can be reduced to physical phenomena, such as neurological activity of the brain (hence the doctrine is known as *physicalism* or *materialism*). Nagel contends that the major difficulty facing reductionist, physicalist theories of mind is the phenomenon of consciousness. Although there may be some way to reduce consciousness to physical states, we are far from knowing how this might be done.

Nagel explains that the fact that an organism (human or nonhuman) has consciousness means that "there is something it is like to *be* that organism—something it is like *for* that organism." Consciousness is by nature a subjective phenomenon, and as such seems impossible to analyze exhaustively in terms of objective, physical phenomena. Subjectivity implies a single point of view, whereas objectivity requires a more universal point of view. Taking the example of a bat as a creature very different from us, Nagel argues that it seems impossible for us to capture in objective analysis the subjective experience of a bat. I might imagine what it would be like *for me* to behave as a bat behaves (hanging upside down by my feet, for example), but I seem unable to know what it is like *for the bat* to be a bat. Even if I had complete knowledge of the working of the bat's neurological system, how could the subjective experience of the bat be reduced to this kind of objective analysis? Nagel points out that he does not claim to have disproved the physicalist claim that mental states are states of the body; he simply claims that the two terms of this alleged equation are so different that we have no idea what it means to say that a mental state "is" a physical state.

[INTRODUCTION]

Consciousness is what makes the mind-body problem really intractable. Perhaps that is why current discussions of the problem give it little attention or get it obviously wrong. The recent wave of reductionist euphoria has produced several analyses of mental phenomena and mental concepts designed to explain the possibility of some variety of materialism, psychophysical identification,[1] or reduction. But the problems dealt with are those common to this type of reduction and other types, and what makes the mind-body problem unique, and unlike the water-H_2O problem or the Turing machine-IBM machine problem or the lightning-electrical discharge problem or the gene-DNA problem or the oak tree-hydrocarbon problem,[2] is ignored.

Every reductionist has his favorite analogy from modern science. It is most unlikely that any of these unrelated examples of successful reduction will shed light on the relation of mind to brain. But philosophers share the general human weakness for explanations of what is incomprehensible in terms suited for what is familiar and well understood, though entirely different. This has led to the acceptance of implausible accounts of the mental largely because they would permit familiar kinds of reduction. I shall try to explain why the usual examples do not help us to understand the relation between mind and body— why, indeed, we have at present no conception of what an explanation of the physical nature of a mental phenomenon would be. Without consciousness the mind-body problem would be much less interesting. With consciousness it seems hopeless. The most important and characteristic feature of conscious mental phenomena is very poorly understood. Most reductionist theories do not even try to explain it. And careful examination will show that no currently available concept of reduction is applicable to it. Perhaps a new theoretical form can be devised for the purpose, but such a solution, if it exists, lies in the distant intellectual future.

[SUBJECTIVITY AND OBJECTIVITY]

Conscious experience is a widespread phenomenon. It occurs at many levels of animal life, though we cannot be sure of its presence in the simpler organisms, and it is very difficult to say in general what provides evidence of it. (Some extremists have been prepared to deny it even of mammals other than man.) No doubt it occurs in countless forms totally unimaginable to us, on other planets in other solar systems throughout the universe. But no matter how the form may vary, the fact that an organism has conscious experience *at all* means, basically, that there is something it is like to *be* that organism. There may be further

---

[1]*psychophysical identification:* the equating of the mind (psyche) with the body. [D. C. ABEL]

[2]Nagel here gives examples of reductionism: water reduced to hydrogen and oxygen, intelligence reduced to computing ability (a *Turing machine* is a kind of computer imagined by the British mathematician Alan Turing [1912–1954]), lightning reduced to the discharge of electricity, genes reduced to DNA, and oak trees reduced to hydrocarbons. [D. C. ABEL]

implications about the form of the experience; there may even (though I doubt it) be implications about the behavior of the organism. But fundamentally an organism has conscious mental states if and only if there is something that it is like to *be* that organism—something it is like *for* the organism.

We may call this the subjective character of experience. It is not captured by any of the familiar, recently devised reductive analyses of the mental, for all of them are logically compatible with its absence. It is not analyzable in terms of any explanatory system of functional states, or intentional states,[3] since these could be ascribed to robots or automata that behaved like people though they experienced nothing. It is not analyzable in terms of the causal role of experiences in relation to typical human behavior—for similar reasons. I do not deny that conscious mental states and events cause behavior, nor that they may be given functional characterizations. I deny only that this kind of thing exhausts their analysis. Any reductionist program has to be based on an analysis of what is to be reduced. If the analysis leaves something out, the problem will be falsely posed. It is useless to base the defense of materialism on any analysis of mental phenomena that fails to deal explicitly with their subjective character. For there is no reason to suppose that a reduction that seems plausible when no attempt is made to account for consciousness, can be extended to include consciousness. Without some idea, therefore, of what the subjective character of experience is, we cannot know what is required of a physicalist theory.

While an account of the physical basis of mind must explain many things, this appears to be the most difficult. It is impossible to exclude the phenomenological[4] features of experience from a reduction in the same way that one excludes the phenomenal[5] features of an ordinary substance from a physical or chemical reduction of it—namely, by explaining them as effects on the minds of human observers. If physicalism is to be defended, the phenomenological features must themselves be given a physical account. But when we examine their subjective character it seems that such a result is impossible. The reason is that every subjective phenomenon is essentially connected with a single point of view, and it seems inevitable that an objective, physical theory will abandon that point of view.

Let me first try to state the issue somewhat more fully than by referring to the relation between the subjective and the objective, or between the *pour soi* and the *en soi*.[6] This is far from easy. Facts about what it is like to be an X are very peculiar, so peculiar that some may be inclined to doubt their reality, or the significance of claims about them. To illustrate the connection between subjectivity and a point of view, and to make evident the importance of subjective features, it will help to explore the matter in relation to an example that brings

---

[3]To analyze conscious experience in terms of *functional states* is to define it in terms of the function it performs; to analyze it in terms of *intentional states* is to define it in terms of its property of referring to objects, of being *about* objects. [D. C. ABEL]

[4]*phenomenological:* relating to *phenomenology,* the study of how things appear to and are experienced by a subject. [D. C. ABEL]

[5]*phenomenal:* involving experienced phenomena. [D. C. ABEL]

[6]the *pour soi* and the *en soi:* the "for itself" and the "in itself" (French). These terms are used by the French philosopher Jean-Paul Sartre to designate, respectively, mere things and consciousness. For a biography of Sartre, see p. 386. [D. C. ABEL]

out clearly the divergence between the two types of conception, subjective and objective.

I assume we all believe that bats have experience. After all, they are mammals, and there is no more doubt that they have experience than that mice or pigeons or whales have experience. I have chosen bats instead of wasps or flounders because if one travels too far down the phylogenetic tree, people gradually shed their faith that there is experience there at all. Bats, although more closely related to us than those other species, nevertheless present a range of activity and a sensory apparatus so different from ours that the problem I want to pose is exceptionally vivid (though it certainly could be raised with other species). Even without the benefit of philosophical reflection, anyone who has spent some time in an enclosed space with an excited bat knows what it is to encounter a fundamentally *alien* form of life.

I have said that the essence of the belief that bats have experience is that there is something that it is like to be a bat. Now we know that most bats (the microchiroptera, to be precise) perceive the external world primarily by sonar, or echolocation, detecting the reflections, from objects within range, of their own rapid, subtly modulated, high-frequency shrieks. Their brains are designed to correlate the outgoing impulses with the subsequent echoes, and the information thus acquired enables bats to make precise discriminations of distance, size, shape, motion, and texture comparable to those we make by vision. But bat sonar, though clearly a form of perception, is not similar in its operation to any sense that we possess, and there is no reason to suppose that it is subjectively like anything we can experience or imagine. This appears to create difficulties for the notion of what it is like to be a bat. We must consider whether any method will permit us to extrapolate to the inner life of the bat from our own case, and if not, what alternative methods there may be for understanding the notion.

Our own experience provides the basic material for our imagination, whose range is therefore limited. It will not help to try to imagine that one has webbing on one's arms, which enables one to fly around at dusk and dawn catching insects in one's mouth; that one has very poor vision, and perceives the surrounding world by a system of reflected high-frequency sound signals; and that one spends the day hanging upside down by one's feet in an attic. Insofar as I can imagine this (which is not very far), it tells me only what it would be like for *me* to behave as a bat behaves. But that is not the question. I want to know what it is like for a *bat* to be a bat. Yet if I try to imagine this, I am restricted to the resources of my own mind, and those resources are inadequate to the task. I cannot perform it either by imagining additions to my present experience, or by imagining segments gradually subtracted from it, or by imagining some combination of additions, subtractions, and modifications.

To the extent that I could look and behave like a wasp or a bat without changing my fundamental structure, my experiences would not be anything like the experiences of those animals. On the other hand, it is doubtful that any meaning can be attached to the supposition that I should possess the internal neurophysiological constitution of a bat. Even if I could by gradual degrees be transformed into a bat, nothing in my present constitution enables me to imagine what the experiences of such a future stage of myself thus metamorphosed would be like. The best evidence would come from the experiences of bats, if we only knew what they were like.

So if extrapolation from our own case is involved in the idea of what it is like to be a bat, the extrapolation must be incompletable. We cannot form more than a schematic conception of what it *is* like. For example, we may ascribe general *types* of experience on the basis of the animal's structure and behavior. Thus we describe bat sonar as a form of three-dimensional forward perception; we believe that bats feel some versions of pain, fear, hunger, and lust, and that they have other, more familiar types of perception besides sonar. But we believe that these experiences also have in each case a specific subjective character, which it is beyond our ability to conceive. And if there is conscious life elsewhere in the universe, it is likely that some of it will not be describable even in the most general experiential terms available to us. (The problem is not confined to exotic cases, however, for it exists between one person and another. The subjective character of the experience of a person deaf and blind from birth is not accessible to me, for example, nor presumably is mine to him. This does not prevent us each from believing that the other's experience has such a subjective character.)

If anyone is inclined to deny that we can believe in the existence of facts like this whose exact nature we cannot possibly conceive, he should reflect that in contemplating the bats we are in much the same position that intelligent bats or Martians would occupy if they tried to form a conception of what it was like to be us. The structure of their own minds might make it impossible for them to succeed, but we know they would be wrong to conclude that there is not anything precise that it is like to be us: that only certain general types of mental state could be ascribed to us (perhaps perception and appetite would be concepts common to us both; perhaps not). We know they would be wrong to draw such a skeptical conclusion because we know what it is like to be us. And we know that while it includes an enormous amount of variation and complexity, and while we do not possess the vocabulary to describe it adequately, its subjective character is highly specific, and in some respects describable in terms that can be understood only by creatures like us. The fact that we cannot expect ever to accommodate in our language a detailed description of Martian or bat phenomenology should not lead us to dismiss as meaningless the claim that bats and Martians have experiences fully comparable in richness of detail to our own. It would be fine if someone were to develop concepts and a theory that enabled us to think about those things; but such an understanding may be permanently denied to us by the limits of our nature. And to deny the reality or logical significance of what we can never describe or understand is the crudest form of cognitive dissonance.

This brings us to the edge of a topic that requires much more discussion than I can give it here—namely, the relation between facts on the one hand and conceptual schemes or systems of representation on the other. My realism[7] about the subjective domain in all its forms implies a belief in the existence of facts beyond the reach of human concepts. Certainly it is possible for a human

---

[7]*realism:* the view that a kind of entity (here, subjective states) really exists. [D. C. ABEL]

being to believe that there are facts that humans never *will* possess the requisite concepts to represent or comprehend. Indeed, it would be foolish to doubt this, given the finiteness of humanity's expectations. After all, there would have been transfinite numbers even if everyone had been wiped out by the Black Death before Cantor[8] discovered them. But one might also believe that there are facts that *could* not ever be represented or comprehended by human beings, even if the species lasted forever—simply because our structure does not permit us to operate with concepts of the requisite type. This impossibility might even be observed by other beings, but it is not clear that the existence of such beings, or the possibility of their existence, is a precondition of the significance of the hypothesis that there are humanly inaccessible facts. (After all, the nature of beings with access to humanly inaccessible facts is presumably itself a humanly inaccessible fact.) Reflection on what it is like to be a bat seems to lead us, therefore, to the conclusion that there are facts that do not consist in the truth of propositions expressible in a human language. We can be compelled to recognize the existence of such facts without being able to state or comprehend them.

I shall not pursue this subject, however. Its bearing on the topic before us (namely, the mind-body problem) is that it enables us to make a general observation about the subjective character of experience. Whatever may be the status of facts about what it is like to be a human being, or a bat, or a Martian, these appear to be facts that embody a particular point of view.

I am not adverting here to the alleged privacy of experience to its possessor. The point of view in question is not one accessible only to a single individual. Rather it is a *type*. It is often possible to take up a point of view other than one's own, so the comprehension of such facts is not limited to one's own case. There is a sense in which phenomenological facts are perfectly objective: One person can know or say of another what the quality of the other's experience is. They are subjective, however, in the sense that even this objective ascription of experience is possible only for someone sufficiently similar to the object of ascription to be able to adopt his point of view—to understand the ascription in the first person as well as in the third, so to speak. The more different from oneself the other experiencer is, the less success one can expect with this enterprise. In our own case we occupy the relevant point of view, but we will have as much difficulty understanding our own experience properly if we approach it from another point of view as we would if we tried to understand the experience of another species without taking up *its* point of view.

This bears directly on the mind-body problem. For if the facts of experience—facts about what it is like *for* the experiencing organism—are accessible only from one point of view, then it is a mystery how the true character of experiences could be revealed in the physical operation of that organism. The latter is a domain of objective facts par excellence—the kind that can be observed and understood from many points of view and by individuals with differing perceptual systems. There are no comparable imaginative obstacles to the acquisition of knowledge about bat neurophysiology by human scientists, and intelligent bats or Martians might learn more about the human brain than we ever will.

---

[8]Georg Cantor (1845–1918) was a German mathematician. [D. C. ABEL]

This is not by itself an argument against reduction. A Martian scientist with no understanding of visual perception could understand the rainbow, or lightning, or clouds as physical phenomena, though he would never be able to understand the human concepts of rainbow, lightning, or cloud, or the place these things occupy in our phenomenal world. The objective nature of the things picked out by these concepts could be apprehended by him because, although the concepts themselves are connected with a particular point of view and a particular visual phenomenology, the things apprehended from that point of view are not: They are observable from the point of view but external to it; hence they can be comprehended from other points of view also, either by the same organisms or by others. Lightning has an objective character that is not exhausted by its visual appearance, and this can be investigated by a Martian without vision. To be precise, it has a *more* objective character than is revealed in its visual appearance. In speaking of the move from subjective to objective characterization, I wish to remain noncommittal about the existence of an end point, the completely objective intrinsic nature of the thing, which one might or might not be able to reach. It may be more accurate to think of objectivity as a direction in which the understanding can travel. And in understanding a phenomenon like lightning, it is legitimate to go as far away as one can from a strictly human viewpoint.

In the case of experience, on the other hand, the connection with a particular point of view seems much closer. It is difficult to understand what could be meant by the *objective* character of an experience, apart from the particular point of view from which its subject apprehends it. After all, what would be left of what it was like to be a bat if one removed the viewpoint of the bat? But if experience does not have, in addition to its subjective character, an objective nature that can be apprehended from many different points of view, then how can it be supposed that a Martian investigating my brain might be observing physical processes that were my mental processes (as he might observe physical processes that were bolts of lightning), only from a different point of view? How, for that matter, could a human physiologist observe them from another point of view?

We appear to be faced with a general difficulty about psychophysical reduction. In other areas the process of reduction is a move in the direction of greater objectivity, toward a more accurate view of the real nature of things. This is accomplished by reducing our dependence on individual or species-specific points of view toward the objective of investigation. We describe it not in terms of the impressions it makes on our senses, but in terms of its more general effects and of properties detectable by means other than the human senses. The less it depends on a specifically human viewpoint, the more objective is our description. It is possible to follow this path because although the concepts and ideas we employ in thinking about the external world are initially applied from a point of view that involves our perceptual apparatus, they are used by us to refer to things beyond themselves—toward which we *have* the phenomenal point of view. Therefore we can abandon it in favor of another, and still be thinking about the same things.

Experience itself, however, does not seem to fit the pattern. The idea of moving from appearance to reality seems to make no sense here. What is the analogue in this case to pursuing a more objective understanding of the same phenomena by abandoning the initial subjective viewpoint toward them in favor of another that is more objective but concerns the same thing? Certainly it *appears* unlikely that we will get closer to the real nature of human experience by leaving behind the particularity of our human point of view and striving for a description in terms accessible to beings that could not imagine what it was like to be us. If the subjective character of experience is fully comprehensible only from one point of view, then any shift to greater objectivity—that is, less attachment to a specific viewpoint—does not take us nearer to the real nature of the phenomenon; it takes us farther away from it.

In a sense, the seeds of this objection to the reducibility of experience are already detectable in successful cases of reduction; for in discovering sound to be, in reality, a wave phenomenon in air or other media, we leave behind one viewpoint to take up another, and the auditory, human or animal viewpoint that we leave behind remains unreduced. Members of radically different species may both understand the same physical events in objective terms, and this does not require that they understand the phenomenal forms in which those events appear to the senses of members of the other species. Thus it is a condition of their referring to a common reality that their more particular viewpoints are not part of the common reality that they both apprehend. The reduction can succeed only if the species-specific viewpoint is omitted from what is to be reduced.

But while we are right to leave this point of view aside in seeking a fuller understanding of the external world, we cannot ignore it permanently, since it is the essence of the internal world, and not merely a point of view on it. Most of the neobehaviorism[9] of recent philosophical psychology results from the effort to substitute an objective concept of mind for the real thing, in order to have nothing left over which cannot be reduced. If we acknowledge that a physical theory of mind must account for the subjective character of experience, we must admit that no presently available conception gives us a clue how this could be done. The problem is unique. If mental processes are indeed physical processes, then there is something it is like, intrinsically, to undergo certain physical processes. What it is for such a thing to be the case remains a mystery.

[CONCLUSION]

What moral should be drawn from these reflections, and what should be done next? It would be a mistake to conclude that physicalism must be false. Nothing is proved by the inadequacy of physicalist hypotheses that assume a faulty objective analysis of mind. It would be truer to say that physicalism is a position we cannot understand because we do not at present have any conception of how it might be true. Perhaps it will be thought unreasonable to require such a conception as a condition of understanding. After all, it might be said, the meaning of physicalism is clear enough: Mental states are states of the body; mental events are physical events. We do not know *which* physical states and events

---

[9]*neobehaviorism:* the view that statements about the mind should be reformulated entirely in terms of physical, observable behavior. [D. C. Abel]

they are, but that should not prevent us from understanding the hypothesis. What could be clearer than the words "is" and "are"?

But I believe it is precisely this apparent clarity of the word "is" that is deceptive. Usually, when we are told that X is Y we know *how* it is supposed to be true, but that depends on a conceptual or theoretical background and is not conveyed by the "is" alone. We know how both "X" and "Y" refer, and the kinds of things to which they refer, and we have a rough idea how the two referential paths might converge on a single thing, be it an object, a person, a process, an event, or whatever. But when the two terms of the identification are very disparate it may not be so clear how it could be true. We may not have even a rough idea of how the two referential paths could converge, or what kind of things they might converge on, and a theoretical framework may have to be supplied to enable us to understand this. Without the framework, an air of mysticism surrounds the identification.

This explains the magical flavor of popular presentations of fundamental scientific discoveries, given out as propositions to which one must subscribe without really understanding them. For example, people are now told at an early age that all matter is really energy. But despite the fact that they know what "is" means, most of them never form a conception of what makes this claim true, because they lack the theoretical background.

At the present time the status of physicalism is similar to that which the hypothesis that matter is energy would have had if uttered by a pre-Socratic philosopher. We do not have the beginnings of a conception of how it might be true. In order to understand the hypothesis that a mental event is a physical event, we require more than an understanding of the word "is." The idea of how a mental and a physical term might refer to the same thing is lacking, and the usual analogies with theoretical identification in other fields fail to supply it. They fail because if we construe the reference of mental terms to physical events on the usual model, we either get a reappearance of separate subjective events as the effects through which mental reference to physical events is secured, or else we get a false account of how mental terms refer (for example, a causal behaviorist one).

Strangely enough, we may have evidence for the truth of something we cannot really understand. Suppose a caterpillar is locked in a sterile safe by someone unfamiliar with insect metamorphosis, and weeks later the safe is reopened, revealing a butterfly. If the person knows that the safe has been shut the whole time, he has reason to believe that the butterfly is or was once the caterpillar, without having any idea in what sense this might be so. (One possibility is that the caterpillar contained a tiny winged parasite that devoured it and grew into the butterfly.)

It is conceivable that we are in such a position with regard to physicalism. Donald Davidson has argued that if mental events have physical causes and effects, they must have physical descriptions. He holds that we have reason to believe this even though we do not—and in fact *could* not—have a general psychophysical theory.[10] His argument applies to intentional mental events, but I think we also have some reason to believe that sensations are physical

---

[10]Donald Davidson, "Mental Events," in *Experience and Theory,* ed. Lawrence Foster and J. W. Swanson (Amherst: University of Massachusetts Press, 1970), pp. 79–101. [T. NAGEL]

processes, without being in a position to understand how. Davidson's position is that certain physical events have irreducibly mental properties, and perhaps some view describable in this way is correct. But nothing of which we can now form a conception corresponds to it; nor have we any idea what a theory would be like that enabled us to conceive of it.

Very little work has been done on the basic question (from which mention of the brain can be entirely omitted) whether any sense can be made of experiences having an objective character at all. Does it make sense, in other words, to ask what my experiences are *really* like, as opposed to how they appear to me? We cannot genuinely understand the hypothesis that their nature is captured in a physical description unless we understand the more fundamental idea that they *have* an objective nature (or that objective processes can have a subjective nature).

I should like to close with a speculative proposal. It may be possible to approach the gap between subjective and objective from another direction. Setting aside temporarily the relation between the mind and the brain, we can pursue a more objective understanding of the mental in its own right. At present we are completely unequipped to think about the subjective character of experience without relying on the imagination—without taking up the point of view of the experiential subject. This should be regarded as a challenge to form new concepts and devise a new method—an objective phenomenology not dependent on empathy or the imagination. Though presumably it would not capture everything, its goal would be to describe, at least in part, the subjective character of experiences in a form comprehensible to beings incapable of having those experiences.

We would have to develop such a phenomenology to describe the sonar experiences of bats; but it would also be possible to begin with humans. One might try, for example, to develop concepts that could be used to explain to a person blind from birth what it was like to see. One would reach a blank wall eventually, but it should be possible to devise a method of expressing in objective terms much more than we can at present, and with much greater precision. The loose intermodal analogies—for example, "Red is like the sound of a trumpet"—that crop up in discussions of this subject are of little use. That should be clear to anyone who has both heard a trumpet and seen red. But structural features of perception might be more accessible to objective description, even though something would be left out. And concepts alternative to those we learn in the first person may enable us to arrive at a kind of understanding even of our own experience that is denied us by the very ease of description and lack of distance that subjective concepts afford.

Apart from its own interest, a phenomenology that is in this sense objective may permit questions about the physical basis of experience to assume a more intelligible form. Aspects of subjective experience that admitted this kind of objective description might be better candidates for objective explanations of a more familiar sort. But whether or not this guess is correct, it seems unlikely that any physical theory of mind can be contemplated until more thought has been given to the general problem of subjective and objective. Otherwise we cannot even pose the mind-body problem without sidestepping it.

B. Personal Identity

READING 22   ## Of Identity and Diversity

John Locke

A biography of John Locke appears on p. 155.

Our selection is from "Of Identity and Diversity," which first appeared as Chapter XXVII of Book II of the second edition of *An Essay Concerning Human Understanding* (1694). Given the obvious fact that people are constantly changing, Locke asks what makes someone the same individual from one moment to the next. He distinguishes two kinds of identity: being the same *human being* ("man" in his terminology) and being the same *person*. "Human being" refers to the physical organization of a human animal, not to the soul or mind. To support this claim, Locke points out that someone with a human body who is irrational is still considered a human being, but a creature without a human body would not be considered a human being even if it had rationality (a rational parrot, for example, would still be a parrot). The criterion for the identity of a human being is the same as that for all other animals: "a participation of the same continued life, by constantly fleeting particles of matter, in succession vitally united to the same organized body." A human being, then, is the same human being if the same life animates his or her constantly changing body.

By the term "person," Locke means "a thinking intelligent being." Locke argues that since consciousness is what makes a thinking being a "self" and distinguishes it from all other "selves," consciousness constitutes personal identity. Having the same consciousness means being the same person, and personal identity extends as far back as one's consciousness (memory) of past experiences. Locke points out, however, that being the same person is not equivalent to being the same *substance*, since the same consciousness (the criterion for personal identity) could exist in a succession of different substances.

6.[1] . . . The identity of the same *man* consists . . . in nothing but a participation of the same continued life, by constantly fleeting particles of matter, in succession vitally united to the same organized body. He that shall place the identity of man in anything else but, like that of other animals, in one fitly organized body taken in any one instant and from thence continued, under one organization of life, in several successively fleeting particles of matter united to it, will find it hard to make an embryo, one of years, mad and sober, the same man by any supposition that will not make it possible for Seth, Ismael, Socrates, Pilate, St. Austin, and Caesar Borgia to be the same man. For if the identity of soul alone makes the same man, and there be nothing in the nature of matter why the same individual spirit may not be united to different bodies, it will be possible

---

[1]The section numbers vary from edition to edition. The numbering here follows the edition of Peter H. Nidditch (New York: Oxford University Press, 1975; 2nd ed., 1979). [D. C. ABEL]

that those men, living in distant ages and of different tempers, may have been the same man—which way of speaking must be from a very strange use of the word *man*, applied to an idea out of which body and shape are excluded. And that way of speaking would agree yet worse with the notions of those philosophers who allow of transmigration[2] and are of opinion that the souls of men may, for their miscarriages,[3] be detruded[4] into the bodies of beasts as fit habitations, with organs suited to the satisfaction of their brutal inclinations. But yet I think nobody, could he be sure that the soul of Heliogabalus were in one of his hogs, would yet say that hog were a man or Heliogabalus. . . .

8. An animal is a living organized body, and consequently the same animal . . . is the same continued life communicated to different particles of matter, as they happen successively to be united to that organized living body. And whatever is talked of other definitions, ingenious[5] observation puts it past doubt that the idea in our minds, of which the sound "man" in our mouths is the sign, is nothing else but of an animal of such a certain form. Since I think I may be confident that whoever should see a creature of his own shape or make, though it had no more reason all its life than a cat or a parrot, would call him still a man; or whoever should hear a cat or a parrot discourse, reason, and philosophize, would call or think it nothing but a cat or a parrot; and say [that] the one was a dull irrational man, and the other a very intelligent rational parrot. . . .

9. This being premised, to find wherein *personal identity* consists, we must consider what *person* stands for—which, I think, is a thinking intelligent being that has reason and reflection and can consider itself as itself the same thinking thing in different times and places; which it does only by that consciousness which is inseparable from thinking and, as it seems to me, essential to it; it being impossible for anyone to perceive without perceiving that he does perceive. When we see, hear, smell, taste, feel, meditate, or will anything, we know that we do so. Thus it is always as to our present sensations and perceptions; and by this everyone is to himself that which he calls *self*—it not being considered, in this case, whether the same self be continued in the same or divers[6] substances. For, since consciousness always accompanies thinking, and it is that which makes everyone to be what he calls self and thereby distinguishes himself from all other thinking things, in this alone consists personal identity—that is, the sameness of a rational being. And as far as this consciousness can be extended backwards to any past action or thought, so far reaches the identity of that person. It is the same self now it was then, and it is by the same self with this present one that now reflects on it, that that action was done.

10. But it is further inquired whether it be the same identical *substance*. This few would think they had reason to doubt of, if these perceptions, with their consciousness, always remained present in the mind, whereby the same thinking

---

[2]*transmigration:* the passage of the soul, at death, from one body to another. [D. C. ABEL]
[3]*miscarriages:* misdeeds. [D. C. ABEL]
[4]*detruded:* forced down. [D. C. ABEL]
[5]*ingenious:* displaying intelligence. [D. C. ABEL]
[6]*divers:* various. [D. C. ABEL]

thing would be always consciously present and, as would be thought, evidently the same to itself. But that which seems to make the difficulty is this, that this consciousness being interrupted always by forgetfulness, there being no moment of our lives wherein we have the whole train of all our past actions before our eyes in one view, but even the best memories losing the sight of one part whilst they are viewing another; and we sometimes (and that the greatest part of our lives) not reflecting on our past selves, being intent on our present thoughts, and in sound sleep having no thoughts at all, or at least none with that consciousness which remarks our waking thoughts—I say, in all these cases, our consciousness being interrupted, and we losing the sight of our past selves, doubts are raised whether we are the same thinking thing, that is, the same *substance* or no. Which, however reasonable or unreasonable, concerns not *personal* identity at all—[this] question being what makes the same person, and not whether it be the same identical substance which always thinks in the same person, which in this case matters not at all. Different substances by the same consciousness (where they do partake in it) [are] united into one person, as well as different bodies by the same life are united into one animal, whose identity is preserved in that change of substances by the unity of one continued life. For, it being the same consciousness that makes a man be himself to himself, personal identity depends on that only— whether it be annexed solely to one individual substance or can be continued in a succession of several substances. For as far as any intelligent being can repeat the idea of any past action with the same consciousness it had of it at first, and with the same consciousness it has of any present action; so far it is the same personal self. For it is by the consciousness it has of its present thoughts and actions that it is self to itself now, and so will be the same self as far as the same consciousness can extend to actions past or to come, and would be, by distance of time or change of substance, no more two persons than a man be two men by wearing other clothes today than he did yesterday, with a long or a short sleep between—the same consciousness uniting those distant actions into the same person, whatever substances contributed to their production.

11. That this is so, we have some kind of evidence in our very bodies, all whose particles, whilst vitally united to this same thinking conscious self, so that we feel when they are touched and are affected by, and conscious of, good or harm that happens to them, as a part of ourselves—that is, our thinking conscious self. Thus, the limbs of his body are to everyone a part of himself; he sympathizes and is concerned for them. Cut off a hand and thereby separate it from that consciousness he had of its heat, cold, and other affections, and it is then no longer a part of that which is himself, any more than the remotest part of matter. Thus we see the substance whereof personal self consisted at one time may be varied at another, without the change of personal identity—there being no question about the same person, though the limbs which but now were a part of it, be cut off. . . .

15. And thus may we be able, without any difficulty, to conceive the same person at the resurrection [of the dead], though in a body not exactly in make or parts the same which he had here—the same consciousness going along with the soul that inhabits it. But yet the soul alone, in the change of bodies, would scarce to anyone but to him that makes the soul the man, be enough to make the

same man. For should the soul of a prince, carrying with it the consciousness of the prince's past life, enter and inform the body of a cobbler, as soon as deserted by his own soul, everyone sees he would be the same *person* with the prince, accountable only for the prince's actions. But who would say it was the same *man?* The body too goes to the making the man, and would, I guess, to everybody determine the man in this case, wherein the soul, with all its princely thoughts about it, would not make another man. But he would be the same cobbler to everyone besides himself. I know that, in the ordinary way of speaking, the *same person* and the *same man* stand for one and the same thing. And indeed everyone will always have a liberty to speak as he pleases, and to apply what articulate sounds to what ideas he thinks fit, and change them as often as he pleases. But yet, when we will inquire what makes the same spirit, man, or person, we must fix the ideas of spirit, man, or person in our minds; and having resolved with ourselves what we mean by them, it will not be hard to determine, in either of them, or the like, when it is the same, and when not.

16. But though the same immaterial substance or soul does not alone, wherever it be, and in whatsoever state, make the same *man;* yet it is plain [that] consciousness, as far as ever it can be extended (should it be to ages past) unites existences and actions very remote in time into the same *person*, as well as it does the existences and actions of the immediately preceding moment: So that whatever has the consciousness of present and past actions is the same person to whom they both belong. Had I the same consciousness that I saw the ark and Noah's flood, as that I saw an overflowing of the [River] Thames last winter, or as that I write now, I could no more doubt that I who write this now, that saw the Thames overflowed last winter, and that viewed the flood at the general deluge, was the same self (place that self in what substance you please) than that I who write this am the same myself now whilst I write (whether I consist of all the same substance, material or immaterial, or no) that I was yesterday. For as to this point of being the same self, it matters not whether this present self be made up of the same or other substances—I being as much concerned and as justly accountable for any action that was done a thousand years since, appropriated to me now by this self-consciousness, as I am for what I did the last moment.

17. Self is that conscious thinking thing (whatever substance made up of, whether spiritual or material, simple or compounded, it matters not) which is sensible[7] or conscious of pleasure and pain, capable of happiness or misery, and so is concerned for itself as far as that consciousness extends. Thus everyone finds that, whilst comprehended under that consciousness, the little finger is as much a part of himself as what is most so. Upon separation of this little finger, should this consciousness go along with the little finger and leave the rest of the body, it is evident the little finger would be the person, the same person; and self then would have nothing to do with the rest of the body. As in this case it is the consciousness that goes along with the substance, when one part is separate from another, which makes the same person and constitutes this inseparable self; so it is in reference to substances remote in time. That with which the consciousness of this present thinking thing can join itself makes the same

---

[7]*sensible:* aware. [D. C. ABEL]

person, and is one self with it, and with nothing else; and so attributes to itself, and owns all the actions of that thing as its own, as far as that consciousness reaches, and no further—as everyone who reflects will perceive.

18. In this personal identity is founded all the right and justice of reward and punishment—happiness and misery being that for which everyone is concerned for himself, and not mattering what becomes of any substance not joined to or affected with that consciousness. For, as it is evident in the instance I gave but now, if the consciousness went along with the little finger when it was cut off, that would be the same self which was concerned for the whole body yesterday, as making part of itself, whose actions then it cannot but admit as its own now. Though, if the same body should still live, and immediately from the separation of the little finger have its own peculiar consciousness, whereof the little finger knew nothing, it would not at all be concerned for it, as a part of itself, or could own any of its actions or have any of them imputed to him.

19. This may show us wherein personal identity consists: not in the identity of substance, but, as I have said, in the identity of consciousness, wherein if Socrates and the present mayor of Queinborough agree, they are the same person. If the same Socrates waking and sleeping do not partake of the same consciousness, Socrates waking and sleeping is not the same person. And to punish Socrates waking for what sleeping Socrates thought and waking Socrates was never conscious of, would be no more of right than to punish one twin for what his brother twin did, whereof he knew nothing, because their outsides were so like, that they could not be distinguished (for such twins have been seen).

20. But yet possibly it will still be objected: "Suppose I wholly lose the memory of some parts of my life, beyond a possibility of retrieving them, so that perhaps I shall never be conscious of them again. Yet am I not the same person that did those actions, had those thoughts that I once was conscious of, though I have now forgot them?" To which I answer that we must here take notice what the word "I" is applied to—which, in this case, is the *man* only. And the same *man* being presumed to be the same *person*, "I" is easily here supposed to stand also for the same person. But if it be possible for the same man to have distinct incommunicable consciousness at different times, it is past doubt the same man would at different times make different persons. Which, we see, is the sense of mankind in the solemnest declaration of their opinions, human laws not punishing the mad man for the sober man's actions, nor the sober man for what the mad man did; thereby making them two persons. Which is somewhat[8] explained by our way of speaking in English when we say such a one is "not himself," or is "beside himself"—in which phrases it is insinuated, as if those who now (or at least first) used them, thought that self was changed: The selfsame person was no longer in that man. . . .

23. Nothing but consciousness can unite remote existences into the same person. The identity of substance will not do it, for whatever substance there is, however framed, without consciousness there is no person. . . .

Could we suppose two distinct incommunicable consciousnesses acting[9] the same body, the one constantly by day, the other by night; and, on the other

---

[8]*somewhat:* something. [D. C. ABEL]
[9]*acting:* actuating, moving to action. [D. C. ABEL]

side, the same consciousness, acting by intervals, two distinct bodies; [then] I ask, in the first case, whether the day- and the night-man would not be two as distinct persons as Socrates and Plato; and whether, in the second case, there would not be one person in two distinct bodies, as much as one man is the same in two distinct clothings? Nor is it at all material[10] to say that this same and this distinct consciousness, in the cases above mentioned, is owing to the same and distinct immaterial substances, bringing it with them to those bodies—which, whether true or no, alters not the case, since it is evident the personal identity would equally be determined by the consciousness, whether that consciousness were annexed to some individual immaterial substance or no. For, granting that the thinking substance in man must be necessarily supposed immaterial, it is evident that immaterial thinking thing may sometimes part with its past consciousness and be restored to it again, as appears in the forgetfulness men often have of their past actions; and the mind many times recovers the memory of a past consciousness which it had lost for twenty years together. Make these intervals of memory and forgetfulness to take their turns regularly by day and night, and you have two persons with the same immaterial spirit, as much as in the former instance two persons with the same body. So that self is not determined by identity or diversity of substance, which it cannot be sure of, but only by identity of consciousness.

---

[10]*material:* pertinent. [D. C. ABEL]

Personal Identity and the Past

Marya Schechtman

Marya Schechtman was born in Chicago in 1960. She did her undergraduate studies at the University of Chicago, receiving her bachelor's degree in philosophy in 1982. She then enrolled in the graduate program in philosophy at Harvard University. Upon completing her doctorate in 1988 with a prize-winning dissertation, she accepted an appointment as assistant professor of philosophy at the University of Illinois at Chicago (UIC). In 1995 Schechtman was promoted to associate professor and began a joint appointment with UIC's Laboratory for Integrative Neuroscience. Since 2004 she has served as associate dean of the Graduate College of UIC. She has held visiting positions at the University of Chicago (1994) and New York University (1996).

Schechtman has published articles on the philosophy of mind in journals such as *The Journal of Philosophy, American Philosophical Quarterly,* and *Philosophical Psychology* and *Social Philosophy and Policy.* She has contributed essays to several anthologies on topics in the philosophy of mind and is the author of *The Constitution of Selves* (1996).

Our reading is from Schechtman's 2005 article "Personal Identity and the Past," in which she proposes a development of the theory of personal identity set forth by English philosopher John Locke in the 17th century. Locke maintains that what makes someone the same person over time is not some physical substance (body) or nonphysical substance (soul), but the continuity of consciousness: "Personal identity consists . . . in the identity of consciousness." Locke seems to be saying that one's *conscious memory* of past actions and experiences is what makes these actions and experiences one's own. This theory leads to the conclusion that past actions and experiences that persons do not consciously remember do not belong to them. Because this conclusion is highly implausible, Locke's theory needs to be modified.

Schechtman agrees with Locke the personal identity is not to be found in the continuity of substance. Some theorists, she explains, try to fix Locke's account of personal identity by stating that psychological continuity requires that we have access to a *sufficient number* of memories to connect us to a past time. Schechtman contends that this additional requirement still fails to give adequate explanation of personhood because it says nothing about the *intelligibility* of these memories. To remedy the problem, Schechtman proposes a "self-understanding view" of personhood. In this view, personal identity requires not only that we *remember* past events, but *understand* how they form part of a meaningful trajectory from our past, to our present, and into the future. Such an understanding "gives us our sense of continuation and coherence as a self, and so provides the kind of self-conception and relation to a particular past that constitutes personal identity." And because personal identity is affected not only by conscious memories (as Locke recognized), but by *unconscious* ones (which Locke failed to recognize), Schechtman's self-understanding theory of personal identity includes both conscious and unconscious memories.

[INTRODUCTION]

In the second edition of the *Essay Concerning Human Understanding*, John Locke takes up the question of what makes someone the same person throughout her entire life.[1] His response to this question has served as the starting point for many of the views of personal identity represented in the philosophical literature today. Locke's important contribution is to argue that the continuation of a person is independent of the continuation of any substance—either physical (the body) or nonphysical (the soul). I am the same person as someone who existed in the past, says Locke, if and only if I can extend my current consciousness back to that person's actions. This assertion is usually interpreted as a "memory theory" of personal identity—the view that whatever actions and experiences a person can remember are, for that reason, her actions and experiences.

In some respects, Locke's view is extremely compelling, but at the same time a simple memory theory is totally implausible. Although Locke's arguments that continuation of substance cannot serve as a viable account of personal identity are powerful, a view that implies that a person can have no experiences that he does not (or cannot easily) remember consciously seems far too strong. Locke might or might not be willing to bite the bullet and accept that no forgotten experiences can be ours, but most philosophers are not. . . .

I propose a . . . development of Locke's insight that emphasizes the importance of self-understanding. This view captures most of what Locke says about why consciousness is so central to personhood and personal identity without being committed to the implausible view that only experiences of which we are conscious can be ours. I begin with a brief review of Locke's view. . . .

LOCKE'S ARGUMENT

Locke's central contribution to work on personal identity is his insistence that identity must be defined in terms of sameness of consciousness rather than sameness of substance. It is not the continuation of either an immaterial soul or a body that constitutes the continuation of the person, he says, but rather the continued flow of consciousness. There are two basic elements of his argument for this claim. To make the claim intuitively plausible, he uses a number of hypothetical cases in which continuation of consciousness is separated from continuation of substance, showing that our judgment in such cases would be that the person goes with the consciousness. He also provides a more theoretical discussion about what it is to be a person, arguing that once we understand this clearly we see that identity must be defined in terms of consciousness rather than substance. It is helpful to review briefly each aspect of his discussion.

---

[1]John Locke, *An Essay Concerning Human Understanding,* "Of Identity and Diversity," which first appeared as Book II, Chapter 27, of the 2nd edition (1694). All quotations from this chapter in this article are taken from the edition of Peter H. Nidditch (2nd ed.; New York: Oxford University Press, 1979), pp. 328–348. Locke (1632–1704) was an English philosopher. [D. C. ABEL]

Locke gets us to see the force of his view through the use of a series of imagined cases. He asks us to imagine, for instance, the mental life of a prince "entering and informing" the body of a cobbler, and argues that everyone would see that the resulting person is the same person as the prince rather than the cobbler. He suggests that we imagine someone who has the same soul as Nestor or Thersites at the siege of Troy, but without consciousness of any of their actions, and tells us that it is obvious that this person is no more the same person as Nestor or Thersites than he would be if his body happened to share some of the same matter that had once composed theirs. He asks us also to imagine a man who has two distinct consciousnesses sharing his body—one by day and one by night—with no communication between them, and says that it is clear that there are two distinct persons sharing one body in such a case.

This view of personal continuation is not, of course, uncontroversial. It is, however, widely accepted, and whether or not this is the final word on what it is to be a person, it undoubtedly captures one important strand of our thought about ourselves. The same basic intuition is expressed, for instance, by William James in *The Principles of Psychology* when he says:

> The soul, however, when closely scrutinized, guarantees no immortality of a sort *we care for*. The enjoyment of the atom-like simplicity of their substance *in saecula saeculorum*[2] would not to most people seem a consummation devoutly to be wished. The substance must give rise to a stream of consciousness continuous with the present stream, in order to arouse our hope, but of this the mere persistence of the substance per se[3] offers no guarantee.[4]

This idea can also be seen when we recognize that there is a real sense in which we would view total, irreversible amnesia as a form of death. Faced with the prospect of such amnesia we might well distribute remembrances, write letters to loved ones, and in other ways act as if we were anticipating death.

The Lockean insight is also seen in the impulse to view multiple personality disorder[5] as a circumstance in which more than one person share a body. Of course, describing this disorder in this way is by no means uncontroversial. . . . It is, I think, at least uncontroversial to claim that in multiple personality disorder we are not presented unproblematically with a single person. The fact that these cases seem to present, at least sometimes, genuinely independent streams of consciousness that may have no awareness of one another, seems reason enough to say that there is some very important sense in which distinct persons co-occupy a body just as Locke took his revolving day and night consciousness to do.

This, then, is the basic intuition behind Locke's view, and it is in many respects a familiar and compelling one. Locke further supports his account of identity by giving a more general definition of the concept of the person revealed in these cases. He tells us that *person* stands for "a thinking intelligent

---

[2]*in saecula saeclorum:* (Latin, "for ages of ages") forever and ever. [D. C. ABEL]
[3]*per se:* (Latin) in itself. [D. C. ABEL]
[4]William James, *The Principles of Psychology* (New York: Dover Publications, 1950), 1:348. [M. SCHECHTMAN] James (1842–1910) was an American philosopher and psychologist. [D. C. ABEL]
[5]*multiple personality disorder:* also called *dissociative identity disorder.* [D. C. ABEL]

being that has reason and reflection and can consider itself as itself the same thinking thing in different times and places." To be a person is to have self-consciousness, viewing oneself as a persisting subject. This means that a person becomes the same person who has past experiences or undertook past actions when her consciousness includes them. "As far as any intelligent being can repeat the idea of any past action with the same consciousness it had of it at first, and with the same consciousness it has of any present action;" says Locke, "so far it is the same personal self." His view in a nutshell, then, is that "personal identity consists, not in the identity of substance, but, as I have said, in the identity of consciousness."

Locke expands on this concept of person by telling us that *person* is a "forensic term appropriating actions and their merit; and so belongs only to intelligent agents capable of a law, and happiness and misery." This characterization sets out two features that Locke takes to be unique to personhood, and that he uses to support his definition of personal identity in terms of sameness of consciousness. First, persons are capable of a special sort of self-interested concern; and second, they are moral agents, capable of taking actions for which they can be held responsible. Both of these capacities, he argues, are linked to consciousness. To care about the unfolding of our lives, we need to have a conscious conception of ourselves as having a future to care about. Moreover, it is through consciousness that we experience pleasure and pain, and so the extent of our concern is the extent of our conscious experience. He puts it this way: "Self is that conscious thinking thing (whatever substance made up of, whether spiritual or material, simple or compounded, it matters not) which is sensible[6] or conscious of pleasure and pain, capable of happiness or misery, and so is concerned for itself as far as that consciousness extends."

He also argues that moral responsibility requires consciousness. To be moral agents, we must be able to plan and to recognize that actions we take now have consequences in the future. Here he taps the intuitions unearthed by the kinds of hypothetical cases described above. He says, for instance, "for suppose a man punished now for what he had done in another life, whereof he could be made to have no consciousness at all—what difference is there between that punishment and being created miserable?" Again the case of multiple personality disorder gives us a real-life example of what Locke has in mind here. Such cases have raised tricky questions in legal contexts about how to assign culpability when the consciousness of the personality who allegedly committed a crime is unavailable to other personalities in the same body.

Locke thus taps into a widely held concept of the person according to which a person is a self-conscious subject. On this picture, personal identity or continuation through time depends on the continuation of consciousness. In particular, if one is conscious of oneself as the same self who existed at some past time, this consciousness actually makes one the same person as that past self. The failure of such self-consciousness, on the other hand, signals the end of the person. Attempting to capture this conception of the person, Locke thus tells us that we become the same person as some past person by extending our consciousness

---

[6]*sensible:* aware. [D. C. ABEL]

back to her experiences because in doing so we become aware not only of those experiences themselves, but of the fact that we are the ones who had them. This awareness gives us consciousness of ourselves as persisting beings, and so constitutes the fact of our identity with the past person—a fact that would not hold were we not conscious of her experiences.

Although there is undoubtedly something very compelling about Locke's view of personal identity, it is problematic as it stands. It is not entirely obvious just what the details of the view are, but it is generally read as a "memory theory"—the view that whatever experiences a person remembers are, for that reason, her experiences. . . .

A simple memory theory, however, is not plausible on its own. It is at the same time too weak and too strong. This theory is *too weak* because it seems that it takes more than simply remembering an experience to make me the person who did it. As many objectors have pointed out, memory is good evidence that a past experience is ours, but on its own it does not seem quite enough to make it ours. To use a variation on a science fiction case that appears often in the literature, the fact that a neurosurgeon may develop a technique whereby she could implant in my brain the recollection of an experience had by her grandmother does not now make me the person who had that experience (namely, her grandmother). The memory theory is *too strong* because even when we are thinking of ourselves as conscious subjects rather than substances, it seems obvious that we can and do forget experiences that are nonetheless ours. If the mind of the prince were, for example, to enter the body of the cobbler but along the way lose the memory of what the prince ate for breakfast or repress the memory of a rather unfortunate interaction with the vice chancellor, we would not want to deny that these were, nonetheless, experiences of the prince and so of the person inhabiting the cobbler's body. To provide a plausible account of identity, then, the simple memory theory needs some development. . . .

AN ALTERNATIVE ACCOUNT

The task of developing the Lockean insight is . . . twofold. First, it is necessary to give an account of the kind of connection to the past that a person must have to develop the type of self-conception that constitutes personal identity. Second, it is necessary to give an account of the attribution of particular actions and experiences that allows for the attribution of unconscious elements as well as conscious ones. It is easiest to begin with the first task.

Locke tells us that we make ourselves selves, and so determine our identity, by forming a self-conscious conception of ourselves as persisting subjects. The exact nature of this self-conception is never really spelled out, however. In the hands of psychological continuity theorists, it becomes the requirement that we have a sufficient number of memories of past experiences to connect us to a past time. Undoubtedly, this is a very important part of how we come to have our self-conceptions, but as a full account, it is rather thin: All that is required to have the appropriate sort of self-conception—the kind that determines personal identity and continuation into the future—is to have knowledge of what some collection of experiences is like from the inside. It is enough, on this view, just to have access to a certain number of memories. There is no further requirement on how these memories are to cohere or to be associated with present states.

The alternative development of the Lockean view I suggest adds to the recognition of the importance of memory and brute self-consciousness a recognition of the importance of being intelligible to ourselves. To have the kind of self-conception that constitutes personal identity on the view I am urging (call it the "self-understanding view"), one must not just know about some collection of past experiences and think of them as hers; she must see her life as unfolding according to an intelligible trajectory, where present states follow meaningfully from past ones, and the future is anticipated to bear certain predictable relations to the present. This does not mean that a person's life course is entirely under her control, only that she can see connections between how things were, how they are, and how they are likely to be. Having a self-conception does not just amount to knowing that one has a past and will have a future, but also involves seeing these as inherently interconnected and rich with implications for one another.

This understanding changes the fundamental nature of the self-awareness that constitutes us as persons. It is no longer a passive knowing that we have had experiences, but a more active attempt to make sense of those experiences and understand where they are leading us. Fully understood, Locke's fundamental insight is that as self-conscious entities we are interested in the character of our experience, and also in what we should do and what kind of person we should be. What this means, however, is that we are constantly self-monitoring, keeping track of how we are feeling, what we are doing, and what we are like. This self-monitoring is mostly implicit. There are many occasions where we introspect and consciously consider the trajectory of our lives and how its episodes fit together, but usually we are caught up in the activity of living, and this work goes on in the background. On the self-understanding view, it is this self-monitoring that gives us our sense of continuation and coherence as a self, and so provides the kind of self-conception and relation to a particular past that constitutes personal identity.

The basic picture of this self-monitoring is nicely developed by Raymond Martin in his book *Self-Concern*.[7] There Martin develops the notion of a "perceiver self." We experience the world, Martin says, as if one part of the self were split off from the flux of events as an observer, watching and recording the stream of our experience. Martin argues that the perceiver-self is an illusion, and of course in some sense it must be; there is no homuncular[8] entity within people who is the observer of their experience. Nevertheless, as Martin indicates, the sense that there is such a self is a robust and pervasive element of experience, and a central feature of human psychological organization. . . .

The "perceiver-self" then should be thought of as a stable observer who views and records the passing flux of experience and recognizes it as part of a

---

[7]Raymond Martin, *Self-Concern: An Experiential Approach to What Matters in Survival* (New York: Cambridge University Press, 1998). [M. Schechtman]

[8]*homuncular:* relating to a *homunculus,* a miniature human being postulated to exist inside human beings, as a way to explain psychological processes. [D . C. Abel]

single life; it need not be an actually persisting agent, or even a truly continuous psychological process, but it is a process that gives rise to the background sense of a stable self of the sort whose existence seems crucial to personal identity on the view we have been exploring. My suggestion is that it is this sense of a stable perceiver-self, rather than a simple knowledge that one has had experiences in the past, that constitutes the continuation of consciousness that constitutes personal identity over time.

One way to make this rather abstract conception more concrete is to connect this self-monitoring to certain capacities. One quite simple implication of having such a self-conception is that a person can generally answer questions such as "Why do I feel this way?" or "Why am I doing this?," should they arise. If she cannot answer them, she should be motivated to look for an answer. Answers to questions of this sort usually involve a number of factors. If one cannot easily make sense of the way one is feeling or choosing to act, however, it is natural to look for external explanations, considering the environment carefully to see if there is some hitherto undetected factor that is exerting an influence. In this way one might notice that it is the gathering clouds outside that are making one gloomy or anxious, even if one had not noticed them before; or that one's mother is constantly sending off subtle signals of disapproval and that this can explain one's guilt.

Sometimes, however, scrutiny of our environment and of our conscious internal states still leaves us baffled about why we feel or act as we do. This unintelligibility threatens our integrity as self-conscious subjects—in the subject, as in the world more generally, there should be no events that are simply uncaused. This does not mean that we must fully understand all of our feelings or motives, but only that we should not be at a loss as to where to start in such self-understanding. This really would undermine the difference between punishment and being created miserable. If we are at a loss, and no overlooked external factors can be found, it is natural to look for occult internal causes—nonconscious memories or impulses. Descartes offers an early example of this strategy with respect to his perceptions in the course of his *Meditations on First Philosophy*.[9] He recognizes that he had previously taken his perceptual images to come from external objects because he was not aware of bringing them about himself. In the context of the meditations, however, he is supposing that there are no external objects, and so wonders if the images might come instead from some unknown part of himself. Although he ultimately decides that they come from an external world via God, his reflections demonstrate nicely the kind of dynamic I have in mind—first, the basic idea that it is our responsibility not only to know the contents of our consciousness but to understand their origins; and second, the willingness to consider that we could, unknowingly, be the cause of our conscious experience. In a context more directly related to the current discussion, Freud's[10] "discovery" of the unconscious follows just this logic, and it is, of course, this insight that is the inspiration of the self-understanding view with its emphasis on the importance of being intelligible to ourselves.

---

[9]René Descartes, *Meditations on First Philosophy,* Sixth Meditation (an excerpt on pp. 207–208 of this book). Descartes (1596–1650) was a French philosopher and mathematician; for a biography, see p. 144. [D. C. ABEL]

[10]Sigmund Freud (1856–1939) was an Austrian neurologist who founded psychoanalysis. [D. C. ABEL]

In postulating inner sources for our experiences and actions we recognize that there are parts of ourselves that we are not conscious of, but that are yet part of our psychological lives in an importantly intimate way. These experiences impact the nature of our conscious experience, and hence should be part of the purview of our self-interested concern. They also influence what we do and lead to experiences of guilt, shame, or pride, and so are connected to our moral agency. To have an identity-constituting self-conception, then, a person must demand (at least implicitly) a kind of coherence and intelligibility to the course of her life. The past should not only be remembered; it should help to explain the present, which in turn should help predict the future. To achieve this intelligibility, we often need to allow for the impact of psychological features and experiences of which we are not directly conscious. The suggestion is thus that the attribution of individual states should be on this basis. Those memories or desires or motivations whose existence, as part of the psychological economy, must be postulated to make sense of a person's experience or the course of her life will be considered her experiences. In this way, we can make room for the attributions of experiences that are nonconscious without violating the fundamental Lockean insight. These experiences still affect us along the dimension of pleasure and pain, and are still connected to our capacities for moral agency. They are part of what determines how our lives will unfold, and what our experience will be like.

The proposed alternative to the psychological continuity theory is thus a view that develops Locke's idea that to be a person is to understand oneself as a persisting being in terms of the demands we make that our lives be intelligible. To be a person on this view is implicitly to keep track of the unfolding of one's life. The particular type of self-concern that Locke takes to be definitive of personhood, as well as the capacity for moral agency, depends on our not just knowing ourselves to persist, but actively seeking to understand how our lives come to be pleasant or unpleasant, learning lessons from the past and applying them to the future. The stream of consciousness that we count as personal continuation involves understanding how the connections between past, present, and future work for us—not just seeing the present as connected to the past, but as flowing from it. This sometimes depends on the recognition of psychological states that play a role in determining our conscious experience, although they are not themselves conscious. It is important to understand that for such states to be attributed to a person, she need not consciously reflect on her history and accept their existence. This is worthy work and may be well worth undertaking for many reasons. For us to say of a person that a nonconscious experience is hers, however, all that is required is that it in fact be necessary to make her psychological life intelligible, whether she recognizes this fact or not.

There is a long-standing idea that memory plays a crucial role in the constitution of personal identity over time. This idea is tied to the Lockean insight about the importance of continuity of consciousness for personal identity. There is also a sense that a person can obviously have experiences she does not remember. This conflict of intuitions seems to be more than simply a conflict over whether persons are to be viewed as psychological subjects or substances. It is also internal to the view of persons as subjects. . . . An alternative account—the self-understanding view—recognizes the original conflict as between intuitions that identify the psychological subject with conscious states and intuitions that see psychological life and the subject itself as involving much that is unconscious as well. We can accommodate this latter understanding of the person and still retain Locke's insight if we simply recognize the fact that unconscious states have a powerful effect on consciousness and self-consciousness. The self-consciousness that Locke is after requires more than memory; it requires a certain level of self-understanding, and this, in turn, leads us to the attribution of psychological elements that help explain how our conscious experience comes to be as it is. The memory theory on its own is obviously too simple to explain what is distinctive about being a person, but the idea that we are what we are—and who we are—because we understand ourselves in a certain way is not. On at least one important conception, to be a person is, as Locke says, to recognize oneself as a person, and here identity is indeed determined by self-understanding. Given that we are ultimately trying to define beings as complex as ourselves, however, it should be no surprise that this self-understanding involves more than a simple act of recollection.

The No-Self Theory: Hume, Buddhism, and Personal Identity

James Giles

James Giles was born in 1958 in Vancouver, Canada. He studied philosophy and psychology at the University of British Columbia, where he completed his bachelor's degree in 1980 and his master's degree in 1983. He then enrolled in the University of Edinburgh, Scotland, receiving his doctorate in 1989. Giles has been tutor at Madingly Hall, Cambridge University, since 1994, and lecturer in philosophy at La Trobe University in Melbourne, Australia, since 2010. He has also held appointments at the University of Guam, the Hawaii College of Kansai Gaidai University, Japan, and three schools in Denmark: Aalborg University, Roskilde University, and the University of Copenhagen.

Giles's publications include *A Study in Phenomenalism* (1994), *No Self to Be Found: The Search for Personal Identity* (1997), *French Existentialism: Consciousness, Ethics, and Relations with Others* (editor, 1999), *Kierkegaard and Freedom* (editor, 2000), *The Nature of Sexual Desire* (2004), and *Kierkegaard and Japanese Thought* (editor, 2008).

Our reading is an excerpt from Giles's 1993 article "The No-Self Theory: Hume, Buddhism, and Personal Identity." (The entire article is the concluding chapter of *No Self to Be Found.*) Giles begins by presenting the no-self theory set forth by Scottish philosopher David Hume (1711–1776) in *A Treatise of Human Nature.* Hume contends that we never experience a self, but only an ever-changing flow of perceptions, and therefore have no legitimate basis for positing the existence of a self, for claiming that persons retain their identity over time. He explains that even though we realize that all objects, including ourselves, are constantly changing, the images we form of an object are so similar from moment to moment that we are misled into thinking there is some unchanging "substance" underlying these changes. In the case of human beings, we call this alleged substance a "self." Hume says that although it is permissible in ordinary discourse to call a changing object (for example, a tree or a person) the same object over time, we should keep in mind that, strictly speaking, there is no identity involved.

Giles proceeds to develop Hume's no-self theory in terms of Buddhist thought. He explains that Buddhism, like Hume, holds that what we call the self is just a bundle of ever-changing elements, and that although it is permissible to speak of a "self" in *conventional* speech (which is established by mutual agreement), the word has no referent in *ultimate* speech.

In the final section of his article, Giles expands the no-self theory by explaining how this doctrine is compatible with the fact that we sometimes have psychological or emotional states that seem to give an instantaneous awareness of self. Giles holds that what we are instantaneously aware of in such states is not some unchanging entity, but a "constructed or condensed self-image"—that is, a composite of related images and meanings referring to how I see and feel about myself at that moment. These moments, Giles argues, are but rare occurrences in consciousness. The constructed self-image, and thus self-awareness, is consequently not part of the fabric of experience. It is rather a secondary phenomenon that experience itself creates.

[INTRODUCTION]

The problem of personal identity is often said to be one of accounting for what it is that gives persons their identity over time. However, once the problem has been construed in these terms, it is plain that too much has already been assumed. For what has been assumed is just that persons do have an identity. To the philosophers who approach the problem with this supposition already accepted, the possibility that there may be no such thing as personal identity is scarcely conceived. As a result, the more fundamental question—whether or not personal identity exists in the first place—remains unasked. Consequently, the no-self theory, that is, the rejection of the notion of personal identity altogether, is never fully considered. . . .

[HUME'S NO-SELF THEORY]

Hume[1] was the first Western philosopher to unmask the confusions attending our idea of personal identity and subsequently to reject the idea as a fiction. It will be worth our while, therefore, to start by conducting a detailed examination of his position. . . .

What, then, is Hume's position? If we attend to the section "Of Personal Identity" in Book I of *A Treatise of Human Nature,* an answer is immediately forthcoming. Hume starts by pointing out that although some philosophers believe we are continuously aware of something we call the self, when we look to our experience there is nothing to substantiate this belief. We are never, says Hume, aware of any constant invariable impression[2] that could answer to the name of self. What we experience, rather, is a continuous flow of perceptions that replace one another in rapid succession. "When I enter most intimately into what I call *myself*," says Hume, "I always stumble on some particular perception or other, of heat or cold, light or shade, love or hatred, pain or pleasure. I never catch *myself* at any time without a perception and never can observe anything but the perception."[3] Within the mind, he continues, these perceptions "successively make their appearance—pass, re-pass, glide away, and mingle in an infinite variety of postures and situations." And there is nothing to the mind but these perceptions. There is consequently never any simplicity within the mind at one time, nor identity at two different times. Nor, says, Hume, do we have any idea of a self; for every real idea must be derived from some one impression; "but self or person is not any one impression, but that to which our several impressions and ideas are supposed to have reference."

---

[1]David Hume (1711–1776) was a Scottish philosopher and historian; for a biography, see p. 46. [D. C. ABEL]

[2]In Hume's philosophy, the mind consists of *perceptions*, of which there two kinds: *impressions*, which are forceful and lively (for example, seeing a tree), and *ideas*, which are less forceful and lively (for example, imagining a tree). An idea is genuine (as Hume explains later in this paragraph) only if it derives from an impression. [D. C. ABEL]

[3]David Hume, *A Treatise of Human Nature*, ed. L. A. Selby-Bigge, 2nd ed., rev. P. H. Nidditch (New York: Oxford University Press, 1978). This and all subsequent quotations from Hume are from the Book I, Part IV, Section VI, "Of Personal Identity," pp. 251–263. [J. GILES]

With this much said against the notion of personal identity, Hume turns to the question of why we have such a proclivity to ascribe identity to our successive perceptions. Prefacing his reply to this question, Hume points out that a distinction must first be made between "personal identity as it regards our thought or imagination, and as it regards our passions or the concern we take in ourselves." His concern here, he says, is with the former. He then starts his answer by distinguishing between the ideas of identity and diversity. In the former case, we have the idea of an object that persists, invariable and uninterrupted, through a particular span of time. It is this that comprises our idea of identity. In the case of diversity we have the "idea of several different objects existing in succession and connected together by a close relation." Now although these two ideas are plainly distinct, it is certain, says Hume, that in our "common way of thinking" we generally confound them. That is, we often claim that an object at one time is identical with an object at another time, when in fact the two are little more than a succession of different objects connected by a close relation. To justify these absurd ascriptions of identity, we either come up with the notion of a substantive self by feigning the continued existence of our perceptions, or we imagine the existence of something mysterious that binds our many perceptions together. Even where we do not do this, we at least have a propensity to do so. We can see, then, says Hume, that because we often assert the existence of such fictions, the problem of personal identity is not merely a verbal dispute.

It is natural to ask, therefore, what it is that induces us mistakenly to attribute identity to something while, being a succession of objects, it is really an instance of diversity. Hume feels that the answer must lie in the workings of the imagination. The reason why we might make such an attribution, says Hume, is that "the passage of thought from the object before the change to the object after it, is so smooth and easy that we scarce perceive the transition and are apt to imagine that it is nothing but a continued survey of the same object." This is especially true when the alteration is either relatively small or when it occurs gradually and insensibly.

From here Hume goes on to consider the various other ways in which we ascribe identity to objects that are variable and interrupted. This lays the ground for his account of personal identity. For the identity of the mind, like that of such changing things as plants, animals, repaired ships, rebuilt churches, and republics, says Hume, is only a fictitious identity. It must therefore be similarly explicable in terms of the workings of the imagination. Hume concludes his account with the important remark that all "nice and subtle" questions concerning personal identity are best considered as grammatical rather than philosophical difficulties. Thus, except where the notion of a fictional entity or principle is involved, all disputes about personal identity are merely verbal disputes and can never possibly be decided. . . .

If we view the section "Of Personal Identity" as a whole, we will see that in the first four paragraphs Hume discusses the actual identity of the self and categorically rejects the notion as untenable. He does, however, feel that we have a natural propensity to ascribe identity to ourselves, and it is to an explanation of this propensity that Hume devotes the rest of his discussion. This division in the text is also attended, for the most part, by a division in the type of language that Hume uses to discuss identity. In the first part, Hume speaks in a categorical way. Thus it is claimed, for example, that "there is no impression constant and invariable," "there is no such idea [of the self]," "I always stumble on some particular perception or other," and, finally, "there is properly no *simplicity* in [the mind] at one time, nor *identity* in different [times]."

However, when we come to the second part of the discussion, the language becomes more psychological than categorical. That is, Hume's concern here is more with how we imagine, suppose, ascribe, or attribute identity rather than with the actual identity of things. And so the second part begins by asking "What then gives us so great a propension[4] to *ascribe* an identity to these successive perceptions and to *suppose* ourselves possessed of an invariable and uninterrupted existence through the whole course of our lives?" This psychological language continues, for the most part, throughout this latter half: The repaired ship "is still *considered* as the same; nor does the difference of the materials *hinder us* from *ascribing* an identity to it"; although plants and animals undergo a total change, "yet *we still attribute* identity to them"; a man who hears an intermittent noise "*says* it is still the same noise"; and because an earlier church is demolished before its successor appears we do not think of them as being different "and for that reason are *less scrupulous* in *calling* them the same." Likewise, when Hume says we can extend our identity beyond our memories, his discussion makes it plain that he is only talking about "the most *established notions* of personal identity"—that is, what is commonly believed to be true about personal identity, and not about personal identity itself.

This use of psychological language to discuss the supposed identity of interrupted and variable objects should keep us alert to the fact that Hume is here discussing only the origin of our belief in such identity, and not the actual identity of what is really an instance of diversity. Once we see this we should not be worried by Hume's occasional use of categorical statements in what is overtly a discussion of psychology. Thus, when, in the second part of the text, Hume states that a seedling that becomes a tree "is still the same oak," all that is before this makes it plain that he can only mean that it is still *called* the same oak, or it is still *supposed* to be the same oak, or some such thing, not that it is actually still the same oak. Likewise, when he says that the infant becomes a man "without any change in his identity," all that he can mean is "without *our attributing* any change to his identity." . . .

Hume even says that a rebuilt church that we only imagine to be the same as an earlier one, can still be called the same as its predecessor "without breach of the propriety of language." He does not, unfortunately, elaborate on this. However, at the end of the section on personal identity something is said that suggests how it might be permissible to call two things the same that in fact are only imagined to be the same. Here Hume states that all disputes about the identity of successive objects "are merely verbal, except so far as the relation of parts gives rise to some fiction or imaginary principle of union." Thus if two persons are arguing about whether or not an earlier church is the same as its

---

[4]*propension:* tendency, inclination. [D. C. ABEL]

rebuilt successor, and neither of them is asserting the existence of a fictional entity or principle of union that somehow unites the two churches, then their dispute will be merely about how the word "same" is to be used in these circumstances. That is, they will not be disputing an actual identity but only the linguistic conventions surrounding our use of identity terms. If we imagine that our disputants finally agree that our linguistic conventions permit us to call the two churches the same (a conclusion to which Hume would give his assent), then we can see why it is permissible to call two things the same that are in fact different. This is because there are two levels at which the notion of identity can be employed: one that deals with questions about identity at the metaphysical or ultimate level, and one that deals with them at the verbal or conventional level.

[BUDDHIST NO-SELF THEORY]

It is disappointing that Hume does not have more to say about the two levels of "disputes." For it is with such an account that we are able to explain why it is acceptable for us to continue to talk in terms of selves and personal identity despite the fact that there are no such things. We can, however, arrive at a fuller understanding of what the two-level account involves by turning to another version of the no-self theory. This is the no-self theory as propounded by the Buddha[5] and various of his followers. The Buddhist theory can offer some insights. For at the very heart of this theory lies the doctrine of the two levels of truth. Although the different schools of Buddhist thought disagree on the exact nature of the distinction to be drawn between the two truths, there are enough similarities—at least in the early Hinayana[6] schools—for us to give a general account. This will . . . allow us . . . to see what Hume might have been getting at. . . . I hasten to add, however, that I am not here attempting a scholarly exposition of Buddhist thought; for my present interests are confined to an exposition of the no-self theory of personal identity. It is just that Buddhism has some valuable contributions to make here. There are, of course, problems involved in the cross-cultural discussion of ideas; Hume and the Buddha, after all, lived their lives in very different social and historical contexts. And yet I do not think that these difficulties need detain us; for when we go to the texts where Buddhist thinkers are grappling with the problem of personal identity, we find their concerns are essentially the same as Hume's.

In the earliest texts of Buddhism, the Pali Canon (about 500 B.C.E.), we come across a distinction drawn between two types of discourse: that of direct meaning and that of indirect meaning. The former type of discourse is said to be one whose meaning is plain while the latter type needs to have its meaning inferred with reference to the former. In the discourses of indirect meaning, words are used

---

[5]The Buddha (born Siddhartha Gautama; about 563–483 B.C.E.) was the Indian philosopher who founded Buddhism. [D. C. ABEL]
[6]Hinayana ("Small Vehicle [to enlightenment]") Buddhism, also called Theravada ("The Teaching of the Elders") Buddhism, is distinguished from a later form called Mahayana ("Great Vehicle") Buddhism. [D. C. ABEL]

that apparently refer to persisting entities such as a self or an I that, according to the Buddha, are merely "expressions, turns of speech, designations in common use in the world that the Tathagata[7] makes use of without being led astray by them."[8] That is, although we may use words like "self" and "I," we should not be led into thinking that they actually refer to something, for they are but grammatical devices. This nondenoting aspect of these expressions is something that must be inferred in light of the discourses of direct meaning. In this latter type of discourse, the nonexistence of anything permanent or enduring, such as the self or I, is asserted, and the misleading features of language—those features that lead us astray into the belief in an I—are made explicit. Here there is no need for inference, since the meaning of such discourse is plain.

As it happens, however, we are apt to confuse the two types of discourse: "There are these two who misrepresent the Tathagata. Which two? He who represents a sutta[9] of indirect meaning as a sutta of direct meaning and he who represents a sutta of direct meaning as a sutta of indirect meaning."[10] Although the Pali Canon does not elaborate here, we can easily see what sorts of errors are being referred to. On the one hand we might think that someone who is using the words "self," I," or "Buddha" (which are mere turns of speech) is in fact denoting a particular entity. Or, on the other hand, we might think that someone who is denying the existence of the self cannot really mean what he or she is saying and so we might be tempted to infer a further meaning that would still allow the existence of the self. We might, for instance, think that the person making this claim is only denying the existence of a certain type of self.

The discussion of the two types of discourse is continued in the various Buddhist commentaries on the Pali Canon, and here we are introduced to the related ideas of two levels of truth. In one commentary it is stated that all "Buddhas[11] have two types of speech: conventional and ultimate. Thus 'being,' 'man,' 'person,' [and the proper names] 'Tissa,' 'Naga' are used as conventional speech. 'Categories,' 'elements.' 'sense-bases' are used as ultimate speech." Because of this division in speech, we are told that the Buddha "declared two truths: the conventional and ultimate; there is no third. Words [used by] mutual agreement are true because of worldly convention; words of ultimate meaning are true because of the existence of elements."[12] Although the various elements are said to be the constituents of which everything else, including what we call the self, is made, it is not because the elements are more basic than the self that the self is said ultimately not to exist. It is simply because there is nothing in the world, not even an assemblage of the elements, that can be identified with the

---

[7]*Tathagata:* (Pali, "one who has thus gone," "one who has thus attained") the perfect one—an epithet of the Buddha that he uses when speaking of himself. [D. C. ABEL]

[8]Pali Canon text (*Dingha Nikaya* I.202) cited in K. N. Jayatilleke, *Early Buddhist Theory of Knowledge* (London, England: George Allen & Unwin, 1963), pp. 319–20. [J. GILES]

[9]*sutta:* discourse. [J. GILES]

[10]Jayatilleke, *Early Buddhist Theory of Knowledge*, p. 361. [J. GILES]

[11]*Buddhas:* enlightened beings. [J. GILES]

[12]Commentary text cited in Steven Collins, *Selfless Persons: Imagery and Thought in Theravada Buddhism* (New York: Cambridge University Press, 1990), p. 154. [J. GILES]

self. Although the Buddha cites various characteristics that something must have if it is to be considered a self, the most important is that of permanence or identity over time. But when we look to our experience, there is nothing but impermanence: Our bodies, feelings, and thoughts are forever coming and going. In this sense the Buddha is in complete agreement with Hume: Where there is diversity there can be no identity. None of this, however, implies that statements that make use of words like "self," "I," "you," "Tissa," or "Buddha" are false or nonsensical at every level of discourse. For they can be true at the conventional level, which means that they can be true because of their being used in accordance with mutual agreement—that is, linguistic convention.

A good illustration of how this distinction is to be drawn is given in a well-known passage from *The Questions of King Menander* (about 100 C.E.).[13] In this dialogue, the Indo-Greek King Menander puts various questions about the nature of the self to the Buddhist monk Nagasena. At the opening of the dialogue, Menander asks "How is your Reverence known, and what is your name?" The somewhat provocative answer given to the king is "I'm known as Nagasena, your Majesty; that's what my fellow monks call me. But though my parents may have given me such a name . . . , it is only a generally understood term, a practical designation. There is no question of a permanent individual implied in the use of the word." Menander is quite astonished by this reply and eventually asks "If your fellow monks call you Nagasena, what then is Nagasena?" He asks whether Nagasena is any part of the body or the mind, or whether he is all of these things taken together, or whether he is anything apart from them. To all of this Nagasena replies merely "No, your Majesty." Menander then exclaims triumphantly: "Then for all my asking I find no Nagasena. Nagasena is a mere sound! Surely what your Reverence has said is false!" But Nagasena is not to be dealt with so swiftly and, in good Socratic[14] fashion, replies by himself asking a question: "Your Majesty, how did you come here—on foot, or in a vehicle?" "In a chariot," says Menander. Nagasena then asks what the chariot is, whether it is the pole, axle, wheels, frame, reins, or yoke, or whether it is all these taken together, or again whether it is something other than the separate parts. Menander replies in the negative. With this Nagasena fires back at the king his own reasoning: "Then for all my asking, your Majesty, I can find no chariot. The chariot is merely a sound. What then is the chariot? Surely what your Majesty has said is false! There is no chariot!" Menander protests that he has not said anything false: "It's on account of all these various components, the pole, axle, wheels, and so on, that the vehicle is called a chariot. It's just a generally understood term, a practical designation." Nagasena's rejoinder is to praise Menander for this remark and to point out that the same holds true of himself. For it is because of his various components that he is

---

[13]Quotations from the *Menander* text come mainly from *Sources of Indian Tradition*, ed. William Theodore de Bary (New York: Columbia University Press, 1958), 1:103–105. However, the editor omits the important final remark made by Nagasena. This line, which I have included, can be found in *The Sacred Books of the Buddhists*, vol. 22, *Milinda's Questions*, vol. 1, trans. I. B. Horner (London, England: Luzac, 1963), pp. 37–38 [J. GILES]. Milinda is another name for Menander. [D. C. ABEL]
[14]Socrates (470–399 B.C.E.) was a Greek philosopher. [D. C. ABEL]

known by the practical designation "Nagasena." However, he adds, in the ultimate sense there is no person to whom the name refers. . . .

Nagasena rejects any notion of a person that exists in the ultimate sense: A person is not ultimately something other than his parts (the strict theory), nor is a person ultimately the sum of his parts (the reductionist theory).[15] This does not mean, however, that the word "Nagasena" is a mere sound, for it is more than that: It is a generally understood term whose proper use is determined by mutual agreement concerning how, when, and where it is to be used. Or, as Nagasena says, it is because of his various components that he is known as "Nagasena," even though "Nagasena" does not refer to anything. . . .

Some will no doubt find it paradoxical that we can use personal language correctly when there is nothing to which these terms ultimately refer. It was reasoning akin to this, it seems, that led Descartes[16] to his famous proclamation "I think, therefore I am." I must exist, reasoned Descartes, because even when I doubt that I exist there is still an I that is doing the doubting. But Descartes has become led astray by his own language, for there is no need for the "I" in "I think" or "I doubt" to refer to anything. What Descartes was aware of, as both Hume and the Buddha would agree, was just thinking, not an I that was doing the thinking. Consequently Descartes might just as well have said (and should have said if his concern was with ultimate rather than conventional truth) "There is thinking, therefore there are thoughts." And such a deduction, if we may call it that, does not suffice to prove the existence of an I.

A possible response here would be to say that although there need be no reference to an I when we use the noun sense of "thinking" or "thoughts," when the verb sense "I think" is employed, then plainly there must be some reference to a subject; for what is it that thinks? To this it can be replied that although the term "think" does require a subject, this is little more than a grammatical requirement. And so we might just as well employ a nonreferring grammatical subject rather than the misleading term "I." This is a point that was recognized by Georg Christoph Lichtenberg, who said about Descartes' dictum: "We should say, 'It thinks,' just as we say 'It thunders.' Even to say *"cogito"*[17] is too much if we translate it with 'I think.' To assume the 'I' to postulate it, is a practical need."[18] Thus, since the use of the verbal sense "thunders" also requires the introduction of a subject, we bring in the word "it" and say "It thunders." But this does not mean that the grammatical subject "it" here refers to anything. All we are saying when we say "It thunders" is "There is thunder." Consequently, since the requirement that the word "thinks" have a subject is also a convention of grammar, or, as we might say with Lichtenberg, a practical need, we could

---

[15]*reductionist theory:* a theory that one kind of thing can be "reduced to" (explained fully in terms of) another kind of thing. [D. C. ABEL]

[16]René Descartes (1596–1650) was a French philosopher and mathematician; for a biography, see p. 144. [D. C. ABEL]

[17]*cogito;* the first-person singular of the Latin verb *cogitare,* "to think," which Descartes used in "Cogito ergo sum," the Latin version of his statement "I think, therefore I am." [D. C. ABEL]

[18]Cited in J. P. Stern, *Lichtenberg: A Doctrine of Scattered Occasions, Reconstructed from His Aphorisms and Reflections* (Bloomington: Indiana University Press, 1959), p. 270. [J. GILES]. Lichtenberg (1742–1799) was a German philosopher and physicist. [D. C. ABEL]

likewise employ "it" to serve this purpose. We could say "It thinks, therefore there are thoughts," and the appearance of "it" here would no more imply a reference to an actual subject than would "it" in "It thunders." . . .

[AN EXPANSION OF THE NO-SELF THEORY]

Hume often speaks in Book II [of *A Treatise of Human Nature*] of our idea or impression of the self as though it were something that occurs instantaneously within our awareness, a singular perception that we experience as the object of pride and humility. But, as Hume has told us, there is no impression or idea of the self; there is only the smooth and uninterrupted progress of thought within our imagination. But how is it that a smooth and uninterrupted progress of thought could appear instantaneously within awareness? The notion of an uninterrupted progress is a temporal notion; it is something that occurs over an extended period of time. Accordingly, it is difficult to see how such a train of perceptions could be an object to which we could, in an instant, direct our emotions. . . .

The way for us to deal with this problem, and so fill out our picture of the no-self theory, is to see that when we enter a psychological or emotional state that seems to depend on an instantaneous awareness of self, what we are doing is not reflecting on a succession of related ideas (which could not be done at any one instant); rather we are latching on to a particular collection of some of these ideas that, by virtue of their being related, can instantaneously present themselves in a condensed form to our awareness. It is with this discovery of a constructed or condensed self-image, as we shall call it, that we are brought to a central point within the no-self theory—namely, that although we may on various occasions have experiences of something that we take to be our self, on closer examination this object of our awareness turns out to be nothing more than a collation of related images. . . .

When I enter a state of self-awareness, the I that is summoned before my consciousness is not a simple entity that infixes itself changelessly in my mind. It is rather a composite of various fading images that will have some reference to how I see and feel about myself. I may, for example, have an image of my face as it appeared to me in the mirror this morning that is nevertheless infused with features of previous images of my face. Thus, although my eyes and lips might appear to me as they did today, my cheeks and the shape of my face might seem more like those of myself of 12 years ago. Or again it might include features of how I would imagine myself to look in 20 years. This composite image of my face might itself be superimposed on some familiar scene, say, the beach where I often go for walks. Here the sand dunes might be incorporated into the cheeks and the rising of the waves into the forming of a smile. And all of this will be presented in a suffusion of affective tones that will exhibit the emotional evaluations I have of myself. Like other of our condensed images, the self-image will have but an ephemeral existence; the constituent images, continuously dissolving as new associations, make their way into the complex. Just what the constituents of the constructed self-image are will naturally be different for each person, since each person will see herself in a different way. While for one person it may consist mainly of idealized images of her physical appearance, for another it may be a mixture of certain sensations or emotions, while for a third it may be images of how others respond to her. To verify that this is so one need only ask different persons to describe what it is they are aware of when they are aware of themselves. It will then be seen that such images vary quite markedly. . . .

We now have to ask what it is that leads someone into perceiving the constructed self-image as being a self. And here again the work of Buddhist philosophers is most helpful. According to Buddhist theory, what we call a person is really just an aggregation of the five *khandhas* or elements. These are: physical form, perceptions, feelings, motives, and consciousness. But none of these elements, whether considered separately or in combination, can rightly be identified with the self, for they lack the various qualities that we attribute to the self.[19] This, however, does not stop one from mistakenly identifying oneself with one or another of the elements, and indeed this is a ubiquitous confusion from which Buddhism hopes to set us free. But what is it that leads a person to this mistaken identification? To answer this we need to refer back to our previous discussion of the conventional and ultimate levels of truth. There we saw that although personal names and personal pronouns do not at the ultimate level refer to anything, at the conventional level it is quite acceptable to use such expressions for pragmatic reasons. Thus the Buddha uses the language of the self as convenient designations without being led astray by them. The problem is that, unlike the Buddha, many of us do get led astray by the expressions we use; that is, in failing to notice that we are using language at the level of convention, we end up thinking that there must be something to which the words "I" or "self" refer. And so we turn our gaze inward (because this is where the self is supposed to exist) and, coming upon one or another of the elements, or a collection of the elements, hasten to identify it with our self.

---

[19]This argument is given in "Lesser Discourse to Saccaka," in *The Collection of the Middle-Length Sayings (Majjhima Nikaya)*, vol. 1, *The First Fifty Discourses (Mulapannasa)* trans. I. B. Horner (London, England: Pali Text Society, 1954), pp. 280–91. [J. Giles]

The Origins of Selves
Daniel C. Dennett

Daniel C. Dennett was born in Boston in 1942. After receiving his bachelor's degree in philosophy from Harvard University in 1963, he went to Oxford University, where he studied under Gilbert Ryle and completed his doctoral studies in 1965. He then accepted a position at the University of California, Irvine. Dennett began teaching at Tufts University in 1971, where he is now university professor, Austin B. Fletcher Professor of Philosophy, and director of the Center for Cognitive Studies. He has been a visiting professor at Harvard University, the University of Pittsburgh, Oxford University, and the Ecole Normale Supérieur in Paris. He has been awarded Guggenheim and Fulbright fellowships and was elected to the American Academy of Arts and Sciences in 1987.

Dennett's publications include *Content and Consciousness* (1969; 2d ed., 1986), *Elbow Room: The Varieties of Free Will Worth Wanting* (1984), *The Intentional Stance* (1987), *Consciousness Explained* (1991), *Darwin's Dangerous Idea: Evolution and the Meanings of Life* (1995), *Kinds of Minds: Toward an Understanding of Consciousness* (1996), *Freedom Evolves* (2003), *Breaking the Spell: Religion as a Natural Phenomenon* (2006), and *Science and Religion: Are They Compatible?* (coauthor with Alvin Plantinga; 2011).

Our reading is Dennett's 1989 article, "The Origins of Selves," which explores the perplexing question of what a "self" is by examining how there came to be creatures that have (or are) selves. The distinction between self and other began with the evolution of living things, which seek *self*-preservation from threats arising from the world outside. A primitive self is not a *thing* inside an organism but an *organization* that "tends to distinguish, control and preserve portions of the world [and] thereby creates and maintains boundaries." The boundaries are drawn on the principle "You are what you control and care for." No fixed boundaries delineate what an organism controls and cares for: The shell that a snail grows becomes part of its self, and the discarded shell that the hermit crab moves into becomes part of its self.

Human beings have a technique of self-preservation much more sophisticated than that of snails and crabs: We have language and preserve ourselves by creating and telling stories about whom we are. Although the human self seems to be the *source* of the narrative we tell, it is in fact not the source but the *product* of this narrative. Using an analogy from physics, Dennett argues that a human self is a "center of narrative gravity": Just as the center of gravity of a physical object is an abstraction yet nonetheless real, so the center of *narrative* gravity is an abstraction yet quite real. (And this center of narrative gravity would account for personal identity.) Dennett develops his theory of the narrative self by examining an aberration from the norm of one self per body: multiple personality disorder (also called dissociative identity disorder).

[INTRODUCTION]

What is a self? Since Descartes[1] in the seventeenth century we have had a vision of the self as a sort of immaterial ghost that owns and controls a body the way you own and control your car.

---

[1]René Descartes (1596–1650) was a French philosopher and mathematician; for a biography, see p. 144. [D. C. ABEL]

More recently, with the rejection of dualism[2] and the rise of materialism—the idea that the mind just *is* the brain—we have gravitated to the view that the self must be a node or module in the brain, the central headquarters responsible for organizing and directing all the subsidiary bureaucracies that keep life and limb together.

Or is the very idea of a self nothing but a compelling fiction, a creed outworn, as some theorists insist, a myth we keep telling ourselves in spite of the advances of science that discredit it?

" . . . a myth we keep telling ourselves." A myth we keep telling *whom?* Is a self something else, perhaps even some hard-to-imagine combination of these very different ideas?

On my first trip to London many years ago I found myself looking for the nearest Underground station. I noticed a stairway in the sidewalk labeled "Subway," which in *my* version of English meant subway train, so I confidently descended the stairs and marched forth looking for the trains. After wandering around in various corridors, I found another flight of stairs, leading up, alas, and somewhat dubiously climbed them to find myself on the other side of the intersection from where I had started. I must have missed a turn, I thought, and walked back downstairs to try again. After what seemed to me to be an exhaustive search for hitherto overlooked turnstiles or side entrances, I emerged back on the sidewalk where I had started, feeling somewhat cheated. It finally dawned on me that a subway in London is just a way of crossing the street underground. Searching for the self can be somewhat like that. You enter the brain through the eye, march up the optic nerve, round and round in the cortex, looking behind every neuron, and then, before you know it, you emerge into daylight on the spike of a motor nerve impulse, scratching your head and wondering where the self is.

That is not the way to find the self, or to understand what a self is. (That's a bit like wandering around Manhattan looking for the Big Apple.) Where then might we look? We might look first to origins. As the British biologist D'Arcy Thompson once said, "Everything is what it is because it got that way."[3]

If selves are anything at all, then they exist. *Now* there are selves. There was a time, millions (or billions) of years ago, when there were none—at least none on this planet. So there has to be—as a matter of logic—a true story to be told about how there came to be creatures with selves. This story will have to tell—as a matter of logic—about a process (or a series of processes) involving the activities or behaviors of things that do not yet *have* selves—or *are* not yet selves—but that eventually yield, as a new product, beings that do have selves. That is the true story I would like to tell, but quite obviously it is now—and probably forever—impossible to *know* the details of that story, so we will have to speculate somewhat, guided as firmly as possible by the available facts.

---

[2]*dualism:* the theory that a human being consists of two substances—body and mind (soul, self). [D. C. ABEL]

[3]D'Arcy Wentworth Thompson, *Growth and Form* (Cambridge, England: Cambridge University Press, 1917). [D. C. DENNETT]

And since this will have to be a brief overview of a rather large and intricate research project, I must resort to simplifications and metaphors to illustrate the outlines without going into the details. That does not mean that I have a different version, right now, for the experts. In fact there are no experts on these topics, and the experts on the details have just as much trouble seeing the overall shape and direction of theory as any novice—perhaps more trouble, since they are so preoccupied with their close-up views of tiny patches of the problem.

BIOLOGY BEGINS IN SELF-PRESERVATION

This story that must be told is analogous to other stories that science is beginning to tell. Compare it, for instance, to the fascinating story of the evolution of sex. There are many organisms today that have no genders and reproduce asexually, and there most certainly was a time when all the organisms that existed did not come in different genders, male and female, and did not engage in *sexual* reproduction. Somehow, by some imaginable series of steps, some of these organisms have to have evolved into organisms that did have genders, and eventually, of course, into us, and the rather exotic—and indeed erotic—transformations and elaborations we have added to the basic biological phenomenon of gender. What sort of conditions were required to foster or necessitate these innovations? Why, in short, did all these changes happen?

There is a nice parallel between the two questions, about the origins of *sex* and the origins of *selves*. There is almost nothing *sexy* (in human terms) about the sex life of insects, oysters, and other simple forms of life, but we can recognize in their mechanical and apparently joyless routines of reproduction the foundations and principles of our much more exciting world of sex. Similarly, there is nothing particularly *selfy* (if I may coin a term) about the primitive precursors of human selves, but they laid the foundations for our particularly human innovations and complications.

The original distinction between self and other is a deep biological principle; one might say it is the deepest principle, for biology begins in self-preservation—in the emergence of entities (the simplest replicators) who resisted destruction and decay, who combated, at least for a short time, the second law of thermodynamics,[4] and passed on their capacity to do this to their descendants.

As soon as something gets into the business of self-preservation, boundaries become important, for if you are setting out to preserve yourself, you don't want to squander effort trying to preserve the whole world; you draw the line. You become, in a word, *selfish*. This primordial form of selfishness (which, as a primordial form, lacks most of the flavors of our brand of human selfishness) is one of the marks of life. Where one bit of granite ends and the next bit begins is a matter of slight moment; the fracture boundary may be real enough, but nothing works to protect the territory, to push back the frontier or retreat. "Me against the world"—this distinction between everything on the *inside* of a closed

---

[4]*second law of thermodynamics:* the law of physics that states that when a system of heat and energy is left alone, its *entropy* (the amount of disorder) tends to increase. [D. C. ABEL]

boundary and everything in the *external world*, is at the heart of all biological processes—not just ingestion and excretion, respiration and transpiration.

Consider, for instance, the immune system, with its millions of different antibodies arrayed in defense of the body against millions of different alien intruders. This army must solve the fundamental problem of recognition: telling one's self (and one's friends) from everything else. And the problem has been solved in much the way human nations and their armies have solved the counterpart problem: by standardized identification-routines. The passports and customs officers in miniature are molecular shapes and shape-detectors. It is important to recognize that this army of antibodies has no generals, no general headquarters with a battle plan, or even a description of the enemy; the antibodies represent their enemies only in the way a million locks represent the keys that open them. Occasionally, misidentifications are made—in autoimmune reactions, for instance, in which a sort of civil war takes place between different factions of what ought to be peacefully coexisting parts of the whole that resides inside the walls.

The distinctions at this level are far from absolute; within the walls of the body are many, many interlopers, ranging from bacteria and viruses through microscopic mites that live like cliff-dwellers in the ecological niche of our skin and scalp, to larger parasites—horrible tapeworms, for instance. These interlopers are all tiny self-protectors in their own right, but some of them, such as the bacteria that populate our digestive systems and without which we would die, are just as essential team members in our quest for self-preservation as the antibodies in our immune systems. Other interlopers are tolerated parasites—not worth the effort to evict, apparently—and still others are indeed the enemy within, deadly if not rooted out and driven out.

This fundamental biological principle of distinguishing self from world, inside from outside, has some remarkable echoes in the highest vaults of our psychology. The psychologist Paul Rozin has shown in a fascinating series of experiments on the nature of *disgust* that there is a powerful and unacknowledged undercurrent of blind resistance to certain acts that, rationally considered, should not trouble us.[5] For example, would you please swallow the saliva in your mouth right now? This act does not fill you with revulsion. But suppose I had handed you a sparkling clean drinking glass and asked you to spit into the glass and then swallow the saliva from the glass. Disgusting! But why? It seems to have to do with our perception that once something is outside of our bodies it is no longer quite part of us anymore; it becomes alien and suspicious; it has renounced its citizenship and becomes something to be rejected.

Border crossings are thus either moments of anxiety or, in a familiar reversal, something to be especially enjoyed: "In addition, they seemed to spend a great deal of time eating and drinking and going to parties, and Frensic, whose appearance tended to limit his sensual pleasure to putting things into himself rather than into other people, was something of a gourmet."[6] Sharpe suggests,

---

[5]Paul Rozin and April E. Fallon, "A Perspective on Disgust," *Psychological Review* 94 (January 1987): 23–41. [D. C. DENNETT]

[6]Tom Sharpe, *The Great Pursuit* (London, England: Secker & Warburg, 1977), p. 6. [D. C. DENNETT]

in this funny but unsettling passage, that when you get right down to it all pleasure consists in playing around with one's own boundary, or someone else's; and these biological reflections of ours suggest that he is on to something—if not the whole truth, then part of the truth.

In any event, the origin of complex life forms on this planet was also the birth of the most primitive sort of self, whatever sort of self is implied by the self-regard that prevents the lobster, when hungry, from eating itself.

Does a lobster have a self? Or, should we say, are there selves that have lobster bodies? This question is obviously the secular descendant of a question that has troubled theologians for several thousand years: Do animals have immortal souls? Do insects? I must say that I much prefer the secular version to the religious, and will not make any attempt—except by implication, no doubt—to express my opinions about the existence of *souls*. Even the most hard-headed materialist/mechanist/scientist, on the other hand, must face the question of how to describe the distinction between the lobster and the rock behind which the lobster crouches—only one of them is designed around the principle of self-regard. So far as *that* property goes, we can make fairly simple robots or automata that also exhibit it, detecting and retreating from dangers, seeking out shelter and striving to renew their energy resources. This is minimal selfhood, but one must start at the beginning.

So a minimal self is not a *thing* inside a lobster or a lark, and it is not the "whole lobster" or "whole lark" either; it is something abstract that amounts just to the existence of an organization that tends to distinguish, control, and preserve portions of the world, an organization that thereby creates and maintains boundaries. To a first approximation the principle that draws the boundary is this slogan: *You are what you control and care for.*

THE SELF HAS FLEXIBLE BOUNDARIES

Every word in this slogan cries out for further refinement, but I prefer to leave it in its simplest form, since the amendments that will already no doubt have occurred to you illustrate my next point. The boundaries of the minimal self are not only permeable, as we have just seen, but flexible as well. The hermit crab finds the discarded shell of another creature and appropriates it as a portable shelter, but by this appropriation that alien shell is moved inside the boundary—just as much as the shell that a snail grows, utilizing materials it likewise finds in its environment, but ingests and then extrudes.

The beaver's dam, by the same token, is so intimately associated with the beaver's fundamental strategies of survival that it should be included inside the boundary as well, as Richard Dawkins argues—I think conclusively—in *The Extended Phenotype.*[7] One might protest that however loyally the beaver cares for its dam, it doesn't *directly* control the shape of its dam (in the way that it directly controls the posture of its limbs), but one could also go on to point out that it

---

[7]Richard Dawkins, *The Extended Phenotype: The Gene as the Unit of Selection* (Oxford, England: Oxford University Press, 1982), pp. 195–208. [D. C. ABEL]

doesn't control its limbs as directly as it controls the motor nerve firings that innervate its limbs—so should we draw the boundary of minimal selfhood inside its limbs? Surely not.

An even more stunning example is the anthill or termite colony, in which there is a boundary not marked by any membrane or even by unbroken proximity of parts. What is particularly striking about the termite colony is that it is an example of a complex system capable of functioning in what seems to be a thoroughly "purposeful and integrated" way simply by having *lots of subsystems doing their own thing* without any central supervision. Indeed, most systems on earth that appear to have central controllers (and are usefully described as having them) do not. The colony as a whole builds elaborate mounds, gets to know its territory, organizes foraging expeditions, sends out raiding parties against other colonies, and so on. The group cohesion and coordination is so remarkable that hardheaded observers have been led to postulate the existence of a colony's "group soul."[8] Yet in fact all this group wisdom results from nothing other than myriads of individual termites, specialized as several different castes, going about their individual business—influenced by each other, but quite uninfluenced by any master plan.

In every beehive or termite colony there is, to be sure, a queen bee or queen termite, but these individuals are more patient than agent, more a treasure to be protected than the chief of the protective forces—in fact their name is more fitting today than in earlier ages, for they are much more like Queen Elizabeth II than Queen Elizabeth I. There is no Margaret Thatcher bee, no George Bush termite, no Oval Office in the anthill.[9]

But enough about the bees and the birds. What about us? I know that there will be some among you who will be sure I am leading you on a wild goose chase; the sort of selfhood we have been examining, you think, is *not at all* the sort of selfhood that you have; a human being's self is *entirely different* from the sort of implied self of the lobster or the ant colony. Yes and no. Of course they are different in important ways; the question is, can we build a bridge of evolution or development between them?

First let's look at a similarity, and then a major difference. Do our selves, our non-minimal *selfy* selves, exhibit permeability and flexibility of boundaries? We have noted the hermit crab's shell and the beaver's dam. What of our own clothes, our houses, our automobiles, and the other paraphernalia we strive to control—our "stuff," as George Carlin[10] calls it? Do we expand our personal boundaries—the boundaries of our selves—to enclose any of this? In general, perhaps, no, but there are certainly times when this seems true, psychologically. For instance, some people own cars and drive them, while other people are *motorists.* The inveterate motorist prefers being a four-wheeled gas-consuming agent to being a two-legged food-consuming agent, and his use of the first-person pronoun betrays this identification: "I'm not cornering

---

[8]Eugène N. Marais, *The Soul of the White Ant* (London, England: Methuen, 1937). [D. C. DENNETT]
[9]When Dennett wrote this article in 1989, Margaret Thatcher was the British prime minister, and George Herbert Walker Bush the U.S. president. [D. C. ABEL]
[10]George Carlin (1937–2008) was an American comedian. [D. C. ABEL]

well on rainy days because my tires are getting bald." So sometimes we enlarge our boundaries; at other times, in response to perceived challenges real or imaginary, we let our boundaries shrink: "I didn't do that! That wasn't the real me talking. Yes, the words came out of my mouth, but I refuse to recognize them as my own." This shrinking tactic has important moral implications. If you make yourself really small, you can externalize virtually everything.[11]

I have reminded you of these familiar speeches to draw out the similarities between our selves and the selves of ants and hermit crabs, but the speeches also draw attention to the most important differences: Ants and hermit crabs don't talk. The hermit crab is designed or organized in such a way as to see to it that it acquires a shell. This organization, we might say, *implies* a shell, and hence, in a *very* weak sense, tacitly *represents the crab as having a shell.* But the crab does not in any stronger sense *represent itself* as having a shell. It doesn't go in for self-representation at all. To whom would it so represent itself and why? It doesn't need to remind it*self* of this aspect of its nature, since its innate design takes care of that problem, and there are no other interested parties in the offing. And the ants, as we have noted, accomplish their communal projects without relying on any explicitly communicated blueprints or edicts.

OUR SELVES ARE THE PRODUCT OF NARRATIVE

We, in contrast, are almost constantly engaged in presenting ourselves to others, and to ourselves, and hence *representing* ourselves—in language and gesture, external and internal. The most obvious difference in our environment that would explain this difference in our behavior is the behavior itself. Our human environment contains not just food and shelter, enemies to fight or flee, and conspecifics[12] with whom to mate, but words, words, words. These words are potent elements of our environment that we readily incorporate, ingesting and extruding them, weaving them like spiderwebs into self-protective strings of *narrative.* Our fundamental tactic of self-protection, self-control, and self-definition is not building dams or spinning webs, but telling stories—and more particularly concocting and controlling the story we tell others, and ourselves, about who we are.

Now we are ready for the strangest idea in my paper, but also, I think, the most important: There is a further similarity between the spiders, the beavers, and us. Spiders don't have to think, consciously and deliberately, about how to spin their webs; that is just something that spider brains are designed to get spiders to do. And even beavers, unlike professional human engineers, do not consciously and deliberately plan the structures they build. And finally, *we* (unlike *professional* human storytellers) do not consciously and deliberately figure out what narratives to tell and how to tell them; like spiderwebs, our tales are *spun by us;* our human consciousness, and our narrative selfhood, is their *product,* not their *source.*

---

[11]See the discussion of the moral implications of the "dimensions of the self" in Daniel C. Dennett, *Elbow Room: The Varieties of Free Will Worth Wanting* (Cambridge, MA: MIT Press, 1984), especially p. 143. [D. C. DENNETT]

[12]*conspecifics:* members of the same species. [D. C. ABEL]

These strings or streams of narrative issue forth *as if* from a single source—not just in the obvious physical sense of flowing from just one mouth, or one pencil or pen, but in a more subtle sense: Their effect on any audience or readers is to encourage them to (try to) posit a unified agent whose words they are, about whom they are—in short, to posit what I call a *center of narrative gravity*.[13] This is yet another abstraction, not a thing in the brain, but still a remarkably robust and almost tangible attractor of properties, the "owner of record" of whatever items and features are lying about unclaimed. Who owns your car? You do. Who owns your clothes? You do. Then who owns your body? You do. When you say "This is my body," you certainly aren't taken as saying "This body owns itself." But what can you be saying, then? If what you say is neither a bizarre and pointless tautology (this body is its own owner, or something like that) nor the metaphysically[14] discredited—or at least highly suspect—claim that you are an immaterial soul or ghost puppeteer who owns and operates this body, what else could you mean? I think we could see more clearly what "This is my body" meant, if we could answer the question: as opposed to what? How about as opposed to this? "No, it isn't; it's mine, and I don't like sharing it!"

If we could see what it would be like for two (or more) selves to vie for control of a single body, we could see better what a single self really is. As scientists of the self, we would like to conduct controlled experiments in which, by varying the initial conditions, we could see just what has to happen, in what order and requiring what resources, for such a talking self to emerge. Are there conditions under which life goes on but no self emerges? Are there conditions under which more than one self emerges? Of course we cannot ethically conduct such experiments, but, as in other scientific investigations of human phenomena, occasionally nature conducts terrible experiments, from which we can cautiously draw conclusions.

ALWAYS ONE SELF TO ONE BODY?

Such an experiment is multiple personality disorder (MPD), in which a single human body *seems* to be shared by several selves—each, typically, with a proper name and an autobiography. Nicholas Humphrey and I have been investigating MPD with an eye to answering these questions about the self.

The idea of multiple personality disorder strikes many people as too outlandish and metaphysically bizarre to believe—a "paranormal" phenomenon to discard along with extrasensory perception, close encounters of the third kind, and witches on broomsticks. I suspect that some of these people have made a simple *arithmetical* mistake: They have failed to notice that two or three or

---

[13]See Daniel C. Dennett, "Why Everyone Is a Novelist," *Times Literary Supplement*, September 16–22, 1988, pp. 1016, 1028–1029. [D. C. DENNETT] Reprinted in a slightly revised form as "The Self as a Center of Narrative Gravity," in *Self and Consciousness: Multiple Perspectives,* ed. Frank S. Kessel, Pamela M. Cole, and Dale L. Johnson (Hillsdale, NJ: Lawrence Erlbaum Associates, 1992), pp. 103–115. [D. C. ABEL]

[14]*metaphysically:* relating to *metaphysics,* the study of the nature and kinds of reality. [D. C. ABEL]

seventeen selves per body is really no more *metaphysically* extravagant than one
self per body. One is bad enough!

"I just saw a car drive by with five selves in it."
"What?? The mind reels! What kind of metaphysical nonsense is this?"
"Well, there were also five bodies in the car."
"Oh, well, why didn't you say so? Then everything is OK."
"Oh maybe only four bodies, or three—but definitely five selves."
"What??!!"

The principle of "one to a customer" certainly captures the normal arrangement, but if a body can have one, why not more than one under abnormal
conditions?

I don't at all mean to suggest that there is nothing shocking or deeply puzzling about MPD. It is, in fact, a phenomenon of surpassing strangeness—not,
I think, because it challenges our presuppositions about what is *metaphysically*
possible, but more because it challenges our presuppositions about what is
humanly possible about the limits of human cruelty and depravity on the one
hand, and the limits of human creativity on the other. For the evidence is now
voluminous that there are not a handful or a hundred but thousands of cases of
MPD in this country, and it almost invariably owes its existence to prolonged
early child abuse, usually sexual, and of sickening severity.

These children have often been kept in such extraordinarily terrifying and
confusing circumstances that I am more amazed that they survive psychologically at all, than I am that they manage to preserve themselves by a desperate
redrawing of their boundaries. What they do, when confronted with overwhelming conflict and pain, is this: They "leave." They create a boundary so
that the horror doesn't happen to *them*; it either happens to no one, or to some
other self, better able to sustain its organization under such an onslaught—at
least this is what they *say* they did, as best they recall.

How can this be? What kind of account could we give, ultimately at the biological level, of such a process of splitting? Does there have to have been a
single, whole self that somehow fissioned, amoeba-like? How could that be if a
self is not a proper physical part of an organism or a brain, but, as I have suggested, an abstraction? The response to the trauma seems so creative, moreover,
that one is inclined at first to suppose that it must be the work of some kind of
supervisor in there—a supervisory brain program, a central controller, or whatever. But we should remind ourselves of the termite colony, which also seemed,
at first, to require a central chief executive to accomplish such clever projects. We
can perhaps convince ourselves of the possibility—no more than that—of such
a creative process by exploring an extended analogy.

DO I RESEMBLE THE U.S.A.?

Consider the United States of America. At one level of description there is surely
nothing wrong with personifying the U.S.A. and talking about it (rather like the
termite colony) as if it had an inner self. The U.S.A. has memories, feelings, likes
and dislikes, hopes, talents, and so on. It hates Communism, is haunted by the

memory of Vietnam, is scientifically creative, socially clumsy, somewhat given to self-righteousness, rather sentimental. But does that mean there is one central agency inside the U.S.A. that embodies all those qualities? Of course not. There is, as it happens, a specific area of the country where much of it comes together. But go to Washington and ask to speak to Mr. American Self, and you'd find there was nobody home; instead you'd find a lot of different agencies (the Defense Department, the Treasury, the courts, the Library of Congress, the National Science Foundation, and so on) operating in relative independence of each other.

To be sure, there is no such thing as Mr. American Self, but as a matter of fact there is in every country on earth a Head of State: a president, queen, chancellor, or some other figurehead. The Head of State may actually be non-executive; certainly he does not himself enact all the subsidiary roles (the U.S. President does not bear arms, sit in the courts, play baseball, or travel to the moon). But nevertheless he is expected at the very least to take an active interest in all these national pursuits. The president is meant to appreciate better than anyone the "state of the Union." He is meant to *represent* different parts of the nation to each other, and to inculcate a common value system. Moreover—and this is most important—he is the "spokesman" when it comes to dealing with other nation states. Other individuals—diplomats and press secretaries—may deliver the actual utterances, but these acts are understood to be relaying his speech acts to the world.

That is not to say that a nation lacking such a figurehead would cease to function day-to-day. But it is to say that in the longer term it may function much better if it does have one. Indeed a good case can be made that nations, unlike termite colonies, require this kind of figurehead as a condition of their political survival—especially given the complexity of international affairs.

The drift of this analogy is obvious. In short, a human being too may need an inner figurehead—especially given the complexities of human social life. If this is accepted (as I think it should be), we can turn to the vexed question of how such a figurehead could be developed or established in the first place. Here the Head of State analogy may seem at first less helpful. For one thing, in the U.S.A. at least, the president is democratically elected by the population. For another, the candidates for the presidency are pre-formed entities, already waiting in the wings.

Yet is this really so? It could equally be argued that the presidential candidates, rather than being pre-formed, are actually brought into being—through a narrative dialectical process—by the very population to which they offer their services as president. Thus the population (or the news media) first try out various fictive versions of what they think their "ideal president" should be, and then the candidates adapt themselves as best they can to fill the bill. To the extent that there is much more than one dominant fiction about "what it means to be American," different candidates mold themselves in different ways. But in the end only one can be elected—and he will of course claim to speak for the whole nation.

In very much a parallel way, Humphrey and I suggest, a human being first creates—unconsciously (the way a spider creates a web)—one or more ideal fictive selves and then elects the best supported of these into office as her Head of Mind. A significant difference in the human case, however, is that there is likely to be considerably more *outside influence*. Parents, friends, and even enemies may all contribute to the image of "what it means to be me" as well as—and maybe over and above—the internal news media. In a multiple personality case, daddy, for example, might lean on the growing child to impose an *invasive* fictive self.

Thus a human being does not start out as single or as multiple—she starts out without any Head of Mind at all. She is poised to fend for herself—just as the lobster or beaver is—but she does not yet have an organization crystallized around one or more centers of narrative gravity. In the normal course of development, she slowly gets acquainted with the various possibilities of selfhood that "make sense"—partly through her own observation, partly through outside influence. In most cases a majority view emerges, strongly favoring one version of "the real me," and it is that version that is installed as her elected Head of Mind. But in some cases the competing fictive selves are so equally balanced, or different constituencies within her are so unwilling to accept the result of the election, that constitutional chaos reigns—and there are snap elections (or coups d'état) all the time.

I think that a model inspired by (underlying, rendering honest) this analogy can account for symptomatology of MPD—the memory black-spots, differences in style, and so forth. Certainly the analogy provides a wealth of detail suggesting so. Once in office, a new Head of State typically downplays certain "unfortunate" aspects of his nation's history (especially those associated with the rival Head of State who immediately preceded him). Moreover he himself, by standing for particular national values, affects the course of future history by encouraging the expression of those values by the population (and so, by a kind of feedback, confirming his own role).

I am still talking in metaphors, however. What translations into the terms of current cognitive science could we formulate? First, what sense can be given to the notion of a "Head of Mind"? The analogy with a spokesman may not be far off the literal truth. The language-producing systems of the brain have to get their instructions from somewhere, and the very demands of pragmatics and grammar would conspire to confer something like Head of Mind authority on whatever subsystem currently controls their input. E. M. Forster[15] once remarked, "How can I tell what I think until I see what I say?" The four "I"s in this sentence are meant to refer to the same thing. But this grammatical tradition may depend—and always has depended—on the fact that the thought expressed in Forster's question is quite literally self-confirming: What "I" (my self) thinks is what "I" (my language apparatus) says.

There can, however, be no guarantee that either the speaker or anyone else who hears him over an extended period will settle on there being just a single "I." Suppose, at different times, different subsystems within the brain produce "clusters" of speech that simply cannot easily be interpreted as the output of a single self. Then—as a Bible scholar may discover when working on the authorship of what is putatively a single-authored text—it may turn out that the clusters make best sense when attributed to different selves.

---

[15]E. M. Forster (1879–1970) was a British novelist. [D. C. ABEL]

Another central feature of MPD is selective amnesia, which is the chief difference between the plight of the MPD sufferer and the rest of us (who have our various personae in the various roles we play day to day). MPD sufferers typically have no memory at all for the events that occur during regimes when they are out of power. To those who have even a passing knowledge of computer information processing, the idea of mutually inaccessible "directories" of stored information will already be familiar. In cognitive psychology, new discoveries about state-dependent learning and other evidence of modularization in the brain have led people to recognize that *failure* of access between different subsystems is the norm rather than the exception. Indeed the old Cartesian[16] picture of the mind "transparent to itself" now appears to be rarely if ever achievable (or even desirable) in practice. In this context the out-of-touchness of different selves no longer looks so startling.

The different "alters"[17] of an MPD sufferer almost always have different attitudes towards life and different emotional characters; one will be prudish and reserved, another sexy, a third angry and violent, for instance. What could be the basis for the different "value systems" associated with these rival Heads of Mind? At another level of analysis, psychopharmacological evidence suggests that the characteristic emotional style of different personalities could correspond to the brain-wide activation or inhibition of neural pathways that rely on different neurotransmitter chemicals. Thus the phlegmatic style of one personality could be associated with low norepinephrine levels, the shift to a carnal style with high norepinephrine, and the out-of-control alter could coincide with low dopamine.

Even the idea of an "election" of the current Head of Mind is not implausible. Events very like elections take place in the brain all the time—whenever coherent patterns of activity compete for control of the same network. Consider what happens, for example, when the visual system receives two conflicting images at the two eyes. First there is an attempt at fusion; but if this proves to be unstable, "binocular rivalry" results, with the input from one eye completely taking over while the other is suppressed. Thus we already have, at the level of visual neurophysiology, clear evidence of the mind's general preference for single-mindedness over completeness.

MPD provides a window into alternative possibilities. In the same way that the force of gravity is well-nigh invisible until you have imagined the weightlessness of outer space, so single-selfedness is hard to discern in a body until you have seen, or imagined, multiple-selfedness.

I have not had time to show you the detailed view through this window, but I hope I have succeeded in opening it for you.

---

[16]*Cartesian:* relating to Descartes. [D. C. ABEL]
[17]*"alters"*: the various personalities of a person with multiple personality disorder (short for "alter egos"—literally, in Latin, "other I's"). [D. C. ABEL]

CHAPTER 5

Free Will and Determinism

It seems an obvious fact of our experience that some of the things we do are the result of our own free choice. For example, you probably believe that you freely chose to read this book now, and that you could have chosen to read it earlier or later—or perhaps never! You probably also believe that you could stop reading right now if you decided to. (If you *did* stop, you would probably believe that you could have *not* stopped if you had so chosen.) When we reflect on *why* we choose what we choose, however, we may start to wonder if any of our choices are actually free. You would probably admit that when you choose something, there is some *reason* why you choose it—that your choice has some sort of *cause.* In fact, it seems to be a basic assumption of both common sense and science that *everything* that happens has a cause; it would seem strange if some events (for example, a loud noise right now) "just happened" without having any cause. If a cause is something that necessarily produces a particular effect and if every choice has a cause, then we necessarily choose whatever we choose; our belief that we are free to choose among alternatives is an illusion.

The view that all events are determined by preceding causes and that we can never act otherwise than we do is called *determinism.* Determinists usually locate the causes of human actions in some combination of genetic, environmental, and psychological factors. There are two kinds of determinism: "hard" and "soft." *Hard determinism* accepts determinism and denies the existence of free will and moral responsibility. *Soft determinism* maintains that, although determinism is true, actions with certain kinds of *internal* causes are free, and we are morally responsible for those actions. Because it defends the compatibility of determinism with free will and moral responsibility, soft determinism is also known as *compatibilism.*

Libertarianism is the theory that determinism is false and that human beings can, in some situations, make free choices. Some libertarians are *indeterminists,* making either the general claim that the universe is such that it contains multiple possibilities, or the more specific claim that some events, including some human actions, simply have no cause. Other libertarians (and some soft determinists) are *self-determinists,* agreeing that all our actions have causes but holding that an action is free if it is caused by the *person as a whole* rather than by some preceding set of conditions. (Libertarian self-determinism is sometimes called the *theory of agency* because its proponents define an "agent" precisely as a cause not determined by prior causes.) Like soft determinists, libertarians defend the notion of moral responsibility; unlike them, they deny that an action can be free and determined at the same time.

This chapter contains six readings, arranged in chronological order. Paul-Henri Thiry, Baron d'Holbach, supports hard determinism: We are completely material beings and therefore subject to the causal laws of nature. Holbach contends that, although we do have a will, our will is not free because it necessarily chooses what it thinks will be most advantageous to us. William James presents an indeterminist defense of libertarianism: Although we can prove neither determinism (whether hard or soft) nor indeterminism, indeterminism is more plausible because it can better account for "judgments of regret"—judgments that something should have been (or should now be) otherwise than it was (or now is). W. T. Stace argues for soft determinism: Although all actions are caused and therefore determined, a particular action is also *free* if it is caused by a psychological state of the agent rather than by an external force. Richard Taylor defends libertarianism with a theory of self-determinism: Human actions are free when they are caused by the person as a whole (the agent). He rejects the soft determinist claim that an action caused by a psychological state of the person (as distinct from the person as a whole) is free. Nancy Holmstrom "firms up" soft determinism to defend it against Taylor's criticism. She modifies Stace's theory so that it claims that an action caused by a psychological state free only if the person has *control* over that state. In the final reading, Galen Strawson contends that, whether or not determinism is true, we have no ultimate moral responsibility for any of our actions because our actions derive ultimately from our heredity and early experience, and we are not morally responsible for these things.

The System of Human Freedom

Paul-Henri Thiry, Baron d'Holbach

Paul-Henri Thiry (the French rendering of his original German name, Paul Heinrich Dietrich), Baron d'Holbach, was born in 1723 in Edesheim, Germany. At the age of 12, Thiry was taken to Paris to be brought up by his uncle, Franciscus Adam d'Holbach. His uncle, who had made a fortune in Paris and had become a French citizen, carefully directed his education. In 1744 Thiry enrolled in the University of Leiden in Holland. He returned to France five years later and became a naturalized citizen. When his uncle died in 1753, Thiry inherited his fortune and his title, Baron d'Holbach. Holbach's home became a gathering place for many prominent French thinkers, including Jean-Jacques Rousseau, Denis Diderot, and Jean Le Rond d'Alembert. His foreign acquaintances included David Hume, Adam Smith, and Benjamin Franklin. Holbach was an atheist, a materialist, and a severe critic of religion, absolute monarchy, and feudalism. To avoid the personal danger that would result from being known as the proponent of such views, Holbach had his books published in Holland under a false name and then had them smuggled back into France. He died in Paris in 1789.

Holbach's major works are *Christianity Unveiled; Being an Examination of the Principles and Effects of Christianity* (1761), *The System of Nature; or, Laws of the Moral and Physical World* (1770), and *Common Sense; or, Natural Ideas Opposed to Supernatural* (1772).

Our selection is from Part I, Chapter 11, of *The System of Nature*, entitled "The System of Human Freedom." Holbach argues that human beings are wholly physical entities and therefore wholly subject to the laws of nature. We have a will (which Holbach views as a modification of the brain), but our will is not free because it necessarily seeks our well-being and self-preservation. Forces independent of us create various desires in us. In any situation, we always act in accordance with our strongest desire—namely, the desire for what we think is most advantageous to us. To use one of Holbach's examples, suppose I am extremely thirsty and come upon a fountain of water but know that the water is poisoned. If I refrain from drinking, it is because of the strength of my desire to avoid being poisoned; if I drink, it is because my present desire for water overpowers the foreseen harm from the poison. Whether I drink or refrain from drinking, my action "is equally necessary; it is the effect of the motive that is more powerful and acts more strongly on the will."

In the latter part of our reading, Holbach responds to several arguments commonly raised by defenders of free will. For example, some argue that we must be free because we deliberate among alternatives. Holbach responds that deliberation is simply the process of stopping to calculate which alternative would be most advantageous. Others try to demonstrate their freedom by performing a simple action such as moving their hand. Holbach replies that the moving of their hand is simply the necessary result of their desire to prove that they are free. Holbach concludes that every human action, just like every other occurrence in nature, "is a necessary consequence of causes, visible or concealed, that are forced to act according to their proper natures."

[INTRODUCTION]

. . . Human beings are [wholly] physical entities. However one considers them, they are bound to universal nature and are subject to the necessary and immutable laws that nature imposes on all the beings it includes, according to the peculiar essence or properties it gives each being, without consulting them. Our life is a line that nature commands us to trace on the face of the earth, and we can never deviate from this line, even for a moment. We are born without our assent, our organization does not depend on us, our ideas come to us involuntarily, our habits are in the power of those who cause us to acquire them, and we are continually changed by causes, both visible and hidden, that necessarily regulate the way we exist, think, and act. We are good or bad, happy or unhappy, wise or foolish, reasonable or unreasonable, without our will having anything to do with these different states. Yet, despite the shackles that constantly bind us, we claim that we are free—that we determine our actions and destiny, independently of the causes that move us. . . .

[THE MECHANISM OF DETERMINISM]

If it is our actual essence to tend to our well-being and to seek self-preservation; if all the movements of our human machine follow necessarily from this primitive impulse; if pain turns us aside from what we should avoid; if pleasure tells us what we should seek; then it is our essence to love what causes agreeable sensations or leads us to expect them, and to hate what causes the opposite sensations or leads us fear that they will occur. We are necessarily attracted, and our will is necessarily determined, by objects we judge useful; and we are necessarily repelled by objects we judge harmful to our permanent or momentary way of existing. It is only by the aid of experience that we acquire the ability to know what we should love or fear. Are our organs sound? If so, our experiences will be true; we will have reason, prudence, and foresight; we will anticipate effects that lie in the distant future; and we will know that sometimes what we judge to be good can become bad through its necessary or probable consequences, and that what we know to be momentarily bad can by its results attain for us a solid and lasting good. Thus it is experience that enables us to know that the amputation of a limb will cause a painful sensation; and therefore we necessarily fear this operation and want to avoid the pain. But if experience has shown us that the momentary pain caused by the operation can save our life, then, since we cherish our preservation, we necessarily submit to this momentary pain in light of the good that outweighs it.

The will . . . is a modification of the brain that disposes the brain to action or prepares it to put into play the organs that it can move. This will is necessarily determined by the good or bad, agreeable or disagreeable, qualities of the object or of the motive that acts on our senses, or the idea of it that remains with us and is supplied by our memory. Consequently, we act necessarily; our action is the result of the impulse that we have received from the motive, the object, or the idea that has modified our brain or disposed our will. When we do not act on this impulse, it is because some new cause, motive, or idea occurs, which modifies our brain in a different manner, gives it a new impulse, a new will—and the will either acts according to this new impulse or it suspends action. Thus, the sight of an agreeable object, or the idea of it, determines our will to action in order to attain this object. But a new object or a new idea can destroy the effect of the initial one and prevent us from acting to attain the object. This is how reflection, experience, and reason necessarily stop or suspend the actions of our will; otherwise our will would necessarily follow the initial impulses that began carrying it toward a desirable object. In all this, we always act according to necessary laws.

[ANSWERS TO OBJECTIONS]

When I am tormented by a strong thirst and create an idea of, or actually perceive, a fountain whose pure waters can quench my thirst, am I master of desiring or not desiring the object that can satisfy such an acute need in my present state? Undoubtedly everyone would agree that is impossible for me not to want to satisfy my thirst. But someone will say, "If someone tells you at that moment that the water you desire is poisoned, you will abstain from drinking it, despite your thirst." And this person would falsely conclude that this shows that I am free. In fact, however, just as thirst necessarily was determining me to drink before I knew that the water had been poisoned, in the same way, this new discovery necessarily determines me not to drink. The desire for self-preservation destroyed or suspended the initial impulse that thirst was imparting to my will. The second motive became stronger than the first; the fear of death necessarily outweighed the painful sensation caused by thirst. "But," someone will say, "if the thirst is very strong, an imprudent person would risk drinking the poisoned water, without regard for the danger." In this case the initial impulse will prevail and will necessarily make the person act, since it will be stronger than the later impulse. Nevertheless, in each case—drinking the water or not drinking it—the action is equally necessary; it is the effect of the motive that is more powerful and acts more strongly on the will.

This example can serve to explain all the phenomena of the will. This will, or rather the brain, is like a ball that, although it has received an impulse that drives it in a straight line, is moved off course as soon as a force greater than the initial one makes it change direction. The person who drinks water that he has been told is poisoned seems to be insane; but the actions of the insane are as necessary as those of the most prudent individuals. The motives that determine the hedonist and the sensualist to risk their health are as powerful, and resulting actions are as necessary, as those that determine wise persons to manage their actions. "But," one will insist, "the sensualist can be led to change his conduct." But this does not mean that he is free; it means only that there are motives sufficiently powerful to destroy the effect of those that previously acted on him. These new motives determine his will to his new conduct as necessarily as the previous motives determined his previous conduct.

We are said to *deliberate* when the action of the will is suspended. This happens when two opposite motives act alternately on us. To deliberate is to love and hate alternately—to be successively attracted and repelled, to be moved sometimes by one motive and sometimes by another. We deliberate only when we do not sufficiently understand the quality of the objects that move us, or when experience has not sufficiently taught us the effects, more or less distant, that our actions will have on us. I want to go outside to get some fresh air, but the weather is uncertain; hence I deliberate, weighing the various motives that press alternately on my will, to go out or not to go out. In the end I am determined by the most probable motive, which takes me from indecision and necessarily draws my will either to go outside or to remain inside. This motive is always the present or future advantage that I find in the action I decide to take.

Our will is often suspended between two objects, the presence or the ideas of which move us alternately. Before acting, we wait until we have contemplated the objects, or the ideas they have left in our brain, that call us to different actions. We then compare these objects or these ideas. But even when we are deliberating, comparing the alternatives of love and hate that follow each other (sometimes with extreme rapidity), we are not free for a single moment; for the good or the evil that we find successively in the objects are the necessitating motives of these momentary acts of the will, these rapid movements of love and fear, that we experience as long as our uncertainty continues. From this it is obvious that deliberation is necessary, that uncertainty is necessary, and that whatever choice we make after deliberation will always necessarily be the one that we have judged, rightly or wrongly, to be probably the most advantageous to us. . . .

Choice in no way proves human freedom. A person deliberates only when he does not yet know which object to choose, among the many that move him; he is then in a quandary that does not end that until his will is determined by idea of the greatest advantage that he believes he will find in the object he chooses or the action he undertakes. So we see that his choice is necessary, because he would not decide on an object or an action unless he believed that he would find some advantage in it. For a person to act freely, he would have to be able to will or choose his motives, or to prevent those motives from acting on his will. Since action is always the effect of our will once is it determined, and since our will can be determined only by a motive that is not in our power, it follows that we are never the master of the determinations of our own will, and that consequently we never act freely. Some have believed that we are free because we have a will and the power to choose, but these people have paid attention to the fact that our will is moved by causes independent of us. . . .

Some have believed that human beings are free, because they imagine that the soul can at will call to mind ideas that sometimes suffice to curb the most passionate desires. Thus, the idea of a distant evil sometimes prevents us from yielding to a present and actual good: A remembrance (which is an imperceptible, slight modification of our brain) destroys at each moment the real objects that act on our will. But we are not master of recalling our ideas at will: These ideas associate independently of us; they are arranged in our brain without our knowledge and despite us, making an impression more or less profound. Our memory itself depends on our organization, and its fidelity depends on the habitual or momentary state in which we find ourselves. When our will is strongly determined to some object or idea that rouses a very lively passion in us, those objects or ideas that would be able to stop our action disappear from our mind. We shut our eyes to the present dangers that threaten us, the ideas of which should restrain us. We march forward headlong toward the object that draws us. Reflection has no effect on us, and we see nothing but the object of our desires. The salutary ideas that would be able to stop us are no longer present, or they become present too weakly or too late to prevent us from acting. Such is the case with all those who, blinded by some strong passion, are not in a state to recall to themselves those motives, the ideas of which would alone would be able to restrain them. The trouble they are in prevents them from judging sanely, from foreseeing the consequences of their actions, from applying their experience, and from using their reason. But these operations suppose a soundness in the manner of associating ideas, and the brain of these people can no more do this, because of the momentary delirium it suffers, than their hand can write when they are doing vigorous exercise.

Our ways of thinking are necessarily determined by our ways of being; they therefore depend on our natural organization and the modification that our machine receives independently of our will. From this we are forced to conclude that our thoughts, our reflections, and the ways we see, feel, judge, and combine ideas are neither voluntary nor free. In short, our soul is master neither of the movements excited in it, nor of representing to itself the images or ideas that would be needed to counterbalance the impulses it receives. This is why we cease to reason when we are in passion: It is as impossible to hear reason, at that time, as when we are in ecstasy or drunk. The wicked are never more than people drunk or delirious; if they reason, it is only when tranquillity is reestablished in their machine, and then the tardy ideas that present themselves to their mind allow them to see the consequence of their actions—and this brings on them the disturbance we call *shame, regret, remorse.* . . .

In short, the actions of human beings are never free; their actions are always the necessary consequence of their temperament, their received ideas, their true or false notions of happiness, and their opinions strengthened by example, education, and daily experience. We see so many crimes in the world only because everything conspires to make human beings vicious and criminal: their religions, their governments, their education, and the examples they see—all these drive them irresistibly to evil. In such cases, morality preaches virtue to them in vain; for virtue would be simply a painful sacrifice of happiness in societies where crimes are continually crowned, esteemed, and rewarded, and where the most hideous disorders are punished only when those who commit them are too weak to have the right to do so with impunity. Such societies punish members of the lower classes for very excesses that they respect in members of the upper classes; and they often have the injustice to sentence to death those were made criminal by the public prejudices that they themselves uphold.

A human being, therefore, is not free at any moment in his life; he is necessarily guided at each step by the advantages—real or fictitious—that he attaches to the objects that rouse his passions. These passions are necessary in a being that tends constantly toward happiness. The energy of these passions is necessary, because it depends on his temperament; a human being's temperament is necessary, because it depends on the physical elements that enter into his composition; the modifications of his temperament are necessary, because they are the infallible and inevitable consequences of the way that physical and moral beings continually act on him.

Despite these clear proofs of the lack of human freedom, some may still insist that this freedom exists. Someone will tell us that if he proposes to move or not to move his hand (actions in the category called "indifferent"),[1] he evidently appears to be master of his choice, and this proves that he is free. My reply is that this example of a person performing an action that he resolves to perform does not prove his freedom: His desire to exhibit his freedom, roused by the dispute, has become a necessary motive that decides his will for moving or not moving his hand. What misleads him, or persuades him that he is free in this case, is that he does not discern the true motive that causes him to act—namely, the desire to convince me. If in the heat of the dispute he insists and asks, "Am I not the master of throwing myself out the window?," I will say no and tell him that, as long as he preserves his reason, there is no probability that the desire to prove to me his freedom will become a motive sufficiently strong to cause him to sacrifice his own life. If my adversary, despite this, would throw himself out the window in order to prove to me that he is free, I would not conclude that he acted freely in doing this, but that the strong force of his temperament led him to this folly. Insanity is a state that is based on the heat of the blood, not on the will. Fanatics and heroes face death as necessarily as cowards flee from it. . . .

CONCLUSION

When we say that a human being is not free, we are not comparing him to a body whose motion is caused by a simple impulse: He contains in himself causes inherent to his existence, and he is moved by an internal organ that has its own laws and is necessarily determined by ideas, by perceptions, and by sensations received from external objects. We do not know the mechanism of these sensations and perceptions or the way ideas are imprinted on our brain, because we cannot discern all these movements, or perceive the chain of operations in our soul, or perceive the motive[2] principle that acts in us. We therefore suppose that this motive principle is free. "Motive principle" means, literally, something that moves itself, that determines itself without a cause—or rather, a term that signifies that we do not know how or why it acts as it does. It is true that people say that the soul has an activity proper to itself, and I agree. But it is certain that this activity would never take place unless some motive or cause put it in a condition to act. At least no one will claim the soul can love or hate without having been moved, without knowing the objects, or without having some idea of the qualities of these objects. Gunpowder undoubtedly has an activity proper to

---

[1]*"indifferent"*: neither morally good nor morally evil. [D. C. ABEL]
[2]*motive*: causing motion. [D. C. ABEL]

itself, but this activity will never take place unless someone applies fire to it, which forces it to act.

It is the great complexity of our movements, the variety of our actions, and the multiplicity of causes that move us (whether simultaneously or successively without interruption) that persuade us that we are free. If all the movements of human beings were simple, if the causes that move us were distinct and not intermingled, and if our machine were less complicated, we would see that all our actions are necessary because we could go back at once to the cause that made us act. . . .

It is, then, because we do not go back to the causes that move us, and because we are unable to analyze and disentangle the complicated movements that occur in us, that we think we are free. It is only because of our ignorance that we have the deep, though illusory, feeling that we are free, and take this feeling as a striking proof of this supposed freedom. If only each person were willing to examine his own actions, and search out his true motives and discover how they are connected, he would remain convinced that the feeling that he has about his own freedom is a mental fabrication that experience must quickly destroy. . . .

From all that has been said in this chapter, it follows that no human being is free at any time during his existence. He is not master of his formation, for this comes from nature. He is not master of his ideas or the modifications of his brain, for these result from causes that, despite himself and without his knowledge, continually act on him. He is not master of loving or desiring what he finds lovable or desirable. He is not master of deliberating in situations in which he is uncertain of the effects that objects will produce on him. He is not master of choosing what he believes to be the most advantageous. He is not master of acting otherwise than he does at the moment when his will is determined by his choice. . . .

In both the physical world and the moral world, everything that happens is a necessary consequence of causes, visible or concealed, that are forced to act according to their proper natures. In a human being, [what we call] freedom is simply necessity contained inside himself.

The Dilemma of Determinism

William James

William James was born in New York City in 1842. As a youth he attended schools in England, France, Switzerland, and Germany. He also learned a great deal from his father (an energetic and unconventional scholar) and from extensive reading. He was interested in both science and art and decided to become a painter. When he was eighteen, he began to study painting, but soon realized that he did not have the talent to become a great artist. The following year he enrolled in the Lawrence Scientific School at Harvard University. In 1864 James transferred to the medical school. He took time out from his studies to accompany naturalist Louis Agassiz on a trip to the Amazon River. He later spent time studying experimental physiology in Germany. James received his medical degree from Harvard in 1869. He had long been in poor health, and he spent the next few years as a semi-invalid at his father's house. In 1873 he began teaching physiology at Harvard. Two years later he began teaching psychology, and four years after that he started teaching philosophy. Except for a two-year period spent recovering from serious illness, he continued teaching at Harvard until his retirement in 1907. James died in 1910 in Chocorua, New Hampshire.

James's principal works are *Principles of Psychology* (1890), *The Will to Believe and Other Essays in Popular Philosophy* (1897), *The Varieties of Religious Experience* (1902), *Pragmatism: A New Name for Some Old Ways of Thinking* (1907), and *A Pluralistic Universe* (1909).

Our reading is from "The Dilemma of Determinism," a lecture James gave in 1884 to students of the Harvard Divinity School. *Determinism,* James explains, is the doctrine that everything happening in the future is already completely predetermined by the way things are now: "Those parts of the universe already laid down absolutely appoint and decree what the other parts shall be." *Indeterminism,* by contrast, allows some "loose play" among the parts of the universe, so that the future holds more than one possibility. According to determinism, the only future that is possible is the one that actually happens; whatever happens, happens by necessity. According to indeterminism, alternative futures are possible; things could have happened differently from the way they did.

James contends that our decision whether to accept determinism or indeterminism will be based on our "postulates of rationality"—whether we think the world is more rational if it is governed by necessity or if it contains multiple possibilities. Determinists are people who think that if chance has a role in the world (that is, if some events are not the product of necessity), the world becomes chaotic and unintelligible. James maintains, however, that an event that happens by chance is just as intelligible as one that happens by necessity. James goes on to argue that the existence of "judgments of regret" (judgments that something should have been or should now be otherwise than it was or now is) makes indeterminism more plausible than determinism. If determinists admit the rationality of judgments of regret, they commit themselves to the pessimistic view that the world, with all its evils, could not be better than it is. If they want to be optimistic, they have to view all judgments of regret as irrational. The only way out of this dilemma is to accept indeterminism.

[INTRODUCTION]

. . . A common opinion prevails that the juice has ages ago been pressed out of the free will controversy, and that no new champion can do more than warm up stale arguments which everyone has heard. This is a radical mistake. I know of no subject less worn out, or in which inventive genius has a better chance of breaking open new ground—not, perhaps, of forcing a conclusion or of coercing assent, but of deepening our consciousness of *what* the issue between the two parties really is, our sense of what hidden implications the ideas of fate and of free will contain. . . .

To begin, then, I must suppose [that] you [are] acquainted with all the usual arguments on the subject. I cannot stop to take up the arguments from causation, from statistics, from the certainty with which we can foretell each other's conduct, from the fixity of character, and all the rest. But there are two *words* which encumber these classical arguments usually, and which we must immediately dispose of, if we are to make any progress. One is the eulogistic word *freedom*, and the other is the opprobrious word *chance*. The word "chance" I wish to keep, but I wish to get rid of the word "freedom." Its eulogistic associations have so far overshadowed all the rest of its meaning that both parties claim the sole right to use it, and determinists today insist that they alone are freedom's champions. Old-fashioned determinism was what we may call *hard* determinism. It did not shrink from such words as fatality, bondage of the will, necessitation, and the like. Nowadays we have a *soft* determinism[1] which abhors harsh words, and, repudiating fatality, necessity, and even determinism, says that its real name is freedom; for freedom is only necessity understood, and bondage to the highest is identical with true freedom. . . .

[DETERMINISM AND INDETERMINISM]

Now, this is all a quagmire of evasion under which the real issue of fact has got entirely smothered up. Freedom in all these senses presents simply no problem at all. No matter what the soft determinist means by it—whether he means acting without external constraint, whether he means acting rightly, or whether he means acquiescing in the law of the whole—who cannot answer him that sometimes we are free and sometimes we are not? But there *is* a problem, an issue of fact and not of words, an issue of the most momentous importance, which is often decided without discussion in one sentence, nay, in one clause of a sentence, by those very writers who spin out whole chapters in their efforts to show what "true" freedom is; and that is the question of determinism, about which we are to talk tonight.

Fortunately, no ambiguities hang about this word or about its opposite, indeterminism. Both designate an outward way in which things may happen,

---

[1] *soft determinism:* the view that although all actions are determined by preceding causes, actions determined by certain kinds of *internal* causes are free and we are morally responsible for these actions. As James explains, he calls this form of determinism "soft" because it backs away from the harsh implications of determinism as ordinarily understood. The harsh implications of ordinary ("hard") determinism include the denial of free will and moral responsibility. [D. C. ABEL]

and their cold and mathematical sound has no sentimental associations that can bribe our partiality either way in advance. Now, evidence of an external kind to decide between determinism and indeterminism is . . . strictly impossible to find. Let us look at the difference between them and see for ourselves. What does determinism profess?

It professes that those parts of the universe already laid down absolutely appoint and decree what the other parts shall be. The future has no ambiguous possibilities hidden in its womb: The part we call the present is compatible with only one totality. Any other future complement than the one fixed from eternity is impossible. The whole is in each and every part, and welds it with the rest into an absolute unity, an iron block, in which there can be no equivocation or shadow of turning.

> With Earth's first Clay They did the Last Man knead,
> And there of the Last Harvest sow'd the Seed:
>   And the first Morning of Creation wrote
> What the Last Dawn of Reckoning shall read.[2]

Indeterminism, on the contrary, says that the parts have a certain amount of loose play on each other, so that the laying down of one of them does not necessarily determine what the others shall be. It admits that possibilities may be in excess of actualities, and that things not yet revealed to our knowledge may really in themselves be ambiguous. Of two alternative futures we now conceive, both now may be really possible; and the one only become impossible at the very moment when the other excludes it by becoming real itself. Indeterminism thus denies the world to be one unbroken, unbending unit of fact. It says there is a certain ultimate pluralism in it; and, so saying, it corroborates our ordinary unsophisticated view of things. To that view, actualities seem to float in a wider sea of possibilities from out of which they are chosen; and, *somewhere*, indeterminism says such possibilities exist, and form a part of truth.

Determinism, on the contrary, says they exist *nowhere*, and that necessity on the one hand and impossibility on the other are the sole categories of truth. Possibilities that fail to get realized are, for determinism, pure illusions: They never were possibilities at all. There is nothing inchoate, it says, about this universe of ours; all that was or is or shall be actual in it, having been from eternity necessarily and virtually there. The cloud of alternatives [that] our minds escort this mass of actuality withal[3] is a cloud of sheer deceptions, to which "impossibilities" is the only name that rightfully belongs.

The issue, it will be seen, is a perfectly sharp one, which no eulogistic terminology can smear over or wipe out. The truth *must* lie with one side or the other, and its lying with one side makes the other false.

The question relates solely to the existence of possibilities, in the strict sense of the term, as things that *may*, but *need* not, be. Both sides admit that a volition, for instance, has occurred. The indeterminists say another volition might have

---

[2]Omar Khayyám, *Rubáiyát*, trans. Edward Fitzgerald, Stanza 79. Omar Khayyám (about 1048–1122) was a Persian poet and astronomer. [D. C. ABEL]
[3]*withal:* with. [D. C. ABEL]

occurred in its place; the determinists swear that nothing could possibly have occurred in its place. Now can *science* be called in to tell us which of these two point-blank contradictors of each other is right? Science professes to draw no conclusions but such as are based on matters of fact, things that have actually happened. But how can any amount of assurance that anything actually happened give us the least grain of information as to whether another thing might or might not have happened in its place? Facts can only prove facts. With things that are possibilities and not facts, they have no concern. If we have no other evidence than the evidence of existing facts, the possibility-question must remain a mystery never to be cleared up.

And the truth is that facts practically have hardly anything to do with making us either determinists or indeterminists. Sure enough, we make a flourish of quoting facts this way or that; and, if we are determinists, we talk about the infallibility with which we can predict each other's conduct, while, if we are indeterminists, we lay great stress on the fact that it is just because we cannot foretell each other's conduct, either in war or statecraft or in any of the great and small intrigues and businesses of men, that life is so intensely anxious and hazardous a game. But who does not see the wretched insufficiency of this so-called objective testimony on both sides? What fills up the gaps in our minds is something not objective, not external. What divides us into possibility men and anti-possibility men is different faiths or postulates—postulates of rationality. To this man the world seems more rational with possibilities in it, to that man more rational with possibilities excluded. And talk as we will about having to yield to evidence, what makes us monists or pluralists,[4] determinists or indeterminists, is at bottom always some sentiment like this.

[DETERMINISM AND CHANCE]

The stronghold of the deterministic sentiment is the antipathy to the idea of chance. As soon as we begin to talk indeterminism to our friends, we find a number of them shaking their heads. This notion of alternative possibility, they say, this admission that any one of several things may come to pass, is, after all, only a roundabout name for *chance;* and chance is something the notion of which no sane mind can for an instant tolerate in the world. What is it, they ask, but barefaced crazy unreason, the negation of intelligibility and law? And, if the slightest particle of it exist anywhere, what is to prevent the whole fabric from falling together, the stars from going out, and chaos from recommencing her topsy-turvy reign?

Remarks of this sort about chance are apt to put an end to discussion about as quickly as anything one can find. I told you a short while ago that "chance" was a word I wished to keep and use. Let us then examine exactly what it means, and see whether it ought to be such a terrible bugbear to us. I fancy that squeezing the thistle boldly will rob it of its sting.

---

[4]*Monists* hold that there is just one kind of ultimate reality; *pluralists* hold that there is more than one kind of ultimate reality. [D. C. ABEL]

The sting of the word "chance" seems to lie in the assumption that it means something positive, and that, if anything happens by chance, it must needs[5] be something of an intrinsically irrational and preposterous sort. Now, chance means nothing of the kind. It is a purely negative and relative term, giving us no information about that of which it is predicated, except that it happens to be disconnected with something else—not controlled, secured, or necessitated by other things in advance of its own actual presence. As this point is the most subtle point of the whole lecture, and at the same time the point on which all the rest hinges, I want to beg you to pay special attention to it. What I say is that it tells us nothing about what a thing may be in itself to call it chance. It may be a bad thing, it may be a good thing. It may be lucidity, transparency, fitness incarnate, matching the whole system of other things, when it has once befallen, in an unimaginably perfect way. All you mean by calling it chance is that this is not *guaranteed*, that it may also fall out otherwise. For the system of other things has no positive hold on the chance thing. Its origin is in a certain fashion negative: It escapes, and says "Hands off!"—coming, when it comes, as a free gift or not at all. . . .

Nevertheless, many people talk as if the minutest dose of disconnectedness of one part with another, the smallest modicum of independence, the faintest tremor of ambiguity about the future, for example, would ruin everything, and turn this goodly universe into a sort of insane sand-heap or nulliverse, no universe at all. Since future human volitions are as a matter of fact the only ambiguous things we are tempted to believe in, let us stop for a moment to make ourselves sure whether their independent and accidental character need be fraught with such direful consequences to the universe as these.

What is meant by saying that my choice of which way to walk home after the lecture is ambiguous and matter of chance as far as the present moment is concerned? It means that both Divinity Avenue and Oxford Street are called; but that only one, and that one *either* one, shall be chosen.[6] Now, I ask you seriously to suppose that this ambiguity of my choice is real and then to make the impossible hypothesis that the choice is made twice over, and each time falls on a different street. In other words, imagine that I first walk through Divinity Avenue, and then imagine that the powers governing the universe annihilate ten minutes of time with all that it contained, and set me back at the door of this hall just as I was before the choice was made. Imagine then that, everything else being the same, I now make a different choice and traverse Oxford Street. You, as passive spectators, look on and see the two alternative universes—one of them with me walking through Divinity Avenue in it, the other with the same me walking through Oxford Street. Now if you are determinists you believe one of these universes to have been from eternity impossible: You believe it to have been impossible because of the intrinsic irrationality or accidentality somewhere involved in it. But, looking outwardly at these universes,

---

[5]*needs:* necessarily. [D. C. ABEL]
[6]James's terms "called" and "chosen" allude to the saying of Jesus, "Many are called, but few are chosen" (Matthew 22:14). [D. C. ABEL]

can you say which is the impossible and accidental one, and which the rational and necessary one? I doubt if the most ironclad determinist among you could have the slightest glimmer of light on this point. In other words, either universe *after the fact* and once there would, to our means of observation and understanding, appear just as rational as the other. There would be absolutely no criterion by which we might judge one necessary and the other matter of chance. Suppose now we relieve the gods of their hypothetical task and assume my choice, once made, to be made forever. I go through Divinity Avenue for good and all. If, as good determinists, you now begin to affirm, what all good determinists punctually do affirm, that in the nature of things I *couldn't* have gone through Oxford Street—had I done so it would have been chance, irrationality, insanity, a horrid gap in nature—I simply call your attention to this, that your affirmation is what the Germans call a *Machtspruch*,[7] a mere conception fulminated as a dogma and based on no insight into details. Before my choice, either street seemed as natural to you as to me. Had I happened to take Oxford Street, Divinity Avenue would have figured in your philosophy as the gap in nature, and you would have so proclaimed it with the best of deterministic consciences.

But what a hollow outcry, then, is this against a chance which, if it were present to us, we could by no sensible[8] empirical character whatever distinguish from a rational necessity. . . .

And this at last brings us within sight of our subject. We have seen what determinism means: We have seen that indeterminism is rightly described as meaning chance; and we have seen that chance, the very name of which we are urged to shrink from, as from a metaphysical[9] pestilence, means only the negative fact that no one part of the world can claim to control absolutely the destinies of the whole. But although, in discussing the word "chance," I may at moments have seemed to be arguing for its real existence, I have not meant to do so yet. We have not yet ascertained whether this *is* a world of chance or not. At most, we have agreed that it *seems* so. And I now repeat what I said at the outset, that from any strict theoretical point of view the question is insoluble. To deepen our theoretic sense of the *difference* between a world with chances in it and a deterministic world is the most I can hope to do. And this I may now at last begin upon, after all our tedious clearing of the way.

[IMPLICATIONS OF DETERMINISM]

I wish first of all to show you just what the notion that this is a deterministic world implies. The implications I call your attention to are all bound up with the fact that it is a world in which we constantly have to make what I shall, with your permission, call judgments of regret. Hardly an hour passes in which we

---

[7]*Machtspruch:* an authoritative decree (literally, in German, "power saying"). [D. C. ABEL]
[8]*sensible:* able to be sensed. [D. C. ABEL]
[9]*metaphysical:* relating to *metaphysics,* the study of the nature and kinds of reality. [D. C. ABEL]

do not wish that something might be otherwise; and happy indeed are those of us whose hearts have never echoed the wish of Omar Khayyám,

> That we might clasp ere closed the Book of Fate,
>   And make The Writer on a fairer leaf
> Inscribe our names, or quite obliterate! . . .
>
> Ah Love! could you and I with Fate conspire
> To grasp this sorry Scheme of Things entire,
>   Would we not shatter it to bits—and then
> Remold it nearer to the Heart's Desire![10]

Now it is undeniable that most of these regrets are foolish and quite on a par in point of philosophic value with the criticisms on the universe of that friend of our infancy, the hero of the fable "The Atheist and the Acorn"—

> Fool! had that bough a pumpkin bore,
> Thy whimsies would have worked no more (and so on).[11]

Even from the point of view of our own ends, we should probably make a botch of remodeling the universe. How much more then from the point of view of ends we cannot see! Wise men therefore regret as little as they can. But still some regrets are pretty obstinate and hard to stifle—regrets for acts of wanton cruelty or treachery, for example, whether performed by others or by ourselves. Hardly anyone can remain *entirely* optimistic after reading the confession of the murderer at Brockton the other day—how, to get rid of the wife whose continued existence bored him, he inveigled her into a desert[12] spot, shot her four times, and then, as she lay on the ground and said to him "You didn't do it on purpose, did you, dear?," replied "No, I didn't do it on purpose" as he raised a rock and smashed her skull. Such an occurrence, with the mild sentence and self-satisfaction of the prisoner, is a field for a crop of regrets, which one need not take up in detail. We feel that, although a perfect mechanical fit to the rest of the universe, it is a bad *moral* fit, and that something else would *really* have been better in its place.

Now for the deterministic philosophy, the murder, the sentence, and the prisoner's optimism were all necessary from eternity; and nothing else for a moment had a ghost of a chance of being put into their place. To admit such a chance, the determinists tell us, would be to make a suicide of reason, so we must steel our hearts against the thought. And here our plot thickens, for we see the first of those difficult implications of determinism and monism which it is my purpose to make you feel. If this Brockton murder was called for by the rest of the universe, if it had to come at its preappointed hour, and if nothing else would have been consistent with the sense of the whole, what are we to think of the universe? Are we stubbornly to stick to our judgment of regret, and say, though it *couldn't* be, yet it *would* have been a better universe with something

---

[10]Omar Khayyám, *Rubáiyát*, Stanza 106, lines 2–4; Stanza 108. [D. C. ABEL]

[11]Anne Finch, Countess of Winchilsea, "The Atheist and the Acorn." Finch (1661–1720) was an English poet. [D. C. ABEL]

[12]*desert:* desolate. [D. C. ABEL]

different from this Brockton murder in it? That, of course, seems the natural and spontaneous thing for us to do. And yet it is nothing short of deliberately espousing a kind of pessimism. The judgment of regret calls the murder bad. Calling a thing bad means, if it means anything at all, that the thing ought *not to be*, that something else ought to be in its stead. Determinism, in denying that anything else *can* be in its stead, virtually defines the universe as a place in which what ought to be is impossible—in other words, as an organism whose constitution is afflicted with an incurable taint, an irremediable flaw. . . . Regret for the murder must transform itself, if we are determinists and wise, into a larger regret. It is absurd to regret the murder alone. Other things being what they are, *it* could not be different. What we should regret is that whole frame of things of which the murder is one member. I see no escape whatever from this pessimistic conclusion, if, being determinists, our judgment of regret is to be allowed to stand at all.

The only deterministic escape from pessimism is *everywhere* to abandon the judgment of regret. That this can be done, history shows to be not impossible. The devil, *quoad existentiam*,[13] may be good. That is, although he be a *principle* of evil, yet the universe with such a principle in it may practically be a better universe than it could have been without. On every hand, in a small way, we find that a certain amount of evil is a condition by which a higher form of good is bought. There is nothing to prevent anybody from generalizing this view, and trusting that if we could but see things in the largest of all ways, even such matters as this Brockton murder would appear to be paid for by the uses that follow in their train. An optimism *quand même*,[14] a systematic and infatuated optimism like that ridiculed by Voltaire[15] in his *Candide,* is one of the possible ideal ways in which a man may train himself to look on life. Bereft of dogmatic hardness and lit up with the expression of a tender and pathetic hope, such an optimism has been the grace of some of the most religious characters that ever lived.

> Throb thine with Nature's throbbing breast,
> And all is clear from east to west.[16]

Even cruelty and treachery may be among the absolutely blessed fruits of time, and to quarrel with any of their details may be blasphemy. The only real blasphemy, in short, may be that pessimistic temper of the soul which lets it take pleasure in such things as regrets, remorse, and grief.

Thus, our deterministic pessimism may become a deterministic optimism at the price of extinguishing our judgments of regret.

But does not this immediately bring us into a curious logical predicament? Our determinism leads us to call our judgments of regret wrong, because they are pessimistic in implying that what is impossible yet ought to be. But how then about the judgments of regret themselves? If they are

---

[13]*quoad existentiam:* (Latin) as far as existence is concerned. [D. C. ABEL]
[14]*quand même:* (French) despite all this. [D. C. ABEL]
[15]Francois-Marie Aroute de Voltaire (1694–1778) was a French writer. [D. C. ABEL]
[16]Ralph Waldo Emerson, "Threnody," lines 207–208. Emerson (1803–1882) was an American essayist and poet. [D. C. ABEL]

wrong, other judgments—judgments of approval presumably—ought to be in their place. But, as they are necessitated, nothing else *can* be in their place; and the universe is just what it was before—namely, a place in which what ought to be appears impossible. We have got one foot out of the pessimistic bog, but the other one sinks all the deeper. We have rescued our actions from the bonds of evil, but our judgments are now held fast. When murders and treacheries cease to be sins, regrets are errors. The theoretic and the active life thus play a kind of see-saw with each other on the ground of evil. The rise of either sends the other down. Murder and treachery can't be good without regret being bad; regret can't be good without treachery and murder being bad. Both, however, are supposed to have been foredoomed, so *something* must be bad in the world. It must be a place of which either sin or error forms a necessary part. . . .

[CONCLUSION]

. . . The only consistent way of representing . . . a world whose parts may affect each other through their conduct being either good or bad is the indeterministic way. What interest, zest, or excitement can there be in achieving the right way, unless we are enabled to feel that the wrong way is also a possible and a natural way—nay, more, a menacing and an imminent way? And what sense can there be in condemning ourselves for taking the wrong way, unless we need have done nothing of the sort, unless the right way was open to us as well? I cannot understand the willingness to act, no matter how we feel, without the belief that acts are really good and bad. I cannot understand the belief that an act is bad, without regret at its happening. I cannot understand regret without the admission of real, genuine possibilities in the world. Only *then* is it other than a mockery to feel, after we have failed to do our best, that an irreparable opportunity is gone from the universe, the loss of which it must forever after mourn. . . .

The world is enigmatical enough in all conscience, whatever theory we may take up toward it. The indeterminism I defend, the free will theory of popular sense based on the judgment of regret, represents that world as vulnerable and liable to be injured by certain of its parts if they act wrong. And it represents their acting wrong as a matter of possibility or accident, neither inevitable nor yet to be infallibly warded off. In all this, it is a theory devoid either of transparency or of stability. It gives us a pluralistic, restless universe, in which no single point of view can ever take in the whole scene; and, to a mind possessed of the love of unity at any cost, it will, no doubt, remain forever inacceptable. A friend with such a mind once told me that the thought of my universe made him sick, like the sight of the horrible motion of a mass of maggots in their carrion bed.

But while I freely admit that the pluralism and the restlessness are repugnant and irrational in a certain way, I find that every alternative to them is irrational in a deeper way. The indeterminism with its maggots, if you please to speak so about it, offends only the native absolutism of my intellect—an absolutism which, after all, perhaps, deserves to be snubbed and kept in check. But the determinism with its necessary carrion, to continue the figure of speech, and with no possible maggots to eat the latter up, violates my sense of moral reality through and through. When, for example, I imagine such carrion as the Brockton murder, I cannot conceive it as an act by which the universe as a Whole logically and necessarily expresses its nature, without shrinking from complicity with such a Whole. And I deliberately refuse to keep on terms of loyalty with the universe by saying blankly that the murder, since it does flow from the nature of the Whole, is *not* carrion. There are *some* instinctive reactions that I, for one, will not tamper with. . . .

Make as great an uproar about chance as you please, I know that chance means pluralism and nothing more. If some of the members of the pluralism are bad, the philosophy of pluralism, whatever broad views it may deny me, permits me, at least, to turn to the other members with a clean breast of affection and an unsophisticated moral sense. And if I still wish to think of the world as a totality, it lets me feel that a world with a *chance* in it of being altogether good, even if the chance never come to pass, is better than a world with no such chance at all. That "chance" whose very notion I am exhorted and conjured to banish from my view of the future as the suicide of reason concerning it, that chance is—what? Just this—the chance that in moral respects the future may be other and better than the past has been. This is the only chance we have any motive for supposing to exist. Shame, rather, on its repudiation and its denial! For its presence is the salt that keeps the world sweet, the air that fills its lungs.

The Problem of Morals

W. T. Stace

W. T. Stace was born in London in 1886. He received his initial education in England and Scotland and then went to Ireland, where he enrolled in Trinity College in Dublin. He was awarded his bachelor's degree in philosophy from Trinity in 1908. He had planned to become a cleric in the Anglican Church but became skeptical of religion and joined the British Civil Service instead. In 1910 Stace began working for the Civil Service in Ceylon (now Sri Lanka), holding various positions—including those of district judge and mayor of Colombo, the capital city. In 1929 he was awarded an honorary doctor of letters degree by Trinity College. In 1932, after serving 22 years in Ceylon, Stace accepted an appointment on the philosophy faculty at Princeton University, where he remained until his retirement in 1955. He died in Cambridge, Massachusetts, in 1967.

Stace's main works are *The Philosophy of Hegel* (1924), *The Theory of Knowledge and Existence* (1932), *The Concept of Morals* (1937), *The Destiny of Western Man* (1942), *Religion and the Modern Mind* (1952), *Time and Eternity* (1952), and *Mysticism and Philosophy* (1960).

Our selection is from the first part of Chapter 11 of *Religion and the Modern Mind*, "The Problem of Morals." Stace explains that since moral rules would be meaningless if we have no freedom to obey or disobey them, a discussion of free will should precede the inquiry into morality. The first part of "The Problem of Morals," consequently, is devoted to the topic of free will. Stace argues here that the longstanding dispute about whether we have free will does not concern a real problem but merely a verbal one—a problem "due to nothing but a confusion about the meanings of words." Philosophers on both sides of the dispute have assumed that "free will" means "indeterminism"—that an action done freely is an action not determined by causes. According to Stace, this definition of free will is incorrect and produces a false dichotomy between freedom and determinism.

Stace holds that the criterion for deciding the correct meaning of a term is common usage. To discover the correct meaning of "free will," Stace presents several examples of ordinary conversations in which people state whether an action they performed was done of their own free will. Some actions are described as free, others as unfree. According to Stace, what distinguishes the two kinds of actions is not *whether* they are determined by a cause, but *what kind* of cause they have. Free actions are caused by the agent's internal psychological states; unfree actions are caused by external physical forces. This ordinary conception of free will is the correct one, and from this conception it is obvious that free will exists and that it is compatible with determinism. Stace goes on to argue that his theory that free actions are determined is compatible with moral responsibility and with the punishment of wrongdoers.

[INTRODUCTION]

. . . If there is no free will there can be no morality. Morality is concerned with what men ought and ought not to do. But if a man has no freedom to choose what he will do, if whatever he does is done under compulsion, then it does not make sense to tell him that he ought not to have done what he did and that he ought to do something different. All moral precepts would in such case be meaningless. Also, if he acts always under compulsion, how can he be held morally responsible for his actions? How can he, for example, be punished for what he could not help doing?

It is to be observed that those learned professors of philosophy or psychology who deny the existence of free will do so only in their professional moments and in their studies and lecture rooms. For when it comes to doing anything practical, even of the most trivial kind, they invariably behave as if they and others were free. They inquire from you at dinner whether you will choose this dish or that dish. They will ask a child why he told a lie, and will punish him for not having chosen the way of truthfulness. All of which is inconsistent with a disbelief in free will. This should cause us to suspect that the problem is not a real one; and this, I believe, is the case. The dispute is merely verbal, and is due to nothing but a confusion about the meanings of words. It is what is now fashionably called a semantic problem.

How does a verbal dispute arise? Let us consider a case that, although it is absurd in the sense that no one would ever make the mistake that is involved in it, yet illustrates the principle that we shall have to use in the solution of the problem. Suppose that someone believed that the word "man" means a certain sort of five-legged animal—in short, that "five-legged animal" is the correct *definition* of man. He might then look around the world, and rightly observing that there are no five-legged animals in it, he might proceed to deny the existence of men. This preposterous conclusion would have been reached because he was using an incorrect definition of "man." All you would have to do to show him his mistake would be to give him the correct definition, or at least to show him that his definition was wrong. Both the problem and its solution would, of course, be entirely verbal. The problem of free will and its solution, I shall maintain, is verbal in exactly the same way. The problem has been created by the fact that learned men, especially philosophers, have assumed an incorrect definition of free will, and then finding that there is nothing in the world that answers to their definition, have denied its existence. As far as logic is concerned, their conclusion is just as absurd as that of the man who denies the existence of men. The only difference is that the mistake in the latter case is obvious and crude, while the mistake that the deniers of free will have made is rather subtle and difficult to detect.

[THE COMPATIBILITY OF DETERMINISM AND FREE WILL]

Throughout the modern period, until quite recently, it was assumed, both by the philosophers who denied free will and by those who defended it, that *determinism is inconsistent with free will*. If a man's actions were wholly determined by chains of causes stretching back into the remote past, so that they could be predicted beforehand by a mind that knew all the causes, it was assumed that they could not in that case be free. This implies that a certain definition of actions done from free will was assumed—namely, that they are actions *not* wholly determined by causes or predictable beforehand. Let us shorten this by saying that free will was defined as meaning indeterminism. This is the incorrect definition that has led to the denial of free will. As soon as we see what the true definition is, we shall find that the question whether the world is deterministic, as Newtonian[1] science implied, or in a measure indeterministic, as current physics teaches, is wholly irrelevant to the problem.

Of course there is a sense in which one can define a word arbitrarily in any way one pleases. But a definition may nevertheless be called correct or incorrect. It is correct if it accords with a *common usage* of the word defined. It is incorrect if it does not. And if you give an incorrect definition, absurd and untrue results are likely to follow. For instance, there is nothing to prevent you from arbitrarily defining a man as a five-legged animal, but this is incorrect in the sense that it does not accord with the ordinary meaning of the word. Also it has the absurd result of leading to a denial of the existence of men. This shows that *common usage is the criterion for deciding whether a definition is correct or not*. And this is the principle that I shall apply to free will. I shall show that indeterminism is not what is meant by the phrase "free will" *as it is commonly used*. And I shall attempt to discover the correct definition by inquiring how the phrase is used in ordinary conversation.

Here are a few samples of how the phrase might be used in ordinary conversation. It will be noticed that they include cases in which the question whether a man acted with free will is asked in order to determine whether he was morally and legally responsible for his acts.

> JONES: I once went without food for a week.
> SMITH: Did you do that of your own free will?
> JONES: No. I did it because I was lost in a desert and could find no food.

But suppose that the man who had fasted was Mahatma Gandhi.[2] The conversation might then have gone:

> GANDHI: I once fasted for a week.
> SMITH: Did you do that of your own free will?
> GANDHI: Yes. I did it because I wanted to compel the British government to give India its independence.

Take another case. Suppose that I had stolen some bread, but that I was as truthful as George Washington. Then, if I were charged with the crime in court, some exchange of the following sort might take place:

> JUDGE: Did you steal the bread of your own free will?
> STACE: Yes. I stole it because I was hungry.

Or in different circumstances the conversation might run:

> JUDGE: Did you steal of your own free will?
> STACE: No. I stole because my employer threatened to beat me if I did not.

---

[1]*Newtonian:* based on the theories of English physicist Isaac Newton (1642–1726). [D. C. ABEL]
[2]Mohandas (later called Mahatma) Gandhi (1869–1948) was an Indian nationalist leader. He sometimes fasted as a way to help achieve his objectives. [D. C. ABEL]

At a recent murder trial in Trenton some of the accused had signed confessions, but afterwards asserted that they had done so under police duress. The following exchange might have occurred:

JUDGE: Did you sign this confession of your own free will?
PRISONER: No. I signed it because the police beat me up.

Now suppose that a philosopher had been a member of the jury. We could imagine this conversation taking place in the jury room.

FOREMAN OF THE JURY: The prisoner says he signed the confession because he was beaten, and not of his own free will.
PHILOSOPHER: This is quite irrelevant to the case. There is no such thing as free will.
FOREMAN: Do you mean to say that it makes no difference whether he signed because his conscience made him want to tell the truth or because he was beaten?
PHILOSOPHER: None at all. Whether he was caused to sign by a beating or by some desire of his own—the desire to tell the truth, for example—in either case his signing was causally determined, and therefore in neither case did he act of his own free will. Since there is no such thing as free will, the question whether he signed of his own free will ought not to be discussed by us.

The foreman and the rest of the jury would rightly conclude that the philosopher must be making some mistake. What sort of a mistake could it be? There is only one possible answer. The philosopher must be using the phrase "free will" in some peculiar way of his own that is not the way in which men usually use it when they wish to determine a question of moral responsibility. That is, he must be using an incorrect definition of it as implying action not determined by causes.

Suppose a man left his office at noon, and were questioned about it. Then we might hear this:

JONES: Did you go out of your own free will?
SMITH: Yes. I went out to get my lunch.

But we might hear:

JONES: Did you leave your office of your own free will?
SMITH: No. I was forcibly removed by the police.

We have now collected a number of cases of actions that, in the ordinary usage of the English language, would be called cases in which people have acted of their own free will. We should also say in all these cases that they *chose* to act as they did. We should also say that they could have acted otherwise, if they had chosen. For instance, Mahatma Gandhi was not compelled to fast; he chose to do so. He could have eaten if he had wanted to. When Smith went out to get his lunch, he chose to do so. He could have stayed and done some more work, if he had wanted to. We have also collected a number of cases of the opposite kind. They are cases in which men were not able to exercise their free will.

They had no choice. They were compelled to do as they did. The man in the desert did not fast of his own free will. He had no choice in the matter. He was compelled to fast because there was nothing for him to eat. And so with the other cases. It ought to be quite easy, by an inspection of these cases, to tell what we ordinarily mean when we say that a man did or did not exercise free will. We ought therefore to be able to extract from them the proper definition of the term. Let us put the cases in a table:

FREE ACTS	UNFREE ACTS
Gandhi fasting because he wanted to free India.	The man fasting in the desert because there was no food.
Stealing bread because one is hungry.	Stealing because one's employer threatened to beat one.
Signing a confession because one wanted to tell the truth.	Signing because the police beat one.
Leaving the office because one wanted one's lunch.	Leaving because forcibly removed.

It is obvious that to find the correct definition of free acts we must discover what characteristic is common to all the acts in the left-hand column and is, at the same time, absent from all the acts in the right-hand column. This characteristic, which all free acts have, and which no unfree acts have, will be the defining characteristic of free will.

Is being uncaused, or not being determined by causes, the characteristic of which we are in search? It cannot be, because although it is true that all the acts in the right-hand column have causes, such as the beating by the police or the absence of food in the desert, so also do the acts in the left-hand column. Mr. Gandhi's fasting was caused by his desire to free India, the man leaving his office by his hunger, and so on. Moreover there is no reason to doubt that these causes of the free acts were in turn caused by prior conditions, and that these were again the results of causes, and so on back indefinitely into the past. Any physiologist can tell us the causes of hunger. What caused Mr. Gandhi's tremendously powerful desire to free India is no doubt more difficult to discover. But it must have had causes. Some of them may have lain in peculiarities of his glands or brain, others in his past experiences, others in his heredity, others in his education. Defenders of free will have usually tended to deny such facts. But to do so is plainly a case of special pleading that is unsupported by any scrap of evidence. The only reasonable view is that all human actions, both those that are freely done and those that are not, are either wholly determined by causes, or at least as much determined as other events in nature. It may be true, as the physicists tell us, that nature is not as deterministic as was once thought. But whatever degree of determinism prevails in the world, human actions appear to be as much determined as anything else. And if this is so, it cannot be the case that what distinguishes actions freely chosen from those that are not free is that the latter are determined by causes while the former are not. Therefore, being uncaused or being undetermined by causes, must be an incorrect definition of free will.

What, then, is the difference between acts that are freely done and those that are not? What is the characteristic that is present to all the acts in the left-hand column and absent from all those in the right-hand column? Is it not obvious that, although both sets of actions have causes, the causes of those in the left-hand column are *of a different kind* from the causes of those in the right-hand column? The free acts are all caused by desires, or motives, or by some sort of internal psychological states of the agent's mind. The unfree acts, on the other hand, are all caused by physical forces or physical conditions outside the agent. Police arrest means physical force exerted from the outside; the absence of food in the desert is a physical condition of the outside world. We may therefore frame the following rough definitions. *Acts freely done are those whose immediate causes are psychological states in the agent. Acts not freely done are those whose immediate causes are states of affairs external to the agent.*

It is plain that if we define free will in this way, then free will certainly exists, and the philosopher's denial of its existence is seen to be what it is—nonsense. For it is obvious that all those actions of men which we should ordinarily attribute to the exercise of their free will, or of that we should say that they freely chose to do them, are in fact actions that have been caused by their own desires, wishes, thoughts, emotions, impulses, or other psychological states.

[ANSWERS TO OBJECTIONS]

In applying our definition we shall find that it usually works well, but that there are some puzzling cases that it does not seem exactly to fit. These puzzles can always be solved by paying careful attention to the ways in which words are used, and remembering that they are not always used consistently. I have space for only one example. Suppose that a thug threatens to shoot you unless you give him your wallet, and suppose that you do so. Do you, in giving him your wallet, do so of your own free will or not? If we apply our definition, we find that you acted freely, since the immediate cause of the action was not an actual outside force but the fear of death, which is a psychological cause. Most people, however, would say that you did not act of your own free will but under compulsion. Does this show that our definition is wrong? I do not think so. Aristotle, who gave a solution of the problem of free will substantially the same as ours (though he did not use the term "free will"), admitted that there are what he called "mixed" or borderline cases in which it is difficult to know whether we ought to call the acts free or compelled. In the case under discussion, though no actual force was used, the gun at your forehead so nearly approximated to actual force that we tend to say the case was one of compulsion. It is a borderline case.

Here is what may seem like another kind of puzzle. According to our view an action may be free though it could have been predicted beforehand with certainty. But suppose you told a lie, and it was certain beforehand that you would tell it. How could one then say, "You could have told the truth"? The answer is that it is perfectly true that you could have told the truth *if* you had wanted to. In fact you would have done so, for in that case the causes producing your action, namely your desires, would have been different, and would therefore have produced different effects. It is a delusion that predictability and free will are incompatible. This agrees with common sense. For if, knowing your character, I predict that you will act honorably, no one would say when you do act honorably, that this shows you did not do so of your own free will.

[THE COMPATIBILITY OF DETERMINISM AND MORAL RESPONSIBILITY]

Since free will is a condition of moral responsibility, we must be sure that our theory of free will gives a sufficient basis for it. To be held morally responsible for one's actions means that one may be justly punished or rewarded, blamed or praised, for them. But it is not just to punish a man for what he cannot help doing. How can it be just to punish him for an action that it was certain beforehand that he would do? We have not attempted to decide whether, as a matter of fact, all events, including human actions, are completely determined. For that question is irrelevant to the problem of free will. But if we assume for the purposes of argument that complete determinism is true, but that we are nevertheless free, it may then be asked whether such a deterministic free will is compatible with moral responsibility. For it may seem unjust to punish a man for an action that it could have been predicted with certainty beforehand that he would do.

But that determinism is incompatible with moral responsibility is as much a delusion as that it is incompatible with free will. You do not excuse a man for doing a wrong act because, knowing his character, you felt certain beforehand that he would do it. Nor do you deprive a man of a reward or prize because, knowing his goodness or his capabilities, you felt certain beforehand that he would win it.

Volumes have been written on the justification of punishment. But so far as it affects the question of free will, the essential principles involved are quite simple. The punishment of a man for doing a wrong act is justified, either on the ground that it will correct his own character, or that it will deter other people from doing similar acts. The instrument of punishment has been in the past— and no doubt still is—often unwisely used, so that it may often have done more harm than good. But that is not relevant to our present problem. Punishment, if and when it is justified, is justified only on one or both of the grounds just mentioned. The question then is how, if we assume determinism, punishment can correct character or deter people from evil actions.

Suppose that your child develops a habit of telling lies. You give him a mild beating. Why? Because you believe that his personality is such that the usual motives for telling the truth do not cause him to do so. You therefore supply the missing cause, or motive, in the shape of pain and the fear of future pain if he repeats his untruthful behavior. And you hope that a few treatments of this kind will condition him to the habit of truth-telling, so that he will come to tell the truth without the infliction of pain. You assume that his actions are determined by causes, but that the usual causes of truth-telling do not in him produce their usual effects. You therefore supply him with an artificially injected motive, pain and fear, which you think will in the future cause him to speak truthfully.

The principle is exactly the same where you hope, by punishing one man, to deter others from wrong actions. You believe that the fear of punishment will cause those who might otherwise do evil to do well.

We act on the same principle with nonhuman, and even with inanimate, things, if they do not behave in the way we think they ought to behave. The rose bushes in the garden produce only small and poor blooms, whereas we want large and rich ones. We supply a cause that will produce large blooms, namely fertilizer. Our automobile does not go properly. We supply a cause that will make it go better, namely oil in the works. The punishment for the man, the fertilizer for the plant, and the oil for the car, are all justified by the same principle and in the same way. The only difference is that different kinds of things require different kinds of causes to make them do what they should. Pain may be the appropriate remedy to apply, in certain cases, to human beings, and oil to the machine. It is, of course, of no use to inject motor oil into the boy or to beat the machine.

Thus we see that moral responsibility is not only consistent with determinism, but requires it. The assumption on which punishment is based is that human behavior is causally determined. If pain could not be a cause of truth-telling, there would be no justification at all for punishing lies. If human actions and volitions were uncaused, it would be useless either to punish or reward, or indeed to do anything else to correct people's bad behavior. For nothing that you could do would in any way influence them. Thus moral responsibility would entirely disappear. If there were no determinism of human beings at all, their actions would be completely unpredictable and capricious, and therefore irresponsible. And this is in itself a strong argument against the common view of philosophers that free will means being undetermined by causes.

Freedom and Determinism

Richard Taylor

Richard Taylor was born in 1919 in Charlotte, Michigan. He attended the University of Illinois, receiving his bachelor's degree in 1941. During World War II, when serving in the U.S. Navy, he became interested in philosophy. After the war he began graduate studies in philosophy at Oberlin College. Taylor received his master's degree in 1947 and then enrolled in the doctoral program at Brown University. In 1951 he completed his doctorate and became a member of the faculty at Brown. In 1959 he was appointed William Herbert Perry Faunce Professor of Philosophy. In 1963 Taylor joined the faculty of Columbia University. Two years later he accepted an appointment at the University of Rochester, where he remained until his retirement in 1985. He held distinguished visiting professorships at Wells College, Hamilton College, and Hobart and William Smith Colleges. He died in 2003 in Trumansburg, New York.

Taylor's books include *Metaphysics* (1963; 4th ed., 1992); *Action and Purpose* (1966); *Good and Evil: A New Direction* (1970); *With Heart and Mind* (1973); *Freedom, Anarchy, and the Law: An Introduction to Political Philosophy* (1973); *Ethics, Faith, and Reason* (1985); and *Virtue Ethics: An Introduction* (2002).

Our reading is from Chapter 5 of *Metaphysics,* "Freedom and Determinism," which addresses the question of whether any of our actions are free. The theory of determinism states that every event—including every human action—is a necessary result of prior causes. Taylor begins by discussing "soft determinism," the theory that some human actions are both determined and free. Soft determinists define a free action as one not impeded by any obstacle and not coerced by any external force. With this definition, they can claim that an action is both determined and free if it is the necessary result of an *internal* force (a desire, for example). Taylor rejects soft determinism because saying that a person's action was free implies that he or she could have acted otherwise. But if determinism is true (as the soft determinist maintains), the internal state that causes the action is *itself* the necessary result of prior causes, and therefore the person could not have acted otherwise. Taylor also rejects "simple indeterminism" (the theory that some actions are free because they have no causes) because it is at odds with our ordinary notion of responsibility: Actions without causes would occur at random and be wholly beyond a person's control.

Taylor's own solution to the problem of freedom and determinism is a "theory of agency." According to this theory, free actions are those caused by the person (agent) herself or himself. A free action is not caused by something within the person (such as a desire) but by the person as a whole. Whereas every other kind of event in nature is the necessary result of an endless series of prior causes, a free action originates with the person. Taylor is somewhat hesitant to postulate such a striking exception to an otherwise deterministic world, but he believes that his theory of agency is justified because it does more justice to our ordinary experience than alternative theories do.

[INTRODUCTION]

. . . We want to learn, if we can, whether determinism is true. . . . It can, like all good questions of philosophy, be answered only on the basis of certain data; that is, by seeing whether or not it squares with certain things that everyone knows, or believes himself to know, or with things everyone is at least more sure about than the answer to the question at issue.

Now I could, of course, simply affirm that I am a morally responsible being, in the sense in which my responsibility for my behavior implies that I could have avoided that behavior. But this would take us into the nebulous realm of ethics, and it is, in fact, far from obvious that I am responsible in that sense. Many have doubted that they are responsible in that sense, and it is in any case not difficult to doubt it, however strongly one might feel about it.

There are, however, two things about myself of which I feel quite certain and that have no necessary connection with morals. The first is that I sometimes deliberate, with the view to making a decision—a decision, namely, to do this thing or that. And the second is that whether or not I deliberate about what to do, it is sometimes up to me what I do. This might all be an illusion, of course; but so also might any philosophical theory, such as the theory of determinism, be false. The point remains that it is far more difficult for me to doubt that I sometimes deliberate, and that it is sometimes up to me what to do, than to doubt any philosophical theory whatever, including the theory of determinism. We must, accordingly, if we ever hope to be wiser, adjust our theories to our data and not try to adjust our data to our theories. . . .

SOFT DETERMINISM

. . . The three claims of soft determinism are (1) that the thesis of determinism is true, and that accordingly all human behavior, voluntary or other, like the behavior of all other things, arises from antecedent conditions, given which no other behavior is possible—in short, that all human behavior is caused and determined; (2) that voluntary behavior is nonetheless free to the extent that it is not externally constrained or impeded; and (3) that, in the absence of such obstacles and constraints, the causes of voluntary behavior are certain states, events, or conditions within the agent himself—namely, his own acts of will or volitions, choices, decisions, desires, and so on.

Thus, on this view, I am free, and therefore sometimes responsible for what I do, provided nothing prevents me from acting according to my own choice, desire, or volition, or constrains me to act otherwise. There may, to be sure, be other conditions for my responsibility—such as, for example, an understanding of the probable consequences of my behavior, and that sort of thing—but absence of constraint or impediment is, at least, one such condition. And, it is claimed, it is a condition that is compatible with the supposition that my behavior is caused—for it is, by hypothesis, caused by my own inner choices, desires, and volitions.

THE REFUTATION OF THIS

The theory of soft determinism looks good at first—so good that it has for generations been solemnly taught from innumerable philosophical chairs and implanted in the minds of students as sound philosophy—but no great acumen is needed to discover that far from solving any problem, it only camouflages it.

My free actions are those unimpeded and unconstrained motions that arise from my own inner desires, choices, and volitions; let us grant this provisionally. But now, whence arise those inner states that determine what my body shall do? Are they within my control or not? Having made my choice or decision and acted upon it, could I have chosen otherwise or not?

Here the determinist, hoping to surrender nothing and yet to avoid the problem implied in that question, bids us not to ask it; the question itself, he announces, is without meaning. For to say that I could have done otherwise, he says, means only that I *would* have done otherwise, *if* those inner states that determined my action had been different; if, that is, I had decided or chosen differently. To ask, accordingly, whether I could have chosen or decided differently is only to ask whether, had I decided to decide differently or chosen to choose differently, or willed to will differently, I *would* have decided or chosen or willed differently. And this, of course, *is* unintelligible nonsense.

But it is not nonsense to ask whether the causes of my actions—my own inner choices, decisions, and desires—are themselves caused. And of course they are, if determinism is true, for on that thesis everything is caused and determined. And if they are, then we cannot avoid concluding that, given the causal conditions of those inner states, I could not have decided, willed, chosen, or desired other than I, in fact, did, for this is a logical consequence of the very definition of determinism. Of course we can still say that, *if* the causes of those inner states, whatever they were, had been different, then their effects, those inner states themselves, would have been different, and that in this hypothetical sense I could have decided, chosen, willed, or desired differently—but that only pushes our problem back still another step. For we will then want to know whether the causes of those inner states were within my control, and so on ad infinitum.[1] We are, at each step, permitted to say "could have been otherwise" only in a provisional sense—provided, that is, that something else had been different—but must then retract it and replace it with "could not have been otherwise" as soon as we discover, as we must at each step, that whatever would have to have been different could not have been different.

EXAMPLES

Such is the dialectic of the problem. The easiest way to see the shadowy quality of soft determinism, however, is by means of examples.

Let us suppose that my body is moving in various ways, that these motions are not externally constrained or impeded, and that they are all

---

[1] *ad infinitum:* (Latin) to infinity. [D. C. ABEL]

exactly in accordance with my own desires, choices, or acts of will, and whatnot. When I will that my arm should move in a certain way, I find it moving in that way, unobstructed and unconstrained. When I will to speak, my lips and tongue move, unobstructed and unconstrained, in a manner suitable to the formation of the words I choose to utter. Now, given that this is a correct description of my behavior, namely, that it consists of the unconstrained and unimpeded motions of my body in response to my own volitions, then it follows that my behavior is free, on the soft determinist's definition of "free." It follows further that I am responsible for that behavior; or at least, that if I am not, it is not from any lack of freedom on my part.

But if the fulfillment of these conditions renders my behavior free—that is to say, if my behavior satisfies the conditions of free action set forth in the theory of soft determinism—then my behavior will be no less free if we assume further conditions that are perfectly consistent with those already satisfied.

We suppose further, accordingly, that while my behavior is entirely in accordance with my own volitions, and thus "free" in terms of the conception of freedom we are examining, my volitions themselves are caused. To make this graphic, we can suppose that an ingenious physiologist can induce in me any volition he pleases, simply by pushing various buttons on an instrument to which, let us suppose, I am attached by numerous wires. All the volitions I have in that situation are, accordingly, precisely the ones he gives me. By pushing one button, he evokes in me the volition to raise my hand; and my hand, being unimpeded, rises in response to that volition. By pushing another, he induces the volition in me to kick, and my foot, being unimpeded, kicks in response to that volition. We can even suppose that the physiologist puts a rifle in my hands, aims it at some passerby, and then, by pushing the proper button, evokes in me the volition to squeeze my finger against the trigger, whereupon the passerby falls dead of a bullet wound.

This is the description of a man who is acting in accordance with his inner volitions, a man whose body is unimpeded and unconstrained in its motions, these motions being the effects of those inner states. It is hardly the description of a free and responsible agent. It is the perfect description of a puppet. To render someone your puppet, it is not necessary forcibly to constrain the motions of his limbs, after the fashion in which real puppets are moved. A subtler but no less effective means of making a person your puppet would be to gain complete control of his inner states, and ensuring, as the theory of soft determinism does ensure, that his body will move in accordance with them.

The example is somewhat unusual, but it is no worse for that. It is perfectly intelligible, and it does appear to refute the soft determinist's conception of freedom. . . . The example can, moreover, be modified in perfectly realistic ways, so as to coincide with actual and familiar cases. One can, for instance, be given a compulsive desire for certain drugs, simply by having them administered over a course of time. Suppose, then, that I do, with neither my knowledge nor consent, thus become a victim of such a desire and act upon it. Do I act freely, merely by virtue of the fact that I am unimpeded in my quest for drugs? In a sense I do, surely, but I am hardly free with respect to whether or not I shall use drugs. I never chose to have the desire for them inflicted upon me.

Nor does it, of course, matter whether the inner states that allegedly prompt all my "free" activity are evoked in me by another agent or by perfectly impersonal forces. Whether a desire that causes my body to behave in a certain way is inflicted upon me by another person, for instance, or derived from hereditary factors, or indeed from anything at all, matters not the least. In any case, if it is in fact the cause of my bodily behavior, I cannot help but act in accordance with it. Wherever it came from, whether from personal or impersonal origins, it was entirely caused or determined, and not within my control. Indeed, if determinism is true, as the theory of soft determinism holds it to be, all those inner states that cause my body to behave in whatever ways it behaves must arise from circumstances that existed before I was born; for the chain of causes and effects is infinite, and none could have been the least different, given those that preceded.

SIMPLE INDETERMINISM

We might at first now seem warranted in simply denying determinism, and saying that, insofar as they are free, my actions are not caused; or that, if they are caused by my own inner states—my own desires, impulses, choices, volitions, and whatnot—then these, in any case, are not caused. This is a perfectly clear sense in which a person's action, assuming that it was free, could have been otherwise. If it was uncaused, then, even given the conditions under which it occurred and all that preceded, some other act was nonetheless possible, and he did not have to do what he did. Or if his action was the inevitable consequence of his own inner states, and could not have been otherwise, given these, we can nevertheless say that these inner states, being uncaused, could have been otherwise, and could thereby have produced different actions.

Only the slightest consideration will show, however, that this simple denial of determinism has not the slightest plausibility. For let us suppose it is true, and that some of my bodily motions—namely, those that I regard as my free acts—are not caused at all or, if caused by my own inner states, that these are not caused. We shall thereby avoid picturing a puppet, to be sure—but only by substituting something even less like a human being; for the conception that now emerges is not that of a free person, but of an erratic and jerking phantom, without any rhyme or reason at all.

Suppose that my right arm is free, according to this conception; that is, that its motions are uncaused. It moves this way and that from time to time, but nothing causes these motions. Sometimes it moves forth vigorously, sometimes up, sometimes down, sometimes it just drifts vaguely about—these motions all being wholly free and uncaused. Manifestly I have nothing to do with them at all; they just happen, and neither I nor anyone can ever tell what this arm will be doing next. It might seize a club and lay it on the head of the nearest bystander, no less to my astonishment than his. There will never be any point in asking why these motions occur, or in seeking any explanation of them, for under the conditions assumed there is no explanation. They just happen, from no causes at all.

This is no description of free, voluntary, or responsible behavior. Indeed, so far as the motions of my body or its parts are entirely uncaused, such motions cannot even be ascribed to me as my behavior in the first place, since I have nothing to do with them. The behavior of my arm is just the random motion of a foreign object. Behavior that is mine must be behavior that is within my control, but motions that occur from no causes are beyond the control of anyone. I can have no more to do with, and no more control over, the uncaused motions of my limbs than a gambler has over the motions of an honest roulette wheel. I can only, like him, idly wait to see what happens.

Nor does it improve things to suppose that my bodily motions are caused by my own inner states, so long as we suppose these to be wholly uncaused. The result will be the same as before. My arm, for example, will move this way and that, sometimes up and sometimes down, sometimes vigorously and sometimes just drifting about, always in response to certain inner states, to be sure. But since these are supposed to be wholly uncaused, it follows that I have no control over them and hence none over their effects. If my hand lays a club forcefully on the nearest bystander, we can indeed say that this motion resulted from an inner club-wielding desire of mine; but we must add that I had nothing to do with that desire, and that it arose, to be followed by its inevitable effect, no less to my astonishment than to his. Things like this do, alas, sometimes happen. We are all sometimes seized by compulsive impulses that arise we know not whence, and we do sometimes act upon these. But because they are far from being examples of free, voluntary, and responsible behavior, we need only to learn that the behavior was of this sort to conclude that it was not free, voluntary, or responsible. It was erratic, impulsive, and irresponsible.

DETERMINISM AND SIMPLE INDETERMINISM AS THEORIES

Both determinism and simple indeterminism are loaded with difficulties, and no one who has thought much on them can affirm either of them without some embarrassment. Simple indeterminism has nothing whatever to be said for it, except that it appears to remove the grossest difficulties of determinism, only, however, to imply perfect absurdities of its own. Determinism, on the other hand, is at least initially plausible. People seem to have a natural inclination to believe in it; it is, indeed, almost required for the very exercise of practical intelligence. And beyond this, our experience appears always to confirm it, so long as we are dealing with everyday facts of common experience, as distinguished from the esoteric researches of theoretical physics. But determinism, as applied to human behavior, has implications that few can casually accept, and they appear to be implications that no modification of the theory can efface.

Both theories, moreover, appear logically irreconcilable to the two items of data that we set forth at the outset; namely, (1) that my behavior is sometimes the outcome of my deliberation, and (2) that in these and other cases it is sometimes up to me what I do. Because these were our data, it is important to see, as must already be quite clear, that these theories cannot be reconciled to them.

I can deliberate only about my own future actions, and then only if I do not already know what I am going to do. If a certain nasal tickle warns me that I am about to sneeze, for instance, then I cannot deliberate whether to sneeze or not; I can only prepare for the impending convulsion. But if determinism is true, then there are always conditions existing antecedently to everything I do, sufficient for my doing just that, and such as to render it inevitable. If I can know what those conditions are and what behavior they are sufficient to produce, then I can in every such case know what I am going to do and cannot then deliberate about it.

By itself this only shows, of course, that I can deliberate only in ignorance of the causal conditions of my behavior; it does not show that such conditions cannot exist. It is odd, however, to suppose that deliberation should be a mere substitute for clear knowledge. Ignorance is a condition of speculation, inference, and guesswork, which have nothing whatever to do with deliberation. A prisoner awaiting execution may not know when he is going to die, and he may even entertain the hope of reprieve, but he cannot deliberate about this. He can only speculate, guess—and wait.

Worse yet, however, it now becomes clear that I cannot deliberate about what I am going to do, if it is even *possible* for me to find out in advance, whether I do in fact find out in advance or not. I can deliberate only with the view to deciding what to do, to making up my mind; and this is impossible if I believe that it could be inferred what I am going to do from conditions already existing, even though I have not made that inference myself. If I believe that what I am going to do has been rendered inevitable by conditions already existing, and could be inferred by anyone having the requisite sagacity, then I cannot try to decide whether to do it or not, for there is simply nothing left to decide. I can at best only guess or try to figure it out myself or, all prognostics failing, I can wait and see; but I cannot deliberate. I deliberate in order to *decide* what *to* do, not to *discover* what it is that I am *going* to do. But if determinism is true, then there are always antecedent conditions sufficient for everything that I do, and this can always be inferred by anyone having the requisite sagacity; that is, by anyone having a knowledge of what those conditions are and what behavior they are sufficient to produce.

This suggests what in fact seems quite clear, that determinism cannot be reconciled with our second datum either, to the effect that it is sometimes up to me what I am going to do. For if it is ever really up to me whether to do this thing or that, then, as we have seen, each alternative course of action must be such that I can do it; not that I can do it in some abstruse or hypothetical sense of "can"; not that I could do it if only something were true that is not true; but in the sense that it is then and there within my power to do it. But this is never so, if determinism is true, for on the very formulation of that theory whatever happens at any time is the only thing that can then happen, given all that precedes it. It is simply a logical consequence of this that whatever I do at any time is the only thing I can then do, given the conditions that precede my doing it. Nor does it help in the least to interpose, among the causal antecedents of my behavior, my own inner states, such as my desires, choices, acts of will, and so on. For even supposing these to be always involved in voluntary behavior—which is highly doubtful in itself—it is a consequence of determinism that these, whatever they are at any time, can never be other than what they then are. . . .

It is even more obvious that our data cannot be reconciled to the theory of simple indeterminism. I can deliberate only about my own actions; this is obvious. But the random, uncaused motion of any body whatever, whether it be a part of my body or not, is no action of mine and nothing that is within my power. I might try to guess what these motions will be, just as I might try to guess how a roulette wheel will behave, but I cannot deliberate about them or try to decide what they shall be, simply because these things are not up to me. Whatever is not caused by anything is not caused by me, and nothing could be more plainly inconsistent with saying that it is nevertheless up to me what it shall be.

THE THEORY OF AGENCY

The only conception of action that accords with our data is one according to which people—and perhaps some other things too—are sometimes, but of course not always, self-determining beings; that is, beings that are sometimes the causes of their own behavior. In the case of an action that is free, it must not only be such that it is caused by the agent who performs it, but also such that no antecedent conditions were sufficient for his performing just that action. In the case of an action that is both free and rational, it must be such that the agent who performed it did so for some reason, but this reason cannot have been the cause of it.

Now, this conception fits what people take themselves to be—namely, beings who act, or who are agents, rather than beings that are merely acted upon, and whose behavior is simply the causal consequence of conditions that they have not wrought. When I believe that I have done something, I do believe that it was I who caused it to be done, I who made something happen, and not merely something within me, such as one of my own subjective states, which is not identical with myself. If I believe that something not identical with myself was the cause of my behavior—some event wholly external to myself, for instance, or even one internal to myself, such as a nerve impulse, volition, or whatnot—then I cannot regard that behavior as being an act of mine, unless I further believe that I was the cause of that external or internal event. My pulse, for example, is caused and regulated by certain conditions existing within me, and not by myself. I do not, accordingly, regard this activity of my body as my action, and would be no more tempted to do so if I became suddenly conscious within myself of those conditions or impulses that produce it. This is behavior with which I have nothing to do, behavior that is not within my immediate control, behavior that is not only not free activity, but not even the activity of an agent to begin with; it is nothing but a mechanical reflex. Had I never learned that my very life depends on this pulse beat, I would regard it with complete indifference, as something foreign to me, like the oscillations of a clock pendulum that I idly contemplate.

Now this conception of activity, and of an agent who is the cause of it, involves two rather strange metaphysical[2] notions that are never applied else-where in nature. The first is that of a *self* or *person*—for example, a man—who is

---

[2]*metaphysical:* relating to *metaphysics*, the study of the nature and kinds of reality. [D. C. ABEL]

not merely a collection of things or events, but a self-moving being. For on this view it is a person, and not merely some part of him or something within him, that is the cause of his own activity. Now, we certainly do not know that a human being is anything more than an assemblage of physical things and processes that act in accordance with those laws that describe the behavior of all other physical things and processes. Even though he is a living being, of enormous complexity, there is nothing, apart from the requirements of this theory, to suggest that his behavior is so radically different in its origin from that of other physical objects, or that an understanding of it must be sought in some metaphysical realm wholly different from that appropriate to the understanding of nonliving things.

Second, this conception of activity involves an extraordinary conception of causation according to which an agent, which is a substance and not an event, can nevertheless be the cause of an event. Indeed, if he is a free agent then he can, on this conception, cause an event to occur—namely, some act of his own—without anything else causing him to do so. This means that an agent is sometimes a cause, without being an antecedent sufficient condition; for if I affirm that I am the cause of some act of mine, then I am plainly not saying that my very existence is sufficient for its occurrence, which would be absurd. If I say that my hand causes my pencil to move, then I am saying that the motion of my hand is, under the other conditions then prevailing, sufficient for the motion of the pencil. But if I then say that I cause my hand to move, I am not saying anything remotely like this, and surely not that the motion of my self is sufficient for the motion of my arm and hand, since these are the only things about me that are moving.

This conception of the causation of events by things that are not events is, in fact, so different from the usual philosophical conception of a cause that it should not even bear the same name, for "being a cause" ordinarily just means "being an antecedent sufficient condition or set of conditions." Instead, then, of speaking of agents as *causing* their own acts, it would perhaps be better to use another word entirely, and say, for instance, that they *originate* them, *initiate* them, or simply that they *perform* them.

Now this is, on the face of it, a dubious conception of what a person is. Yet it is consistent with our data, reflecting the presuppositions of deliberation, and appears to be the only conception that is consistent with them, as determinism and simple indeterminism are not. The theory of agency avoids the absurdities of simple indeterminism by conceding that human behavior is caused, while at the same time avoiding the difficulties of determinism by denying that every chain of causes and effects is infinite. Some such causal chains, on this view, have beginnings, and they begin with agents themselves. Moreover, if we are to suppose that it is sometimes up to me what I do, and understand this in a sense that is not consistent with determinism, we must suppose that I am an agent or a being who initiates his own actions, sometimes under conditions that do not determine what action I shall perform. Deliberation becomes, on this view, something that is not only possible but quite rational, for it does make sense to deliberate about activity that is truly my own and that depends in its outcome upon me as its author, and not merely upon something more or less esoteric that is supposed to be intimately associated with me, such as my thoughts, volitions, choices, or whatnot.

One can hardly affirm such a theory of agency with complete comfort, however, and not wholly without embarrassment, for the conception of agents and their powers that is involved in it is strange indeed, if not positively mysterious. In fact, one can hardly be blamed here for simply denying our data outright, rather than embracing this theory to which they do most certainly point. Our data—to the effect that we do sometimes deliberate before acting, and that, when we do, we presuppose among other things that it is up to us what we are going to do—rest upon nothing more than fairly common consent. These data might simply be illusions. It might, in fact, be that no one ever deliberates but only imagines that he does, that from pure conceit he supposes himself to be the master of his behavior and the author of his acts. Spinoza[3] has suggested that if a stone, having been thrown into the air, were suddenly to become conscious, it would suppose itself to be the source of its own motion, being then conscious of what it was doing but not aware of the real cause of its behavior. Certainly we are *sometimes* mistaken in believing that we are behaving as a result of choice deliberately arrived at. A man might, for example, easily imagine that his embarking upon matrimony is the result of the most careful and rational deliberation, when in fact the causes, perfectly sufficient for that behavior, might be of an entirely physiological, unconscious origin. If it is sometimes false that we deliberate and then act as the result of a decision deliberately arrived at, even when we suppose it to be true, it might always be false. . . .

These are, then, dubitable conceptions, despite their being so well implanted in common sense. . . . Perhaps here, as elsewhere in metaphysics, we should be content with discovering difficulties, with seeing what is and what is not consistent with such convictions as we happen to have, and then drawing such satisfaction as we can from the realization that, no matter where we begin, the world is mysterious and that we who try to understand it are even more so. This realization can, with some justification, make one feel wise, even in the full realization of his ignorance.

---

[3]Baruch (Benedict de) Spinoza (1632–1677) was a Dutch philosopher. [D. C. ABEL]

Firming Up Soft Determinism

Nancy Holmstrom

Nancy Holmstrom was born in 1943 in New York City. She received her bachelor's degree in philosophy from City College of the City University of New York in 1964 and her doctorate in philosophy from the University of Michigan in 1970. She then accepted a position at the University of Wisconsin–Madison. In 1977 she joined the faculty at Rutgers State University in Newark, New Jersey, where she is associate professor of philosophy. Holmstrom has held visiting professorships at the University of Illinois at Chicago (formerly called University of Illinois at Chicago Circle), the University of Hawaii at Hilo, and other schools. Since the 1960s Holmstrom has been active in radical movements and committed to social justice. She was a founding member of the Society for Women in Philosophy and of the Radical Philosophical Association.

Holmstrom's involvement in political activity led to a gradual shift in her philosophical work from topics in the philosophy of mind and metaphysics to issues in political and social philosophy, especially feminist and Marxist theory. In addition to publishing a variety of articles on these topics, Holmstrom is coeditor (with Anatole Anton and Milton Fisk) of *Not for Sale: In Defense of Public Goods* (2000) and editor of *The Socialist Feminist Project: A Contemporary Reader in Theory and Politics* (2002).

In her 1977 article, "Firming Up Soft Determinism," Holmstrom discusses *soft determinism,* the view that determinism is compatible with free will and moral responsibility. (*Hard determinism* denies this compatibility.) This theory (also called *compatibilism*) accepts the determinist thesis that all actions are determined because they result from preceding causes, but it also holds that if a particular action is caused by the agent's beliefs and desires, the action is free and the agent is responsible for performing it. Holmstrom finds this theory inadequate as it stands, since it does not consider the *sources* of the agent's beliefs and desires. For example, an action resulting from desire induced by brainwashing or subliminal advertising is not free.

Holmstrom seeks to remedy this inadequacy in the theory of soft determinism by postulating that an action is free only to the extent that the agent has *control* over the beliefs and desires that cause the performance of the action. Control need not be all or nothing; it is often a matter of degree. Since we have at least some control over many of our beliefs and desires, many of our actions are free to some extent. "There is a continuum between free and unfree, with many or most acts lying somewhere in between." The degree of control depends on the degree to which the source of our desire or belief does not operate on us against our will, and on the degree of our awareness *that* the source is operating on us and *how* and *why* it does so. After developing her views of freedom and control, Holmstrom reflects on how free most people are today.

I

An important position on the question of freedom and determinism holds that determinism and predictability per se constitute no threat to the freedom and responsibility of an agent. What matters, according to this view, called soft determinism, is the basis on which the prediction is made or the nature of the conditions such that, given those conditions, the agent will do what he/she does. When the agent does what he does because of his beliefs and desires[1] to do it, then what the agent does is "up to him"; the causal chain goes through the person or the self, as it were. In such cases the agent can be said to be the cause of the action. Such actions are free. On the other hand, when the causes of an action, or, more generally, of what a person does, are not his/her beliefs and desires to do that action, then what happens is not "up to him" and the action is not free. However, it may not be compelled either. It is where the action is in contradiction to what the agent wants that the act can be said to be compelled. The agent is not responsible for the action because the action occurs in spite of him.

Among the objections that have been raised to this account of the distinction between free and unfree acts is that it provides an insufficient account of what it is for an agent to do an act freely. The problem is the source of the sources of one's allegedly free actions, that is, the sources of one's beliefs and desires. Many philosophers have felt that if an agent's beliefs and desires are themselves determined, then actions proceeding from them must be as unfree as actions that are not caused by the agent's beliefs and desires. For example, Richard Taylor bids us to suppose that

> while my behavior is entirely in accordance with my own volitions, and thus "free" in terms of the conception of freedom we are examining, my volitions themselves are caused. To make this graphic, we can suppose that an ingenious physiologist can induce in me any volition he pleases, simply by pushing various buttons on an instrument to which, let us suppose, I am attached by numerous wires. All the volitions I have in that situation are, accordingly, precisely the ones he gives me. . . .
>
> This is the description of a man who is acting in accordance with his inner volitions, a man whose body is unimpeded and unconstrained in its motions, these motions being the effects of those inner states. It is hardly the description of a free and responsible agent. It is the perfect description of a puppet.[2]

The same point can be made by examples of beliefs and desires acquired by brainwashing, hypnosis, subliminal advertising, and so on. If a person acts because of beliefs and desires acquired in such ways, the action is clearly not free even though the action was done because of the agent's beliefs and desires. This shows that it is not the case that an act is free just because it is caused by the beliefs and desires of the agent to do the act. The standard soft determinist position is inadequate as it stands.

One way of dealing with the objection might be to distinguish freedom of action and freedom of will and to maintain that the act was free but the will was not. However, I think such examples show that these concepts cannot be so easily separated. Because the "will" is unfree in such cases, we would not call the

---

[1]I intend "beliefs" and "desires" to cover all mental sources of action, whatever exactly these are. [N. HOLMSTROM]

[2]Richard Taylor, *Metaphysics* (Englewood Cliffs, NJ: Prentice-Hall, 1963), p. 45. [N. HOLMSTROM] This passage from Taylor appears on p. 297 of this book. [D. C. ABEL]

act free. Taylor thinks his point applies much more generally than just to these sorts of examples and concludes that the standard conception of determinism cannot apply to a free act. He introduces, instead, a special notion of "agent causality."[3] I prefer to explore a response to the above objection that remains within the standard compatibilist framework.

I think that the objection I raised to soft determinism shows that soft determinists have too limited a notion of what is required for an agent to be the source of his/her actions. All that they require is that the agent do what he or she pleases. They ignore the question of whether the agent has control over the sources of the actions, his/her desires and beliefs. Taylor inferred that if the desires causing an action are themselves caused then the action is not free. This does not follow. Just because some causes of desires and beliefs, such as brainwashing, make actions resulting from them unfree, it does not follow that any cause of desires and beliefs has the same implications for the freedom of actions resulting from them.

Since the notion of having control is the heart of the notion of freedom for me, let me stop to clarify the concept briefly. If I have control over x then x depends on what I do or do not do. I am an important part of the causal process producing x, such that if I did something different x would be different. Moreover, I must be conscious of x's dependence on me in order for x to be under my control. Whether some insect lives or not depends on whether or not I step on him as I walk down the street. But if I do not know he is there his life is not under my control. So for x to be under my control what I do or do not do must be an important part of the cause of x and I must know this. X therefore must depend on what I want or on my "will" in order for x to be under my control. Now since one can make more or less of a difference, be more or less important a part of the causal process, it therefore follows that one can have more or less control over something. The more control a person has the freer that person is. Clearly, then, a person is not simply free or unfree. Nor is every action simply free or unfree. Rather, there is a continuum between free and unfree, with many or most acts lying somewhere in between. When I say that an act is free what I mean is that the act falls on the free side of the continuum. Or, since there is no line in the middle of a continuum, it might be clearer to say that a free act falls in the direction of the free end of the continuum. Acts are more or less free according to how close they are to the free end of the continuum.

What I want to argue in this paper is that people can have differing amounts of control over what they desire and what they believe. People can be more or less important a part of the causal process leading to their having the desires and beliefs that they do. Our discussion thus far shows that only if they have control over their beliefs and desires do they really have control over their actions. The key question, then, is whether this idea of having control over one's beliefs and desires makes any sense and whether in fact we do have such control. Many people would probably say that while what we do is often up to us, what we believe and desire depends on factors completely beyond our control. Speaking generally, it depends on the way the world is;

---

[3]Ibid., pp. 50–53; pp. 301–303 of this book. [D. C. ABEL]

more specifically, it depends on our biological and psychological natures, the society in which we live, and our particular portion of it (that is, our class, race, ethnic group, and so on). Others would object that it makes no sense to separate the person or self from his/her desires and beliefs, and hence makes no sense to talk of the person having control over his/her desires and beliefs. My major purpose in this paper will be to give substance to the idea that people can have control over the sources of their actions—that is, have control over their desires and beliefs.

If an agent can be said to be the source of his/her beliefs and desires, then it makes sense to say that the agent is a self-determining being. This is a concept that many have taken to be at the heart of freedom, whether they be determinists, indeterminists, or hold to the idea of "agent causality." If we can give substance to this notion of a person having control over his desires and beliefs, we will have given substance to the notion of a self-determining being.

II

Before turning directly to the central task, I wish to raise another sort of counter-example to soft determinism. Some acts that are done because of the agent's desires and beliefs to do them are nevertheless unfree, but for reasons other than the source of those desires and beliefs. However, we will see that these counter-examples do not challenge the fundamental thrust of soft determinism because the examples are all such that we have reason to say that the actions in the examples are not truly self-determined.

A heroin addict steals some money and uses it to buy heroin, which he then takes. It might be said that all three acts (stealing, buying the drug, and taking it) are done because of the addict's desire to achieve a certain state and the belief that these are ways of achieving it. If we imagine that this addict does not want to be an addict, as is the case with most addicts, then these acts of his are crucially different from most acts done because of the agent's beliefs and desires. While the addict wants the heroin he also wants to not take the drug. Moreover, he wants a great number of things that he believes to be incompatible with taking the drug—for example, health, self-respect, an ordinary life, and so on. These contrary desires, values, and beliefs are greater in number and also are part of an integrated whole. The desire to take the drug is not part of such an integrated whole, but nevertheless it outweighs all these contrary desires and beliefs. A kleptomaniac's desire to steal would probably be similar. Most actions done because of the agent's desires are not in conflict with a greater number of his/her integrated desires and beliefs. I think it is this factor that leads compatibilists to reject such cases as not really counterexamples to their analysis of a free act as one resulting from the wants of the agent. An act resulting from such a conflict does not seem to proceed from the self as a free act must: It occurs in spite of the person. Moritz Schlick says, "We consider the man to be more or less unfree, and hold him less accountable, because we rightly view the influence of the drug as 'external,' even though it is found within the body; it prevents him from making decisions in the manner peculiar to his nature."[4] This integrated set of desires, beliefs, and values might be said to constitute the person's nature or self as it is at that time. Acts proceeding from desires that are external to this and yet dominant would seem to be unfree. There are certain exceptions to this, however, which we will discover as we progress.

III

I wish at this point to introduce the notion of a second-order volition as discussed by Harry Frankfurt in "Freedom of the Will and the Concept of a Person."[5] Someone has a volition of the second-order when he wants to have a certain desire[6] and, moreover, wants that desire to be his effective desire—that is, his *will*, in Frankfurt's terminology. The addict in our example may simply suffer from a conflict between the desire to take the drug and a number of contradictory or incompatible desires. However, he may, further, want that the latter desires be his effective desires. If so, then the addict's desire to take the drug is in conflict not only with a greater number of integrated desires and beliefs, but with a second-order volition as well. Yet it still determines the addict's actions. By being in conflict with the will he wants to have, it is in conflict with the want with which he has thereby identified himself. Hence, when this desire determines action, the action is in sharp contrast to most acts done because of the agent's beliefs and desires. Instead of being an act that depends on the agent, that is "up to him," it happens against his will. This provides further grounds for saying that the act does not proceed from the self. Quite aside from the nature of the desire that is in conflict with the second-order volition in our example (that is, the desire to take heroin), it would seem plausible to take as a sufficient condition for making an act unfree that it proceed from beliefs and desires that are in conflict with a second-order volition. A necessary condition, then, of a free act is that it proceed from desires and beliefs that are consistent with second-order volitions. This should be seen as a development of the compatibilist account of a free act as one caused by the self, specifically the agent's beliefs and desires.

IV

Consistency with an integrated set of beliefs and desires and with second-order volitions is not sufficient for an act to be free. We saw at the outset that the source of the beliefs and desires causing an act is relevant to the freedom of that

---

[4]Moritz Schlick, "When Is a Man Responsible?," in *Free Will and Determinism*, ed. Bernard Berofsky (New York: Harper & Row, 1966), p. 59. [N. HOLMSTROM] Schlick (1882–1936) was a German philosopher. [D. C. ABEL]

[5]Harry Frankfurt, "Freedom of the Will and the Concept of a Person," *The Journal of Philosophy* 68 (January 1971), pp. 5–20. [N. HOLMSTROM]

[6]In Frankfurt's terminology, the original desire is a *first-order* volition; the desire to have this desire is a *second-order* volition. [D. C. ABEL]

act. The sorts of examples that first showed us that the soft determinist position was unsatisfactory as thus far presented were examples of acts done because of beliefs and desires that seemed in some way to have been forced upon the agent. Whether the person acquired beliefs and desires (volitions or the reasons for doing what he/she does) by being hooked up to a machine someone else controls, or by being brainwashed or exposed to subliminal advertising, the following is true. The beliefs and desires were acquired by measures taken by others in order to induce them, which measures were taken either explicitly against the person's will (brainwashing), and/or without his/her knowledge (subliminal advertising). (Taylor's case could be either.) Being ignorant of the measures taken to induce the beliefs and desires, the person is as much lacking in control over them as if they were taken explicitly against his/her will. In both cases the person, as an active determining being, is irrelevant to what happens. He/she has no control, and—more importantly—no possibility of control over the beliefs and desires he/she acquires. Actions done because of beliefs and desires acquired under such conditions are not free.

Now is it really necessary that a person's beliefs and desires be caused by other people in order for it to be the case that they were forced upon him/her? Although it was true of our original examples, I do not think it is a necessary condition. While it may sound odd to say they were the result of force or coercion where no persons were the cause, it can certainly be said that the desires were not acquired freely, or even that they were acquired under coercive conditions. The issue about causation of beliefs and desires that is crucial to the freedom of acts resulting from them is whether the person enters into the causal process as an active determinant. If the person does not, then the beliefs and desires were not acquired freely, and acts resulting from them are not free because not self-determined. If, on the contrary, the beliefs and desires are opposed to the person's desires, first or second-order, then acts resulting from them are unfree or compelled. All this can be true even though the causes of the beliefs and desires were not measures taken by others to induce them. Suppose that a person lives under conditions of economic scarcity, which entails that not everyone will get what he/she needs and wants. A consequence of a person getting enough for himself and his family is that others will not have enough. A person in these conditions might, partly as a survival mechanism, come to desire that others not have enough—and might act on this desire. If this occurred, it seems to me that such an act would be an unfree one (although perhaps not at the very end of the continuum). If the person did not want to want that others not have enough, if in fact he/she wanted not to want this, then the desire would conflict with a second-order volition. Acts resulting from such desires are unfree. However, in the absence of a conflicting or reinforcing second-order volition, I would still wish to put the act on the unfree end of the continuum because the desires causing the act were produced under coercive conditions. The conditions were coercive because the person had no control over them, their existence was contrary to his/her desires, and his/her personality and character had little or no effect on their influence. Remove economic scarcity and the desire would be removed (although perhaps not immediately). Similar examples could be given of beliefs and desires caused by particular social systems and particular institutions within a social system.

V

Let us examine in some greater detail the conditions I have given under which desires could be said to have been acquired unfreely or coercively. It might be thought that my conditions apply too widely and would make too many desires turn out to have been unfreely acquired. For example, suppose a person has a strong desire to hear Bach because her parents regularly played Bach records in order to induce that desire. Her desire was acquired because of her parents' efforts to induce the desire. Their efforts consisted of intensively exposing her to the object they wished her to desire. If my conditions apply to such cases then her going to a concert as an adult because she wants to hear Bach played would be unfree—and this is an unattractive conclusion. However, my conditions do not lead to this conclusion, because the conditions I set are not met in the example. The child was not unaware of the causes of her later desire, which is what my condition requires; in fact it was by being aware of the music that was regularly played that she came to desire to hear it. Conceivably, but improbably, she was unaware that hearing the music was the cause of her later desire or that her parents regularly played it in order to produce that desire in her. However, these are different conditions from the one I gave. In general, where the measures taken to induce a desire simply amount to exposing a person to the object of the hoped-for desire, this does not meet my conditions, because the person cannot be unaware of the causes of the desire (although he/she may be unaware that they are the causes).

I am inclined to think that my conditions as they stand thus far are in need of revision in the other direction, that is, to make them apply more widely. Suppose that what was done to induce the desire was not mere exposure to the object, but rather conditioning. If they had conditioned her, the parents would have accompanied the playing of the music with pleasurable stimuli and they would have negatively reinforced any expressions of negative feeling toward the music. If this had been done, the desire would be the result of more than the interrelation of the person and the object of the desire, as is the case when the desire for something comes into being because of exposure to it. A desire that is the result of conditioning is the result of pleasures and pains that accompany the object, but are external to the person, the object, and the relation between them. When a person acquires desires and aversions for things because of pleasures and pains that are intrinsic to those things, such as the pleasures of eating good food, the pains of overeating, then those desires and aversions are freely acquired. Where the pleasures and pains are external, the *person* (that is, his/her personality, reasoning capacities, and so on) is bypassed in the process. This should make the process coercive. However, as my conditions stand they do not give this result. The person could be aware of the elements of the conditioning process (the music, the accompanying pleasures and pains), though unaware of the connections between them, the purposes behind them, and their effect. She was aware of the measures taken and therefore, if it were not explicitly against her will, the conditioning would not be coercive according to what I have said about coercion thus far. I take this to indicate that something more must be said.

In the hopes of working out how conditioning differs from mere exposure, let us go back to the example of the person who acquired a desire to hear the music of Bach because of repeated exposure to his music as a child. Whether the exposure was the deliberate work of others, as in our example, or not, acquisition of a desire through exposure differs from clearly coercive ways of acquiring desires. When people acquire a desire through being acquainted with the object or experience, they have the possibility of coming to have that desire or not. Whether they do or not will depend on facts about them: their aptitudes, beliefs, personality, other desires, and so on. Where this is the case they can be said to have control, or at least the possibility of control, over the desires they acquire. Where, on the other hand, the causes of their beliefs and desires would exist and would effectively operate regardless of the fact that their personality, character, other beliefs and desires are opposed to these causes, then they obviously have no chance of controlling what beliefs and desires they come to have.

We can distinguish, then, between cases where people can have control over their beliefs and desires and those where they cannot. Knowledge is necessary in order that a person have this possibility of control. In the account I gave of when a person could be said to have freely acquired his/her desires, I only required that the person have knowledge of the causes (and also that they not be against the person's will) in order that the causes not be coercive. Oftentimes, however, one needs to have more than simple knowledge of the causes. Conditioning is a case where the person being conditioned might know the causes, that is, might know the elements of the causal process, but might not know their interconnections or the purposes behind them. The person is acquainted with the causes but unaware that they are the causes or how and why they operate. If conditioning would operate regardless of whether a person knew the latter, then it is a causal process that the person cannot have any control over. Hence it is coercive.

Sometimes the efficacy of causal conditions depends on people's ignorance of them, that they are or may be causes, and how and why they operate. In such cases, people's ignorance of these facts would deprive them of whatever control knowledge might give them. People are less free to the extent that they operate on unconscious motives. Successful psychoanalysis can increase the patient's control and therefore freedom, by making conscious things that had hitherto been unconscious. Sometimes just knowing the purposes behind potential causes (for example, that it is designed to convince you, scare you, buy you off, or get you to buy something) can make a difference to whether those purposes are realized. Without the knowledge, one's attitudes towards these purposes cannot come into play and one cannot exercise any control over them. If the efficacy of the causes depends on one's ignorance of such facts about the causes, then the causes are coercive. It is where knowledge about the causes would have made a difference that ignorance makes the causes coercive. Causes of beliefs and desires are coercive where they operate contrary to the person's other beliefs, desires, character, and personality. This is so when the causes are explicitly against the person's will, or unknown to the person, or when they depend for their efficacy on the person's ignorance of certain facts about them. According to these conditions, conditioning would usually be coercive, which, I think, is as it should be.

Suppose one came to know that one was being conditioned and the knowledge made no difference to the efficacy of the causes. Is this a coercive way of acquiring desires? The answer depends on whether the conditioning process was against the person's will. If the causes operate against his/her will then they are coercive. On the other hand, suppose they are not operating against the person's will; in other words, suppose a person voluntarily chooses to be conditioned. A person might deliberately expose himself to conditions that will cause him to have (or not have) certain desires, for example, not to smoke. Once he puts himself into the situation, the causes operate independent of his other beliefs and desires, personality, and so on. His new effective desire not to smoke will be the result of conditioning, and we have said that conditioning is a form of coercion. However, I think that the circumstances of this kind of case make a significant difference. The person's self does enter into the causal process as an active determinant, whereas in most cases of conditioning this is not so. The person in our example who voluntarily has himself conditioned has a second-order volition not to smoke, which is in conflict with his or her volition to smoke. If the second-order volition were sufficiently strong to outweigh the first-order volition by itself, then the new effective desire would be acquired in a completely free manner. However, it is not sufficiently strong to do this by itself. Causes that are independent of the person are necessary to change his desire. However, these other causes come into play only because of his second-order volition. He had himself conditioned because he has a desire not to desire to smoke. So I think we can say that the cause of his new effective desire not to smoke is his second-order volition. The new desire is not the result of coercion; it does spring from the self. However, it does not only spring from the self. It was not acquired in as free a manner as if the second-order volition was sufficient by itself to cause it, but I would still put it towards the free end of the continuum.

What we have come up with is what we started with—and that is, to the extent that the causes of one's actions are themselves caused by things over which people have no control (even with knowledge of them), to that extent one's actions are unfree. What I have tried to do is to make sense of the idea of having control over one's desires. In order to say that one has control over one's desires it is necessary that what we identify as the self determines what one desires and what desires one acts on. To put together the criteria elaborated thus far: In order for actions caused by desires to be free, these desires must first of all not have been coercively acquired. What this means has been explained. Knowledge was seen to be a key factor. Secondly, they must not be contrary to the person's second-order volitions. This second condition implies that the person has second-order volitions. We will not be able to say that these desires are the desires the person wants to have unless (a) he/she has second-order volitions and unless (b) these volitions outweigh first-order volitions in the case of a conflict. Thirdly, the desire must be in harmony with an integrated set of desires and beliefs—hence one's self—at that given time. This third requirement must be qualified. A desire causing a free action may be inconsistent with this integrated set if the set does not meet one of the necessary conditions and the desire fulfills both the conditions. If the set was coercively acquired and the conflicting desire was not, or if the conflicting desire is supported by a second-order volition and the set is not, then an action caused by the conflicting desire would be free. Any person missing second-order volitions is missing an important kind of control over his/her actions, and hence an important dimension of freedom. That is why an action that proceeds from a conflicting desire that is supported by a second-order volition is freer than one that proceeded from the integrated set, where there are no effective second-order volitions. This sort of situation could lead to a revision of the set—a restructuring of the self. However, lacking an integrated set that is responsible for his/her actions, the person is divided, and it is less possible for that person to be a self-determining being. Therefore, the person is most free when there is an integrated set that is in accordance with his/her second-order volitions. Then we can say that this is a self-determining person.

VI

An objection that will almost certainly be raised to what I have said thus far is that I have failed to carry through the logic of my argument. If, in order to have control over one's actions (that is, for one's actions to be free), it is necessary to have control over the causes of one's actions (that is, one's desires), then in order to have control over them, it is also necessary to have control over *their* causes, and in order to have control over them, it is necessary . . . In short, we are led to an infinite regress, or at least to a point where the person cannot possibly have any control—namely, a point before they are born. If it leads back to this point, then we can never have control over what we do. And so it seems we are led back to a choice of hard determinism, indeterminism, or a position like Taylor's.

I do not agree that the logic of my argument has to lead back to this point. In order to take this same analysis further back, one would have to make sense of having control over both (a) the integrated set of beliefs and desires and also over (b) one's second-order volitions. Taking the former first, one way of having control over this integrated act would be to have effective second-order volitions with respect to it. This is already part of my account. Aside from having effective second-order volitions with respect to the integrated set of beliefs, desires, and so on, is there any other way in which one might be said to have or lack control over it? To give any other sense to how one might have control over this integrated set would require that some person or self be found to have control over it. But in the absence of a higher-order volition, where and what is this entity that might but does not control this set? Unless some sense can be made of such an entity the idea remains incoherent, and my account thus far has not been shown to lead too far back.

To turn to (b), having control over one's second-order volitions, we can make sense of this if we bring in the idea of third-order volitions (wanting to want to want), and we could bring in volitions of still higher orders. I am not opposed to this but it is an empirical question just how far back we can go in any given case. Frankfurt deals with the point in the following way:

> There is no *theoretical* [my emphasis] limit to the length of the series of desires of higher and higher orders; nothing but common sense and, perhaps, a saving fatigue. . . . The tendency to generate such a series of acts of forming desires . . . leads to the destruction of a person. . . . It is possible, however, to terminate such a series of acts without cutting it off arbitrarily. When a person identified himself *decisively* with one of his first-order desires, this commitment "resounds" throughout the potentially endless array of higher orders. . . . The decisiveness of the commitment he has made means that he has decided that no further question about his second-order volition, at any higher order, remains to be asked. It is relatively unimportant whether we explain this by saying that the commitment implicitly generates an endless series of confirming desires of higher orders, or by saying that the commitment is tantamount to a dissolution of the pointedness of all questions concerning higher orders of desire.[7]

A person does not have an indefinite number of orders of volition with respect to a given desire. Once we have reached the point where a person has identified him/herself with a particular volition, the idea of that person having control over his/her desires of that order through volitions of a higher order seems to make no sense, because that person does not go further back. The person, a discriminating being capable of choice among desires, has committed and identified him/herself with a particular volition. To go further back is to leave the person behind. To speak of identifying oneself with a volition requires the possibility of desires of more than one order, but it does not require an indefinite series.

Let us approach the question from a slightly different angle. A second-order volition might be the result of a higher-order volition, or of coercion, or of neither of these. If a second-order volition results from a volition of a higher order, then the person can be said to have control over that [second-order] volition. Suppose now that the person's second-order volition was not the result of a higher-order volition, but neither was it the result of coercion. This would be true where the person had no higher-order volitions relevant to the second-order volition, but where the causes would not have operated if there had been second-order volitions in conflict [with those causes]. (If they would have operated anyway then they would be coercive.) In such cases, it seems to me that the volitions should be said to have been acquired freely. It certainly was not acquired unfreely. The person did not *lack* control, and would have had control if there had been higher-order volitions. A person can be said to have acquired a second-order volition through coercion if the person has conflicting volitions of a still higher order that are ineffective against these causes. The person then lacks control over his/her second-order volitions in an obvious way. Where the person has no volitions of a higher order, or where the person has decisively identified him/herself with the volition, Frankfurt and I have argued that something is wrong with saying that the person lacks control, because the person does not go further back. However, suppose that, if there were a conflicting

---

[7]Frankfurt, "Freedom of the Will and the Concept of a Person," pp. 16–17. [N. Holmstrom]

higher-order volition (although there isn't one), it would be ineffective. I am inclined to say that in this case as well, the person lacks control over his/her volitions and the causes are coercive. If this is correct, then a person lacks control over second-order volitions if conflicting higher-order volitions (whether the person has any or not) would be ineffective against them.

One might argue that because a person lacks control over his/her second-order volitions it does not follow that he/she lacks control over his/her first-order volitions or over his/her actions. I would want to distinguish between two sorts of cases. Recall that I distinguished two kinds of cases of second-order volitions acquired through coercion: (a) ones in which there were conflicting volitions of a higher order, and (b) ones in which there were no volitions of a higher order, but if there had been they would have been ineffective. It seems to me that where the second-order volitions result from coercion in the latter sort of case, actions proceeding from them are still free. The sense in which the second-order volitions were coerced is a more extended hypothetical sense, and I therefore see little need to infer that the person's first-order volitions and actions must also have been coerced. On the other hand, if the person's second-order volitions are coerced as described in (a), the person lacked control and was coerced in more obvious and direct ways. Although it does not strictly follow, it seems more consistent with what I have been arguing to conclude that in such cases the person should be said to lack control over his/her first-order volitions and his/her actions. I have argued that people have control over their actions when they have control over their causes (beliefs and desires), and that they have control over these when they are caused by second-order volitions. If there are higher-order volitions that are ineffective against the causes of the second-order volitions, then the person has no control over these second-order volitions. And it seems closer to the general line of argument I have been using, to conclude that in such cases they also have no control over their first-order volitions and actions.

VII

As a prelude to concluding, I wish to consider the implications of my general and abstract analysis to the concrete question of just how free most people are today. We shall see that although my view implies that people can be free, though determined, it is also an implication of my view that most people are quite unfree today. The answer to this question of how free people are is not one that applies to all people just in virtue of their being human, but rather depends on who the people are and where and when they are living. It turns out, then, on my view, that human freedom is closely tied to social and political freedom and is not a distinct metaphysical[8] question. (In considering this part of the philosophical question we are inevitably drawn into empirical issues, including political ones, so my own opinion on these matters will certainly intrude.)

---

[8]*metaphysical:* relating to *metaphysics,* the study of the nature and kinds of reality. [D. C. ABEL]

Desires arise in us because of a whole complex set of conditions that affect one another. (Neither they nor their influence can actually be separated, so the following remarks are unavoidably artificial.) These determining conditions include physical and psychological conditions that to some extent we share with others, but that also differ from person to person. People today are capable of some but not much control over these conditions. Greater knowledge, aided by money, gives a person greater possibilities of control, but there are still very definite limits that no one today is capable of transcending. Greater knowledge will give greater possibilities of human control, but it is probable that there will always be limits that one cannot transcend. What is possible is for a person to exercise some control over the form of the desires these conditions tend to produce, and also over whether and how these desires are acted upon.

How much control a person can exercise over the social and political conditions causing his/her desires depends on the particular social system in which the person lives, and also the place that the person occupies in the system. Some changes are possible in the latter in most societies but usually quite little. In any case, it is only within the framework allowed by that system and it is not possible within the framework of *any* present society for *most* people to change their positions within that framework. As for the framework itself, one cannot change the time in which one lives, and since what social systems are possible depends on the time and place, there is a certain inevitable limitation. However, there are many fewer inevitable limitations on the degree of control one can exercise over social causes than over physical causes—in the future, but also in the present. Given the limitations of time and place, there is great potential today for people to collectively control the social conditions under which they live, and hence the beliefs and desires these conditions tend to produce, even if there are some conditions they still would not be able to control. However, with some notable exceptions, the ability to control the social conditions in which one lives is only potential today, not actual. This is partially because people do not realize they have this ability. This lack of realization is strongly supported, of course, by the social system in which they live and by those who do control it. There is, again, the possibility of exercising some control over the form of the desires likely to be produced by these conditions, and also over whether and how these desires are acted upon. However, so long as one does not control the social causes of one's beliefs and desires, one does not have much chance of controlling the actual beliefs and desires one comes to have.

Leaving aside the nature of the influence, what is necessary in order to be able to exercise control over the influences acting upon one, is to be a certain kind of person, as well as to have knowledge and the cooperation of others. A person who is critical and discriminating and sees him/herself as actively shaping the world, history, and also him/herself, is capable of doing just that—not alone, but in cooperation with others. There are, of course, varying conditions where people may be more or less aware and/or more or less able not to be passive products. However, it seems that most people today are quite uncritical and undiscriminating and lack this self-conception. Many feel themselves to be more like passive products of history and their own particular environment—and their environment makes them feel that way. However, in the course of struggle against the oppressive aspects of their environment, they can come to realize their potential to bring the world under their conscious collective control. The realization of this is a first step towards changing the framework that keeps them without control. This capacity to change the world and consequently their own nature is unique to human beings. It gives them the potential of being free in the fullest sense that is possible in a deterministic world.

The Impossibility of Ultimate Moral Responsibility[1]

Galen Strawson

Galen Strawson was born in 1952 in Oxford, England. After earning a master's degree in art from Trinity Hall, Cambridge University, he pursued further graduate work at Wolfson College, Oxford University, where he completed his bachelor's degree in philosophy in 1977 and his doctorate in philosophy in 1983. During the 1977–1978 academic year he attended the Ecole Normale Superior in Paris as a French government scholar. From 1979 to 1990 Strawson taught at Oxford University, where he held successive posts as lecturer in philosophy at University College, Exeter College, St. Hugh's College, New College, and St. Hilda's College, and as fellow and tutor in philosophy at Jesus College. He has held visiting appointments at Australian National University, New York University, and Rutgers University. Strawson is currently professor of philosophy at Reading University, England, and distinguished professor of philosophy at the City University of New York Graduate Center. He received the T. H. Green Prize for Moral Philosophy from Oxford University in 1983 and has been an editor of the *Times Literary Supplement* (London, England) since 1988.

Strawson's publications include *Freedom and Belief* (1986; 2nd ed., 2010); *The Secret Connexion: Causation, Realism, and David Hume* (1989); *Mental Reality* (1994; 2nd ed., 2010); *Real Materialism and Other Essays* (2008); and *Selves: An Essay in Revisionary Metaphysics* (2009).

Our reading is from Strawson's 1994 article "The Impossibility of Ultimate Moral Responsibility" (reprinted in *Real Materialism and Other Essays*), in which Strawson presents and defends what he terms the "Basic Argument." According to the Basic Argument, we have no ultimate moral responsibility for any of our actions—that is, praise or blame, or reward and punishment for our actions can never be ultimately just. (Strawson points out that it makes no difference to the Basic Argument whether determinism—the doctrine that all our actions are determined by preceding causes and we can never act otherwise than we do—is true or false. For even if some changes in the way we are are influenced by events that are random or undetermined by causes, we are clearly not morally responsible for random or undetermined events.) The reason we are not ultimately morally responsible is that our actions derive from how we are; and how we are derives ultimately from our heredity and early experience; and we are not morally responsible for our heredity or early experience. Later on in life we can try to change the way we are, but our decision and efforts to do so are *themselves* determined by our heredity and previous experience.

In the latter part of his article, Strawson gives his response to three prominent theoretical positions on free will that defend the notion of moral responsibility: *compatibilism*, which holds that we can be morally responsible for actions even if we cannot act otherwise than we do; *libertarianism*, which holds that we can sometimes act otherwise than we do; and the *self theory*, which holds that even though we are not ultimately responsible our

---

[1]The title of the original journal article (1994) was "The Impossibility of Moral Responsibility." Strawson expanded the title when the article was reprinted in his book *Real Materialism, and Other Essays* (New York: Oxford University Press, 2008). [D. C. ABEL]

318

character, personality, or motivational structure, we are morally responsible for our choices because we have a "self" that can make choices independently of these three elements. Strawson argues that none of these theories successfully refutes the Basic Argument.

1

There is an argument, which I will call the Basic Argument, that appears to prove that we cannot be truly or ultimately morally responsible for our actions. According to the Basic Argument, it makes no difference whether determinism[2] is true or false. We cannot be truly or ultimately morally responsible for our actions in either case.

The Basic Argument has various expressions in the literature of free will, and its central idea can be quickly conveyed:

(1) Nothing can be *causa sui*—nothing can be the cause of itself.

(2) In order to be truly morally responsible for one's actions one would have to be *causa sui*, at least in certain crucial mental respects.

(3) Therefore nothing can be truly morally responsible.

In this paper I want to reconsider the Basic Argument, in the hope that anyone who thinks that we can be truly or ultimately morally responsible for our actions will be prepared to say exactly what is wrong with it. I think that the point that it has to make is obvious, and that it has been underrated in recent discussion of free will—perhaps because it admits of no answer. I suspect that it is obvious in such a way that insisting on it too much is likely to make it seem less obvious than it is, given the innate contrasuggestibility of human beings in general and philosophers in particular. But I am not worried about making it seem less obvious than it is so long as it gets adequate attention. As far as its validity is concerned, it can look after itself. . . .

The same argument can be given in [the following] form:

(1) It is undeniable that one is the way one is, initially, as a result of heredity and early experience, and it is undeniable that these are things for which one cannot be held to be in any responsible (morally or otherwise).

(2) One cannot at any later stage of life hope to accede to true moral responsibility for the way one is by trying to change the way one already is as a result of heredity and previous experience. For:

(3) Both the particular way in which one is moved to try to change oneself, and the degree of one's success in one's attempt at change, will be determined by how one already is as a result of heredity and previous experience. And:

(4) Any further changes that one can bring about only after one has brought about certain initial changes will in turn be determined, via the initial changes, by heredity and previous experience.

---

[2]*determinism:* the doctrine that all events are determined by preceding causes and that we can never act otherwise than we do. [D. C. ABEL]

(5) This may not be the whole story, for it may be that some changes in the
     way one is are traceable not to heredity and experience but to the influ-
     ence of indeterministic³ or random factors. But it is absurd to suppose
     that indeterministic or random factors, for which one is ex hypothesi⁴ in
     no way responsible, can in themselves contribute in any way to one's
     being truly morally responsible for how one is.

The claim, then, is not that people cannot change the way they are. They can,
in certain respects (which tend to be exaggerated by North Americans and
underestimated, perhaps, by Europeans). The claim is only that people cannot be
supposed to change themselves in such a way as to be or become truly or ultimately morally responsible for the way they are, and hence for their actions. . . .

3

. . . It is important to try to be precise about what sort of responsibility is under
discussion. What sort of "true" moral responsibility is being said to be both
impossible and widely believed in?
     An old story is very helpful in clarifying this question. This is the story of
heaven and hell. As I understand it, true moral responsibility is responsibility
of such a kind that, if we have it, then it *makes sense,* at least, to suppose that it
could be just to punish some of us with (eternal) torment in hell and reward
others with (eternal) bliss in heaven. The stress on the words "makes sense" is
important, for one certainly does not have to believe in any version of the story
of heaven and hell in order to understand the notion of true moral responsibility that it is being used to illustrate. Nor does one have to believe in any version of the story of heaven and hell in order to believe in the existence of true
moral responsibility. On the contrary: Many atheists have believed in the existence of true moral responsibility. The story of heaven and hell is useful simply
because it illustrates, in a peculiarly vivid way, the *kind* of absolute or ultimate
accountability or responsibility that many have supposed themselves to have,
and that many do still suppose themselves to have. It very clearly expresses its
scope and force.
     But one does not have to refer to religious faith in order to describe the sorts
of everyday situation that are perhaps primarily influential in giving rise to our
belief in true responsibility. Suppose you set off for a shop on the evening of a
national holiday, intending to buy a cake with your last ten-pound note. On the
steps of the shop someone is shaking an Oxfam⁵ tin. You stop, and it seems completely clear to you that it is entirely up to you what you do next. That is, it
seems to you that you are truly, radically free to choose, in such a way that you
will be ultimately morally responsible for whatever you do choose. Even if you

---

³*indeterministic:* relating to *indeterminism,* the doctrine that some or all events are not determined by
preceding causes. [D. C. ABEL]
⁴*ex hypothesi:* (Latin) by hypothesis. [D. C. ABEL]
⁵*Oxfam:* a confederation of organizations dedicated to ending poverty and injustice. [D. C. ABEL]

believe that determinism is true, and that you will in five minutes time be able to look back and say that what you did was determined, this does not seem to undermine your sense of the absoluteness and inescapability of your freedom, and of your moral responsibility for your choice. The same seems to be true even if you accept the validity of the Basic Argument stated in Section 1, which concludes that one cannot be in any way ultimately responsible for the way one is and decides. In both cases, it remains true that as one stands there, one's freedom and true moral responsibility seem obvious and absolute to one.

Large and small, morally significant or morally neutral, such situations of choice occur regularly in human life. I think they lie at the heart of the experience of freedom and moral responsibility. They are the fundamental source of our inability to give up belief in true or ultimate moral responsibility. . . .

5

Let me now restate the Basic Argument in very loose—as it were, conversational— terms. New forms of words allow for new forms of objection, but they may be helpful nonetheless.

(1) You do what you do, in any situation in which you find yourself, because of the way you are. So:
(2) To be truly morally responsible for what you do, you must be truly responsible for the way you are—at least in certain crucial mental respects.

Or:

(1) What you intentionally do, given the circumstances in which you (believe you) find yourself, flows necessarily from how you are. Hence:
(2) You have to get to have some responsibility for how you are in order to get to have some responsibility for what you intentionally do, given the circumstances in which you (believe you) find yourself.

Comment. Once again the qualification about "certain mental respects" is one I will take for granted. Obviously one is not responsible for one's sex, one's basic body pattern, one's height, and so on. But if one were not responsible for anything about oneself, how one could be responsible for what one did, given the truth of (1)? This is the fundamental question, and it seems clear that if one is going to be responsible for any aspect of oneself, it had better be some aspect of one's mental nature.

I take it that (1) is incontrovertible, and that it is (2) that must be resisted. For if (1) and (2) are conceded, the case seems lost, because the full argument runs as follows:

(1) You do what you do because of the way you are. So:
(2) To be truly morally responsible for what you do you must be truly responsible for the way you are—at least in certain crucial mental respects. But:
(3) You cannot be truly responsible for the way you are, so you cannot be truly responsible for what you do. Why can't you be truly responsible for the way you are? Because:

(4) To be truly responsible for the way you are, you must have intentionally brought it about that you are the way you are, and this is impossible. Why is it impossible? Well, suppose it is not. Suppose that:

(5) You have somehow intentionally brought it about that you are the way you now are, and that you have brought this about in such a way that you can now be said to be truly responsible for being the way you are now. For this to be true:

(6) You must already have had a certain nature N in the light of which you intentionally brought it about that you are as you now are. But then:

(7) For it to be true that you and you alone are truly responsible for how you now are, you must be truly responsible for having had the nature N in the light of which you intentionally brought it about that you are the way you now are. So:

(8) You must have intentionally brought it about that you had that nature N, in which case you must have existed already with a prior nature in the light of which you intentionally brought it about that you had the nature N in the light of which you intentionally brought it about that you are the way you now are. . . .

Here one is setting off on the regress. Nothing can be *causa sui* in the required way. Even if such causal "aseity"[6] is allowed to belong unintelligibly to God, it cannot be plausibly be supposed to be possessed by ordinary finite human beings. "The *causa sui* is the best self-contradiction that has been conceived so far," as Nietzsche remarked in 1886:

> It is a sort of rape and perversion of logic. But the extravagant pride of man has managed to entangle itself profoundly and frightfully with just this nonsense. The desire for "freedom of the will" in the superlative metaphysical[7] sense, which still holds sway, unfortunately, in the minds of the half-educated; the desire to bear the entire and ultimate responsibility for one's actions oneself, and to absolve God, the world, ancestors, chance, and society involves nothing less than to be precisely *causa sui* and, with more than Baron Münchhausen's[8] audacity, to pull oneself up into existence by the hair, out of the swamps of nothingness.[9]

The rephrased argument is essentially exactly the same as before, although the first two steps are now more simply stated. It may seem pointless to repeat it, but the questions remain. Can the Basic Argument simply be dismissed? It is really of no importance in the discussion of free will and moral responsibility? (No and No.) Shouldn't any serious defense of free will and moral responsibility thoroughly acknowledge the respect in which the Basic Argument is valid before going on to try to give its own positive account of the nature of free will and moral responsibility? Doesn't the argument go to the heart of things if the

---

[6]*aseity:* the property whereby something exists from and of itself. [D. C. ABEL]

[7]*metaphysical:* relating to *metaphysics,* the study of the nature and kinds of reality. [D. C. ABEL]

[8]Karl Friedrich Hieronymous von Münchhausen (1720–1797) was a German soldier and teller of tall tales. [D. C. ABEL]

[9]Friedrich Nietzsche, *Beyond Good and Evil,* trans. Walter Kaufman (New York: Vintage Books, 1966), Part One, Section 21, p. 28. [G. STRAWSON]

heart of the free will debate is a concern about whether we can be truly morally responsible in the absolute way that we ordinarily suppose? (Yes and Yes.)

We are what we are, and we cannot be thought to have made ourselves *in such a way* that we can be held to be free in our actions *in such a way* that we can be held to be morally responsible for our actions *in such a way* that any punishment or reward for our actions is ultimately just or fair. Punishments and rewards may seem deeply appropriate or intrinsically "fitting" to us in spite of this argument, and many of the various institutions of punishment and reward in human society appear to be practically indispensable in both their legal and non-legal forms. But if one takes the notion of justice that is central to our intellectual and cultural tradition seriously, then the evident consequence of the Basic Argument is that there is a fundamental sense in which no punishment or reward is ever ultimately just. It is exactly as just to punish or reward people for their actions as it is to punish or reward them for the (natural) color of their hair or the (natural) shape of their faces. The point seems obvious, and yet it contradicts a fundamental part of our natural self-conception, and there are elements in human thought that move very deeply against it. When it comes to questions or responsibility, we tend to feel that we are somehow responsible for the way we are. Even more importantly, perhaps, we tend to feel that our explicit self-conscious awareness of ourselves as agents who are able to deliberate about what to do, in situations of choice, suffices to constitute us as morally responsible free agents in the strongest sense, whatever the conclusion of the Basic Argument.

6

I have suggested that it is step (2) of the restated Basic Argument that must be rejected, and of course it can be rejected, because the phrases "truly responsible" and "truly morally responsible" can be defined in many ways. I will briefly consider three sorts of response to the Basic Argument, and I will concentrate on their more simple expressions, in the belief that truth in philosophy, especially in areas of philosophy like the present one, is almost never very complicated.

(i) The first is *compatibilist.* Compatibilists believe that one can be a free and morally responsible agent even if determinism is true. Roughly, they claim, with many variations of detail, that one may correctly be said to be truly responsible for what one does when one acts, just so long as one is not caused to act by any of a certain set of constraints (kleptomaniac impulses, obsessional neuroses, desires that are experienced as alien, post-hypnotic commands, threats, instances of *force majeure,*[10] and so on). Clearly, this sort of compatibilist responsibility does not require that one should be truly responsible for how one is in any way at all, and so step (2) of the Basic Argument comes out as false. One can have compatibilist responsibility even if the way one is is totally determined by factors entirely outside one's control.

It is for this reason, however, that compatibilist responsibility famously fails to amount to any sort of true *moral* responsibility, given the natural, strong

---

[10]*force majeure:* (French, "greater force") an irresistible force. [D. C. ABEL]

understanding of the notion of true moral responsibility (characterized above by reference to the story of heaven and hell). One does what one does entirely because of the way one is, and one is in no way ultimately responsible for the way one is. So how can one be justly punished for anything one does? Compatibilists have given increasingly refined accounts of the circumstances in which punishment may be said to be appropriate or intrinsically fitting. But they can do nothing against this basic objection.

Many compatibilists have never supposed otherwise. They are happy to admit the point. They observe that the notions of true moral responsibility and justice that are employed in the objection cannot possibly have application to anything real, and suggest that the objection is therefore not worth considering. In response, proponents of the Basic Argument agree that the notions of true moral responsibility and justice in question cannot have application to anything real; but they make no apologies for considering them. They consider them because they are central to ordinary thought about moral responsibility and justice. So far as most people are concerned, they are the subject, if the subject is moral responsibility and justice.

(ii) The second response is *libertarian*. Incompatibilists believe that freedom and moral responsibility are incompatible with determinism, and some of them are libertarians, who believe that we are free and morally responsible agents, and that determinism is therefore false. In an ingenious statement of the incompatibilist-libertarian case, Robert Kane argues that agents in an undetermined world can have free will, for they can "have the power to make choices for which they have ultimate responsibility." That is, they can "have the power to make choices that can only and finally be explained in terms of their own wills (that is, character, motives, and efforts of will)."[11] Roughly, Kane sees this power as grounded in the possible occurrence, in agents, of efforts of will that have two main features: first, they are partly indeterministic in their nature, and hence indeterminate in their outcome; second, they occur in cases in which agents are trying to make a difficult choice between the options that their characters dispose them to consider. (The paradigm cases will be cases in which they face a conflict between moral duty and nonmoral desire.)

But the old objection to libertarianism recurs. How can this indeterminism help with moral responsibility? Granted that the truth of determinism rules out true moral responsibility, how can the falsity of determinism help? How can the occurrence of partly random or indeterministic events contribute in any way to one's being truly morally responsible either for one's actions or for one's character? If my efforts of will shape my character in an admirable way, and in so doing are partly indeterministic in nature, while also being shaped (as Kane grants) by my already existing character, why am I not merely lucky?

The general objection applies equally whether determinism is true or false, and can be restated as follows. We are born with a great many genetically determined predispositions for which we are not responsible. We are subject to many early influences for which we are not responsible. These decisively shape

---

[11]Robert Kane, "Two Kinds of Incompatibilism," *Philosophy and Phenomenological Research* 50 (December 1989): 254. I have omitted some italics. [G. STRAWSON]

our characters, our motives, the general bent and strength of our capacity to make efforts of will. We may later engage in conscious and intentional shaping procedures—call them S-procedures—designed to affect and change our characters, motivational structure, and wills. Suppose we do. The question is then why we engage in the particular S-procedures that we do engage in, and why we engage in them in the particular way that we do. The general answer is that we engage in the particular S-procedures that we do engage in, given the circumstances in which we find ourselves, because of certain features of the way we already are. (Indeterministic factors may also play a part in what happens, but these will not help to make us responsible for what we do.) And these features of the way we already are—call them character features, or C-features—are either wholly the products of genetic or environmental influences, deterministic or random, for which we are not responsible, or are at least partly the result of earlier S-procedures, which are in turn either wholly the product of C-features for which we are not responsible, or are at least partly the product of still earlier S-procedures, which are in turn either the products of C-features for which we are not responsible, or the product of such C-features together with still earlier S-procedures—and so on. In the end, we reach the first S-procedure, and this will have been engaged in, and engaged in the particular way in which it was engaged in, as a result of genetic or environmental factors, deterministic or random, for which we were not responsible.

Moving away from the possible role of indeterministic factors in character or personality formation, we can consider their possible role in particular instances of deliberation and decision. Here too it seems clear that indeterministic factors cannot, in influencing what happens, contribute to true moral responsibility in any way. In the end, whatever we do, we do it either as a result of random influences for which we are not responsible, or as a result of nonrandom influences for which we are not responsible, or as a result of influences for which we are proximally responsible but not ultimately responsible. The point seems obvious. Nothing can be ultimately *causa sui* in any respect at all. Even if God can be, we can't be. . . .

(iii) The third option begins by accepting that one cannot be held to be ultimately responsible for one's character or personality or motivational structure. It accepts that this is so whether determinism is true or false. It then directly challenges step (2) of the Basic Argument. It appeals to a certain picture of the self in order to argue that one can be truly free and morally responsible in spite of the fact that one cannot be held to be ultimately responsible for one's character or personality or motivational structure. This picture has some support in the "phenomenology"[12] of human choice—we sometimes experience our choices and decisions as if the picture were an accurate one. But it is easy to show that it cannot be accurate in such a way that we can be said to be truly or ultimately morally responsible for our choices or actions.

It can be set out as follows. One is free and truly morally responsible because one's self is, in a crucial sense, independent of one's character or

---

[12]*phenomenology:* the study of how things appear to and are experienced by a knowing subject. [D. C. ABEL]

personality or motivational structure—one's CPM, for short. Suppose one is in a situation that one experiences as a difficult choice between A, doing one's duty, and B, following one's nonmoral desires. Given one's CPM, one responds in a certain way. One's desires and beliefs develop and interact and constitute reasons for both A and B. One's CPM makes one tend towards A or B. So far the problem is the same as ever: Whatever one does, one will do what one does because of the way one's CPM is, and since one neither is nor can be ultimately responsible for the way one's CPM is, one cannot be ultimately responsible for what one does.

Enter one's self, S. S is imagined to be in some way independent of one's CPM. S (that is, one) considers the deliverances of one's CPM and decides in the light of them, but it—S—incorporates a power of decision that is independent of one's CPM in such a way that one can after all count as truly and ultimately morally responsible in one's decisions and actions, even though one is not ultimately responsible for one's CPM. Step (2) of the Basic Argument is false because of the existence of S.

The trouble with the picture is obvious. S (that is, one) decides on the basis of the deliverances of one's CPM. But whatever S decides, it decides as it does because of the way it is (or else partly or wholly because of the occurrence in the decision process of indeterministic factors for which it—that is, one—cannot be responsible, and that cannot plausibly be thought to contribute to one's true moral responsibility). And this returns us to where we started. To be a source of true or ultimate responsibility, S must be responsible for being the way it is. But this is impossible, for the reasons given in the Basic Argument.

The story of S and CPM adds another layer to the description of the human decision process, but it cannot change the fact that human beings cannot be ultimately self-determining in such a way as to be ultimately morally responsible for how they are, and thus for how they decide and act. The story is crudely presented, but it should suffice to make clear that no move of this sort can solve the problem.

"Character is destiny," as Novalis is often reported as saying.[13] The remark is inaccurate because external circumstances are part of destiny, but the point is well taken when it comes to the question of moral responsibility. Nothing can be *causa sui*, and in order to be truly morally responsible for one's actions one would have to be *causa sui*, at least in certain crucial mental respects. One cannot institute oneself in such a way that one can take over true or assume moral responsibility for how one is in such a way that one can indeed be truly morally responsible for what one does. This fact is not changed by the fact that we may be unable not to think of ourselves as truly morally responsible in ordinary circumstances. Nor is it changed by the fact that it may be a very good thing that we have this inability—so that we might wish to take steps to preserve it, if it looked to be in danger of fading. As already remarked, many human beings are

---

[13]For example, by George Eliot in *The Mill on the Floss*, Book 6, Chapter 6. [G. STRAWSON] Novalis was the pseudonym of German poet and theorist Georg Philipp Friedrich Freiherr von Hardenberg (1772–1801); George Eliot was the pseudonym of English novelist Mary Anne (or Marian) Evans (1819–1880). [D. C. ABEL]

unable to resist the idea that it is their capacity for fully explicit self-conscious deliberation, in a situation of choice, that suffices to constitute them as truly morally responsible agents in the strongest possible sense. The Basic Argument shows that this is a mistake. However self-consciously aware we are, as we deliberate and reason, every act and operation of our mind happens as it does as a result of features for which we are ultimately in no way responsible. But the conviction that self-conscious awareness of one's situation can be a sufficient foundation of strong free will is very powerful. It runs deeper than rational argument, and it survives untouched, in the everyday conduct of life, even after the validity of the Basic Argument has been admitted.

CHAPTER 6

Ethics

All of us could name certain actions that we think are morally right and others that we think are morally wrong. But what is it that makes an action morally right or wrong? Is it the way it affects other people? If so, what kinds of effects are good and what kinds are bad? Is it the intention behind our action? If so, what kinds of intentions are good and what kinds are bad? Is the goodness or evil of an action determined by whether it follows some rule of conduct? If so, how do we know whether the rule itself is good? Even if the rule *is* good, might it be morally better to make an exception to it in a particular situation? Can morality be adequately defined in terms of actions and rules, or does morality depend more on the *kind of person* we are? If so, what kind of qualities make a person good and what kind make a person bad? To ask a more radical question, are all judgments of moral good and evil—whether we are speaking of actions or personal qualities—simply a matter of opinion?

These are some of the questions addressed by the philosophical discipline of ethics. The word "ethics" derives from the Greek *ēthos,* which means "custom" in the singular and "character" in the plural *(ēthē).* The word "morality" has a parallel origin: It derives from the Latin *mos,* which—exactly like the Greek *ēthos*—means "custom" in the singular and "character" in the plural *(mores).* These root meanings indicate that ethics (morality) is concerned with what we do (custom) and with the kind of person we are (character). What we do is, of course, closely connected with the kind of person we are, because our character is formed largely by the way we habitually act. Using the root meanings as a guide, we can define ethics as the study of how we should live our life and what kind of person we should be. More succinctly, ethics is the study of right conduct and character.

Philosophy is not the only discipline to propose theories about proper conduct and character; theology also sets forth such theories. The principal difference between philosophical ethics and theological ethics is that the former bases its answers on reason and experience, and the latter appeals ultimately to faith and divine revelation. In philosophical ethics, all questions about morality are open to debate— even the question of whether there *is* a correct morality. Theological ethics, by contrast, assumes that the answers given by revelation are true; to call these answers into question is to leave the realm of theological ethics. Although theologians may disagree about the precise *meaning* of revealed moral directives (for example, "Thou shalt not kill"), they do not question their *truth*. The readings in this book, of course, are confined to philosophical ethics.

Our first section of readings, "Classical Ethical Theories," presents selections from four thinkers whose ethical doctrines have become central to the Western philosophical tradition. Aristotle argues that we all ultimately seek happiness and that we should live in a way that leads to happiness. He claims that being happy means living rationally and that living rationally means acting in accordance with excellences (virtues) of intellect and of character. To attain happiness, therefore, we must acquire these excellences. Thomas Aquinas maintains that we should live our lives in a way that conforms to "natural law"—the moral law that derives from the basic inclinations of our human nature. Immanuel Kant contends that being moral means acting out of duty, which in turn means following the "categorical imperative." The categorical imperative states that we may perform an action only if we can consistently will that *everyone* follow the policy upon which our action is based. The final classical theory presented here is that of John Stuart Mill. Mill explains and defends the theory of utilitarianism, the doctrine that we should always act in a way that promotes utility. By "utility" he means the greatest good of the greatest number. Mill defines "good" as pleasure and the absence of pain; he includes in the "greatest number" all creatures capable of feeling pleasure and pain.

The five authors in the second group of readings, "Critiques of Classical Theories," call into question some of the fundamental assumptions of traditional Western ethics.

Søren Kierkegaard argues that ethics exalts the universal, subordinating the individual person to universal norms of conduct. Religious faith, however, transports us to a higher sphere of existence, where the individual is superior to the universal. Friedrich Nietzsche characterizes traditional morality as "slave morality" and argues that the qualities that traditional morality classifies as virtues (for example, kindness and selflessness) are actually life-denying vices. He believes that true morality is "master morality," which affirms life by exercising the "will to power." Jean-Paul Sartre rejects the claim that ethics can be based on human nature, because he holds that there *is* no human nature. Our ethical task is to create our nature through our choices. For Sartre, we do not choose something because it is good; it is good because we choose it. James Rachels and Stuart Rachels discuss the challenge to traditional ethics posed by cultural relativism, the doctrine that moral values derive entirely from individual cultural codes and that there are no objective, independently valid moral values. They present the arguments given to support this doctrine and point out their weaknesses. The final reading is from Rita C. Manning, who approaches ethics from a feminist perspective. She proposes an "ethic of care," arguing that morality consists essentially in having a disposition to care and in expressing this disposition in concrete actions.

A. Classical Ethical Theories

READING 32
Nicomachean Ethics
Aristotle

Aristotle was born in the town of Stagira in northern Greece in 384 B.C.E. At the age of 17, he went to Athens to study at Plato's Academy, where he remained until Plato's death 20 years later. He then spent three years in the city of Assos in Asia Minor and two years in Mytilene on the island of Lesbos. In 343 or 342 he accepted the invitation of King Philip II of Macedon to become the tutor of his 13-year-old son, Alexander (later known as Alexander the Great). After a few years at the royal court in Pella, Aristotle returned to Stagira. In 335 he went back to Athens, where he founded a school called the Lyceum. When Alexander died in 323, strong anti-Macedonian sentiment arose in Athens. Because of his connections with Macedon, Aristotle thought it prudent to leave Athens. He went to Chalcis on the island of Euboea, where he died the following year of a stomach ailment.

Aristotle is the author of two very different kinds of philosophical writings: polished works intended for the general reading public, and notes from which he lectured, intended for circulation among his students and associates. The polished works have been entirely lost except for a few fragments; what have survived are the notes from his lectures on a wide variety of topics, including logic, biology, physics, psychology, metaphysics, and ethics.

Our selection is taken from the set of notes known as the *Nicomachean Ethics.* Here Aristotle argues that the ultimate goal everyone seeks is happiness and that being moral is a necessary part of a happy life. Happiness, Aristotle contends, consists in living rationally. Living rationally requires that two parts of a person's soul function well: the part that is rational in the proper sense (the intellectual part, which *has* reason) and the part containing appetites and desires (appetites and desires are not rational in themselves, but they are capable of *listening to and obeying* reason).

These two parts of the soul function well if they possess their respective excellences (virtues, good inner dispositions). *Intellectual excellences* are those that enable reason in the proper sense to carry out its function; *excellences of character* are those qualities that enable appetites and desires to fulfill their functions. Aristotle argues that a person who lives in accordance with intellectual excellences and excellences of character attains happiness and is moral.

Intellectual excellences include such qualities as good sense and wisdom; excellences of character include such traits as courage and moderation. Aristotle defines excellences of character as dispositions to seek the intermediate between the two extremes of excess and deficiency—the intermediate with regard to both affections (emotions) and actions. For example, the excellence of the affection of boldness is *courage,* which lies between rashness and cowardice; the excellence of the action of giving and receiving money is *open-handedness* (generosity), which is intermediate between wastefulness and avarice. Aristotle explains that the way to acquire an excellence of character is to perform the appropriate acts repeatedly. To become a courageous person, for example, one must do courageous things.

BOOK I

Chapter 1

Every sort of expert knowledge and every inquiry, and similarly every action and undertaking, seems to seek some good. Because of that, people are right to affirm that the good is "that which all things seek." But there appears to be a certain difference among ends:[1] Some are activities, while others are products of some kind, over and above the activities themselves. Where there are ends over and above the activities, in these cases the products are by their nature better than the activities.

Since there are many sorts of action, and of expertise and knowledge, their ends turn out to be many, too. Thus health is the end of medicine, a ship of shipbuilding, victory of generalship, wealth of household management. But in every case where such activities fall under some single capacity, just as bridle-making falls under horsemanship, along with all the others that produce the equipment for horsemanship, and horsemanship along with every action that has to do with expertise in warfare falls under generalship—so in the same way others fall under a separate one. And in all activities the ends of the controlling ones are more desirable than the ends under them, because it is for the sake of the former that the latter too are pursued. It makes no difference—as in the case of the sorts of knowledge mentioned—whether the ends of the actions are the activities themselves or some other thing over and above these.

Chapter 2

If then there is some end in our practical projects that we wish for because of itself, while wishing for the other things we wish for because of it, and we do not choose everything because of something else (for if *that* is the case, the sequence will go on to infinity, making our desire empty and vain), it is clear that this will be the good, that is, the chief good. So in relation to life, too, knowing it will have great weight. And, like archers with a target, would we not be more successful in hitting the point we need to hit if we had this knowledge?

If so, then one must try to grasp it at least in outline—that is, what it might be and to which sort of expertise or productive capacity it belongs. It would seem to belong to the most sovereign expertise, the most architectonic.[2] Political expertise appears to be like this, for it is this expertise that sets out which of the expertises there needs to be in cities, and what sorts of expertise each group of people should learn, and up to what point. And we see even the most prestigious of the productive capacities falling under it, for example generalship, household management, and rhetoric. Since it makes use of the practical expertises that remain, and furthermore legislates about what one must do and what things one must abstain from doing, the end of this expertise will contain those of the rest; so that this end will be the human good. For even if the good is the

---

[1]*ends:* goals. [D. C. Abel]
[2]*architectonic:* superior in a hierarchy and directing subordinate members. [D. C. Abel]

same for a single person and for a city, the good of the city is a greater and more complete thing both to achieve and to preserve; for while to do so for one person on his own is satisfactory enough, to do it for a nation or for cities is finer and more godlike. So our inquiry seeks these things, being a political inquiry in a way.

Chapter 3

Our account would be adequate if we achieved a degree of precision appropriate to the underlying material, for precision must not be sought to the same degree in all accounts of things, any more than it is by craftsmen in the things they are producing. Fine things and just things, which are what political expertise inquires about, involve great variation and irregularity, so that they come to seem fine and just by convention alone, and not by nature. Something like this lack of regularity is found also in good things, because of the fact that they turn out to be a source of damage to many people: Some in fact have perished because of wealth, others because of courage. We must be content then, when talking about things of this sort and starting from them, to show what is true about them roughly and in outline, and when talking about things that are for the most part, and starting from these, to reach conclusions too of the same sort. It is in this same way, then, that one must also receive each sort of account, for it is a mark of an educated person to look for precision in each kind of inquiry just to the extent that the nature of the subject allows it. It looks like the same kind of mistake to accept a merely persuasive account from a mathematician and to demand demonstrations[3] from an expert in oratory. . . .

Chapter 4

Let us then resume the argument: Since every sort of knowledge and every undertaking seeks after some good, let us say what it is that we say political expertise seeks, and what the topmost of all achievable goods is. Pretty well most people are agreed about what to call it: Both ordinary people and people of quality say "happiness," and suppose that living well and doing well are the same thing as being happy. But they are in dispute about what happiness actually is, and ordinary people do not give the same answer as intellectuals. The first group identifies it with one of the obvious things that anyone would recognize, like pleasure or wealth or honor, while some pick some other thing and others another (often, too, the same person picks a different thing—when he falls ill, it's health, and if he is poor, it's wealth). But out of consciousness of their own ignorance they are in awe of those who say something impressive and over their heads. Some people used to think that besides these many goods there is another one, existing by itself, which is cause for all of these too of their being good.[4] Now it is presumably rather otiose to examine all these opinions, and enough to examine those that are most widely held, or seem to have some justification. . . .

---

[3]*demonstrations:* proofs whose conclusions are logically certain. [D. C. ABEL]
[4]Aristotle here refers primarily to Plato, under whom he studied for 20 years. [D. C. ABEL]

Chapter 5

. . . To judge from their lives, most people (that is, the most vulgar) seem, not unreasonably, to suppose [happiness] to be pleasure; that is just why they favor the life of consumption. The kinds of lives that stand out here are especially three: the one just mentioned, the political life, and the life of reflection.

Now most of the utterly slavish sort of people obviously decide in favor of a life that belongs to grazing cattle—and not without reason, given that many of those in high places behave like Sardanapallus.[5] People of quality, for their part, those who tend towards a life of action, go for honor, for pretty much this is the end of the political life. But it appears more superficial than what we are looking for, as it seems to be located in those doing the honoring rather than in the person receiving it, and our hunch is that the good is something that belongs to a person and is difficult to take away from him. Again, people seem to pursue honor in order to be convinced that they themselves are good; at any rate they seek to be honored by people of discernment, and among those who know them, and to be honored for excellence. So it is clear, at any rate according to them, that excellence is of greater value. In fact, perhaps one might suppose that this is even more the end of the political life than honor is. But excellence too appears somewhat incomplete, for it seems to be possible actually to be asleep while having one's excellence, or to spend one's life in inactivity, and furthermore to suffer, and to meet with the greatest misfortunes—and no one would call the person who lived this kind of life happy, unless to defend a debating position. . . . Third of the three lives in question, then, is the life of reflection, about which we shall make our investigation in what follows.[6]

The life of the moneymaker is of a sort that is chosen under compulsion of need, and wealth is clearly not the good we are looking for, since it is useful, and for the sake of something else. Hence one might be more inclined to take as ends the things mentioned before, because they are valued for themselves. But it appears that they are not what we are looking for either; and yet there are many established arguments that focus on them. Let these things, then, be set aside. . . .

Chapter 7

Let us go back to the good we are looking for—what might it be? For it appears to be one thing in one activity or sphere of expertise, another in another: It is different in medicine and in generalship, and likewise in the rest. What then is the good that belongs to each? Or is it that for which everything else is done? In medicine this is health, in generalship victory, in housebuilding a house, in some other sphere some other thing, but in every activity and undertaking it is the end; for it is for the sake of this that they all do the rest. The consequence is that if there is some one end of all practical undertakings, this will be the practicable[7] good,

---

[5]*Sardanapallus:* the Hellenized name of King Ashurbanipal of Assyria (668–627 B.C.E.), who was famous for his sensual indulgence. [D. C. ABEL]
[6]Aristotle discusses this in Book X of the *Nicomachean Ethics* (not included in our reading). [D. C. ABEL]
[7]*practicable:* attainable by action. [D. C. ABEL]

and if there are more than one, it will be these. Thus as the argument turns in its course, it has arrived at the same point; but we must try even more to achieve precision in this matter.

Since, then, the ends are evidently more than one, and of these we choose some because of something else, as we do wealth, flutes, and instruments in general, it is clear that not all are complete; and the best is evidently something complete. So that if there is some one thing alone that is complete, this will be what we are looking for, and if there are more such things than one, the most complete of these. Now we say that what is worth pursuing for itself is more complete than what is worth pursuing because of something else, and what is never desirable because of something else is more complete than those things that are desirable both for themselves and because of it; while what is complete *without qualification* is what is always desirable in itself and never because of something else. Happiness seems most of all to be like this; for this we do always choose because of itself and never because of something else, while as for honor, pleasure, intelligence, and every excellence, we do choose them because of themselves (since if nothing resulted from them, we would still choose each of them), but we also choose them for the sake of happiness, supposing that we shall be happy through them. But happiness no one chooses for the sake of these things, nor in general because of something else.

The same appears also to follow from considerations of self-sufficiency, for the complete good seems to be self-sufficient. By "self-sufficient" we do not mean sufficient for oneself alone . . . but also for one's parents, children, wife, and generally those one loves, and one's fellow citizens, since man is by nature a civic being. But there must be some limit found here: If the point is extended to ancestors and descendants and loved ones' loved ones, an infinite series will result. But this we must look at on another occasion. The "self-sufficient" we posit [is] what in isolation makes life desirable and lacking in nothing, and we think happiness is like this—and moreover most desirable of all things, it not being counted with other goods. Clearly, if it *were* so counted in with the least of other goods, we would think it more desirable [by the addition of these other goods], for what is added becomes an extra quantity of goods, and the larger total amount of goods is always more desirable. So happiness is clearly something complete and self-sufficient, being the end of our practical undertakings.

But perhaps it appears somewhat uncontroversial to say that happiness is the chief good, and a more distinct statement of what it is is still required. Well, perhaps this would come about if one established the *function* of human beings. For just as for a flute player or a sculptor or any expert, and generally for all those who have some characteristic function or activity, the good—their doing well—seems to reside in their function, so too it would seem to be for the human being, if indeed there is some function that belongs to him. So does a carpenter or a shoemaker have certain functions and activities, while a human being has none, and is by nature a do-nothing? Or just as an eye, a hand, a foot, and generally each and every part of the body appears as having some function, in the same way would one not posit a characteristic function for a human being too, alongside all of these? What, then, should we suppose this to be? Being alive is obviously shared by plants too, and we are looking for what is peculiar to human beings. In that case we must divide off the kind of life that consists in taking in nutriment and growing. Next to consider would be some sort of life of perception, but this too is evidently shared by horses, oxen, and every other animal. There remains a practical sort of life of what possesses reason; and of this, one element "possesses reason" insofar as it is *obedient to* reason, while the other possesses it insofar as it actually *has* it, and itself thinks. Since this life, too, is spoken of in two ways,[8] we must posit the *active* life; for this seems to be called a practical life in the more proper sense.

If the function of a human being is activity of soul in accordance with reason, or not apart from reason, and the function, we say, of a given sort of practitioner and a good practitioner of that sort is generically the same, as for example in the case of a cithara player and a good cithara player, and this is so without qualification in all cases, when a difference in respect of excellence is added to the function (for what belongs to the citharist is to play the cithara, to the good citharist to play it well)—if all this is so, and a human being's function we posit as being a kind of life, and this life [is] activity of soul and actions accompanied by reason, and it belongs to a good man to perform these well and finely, and each thing is completed well when it possesses its proper excellence—if all this is so, the human good turns out to be activity of soul in accordance with excellence (and if there are more excellences than one, in accordance with the best and the most complete). But furthermore it will be this in a complete life. For a single swallow does not make spring, nor does a single day; in the same way, neither does a single day, or a short time, make a man blessed and happy. . . .

Chapter 13

Since happiness is some activity of soul in accordance with complete excellence, we should discuss the subject of excellence; for perhaps in this way we shall get a better view of happiness too. . . .

One aspect of soul is nonrational, while another possesses reason . . . Of the nonrational, one grade looks likely to be shared, and to have to do with growth—by which I mean what is responsible for the taking in of food and for increase in size; for this sort of capacity of soul one would posit as being in all things that take in food, and in embryos, and this same one too as being in them when they are full-grown, for it is more reasonable to suppose the presence of this one than of any other. Excellence in the exercise of this capacity, then, appears to be something shared and not distinctively human. . . .

But another kind of soul also seems to be nonrational, although participating in a way in reason. Take those with and without self-control: We praise their reason and the aspect of their soul that possesses reason; it gives the right encouragement in the direction of what is best. But there appears to be something else besides reason that is naturally in them, which fights against reason and resists it. . . . But this part too seems to participate in reason, as we have said. At any rate, in the self-controlled person it is obedient to reason—and in the

---

[8]*in two ways:* The practical life of reason can be spoken of in a *passive* sense, as merely possessing the ability to reason, or in an *active* sense, as actually exercising this ability. [D. C. ABEL]

moderate and courageous person it is presumably still readier to listen, for in him it always chimes with reason.

The nonrational, then, too, appears to be double in nature. For the plant-like aspect of soul does not share in reason in any way, while the appetitive and generally desiring part does participate in it in a way, that is, insofar as it is capable of listening to it and obeying it. It is the way one is reasonable when one *takes* account of advice from one's father or loved ones, not when one *has* an account of things, as for example in mathematics. That the nonrational is in a way persuaded by reason is indicated by our practice of admonishing people, and all the different forms in which we reprimand and encourage them. If one should call this too "possessing reason," then the aspect of soul that possesses reason will also be double in nature: One element of it will have it in the proper sense and in itself, another as something capable of listening as if to one's father.

Excellence too is divided according to this difference; for we call some of them intellectual excellences, others excellences of character—intellectual accomplishment, good sense, wisdom on the one hand counting on the side of the intellectual excellences, open-handedness and moderation counting among those of character. For when we talk about character, we do not say that someone is accomplished in a subject or has a good sense of things, but rather that he is mild or moderate. But we do also praise someone accomplished in something for his disposition, and the dispositions we praise are the ones we call excellences.

BOOK II

Chapter 1

Excellence being of two sorts, then, the one intellectual and the other of character, the intellectual sort mostly both comes into existence and increases as a result of teaching (which is why it requires experience and time), whereas excellence of character results from habituation—which is in fact the source of the name it has acquired [*ēthikē*], the word for "character trait" [*ēthos*] being a slight variation of that for "habituation" [*ethos*]. This makes it quite clear that none of the excellences of character come about in us by nature, for no natural way of being is changed through habituation. For example, the stone that by nature moves downwards will not be habituated into moving upwards, even if someone tries to make it so by throwing it upwards ten thousand times, nor will fire move downwards, nor will anything else that is by nature one way be habituated into behaving in another. In that case the excellences develop in us neither by nature nor contrary to nature, but because we are naturally able to receive them and are brought to completion by means of habituation.

Again, in the case of those things that accrue to us by nature, we possess the capacities for them first, and display them in actuality later (something that is evident in the case of the senses: we did not acquire our senses as a result of repeated acts of seeing, or repeated acts of hearing, but rather the other way round—we used them because we had them, rather than acquired them because we used them); whereas we acquire the excellences through having first engaged in the activities. [This] is also the case with the various sorts of expert knowledge—for the way we learn the things we should do, knowing how to do them, is by doing them. For example, people become builders by building, and cithara players by playing the cithara. So too, then, we become just by doing just things, moderate by doing moderate things, and courageous by doing courageous things. What happens in cities testifies to this: Lawgivers make the citizens good through habituation, and this is what every lawgiver aims at, but those who do it badly miss their mark—and this is what makes one constitution different from another, a good one from a bad one.

Again, it is from the same things and through the same things that every excellence is both produced and destroyed, and similarly every expertise; for it is from playing the cithara that both the good and the bad cithara players come about. So too both with builders and the rest: Good building will result in good builders, bad building in bad ones. If it were not like this, there would be no need at all of anyone to teach them, and instead everyone would just become a good builder or a bad one. This, then, is how it is with the excellences too; for it is through acting as we do in our dealings with human beings that some of us become just and others unjust, and through acting as we do in frightening situations, and through becoming habituated to fearing or being confident, that some of us become courageous and some of us cowardly. A similar thing holds too with situations relating to the appetites, and with those relating to temper: Some people become moderate and mild-tempered, others self-indulgent and irascible, the one group as a result of behaving one way in such circumstances, the other as a result of behaving another way.

We may sum up by saying just that dispositions come about from activities of a similar sort. This is why it is necessary to ensure that the activities be of a certain quality, for the varieties of these are reflected in the dispositions. So it does not make a small difference whether people are habituated to behave in one way or in another way from childhood on, but a very great one; or rather, it makes all the difference in the world. . . .

Chapter 4

But someone may raise a problem about how we can say that to become just, people need to do what is just, and to do what is moderate in order to become moderate; for if they are doing what is just and moderate, they are already just and moderate, in the same way in which, if people are behaving literately and musically, they are already expert at reading and writing and in music.

Or does this fail to hold, in fact, even for skills? One can do something literate both by chance and at someone else's prompting. One will only count as literate, then, if one both does something literate and does it in the way a literate person does it; and this is a matter of doing it in accordance with one's own expert knowledge of letters.

Again, neither do the case of the skills and that of the excellences resemble each other: The things that come about through the agency of skills contain in themselves the mark of their being done well, so that it is enough if they turn out in a certain way, whereas the things that come about in accordance with the excellences count as done justly or moderately not merely because they themselves are of a certain kind, but also because of facts about the agent doing them—first if he does them knowingly, secondly if he decides to do them and decides to do them for themselves, and thirdly if he does them from a firm and unchanging disposition. When it is a matter of having skills, these conditions are not relevant, except for knowledge itself; but when it comes to having the excellences, knowledge makes no difference, or a small one, whereas the force of the other conditions is not small but counts for everything, and it is these that result from the repeated performance of just and moderate actions. So things done are called just and moderate whenever they are such that the just person or the moderate person would do them; whereas a person is not just and moderate because he does these things, but also because he does them in the way in which just and moderate people do them. . . .

Chapter 6

. . . Every excellence, whatever it is an excellence of, both gives that thing the finish of a good condition and makes it perform its function well, as for example the eye's excellence makes both it and its functioning excellent; for it is through the excellence of the eye that we see well. Similarly the excellence of a horse both makes it an excellent horse and good at running, carrying its rider, and facing the enemy. If, then, this is so in all cases, the excellence of a human being too will be the disposition whereby he becomes a good human being and from which he will perform his own function well. In what way this will be, we have already said, but it will also be clear in this way too—that is, if we consider what sort of nature excellence has.

Now with everything continuous and divisible it is possible to take a greater and a lesser and an equal amount, and these either with reference to the object itself or relative to us. The equal is a kind of intermediate between what exceeds and what falls short. By intermediate "with reference to the object" I mean what is equidistant from each of its two extremes, which is one and the same for all; whereas by intermediate "relative to us" I mean the sort of thing that neither goes to excess nor is deficient—and this is not one thing, nor is it the same for all. So for example if ten count as many and two as few, six is what people take as intermediate with reference to the object, since it exceeds and is exceeded by the same amount; and this is intermediate in terms of arithmetical proportion. But the intermediate relative to us should not be taken in this way; for if ten minas[9] in weight is a large amount for a particular person to eat and two a small amount, the trainer will not prescribe six minas, because perhaps this too is large for the person who will be taking it, or small—small for Milo,[10] large for the person just beginning his training. Similarly with running and wrestling. It is in this way, then, that every expert tries to avoid excess and deficiency, and looks instead for the intermediate and chooses this—the intermediate, that is, not in the object, but relative to us.

---

[9]*minas:* units of weight equivalent to approximately 1 pound. [D. C. ABEL]

[10]Milo of Croton was a famous Greek wrestler of the 6th century B.C.E. [D. C. ABEL]

If, then, it is in this way that every kind of expert knowledge completes its function well, by looking to the intermediate and guiding what it produces by reference to this (which is why people are used to saying about products of good quality that nothing can either be taken away from them or added to them, because they suppose that excess and deficiency destroy good quality, while intermediacy preserves it—and skilled experts, as we say, work by looking to this), and if excellence is more precise and better than any expertise, just as nature is, excellence will be effective at hitting upon what is intermediate. I mean excellence of character; for this has to do with affections and actions, and it is in these that there is excess and deficiency, and the intermediate. So, for example, it is possible on occasion to be affected by fear, boldness, appetite, anger, pity, and pleasure and distress in general both too much and too little, and neither is good; but to be affected when one should, at the things one should, in relation to the people one should, for the reasons one should, and in the way one should, is both intermediate and best, which is what belongs to excellence.

In the same way with actions too there is excess, deficiency, and the intermediate. Excellence has to do with affections and actions—things in which excess and deficiency go astray, while what is intermediate is praised and gets it right. . . .

Excellence, then, is a disposition issuing in decisions, depending on intermediacy of the kind relative to us, this being determined by rational prescription and in the way in which the wise person would determine it. And it is intermediacy [because it lies] between two bad states, one involving excess, the other involving deficiency; and also because one set of bad states is deficient, the other excessive, in relation to what is required both in affections and in actions—whereas excellence both finds and chooses the intermediate. Hence excellence, in terms of its essence and the definition that states what it is for excellence to be, is intermediacy; but in terms of what is best, and good practice, it is extremity.

But not every action admits of intermediacy, nor does every affection; for in some cases they have been named in such a way that they are combined with badness from the start, as for example with malice, shamelessness, and grudging ill will; and in the case of actions, fornication, theft, and murder. All these, and others like them, owe their names to the fact that they themselves—not excessive versions of them, or deficient ones—are bad. It is not possible, then, ever to get it right with affections and actions like these, but only to go astray; nor does good practice or the lack of it in relation to such things consist in (for example) fornicating with the woman one should, when one should, and how. Rather, simply doing any one of these things is going astray. . . .

Chapter 7

But we should not simply state this in general terms; we should also show how it fits the particular cases. For with discussions that relate to actions, those of a general sort have a wider application, but those that deal with the subject bit by bit are closer to the truth; for actions have to do with particulars, and the requirement is that we should be in accord on these. So we should take these cases from the chart.[11] Thus with regard to feelings of *fear and boldness,* courage is the intermediate state; while of those people who go to excess, the one who is excessively fearless has no name (many cases are nameless), the one who is excessively bold is rash, and the one who is excessively fearful and deficiently bold is cowardly. With regard to *pleasures and pains*—not all of them, and still less with regard to all pains—the intermediate state is moderation, the excessive state self-indulgence. As for people deficient with regard to pleasures, they hardly occur; which is why people like this, too, have even failed to acquire a name. But let us put them down as "insensate." With regard to the *giving and receiving of money* the intermediate state is open-handedness, while the excessive and deficient states are wastefulness and avariciousness. But in these states excess and deficiency work in opposite ways: The wasteful person is excessive in handing money out and deficient in taking it, while the avaricious person is excessive in taking it and deficient when it comes to giving it out.

---

[11]Aristotle evidently refers to a chart that he used when presenting this material to his students. [D. C. ABEL]

Treatise on Law

Thomas Aquinas

A biography of Thomas Aquinas appears on p. 39.

This reading is from Aquinas's "Treatise on Law," a section of the First Part of Part Two of the *Summa Theologiae*. Aquinas argues that to be moral means to follow the "natural law." By "natural law" he does not mean the laws of nature, such as the law of gravity, but the moral law that follows from the nature of human beings. Natural law is a subset of eternal law—the law by which God governs the entire universe. According to Aquinas, God directs all creatures by instilling in them natural inclinations. But human beings are subject to eternal law in a special way: Unlike other material creatures, they have reason and free will, which enable them to decide whether and how to fulfill their natural tendencies.

The first precept (command) of the natural law is that "we should do and seek good, and shun evil." To specify what the good is for human beings, Aquinas distinguishes among three levels of natural human inclination. As a substance (thing), we are inclined to preserve our own existence; as an animal, to preserve the existence of our species; as a *rational* animal, to know the truth and live harmoniously with others. Consequently, the natural law dictates that we should (1) preserve our own lives, (2) preserve our species, and (3) seek the truth and live peacefully in society. To be moral is to follow these commands. As Aquinas explains elsewhere, if the commands come into conflict in some situation, we must use the virtue of prudence to decide which one to follow. Aquinas maintains that these precepts are written in the hearts of all human beings, but that strong emotions, evil customs, or corrupt habits can prevent a person from knowing the conclusions properly drawn from them.

QUESTION 91. ON DIFFERENT KINDS OF LAW

First Article. Is There an Eternal Law?

. . . Law is simply a dictate of practical reason[1] by a ruler who governs a [complete] community. But supposing that God's providence rules the world . . . , his reason evidently governs the entire community of the universe. And so the plan of governance of the world existing in God as the ruler of the universe has the nature of law. And since God's reason conceives eternally, as Proverbs 8:23 says, not temporally, we need to say that such law is eternal. . . .

---

[1]*practical reason:* reason as used to direct practical activity. Practical reason is contrasted with *theoretical reason,* which is reason as directed toward knowing the truth for its own sake. As Aquinas explains later on, the first thing that falls within the understanding of practical reason is the *good* (the goal of every practical action), whereas the first thing that falls within the understanding of theoretical reason is *being* (the goal of our desire to know reality). [D. C. ABEL]

Second Article. Is There a Natural Law in Us?

. . . Law, since it is a rule or measure, can belong to things in two ways: in one way to those who rule and measure; in a second way to those ruled and measured, since things are ruled or measured insofar as they partake of the rule or measure. But the eternal law rules and measures everything subject to God's providence . . . And so everything evidently shares in some way in the eternal law, namely, insofar as all things have inclinations to their own acts and ends[2] from its imprint on them. But the rational creature is subject to God's providence in a more excellent way than other things, since such a creature also shares in God's providence in providing for itself and others. And so it shares in the eternal plan whereby it has its natural inclination to its requisite activity and end. And we call such participation in the eternal law by rational creatures the natural law. And so Psalm 4:6, after saying "Offer just sacrifices," asks "Who shows us just things?" and replies: "The light of your countenance, O Lord, has been inscribed on us." The Psalmist thus signifies that the light of natural reason whereby we discern good and evil is simply the imprint of God's light in us. And so it is clear that the natural law is simply rational creatures' participation in the eternal law. . . .

QUESTION 94. ON THE NATURAL LAW

Second Article. Does the Natural Law Include Several Precepts or Only One?

. . . There is a priority regarding the things that fall within the understanding of all persons. For what first falls within our understanding is *being*, the understanding of which is included in everything that one understands. And so the first indemonstrable principle[3] is that one cannot at the same time affirm and deny the same thing. And this principle is based on the nature of being and nonbeing, and all other principles are based on it, as the *Metaphysics* says.[4] And as being is the first thing that without qualification falls within our understanding, so *good* is the first thing that falls within the understanding of practical reason. And practical reason is ordered to action, since every efficient cause[5] acts for the sake of an end, which has the nature of good. And so the first principle in practical reason is one based on the nature of good, namely, that good is what all things seek.[6] Therefore, the first precept of the natural law is that we should do and seek good, and shun evil. And all the other precepts of the natural law are based on that precept, so that all the things that practical reason by nature understands to be human goods or evils belong to precepts of the natural law as things to be done or shunned.

---

[2]*ends:* goals. [D. C. ABEL]
[3]*indemonstrable principle:* a principle that cannot be proved (demonstrated) because there is nothing more fundamental on which to base a proof. [D. C. ABEL]
[4]Aristotle, *Metaphysics*, Book III, Chapter 3. [R. J. REGAN, TRANSLATOR]
[5]*efficient cause:* an agent that brings something into being or imparts change. [D. C. ABEL]
[6]This definition of *good* is given by Aristotle in *Nicomachean Ethics,* Book I, Chapter 1. The text appears on p. 332 of this book. [D. C. ABEL]

And since good has the nature of end, and evil the nature of the contrary, reason by nature understands to be good all the things for which human beings have a natural inclination, and so to be things to be actively sought, and understands contrary things as evil and to be shunned. Therefore, the ordination of our natural inclinations ordains the precepts of the natural law.

First, for example, human beings have an inclination for good by the nature they share with all substances, namely, as every substance by nature seeks to preserve itself. And regarding this inclination, means that to preserve our human life and to prevent the contrary belong to the natural law.

Second, human beings have more particular inclinations by the nature they share with other animals. And so the *Digest* says that things "that nature has taught all animals"[7]—such as the sexual union of male and female, and the upbringing of children, and the like—belong to the natural law.

Third, human beings have inclinations for good by their rational nature, which is proper to them. For example, human beings by nature have inclinations to know truths about God and to live in society with other human beings. And so things that relate to such inclinations belong to the natural law—for example, that human beings shun ignorance, that they not offend those with whom they ought to live sociably, and other such things regarding those inclinations.

Fourth Article. Is the Natural Law the Same for All Human Beings?

. . . Things to which nature inclines human beings belong to the natural law, as I have said before, and one of the things proper to human beings is that their nature inclines them to act in accord with reason. And it belongs to reason to advance from the general to the particular, as the *Physics* makes clear.[8] And regarding that process, theoretical reason proceeds in one way, and practical reason in another way. For inasmuch as theoretical reason is especially concerned about necessary things, which cannot be otherwise disposed, its particular conclusions, just like its general principles, are true without exception. But practical reason is concerned about contingent[9] things, which include human actions. And so the more reason goes from the general to the particular, the more exceptions we find, although there is some necessity in the general principles. Therefore, truth in theoretical matters, both first principles and conclusions, is the same for all human beings, although some know only the truth of the principles, which we call universal propositions, and not the truth of the conclusions. But truth in practical matters, or practical rectitude, is the same for all human beings only regarding the general principles, not regarding the particular conclusions. And not all of those with practical rectitude regarding particulars know the truth in equal measure.

---

[7]*Digest,* Book I, Title 1, no. 1. The *Digest* is a codification of the works of classical jurists published by the Roman emperor Justinian in 533. The quotation cited here is attributed to the Roman jurist Ulpian (died 228 C.E.). [D. C. ABEL]

[8]Aristotle, *Physics,* Book I, Chapter 1. [R. J. REGAN]

[9]*contingent:* capable of being otherwise. [D. C. ABEL]

Therefore, the truth or rectitude regarding the general principles of both theoretical and practical reason is the same for all persons and known in equal measure by all of them. And the truth regarding the particular conclusions of theoretical reason is the same for all persons, but some know such truth less than others. For example, it is true for all persons that triangles have three angles equal to two right angles, although not everybody knows this.

But the truth or rectitude regarding particular conclusions of practical reason is neither the same for all persons nor known in equal measure even by those for whom it is the same. For example, it is correct and true for all persons that they should act in accord with reason. And it follows as a particular conclusion from this principle that those holding goods in trust should return the goods to the goods' owners. And this is indeed true for the most part, but it might in particular cases be injurious, and so contrary to reason, to return the goods (for example, if the owner should be seeking to attack one's country). And the more the particular conclusion goes into particulars, the more exceptions there are (for example, if one should declare that entrusted goods should be returned to their owners with such and such safeguards or in such and such ways). For the more particular conditions are added to the particular conclusion, the more ways there may be exceptions, so that the conclusion about returning or not returning entrusted goods is erroneous.

Therefore we should say that the natural law regarding general first principles is the same for all persons both as to their rectitude and as to knowledge of them. And the natural law regarding particulars, which are, as it were, conclusions from the general principles, is for the most part the same for all persons both as to its rectitude and as to knowledge of it. Nonetheless, it can be wanting in rather few cases both as to its rectitude and as to knowledge of it. As to rectitude, the natural law can be wanting because of particular obstacles, just as natures that come to be and pass away are wanting in rather few cases because of obstacles. And also as to knowledge of the natural law, the law can be wanting because emotions or evil habituation or evil natural disposition has perverted the reason of some. For example, the Germans of old did not consider robbery wicked, as Caesar's *Gallic Wars* relates,[10] although robbery is expressly contrary to the natural law.

Fifth Article. Can the Natural Law Vary?

. . . We can understand the mutability of the natural law in two ways. We can understand it in one way by things being added to it. And then nothing prevents the natural law changing, since both divine law and human laws add to natural law many things beneficial to human life.

We can understand the mutability of the natural law in a second way by way of substraction, namely, that things previously subject to the law cease to be so. And then the natural law is altogether immutable as to its first principles. And as to its secondary precepts, which we said are proper proximate conclusions, as it

---

[10]Gaius Julius Caesar, *Gallic Wars,* Book VI, Chapter 23. [R. J. REGAN] Caesar (100–44 B.C.E.) was a Roman general, politician, and author. [D. C. ABEL]

were, from the first principles, the natural law is not so changed that what it prescribes is not for the most part completely correct. But it can be changed regarding particulars and in rather few cases, due to special causes that prevent observance of such precepts, as I have said before.

Sixth Article. Can the Natural Law Be Excised from the Hearts of Human Beings?

. . . As I have said before, there belong to the natural law, indeed primarily, very general precepts, precepts that everyone knows; and more particular, secondary precepts, which are like proximate conclusions from first principles. Therefore, regarding the general principles, the natural law in general can in no way be excised from the hearts of human beings. But the natural law is wiped out regarding particular actions insofar as desires or other emotions prevent reason from applying the general principles to particular actions, as I have said before.

And the natural law can be excised from the hearts of human beings regarding the other, secondary precepts, either because of wicked opinions, just as errors in theoretical matters happen regarding necessary conclusions, or because of evil customs or corrupt habits. For example, some did not think robbery a sin, or even sins against nature to be sinful, as the Apostle [Paul] also says in Romans 1:24–28.

Groundwork of the Metaphysics of Morals

Immanuel Kant

A biography of Immanuel Kant appears on p. 175.

This reading is taken from Kant's *Groundwork of the Metaphysics of Morals,* a work whose aim, Kant explains in his preface, is "to seek out and establish the supreme principle of morality." According to Kant, the moral worth of an action is determined by one's motive, not by the consequences of the action. And the proper motive (what makes a will a *good* will) is to do one's duty simply because it is one's duty. To act out of duty means to act out of respect for the law, and to act out of respect for the law means to follow the "categorical imperative." This imperative states that our action should be "universalizable," which means that the personal policy (maxim) on which our action is based must be one that we could consistently will that all persons follow. If our maxim cannot be universalized, the action is immoral. For example, the maxim of making a false promise to escape a difficulty cannot consistently be universalized because, if everyone followed it, promises would no longer be able to function as promises because no one would believe them. The categorical imperative is, for Kant, the ultimate criterion for determining the morality of any action.

According to Kant, the categorical imperative can be expressed in various equivalent ways, including the injunction that we should always treat persons (including ourselves) as ends in themselves, and never simply as means to an end. Returning to his example of making a false promise, he explains that such a promise is immoral because it uses the person lied to merely as means to obtain one's end.

SECTION I. TRANSITION FROM COMMON RATIONAL TO PHILOSOPHIC MORAL COGNITION

It is impossible to think of anything at all in the world, or indeed even beyond it, that could be considered good without limitation except a *good will.* Understanding, wit, judgment and the like, whatever such talents of mind may be called, or courage, resolution, and perseverance in one's plans, as qualities of temperament, are undoubtedly good and desirable for many purposes, but they can also be extremely evil and harmful if the will that is to make use of these gifts of nature, and whose distinctive constitution is therefore called *character,* is not good. It is the same with gifts of fortune. Power, riches, honor, even health and that complete well-being and satisfaction with one's condition called *happiness,* produce boldness and thereby often arrogance as well unless a good will is present that corrects the influence of these on the mind and, in so doing, also corrects the whole principle of action and brings it into conformity with universal ends[1]—not to mention that an impartial rational spectator can take no delight in seeing the uninterrupted prosperity of a being graced with no feature of a pure and good will, so that a good will seems to constitute the indispensable condition even of worthiness to be happy.

---

[1]*ends:* goals. [D. C. ABEL]

Some qualities are even conducive to this good will itself and can make its work much easier. Despite this, however, they have no inner unconditional worth but always presuppose a good will, which limits the esteem one otherwise rightly has for them and does not permit their being taken as absolutely good. Moderation in affects and passions, self-control, and calm reflection are not only good for all sorts of purposes but even seem to constitute a part of the inner worth of persons. But they lack much that would be required to declare them good without limitation (however unconditionally they were praised by the ancients), for without the basic principles of a good will they can become extremely evil, and the coolness of a scoundrel makes him not only far more dangerous but also immediately more abominable in our eyes than we would have taken him to be without it.

A good will is not good because of what it effects or accomplishes, because of its fitness to attain some proposed end, but only because of its volition—that is, it is good in itself and, regarded for itself, is to be valued incomparably higher than all that could merely be brought about by it in favor of some inclination and indeed, if you will, of the sum of all inclinations. Even if, by a special disfavor of fortune or by the [stingy] provision of a stepmotherly nature, this will should wholly lack the capacity to carry out its purpose—if with its greatest efforts it should yet achieve nothing and only the good will were left (not, of course, as a mere wish but as the summoning of all means insofar as they are in our control)—then, like a jewel, it would still shine by itself, as something that has its full worth in itself. Usefulness or fruitlessness can neither add anything to this worth nor take anything away from it. Its usefulness would be, as it were, only the setting to enable us to handle it more conveniently in ordinary commerce or to attract to it the attention of those who are not yet expert enough, but not to recommend it to experts or to determine its worth. . . .

We have, then, to explicate the concept of a will that is to be esteemed in itself and that is good apart from any further purpose, as it already dwells in natural sound understanding and needs not so much to be taught as only to be clarified—this concept that always takes first place in estimating the total worth of our actions and constitutes the condition of all the rest. In order to do so, we shall set before ourselves the concept of *duty,* which contains that of a good will though under certain subjective limitations and hindrances—which, however, far from concealing it and making it unrecognizable, rather bring it out by contrast and make it shine forth all the more brightly.

I here pass over all actions that are already recognized as contrary to duty, even though they may be useful for this or that purpose; for in their case the question whether they might have been done *from duty* never arises, since they even conflict with it. I also set aside actions that are really in conformity with duty but to which human beings have *no inclination immediately* and which they still perform because they are impelled to do so through another inclination. For in this case it is easy to distinguish whether an action in conformity with duty is done from duty or from a self-seeking purpose. It is much more difficult to note this distinction when an action conforms with duty and the subject has, besides, an *immediate inclination* to it. For example, it certainly conforms with duty that a shopkeeper not overcharge an inexperienced customer, and where there is a good deal of trade a prudent merchant does not overcharge but keeps a fixed general price for everyone, so that a child can buy from him as well as everyone else. People are thus served honestly, but this is not nearly enough for us to believe that the merchant acted in this way from duty and basic principles of honesty. His advantage required it; it cannot be assumed here that he had, besides, an immediate inclination toward his customers, so as from love, as it were, to give no one preference over another in the matter of price. Thus the action was done neither from duty nor from immediate inclination but merely for purposes of self-interest.

On the other hand, to preserve one's life is a duty, and besides everyone has an immediate inclination to do so. But on this account the often anxious care that most people take of it still has no inner worth and their maxim[2] has no moral content. They look after their lives *in conformity with duty* but not *from duty*. On the other hand, if adversity and hopeless grief have quite taken away the taste for life; if an unfortunate man, strong of soul and more indignant about his fate than despondent or dejected, wishes for death and yet preserves his life without loving it, not from inclination or fear but from duty, then his maxim has moral content.

To be beneficent where one can is a duty, and besides there are many souls so sympathetically attuned that, without any other motive of vanity or self-interest they find an inner satisfaction in spreading joy around them and can take delight in the satisfaction of others so far as it is their own work. But I assert that in such a case an action of this kind, however it may conform with duty and however amiable it may be, has nevertheless no true moral worth but is on the same footing with other inclinations, for example, the inclination to honor, which, if it fortunately lights upon what is in fact in the common interest and in conformity with duty and hence honorable, deserves praise and encouragement but not esteem—for the maxim lacks moral content, namely, that of doing such actions not from inclination but from duty. Suppose, then, that the mind of this philanthropist were overclouded by his own grief, which extinguished all sympathy with the fate of others, and that while he still had the means to benefit others in distress their troubles did not move him because he had enough to do with his own; and suppose that now, when no longer incited to it by any inclination, he nevertheless tears himself out of this deadly insensibility and does the action without any inclination, simply from duty; then the action first has its genuine moral worth. Still further: If nature had put little sympathy in the heart of this or that man; if (in other respects an honest man) he is by temperament cold and indifferent to the sufferings of others, perhaps because he himself is provided with the special gift of patience and endurance toward his own sufferings and presupposes the same in every other or even requires it; if nature had not properly fashioned such a man (who would in truth not be its worst product) for a philanthropist, would he not still find within himself a source from which to give himself a far higher worth than what a mere

---

[2]*maxim:* the personal policy that motivates one's action. In the case described here, the maxim would be to follow one's inclination to preserve one's life. Kant later contrasts a maxim with a *universal law,* which binds all rational creatures. [D. C. ABEL]

good-natured temperament might have? By all means! It is just then that the worth of character comes out that is moral and incomparably the highest, namely, that he is beneficent not from inclination but from duty. . . .

The second proposition[3] is this: An action from duty has its moral worth not in the purpose to be attained by it but in the maxim in accordance with which it is decided upon, and therefore does not depend upon the realization of the object of the action but merely upon the *principle of volition* in accordance with which the action is done, without regard for any object of the faculty of desire. That the purposes we may have for our actions, and their effects as ends and incentives of the will, can give actions no unconditional and moral worth is clear from what has gone before. In what, then, can this worth lie, if it is not to be in the will in relation to the hoped-for effect of the action? It can lie nowhere else than in the principle of the will, without regard for the ends that can be brought about by such an action. For the will stands between its a priori principle, which is formal, and its a posteriori incentive, which is material,[4] as at a crossroads; and since it must still be determined by something, it must be determined by the formal principle of volition as such when an action is done from duty, where every material principle has been withdrawn from it.

The third proposition, which is a consequence of the two preceding, I would express as follows: Duty is the necessity of an action from respect for law. For an object as the effect of my proposed action I can indeed have *inclination* but never *respect*, just because it is merely an effect and not an activity of a will. In the same way, I cannot have respect for inclination as such, whether it is mine or that of another; I can at most in the first case approve it and in the second sometimes even love it, that is, regard it as favorable to my own advantage. Only what is connected with my will merely as ground and never as effect, what does not serve my inclination but outweighs it or at least excludes it altogether from calculations in making a choice—hence the mere law for itself—can be an object of respect and so a command. Now an action from duty [must] put aside entirely the influence of inclination and with it every object of the will; hence there is left for the will nothing that could determine it except objectively the law and sub- jectively pure respect for this practical law, and [consequently] the maxim of complying with such a law even if it infringes upon all my inclinations.

Thus the moral worth of an action does not lie in the effect expected from it and so too does not lie in any principle of action that needs to borrow its motive from this expected effect. For all these effects (agreeableness of one's condition, indeed even promotion of others' happiness) could have been also brought about by other causes, so that there would have been no need, for this, of the will of a rational being—in which, however, the highest and unconditional good

---

[3]Kant did not label the first proposition, but it is implicit in the preceding paragraphs: An action must be done from duty in order to have moral worth. [D. C. ABEL]

[4]*A priori* means "independent of experience" (literally, in Latin, "from what comes earlier"); *a poste- riori* means "dependent on experience" ("from what comes later"). Duty is an a priori principle of the will because it binds prior to any experience; the incentive of an action is a posteriori because it depends on the person's experience. Kant here draws a further contrast between duty and incen- tive: Duty is a *formal* principle because it refers to the general form any action should take; incentive is *material* because it involves the situation ("matter") of a particular action. [D. C. ABEL]

alone can be found. Hence nothing other than the *representation of the law* in itself, which can of course occur only in a rational being, insofar as it and not the hoped-for effect is the determining ground of the will, can constitute the pre-eminent good we call moral, which is already present in the person himself who acts in accordance with this representation and need not wait upon the effect of his action.

But what kind of law can that be, the representation of which must deter-mine the will, even without regard for the effect expected from it, in order for the will to be called good absolutely and without limitation? Since I have deprived the will of every impulse that could arise for it from obeying some law, nothing is left but the conformity of actions as such with universal law, which alone is to serve the will as its principle, that is, *I ought never to act except in such a way that I could also will that my maxim should become a universal law.* Here mere conformity to law as such, without having as its basis some law determined for certain actions, is what serves the will as its principle, and must so serve it, if duty is not to be everywhere an empty delusion and a chimerical[5] concept. Common human reason also agrees completely with this in its practical appraisals and always has this principle before its eyes. Let the question be, for example: May I, when hard pressed, make a promise with the intention not to keep it? Here I easily distinguish two significations the question can have: whether it is *prudent,* or whether it is in *conformity with duty,* to make a false promise. The first can undoubtedly often be the case. I see very well that it is not enough to get out of a present difficulty by means of this subterfuge, but that I must reflect carefully whether this lie may later give rise to much greater incon-venience for me than that from which I now extricate myself. And since, with all my supposed cunning, the results cannot be so easily foreseen, but once confi-dence in me is lost this could be far more prejudicial to me than all the troubles I now think to avoid, I must reflect whether the matter might be handled more prudently by proceeding on a general maxim and making it a habit to promise nothing except with the intention of keeping it. But it is soon clear to me that such a maxim will still be based only on results feared. To be truthful from duty, however, is something entirely different from being truthful from anxiety about detrimental results, since in the first case the concept of the action in itself already contains a law for me, while in the second I must first look about else-where to see what effects on me might be combined with it. For if I deviate from the principle of duty this is quite certainly evil; but if I am unfaithful to my maxim of prudence this can sometimes be very advantageous to me, although it is certainly safer to abide by it. However, to inform myself in the shortest and yet infallible way about the answer to this problem, whether a lying promise is in conformity with duty, I ask myself: Would I indeed be content that my maxim (to get myself out of difficulties by a false promise) should hold as a universal law (for myself as well as for others)? And could I indeed say to myself that everyone may make a false promise when he finds himself in a difficulty he can get out of in no other way? Then I soon become aware that I could indeed will the lie, but by no means a universal law to lie; for in accordance with such a law

---

[5]*chimerical:* produced by mental fabrication. [D. C. Abel]

there would properly be no promises at all, since it would be futile to avow my will with regard to my future actions to others who would not believe this avowal or, if they rashly did so, would pay me back in like coin; and thus my maxim, as soon as it were made a universal law, would have to destroy itself.

I do not therefore need any penetrating acuteness to see what I have to do in order that my volition be morally good. Inexperienced in the course of the world, incapable of being prepared for whatever might come to pass in it, I ask myself only: Can you also will that your maxim become a universal law? If not, then it is to be repudiated, and that not because of a disadvantage to you or even to others forthcoming from it but because it cannot fit as a principle into a possible giving of universal law. Reason, however, forces from me immediate respect for such lawgiving. Although I do not yet see what this respect is based upon (this the philosopher may investigate), I at least understand this much: that it is an estimation of a worth that far outweighs any worth of what is recommended by inclination, and that the necessity of my action from pure respect for the practical law is what constitutes duty, to which every other motive must give way because it is the condition of a will good in itself, the worth of which surpasses all else. . . .

SECTION II. TRANSITION FROM POPULAR MORAL PHILOSOPHY TO THE METAPHYSICS OF MORALS

. . . In order to advance by natural steps in this study—not merely from common moral appraisal (which is here very worthy of respect) to philosophic, as has already been done, but from a popular philosophy, which goes no further than it can by groping with the help of examples, to metaphysics (which no longer lets itself be held back by anything empirical and, since it must measure out the whole sum of rational cognition of this kind, goes if need be all the way to ideas, where examples themselves fail us)—we must follow and present distinctly the practical faculty of reason, from its general rules of determination to the point where the concept of duty arises from it.

Everything in nature works in accordance with laws. Only a rational being has the capacity to act in accordance with the *representation of laws*—that is, in accordance with principles—or has a *will*. Since reason is required for the derivation of actions from laws, the will is nothing other than practical reason. If reason infallibly determines the will, the actions of such a being that are cognized as objectively necessary are also subjectively necessary—that is, the will is a capacity to choose only that which reason independently of inclination cognizes as practically necessary, that is, as good. However, if reason solely by itself does not adequately determine the will; if the will is exposed also to subjective conditions (certain incentives) that are not always in accord with the objective ones; in a word, if the will is not in itself completely in conformity with reason (as is actually the case with human beings), then actions that are cognized as objectively necessary are subjectively contingent,[6] and the determination of such a will in conformity with objective laws is *necessitation*—that is to say, the relation

---

[6]*contingent:* capable of being otherwise. [D. C. ABEL]

of objective laws to a will that is not thoroughly good is represented as the determination of the will of a rational being through grounds of reason, indeed, but grounds to which this will is not by its nature necessarily obedient.

The representation of an objective principle, insofar as it is necessitating for a will, is called a *command* (of reason), and the formula of the command is called an *imperative.* . . .

All imperatives command either *hypothetically* or *categorically.* The former represent the practical necessity of a possible action as a means to achieving something else that one wills (or that it is at least possible for one to will). The categorical imperative would be that which represented an action as objectively necessary of itself, without reference to another end.

Since every practical law represents a possible action as good and thus as necessary for a subject practically determinable by reason, all imperatives are formulas for the determination of action that is necessary in accordance with the principle of a will that is good in some way. Now if the action would be good merely as a means *to something else*, the imperative is *hypothetical*; if the action is represented as *in itself* good, hence as necessary in a will in itself conforming to reason as its principle, then it is *categorical.* . . .

When I think of a hypothetical imperative in general, I do not know beforehand what it will contain; I do not know this until I am given the condition. But when I think of a categorical imperative, I know at once what it contains. For, since the imperative contains, beyond the law, only the necessity that the maxim be in conformity with this law, while the law contains no condition to which it would be limited, nothing is left with which the maxim of action is to conform but the universality of a law as such; and this conformity alone is what the imperative properly represents as necessary.

There is, therefore, only a single categorical imperative and it is this: *Act only in accordance with that maxim through which you can at the same time will that it become a universal law.*

Now if all imperatives of duty can be derived from this single imperative as from their principle, then, even though we leave it undecided whether what is called duty is not as such an empty concept, we shall at least be able to show what we think by it and what the concept wants to say.

Since the universality of law in accordance with which effects take place constitutes what is properly called *nature* in the most general sense (as regards its form)—that is, the existence of things insofar as it is determined in accordance with universal laws—the universal imperative of duty can also go as follows: *Act as if the maxim of your action were to become by your will a universal law of nature.*

We shall now enumerate a few duties in accordance with the usual division of them into duties to ourselves and to other human beings and into perfect and imperfect duties.[7]

---

[7]In Kant's terminology, a *perfect duty* is one that prohibits a specific kind of action, without exception; an *imperfect duty* commands us to achieve some general goal without specifying what means we are to use. Kant's following four examples illustrate, respectively: (1) a perfect duty to ourselves (not to commit suicide), (2) a perfect duty to others (not to make false promises), (3) an imperfect duty to ourselves (to develop our talents), and (4) an imperfect duty to others (to help those in need). [D. C. ABEL]

1. Someone feels sick of life because of a series of troubles that has grown to the point of despair, but is still so far in possession of his reason that he can ask himself whether it would not be contrary to his duty to himself to take his own life. Now he inquires whether the maxim of his action could indeed become a universal law of nature. His maxim, however, is: From self-love I make it my principle to shorten my life when its longer duration threatens more troubles than it promises agreeableness. The only further question is whether this principle of self-love could become a universal law of nature. It is then seen at once that a nature whose law it would be to destroy life itself by means of the same feeling whose destination is to impel toward the furtherance of life would contradict itself and would therefore not subsist as nature. Thus that maxim could not possibly be a law of nature and, accordingly, altogether opposes the supreme principle of all duty.

2. Another finds himself urged by need to borrow money. He well knows that he will not be able to repay it but sees also that nothing will be lent him unless he promises firmly to repay it within a determinate time. He would like to make such a promise, but he still has enough conscience to ask himself: Is it not forbidden and contrary to duty to help oneself out of need in such a way? Supposing that he still decided to do so, his maxim of action would go as follows: When I believe myself to be in need of money I shall borrow money and promise to repay it, even though I know that this will never happen. Now this principle of self-love or personal advantage is perhaps quite consistent with my whole future welfare, but the question now is whether it is right. I therefore turn the demand of self-love into a universal law and put the question as follows: How would it be if my maxim became a universal law? I then see at once that it could never hold as a universal law of nature and be consistent with itself, but must necessarily contradict itself. For the universality of a law that everyone, when he believes himself to be in need, could promise whatever he pleases with the intention of not keeping it, would make the promise and the end one might have in it itself impossible, since no one would believe what was promised him but would laugh at all such expressions as vain pretenses.

3. A third finds in himself a talent that by means of some cultivation could make him a human being useful for all sorts of purposes. However, he finds himself in comfortable circumstances and prefers to give himself up to pleasure than to trouble himself with enlarging and improving his fortunate natural predispositions. But he still asks himself whether his maxim of neglecting his natural gifts, besides being consistent with his propensity to amusement, is also consistent with what one calls duty. He now sees that a nature could indeed always subsist with such a universal law, although (as with the South Sea Islanders) the human being should let his talents rust and be concerned with devoting his life merely to idleness, amusement, procreation—in a word, to enjoyment. Only he cannot possibly *will* that this become a universal law or be put in us as such by means of natural instinct, for as a rational being he necessarily wills that all the capacities in him be developed, since they serve him and are given to him for all sorts of possible purposes.

4. Yet a fourth, for whom things are going well while he sees that others (whom he could very well help) have to contend with great hardships, thinks: "What is it to me? Let each be as happy as heaven wills or as he can make

himself; I shall take nothing from him nor even envy him. Only I do not care to contribute anything to his welfare or to his assistance in need." Now if such a way of thinking were to become a universal law, the human race could admittedly very well subsist, no doubt even better than when everyone prates about sympathy and benevolence and even exerts himself to practice them occasionally, but on the other hand also cheats where he can, sells the rights of human beings, or otherwise infringes upon them. But although it is possible that a universal law of nature could very well subsist in accordance with such a maxim, it is still impossible to *will* that such a principle hold everywhere as a law of nature, for a will that decided this would conflict with itself, since many cases could occur in which one would need the love and sympathy of others and in which, by such a law of nature arisen from his own will, he would rob himself of all hope of the assistance he wishes for himself.

These are a few of the many actual duties, or at least of what we take to be such, whose derivation from the one principle cited above is clear. We must be able to will that a maxim of our action become a universal law; this is the canon of moral appraisal of action in general. Some actions are so constituted that their maxim cannot even be *thought* without contradiction as a universal law of nature, far less could one *will* that it should become such. In the case of others that inner impossibility is indeed not to be found, but it is still impossible to will that their maxim be raised to the universality of a law of nature because such a will would contradict itself. It is easy to see that the first is opposed to strict or narrower (unremitting) duty, the second only to wide (meritorious) duty;[8] and so all duties, as far as the kind of obligation (not the object of their action) is concerned, have by these examples been set out completely in their dependence upon the one principle. . . .

The human being and in general every rational being exists as an end in itself, not merely as a means to be used by this or that will at its discretion; instead he must in all his actions, whether directed to himself or also to other rational beings, always be regarded at the same time as an end. All objects of the inclinations have only a conditional worth, for if there were not inclinations and the needs based on them, their object would be without worth. But the inclinations themselves, as sources of needs, are so far from having an absolute worth [that] makes one wish to have them, that it must instead be the universal wish of every rational being to be altogether free from them. Thus the worth of any object to be acquired by our action is always conditional. Beings the existence of which rests not on our will but on nature, if they are beings without reason, still have only a relative worth, as means, and are therefore called *things*, whereas rational beings are called *persons* because their nature already marks them out as ends in themselves—that is, as something that may not be used merely as a means—and hence so far limits all choice (and is an object of respect). These therefore are not merely subjective ends, the existence of which as an effect of our action has a worth *for us*, but rather *objective ends*—that is, beings the existence of which is in itself an end, and indeed one such that no other end, to

---

[8]An *unremitting* duty is a perfect duty and is *necessary*; a *meritorious* duty is an imperfect duty and is *contingent* (see footnotes 6 and 7). [D. C. ABEL]

which they would serve merely as means, can be put in its place, since without it nothing of absolute worth would be found anywhere. But if all worth were conditional and therefore contingent, then no supreme practical principle for reason could be found anywhere.

If, then, there is to be a supreme practical principle and, with respect to the human will,[9] a categorical imperative, it must be one such that, from the representation of what is necessarily an end for everyone because it is an end in itself, it constitutes an objective principle of the will and thus can serve as a universal practical law. The ground of this principle is: *Rational nature exists as an end in itself.* The human being necessarily represents his own existence in this way; so far it is thus a *subjective* principle of human actions. But every other rational being also represents his existence in this way consequent on just the same rational ground that also holds for me; thus it is at the same time an *objective* principle from which, as a supreme practical ground, it must be possible to derive all laws of the will. The practical imperative will therefore be the following: *So act that you use humanity, whether in your own person or in the person of any other, always at the same time as an end, never merely as a means.* We shall see whether this can be carried out.

To keep to the preceding examples:

First, as regards the concept of necessary duty to oneself, someone who has suicide in mind will ask himself whether his action can be consistent with the idea of humanity as an end in itself. If he destroys himself in order to escape from a trying condition, he makes use of a person merely as a means to maintain a tolerable condition up to the end of life. A human being, however, is not a thing and hence not something that can be used merely as a means, but must in all his actions always be regarded as an end in itself. I cannot, therefore, dispose of a human being in my own person by maiming, damaging, or killing him. (I must here pass over a closer determination of this principle that would prevent any misinterpretation, for example, as to having limbs amputated in order to preserve myself, or putting my life in danger in order to preserve my life, and so forth; that belongs to morals proper.)

Second, as regards necessary duty to others, or duty owed them, he who has it in mind to make a false promise to others sees at once that he wants to make use of another human being merely as a means, without the other at the same time containing in himself the end; for he whom I want to use for my purposes by such a promise cannot possibly agree to my way of behaving toward him, and so himself contain the end of this action. This conflict with the principle of other human beings is seen more distinctly if examples of assaults on the freedom and property of others are brought forward. For then it is obvious that he who transgresses the rights of human beings intends to make use of the person of others merely as means, without taking into consideration that, as rational beings, they are always to be valued at the same time as ends, that is, only as beings who must also be able to contain in themselves the end of the very same action.

---

[9]The categorical imperative applies only to a will that is not perfectly good, such as the human will. A "holy will," such as the divine will, does not need an imperative because it automatically wills the good. [D. C. ABEL]

Third, with respect to contingent (meritorious) duty to oneself, it is not enough that the action does not conflict with humanity in our person as an end in itself; it must also *harmonize* with it. Now there are in humanity predispositions to greater perfection, which belong to the end of nature with respect to humanity in our subject. To neglect these might admittedly be consistent with the *preservation* of humanity as an end in itself, but not with the *furtherance* of this end.

Fourth, concerning meritorious duty to others, the natural end that all human beings have is their own happiness. Now humanity might indeed subsist if no one contributed to the happiness of others but yet did not intentionally withdraw anything from it; but there is still only a negative and not a positive agreement with humanity as an end in itself unless everyone also tries, as far as he can, to further the ends of others. For the ends of a subject who is an end in itself must as far as possible be also *my* ends, if that representation is to have its full effect in me.

Utilitarianism

John Stuart Mill

John Stuart Mill was born in London in 1806. He was educated personally by his father, the Scottish economist and philosopher James Mill, who put him through a rigorous program of study from his earliest years. Mill was reading Greek at age three and Latin at age eight. As a boy he read works of many classical authors in the original language, including works by Plato and Aristotle. When he was 13, he began studying the economic theories of Adam Smith and David Ricardo. The following year he traveled to France and spent a year with the family of Samuel Bentham (brother of English jurist and philosopher Jeremy Bentham). After returning to England, he began to study Roman law, with a view to possibly becoming a lawyer. But in 1823, when he was 17, he took a job at the British East India Company, where he was employed for the next 35 years. Mill was elected to Parliament in 1865, but failed to gain reelection in 1868. After his defeat he retired to Avignon, France, where he died in 1873.

Mill's major writings include *A System of Logic* (1843), *Principles of Political Economy* (1848), *On Liberty* (1859), *Utilitarianism* (published serially in *Fraser's Magazine* in 1861, separately in 1863), and *The Subjection of Women* (written in 1861, published in 1869).

Our reading is from *Utilitarianism,* the work that has become the most popular and influential treatment of utilitarianism. Utilitarianism is the moral theory that was first set forth by Jeremy Bentham. It claims that the morality of an action is determined by how well it promotes "utility," which is defined as the greatest good for the greatest number. Utilitarians differ, however, on how to define "good" and whom to include in the "greatest number."

According to Mill, "good" means happiness, and happiness means pleasure and the absence of pain; the "greatest number" includes not only human beings but all creatures capable of feeling pleasure and pain. Mill's version of utilitarianism, therefore, claims that the moral thing to do in any situation is the action that causes the greatest sum total of pleasure for all the sentient beings involved. Mill typically says that utility is to be determined wholly on the basis of the *individual action,* but at times he seems to endorse the view that one should always follow the *rule* (for example, "Don't kill innocent people") that, when universally followed, would promote the greatest utility—even if, in a particular situation, following the rule would not do so. Philosophers have come to call these two versions of utilitarianism, respectively, *act utilitarianism* and *rule utilitarianism.*

In our selection from Chapter II, "What Utilitarianism Is," Mill briefly describes his theory and then defends it against several objections. In the selection from Chapter IV, "Of What Sort of Proof the Principle of Utility Is Susceptible," he explains in what sense one can prove that the happiness (pleasure) of the individual and the group are desirable and are the only things desirable.

CHAPTER II. WHAT UTILITARIANISM IS

[The Doctrine of Utilitarianism]

... The creed which accepts as the foundation of morals, utility, or the greatest happiness principle, holds that actions are right in proportion as they tend to promote happiness, wrong as they tend to produce the reverse of happiness.

By happiness is intended pleasure and the absence of pain; by unhappiness, pain and the privation of pleasure. To give a clear view of the moral standard set up by the theory, much more requires to be said—in particular, what things it includes in the ideas of pain and pleasure, and to what extent this is left an open question. But these supplementary explanations do not affect the theory of life on which this theory of morality is grounded—namely, that pleasure and freedom from pain are the only things desirable as ends;[1] and that all desirable things (which are as numerous in the utilitarian as in any other scheme) are desirable either for the pleasure inherent in themselves, or as means to the promotion of pleasure and the prevention of pain.

Now such a theory of life excites in many minds, and among them in some of the most estimable in feeling and purpose, inveterate dislike. To suppose that life has (as they express it) no higher end than pleasure—no better and nobler object of desire and pursuit—they designate as utterly mean and grovelling; as a doctrine worthy only of swine, to whom the followers of Epicurus[2] were, at a very early period, contemptuously likened; and modern holders of the doctrine are occasionally made the subject of equally polite comparisons by its German, French, and English assailants.

When thus attacked, the Epicureans have always answered that it is not they, but their accusers, who represent human nature in a degrading light, since the accusation supposes human beings to be capable of no pleasures except those of which swine are capable. If this supposition were true, the charge could not be gainsaid, but would then be no longer an imputation; for if the sources of pleasure were precisely the same to human beings and to swine, the rule of life which is good enough for the one would be good enough for the other. The comparison of the Epicurean life to that of beasts is felt as degrading, precisely because a beast's pleasures do not satisfy a human being's conceptions of happiness. Human beings have faculties more elevated than the animal appetites, and when once made conscious of them, do not regard anything as happiness which does not include their gratification. I do not, indeed, consider the Epicureans to have been by any means faultless in drawing out their scheme of consequences from the utilitarian principle. To do this in any sufficient manner, many Stoic,[3] as well as Christian elements, require to be included. But there is no known Epicurean theory of life which does not assign to the pleasures of the intellect, of the feelings and imagination, and of the moral sentiments, a much higher value as pleasures than to those of mere sensation. It must be admitted, however, that utilitarian writers in general have placed the superiority of mental over bodily pleasures chiefly in the greater permanency, safety, uncostliness, and so on, of the former—that is, in their circumstantial advantages rather than in their intrinsic nature.[4]

---

[1]*ends:* goals. [D. C. ABEL]

[2]Epicurus (341–270 B.C.E.) was a Greek philosopher. [D. C. ABEL]

[3]*Stoic:* relating to Stoicism, the school of philosophy founded by the Greek philosopher Zeno of Citium (about 335–263 B.C.E.). [D. C. ABEL]

[4]Mill refers here primarily to Jeremy Bentham (1748–1832), and English jurist and philosopher, who first proposed the theory of utilitarianism. [D. C. ABEL]

And on all these points utilitarians have fully proved their case; but they might have taken the other, and, as it may be called, higher ground, with entire consistency. It is quite compatible with the principle of utility to recognize the fact that some *kinds* of pleasure are more desirable and more valuable than others. It would be absurd that while in estimating all other things, quality is considered as well as quantity, the estimation of pleasures should be supposed to depend on quantity alone.

If I am asked what I mean by difference of quality in pleasures, or what makes one pleasure more valuable than another, merely as a pleasure, except its being greater in amount, there is but one possible answer. Of two pleasures, if there be one to which all or almost all who have experience of both give a decided preference, irrespective of any feeling of moral obligation to prefer it, that is the more desirable pleasure. If one of the two is, by those who are competently acquainted with both, placed so far above the other that they prefer it, even though knowing it to be attended with a greater amount of discontent, and would not resign it for any quantity of the other pleasure which their nature is capable of, we are justified in ascribing to the preferred enjoyment a superiority in quality, so far outweighing quantity as to render it, in comparison, of small account.

Now it is an unquestionable fact that those who are equally acquainted with and equally capable of appreciating and enjoying both, do give a most marked preference to the manner of existence which employs their higher faculties. Few human creatures would consent to be changed into any of the lower animals for a promise of the fullest allowance of a beast's pleasures. No intelligent human being would consent to be a fool, no instructed person would be an ignoramus, no person of feeling and conscience would be selfish and base, even though they should be persuaded that the fool, the dunce, or the rascal is better satisfied with his lot than they are with theirs. They would not resign what they possess more than he for the most complete satisfaction of all the desires which they have in common with him. If they ever fancy they would, it is only in cases of unhappiness so extreme that to escape from it they would exchange their lot for almost any other, however undesirable in their own eyes. A being of higher faculties requires more to make him happy, is capable probably of more acute suffering, and is certainly accessible to it at more points, than one of an inferior type. But in spite of these liabilities, he can never really wish to sink into what he feels to be a lower grade of existence. We may give what explanation we please of this unwillingness; we may attribute it to pride, a name which is given indiscriminately to some of the most and to some of the least estimable feelings of which mankind are capable; we may refer it to the love of liberty and personal independence, an appeal to which was with the Stoics one of the most effective means for the inculcation of it; to the love of power, or to the love of excitement, both of which do really enter into and contribute to it. But its most appropriate appellation is a sense of dignity, which all human beings possess in one form or other and in some, though by no means in exact, proportion to their higher faculties; and which is so essential a part of the happiness of those in whom it is strong, that nothing which conflicts with it could be, otherwise than momentarily, an object of desire to them. Whoever supposes that this preference takes place at a sacrifice of happiness—that the superior being, in anything like equal circumstances, is not happier than the inferior—confounds the two very different ideas of happiness and content. It is indisputable that the being whose capacities of enjoyment are low has the greatest chance of having them fully satisfied; and a highly-endowed being will always feel that any happiness which he can look for, as the world is constituted, is imperfect. But he can learn to bear its imperfections, if they are at all bearable; and they will not make him envy the being who is indeed unconscious of the imperfections, but only because he feels not at all the good which those imperfections qualify. It is better to be a human being dissatisfied than a pig satisfied; better to be Socrates dissatisfied than a fool satisfied. And if the fool or the pig is of a different opinion, it is because they only know their own side of the question. The other party to the comparison knows both sides. . . .

I have dwelt on this point, as being a necessary part of a perfectly just conception of utility or happiness, considered as the directive rule of human conduct. But it is by no means an indispensable condition to the acceptance of the utilitarian standard—for that standard is not the agent's own greatest happiness, but the greatest amount of happiness altogether. And if it may possibly be doubted whether a noble character is always the happier for its nobleness, there can be no doubt that it makes other people happier and that the world in general is immensely a gainer by it. Utilitarianism, therefore, could only attain its end by the general cultivation of nobleness of character, even if each individual were only benefited by the nobleness of others, and his own, so far as happiness is concerned, were a sheer deduction from the benefit. But the bare enunciation of such an absurdity as this last, renders refutation superfluous.

According to the greatest happiness principle, as above explained, the ultimate end, with reference to and for the sake of which all other things are desirable (whether we are considering our own good or that of other people), is an existence exempt as far as possible from pain, and as rich as possible in enjoyments, both in point of quantity and quality—the test of quality, and the rule for measuring it against quantity, being the preference felt by those who, in their opportunities of experience, to which must be added their habits of self-consciousness and self-observation, are best furnished with the means of comparison. This, being according to the utilitarian opinion the end of human action, is necessarily also the standard of morality, which may accordingly be defined [as] the rules and precepts for human conduct, by the observance of which an existence such as has been described might be, to the greatest extent possible, secured to all mankind; and not to them only, but, so far as the nature of things admits, to the whole sentient creation. . . .

[Responses to Objections]

I must again repeat what the assailants of utilitarianism seldom have the justice to acknowledge, that the happiness which forms the utilitarian standard of what is right in conduct is not the agent's own happiness, but that of all concerned. As between his own happiness and that of others, utilitarianism requires him to be as strictly impartial as a disinterested and benevolent spectator. In the golden rule of Jesus of Nazareth, we read the complete spirit of the ethics of utility. To do as one would be done by,[5] and to love one's neighbor as oneself,[6] constitute the ideal perfection of utilitarian morality. As the means of making the nearest approach to this ideal, utility would enjoin, first, that laws and social arrangements should place the happiness, or (as speaking practically it may be called) the interest, of every individual, as nearly as possible in harmony with the interest of the whole; and secondly, that education and opinion, which have so vast a power over human character, should so use that power as to establish in the mind of every individual an indissoluble association between his own happiness and the good of the whole—especially between his own happiness and the practice of such modes of conduct, negative and positive, as regard for the universal happiness prescribes, so that not only he may be unable to conceive the possibility of happiness to himself consistently with conduct opposed to the general good, but also that a direct impulse to promote the general good may be in every individual one of the habitual motives of action, and the sentiments connected therewith may fill a large and prominent place in every human being's sentient existence. If the impugners of the utilitarian morality represented it to their own minds in this its true character, I know not what recommendation possessed by any other morality they could possibly affirm to be wanting to it; what more beautiful or more exalted developments of human nature any other ethical system can be supposed to foster or what springs of action, not accessible to the utilitarian, such systems rely on for giving effect to their mandates.

The objectors to utilitarianism cannot always be charged with representing it in a discreditable light. On the contrary, those among them who entertain anything like a just idea of its disinterested character sometimes find fault with its standard as being too high for humanity. They say it is exacting too much to require that people shall always act from the inducement of promoting the general interests of society. But this is to mistake the very meaning of a standard of morals and to confound the rule of action with the motive of it. It is the business of ethics to tell us what are our duties, or by what test we may know them; but no system of ethics requires that the sole motive of all we do shall be a feeling of duty. On the contrary, ninety-nine hundredths of all our actions are done from other motives, and rightly so done, if the rule of duty does not condemn them. It is the more unjust to utilitarianism that this particular misapprehension should be made a ground of objection to it, inasmuch as utilitarian moralists have gone beyond almost all others in affirming that the motive has nothing to do with the morality of the action, though much with the worth of the agent. He who saves a fellow creature from drowning does what is morally right, whether his motive be duty or the hope of being paid for his trouble; he who betrays the friend that trusts him is guilty of a crime, even if his object be to serve another friend to whom he is under greater obligations. But to speak only of actions done from the motive of duty and in direct obedience to principle: It is a misapprehension of the utilitarian mode of thought, to conceive it as implying that people should fix their minds upon so wide a generality as the world, or society

---

[5]Matthew 7:21; Luke 6:31. [D. C. ABEL]
[6]Matthew 22:39. [D. C. ABEL]

at large. The great majority of good actions are intended not for the benefit of the world, but for that of individuals, of which the good of the world is made up. And the thoughts of the most virtuous man need not on these occasions travel beyond the particular persons concerned, except so far as is necessary to assure himself that in benefiting them he is not violating the rights—that is, the legitimate and authorized expectations—of anyone else. The multiplication of happiness is, according to the utilitarian ethics, the object of virtue. The occasions on which any person (except one in a thousand) has it in his power to do this on an extended scale, in other words, to be a public benefactor, are but exceptional; and on these occasions alone is he called on to consider public utility. In every other case, private utility, the interest or happiness of some few persons, is all he has to attend to. Those alone the influence of whose actions extends to society in general, need concern themselves habitually about so large an object. In the case of abstinences indeed—of things which people forbear to do, from moral considerations, though the consequences in the particular case might be beneficial—it would be unworthy of an intelligent agent not to be consciously aware that the action is of a class which, if practiced generally, would be generally injurious, and that this is the ground of the obligation to abstain from it. The amount of regard for the public interest implied in this recognition is no greater than is demanded by every system of morals, for they all enjoin to abstain from whatever is manifestly pernicious to society. . . .

We not uncommonly hear the doctrine of utility inveighed against as a *godless* doctrine. If it be necessary to say anything at all against so mere an assumption, we may say that the question depends upon what idea we have formed of the moral character of the Deity. If it be a true belief that God desires, above all things, the happiness of his creatures, and that this was his purpose in their creation, utility is not only not a godless doctrine, but more profoundly religious than any other. If it be meant that utilitarianism does not recognize the revealed will of God as the supreme law of morals, I answer that a utilitarian who believes in the perfect goodness and wisdom of God necessarily believes that whatever God has thought fit to reveal on the subject of morals, must fulfill the requirements of utility in a supreme degree. . . .

Again, defenders of utility often find themselves called upon to reply to such objections as this—that there is not time, previous to action, for calculating and weighing the effects of any line of conduct on the general happiness. This is exactly as if anyone were to say that it is impossible to guide our conduct by Christianity because there is not time, on every occasion on which anything has to be done, to read through the Old and New Testaments. The answer to the objection is that there has been ample time, namely the whole past duration of the human species. During all that time mankind have been learning by experience the tendencies of actions, on which experience all the prudence, as well as all the morality of life, is dependent. People talk as if the commencement of this course of experience had hitherto been put off, and as if, at the moment when some man feels tempted to meddle with the property or life of another, he had to begin considering for the first time whether murder and theft are injurious to human happiness. Even then I do not think that he would find the question very puzzling; but, at all events, the matter is now done to his hand.[7] It is truly a whimsical supposition that if mankind were agreed to considering utility to be the test of morality, they would remain without any agreement as to what *is* useful, and would take no measures for having their notions on the subject taught to the young and enforced by law and opinion. There is no difficulty in proving any ethical standard whatever to work ill, if we suppose universal idiocy to be conjoined with it. But on any hypothesis short of that, mankind must by this time have acquired positive beliefs as to the effects of some actions on their happiness; and [the] beliefs which have thus come down are the rules of morality for the multitude, and for the philosopher until he has succeeded in finding better. . . .

CHAPTER IV. OF WHAT SORT OF PROOF THE PRINCIPLE OF UTILITY IS SUSCEPTIBLE

[The Desirability of the General Happiness]

. . . Questions of ultimate ends do not admit of proof, in the ordinary acceptation of the term. To be incapable of proof by reasoning is common to all first principles—to the first premises of our knowledge, as well as to those of our conduct. But the former, being matters of fact, may be the subject of a direct appeal to the faculties which judge of fact, namely our senses and our internal consciousness. Can an appeal be made to the same faculties on questions of practical ends? Or by what other faculty is cognizance taken of them?

Questions about ends are, in other words, questions about what things are desirable. The utilitarian doctrine is that happiness is desirable, and the only thing desirable, as an end; all other things being only desirable as means to that end. What ought to be required of this doctrine—what conditions is it requisite that the doctrine should fulfill—to make good its claim to be believed?

The only proof capable of being given that an object is visible, is that people actually see it. The only proof that a sound is audible, is that people hear it—and so of the other sources of our experience. In like manner, I apprehend, the sole evidence it is possible to produce that anything is desirable, is that people do actually desire it. If the end which the utilitarian doctrine proposes to itself were not, in theory and in practice, acknowledged to be an end, nothing could ever convince any person that it was so. No reason can be given why the general happiness is desirable, except that each person, so far as he believes it to be attainable, desires his own happiness. This, however, being a fact, we have not only all the proof which the case admits of, but all which it is possible to require, that happiness is a good: that each person's happiness is a good to that person, and the general happiness, therefore, a good to the aggregate of all persons. Happiness has made out its title as *one* of the ends of conduct, and consequently one of the criteria of morality.

---

[7]*done to his hand:* done for him. [D. C. ABEL]

[The Desirability of Other Things]

But it has not, by this alone, proved itself to be the sole criterion. To do that, it would seem, by the same rule, necessary to show not only that people desire happiness, but that they never desire anything else. Now it is palpable that they do desire things which, in common language, are decidedly distinguished from happiness. They desire, for example, virtue and the absence of vice, no less really than pleasure and the absence of pain. The desire of virtue is not as universal, but it is as authentic a fact, as the desire of happiness. And hence the opponents of the utilitarian standard deem that they have a right to infer that there are other ends of human action besides happiness, and that happiness is not the standard of approbation and disapprobation.

But does the utilitarian doctrine deny that people desire virtue, or maintain that virtue is not a thing to be desired? The very reverse. It maintains not only that virtue is to be desired, but that it is to be desired disinterestedly, for itself. Whatever may be the opinion of utilitarian moralists as to the original conditions by which virtue is made virtue; however they may believe (as they do) that actions and dispositions are only virtuous because they promote another end than virtue; yet this being granted, and it having been decided, from considerations of this description, what *is* virtuous, they not only place virtue at the very head of the things which are good as means to the ultimate end, but they also recognize as a psychological fact the possibility of its being, to the individual, a good in itself, without looking to any end beyond it; and hold that the mind is not in a right state, not in a state conformable to utility, not in the state most conducive to the general happiness, unless it does love virtue in this manner—as a thing desirable in itself, even although, in the individual instance, it should not produce those other desirable consequences which it tends to produce, and on account of which it is held to be virtue. This opinion is not, in the smallest degree, a departure from the happiness principle. The ingredients of happiness are very various and each of them is desirable in itself, and not merely when considered as swelling an aggregate. The principle of utility does not mean that any given pleasure, as music, for instance, or any given exemption from pain, as for example health, are to be looked upon as means to a collective something termed happiness, and to be desired on that account. They are desired and desirable in and for themselves; besides being means, they are a part of the end. Virtue, according to the utilitarian doctrine, is not naturally and originally part of the end, but it is capable of becoming so; and in those who love it disinterestedly it has become so, and is desired and cherished, not as a means to happiness, but as a part of their happiness. . . .

We have now, then, an answer to the question, of what sort of proof the principle of utility is susceptible. If the opinion which I have now stated is psychologically true—if human nature is so constituted as to desire nothing which is not either a part of happiness or a means of happiness—we can have no other proof, and we require no other, that these are the only things desirable. If so, happiness is the sole end of human action, and the promotion of it the test by which to judge of all human conduct—from whence it necessarily follows that it must be the criterion of morality, since a part is included in the whole.

And now to decide whether this is really so, whether mankind do desire nothing for itself but that which is a pleasure to them, or of which the absence is a pain—we have evidently arrived at a question of fact and experience, dependent, like all similar questions, upon evidence. It can only be determined by practiced self-consciousness and self-observation, assisted by observation of others. I believe that these sources of evidence, impartially consulted, will declare that desiring a thing and finding it pleasant, aversion to it and thinking of it as painful, are phenomena entirely inseparable, or rather two parts of the same phenomenon; in strictness of language, two different modes of naming the same psychological fact; that to think of an object as desirable (unless for the sake of its consequences) and to think of it as pleasant are one and the same thing; and that to desire anything, except in proportion as the idea of it is pleasant, is a physical and metaphysical[8] impossibility.

---

[8]*metaphysical:* relating to *metaphysics,* the study of the nature and kinds of reality. [D. C. ABEL]

B. Critiques of Classical Theories

READING 36

Is There a Teleological Suspension of the Ethical?

Søren Kierkegaard

Søren Kierkegaard was born in 1813 in Copenhagen, Denmark. His father was plagued by a sense of guilt for having cursed God, and Kierkegaard inherited his father's anxiety-filled piety. He enrolled in the University of Copenhagen in 1830, first taking a wide variety of courses in the liberal arts and then concentrating on theology and philosophy. His father died in 1838, leaving him a fortune large enough to support the continuation of his studies at the University of Copenhagen and, after that, a life devoted to reflection and writing. Kierkegaard completed his degree in theology in 1840. Later that year he proposed marriage to a young woman named Regine Olsen. But he came to believe that his unique philosophical and religious vocation would be incompatible with marriage, and in 1841 he made the anguished decision to break the engagement. Kierkegaard then retreated to Berlin. Six months later he returned to Copenhagen, where he spent his remaining years reflecting on his Christian faith and exploring philosophical questions. He died in Copenhagen in 1855 at the age of 42.

Kierkegaard's major works include *Either/Or* (1843), *Fear and Trembling* (1843), *Philosophical Fragments* (1844), *Stages on Life's Way* (1845), *Concluding Unscientific Postscript* (1846), *Works of Love* (1847), and *The Sickness unto Death* (1849).

Our selection is from *Fear and Trembling,* a book whose title is taken from the passage in which Paul tells the Philippians to work out their salvation "in fear and trembling" (Philippians 1:12). The book presents Kierkegaard's reflection on the biblical story of Abraham being commanded by God to sacrifice Isaac, his only son (Genesis 22:1–18). Even though Abraham did not end up slaying Isaac (because, as he was about to do so, God intervened and told him to sacrifice a ram instead), Abraham's willingness to obey the terrible divine command made him "the father of faith." Because killing one's son violates a fundamental ethical precept, Abraham's obedience to God raises, for Kierkegaard, the question "Is there a teleological suspension of the ethical?"—which is the title of Problem 1 of *Fear and Trembling,* which constitutes our reading. (*Teleological,* which derives from the Greek noun *telos* [end, goal], here means "explainable in terms of a higher goal.")

By "the ethical," Kierkegaard means universal norms of conduct, derived from reason. In ethics, the universal is higher than the particular individual, and has its telos in itself: The individual is to follow ethical rules because they are ethical. A "teleological suspension" of the ethical would be the subordination of the ethical to a higher telos, one that places the individual higher than the universal. Kierkegaard argues that Abraham's personal relation with God, which places him in "an absolute relation to the absolute," suspends and transcends the ethical realm. Abraham is not a tragic hero, because the actions of a tragic hero can be explained ethically and rationally. Abraham "acts by virtue of the absurd, for it is precisely the absurd that he as the single individual is higher than the universal." Abraham is a "knight of faith" who has crossed over from the ethical sphere of human existence to the higher, religious sphere.

[THE PARADOX OF FAITH]

The ethical as such is the universal, and as the universal it applies to everyone, which from another angle means that it applies at all times. It rests immanent in itself, has nothing outside itself that is its telos,[1] but is itself the telos for everything outside itself, and when the ethical has absorbed this into itself, it goes no further. The single individual, sensately[2] and psychically qualified in immediacy, is the individual who has his telos in the universal, and it is his ethical task continually to express himself in this, to annul his singularity in order to become the universal. As soon as the single individual asserts himself in his singularity before the universal, he sins, and only by acknowledging this can he be reconciled again with the universal. Every time the single individual, after having entered the universal, feels an impulse to assert himself as the single individual, he is in a spiritual trial from which he can work himself only by repentantly surrendering as the single individual in the universal. If this is the highest that can be said of man and his existence, then the ethical is of the same nature as a person's eternal salvation, which is his telos forevermore and at all times, since it would be a contradiction for this to be capable of being surrendered (that is, teleologically suspended), because as soon as this is suspended it is relinquished, whereas that which is suspended is not relinquished but is preserved in the higher, which is its telos.

If this is the case, then Hegel is right in "The Good and Conscience,"[3] where he qualifies man only as the individual and considers this qualification as a "moral form of evil" that must be annulled in the teleology of the moral in such a way that the single individual who remains in that stage either sins or is immersed in spiritual trial. But Hegel is wrong in speaking about faith; he is wrong in not protesting loudly and clearly against Abraham's enjoying honor and glory as a father of faith when he ought to be sent back to a lower court and shown up as a murderer.

Faith is namely this paradox, that the single individual is higher than the universal—yet, please note, in such a way that the movement repeats itself, so that after having been in the universal he as the single individual isolates himself as higher than the universal. If this is not faith, then Abraham is lost, then faith has never existed in the world precisely because it has always existed. For if the ethical—that is, social morality—is the highest and if there is in a person no residual incommensurability in some way such that this incommensurability is not evil (that is, the single individual, who is to be expressed in the universal), then no categories are needed other than what Greek philosophy had or what

---

[1]*telos:* end, goal. [D. C. ABEL]

[2]*sensately:* in a manner relating to the senses. [D. C. ABEL]

[3]Georg Wilhelm Friedrich Hegel, *Philosophy of Right,* Part Two, Section 3 (paragraphs 129–41). Hegel (1770–1831) was a German philosopher. [D. C. ABEL]

can be deduced from them by consistent thought. Hegel should not have concealed this, for, after all, he had studied Greek philosophy.

People who are profoundly lacking in learning and are given to clichés are frequently heard to say that a light shines over the Christian world, whereas darkness enshrouds paganism. This kind of talk has always struck me as strange, inasmuch as every more thorough thinker, every more earnest artist still regenerates himself in the eternal youth of the Greeks. The explanation for such a statement is that one does not know what one should say but only that one must say something. It is quite right to say that paganism did not have faith, but if something is supposed to have been said thereby, then one must have a clearer understanding of what faith is, for otherwise one falls into such clichés. It is easy to explain all existence, faith along with it, without having a conception of what faith is, and the one who counts on being admired for such an explanation is not such a bad calculator; for it is as Boileau says, *"Un sot trouve toujours un plus sot, qui l'admire."*[4] Faith is precisely the paradox that the single individual as the single individual is higher than the universal, is justified before it, not as inferior to it but as superior—yet in such a way, please note, that it is the single individual who, after being subordinate as the single individual to the universal, now by means of the universal becomes the single individual who as the single individual is superior, that the single individual as the single individual stands in an absolute relation to the absolute. This position cannot be mediated, for all mediation takes place only by virtue of the universal; it is and remains for all eternity a paradox, impervious to thought. And yet faith is this paradox, or else (and I ask the reader to bear these consequences *in mente*[5] even though it would be too prolix for me to write them all down) or else faith has never existed simply because it has always existed, or else Abraham is lost.

It is certainly true that the single individual can easily confuse this paradox with spiritual trial, but it ought not to be concealed for that reason. It is certainly true that many persons may be so constituted that they are repulsed by it, but faith ought not therefore to be made into something else to enable one to have it, but one ought rather to admit to not having it, while those who have faith ought to be prepared to set forth some characteristics whereby the paradox can be distinguished from a spiritual trial.

[ABRAHAM AND ISAAC]

The story of Abraham contains just such a teleological suspension of the ethical. There is no dearth of keen minds and careful scholars who have found analogies to it. What their wisdom amounts to is the beautiful proposition that basically everything is the same. If one looks more closely, I doubt very much that anyone in the whole wide world will find one single analogy, except for a later one, which proves nothing if it is certain that Abraham represents faith and that it is

---

[4]"A fool always finds a greater fool to admire him." Nicolas BoileauDespréaux, *L'Art poétique,* Canto I, line 232. Boileau (1636–1711) was a French critic. [D. C. ABEL]

[5]*in mente:* (Latin) "in mind." [D. C. ABEL]

manifested normatively in him, whose life not only is the most paradoxical that can be thought but is also so paradoxical that it simply cannot be thought. He acts by virtue of the absurd, for it is precisely the absurd that he as the single individual is higher than the universal. This paradox cannot be mediated, for as soon as Abraham begins to do so, he has to confess that he was in a spiritual trial, and if that is the case, he will never sacrifice Isaac, or if he did sacrifice Isaac, then in repentance he must come back to the universal. He gets Isaac back again by virtue of the absurd. Therefore, Abraham is at no time a tragic hero but is something entirely different, either a murderer or a man of faith. Abraham does not have the middle term[6] that saves the tragic hero. This is why I can understand a tragic hero but cannot understand Abraham, even though in a certain demented sense I admire him more than all others.

In ethical terms, Abraham's relation to Isaac is quite simply this: The father shall love the son more than himself. But within its own confines the ethical has various gradations. We shall see whether this story contains any higher expression for the ethical that can ethically explain his behavior, can ethically justify his suspending the ethical obligation to the son, but without moving beyond the teleology of the ethical.

[THREE TRAGIC HEROES]

When an enterprise of concern to a whole nation[7] is impeded, when such a project is halted by divine displeasure, when the angry deity sends a dead calm that mocks every effort, when the soothsayer carries out his sad task and announces that the deity demands a young girl as sacrifice—then the father must heroically bring this sacrifice.[8] He must nobly conceal his agony, even though he could wish he were "the lowly man who dares to weep"[9] and not the king who must behave in a kingly manner. Although the lonely agony penetrates his breast and there are only three persons in the whole nation who know his agony, soon the whole nation will be initiated into his agony and also into his deed, that for the welfare of all he will sacrifice her, his daughter, this lovely young girl. "O bosom! O fair cheeks, flaxen hair."[10] And the daughter's tears will agitate him, and the father will turn away his face, but the hero must raise the knife. And when the news of it reaches the father's house, the beautiful Greek maidens will blush with enthusiasm, and if the daughter was engaged, her betrothed will not be angry but will be proud to share in the father's deed, for the girl belonged more tenderly to him than to the father.

---

[6]*middle term:* in logic, that which connects two elements and allows one to make an inference about the relation of those elements. [D. C. ABEL]

[7]*whole nation:* the Greeks, who were fighting the Trojans. [D. C. ABEL]

[8]When the adverse winds ceased and prevented the Greek fleet from sailing for Troy, the soothsayer Calchas announced that favorable winds would blow only if King Agamemnon sacrificed his daughter Iphigenia to the goddess Artemis. [D. C. ABEL]

[9]A paraphrase of Euripides, *Iphigenia at Aulis,* line 448. Euripides (484–406 B.C.E.) was a Greek dramatist. [D. C. ABEL]

[10]Euripides, *Iphigenia at Aulis,* line 681. [D. C. ABEL]

When the valiant judge[11] who in the hour of need saved Israel binds God and himself in one breath by the same promise, he will heroically transform the young maiden's jubilation, the beloved daughter's joy to sorrow, and all Israel will sorrow with her over her virginal youth. But every freeborn man will understand, every resolute woman will admire Jephthah, and every virgin in Israel will wish to behave as his daughter did, because what good would it be for Jephthah to win the victory by means of a promise if he did not keep it—would not the victory be taken away from the people again?

When a son forgets his duty,[12] when the state entrusts the sword of judgment to the father, when the laws demand punishment from the father's hand, then the father must heroically forget that the guilty one is his son, he must nobly hide his agony. But no one in the nation, not even the son, will fail to admire the father, and every time the Roman laws are interpreted, it will be remembered that many interpreted them more learnedly but no one more magnificently than Brutus.

But if Agamemnon, while a favorable wind was taking the fleet under full sail to its destination, had dispatched that messenger who fetched Iphigenia to be sacrificed; if Jephthah, without being bound by any promise that decided the fate of the nation, had said to his daughter: Grieve now for two months over your brief youth, and then I will sacrifice you; if Brutus had had a righteous son and yet had summoned the lictors[13] to put him to death—who would have understood them? If, on being asked why they did this, these three men had answered: It is an ordeal in which we are being tried—would they have been better understood?

When in the crucial moment Agamemnon, Jephthah, and Brutus heroically have overcome the agony, heroically have lost the beloved, and have only to complete the task externally, there will never be a noble soul in the world without tears of compassion for their agony, of admiration for their deed. But if in the crucial moment these three men were to append to the heroic courage with which they bore the agony the little phrase, "But it will not happen anyway"— who then would understand them? If they went on to explain, "This we believe by virtue of the absurd"—who would understand them any better? For who would not readily understand that it was absurd, but who would understand that one could then believe it?

[THE TELEOLOGICAL SUSPENSION OF THE ETHICAL]

The difference between the tragic hero and Abraham is very obvious. The tragic hero is still within the ethical. He allows an expression of the ethical to have its telos in a higher expression of the ethical; he scales down the ethical relation

---

[11]Jephthah; see Judges 11:30–40. [H. V. HONG AND E. H. HONG, TRANSLATORS]. Jephthah sacrificed his daughter, his only child, in fulfillment of a vow he made to God if God would grant him military victory over the Ammonites. [D. C. ABEL]

[12]When Marcus Junius Brutus (85–42 B.C.E.) was consul of Rome, his sons took part in a conspiracy to restore the king whom he had expelled. Brutus ordered the execution of his sons. [D. C. ABEL]

[13]*lictors:* Roman officials who attended chief magistrates and administered punishments. [D. C. ABEL]

between father and son or daughter and father to a feeling that has its dialectic in its relation to the idea of moral conduct. Here there can be no question of a teleological suspension of the ethical itself.

Abraham's situation is different. By his act he transgressed the ethical altogether and had a higher telos outside it, in relation to which he suspended it. For I certainly would like to know how Abraham's act can be related to the universal, whether any point of contact between what Abraham did and the universal can be found other than that Abraham transgressed it. It is not to save a nation, not to uphold the idea of the state that Abraham does it; it is not to appease the angry gods. If it were a matter of the deity's being angry, then he was, after all, angry only with Abraham, and Abraham's act is totally unrelated to the universal, is a purely private endeavor. Therefore, while the tragic hero is great because of his moral virtue, Abraham is great because of a purely personal virtue. There is no higher expression for the ethical in Abraham's life than that the father shall love the son. The ethical in the sense of the moral is entirely beside the point. Insofar as the universal was present, it was cryptically in Isaac, hidden, so to speak, in Isaac's loins, and must cry out with Isaac's mouth, "Do not do this! You are destroying everything."

Why, then, does Abraham do it? For God's sake and—the two are wholly identical—for his own sake. He does it for God's sake because God demands this proof of his faith; he does it for his own sake so that he can prove it. The unity of the two is altogether correctly expressed in the word already used to describe this relationship: It is an ordeal, a temptation. A temptation—but what does that mean? As a rule, what tempts a person is something that will hold him back from doing his duty, but here the temptation is the ethical itself, which would hold him back from doing God's will. But what is duty? Duty is simply the expression for God's will.

Here the necessity of a new category for the understanding of Abraham becomes apparent. Paganism does not know such a relationship to the divine. The tragic hero does not enter into any private relationship to the divine, but the ethical is the divine, and thus the paradox therein can be mediated in the universal.

Abraham cannot be mediated; in other words, he cannot speak. As soon as I speak, I express the universal, and if I do not do so, no one can understand me. As soon as Abraham wants to express himself in the universal, he must declare that his situation is a spiritual trial, for he has no higher expression of the universal that ranks above the universal he violates.

Therefore, although Abraham arouses my admiration, he also appalls me. The person who denies himself and sacrifices himself because of duty gives up the finite in order to grasp the infinite and is adequately assured; the tragic hero gives up the certain for the even more certain, and the observer's eye views him with confidence. But the person who gives up the universal in order to grasp something even higher that is not the universal—what does he do? Is it possible that this can be anything other than a spiritual trial? And if it is possible, but the individual makes a mistake, what salvation is there for him? He suffers all the agony of the tragic hero, he shatters his joy in the world, he renounces everything, and perhaps at the same time he barricades himself from the sublime joy that was so precious to him that he would buy it at any price. The observer cannot understand him at all; neither can his eye rest upon him with confidence. Perhaps the believer's intention cannot be carried out at all, because it is inconceivable. Or if it could be done but the individual has misunderstood the deity—what salvation would there be for him? The tragic hero needs and demands tears, and where is the envious eye so arid that it could not weep with Agamemnon? But where is the soul so gone astray that it has the audacity to weep for Abraham? The tragic hero finishes his task at a specific moment in time, but as time passes he does what is no less significant: He visits the person encompassed by sorrow, who cannot breathe because of his anguished sighs, whose thoughts oppress him, heavy with tears. He appears to him, breaks the witchcraft of sorrow, loosens the bonds, evokes the tears, and the sufferer forgets his own sufferings in those of the tragic hero. One cannot weep over Abraham. One approaches him with a *horror religiosus*,[14] as Israel approached Mount Sinai.[15] What if he himself is distraught, what if he had made a mistake, this lonely man who climbs Mount Moriah,[16] whose peak towers sky-high over the flatlands of Aulis;[17] what if he is not a sleepwalker safely crossing the abyss while the one standing at the foot of the mountain looks up, shakes with anxiety, and then in his deference and horror does not even dare to call to him? Thanks, and once again thanks, to a man who, to a person overwhelmed by life's sorrows and left behind naked, reaches out the words, the leafage of language by which he can conceal his misery. Thanks to you, great Shakespeare, you who can say everything, everything, everything just as it is. And yet, why did you never articulate this torment? Did you perhaps reserve it for yourself, like the beloved's name that one cannot bear to have the world utter, for with his little secret that he cannot divulge the poet buys this power of the word to tell everybody else's dark secrets. A poet is not an apostle; he drives out devils only by the power of the devil.

But if the ethical is teleologically suspended in this manner, how does the single individual in whom it is suspended exist? He exists as the single individual in contrast to the universal. Does he sin, then? For from the point of view of the idea, this is the form of sin. Thus, even though the child does not sin, because it is not conscious of its existence as such, its existence, from the point of view of the idea, is nevertheless sin, and the ethical makes its claim upon it at all times. If it is denied that this form can be repeated in such a way that it is not sin, then judgment has fallen upon Abraham. How did Abraham exist? He had faith. This is the paradox by which he remains at the apex, the paradox that he cannot explain to anyone else, for the paradox is that he as the single individual places himself in an absolute relation to the absolute. Is he justified? Again, his justification is the paradoxical, for if he is, then he is justified not by virtue of being something universal but by virtue of being the single individual.

How does the single individual reassure himself that he is legitimate? It is a simple matter to level all existence to the idea of the state or the idea of a society.

---

[14]*horror religiousus:* (Latin) "religious dread, awe." [D. C. ABEL]
[15]See Exodus 19:12. [H. V. HONG AND E. H. HONG]
[16]*Mount Moriah:* the place where Abraham was to sacrifice Isaac. [D. C. ABEL]
[17]*Aulis:* the place in Greece where Agamemnon nearly sacrificed his daughter. [D. C. ABEL]

If this is done, it is also simple to mediate, for one never comes to the paradox that the single individual as the single individual is higher than the universal—something I can also express symbolically in a statement by Pythagoras[18] to the effect that the odd number is more perfect than the even number. If occasionally there is any response at all these days with regard to the paradox, it is likely to be: One judges it by the result. Aware that he is a paradox who cannot be understood, a hero who has become a *skandalon*[19] to his age will shout confidently to his contemporaries, "The result will indeed prove that I was justified." This cry is rarely heard in our age, inasmuch as it does not produce heroes—this is its defect—and it likewise has the advantage that it produces few caricatures. When in our age we hear the words "It will be judged by the result," then we know at once with whom we have the honor of speaking. Those who talk this way are a numerous type whom I shall designate under the common name of assistant professors. With security in life, they live in their thoughts; they have a *permanent* position and a *secure* future in a well-organized state. They have hundreds—yes, even thousands—of years between them and the earthquakes of existence. They are not afraid that such things can be repeated, for then what would the police and the newspapers say? Their life task is to judge the great men, judge them according to the result. Such behavior toward greatness betrays a strange mixture of arrogance and wretchedness—arrogance because they feel called to pass judgment, wretchedness because they feel that their lives are in no way allied with the lives of the great. Anyone with even a smattering *erectioris ingenii*[20] never becomes an utterly cold and clammy worm, and when he approaches greatness, he is never devoid of the thought that since the creation of the world it has been customary for the result to come last, and that if one is truly going to learn something from greatness one must be particularly aware of the beginning. If the one who is to act wants to judge himself by the result, he will never begin. Although the result may give joy to the entire world, it cannot help the hero, for he would not know the result until the whole thing was over, and he would not become a hero but by making a beginning.

Moreover, in its dialectic the result (insofar as it is finitude's response to the infinite question) is altogether incongruous with the hero's existence. Or should Abraham's receiving Isaac by a *marvel*[21] be able to prove that Abraham was justified in relating himself as the single individual to the universal? If Abraham actually had sacrificed Isaac, would he therefore have been less justified?

But we are curious about the result, just as we are curious about the way a book turns out. We do not want to know anything about the anxiety, the distress, the paradox. We carry on an aesthetic flirtation with the result. It arrives just as unexpectedly but also just as effortlessly as a prize in a lottery; and when we have heard the result, we have built ourselves up. And yet no manacled robber of churches is so despicable a criminal as the one who plunders holiness in this

---

[18]Pythagoras (about 580–500 B.C.E.) was a Greek philosopher and mathematician. [D. C. ABEL]

[19]*skandalon:* (Greek) "stumbling block, offense." [D. C. ABEL]

[20]*erectioris ingenii:* (Latin) "of a nobler nature." [D. C. ABEL]

[21]God enabled Abraham's wife, Sarah, to conceive Isaac when Abraham was 99 years old and Sarah was 90 (Genesis 17). [D. C. ABEL]

way. And not even Judas, who sold his Lord for 30 pieces of silver, is more contemptible than someone who peddles greatness in this way.

It is against my very being to speak inhumanly about greatness, to make it a dim and nebulous far-distant shape or to let it be great but devoid of the emergence of the humanness without which it ceases to be great. For it is not what happens to me that makes me great, but what I do; and certainly there is no one who believes that someone became great by winning the big lottery prize. A person might have been born in lowly circumstances, but I would still require him not to be so inhuman toward himself that he could imagine the king's castle only at a distance and ambiguously dream of its greatness, and destroy it at the same time he elevates it because he elevated it so basely. I require him to be man enough to tread confidently and with dignity there as well. He must not be so inhuman that he insolently violates everything by barging right off the street into the king's hall—he loses more thereby than the king. On the contrary, he should find a joy in observing every bidding of propriety with a happy and confident enthusiasm, which is precisely what makes him a free spirit. This is merely a metaphor, for that distinction is only a very imperfect expression of the distance of spirit. I require every person not to think so inhumanly of himself that he does not dare to enter those palaces where the memory of the chosen ones lives, or even those where they themselves live. He is not to enter rudely and foist his affinity upon them. He is to be happy for every time he bows before them, but he is to be confident, free of spirit, and always more than a charwoman, for if he wants to be no more than that, he will never get in. And the very thing that is going to help him is the anxiety and distress in which the great were tried; for otherwise, if he has any backbone, they will only arouse his righteous envy. And anything that can be great only at a distance, that someone wants to make great with empty and hollow phrases—is destroyed by that very person.

Who was as great in the world as that favored woman, the mother of God, the Virgin Mary? And yet how do we speak of her? That she was the favored one among women does not make her great, and if it would not be so very odd for those who listen to be able to think just as inhumanly as those who speak, then every young girl might ask, "Why am I not so favored?" And if I had nothing else to say, I certainly would not dismiss such a question as stupid—because, viewed abstractly, vis-à-vis a favor, every person is just as entitled to it as the other. We leave out the distress, the anxiety, the paradox. My thoughts are as pure as anybody's, and he who can think this way surely has pure thoughts, and, if not, he can expect something horrible—for anyone who has once experienced these images cannot get rid of them again, and if he sins against them, they take a terrible revenge in a silent rage, which is more terrifying than the stridency of ten ravenous critics. To be sure, Mary bore the child wondrously, but she nevertheless did it "after the manner of women,"[22] and such a time is one of anxiety, distress, and paradox. The angel was indeed a ministering spirit, but he was not a meddlesome spirit who went to the other young maidens in Israel and said, "Do not scorn Mary; the extraordinary is happening to her." The

---

[22]Genesis 18:11. [H. V. Hong and E. H. Hong]

angel went only to Mary, and no one could understand her. Has any woman been as infringed upon as was Mary, and is it not true here also that the one whom God blesses he curses in the same breath? This is the spirit's view of Mary, and she is by no means—it is revolting to me to say it but even more so that people have inanely and unctuously made her out to be thus—she is by no means a lady idling in her finery and playing with a divine child. When, despite this, she said. "Behold, I am the handmaid of the Lord"[23]—then she is great, and I believe it should not be difficult to explain why she became the mother of God. She needs worldly admiration as little as Abraham needs tears, for she was no heroine and he was no hero, but both of them became greater than these, not by being exempted in any way from the distress and the agony and the paradox, but became greater by means of these.

It is great when the poet in presenting his tragic hero for public admiration dares to say, "Weep for him, for he deserves it." It is great to deserve the tears of those who deserve to shed tears. It is great that the poet dares to keep the crowd under restraint, dares to discipline men to examine themselves individually to see if they are worthy to weep for the hero—for the slop water of the snivelers is a debasement of the sacred. But even greater than all this is the knight of faith's daring to say to the noble one who wants to weep for him, "Do not weep for me, but weep for yourself."[24]

We are touched, we look back to those beautiful times. Sweet sentimental longing leads us to the goal of our desire, to see Christ walking about in the promised land. We forget the anxiety, the distress, the paradox. Was it such a simple matter not to make a mistake? Was it not terrifying that this man walking around among the others was God? Was it not terrifying to sit down to eat with him? Was it such an easy matter to become an apostle? But the result, the eighteen centuries [since the time of Christ]—that helps, that contributes to this mean deception whereby we deceive ourselves and others. I do not feel brave enough to wish to be contemporary with events like that, but I do not for that reason severely condemn those who made a mistake, nor do I depreciate those who saw what was right.

[CONCLUSION]

But I come back to Abraham. During the time before the result, either Abraham was a murderer every minute, or we stand before a paradox that is higher than all mediations.

The story of Abraham contains, then, an teleological suspension of the ethical. As the single individual he became higher than the universal. This is the paradox, which cannot be mediated. How he entered into it is just as inexplicable as how he remains in it. If this is not Abraham's situation, then Abraham is not even a tragic hero but a murderer. It is thoughtless to want to go on calling him

---

[23]Luke 1:38. [H. V. Hong and E. H. Hong]

[24]On his way to his crucifixion, Jesus tells the women following him, "Do not weep for me; weep for yourselves and for your children" (Luke 23:28). [D. C. Abel]

the father of faith, to speak of it to men who have an interest only in words. A person can become a tragic hero through his own strength—but not a knight of faith. When a person walks what is in one sense the hard road of the tragic hero, there are many who can give him advice, but he who walks the narrow road of faith has no one to advise him—no one understands him. Faith is a marvel, and yet no human being is excluded from it; for that which unites all human life is passion, and faith is a passion.

Beyond Good and Evil

Friedrich Nietzsche

Friedrich Nietzsche was born in Röcken, Prussia, in 1844. After graduating from the Lutheran boarding school at Pforta in 1864, he enrolled in the University of Bonn to study theology. There he began to doubt his Christian faith (he eventually became an atheist and harsh critic of Christianity) and in 1865 transferred to the University of Leipzig to study classical philology (Greek and Latin language and literature) and music. He was recognized as a brilliant student of philology, and at the age of 24, before he had even finished his doctorate, he was offered the chair of classical philology at the University of Basel in Switzerland. The University of Leipzig quickly granted his degree, and Nietzsche assumed the professorship at Basel in 1869. Ten years later, because of his increasingly bad health, Nietzsche resigned his position. For the next 10 years, half blind and in unremitting pain, he wandered through Switzerland, Germany, and Italy in search of a cure. His mental health began to deteriorate as well; in 1889 he collapsed on the streets of Turin, Italy, completely insane. He died in Weimar in 1900.

Nietzsche's principal works are *The Birth of Tragedy out of the Spirit of Music* (1872); *Human, All Too Human* (1878); *The Gay Science* (1882); *Thus Spoke Zarathustra* (1883–1885); *Beyond Good and Evil* (1886); and *On the Genealogy of Morals* (1887).

Our selection is from *Beyond Good and Evil,* a book consisting of about three hundred sections, which are organized according to nine topics. The topic of Part 9, from which our reading comes, is "What Is Noble?" According to Nietzsche, to be noble means to see oneself as the center and origin of all value. In fact, the terms "good" and "bad" originally designated simply what the aristocracy did and did not value. For Nietzsche, "life *is* precisely will to power," and historically members of the aristocracy exercised their will to power by exploiting common people and using them as they saw fit. Nietzsche calls the morality of the ruling aristocracy a "master morality." He contrasts this kind of morality with "slave morality," which arose when common people tried to make their inferior and despicable lives more bearable by exalting as virtues such qualities as kindness, sympathy, selflessness, patience, and humility (the cornerstones of Christian morality). Slave morality gave rise to the pair of terms "good" and "evil," which Nietzsche contrasts with the "good" and "bad" of master morality. In slave morality, "good" refers to the slaves' (false) values, and "evil" to the (legitimate and noble) values of the rulers. Since rulers are not in the inferior position of slaves, they need not subscribe to slave values and are "beyond good and evil."

Nietzsche bemoans the fact that modern civilization, with its democratic and egalitarian tendencies, is replacing life-affirming master morality with life-denying slave morality. Yet there are still elements of master morality in some souls, and it is to these souls that Nietzsche's praise of "what is noble" is addressed.

PART 9. WHAT IS NOBLE?

257

Every enhancement so far in the type "man" has been the work of an aristocratic society—and that is how it will be, again and again, since this sort of society believes in a long ladder of rank order and value distinctions between men, and in some sense needs slavery. Without the *pathos of distance* as it grows out of the ingrained differences between stations, out of the way the ruling caste maintains an overview and keeps looking down on subservient types and tools, and out of this caste's equally continuous exercise in obeying and commanding, in keeping away and below—without *this* pathos, that *other,* more mysterious pathos could not have grown at all, that demand for new expansions of distance within the soul itself, the development of states that are increasingly high, rare, distant, tautly drawn and comprehensive, and in short, the enhancement of the type "man," the constant "self-overcoming of man" (to use a moral formula in a supramoral sense). Of course, you cannot entertain any humanitarian illusions about how an aristocratic society originates (and any elevation of the type "man" will presuppose an aristocratic society): The truth is harsh. Let us not be deceived about how every higher culture on earth has *begun!* Men whose nature was still natural, barbarians in every terrible sense of the word, predatory people who still possessed an unbroken strength of will and lust for power, threw themselves on weaker, more civilized, more peaceful races of tradesmen perhaps, or cattle breeders; or on old and mellow cultures in which the very last life-force was flaring up in brilliant fireworks of spirit and corruption. The noble caste always started out as the barbarian caste. Their supremacy was in psychic, not physical strength—they were *more complete* people (which at any level amounts to saying "more complete beasts").

258

Corruption, as an expression of the fact that anarchy threatens inside the instincts and that the foundation of the affects, which we call "life," has been shaken—corruption means fundamentally different things, depending on the life-form in which it manifests itself. When, for instance, an aristocracy like that in France at the beginning of the Revolution[1] throws away its privileges with a sublime disgust and sacrifices itself to an excess of its moral feeling, then this is corruption. It was really just the final act of that centuries-long corruption in which the aristocracy gradually relinquished its dominant authority and was reduced to a mere *function* of the kingdom (and, in the end, to its trinket and showpiece). But the essential feature of a good, healthy aristocracy is that it does *not* feel that it is a function (whether of the kingdom or of the community) but instead feels itself to be the *meaning* and highest justification (of the kingdom or community)—and, consequently, that it accepts in good conscience the sacrifice of countless people who have to be pushed down and shrunk into incomplete human beings, into slaves, into tools, all *for the sake of the aristocracy.* Its fundamental belief must always be that society *cannot* exist for the sake of society, but only as the substructure and framework for raising an exceptional type of being up to its higher duty and to a higher state of *being.* In the same way, the sun-seeking, Javanese climbing plant called the *Sipo matador* will wrap its arms

---

[1]The French Revolution began in 1789 and ended in 1799. [D. C. Abel]

around an oak tree so often and for such a long time that finally, high above the oak, although still supported by it, the plant will be able to unfold its highest crown of foliage and show its happiness in the full, clear light.

259

Mutually refraining from injury, violence, and exploitation, placing your will on par with the other's—in a certain, crude sense, these practices can become good manners between individuals when the right conditions are present (namely, that the individuals have genuinely similar quantities of force and measures of value, and belong together within a single body). But as soon as this principle is taken any further, and maybe even held to be the *fundamental principle of society*, it immediately shows itself for what it is: the will to *negate* life, the principle of disintegration and decay. Here we must think things through thoroughly and ward off any sentimental weakness: Life itself is *essentially* a process of appropriating, injuring, overpowering the alien and the weaker, oppressing, being harsh, imposing your own form, incorporating, and at least, the very least, exploiting. But what is the point of always using words that have been stamped with slanderous intentions from time immemorial? Even a body within which (as we presupposed earlier) particular individuals treat each other as equal (which happens in every healthy aristocracy)—if this body is living and not dying, it will have to treat other bodies in just those ways that the individuals it contains *refrain* from treating each other. It will have to be the embodiment of will to power, it will want to grow, spread, grab, win dominance—not out of any morality or immorality, but because it is *alive*, and because life *is* precisely will to power.

But there is no issue on which the base European consciousness is less willing to be instructed than this. These days, people everywhere are lost in rapturous enthusiasms, even in scientific disguise, about a future state of society where "the exploitative character" will fall away. To my ears, that sounds as if someone is promising to invent a life that dispenses with all organic functions. "Exploitation" does not belong to a corrupted or imperfect, primitive society: It belongs to the *essence* of being alive as a fundamental organic function; it is a result of genuine will to power, which is just the will of life. Although this is an innovation at the level of *theory*, at the level of *reality*, it is the *primal fact* of all history. Let us be honest with ourselves to this extent at least!

260

As I was wandering through the many subtle and crude moralities that have been dominant or that still dominate over the face of the earth, I found certain traits regularly recurring together and linked to each other. In the end, two basic types became apparent to me and a fundamental distinction leaped out. There is a *master morality* and a *slave morality*. I will immediately add that in all higher and more mixed cultures, attempts to negotiate between these moralities also appear, although more frequently the two are confused and there are mutual misunderstandings. In fact, you sometimes find them sharply juxtaposed—inside the same person even, within a single soul.

Moral value distinctions have arisen within either a dominating type that, with a feeling of well-being, was conscious of the difference between itself and those who were dominated—or alternatively, these distinctions arose among the dominated people themselves, the slaves and dependents of every rank. In the first case, when dominating people determine the concept of "good," it is the elevated, proud states of soul that are perceived as distinctive and as determining rank order. The noble person separates himself off from creatures in which the opposite of such elevated, proud states is expressed: He despises them. It is immediately apparent that, in this first type of morality, the contrast between "good" and "bad" amounts to one between "noble" and "despicable" (the contrast between "good" and "*evil*" has a different lineage). People who were cowardly, apprehensive, and petty; people who thought narrowly in terms of utility— these were the ones despised. But the same can be said about distrustful people with their uneasy glances, about grovelers, about dog-like types of people who let themselves be mistreated, about begging flatterers and, above all, about liars—it is a basic belief of aristocrats that base peoples are liars. "We who are truthful"—that is what the nobility of ancient Greece called themselves.

It is obvious that moral expressions everywhere were first applied to *people* and then, only later and derivatively, to *actions* (which is why it is a tremendous mistake when historians of morality take their point of departure from questions such as "Why do acts of pity get praised?"). The noble type of person feels that *he* determines value, he does not need anyone's approval, he judges that "what is harmful to me is harmful in itself," he knows that he is the one who gives honor to things in the first place, he *creates values*. He honors everything he sees in himself: This sort of morality is self-glorifying. In the foreground, there is the feeling of fullness, of power that wants to overflow, the happiness associated with a high state of tension, the consciousness of a wealth that wants to make gifts and give away. The noble person helps the unfortunate too, although not (or hardly ever) out of pity, but rather more out of an impulse generated by the overabundance of power.

In honoring himself, the noble man honors the powerful as well as those who have power over themselves, who know how to speak and be silent, who joyfully exercise severity and harshness over themselves, and have respect for all forms of severity and harshness. "Wotan[2] has put a hard heart in my breast," reads a line from an old Scandinavian saga; this rightly comes from the soul of a proud Viking. This sort of a man is even proud of *not* being made for pity, which is why the hero of the saga adds, by way of warning, "If your heart is not hard when you are young, it will never be hard." The noble and brave types of people who think this way are the furthest removed from a morality that sees precisely pity, actions for others, and *désintéressement*[3] as emblematic of morality. A faith in yourself, pride in yourself, and a fundamental hostility and irony with respect to "selflessness" belong to a noble morality just as certainly as does a slight disdain and caution towards sympathetic feelings and "warm hearts."

---

[2]Wotan (Woden, Odin) is the supreme god of Norse mythology. [D. C. ABEL]
[3]*désintéressement:* (French) unselfishness. [D. C. ABEL]

The powerful are the ones who *know* how to honor; it is their art, their realm of invention. A profound reverence for age and origins—the whole notion of justice is based on this double reverence—a faith and a prejudice in favor of fore-fathers and against future generations is typical of the morality of the powerful. And when, conversely, people with "modern ideas" believe almost instinctively in "progress" and "the future" and show a decreasing respect for age, this gives sufficient evidence of the ignoble origin of these "ideas." But, most of all, the morality of dominating types is foreign and painful to contemporary taste due to its stern axiom that people have duties only towards their own kind; that when it comes to creatures of a lower rank, to everything alien, people are allowed to act as they see fit or "from the heart," and in any event, "beyond good and evil." Things like pity might have a place here. The capacity and duty to experience extended gratitude and vengefulness (both only among your own kind), subtlety in retaliation, refinement in concepts of friendship, a certain need to have enemies (as flue holes, as it were, for the affects of jealousy, irascibility, arrogance—basically in order to be a good *friend*)—all these are characteristic features of noble morality, which, as I have suggested, is not the morality of "modern ideas," and this makes it difficult for us to relate to, and also difficult for us to dig it up and lay it open.

It is different with the second type of morality, *slave morality.* What if people who were violated, oppressed, suffering, unfree, exhausted, and unsure of themselves were to moralize—what type of moral valuations would they have? A pessimistic suspicion of the whole condition of humanity would probably find expression, perhaps a condemnation of humanity would probably find expression, perhaps a condemnation of humanity along with its condition. The slave's gaze resents the virtues of the powerful. It is skeptical and distrustful, it has a *subtle* mistrust of all the "good" that is honored there—it wants to convince itself that even happiness is not genuine there. Conversely, qualities that serve to alleviate existence for suffering people are pulled out and flooded with light: pity, the obliging, helpful hand, the warm heart, patience, industrious-ness, humility, and friendliness receive full honors here, since these are the most useful qualities and practically the only way of holding up under the pressure of existence. Slave morality is essentially a morality of utility.

Here we have the point of origin for that famous opposition between "good" and *"evil."* Evil is perceived as something powerful and dangerous; it is felt to contain a certain awesome quality, a subtlety and strength that block any incipi-ent contempt. According to the slave morality then, "evil" inspires fear; but according to the master morality, it is *"good"* that inspires and wants to inspire fear, while the "bad" man is seen as contemptible. The opposition comes to a head when, following the logic of slave morality, a hint of contempt (however slight and well disposed) finally comes to be associated with even its idea of "good," because within the terms of slave morality, the good man must always be *unthreatening:* He is good-natured, easy to deceive, maybe a bit stupid, *un bonhomme.*[4] Wherever slave morality holds sway, language shows a tendency for the words "good" and "stupid" to come closer together.

---

[4]*un bonhomme:* (French) a simpleminded person; literally, "a good person." [D. C. ABEL]

A final fundamental distinction: The desire for *freedom*, the instinct for happiness, and subtleties in the feeling of freedom necessarily belong to slave morals and morality, just as an artistry and enthusiasm in respect and devotion are invariant symptoms of an aristocratic mode of thinking and valuing. This clearly shows why love *as passion* (our European specialty) must have had a purely noble descent: It is known to have been invented in the knightly poetry of Provence, by those magnificent, inventive men of the *"gai saber."*[5] Europe is indebted to these men for so many things, almost for itself.

261

Vanity is perhaps one of the most difficult things for a noble person to comprehend: He will be tempted to keep denying it when a different type of man will almost be able to feel it in his hands. He has difficulty imagining creatures who would try to inspire good opinions about themselves that they themselves do not hold—and consequently do not "deserve" either—and who would then end up *believing* these good opinions. For one thing, this strikes the noble as being so tasteless and showing such a lack of self-respect, and, for another thing, it seems so baroque and unreasonable to him, that he would gladly see vanity as an exception and stay skeptical in most of the cases where it is brought up. For example, he will say: "I can be wrong about my own worth and still insist that other people acknowledge it to be what I say it is—but that is not vanity (instead, it is arrogance or, more frequently, it is what they call 'humility' or 'modesty')." Or alternatively: "There are many reasons why I can enjoy other people's good opinions, perhaps because I love and honor them and rejoice in each of their joys, and perhaps also because their good opinions confirm and reinforce my faith in my own good opinion of myself, perhaps because other people's good opinions are useful or look as though they could be useful to me, even when I don't agree with them—but none of that is vanity."

It is only when forced (namely with the help of history) that the noble person realizes that from time immemorial, in all strata of people who are in some way dependent, base people *were* only what they were *considered to be:* Not being at all accustomed to positing values, the only value the base person attributes to himself is the one his masters have attributed to him (creating values is the true *right of masters*). We can see it as the result of a tremendous atavism[6] that, to this day, ordinary people still *wait* for an opinion to be pronounced about themselves before instinctively deferring to it. And this is by no means only the case with "good" opinions—they defer to bad and unfair ones as well (for instance, just think about most of the self-estimations and self-underestimations that devout women accept from their father confessors and, in general, that devout Christians accept from their church).

As a matter of fact, in keeping with the slow approach of a democratic order of things (and its cause, the mixing of blood between masters and slaves), the

---

[5]*gai saber:* the art of the troubadours (a 14th-century French term that means, literally, "the merry science"). [D. C. ABEL]

[6]*atavism:* the recurrence of a trait that appeared in one's remote ancestors. [D. C. ABEL]

originally rare and noble urge to ascribe to yourself a value that comes *from* yourself, and to "think well" of yourself is now increasingly widespread and encouraged. But in every age it is opposed by an older, broader, and more thoroughly ingrained tendency—and in the phenomenon of "vanity," this older tendency gains mastery over the younger. The vain take pleasure in *every* good opinion they hear about themselves (abstracted entirely from the point of view of utility, and just as much removed from truth or falsity), just as they suffer from every bad opinion. This is because they submit—they *feel* submissive—to both good and bad opinions out of that oldest instinct of submissiveness that erupts within them. This is "the slave" in the blood of the vain, a remnant of the mischief of the slave. And how much "slave" is still left over in women, for instance!—they try to *seduce* people into having good opinions of them. By the same token, it is the slave who submits to these opinions immediately afterwards, as if he were not the one who had just called for them. And to say it again: Vanity is an atavism. . . .

265

At the risk of annoying innocent ears I will propose this: Egoism belongs to the essence of the noble soul. I mean that firm belief that other beings will, by nature, have to be subordinate to a being "like us" and will have to sacrifice themselves. The noble soul accepts this fact of its egoism without any question mark, and also without feeling any harshness, compulsion, or caprice in it, but rather as something that may well be grounded in the primordial law of things. If the noble soul were to try to name this phenomenon, it would call it "justice itself." It admits to itself, under certain circumstances (that at first give it pause), that there are others with rights equal to its own. As soon as it is clear about this question of rank, it will move among these equals and "equally righted" ones with an assured modesty and a gentle reverence equal to how it treats itself, in accordance with an inborn, celestial mechanics that all stars know so well. This is just *another* piece of its egoism, this finesse and self-limitation in dealing with equals—every star is an egoist of this sort. And the noble soul honors *itself* in them and in the rights that it gives them; it has no doubt that the exchange of rights and honors belongs to the natural state of things too, as the *essence* of all interaction. The noble soul gives as it takes, out of the passionate and sensitive instinct of retribution that is so fundamental to it. The concept of "mercy" is senseless and noisome *inter pares*.[7] There might be a sublime way of letting gifts fall down on you from above, as it were, and lapping them up like raindrops; but the noble soul has no talent for this art and conduct. Its egoism gets in the way: It does not generally like looking "upwards," but rather *ahead*, horizontally and slowly, or downwards; *it knows that it is high up*. . . .

272

Signs of nobility: never thinking about debasing our duties into duties for everyone; not wanting to relinquish, not wanting to share your own responsibility; considering privileges and the exercise of these privileges as a *duty*. . . .

---

[7]*inter pares:* (Latin) among equals. [D. C. ABEL]

287

What is noble? What does the word "noble" still mean to us today? How do noble people reveal who they are, how can they be recognized under this heavy, overcast sky of incipient mob rule that makes everything leaden and opaque? There are no actions that prove who they are—actions are always ambiguous, always unfathomable—and there are no "works" either. Among artists and scholars these days, you will find plenty of people whose works reveal them to be driven by a deep desire for nobility. But this very need *for* nobility is fundamentally different from the needs *of* the noble soul itself, and almost serves as an eloquent and dangerous testimony to the absence of such needs. It is not works, it is *faith* that is decisive here, faith that establishes rank order (this old, religious formula now acquires a new and deeper meaning): some fundamental certainty that a noble soul has about itself, something that cannot be looked for, cannot be found, and perhaps cannot be lost either. *The noble soul has reverence for itself.*

Existentialism Is a Humanism

Jean-Paul Sartre

Jean-Paul Sartre was born in Paris in 1905. At the age of 19 he began studying philosophy at the Ecole Normale Supérieure in Paris. After receiving his graduate degree in 1929, he served in the military for a little over a year. He then began teaching philosophy at Le Havre. Sartre spent the 1933–1934 academic year doing research at the Institut Français in Berlin. Upon returning to France, he taught at Le Havre and other French schools until 1939, when he was drafted by the army to fight in World War II. He was captured by the Germans in 1940, but escaped the following year. Sartre then went to Paris, where he resumed teaching and participated in the resistance movement against the Nazi occupation of France. During the occupation he wrote his main philosophical work, *Being and Nothingness: An Essay in Phenomenological Ontology.* When the war ended, he gave up teaching to devote himself entirely to writing. He was sympathetic to Marxism, and he traveled to a number of Communist countries, often meeting with heads of state. Sartre died in Paris in 1980; his funeral was attended by 25,000 people.

Sartre's major works, in addition to *Being and Nothingness* (1943), include *Nausea* (a novel, 1938), *The Psychology of Imagination* (1940), *Existentialism Is a Humanism* (1946), *The Ways of Freedom* (a three-volume novel, 1945–1949), *Critique of Dialectical Reason* (1960; only the first volume of a projected longer work was completed), *The Words* (his autobiography, 1964), and *The Family Idiot* (a three-volume biography of Gustave Flaubert, 1971–1972).

Our reading is from *Existentialism Is a Humanism,* which was delivered as a public lecture in Paris in 1945 and published the following year. By 1945 Sartre had become known as an "existentialist" thinker, and the purpose of his lecture was to explain, in an accessible way, some basic tenets of his version of existentialism. He makes clear that the basic concept in his existentialist philosophy is human freedom. We are radically free, and through our choices we create our own "essence," making ourselves into the kind of person we are. No preexistent pattern of human nature can guide us in making choices and no God with a plan for us to follow (Sartre is an atheist); each of us is free to fashion our essence in any way we wish. This freedom brings with it burdensome responsibility: We alone are responsible for who we are—not our genetic inheritance, our psychological makeup, or environmental influences.

What should we choose? We would all like to know the "right" thing to choose, but unfortunately there is no objective basis for determining what is "right": We cannot base our choices either on human nature or on God's will, for there is no human nature and there is no God. Ironically, things receive value simply from the fact that we choose them. The only ethical guideline Sartre offers is that we should value freedom above all else. He argues that to value our own freedom requires that we also value the freedom of others.

[WHAT EXISTENTIALISM IS]

. . . What, then, is "existentialism"?

Most people who use this word would be at a loss to explain what it means. For now that it has become fashionable, people like to call this musician or that painter an "existentialist." A columnist in *Clartés* goes by the pen name "The

Existentialist." Indeed, the word is being so loosely applied to so many things that it has come to mean nothing at all. It would appear that, for lack of an avant-garde doctrine analogous to surrealism, those who thrive on the latest scandal or fad have seized upon a philosophy that hardly suits their purpose. The truth is that of all doctrines, this is the least scandalous and the most austere: It is strictly intended for specialists and philosophers. Yet it can be easily defined. What complicates the matter is that there are two kinds of existentialists: on one hand, the Christians, among whom I would include Karl Jaspers and Gabriel Marcel,[1] both professed Catholics; and, on the other, the atheistic existentialists, among whom we should place Heidegger,[2] as well as the French existentialists and myself. What they have in common is simply their belief that existence precedes essence; or, if you prefer, that subjectivity must be our point of departure. What exactly do we mean by that?

If we consider a manufactured object, such as a book or a paper-knife,[3] we note that this object was produced by a craftsman who drew his inspiration from a concept: He referred both to the concept of what a paper-knife is, and to a known production technique that is a part of that concept and is, by and large, a formula. The paper-knife is thus both an object produced in a certain way and one that, on the other hand, serves a definite purpose. We cannot suppose that a man would produce a paper-knife without knowing what purpose it would serve. Let us say, therefore, that the essence of the paper-knife—that is, the sum of formulas and properties that enable it to be produced and defined—precedes its existence. Thus the presence before my eyes of that paper-knife or book is determined. Here, then, we are viewing the world from a technical standpoint, whereby we can say "production precedes essence."

When we think of God the Creator, we usually conceive of him as a superlative artisan. Whatever doctrine we may be considering, say Descartes' or Leibniz's,[4] we always agree that the will more or less follows understanding, or at the very least accompanies it, so that when God creates he knows exactly what he is creating. Thus the concept of man, in the mind of God, is comparable to the concept of the paper-knife in the mind of the manufacturer: God produces man following certain techniques and a conception, just as the craftsman, following a definition and a technique, produces a paper-knife. Thus each individual man is the realization of a certain concept within the divine intelligence. . . .

Atheistic existentialism, which I represent, is more consistent. It states that if God does not exist, there is at least one being in whom existence

---

[1]Karl Jaspers (1883–1968) was a German philosopher; Marcel (1889–1973) was a French philosopher. [D. C. ABEL]

[2]Martin Heidegger (1889–1976) was a German philosopher. In a 1946 work he stated that his philosophy is neither theistic nor atheistic ("Letter on Humanism," trans. Frank A. Cappuzi and J. Glenn Gray, in Martin Heidegger, *Basic Writings: From Being and Time (1927) to The Task of Thinking (1964)*, ed. David Farrell Krell [New York: Harper & Row, 1977]), pp. 229–30. [D. C. ABEL]

[3]*paper-knife:* a flat knife used mainly to cut apart pages of books (pages of some French books are folded together but not pre-cut). [D. C. ABEL]

[4]René Descartes (1596–1650) was a French philosopher and mathematician; for a biography, see p. 144. Gottfried Wilhelm Leibniz (1646–1716) was a German philosopher and mathematician. [D. C. ABEL]

precedes essence—a being whose existence comes before its essence, a being who exists before he can be defined by any concept of it. That being is man, or, as Heidegger put it, the human reality. What do we mean here by "existence precedes essence"? We mean that man first exists: He materializes in the world, encounters himself, and only afterward defines himself. If man as existentialists conceive of him cannot be defined, it is because to begin with he is nothing. He will not be anything until later, and then he will be what he makes of himself. Thus, there is no human nature since there is no God to conceive of it. Man is not only that which he conceives himself to be, but that which he wills himself to be, and since he conceives of himself only after he exists, just as he wills himself to be after being thrown into existence, man is nothing other than what he makes of himself. This is the first principle of existentialism.

It is also what is referred to as "subjectivity," the very word used as a reproach against us. But what do we mean by that, if not that man has more dignity than a stone or a table? What we mean to say is that man first exists; that is, that man primarily exists—that man is, before all else, something that projects itself into a future, and is conscious of doing so. Man is indeed a project that has a subjective existence, rather unlike that of a patch of moss, a spreading fungus, or a cauliflower. Prior to that projection of the self, nothing exists, not even in the divine intelligence, and man shall attain existence only when he is what he projects himself to be—not what he would *will* to be. What we usually understand by "will" is a conscious decision that most of us take after we have made ourselves what we are. I may will to join a party, write a book, or get married—but all of that is only a manifestation of an earlier and more spontaneous choice than what is known as "will." If, however, existence truly does precede essence, man is responsible for what he is. Thus, the first effect of existentialism is to make every man conscious of what he is, and to make him solely responsible for his own existence. And when we say that man is responsible for himself, we do not mean that he is responsible only for his own individuality, but that he is responsible for all men.

The word "subjectivism" has two possible interpretations, and our opponents play with both of them, at our expense. Subjectivism means, on the one hand, the freedom of the individual subject to choose what he will be, and, on the other, man's inability to transcend human subjectivity. The fundamental meaning of existentialism resides in the latter. When we say that man chooses himself, not only do we mean that each of us must choose himself, but also that in choosing himself, he is choosing for all men. In fact, in creating the man each of us wills ourselves to be, there is not a single one of our actions that does not at the same time create an image of man as we think he *ought* to be. Choosing to be this or that is to affirm at the same time the value of what we choose, because we can never choose evil. We always choose the good, and nothing can be good for any of us unless it is good for all. If, moreover, existence precedes essence and we will to exist at the same time as we fashion our image, that image is valid for all and for our whole era.

Our responsibility is thus much greater than we might have supposed, because it concerns all mankind. If I am a worker and I choose to join a Christian trade union rather than to become a Communist, and if, by that membership, I choose to signify that resignation is, after all, the most suitable solution for man, and that the kingdom of man is not on this earth, I am not committing myself alone—I am choosing to be resigned on behalf of all—consequently my action commits all mankind. Or, to use a more personal example, if I decide to marry and have children—granted such a marriage proceeds solely from my own circumstances, my passion, or my desire—I am nonetheless committing not only myself, but all of humanity, to the practice of monogamy. I am therefore responsible for myself and for everyone else, and I am fashioning a certain image of man as I choose him to be. In choosing myself, I choose man.

This allows us to understand the meaning behind some rather lofty-sounding words such as "anguish," "abandonment," and "despair." As you are about to see, it is all quite simple.

[EXISTENTIAL EMOTIONS]

[A. Anguish]

First, what do we mean by anguish? Existentialists like to say that man is in anguish. This is what they mean: A man who commits himself, and who realizes that he is not only the individual that he chooses to be, but also a legislator choosing at the same time what humanity as a whole should be, cannot help but be aware of his own full and profound responsibility. True, many people do not appear especially anguished, but we maintain that they are merely hiding their anguish or trying not to face it. Certainly, many believe that their actions involve no one but themselves, and were we to ask them "But what if everyone acted that way?," they would shrug their shoulders and reply "But everyone does not act that way." In truth, however, one should always ask oneself "What would happen if everyone did what I am doing?" The only way to evade that disturbing thought is through some kind of bad faith. Someone who lies to himself and excuses himself by saying "Everyone does not act that way" is struggling with a bad conscience, for the act of lying implies attributing a universal value to lies. . . .

[B. Abandonment]

When we speak of "abandonment"—one of Heidegger's favorite expressions—we merely mean to say that God does not exist, and that we must bear the full consequences of that assertion. Existentialists are strongly opposed to a certain type of secular morality that seeks to eliminate God as painlessly as possible. Around 1880, when some French professors attempted to formulate a secular morality, they expressed it more or less in these words: God is a useless and costly hypothesis, so we will do without it. However, if we are to have a morality, a civil society, and a law-abiding world, it is essential that certain values be taken seriously; they must have an a priori[5] existence ascribed to them. It must be considered mandatory a priori for people to be honest, not to lie, not to beat their wives, to raise children, and so forth. We therefore will need to do a little

---

[5] *a priori:* independent of personal experience or judgment (literally, in Latin, "from what comes earlier"). [D. C. ABEL]

more thinking on this subject in order to show that such values exist all the same, and that they are inscribed in an intelligible heaven, even though God does not exist. In other words—and I think this is the gist of everything that we in France call "radicalism"—nothing will have changed if God does not exist; we will encounter the same standards of honesty, progress, and humanism, and we will have turned God into an obsolete hypothesis that will die out quietly on its own.

Existentialists, on the other hand, find it extremely disturbing that God no longer exists, for along with his disappearance goes the possibility of finding values in an intelligible heaven. There could no longer be any a priori good, since there would be no infinite and perfect consciousness to conceive of it. Nowhere is it written that good exists, that we must be honest or must not lie, since we are on a plane shared only by men. Dostoyevsky[6] once wrote: "If God does not exist, everything is permissible." This is the starting point of existentialism. Indeed. everything is permissible if God does not exist, and man is consequently abandoned, for he cannot find anything to rely on—neither within nor without. First, he finds there are no excuses. For if it is true that existence precedes essence, we can never explain our actions by reference to a given and immutable human nature. In other words, there is no determinism[7]—man is free, man is freedom. If, however, God does not exist, we will encounter no values or orders that can legitimize our conduct. Thus, we have neither behind us nor before us, in the luminous realm of values, any means of justification or excuse. We are left alone and without excuse. That is what I mean when I say that man is condemned to be free: condemned, because he did not create himself, yet nonetheless free, because once cast into the world, he is responsible for everything he does. Existentialists do not believe in the power of passion. They will never regard a great passion as a devastating torrent that inevitably compels man to commit certain acts and which, therefore, is an excuse. They think that man is responsible for his own passion. Neither do existentialists believe that man can find refuge in some given sign that will guide him on earth; they think that man interprets the sign as he pleases and that man is therefore without any support or help, condemned at all times to invent man. In an excellent article, Ponge once wrote: "Man is the future of man."[8] This is absolutely true. However, if we were to interpret this to mean that such a future is inscribed in heaven, and that God knows what it is, that would be false, for then it would no longer even be a future. If, on the other hand, it means that whatever man may appear to be, there is a future waiting to be created—a virgin future—then the saying is true. But for now, we are abandoned.

To give you an example that will help you to better understand what we mean by abandonment, I will mention the case of one of my students, who sought me out under the following circumstances. His father had broken off with his mother and, moreover, was inclined to be a "collaborator."[9] His older

---

[6]Fyodor Dostoyevsky (1821–1881) was a Russian novelist. [D. C. ABEL]

[7]*determinism:* the doctrine that all human actions are determined by preceding causes and that we can never act otherwise than we do. [D. C. ABEL]

[8]Francis Ponge, "Notes premières de l'homme," *Les Temps modernes* 1 (October 1945): 75. [C. MACOMBER, TRANSLATOR] Ponge (1889–1988) was a French poet and essayist. [D. C. ABEL]

[9]*collaborator:* one who collaborated the Nazis during their occupation of France during World War II. [D. C. ABEL]

brother had been killed in the German offensive of 1940, and this young man, with primitive but noble feelings, wanted to avenge him. His mother, living alone with him and deeply hurt by the partial betrayal of his father and the death of her oldest son, found her only comfort in him. At the time, the young man had the choice of going to England to join the Free French Forces—which would mean abandoning his mother—or remaining by her side to help her go on with her life. He realized that his mother lived only for him and that his absence—perhaps his death—would plunge her into utter despair. He also realized that, ultimately, any action he might take on her behalf would provide the concrete benefit of helping her to live, while any action he might take to leave and fight would be of uncertain outcome and could disappear pointlessly like water in sand. For instance, in trying to reach England, he might pass through Spain and be detained there indefinitely in a camp; or, after arriving in England or Algiers, he might be assigned to an office to do paperwork. He was therefore confronted by two totally different modes of action: one mode that was concrete and immediate, but directed toward only one individual; the other involving an infinitely vaster group—a national corps—but a mode that was more ambiguous, for that very reason, and could be interrupted before being carried out. And, at the same time, he was vacillating between two kinds of morality: a morality motivated by sympathy and individual devotion, and another morality with a broader scope, but less likely to be fruitful. He had to choose between the two.

What could help him make that choice? The Christian doctrine? No. The Christian doctrine tells us we must be charitable, love our neighbor, sacrifice ourselves for others, choose the "narrow way," and so on. But what is the narrow way? Whom should we love like a brother—the soldier or the mother? Which is the more useful aim—the vague one of fighting as part of a group, or the more concrete one of helping one particular person keep on living? Who can decide that a priori? No one. No code of ethics on record answers that question. Kantian morality instructs us to never treat another as a means, but always as an end.[10] Very well; therefore, if I stay with my mother, I will treat her as an end, not as a means. But by the same token, I will be treating those who are fighting on my behalf as a means. Conversely, if I join those who are fighting, I will treat them as an end, and, in so doing, risk treating my mother as a means.

If values are vague and if they are always too broad in scope to apply to the specific and concrete case under consideration, we have no choice but to rely on our instincts. That is what this young man tried to do, and when I last saw him, he was saying: "All things considered, it is feelings that matter; I should choose what truly compels me to follow a certain path. If I feel that I love my mother enough to sacrifice everything else for her—my desire for vengeance, my desire for action, my desire for adventure—then I should stay by her side. If, to the contrary, I feel that my love for my mother is not strong enough, I should go." But how can we measure the strength of a feeling? What gave any value to the young man's feelings for his mother? Precisely the fact that he chose to stay with her. I may say that I love a friend well enough to sacrifice a certain sum of money

---

[10]This moral doctrine of the German philosopher Immanuel Kant (1724–1804) appears in this book, pp. 347–357. For a biography of Kant, see p. 175. [D. C. Abel]

for his sake, but I can claim that only if I have done so. I can say that I love my mother enough to stay by her side only if I actually stayed with her. The only way I can measure the strength of this affection is precisely by performing an action that confirms and defines it. However, since I am depending on this affection to justify my action, I find myself caught in a vicious circle.

Moreover, as Gide[11] once pointed out, it is almost impossible to distinguish between playacting and true feelings. To decide that I love my mother and will stay with her, or to stay with her by putting on a charade, amount to the same thing. In other words, feelings are developed through the actions we take; therefore I cannot use them as guidelines for action. This means that I shouldn't seek within myself some authentic state that will compel me to act, any more than I can expect any morality to provide the concepts that will enable me to act. You may say "Well, he went to see a professor for advice." But if you consult a priest, for instance, it's you who has chosen to consult him, and you already know in your heart, more or less, what advice he is likely to give. In other words, to choose one's adviser is only another way to commit oneself. This is demonstrated by the fact that, if you are Christian, you will say: "Consult a priest." But there are collaborating priests, temporizing priests, and priests connected to the Resistance:[12] Which do you choose? Had this young man chosen to consult a priest connected to the Resistance, or a collaborating priest, he would have decided beforehand what kind of advice he was to receive. Therefore, in seeking me out, he knew what my answer would be, and there was only one answer I could give him: "You are free, so choose; in other words, invent. No general code of ethics can tell you what you ought to do; there are no signs in this world."

Catholics will reply: "But there *are* signs!" Be that as it may, it is I who choose what those signs mean. When I was in a German prison camp, I met a rather remarkable man, who happened to be a Jesuit.[13] This is how he came to join the order: He had experienced several frustrating setbacks in his life. His father died while he was still a child, leaving him in poverty, but he was awarded a scholarship to a religious institution where he was constantly reminded that he had been accepted only out of charity. He was subsequently denied a number of distinctions and honors that would have pleased any child. Then, when he was about 18 years old, he had an unfortunate love affair that broke his heart. Finally, at the age of 22, what should have been a trifle was actually the last straw: He flunked out of military training school. This young man had every right to believe he was a total failure. It was a sign—but a sign of what? He could have sought refuge in bitterness or despair. Instead—and it was very clever of him—he chose to take it as a sign that he was not destined for secular success, and that his achievements would be attained only in the realms of religion, sanctity, and faith. He saw in all of this a message from God, and so he joined the order. Who can doubt that the meaning of the sign was determined by him, and by him alone? We might have concluded something

---

[11]André Gide (1859–1951) was a French novelist, essayist, and critic. [D. C. ABEL]

[12]*Resistance:* an underground movement that resisted the Nazi occupation of France during World War II. [D. C. ABEL]

[13]*Jesuit:* a member of the Society of Jesus, a Roman Catholic religious order. [D. C. ABEL]

quite different from this set of reversals—for example, that he might have been better off training to be a carpenter or a revolutionary. He therefore bears the full responsibility for his interpretation of the sign. This is what "abandonment" implies: It is we ourselves who decide who we are to be. Such abandonment entails anguish.

[C. Despair]

As for "despair," it has a very simple meaning: It means that we must limit ourselves to reckoning only with those things that depend on our will, or on the set of probabilities that enable action. Whenever we desire something, there are always elements of probability. If I am counting on a visit from a friend who is traveling by train or trolley, then I assume that the train will arrive on time, or that the trolley will not derail. I operate within a realm of possibilities. But we credit such possibilities only to the strict extent that our action encompasses them. From the moment that the possibilities I am considering cease to be rigorously engaged by my action, I must no longer take interest in them, for no God or greater design can bend the world and its possibilities to my will. In the final analysis, when Descartes said "Conquer yourself rather than the world," he actually meant the same thing: We should act without hope. Marxists,[14] with whom I have discussed this, reply: "Obviously, your action will be limited by your death; but you can rely on the help of others. You can count both on what others are doing elsewhere, in China, in Russia, to help you, and on what they will do later—that is, after your death—to carry on your work and bring it to fruition, which will be the revolution. What is more, you *must* rely on it; not to do so would be immoral."

My initial response to this is that I will always depend on my comrades-in-arms in the struggle, inasmuch as they are committed, as I am, to a definite common cause, in the solidarity of a party or a group that I can more or less control—that is to say, a party that I joined as a militant and whose every move is familiar to me. In that context, counting on the solidarity and will of this party is exactly like counting on the fact that the train will arrive on time, or that the trolley will not derail. But I cannot count on men whom I do not know based on faith in the goodness of humanity or in man's interest in society's welfare, given that man is free and there is no human nature in which I can place my trust. I do not know where the Russian Revolution might lead. I can admire it and hold it up as an example to the extent that it is clear, to date, that the proletariat[15] plays a part in Russia that it has attained in no other nation. But I cannot assert that this Revolution will necessarily lead to the triumph of the proletariat; I must confine myself to what I can see. Nor can I be certain that comrades-in-arms will carry on my work after my death and bring it to completion, seeing that those men are free and will freely choose, tomorrow, what man is to become. Tomorrow, after

---

[14]*Marxists:* followers of the socialist doctrine of the German philosopher Karl Marx. For a biography of Marx, see p. 466. [D. C. ABEL]

[15]*proletariat:* wage-laborers; contrasted in Marxism with the *bourgeoisie* (capitalists, who own the means of production). For Marx's discussion of these classes, see pp. 467–473. [D. C. ABEL]

my death, men may choose to impose fascism, while others may be cowardly or distraught enough to let them get away with it. Fascism will then become humanity's truth, and so much the worse for us. In reality, things will be what men have chosen them to be. Does that mean that I must resort to quietism?[16] No. First, I must commit myself, and then act according to the old adage "No hope is necessary to undertake anything." This does not mean that I cannot belong to a party, just that I should have no illusions and do whatever I can. For instance, if I were to ask myself "Will collectivization ever be a reality?," I have no idea. All I know is that I will do everything in my power to make it happen. Beyond that, I cannot count on anything.

[QUIETISM]

Quietism is the attitude of people who say "Others can do what I cannot do." The doctrine that I am presenting to you is precisely the opposite of quietism, since it declares that reality exists only in action. It ventures even further than that, since it adds: " Man is nothing other than his own project. He exists only to the extent that he realizes himself; therefore he is nothing more than the sum of his actions, nothing more than his life." In view of this, we can clearly understand why our doctrine horrifies many people. For they often have no other way of putting up with their misery than to think: "Circumstances have been against me; I deserve a much better life than the one I have. Admittedly, I have never experienced a great love or extraordinary friendship, but that is because I never met a man or woman worthy of it. If I have written no great books, it is because I never had the leisure to do so; if I have had no children to whom I could devote myself, it is because I did not find a man with whom I could share my life. So I have within me a host of untried but perfectly viable abilities, inclinations, and possibilities that endow me with worthiness not evident from any examination of my past actions." In reality, however, for existentialists there is no love other than the deeds of love; no potential for love other than that which is manifested in loving. There is no genius other than that which is expressed in works of art; the genius of Proust[17] resides in the totality of his works; the genius of Racine[18] is found in the series of his tragedies, outside of which there is nothing. Why should we attribute to Racine the ability to write yet another tragedy when that is precisely what he did not do? In life, a man commits himself and draws his own portrait, outside of which there is nothing.

No doubt this thought may seem harsh to someone who has not made a success of his life. But on the other hand, it helps people to understand that reality alone counts, and that dreams, expectations, and hopes only serve to define a man as a broken dream, aborted hopes, and futile expectations—in other words, they define him negatively, not positively. Nonetheless, saying "You are nothing but your life" does not imply that the artist will be judged solely by his works

---

[16]*quietism:* the attitude of being passive, of not getting involved. [D. C. ABEL]
[17]Marcel Proust (1871–1922) was a French novelist. [D. C. ABEL]
[18]Jean Racine (1639–1699) was a French dramatist. [D. C. ABEL]

of art, for a thousand other things also help to define him. What we mean to say is that a man is nothing but a series of enterprises, and that he is the sum, organization, and aggregate of the relations that constitute such enterprises.

[OPTIMISM]

In light of all this, what people reproach us for is not essentially our pessimism, but the sternness of our optimism. If people criticize our works of fiction, in which we describe characters who are spineless, weak, cowardly, and some-times even frankly evil, it is not just because these characters are spineless, weak, cowardly, or evil. For if, like Zola,[19] we were to blame their behavior on their heredity, environmental influences, their society, or factors of an organic or psychological nature, people would be reassured and would say: "That is the way we are. No one can do anything about it." But when an existentialist describes a coward, he says that the coward is responsible for his own cow-ardice. He is not the way he is because he has a cowardly heart, lung, or brain. He is not like that as the result of his physiological makeup; he is like that because he has made himself a coward through his actions. There is no such thing as a cowardly temperament; there are nervous temperaments, or "poor blood," as ordinary folks call it, or "rich temperaments," but just because a man has poor blood does not make him a coward, for what produces cowardice is the act of giving up, or giving in. A temperament is not an action; a coward is defined by the action he has taken. What people are obscurely feeling, and what horrifies them, is that the coward, as we present him, is guilty of his cowardice. People would prefer to be born a coward or be born a hero. . . .

[FREEDOM]

When I affirm that freedom, under any concrete circumstance, can have no other aim than itself, and that once a man realizes, in his state of abandonment, that it is he who imposes values, he can will but one thing: freedom as the foundation of all values. That does not mean that he wills it in the abstract; it simply means that the ultimate significance of the actions of men of good faith is the quest of freedom in itself. A man who joins a communist or revolutionary group wills cer-tain concrete aims that imply an abstract will to freedom, yet that freedom must always be exercised in a concrete manner. We will freedom for freedom's sake through our individual circumstances. And in thus willing freedom, we discover that it depends entirely on the freedom of others, and that the freedom of others depends on our own. Of course, freedom as the definition of man does not depend on others, but as soon as there is commitment, I am obliged to will the freedom of others at the same time as I will my own. I cannot set my own free-dom as a goal without also setting the freedom of others as a goal. Consequently, when, operating on the level of complete authenticity, I have acknowledged

---

[19]Emile Zola (1849–1902) was a French novelist. [D. C. ABEL]

that existence precedes essence, and that man is a free being who, under any circumstances, can only ever will his freedom, I have at the same time acknowledged that I must will the freedom of others. Therefore, in the name of this will to freedom, implied by freedom itself, I can pass judgment on those who seek to conceal from themselves the complete arbitrariness of their existence, and their total freedom. Those who conceal from themselves this total freedom, under the guise of solemnity, or by making determinist excuses, I will call cowards.

The Challenge of Cultural Relativism

James Rachels and Stuart Rachels

James Rachels was born in Columbus, Georgia, in 1941. He attended Mercer University in Macon and received his bachelor's degree in 1962. He then began doctoral studies in philosophy at the University of North Carolina at Chapel Hill, completing his Ph.D. in 1967. Rachels held appointments at the University of Richmond (1966–1968), New York University (1968–1972), and the University of Miami (1972–1977). In 1977 he accepted an appointment at the University of Alabama at Birmingham, and the following year began a five-year term as Dean of the School of Arts and Humanities. After serving as acting academic vice president from 1983 to 1984, he was named university professor of philosophy, a position he held until his death in Birmingham in 2003.

James Rachels's publications include *Understanding Moral Philosophy* (1976), *The End of Life: Euthanasia and Morality* (1986), *The Elements of Moral Philosophy* (1986; 4th ed., 2003), *The Right Thing to Do: Readings in Moral Philosophy* (editor, 1989; 3d ed., 2003), and *Created from Animals: The Moral Implications of Darwinism* (1990).

Stuart Rachels, son of James Rachels, was born in New York City in 1969. After completing his undergraduate degree in philosophy at Emory University in 1991, he enrolled in Oxford University, where he earned a bachelor's degree in philosophy and politics in 1993. He then entered the graduate program in philosophy at Syracuse University, completing his doctorate in 1998. After teaching for a year at the University of Colorado at Boulder, he accepted an appointment as assistant professor of philosophy at the University of Alabama at Tuscaloosa. He was promoted to associated professor in 2004.

Stuart Rachels has published articles on ethical theory in such journals as *The Australasian Journal of Philosophy, Bioethics, Nous,* and *Philosophical Studies*. After his father's death, he produced revised editions of *The Elements of Moral Philosophy* (5th ed., 2007) and *The Right Thing to Do* (4th ed., 2007).

Our reading is from Chapter 2 of *The Elements of Moral Philosophy,* "The Challenge of Cultural Relativism." Cultural relativism is the doctrine that all moral values derive entirely from individual cultural codes, and that there are no objective, independently correct moral values. In other words, there are no *absolute* truths about what is right and wrong because judgments of right and wrong are all *relative* to a given culture. The authors explain that many thinkers conclude that because different cultures have different moral codes, cultural relativism must be true. They point out, however, that the existence of cultural differences of opinion does not prove that there are no objectively correct answers about what is right and wrong. They show that if we accept cultural relativism, we are committed to several implausible consequences. They then argue that differences in cultural values are less drastic than they at first appear to be, and that certain basic values are common to all cultures.

HOW DIFFERENT CULTURES HAVE DIFFERENT MORAL CODES

Darius, a king of ancient Persia, was intrigued by the variety of cultures he encountered in his travels. He had found, for example, that the Callatians (a tribe of Indians) customarily ate the bodies of their dead fathers. The Greeks, of course, did not do that—the Greeks practiced cremation and regarded the funeral pyre as the natural and fitting way to dispose of the dead. Darius thought that a sophisticated understanding of the world must include an appreciation of such differences between cultures. One day, to teach this lesson, he summoned some Greeks who happened to be present at his court and asked them what they would take to eat the bodies of their dead fathers. They were shocked, as Darius knew they would be, and replied that no amount of money could persuade them to do such a thing. Then Darius called in some Callatians, and while the Greeks listened asked them what they would take to burn their dead fathers' bodies. The Callatians were horrified and told Darius not even to mention such an awful thing.

This story, recounted by Herodotus in his *Histories*,[1] illustrates a recurring theme in the literature of social science: Different cultures have different moral codes. What is thought right within one group may be utterly abhorrent to the members of another group, and vice versa. Should we eat the bodies of the dead or burn them? If you were a Greek, one answer would seem obviously correct; but if you were a Callatian, the opposite would seem equally certain.

It is easy to give additional examples of the same kind. Consider the Eskimos. The Eskimos are the indigenous peoples of northern Canada, Greenland, and northeastern Siberia. (Today, none of these peoples call themselves "Eskimos"; however, I'll use that term because it's the only one that refers to this scattered Arctic population.) Traditionally Eskimos have lived in small settlements, separated by great distances. Prior to the twentieth century, the outside world knew little about them. Then explorers began to bring back strange tales.

Eskimo customs turned out to be very different from our own. The men often had more than one wife, and they would share their wives with guests, lending them for the night as a sign of hospitality. Moreover, within a community a dominant male might demand—and get—regular sexual access to other men's wives. The women however, were free to break these arrangements simply by leaving their husbands and taking up with new partners—free, that is, so long as their former husbands chose not to make trouble. All in all, the Eskimo practice was a volatile scheme that bore little resemblance to what we call marriage.

But it was not only their marriage and sexual practices that were different. The Eskimos also seemed to have less regard for human life. Infanticide, for example, was common. Knud Rasmussen, one of the most famous early explorers, reported that he met one woman who had borne 20 children but had killed ten of them at birth. Female babies, he found, were especially liable to be destroyed, and this was permitted simply at the parents' discretion, with no social stigma attached to it. Old people also, when they became too feeble to

---

[1]Herodotus, *The Histories*, trans. Aubrey de Sélincourt, rev. A. R. Burn (Harmondsworth, England: Penguin, 1972), pp. 219–220. [J. RACHELS] Herodotus (about 484–425 B.C.E.) was a Greek historian. [D. C. ABEL]

contribute to the family, were left out in the snow to die. So there seemed to be, in this society, remarkably little respect for life.

To most Americans, these were disturbing revelations. Our own way of living seems so natural and right that for many of us it is hard to conceive of others living so differently. And when we do hear of such things, we tend immediately to categorize the other peoples as "backward" or "primitive." But to anthropologists, there was nothing particularly surprising about the Eskimos. Since the time of Herodotus, enlightened observers have been accustomed to the idea that conceptions of right and wrong differ from culture to culture. If we assume that our ethical ideas will be shared by all peoples at all times, we are merely naive.

CULTURAL RELATIVISM

To many thinkers, this observation—"different cultures have different moral codes"—has seemed to be the key to understanding morality. The idea of universal truth in ethics, they say, is a myth. The customs of different societies are all that exist. These customs cannot be said to be "correct" or "incorrect," for that implies we have an independent standard of right and wrong by which they may be judged. But there is no such independent standard; every standard is culture-bound. The great pioneering sociologist William Graham Sumner, writing in 1906, put it like this:

> The "right" way is the way that the ancestors used and that has been handed down. The tradition is its own warrant. It is not held subject to verification by experience. The notion of right is in the folkways. It is not outside of them, of independent origin, and brought to test them. In the folkways, whatever is, is right. This is because they are traditional and therefore contain in themselves the authority of the ancestral ghosts. When we come to the folkways we are at the end of our analysis.[2]

This line of thought has probably persuaded more people to be skeptical about ethics than any other single thing. *Cultural relativism,* as it has been called, challenges our ordinary belief in the objectivity and universality of moral truth. It says, in effect, that there is no such thing as universal truth in ethics; there are only the various cultural codes, and nothing more. Moreover, our own code has no special status; it is merely one among many. As we shall see, this basic idea is really a compound of several different thoughts.

It is important to distinguish the various elements of cultural relativism because, on analysis, some parts turn out to be correct, while others seem to be mistaken. The following claims have all been made by cultural relativists:

1. Different societies have different moral codes.
2. The moral code of a society determines what is right within that society; that is, if the moral code of a society says that a certain action is right, then that action *is* right, at least within that society.
3. There is no objective standard that can be used to judge one society's codes better than another's. In other words, there is no "universal

---

[2]William Graham Summer, *Folkways* (Boston: Ginn, 1906), p. 28. [J. RACHELS]

truth" in ethics; there are no moral truths that hold for all people at all times.

4. The moral code of our own society has no special status; it is merely one among many.
5. It is mere arrogance for us to try to judge the conduct of other peoples. We should adopt an attitude of tolerance toward the practices of other cultures.

These five propositions may seem to go together, but they are independent of one another, in the sense that some of them might be false even if others are true. Indeed, two of them appear to be inconsistent with each other. The second proposition says that right and wrong are determined by the norms of a society; the fifth proposition says that we should always be tolerant of other cultures. But what if the norms of a society favor intolerance? For example, when the Nazi army marched into Poland on September 1, 1939, thus beginning World War II, this was an intolerant action of the first order. But what if it was in line with Nazi ideals? A cultural relativist, it seems, cannot criticize the Nazis for being intolerant, if all they're doing is following their own moral code.

Given that cultural relativists take pride in their tolerance, it would be ironic if their theory actually supported people in intolerant cultures being intolerant of other cultures. However, it need not have that implication. Properly understood, cultural relativism holds that the norms of a culture reign supreme *within the bounds of the culture itself*. Thus, once the German soldiers entered Poland, they became bound by the norms of Polish society—norms that obviously excluded the mass slaughter of innocent Poles. "When in Rome," the old saying goes, "do as the Romans do." Cultural relativists agree.

THE CULTURAL DIFFERENCES ARGUMENT

Cultural relativism is a theory about the nature of morality. At first blush it seems quite plausible. However, like all such theories, it may be evaluated by subjecting it to rational analysis; and when we analyze cultural relativism, we find that it is not so plausible as it first appears to be.

The first thing to notice is that at the heart of cultural relativism there is a certain *form of argument*. Cultural relativists argue from facts about the differences between cultural outlooks to a conclusion about the status of morality. Thus, we are invited to accept this reasoning:

(1) The Greeks believed it was wrong to eat the dead, whereas the Callatians believed it was right to eat the dead.
(2) Therefore, eating the dead is neither objectively right nor objectively wrong. It is merely a matter of opinion, which varies from culture to culture.

Or, alternatively:

(1) The Eskimos see nothing wrong with infanticide, whereas Americans believe infanticide is immoral.
(2) Therefore, infanticide is neither objectively right nor objectively wrong. It is merely a matter of opinion, which varies from culture to culture.

Clearly, these arguments are variations of one fundamental idea. They are both special cases of a more general argument, which says:

(1) Different cultures have different moral codes.

(2) Therefore, there is no objective "truth" in morality. Right and wrong are only matters of opinion, and opinions vary from culture to culture.

We may call this the *cultural differences argument*. To many people, it is persuasive. But from a logical point of view, is it [a] sound [argument]?

It is not sound. The trouble is that the conclusion does not follow from the premise—that is, even if the premise is true, the conclusion still might be false. The premise concerns what people *believe*—in some societies, people believe one thing; in other societies, people believe differently. The conclusion, however, concerns what *really is the case:* The trouble is that this sort of conclusion does not follow logically from this sort of premise.

Consider again the example of the Greeks and Callatians. The Greeks believed it was wrong to eat the dead; the Callatians believed it was right. Does it follow, *from the mere fact that they disagreed,* that there is no objective truth in the matter? No, it does not follow; it could be that the practice was objectively right (or wrong) and that one of them was simply mistaken.

To make the point clearer, consider a different matter. In some societies, people believe the earth is flat. In other societies, such as our own, people believe the earth is (roughly) spherical. Does it follow, from the mere fact that people disagree, that there is no "objective truth" in geography? Of course not; we would never draw such a conclusion because we realize that, in their beliefs about the world, the members of some societies might simply be wrong. There is no reason to think that if the world is round everyone must know it. Similarly, there is no reason to think that if there is moral truth everyone must know it. The fundamental mistake in the cultural differences argument is that it attempts to derive a substantive conclusion about a subject from the mere fact that people disagree about it.

This is a simple point of logic, and it is important not to misunderstand it. We are not saying that the conclusion of the argument is false. That is still an open question. The logical point is merely that the conclusion does not follow from the premise. This is important, because in order to determine whether the conclusion is true, we need arguments in its support. Cultural relativism proposes this argument, but it is fallacious. So it proves nothing.

THE CONSEQUENCES OF TAKING CULTURAL RELATIVISM SERIOUSLY

Even if the cultural differences argument is unsound, cultural relativism might still be true. What would it be like if it were true?

In the passage quoted above, William Graham Sumner summarizes the essence of cultural relativism. He says that there is no measure of right and wrong other than the standards of one's society: "The notion of right is in the folkways. It is not outside of them, of independent origin, and brought to test them. In the folkways, whatever is, is right." Suppose we took this seriously. What would be some of the consequences?

1. *We could no longer say that the customs of other societies are morally inferior to our own.* This, of course, is one of the main points stressed by cultural relativism. We would have to stop condemning other societies merely because they are "different." So long as we concentrate on certain examples, such as the funerary practices of the Greeks and Callatians, this may seem to be a sophisticated, enlightened attitude.

However, we would also be stopped from criticizing other, less benign practices. For example, the Chinese government has a long tradition of suppressing political dissent within its own borders. At any given time, thousands of political prisoners in China are doing hard labor, and in the Tiananmen Square episode of 1989, Chinese troops slaughtered hundreds, if not thousands, of peaceful protesters. Cultural relativism would preclude us from saying that the Chinese government's policies of oppression are wrong. (We could not even say that a society that respects free speech is *better* than Chinese society, for that would imply a universal standard of comparison.) The failure to condemn *these* practices does not seem enlightened; on the contrary, political oppression seems wrong wherever it occurs. Nevertheless, if we accept cultural relativism, we have to regard such political practices as immune from criticism.

2. *We could decide whether actions are right or wrong just by consulting the standards of our society.* Cultural relativism suggests a simple test for determining what is right and what is wrong: All we need do is ask whether the action is in accordance with the code of the society in question. Suppose a resident of India wonders if her society's caste system—a system of rigid social hierarchy—is morally correct. All she has to do is ask whether this policy conforms to her society's moral code. If it does, there is nothing to worry about, at least from a moral point of view.

This implication of cultural relativism is disturbing because few of us think that our society's code is perfect—we can think of all sorts of ways in which it might be improved. Yet cultural relativism not only forbids us from criticizing the codes of *other* societies; it also stops us from criticizing our own. After all, if right and wrong are relative to culture, this must be true for our own culture just as much as for other cultures.

3. *The idea of moral progress is called into doubt.* We think that at least some social changes are for the better. Throughout most of Western history the place of women in society was narrowly circumscribed. They could not own property; they could not vote or hold political office; and generally they were under the almost absolute control of their husbands. Recently much of this has changed, and most people think of it as progress.

But if cultural relativism is correct, can we legitimately view this as progress? Progress means replacing a way of doing things with a better way. But by what standard do we judge the new ways as better? If the old ways were in accordance with the social standards of their time, then cultural relativism would say it is a mistake to judge them by the standards of a different time. Eighteenth-century society was a different society from the one we have now. To say that we have made progress implies a judgment that present-day society is better—just the sort of transcultural judgment that, according to cultural relativism, is unacceptable.

Our ideas about social *reform* will also have to be reconsidered. Reformers such as Martin Luther King, Jr., have sought to change their societies for the better. Within the constraints imposed by cultural relativism, there is one way this might be done. If a society is not living up to its own ideals, the reformer may be regarded as acting for the best in promoting those ideals. After all, those ideals are the standards by which we judge his or her proposals. But no one may challenge the ideals themselves, for those ideals are by definition correct. According to cultural relativism, then, the idea of social reform makes sense only in this limited way.

These three consequences of cultural relativism have led many thinkers to reject it as implausible on its face. It does make sense, they say, to condemn some practices, such as slavery and anti-Semitism, wherever they occur. It makes sense to think that our own society has made some moral progress, while admitting that it is still imperfect and in need of reform. Because cultural relativism implies that these judgments make no sense, the argument goes, it cannot be right.

WHY THERE IS LESS DISAGREEMENT THAN IT SEEMS

The original impetus for cultural relativism comes from the observation that cultures differ dramatically in their views of right and wrong. But just how much do they differ? It is true that there are differences. However, it is easy to overestimate the extent of those differences. Often, when we examine what seems to be a dramatic difference, we find that the cultures do not differ nearly as much as it appears.

Consider a culture in which people believe it is wrong to eat cows. This may even be a poor culture, in which there is not enough food; still, the cows are not to be touched. Such a society would appear to have values very different from our own. But does it? We have not yet asked *why* these people will not eat cows. Suppose it is because they believe that after death the souls of humans inhabit the bodies of animals, especially cows, so that a cow may be someone's grandmother. Now shall we say that their values are different from ours? No; the difference lies elsewhere. The difference is in our belief systems, not in our values. We agree that we shouldn't eat Grandma; we simply disagree about whether the cow is (or could be) Grandma.

The point is that many factors work together to produce the customs of a society. The society's values are only one of them. Other matters, such as the religious and factual beliefs held by its members, and the physical circumstances in which they must live, are also important. We cannot conclude, then, merely because customs differ, that there is a disagreement about values. The difference in customs may be attributable to some other aspect of social life. Thus there may be less disagreement about values than there appears to be.

Consider again the Eskimos, who often kill perfectly normal infants, especially girls. We do not approve of such things; in our society, a parent who killed a baby would be locked up. Thus there appears to be a great difference in the values of our two cultures. But suppose we ask why the Eskimos do this. The explanation is not that they have less affection for their children or less respect for human life. An Eskimo family will always protect its babies if conditions permit. But they live in a harsh environment, where food is in short supply. A fundamental postulate of Eskimo thought is: "Life is hard, and the margin of safety small." A family may want to nourish its babies but be unable to do so.

As in many traditional societies, Eskimo mothers would nurse their infants over a much longer period than mothers in our culture—for four years, and perhaps even longer. So, even in the best of times, there were limits to the number of infants one mother could sustain. Moreover, Eskimos were nomadic; unable to farm, they had to move about in search of food. Infants had to be carried, and a mother could carry only one baby in her parka as she traveled and went about her outdoor work.

Infant girls were more readily disposed of for two reasons. First, in Eskimo society the males were the primary food providers—they were the hunters— and it is obviously important to maintain a sufficient number of food providers. But there was an important second reason as well. Because the hunters suffered a large casualty rate, the adult men who died prematurely far outnumbered the women who died early. If male and female infants had survived in equal numbers, the female adult population would have greatly outnumbered the adult male population. Examining the available statistics, one writer concluded that "were it not for female infanticide . . . there would be approximately one-and-a-half times as many females in the average Eskimo local group as there are food-producing males."[3]

So among the Eskimos, infanticide did not signal a fundamentally different attitude toward children. Instead, it arose from the recognition that drastic measures are sometimes needed to ensure the family's survival. Even then, however, killing the baby was not the first option considered. Adoption was common; childless couples were especially happy to take a more fertile couple's "surplus." Killing was the last resort. I emphasize this in order to show that the raw data of the anthropologists can be misleading; it can make the differences in values between cultures appear greater than they are. The Eskimos' values were not all that different from our own. It is only that life forced upon them choices that we do not have to make.

HOW ALL CULTURES HAVE SOME VALUES IN COMMON

It should not be surprising that, despite appearances, the Eskimos were protective of their children. How could it be otherwise? How could a group survive that did not value its young? It is easy to see that, in fact, all cultural groups must protect their infants. Babies are helpless and cannot survive if they are not given extensive care for a period of years. Therefore, if a group did not care for its young, the young would not survive, and the older members of the group

---

[3]E. Adamson Hoebel, *The Law of Primitive Man: A Study in Comparative Legal Dynamics* (Cambridge, MA: Harvard University Press, 1954), p. 76. [J. RACHELS]

would not be replaced. After a while, the group would die out. This means that any cultural group that continues to exist must care for its young. Infants that are not cared for must be the exception rather than the rule.

Similar reasoning shows that other values must be more or less universal. Imagine what it would be like for a society to place no value at all on truth telling. When one person spoke to another, there would be no presumption that she was telling the truth, for she could just as easily be speaking falsely. Within that society, there would be no reason to pay attention to what anyone says. (I ask you what time it is, and you say "Four o'clock." But there is no presumption that you are speaking truly; you could just as easily have said the first thing that came into your head. So I have no reason to pay attention to your answer. In fact, there was no point in my asking you in the first place.) Communication would then be extremely difficult, if not impossible. And because complex societies cannot exist without communication among their members, society would become impossible. It follows that in any complex society there must be a presumption in favor of truthfulness. There may of course be exceptions to this rule: There may be situations in which it is thought to be permissible to lie. Nevertheless, these will be exceptions to a rule that *is* in force in the society.

Here is one more example of the same type. Could a society exist in which there was no prohibition on murder? What would this be like? Suppose people were free to kill other people at will, and no one thought there was anything wrong with it. In such a "society," no one could feel safe. Everyone would have to be constantly on guard, and to survive they would have to avoid other people as much as possible. This would inevitably result in individuals trying to become as self-sufficient as possible—after all, associating with others would be dangerous. Society on any large scale would collapse. Of course, people might band together in smaller groups with others that they could trust not to harm them. But notice what this means: They would be forming smaller societies that did acknowledge a rule against murder. The prohibition of murder, then, is a necessary feature of all societies.

There is a general theoretical point here, namely, that *there are some moral rules that all societies must have in common, because those rules are necessary for society to exist.* The rules against lying and murder are two examples. And in fact, we do find these rules in force in all viable cultures. Cultures may differ in what they regard as legitimate exceptions to the rules, but this disagreement exists against a broad background of agreement. Therefore, it is a mistake to overestimate the amount of difference between cultures. Not every moral rule can vary from society to society.

JUDGING A CULTURAL PRACTICE TO BE UNDESIRABLE

In 1996, a 17-year-old girl named Fauziya Kassindja arrived at Newark International Airport and asked for asylum. She had fled her native country of Togo, a small west African nation, to escape what people there call "excision." Excision is a permanently disfiguring procedure that is sometimes called "female circumcision," although it bears little resemblance to the Jewish practice.

More commonly, at least in Western newspapers, it is referred to as "female genital mutilation."

According to the World Health Organization, the practice is widespread in 26 African nations, and two million girls each year are "excised." In some instances, excision is part of an elaborate tribal ritual, performed in small traditional villages, and girls look forward to it because it signals their acceptance into the adult world. In other instances, the practice is carried out by families living in cities on young women who desperately resist.

Fauziya Kassindja was the youngest of five daughters in a devoutly Muslim family. Her father, who owned a successful trucking business, was opposed to excision, and he was able to defy the tradition because of his wealth. His first four daughters were married without being mutilated. But when Fauziya was 16, he suddenly died. Fauziya then came under the authority of her aunt, who arranged a marriage for her and prepared to have her excised. Fauziya was terrified, and her mother and oldest sister helped her escape.

In America, Fauziya was imprisoned for nearly 18 months while the authorities decided what to do with her. During this time, she was subjected to humiliating strip searches, denied medical treatment for her asthma, and generally treated like a dangerous criminal. Finally, she was granted asylum, but not before she became the center of a controversy about how we should regard the cultural practices of other peoples. A series of articles in *The New York Times*[4] encouraged the idea that excision is a barbaric practice that should be condemned. Other observers were reluctant to be so judgmental. Live and let live, they said; after all, our culture probably seems just as strange to them.

Suppose we are inclined to say that excision is bad. Would we merely be imposing the standards of our own culture? If cultural relativism is correct, that is all we can do, for there is no culture-neutral moral standard to which we may appeal. But is that true?

Is There a Culture-Neutral Standard of Right and Wrong?

There is much that can be said against excision. Excision is painful and it results in the permanent loss of sexual pleasure. Its short-term effects include hemorrhage, tetanus, and septicemia. Sometimes the woman dies. Long-term effects include chronic infection, scars that hinder walking, and continuing pain.

Why, then, has it become a widespread social practice? It is not easy to say. Excision has no apparent social benefits. Unlike Eskimo infanticide, it is not necessary for the group's survival. Nor is it a matter of religion. Excision is practiced by groups with various religions, including Islam and Christianity, neither of which commends it.

Nevertheless, a number of reasons are given in its defense. Women who are incapable of sexual pleasure are said to be less likely to be promiscuous; thus there will be fewer unwanted pregnancies in unmarried women. Moreover, wives for whom sex is only a duty are less likely to be unfaithful to their husbands; and

---

[4]The *New York Times*, April 15, 25; May 2, 3; July 8; September 11; October 5, 12; December 28, 1996; articles written mainly by Celia W. Dugger. [J. RACHELS]

because they will not be thinking about sex, they will be more attentive to the needs of their husbands and children. Husbands, for their part, are said to enjoy sex more with wives who have been excised. (The women's own lack of enjoyment is said to be unimportant.) Men will not want unexcised women, as they are unclean and immature. And above all, it has been done since antiquity, and we may not change the ancient ways.

It would be easy, and perhaps a bit arrogant, to ridicule these arguments. But we may notice an important feature of this whole line of reasoning: It attempts to justify excision by showing that excision is beneficial—men, women, and their families are said to be better off when women are excised. Thus we might approach this reasoning, and excision itself, by asking whether this is true: Is excision, on the whole, helpful or harmful?

In fact, this is a standard that might reasonably be used in thinking about any social practice whatever: We may ask *whether the practice promotes or hinders the welfare of the people whose lives are affected by it.* And, as a corollary, we may ask if there is an alternative set of social arrangements that would do a better job of promoting their welfare. If so, we may conclude that the existing practice is deficient.

But this looks like just the sort of independent moral standard that cultural relativism says cannot exist. It is a single standard that may be brought to bear in judging the practices of any culture, at any time, including our own. Of course, people will not usually see this principle as being "brought in from the outside" to judge them, because viable cultures value human happiness.

Why, Despite All This, Thoughtful People May Be Reluctant to Criticize Other Cultures

Although they are personally horrified by excision, many thoughtful people are reluctant to say it is wrong, for at least three reasons. First, there is an understandable nervousness about "interfering in the social customs of other peoples." Europeans and their cultural descendants in America have a shabby history of destroying native cultures in the name of Christianity and the Enlightenment.[5] Recoiling from this record, some people refuse to make any negative judgments about other cultures, especially cultures that resemble those that have been wronged in the past. We should notice, however, that there is a difference between (a) judging a cultural practice to be deficient, and (b) thinking that we should announce the fact, conduct a campaign, apply diplomatic pressure, or send in the troops. The first is just a matter of trying to see the world clearly, from a moral point of view. The second is another matter altogether. Sometimes it may be right to "do something about it," but often it will not be.

Second, people also feel, rightly enough, that they should be tolerant of other cultures. Tolerance is, no doubt, a virtue—a tolerant person is willing to live in peaceful cooperation with those who see things differently. But there is

---

[5]*Enlightenment:* an 18th-century philosophical movement that had great confidence in the use of the power of reason to understand the universe and improve the human condition. [D. C. ABEL]

nothing in the nature of tolerance that requires us to say that all beliefs, all religions, and all social practices are equally admirable. On the contrary, if we did not think that some were better than others, there would be nothing for us to tolerate.

Finally, people may be reluctant to judge because they do not want to express contempt for the society being criticized. But again, this is misguided: To condemn a particular practice is not to say that the culture is on the whole contemptible or that it is generally inferior to any other culture, including one's own. It could have many admirable features. In fact, we should expect this to be true of most human societies—they are mixes of good and bad practices. Excision happens to be one of the bad ones.

WHAT CAN BE LEARNED FROM CULTURAL RELATIVISM

So far, in discussing cultural relativism, I have dwelled on its mistakes. I have said that it rests on an unsound argument, that it has implausible consequences, and that the extent of moral disagreement is far less than it suggests. This all adds up to a rather thorough repudiation of the theory. Nevertheless, it is still an appealing idea, and you may have the feeling that all this is a little unfair. The theory must have something going for it—why else has it been so influential? In fact, I think there is something right about cultural relativism, and there are two lessons we should learn from the theory, even if we ultimately reject it.

First, cultural relativism warns us, quite rightly, about the danger of assuming that all our preferences are based on some absolute rational standard. They are not. Many (but not all) of our practices are merely peculiar to our society, and it is easy to lose sight of that fact. In reminding us of it, the theory does a service.

Funerary practices are one example. The Callatians, according to Herodotus, were "men who eat their fathers"—a shocking idea, to us at least. But eating the flesh of the dead could be understood as a sign of respect. It could be taken as a symbolic act that says: We wish this person's spirit to dwell within us. Perhaps this was the understanding of the Callatians. On such a way of thinking, burying the dead could be seen as an act of rejection, and burning the corpse as positively scornful. If this is hard to imagine, then we may need to have our imaginations stretched. Of course we may feel a visceral repugnance at the idea of eating human flesh in any circumstances. But what of it? This repugnance may be, as the relativists say, only a matter of what is customary in our particular society.

There are many other matters that we tend to think of in terms of objective right and wrong that are really nothing more than social conventions. During the 2004 Super Bowl halftime show, Justin Timberlake ripped off part of Janet Jackson's costume, thus exposing one of her breasts to the audience. CBS quickly cut to an aerial view of the stadium, but as far as the country was concerned, the damage had been done. Half a million viewers complained, and the federal government fined CBS $550,000. In America, a publicly exposed breast is scandalous. In other cultures, however, such displays are common. Objectively speaking, the display of a woman's breast is neither right nor wrong. Cultural relativism begins with the valuable insight that many of our practices are like this; they are only cultural products. Then it goes wrong by inferring that, because some practices are like this, all must be.

The second lesson has to do with keeping an open mind. In the course of growing up, each of us has acquired some strong feelings: We have learned to think of some types of conduct as acceptable, and we have learned to reject others. Occasionally, we may find those feelings challenged. For example, we may have been taught that homosexuality is immoral, and we may feel quite uncomfortable around gay people and see them as alien and perverted. But then someone suggests that this may be a mere prejudice; that there is nothing evil about homosexuality; that gay people are just people, like anyone else, who happen, through no choice of their own, to be attracted to others of the same sex. Because we feel so strongly about the matter, we may find it hard to take this seriously. Even after we listen to the arguments, we may still have the unshakable feeling that homosexuals must be unsavory.

Cultural relativism provides an antidote for this kind of dogmatism. When he tells the story of the Greeks and Callatians, Herodotus adds:

> For if anyone, no matter who, were given the opportunity of choosing from among all the nations of the world the set of beliefs that he thought best, he would inevitably, after careful consideration of their relative merits, choose that of his own country. Everyone without exception believes his own native customs, and the religion he was brought up in, to be the best.[6]

Realizing this can help us broaden our minds. We can see that our feelings are not necessarily perceptions of the truth—they may be nothing more than the result of cultural conditioning. Thus, when we hear it suggested that some element of our social code is *not* really the best, and we find ourselves instinctively resisting the suggestion, we might stop and remember this. Then we may be more open to discovering the truth, whatever that might be.

We can understand the appeal of cultural relativism, then, even though the theory has serious shortcomings. It is an attractive theory because it is based on a genuine insight: that many of the practices and attitudes we think so natural are really only cultural products. Moreover, keeping this thought firmly in view is important if we want to avoid arrogance and keep an open mind. These are important points, not to be taken lightly. But we can accept them without accepting the whole theory.

---

[6]Herodotus, *Histories*, p. 219. [J. RACHELS]

Just Caring

Rita C. Manning

Rita C. Manning received her bachelor's degree in philosophy from the University of Massachusetts, Boston, in 1977. She then enrolled in the graduate program in philosophy at the University of California at Riverside, completing her master's degree in 1979 and her doctorate in 1982. She taught at California State University, San Bernardino, from 1979 to 1984 and at California State University, Hayward, during the 1984–1985 academic year. Manning then was appointed professor of philosophy at San José State University. In 1994–1995 she was visiting professor at the United States Military Academy in West Point, New York. Since 2003 she has served as department chair at San José State.

Manning has published articles on various topics in ethical theory and applied ethics, and two books: *Speaking from the Heart: A Feminist Perspective on Ethics* (1992) and *Social Justice in a Diverse Society* (coeditor with René Trujillo, 1996).

Our reading is from Chapter 4 of *Speaking from the Heart,* entitled "Just Caring." Manning proposes and defends an "ethic of caring." This ethic has two components: a disposition to care (a willingness to be open to others and give lucid attention to their needs) and an obligation to "care for" (to express our caring disposition in concrete actions). The objects of care include not only persons and animals, but also values, institutions, and all entities that cannot meet a need without help. How one carries out an ethic of caring with regard to these objects "depends upon one's ability to care for, one's obligation to care for oneself, and one's sense of the appropriateness of the need and the best way to meet it."

Manning explains that caring rests on our natural human capacity for empathy: When we see someone suffering, we feel the suffering almost as our own and want to do something to alleviate it. But since the range of our natural empathy is limited, our caring must be expanded by considerations of justice, by rules and rights (hence the title of Manning's chapter, "Just Caring").

Manning presents arguments to show that we have a general obligation to care and then discusses limitations on this obligation, such as the need to avoid "caring burnout," which limits our ability to care in the future. She concludes by examining how the ethic of caring is related to other ethical theories.

[INTRODUCTION]

. . . An ethic of caring, as I shall defend it, includes two elements. First is a disposition to care. This is a willingness to receive others, a willingness to give the lucid attention required to appropriately fill the needs of others. In this sense, an ethic of care is contextual; my actions must be guided by this lucid attention. I see this disposition to care as nourished by a spiritual awareness similar to the awareness argued for by proponents of the women's spirituality movement. As Starhawk describes this awareness: "Immanent justice rests on the first principle of magic: All things are interconnected. All is relationship. Perhaps the ultimate ethic of immanence is to choose to make that relationship one of love . . . ; love for all the eternally self-creating world, love of the light and the mysterious darkness, and raging love against all that would diminish the unspeakable beauty of the world."[1]

This disposition to care assumes a commitment to an ideal of caring; the ethically preferred world is one in which creatures are caring and cared for. Its institutions support and sustain caring while simultaneously reducing the need for care by eliminating the poverty, despair, and indifference that create a need for care.

Second, in addition to being sensitive to one's place in the world and to one's general obligation to be a caring person, one is also obligated to care for. (I am following Noddings[2] in using "care for" to indicate caring as expressed in action.) In the paradigm case, caring for involves acting in some appropriate way to respond to the needs of persons and animals, but can also be extended to responding to the needs of communities, values, or objects.

We are obligated to adopt this model of caring, insofar as we can, in our moral deliberations. This qualification refers not only to physical, emotional, and psychological incapacity, but to the larger inability to simply adopt a moral life that is radically different from the way of life we have participated in all our lives. This is a kind of incapacity that we all share. We simply cannot choose to have another's moral sensibilities, even if we are convinced that they are finer in some sense than our own. It doesn't follow that we have no obligations to become more morally sensitive; the point here is that we cannot simply will ourselves to begin to see the moral universe in some radically new way. But even where we can adopt a model of caring, we are morally permitted and sometimes morally obliged to appeal to rules and rights. In Gilligan's idiom,[3] we are required to listen to the voices of both care and justice.

In what follows, I shall first fill in some of the details of this model. Specifically, I shall discuss what it is to care for someone or something and when we are obligated to care for. Next, I shall say something about the role of rules and rights in this model.

I. CARING

I have often wondered if taking a class in moral philosophy was the best way for students to become sensitive to moral concerns. It seemed to me that a better way would be to have students work in soup kitchens or shelters for the homeless. Taking care of my children has made me more open to moral concerns. In taking care of the hungry, homeless, and helpless, we are engaged in caring for. In the standard case, caring for is immediate; it admits of no surrogates. When we directly care for some creature, we are in physical contact. Our eyes meet, our hands touch. However, not every need can be met in this immediate way, and sometimes we must accept surrogates. Not every need can be met by individual

---

[1]Starhawk, *Dreaming the Dark: Magic, Sex and Politics* (Boston: Beacon Press, 1982), p. 44. [R. C. MANNING]

[2]Nel Noddings, *Caring: A Feminine Approach to Ethics and Moral Education* (Berkeley: University of California Press, 1984). [R. C. MANNING]

[3]Carol Gilligan, *In a Different Voice: Psychological Theory and Women's Development* (Cambridge, MA: Harvard University Press, 1982). [R. C. MANNING]

action; in such cases, we must seek collective action. But when we can do the caring for directly, we ought to do so, at least some of the time. The need of the other may sometimes require that a particular person do the caring for. If my child needs my attention, I cannot meet this need by sending her to a therapist. Even when the needs of the other do not require our personal attention, we must provide some of the caring for directly in order to develop and sustain our ability to care.

Day-to-day interactions with other persons create a web of reciprocal caring. In these interactions, one is obliged to be a caring person. One is free, to a certain extent, to choose when and how to care for these others. One's choice is limited by one's relationships with these others and by their needs. A pressing need calls up an immediate obligation to care for; roles and responsibilities call up an obligation to respond in a caring manner. In the first case, one is obligated (though this obligation can be limited by a principle of supererogation)[4] to respond; in the second, one can choose, within limits, when and how to care.

A creature in need who is unable to meet this need without help calls for a caring response on my part. This response need not always be direct. Sometimes it is better to organize a political response. (Many, for example, who are confronted on the street by homeless people are unsure about how to respond, convinced that their immediate response will not be enough, and might even be counterproductive.) Certain relationships obligate us to provide direct caring for. When my daughter falls and asks me to "kiss it and make it better," I can't send her to my neighbor for the kiss.

Our roles (for example, as mother, as teacher, as volunteer) put us in particular relationships to others. These roles require and sustain caring. Obligations to infant children and animals involve meeting their basic needs for physical sustenance (food, shelter, clothing, health care) and for companionship and love. Obligations to students are grounded upon roles of teacher and philosopher and the students' psychological needs to discover who they are and how they can live with integrity. Here, one ought to feel a connection with the students but also with teaching and philosophy. But if a student needs another kind of care, we may be obligated to provide it, though not single-handedly. The response depends upon one's ability to care for, one's obligation to care for oneself, and one's sense of the appropriateness of the need and the best way to meet it.

In discharging obligations to care for, which are based on role responsibility, one should be conscious of the need to fill those roles conscientiously. The role of teacher, for example, requires a certain impartiality; the role of mother requires a fierce devotion to each particular child. But one is free, to a certain extent, to choose roles. In adopting or reshaping roles, one should be sensitive to the need to be cared for as well as the capacity to care. In critiquing socially designed and assigned roles, we should aim for roles and divisions of roles that make caring more likely to occur.

Caring for can involve a measure of self-sacrifice. The rescuers of Jessica McClure, the little girl who fell into a well,[5] who went without sleep for days,

---

[4]*supererogation:* doing more than required by duty or obligation. [D. C. Abel]

[5]In 1987 baby Jessica McClure was rescued after being trapped for nearly 60 hours in a 22-foot well into which she had fallen in Midland, Texas. [D. C. Abel]

and the parents of an infant who go without uninterrupted sleep for months, are involved in caring for.

Caring for involves an openness to the one cared for; it requires seeing the real need and satisfying it insofar as we are able. In satisfying it, we should be sensitive not just to the need but to the feelings of those in need.

Caring for does not require feeling any particular emotion toward the one cared for, but an openness to the possibility that some emotional attachment may form in the process of caring for. Nor does it require an ongoing relationship with the one cared for. One may meet the one cared for as stranger, though the caring for will change that.

Obviously, a model of caring along the lines I am defending must include an account of needs. An account of needs must recognize that needs are in some sense social, so identifying needs requires an understanding of biology, psychology, and other relevant social sciences.

Such an account would draw a distinction between subsistence needs and psychological needs. Subsistence needs will usually be needs that must be filled if physical existence is to continue, while psychological needs are needs that must be filled if human flourishing is to occur. Filling subsistence needs does not automatically benefit both the carer and the cared for. Rather, the carer is likely to feel burdened by filling such needs, though the recognition that one has filled such needs often creates a sense of virtue in the carer. Filling psychological needs can often be more fulfilling. It is more likely to be done in a reciprocal relationship, and in such a relationship filling psychological needs requires that both parties share the roles of carer and cared for.

Finally, one need not respond to every need. In choosing how and when to respond, one should consider the seriousness of the need, the benefit to the one needing care of filling this particular need, one's own capacity to fill the need, and the competing needs of others, including oneself, that will be affected by filling this particular need.

II. OBJECTS OF CARE

One can care for persons, animals, ideas, values, institutions, and objects. Later, I will discuss caring for persons and animals in some detail, but here I want to make some brief remarks about caring for ideas, values, institutions, and objects. In caring for ideas, values, and institutions, one devotes oneself to their survival, growth, and flourishing in much the same way as we devote ourselves to the growth and flourishing of a child. In doing so, we are caring for ourselves (insofar as these are our ideas and values) and persons and animals (insofar as these ideas and values support a network of care that embraces persons and animals). In caring for objects, one is devoted primarily to their survival (although some objects, trees, for example, can be said to grow and flourish). The choice of objects of care should reflect our own need to be cared for and our capacity to care. But decisions about what to care for should not depend exclusively upon our own needs and capacities. We should also be sensitive to the needs that summon the obligation to care for. If we understand our obligation to care for as following from the existence of need and helplessness, we should care for ideas, institutions, values, objects, and practices that would diminish such needs. One might argue that we could virtually eliminate the need to care for by creating appropriate institutions, values, and practices and hence undermine our capacity to care. But even in a perfectly just world, children would need care, and people and animals would get sick. Furthermore, human needs include more than needs for physical sustenance. Human needs for companionship and intimacy would exist even in a world free from the horrors of war, homelessness, sickness, and disease. . . .

IV. KNOWING HOW AND WHEN TO CARE

It is not unreasonable to expect an ethic to give us some guidance about how to act, though, as I have argued [earlier in this book], it is unreasonable to expect a calculus. An ethic of care, then, ought to give us some guidance about how and when to care.

Noddings explicitly acknowledges her great debt to Hume,[6] as do I. It seems reasonable then to begin by looking at Hume's answer to this question. Hume saw morality as resting upon a human capacity for sympathetic identification with others.[7] When we see someone suffering, for example, we feel the suffering almost as if it were our own. Our desire to do something to relieve the suffering springs naturally from this empathic response. This natural sentiment is supplanted by an appeal to justice when the sentiment is lacking. Suppose, for example, that the suffering is taking place in a distant place and we are merely aware of it. Our awareness does not excite in us the same empathic response that the immediate perception of the suffering would. What we must do in this case is remind ourselves that although we do not know the sufferer, we can assume that the sufferer shares essential characteristics with someone who is close to us. Since we cannot find any reason to reject the appeal of the one while desiring to respond to the other, we recognize the demands made on us by the absent sufferer. Here what we see is sentiment, colored by reflection. This reflection results in rather general principles, though the principles are seen as derivative of our experience and our sentiments.

Noddings makes a similar move when she distinguishes natural from ethical caring.[8] Natural caring is the caring that one is inclined to do, that springs from ties of affection to others. In the absence of such inclination, one must summon up ethical caring. Both Hume and Noddings are vague about precisely what caring demands in any particular situation. Hume suggests that, at least with respect to general principles, we let experience be our guide; we look for those principles that will make the world more comfortable for the social creatures we are.

---

[6]David Hume (1711–1776) was a Scottish philosopher and historian; for a biography, see p. 46. [D. C. ABEL]
[7]David Hume, *An Enquiry Concerning the Principles of Morals*, ed. L. A. Selby-Bigge, 2nd ed. (Oxford, England: Clarendon Press, 1962), Section 3; *A Treatise of Human Nature*, ed. L. A. Selby-Bigge (Oxford, England: Oxford University Press, 1964), Part III, Section 1. [R. C. MANNING]
[8]Nel Noddings, *Caring*, Chapter 4. [R. C. MANNING]

Noddings rejects an appeal to general principles, but offers instead a strategy for deciding what to do. When natural caring is absent, one should ask oneself what the ideal caring self would do in this situation. She is not suggesting that we appeal to an impartial observer here. Instead, she asks us to remember a situation in which we were ideally caring; we appeal here to our own ideal of caring.

What is implied in both Hume and Noddings is that when sentiment and natural caring do motivate us, we freely follow their dictates. Both of them admit that this capacity can stagnate and die or it can flourish, and, accordingly, we have an obligation to support this capacity in ourselves. Noddings argues that we can only learn to care if we have been cared for as children, and if we have been given opportunities to care. If we have been, then, as adults, we sustain and enrich this capacity by continuing to seek opportunities to care actively for others.

Assuming we are caring persons, both Hume and Noddings suggest that we can trust our impulses; our instincts will guide us toward proper caring, at least when we are caring in the context of a fully present other. There is, of course, an additional requirement that Noddings in particular pays attention to: that we know how the other feels and what the other wants and how the other is likely to be affected by our actions.

Martha Nussbaum combines both sentiment and awareness in her notion of moral imagination. She describes moral imagination as the ability to see "a complex concrete reality in a highly lucid and richly responsive way; . . . taking in what is there, with imagination and feeling."[9]

I agree with Hume, Noddings, and Nussbaum that our interactions with others can and should be guided by our moral imaginations, by our sentiments balanced by our rich understanding of the context. Obviously our responses to strangers will not be guided by the same degree of understanding and sentiment as our responses to those close to us. However, Hume and Noddings are right to suggest that we imagine ourselves in contact with them, that we try to become as aware as we can be of their situations, that we allow this awareness to occasion an emotional response, and that we act, in the full knowledge that our actions, based as they are on insufficient understanding and often less than vibrant sentiment, might not be the right ones. I also agree with Nussbaum and Hume that general principles have a role to play. We appeal to our experiences with intimate others to generate a set of general principles, though we keep in mind that these are merely rules of thumb, based on past experience. But in the absence of understanding and rich emotional response, this might be the only way to guide our actions toward strangers.

V. DEFENSE OF A GENERAL OBLIGATION TO CARE

I am inclined to see the obligation to care as moral bedrock. If it can be said to rest on anything, it rests on our human capacity for caring interaction. Rather than offer a defense of care in terms of appeals to general principles, I would offer a

---

[9]Martha Nussbaum, "'Finely Aware and Richly Responsible': Literature and the Moral Imagination," *The Journal of Philosophy* 82 (October 1985): 521. [R. C. MANNING]

defense of something like general principles in terms of care. Still, for those who find the appeal to general principles more compelling than the obligation to care, I offer a defense of care in terms of such suitably general principles.

The obligation to respond as carer when appropriate can be defended on three grounds. The first is the need. Here one might appeal to Peter Singer's principle, "If it is in our power to prevent something very bad happening without thereby sacrificing anything of comparable moral significance, we ought to do it."[10]

The second is the recognition that human relationships require a continuous kind of caring. This caring involves three components: being receptive to the other, being accepting of the other, and being on call for the other when he/she is in need.[11] Unless we want to do away with human relationships, we must be open to the demands of caring that such relationships require. But caring in human relationships is, as human relationships are, reciprocal.

The third defense is that we cannot develop and sustain the ability to care unless we do some active caring. This is an empirical claim, and we must look both to social science and to our own experience in evaluating it, but there is an obvious way in which caring for enhances our ability to care. When we make the real attempt to care for, we must understand the needs of the one cared for. We must also see how that one wants the needs to be addressed. This ability to notice needs and wants and to empathize as well as sympathize is developed through caring. Of course, one might ask here why one should want to develop this capacity to care. It seems to me that the right response is to point out that human lives devoid of caring impulses and responses would be nasty, brutish, short, and lonely.[12]

Nel Noddings offers a different defense of the general obligation to care, one that seems to offer some problematic consequences. Noddings's theory is that morality essentially involves one obligation: the obligation to care. Caring involves two elements, natural caring and ethical caring. Natural caring requires engrossment in the other, "seeing the other's reality as possible for me,"[13] and the motivation to act "based on recognition of the other's wants and desires and . . . the objective elements of his problematic situation."[14] Ethical caring involves summoning natural caring by remembering "our most caring and tender moments" and recognizing that these moments represent our best self. Ethical caring can only be achieved in situations where dynamic, mutual relationships are possible.

[10]Peter Singer, *Practical Ethics* (Cambridge, England: Cambridge University Press, 1979), p. 168. [R. C. MANNING]

[11]This analysis is from Milton Mayeroff, *On Caring* (New York: Harper & Row, 1971). [R. C. MANNING]

[12]Manning refers here to the famous remark by the English philosopher Thomas Hobbes (1588–1679) that before the formation of society and government, human life was "solitary, poor, nasty, brutish, and short" (*Leviathan*, Part I, Chapter XIII). For a biography of Hobbes, see p. 436 of this book; the quotation is on p. 438. [D. C. ABEL]

[13]Noddings, *Caring*, p. 14. [R. C. MANNING]

[14]Ibid., p. 24. The remaining passages from *Caring* cited in Section V are taken from pp. 86–89. [R. C. MANNING]

This analysis provides, according to Noddings, an analysis of obligation.

I can be obligated to P if: (1) there exists or is potential a relation between P and me; (2) there exists the dynamic potential for growth in relation, including the potential for increased reciprocity and mutuality.

We are only obligated when these conditions obtain because, in her view, it is only under these conditions that caring can occur. Noddings denies that "universal caring" is a possibility and admits to the following three consequences of her analysis. First, "I am not obligated to starving children in Africa." Her argument for this is not exactly clear, but it appears that she would want to say that my ongoing relationships confer obligations that are primary. She says that fulfilling obligations to the starving children in Africa would require me to "abandon my obligations" to those to whom I am already related. Second, we have no obligations to animals because there is no possibility for genuine mutuality from animals. Third, the life of one caring (the ethically preferred life for all according to Noddings) must, in some sense, be a private life. "Her public life is limited by her insistence upon meeting the other as one caring. . . . When . . . reaching out destroys or drastically reduces her actual caring, she retreats and renews her contact with those who address her."

I want to take issue with each of these consequences, but I don't think that by doing so I am rejecting Noddings's account. Indeed, I am puzzled about why Noddings thought she was committed to them. It seems to me that a sympathetic reading of her could justify the exactly opposite conclusions.

Noddings needn't grant that helping the starving in Africa requires abandoning obligations to those to whom one is related. However, I suspect that she would still want to insist that I am not obligated to the starving in Africa. There is no present relationship between me and the starving children in Africa, nor is it likely that such a relationship will begin in the future. She gives us the example of a missionary who decides to go to Africa to help the starving. She says that this person might well have such obligations because this person will begin to have such relationships.

I don't agree that we have no obligations to the starving in Africa, in part because I don't accept Noddings's assumption about the primacy of current obligations. It seems to me that we have self-interested reasons for wanting to meet the obligations to those with whom we share a relationship. First, the possibility and hence the expectation of reciprocity gives us a self-interested reason for meeting these obligations first. Second, if we are truly "engrossed" by the persons for whom we care, we will receive some pleasure in meeting these obligations. I don't want to argue that no moral reasons can be offered where reasons of self-interest naturally obtain, but I do think that we should be suspicious of ethical theories that restrict our obligations to those duties that we have a self-interested reason to perform.

Noddings might have argued that we can have mutually reciprocal relationships with animals, or she might have taken the same stance with regard to animals that she takes with regard to abortion. In the latter case, she argues that the prospective mother can grant "sanctity" to the first-trimester fetus by viewing it as a "product of love between a man deeply cared for and me," and, as such, "joined to others through formal chains of caring." Because the caring exists for this mother, abortion would be immoral. If the mother chooses not to sanctify the fetus, no such relationship exists in the first trimester, and hence abortion would not be immoral. As the fetus begins to develop, it becomes "more nearly capable of response as cared for." At this point the relationship begins to exist and grow, and abortion is again immoral. It sounds like she is saying that if I choose to view myself as involved in a relationship with a fetus, then I have obligations toward it, even if it is not now capable of having a mutually reciprocal relationship with me. Why can't I then choose to see myself as involved in a relationship with animals, or at least with some animals? If I choose to see the animal this way, then I do have an obligation toward the animal. But this is not a very satisfactory consequence for a defender of animal rights; according to this view, if I don't choose to view myself as in a relationship with animals, I am free to treat them any way I want. I would be inclined to say that if we do have obligations toward animals—and I think we do—it is in virtue of qualities that the animals possess, for example the ability to suffer, and not in virtue of our willingness to recognize such qualities.

The claim that one must withdraw from the public sphere and retreat to the private when neglecting those to whom one is already related strikes me as a classic defense of the stereotypical role of the housewife. It tends to reinforce both self-interest and moral cowardice in the face of injustice, inequality, and suffering outside our own little worlds.

What is objectionable about all these consequences is the implication that one can choose all one's obligations. While obligations are created through voluntary commitments, this does not exhaust the possibilities. Further, Noddings's desire to thus limit our obligations is incompatible with the distinction she makes between natural and ethical caring. If one is obligated to do some ethical caring, and this involves calling upon one's ideal caring self, won't this ideal caring self feel some obligation toward animals and starving children in Africa? I'm convinced that it would, for much the same reasons that Hume thinks that the demands of justice will assert themselves after some reflection. We can come to recognize that the starving children in Africa share crucial characteristics with the children we know and love; we can see that animals share important characteristics as well. Surely, our ideal caring selves will not ignore this.

VI. LIMITATIONS ON OBLIGATIONS TO CARE

I don't think that we are obligated to be like Mother Teresa,[15] who cares for continuously. But how are we to limit our obligation to care? One strategy for limiting our obligation to care for focuses on the defenses of this obligation. First, we have a prima facie obligation[16] to care for when we come across a

---

[15]Mother Teresa (1910–1997) was an Albanian-born Roman Catholic nun who devoted her life to caring for the poor and dying in India. [D. C. ABEL]

[16]*prima facie obligation:* an obligation that holds unless it is overridden by another, stronger obligation. [D. C. ABEL]

creature in need who is unable to meet that need without help, when our caring is called upon as a part of a reciprocal relationship, or when caring is indicated as part of our role responsibility. Actual obligations rest upon the seriousness of the need, the assessment of the appropriateness of filling the need, and the ability to do something about filling it. But we must also recognize that we are persons who must be cared for and who deserve such care. The continuous caring for required to respond to needs for physical sustenance is, for most of us, incompatible with caring for ourselves. But not all caring for involves responding to physical needs. The caring for required to sustain relationships, which is usually reciprocal, can be a source of great strength to the person doing the caring for. And finally, allowing ourselves to suffer caring burnout also diminishes our ability to care for others in the future. I don't mean to argue that caring for requires no sacrifice. Indeed, where the need is great and the ability to meet it sufficient, we are required to sacrifice. But one is not required to adopt this as a form of life.

The obligation to care for is not an all-or-nothing thing. Being unable to care for now does not eliminate the possibility that one may be obligated to meet this need later. This is a general point about obligations. I might owe someone money and be unable to pay it back now, through no fault of my own. If I later come into a windfall, I am obligated to pay the money back then. In addition, there is no one right way to care for. Our assessment of the appropriateness of the need, our ability to meet the need, and our sense of the most successful way of doing so provide some guidance here. Perhaps immediate caring for is the best way to meet a need in one case, and cooperative political activity the most successful way of meeting other needs. I would want to leave these kinds of choices up to the agent. . . .

VIII. CARING AND OTHER ETHICAL THEORIES

. . . Caring, as I describe it, is not an ethical theory in any full-blown sense. I have just now argued that it is not an ethical theory in the sense of a set of rules to be rigidly applied. Still, one might wonder if it could be compared to virtue theory,[17] or to what I call perspectivism.

Hume's influence is broad and obvious. I have adopted both his picture of what a moral philosophy should be (the art of suggesting and testing moral strategies in light of our real-world experience) and his conviction that humans have a capacity for care and that this capacity explains the force morality has for humans (and perhaps other animals).

One might think that I am simply defending virtue ethics, but I don't believe so. Virtue ethics requires that the virtue not enter into the deliberations of the virtuous person: The brave person does not do an act because it is the act that would be chosen by a brave person; she does it because she thinks it is the right thing to do and because she is more interested in the rightness of the act

---

[17] *virtue theory:* ethical theory in which the virtue of the agent is the primary factor in morality, rather than the consequences of actions or an intrinsic quality of actions (also called *virtue ethics*). [D. C. ABEL]

than the personal consequences of doing so. In Noddings's and my view, caring does and must enter into the deliberation of the caring person. The caring person must sometimes ask herself what her ideal caring self would do in the situation. Still, an ethic of care has much in common with virtue theory. They both emphasize the importance of habit and inclination. Neither pretends to provide a calculus for moral decision making; rather they insist that the context coupled with the character of the actor and some general rules of thumb will provide all the cues.

Nietzsche[18] offers a model that is similar in some respects to an ethic of care. Both Nietzsche and an ethic of care suggest that we answer questions about how to live our lives by taking a particular perspective. He advocates taking an "eternal recurrence" perspective. He invites us to imagine living our lives over and over again, eternally. We can then ask ourselves, "If I were to live this moment over, eternally, what would I have wanted to do?" An ethic of care invites us to take the perspective of our ideal caring selves. Both views share with the virtue tradition the belief that the ideal moral agent should internalize this perspective to a certain extent so that one's actions flow naturally from a settled disposition. Nietzsche's view is broader than an ethic of care because he is concerned with how we live our lives and not just how we make moral decisions.

The next ethic I wish to consider is the land ethic, first described by Aldo Leopold and recently elaborated and defended by J. Baird Callicott.[19] As Leopold puts it: "A thing is right when it tends to preserve the integrity, stability, and beauty of the biotic community. It is wrong when it tends otherwise."[20] An ethic of care is similar to a land ethic in two ways. First, they are both holistic ethics; second, they share a commitment to the sacredness of the natural world.

A land ethic is holistic in the following sense: The good of any part is defined in terms of the good of the whole. Callicott draws many implications from this view, one being that right now humans are a blight upon the earth because they are squeezing out other species. The land ethic's commitment to the sacredness of the natural world is shown by this definition of the good in terms of what is good for the whole, the whole being the natural world.

An ethic of care is holistic in two ways. First, it recognizes that we are embedded in connections of care and that our self-identity is, in large part, a function of our role in these complex interconnections. In this sense, we see ourselves as part of a larger whole, and inseparable from this whole. An ethic of care, as I conceive it, is holistic in a larger sense as well. It assumes an underlying picture of the earth as one body, and of ourselves as part of this body. It sees an attitude of awe as the appropriate response to the recognition that we are part of this sacred body. Not every version of an ethic of care need be holistic in this second sense. Noddings, for example, is not committed to this. But I think it allows us to escape from the parochialism of an ethic of care that is grounded only in human attachments.

---

[18]Friedrich Nietzsche (1844–1900) was a German philosopher; for a biography, see p. 378. [D. C. ABEL]

[19]J. Baird Callicott, *In Defense of the Land Ethic* (Albany: State University of New York Press, 1989). [R. C. MANNING]

[20]Aldo Leopold, *A Sand County Almanac* (New York: Oxford University Press, 1949), pp. 224–25. [R. C. MANNING]

So, while both ethics are holistic, they are holistic in different ways. There is a second way in which they differ. A land ethic, as Callicott describes it, is indifferent to the value that humans put on other humans and certain animals.

Both a land ethic and an ethic of care are ethics for and from the perspective of humans. In this sense, neither can escape from human psychology. If an ethic is seen as providing guidance for living a good human life, then we must recognize important features of human psychology—the attachments of humans to other humans and certain animals, for example. While Callicott tries to ignore this, an ethic of care takes it as central.

IX. CONCLUSION

An ethic of care has many advantages. It allows us to reconceptualize, and thereby better understand, many moral quandaries, such as that of the porcupine and the moles.[21] It strikes many, and women in particular, as a truer picture of their own moral intuitions. It assumes a theory of human nature that is an improvement upon abstract individualism. It generates a theory of moral education that focuses on the enhancement of the capacity to care. Finally, and most importantly, it might, if widely adopted, make the world a better place.

---

[21]In the story of the porcupine and the moles, a family of moles allows a porcupine to move into their cave for the winter. But the cave is small, and when the porcupine moves around, his quills scratch the moles. The moles ask the porcupine to leave, but he refuses. [D. C. ABEL]

CHAPTER 7

Political and Social
Philosophy

Most of us would agree that we have a certain obligation
to obey the laws passed by our government. But what gives
government the authority to tell us what to do? And what
is the extent of its authority? Most of us would assert that
individuals have certain fundamental rights that no government has the authority to violate. But what are these rights
and where do they come from? Does *society* have rights
also? Does it have the right to demand that I sacrifice my
self-interest for the good of society as a whole? If I live in a
society, am I obliged to obey *all* its laws, or only those that
I consider just? What standard can I use to determine
whether a law—or a society—is just? These are some of the
questions explored by political and social philosophy.

Political philosophy and social philosophy are so closely
related that they are sometimes considered a single field.
Strictly speaking, however, political philosophy is a part of
social philosophy. Social philosophy deals with any group
of "associates" (*socii* in Latin, the root of the word "social"),
whereas political philosophy deals with one specific kind
of association, namely the state (*polis* in Greek, the root of
the word "political"). Social and political matters are, of
course, studied by sociologists and political scientists as
well as by philosophers. The main difference is that sociologists and political scientists focus on the actual structure
and workings of social and political institutions; social and
political philosophers theorize about the way social and
political institutions *should* be structured and about the
nature and grounds of authority, justice, and rights.

The first group of readings, "Classical Political Theories,"
consists of six readings, chronologically arranged. In the

first reading, Plato (expressing his views in a dialogue between Socrates and Crito) maintains that by living in a society and accepting its benefits we enter into a tacit agreement to obey its laws, and that we are obligated to keep our agreement. In the next reading, Thomas Hobbes argues that human beings originally lived in a "state of nature" in which there was no society and no government. Because life in the state of nature was filled with fear and insecurity, human beings formed a "social contract" by which they transferred their rights to a common power and gave this "leviathan" (Hobbes's reference is to a biblical sea monster) absolute power to enforce the terms of the contract. John Locke, like Hobbes, maintains that political society began when human beings left the state of nature by initiating a social contract. However, the state of nature he depicts is less bleak than Hobbes's, and the government established by the social contract has limited rather than absolute authority. Mary Wollstonecraft argues that society treats women unjustly by denying their rationality and failing to provide them with the same kind of education that men receive—an education that develops one's rational abilities and thereby enables one to reach one's full human potential. Karl Marx and Friedrich Engels contend that eventually there will be no need for government. The class struggle between capitalists (owners of the means of production) and workers will result in the victory of the workers. After capitalism has been destroyed and power has shifted temporarily from the capitalists to the workers, the equality of all people will be achieved, human fulfillment will be possible, and political power will be unnecessary. John Stuart Mill argues that the only legitimate reason for government to exercise power over an individual is to prevent that person from harming others; individuals should have the liberty to do anything they wish, provided others are not harmed.

The second set of readings, "Contemporary Social Issues," examines two topics: social justice and multiculturalism. Martin Luther King, Jr., defends his use of nonviolent protest as a way to help African-Americans gain the civil rights and fair treatment that American society for centuries refused to extend to them. He argues that nonviolent protest can be justified even when it is illegal: There is no obligation to obey an unjust law, and even a *just* law may be violated if it is used for unjust purposes. John Rawls presents a general theory of social justice: A society will be just if each person has the greatest liberty compatible with a similar liberty for others, and if social and economic inequalities are arranged in a way likely to work to everyone's advantage. Joseph Raz explores the nature and necessity of multiculturalism in the contemporary world. He suggests several political policies that would acknowledge and respect diverse cultural groups. In the final reading, Anne Phillips maintains that a proper multiculturalism must find a middle path between the view that all moral values are valid for all cultures and the view that the differences among cultures imply that all moral values are relative to culture. She then examines gender equality and the autonomy and cultural coercion of women.

A. Classical Political Theories

READING 41 # Crito

Plato

A biography of Plato appears on p. 5.

Our reading is the *Crito,* a conversation between Socrates and his longtime friend Crito. The scene is Socrates' prison cell: He has been sentenced to death and will be executed as soon as the Athenian ship returns from its religious expedition to the island of Delos. Crito, who has been regularly visiting Socrates in prison, brings the news that the ship has been sighted and will soon arrive. Crito urges Socrates, one last time, to escape and save his life; all the arrangements have been made. Because Socrates seems unwilling to escape, despite his innocence of the charges for which he was condemned, Crito gives Socrates several reasons for escaping. Socrates replies that he will escape only if it would be moral to do so. He then states two moral principles that he and Crito have long agreed are valid: One should never willingly wrong or mistreat others, even if wronged or mistreated by them, and one should fulfill one's just agreements.

To determine whether his escape would violate these moral principles, Socrates imagines the laws of Athens addressing him. Their speech convinces Socrates that to escape would be wrong because Socrates would be breaking both principles. First, Socrates would be mistreating another, namely the laws. The laws, moreover, had benefited Socrates and had never mistreated him (at his trial, it was the *jurors* who were unjust, not the laws). Second, Socrates would be breaking a just agreement—his agreement to abide by the laws of Athens. Socrates argues that when we live in a society and accept its benefits, we enter into a tacit agreement to obey its laws and are obligated to keep our agreement.

Socrates' conversation with Crito not only sets forth his theory of political obligation; it also illustrates his conviction that philosophy requires one to act in accordance with one's principles, no matter what the cost. To violate a moral principle is to harm one's soul, and no bodily benefit gained by an unjust action can outweigh the damage that injustice does to one's soul.

[INTRODUCTION]

> SOCRATES: Why have you come so early, Crito? Or is it not still early?
> CRITO: It certainly is.
> SOCRATES: How early?
> CRITO: Early dawn.
> SOCRATES: I am surprised that the warder was willing to listen to you.
> CRITO: He is quite friendly to me by now, Socrates. I have been here often and I have given him something.
> SOCRATES: Have you just come, or have you been here for some time?

CRITO: A fair time.

SOCRATES: Then why did you not wake me right away but sit there in silence?

CRITO: By Zeus no, Socrates. I wish I myself were not in distress and awake so long. I have been surprised to see you so peacefully asleep. It was on purpose that I did not wake you, so that you should spend your time most agreeably. Often in the past throughout my life, I have considered the way you live happily, and especially so now that you bear your present misfortune so easily and lightly.

SOCRATES: It would not be fitting at my age to resent the fact that I must die now.

CRITO: Other men of your age are caught in such misfortunes, but their age does not prevent them resenting their fate.

SOCRATES: That is so. Why have you come so early?

CRITO: I bring bad news, Socrates—not for you, apparently, but for me and all your friends the news is bad and hard to bear. Indeed, I would count it among the hardest.

SOCRATES: What is it? Or has the ship arrived from Delos, at the arrival of which I must die?[1]

CRITO: It has not arrived yet, but it will, I believe, arrive today, according to a message some men brought from Sunium,[2] where they left the ship. This makes it obvious that it will come today, and that your life must end tomorrow.

SOCRATES: May it be for the best. If it so please the gods, so be it. However, I do not think it will arrive today.

CRITO: What indication have you of this?

SOCRATES: I will tell you. I must die the day after the ship arrives.

CRITO: That is what those in authority say.

SOCRATES: Then I do not think it will arrive on this coming day, but on the next. I take as witness of this a dream I had a little earlier during this night. It looks as if it was the right time for you not to wake me.

CRITO: What was your dream?

SOCRATES: I thought that a beautiful and comely woman dressed in white approached me. She called me and said: "Socrates, may you arrive at fertile Phthia on the third day."[3]

CRITO: A strange dream, Socrates.

SOCRATES: But it seems clear enough to me, Crito.

---

[1]Delos is an island in the Aegean Sea, about 85 miles from Athens. It was sacred to the god Apollo, and every year the Athenians sent a ship there in thanksgiving to him. Socrates's execution had been delayed because ritual purity required that no one be executed during the religious expedition. [D. C. ABEL]

[2]*Sunium:* a promontory overlooking the Saronic Gulf of the Aegean Sea, about 30 miles from Athens. [D. C. ABEL]

[3]This verse parallels the words of the Greek hero Achilles in Homer's *Iliad*, "I shall reach fertile Phthia on the third day" (Book IX, line 363). Phthia is Achilles' homeland; hence Socrates interprets his dream to mean that he will die (his soul will arrive in the next world, its true home) in two days. ("On the third day" means "in two days," since the Greeks, when counting a series, began with the present member of the series.) [D. C. ABEL]

[CRITO'S ARGUMENTS FOR ESCAPING]

CRITO: Too clear it seems, my dear Socrates, but listen to me even now and be saved. If you die, it will not be a single misfortune for me. Not only will I be deprived of a friend, the like of whom I shall never find again, but many people who do not know you or me very well will think that I could have saved you if I were willing to spend money, but that I did not care to do so. Surely there can be no worse reputation than to be thought to value money more highly than one's friends, for the majority will not believe that you yourself were not willing to leave prison while we were eager for you to do so.

SOCRATES: My good Crito, why should we care so much for what the majority think? The most reasonable people, to whom one should pay more attention, will believe that things were done as they were done.

CRITO: You see, Socrates, that one must also pay attention to the opinion of the majority. Your present situation makes clear that the majority can inflict not the least but pretty well the greatest evils if one is slandered among them.

SOCRATES: [I wish] that the majority could inflict the greatest evils, for they would then be capable of the greatest good, and that would be fine, but now they cannot do either. They cannot make a man either wise or foolish, but they inflict things haphazardly.

CRITO: That may be so. But tell me this, Socrates, are you anticipating that I and your other friends would have trouble with the informers if you escape from here, as having stolen you away, and that we should be compelled to lose all our property or pay heavy fines and suffer other punishment besides? If you have any such fear, forget it. We would be justified in running this risk to save you, and worse, if necessary. Do follow my advice, and do not act differently.

SOCRATES: I do have these things in mind, Crito, and also many others.

CRITO: Have no such fear. It is not much money that some people require to save you and get you out of here. Further, do you not see that those informers are cheap, and that not much money would be needed to deal with them? My money is available and is, I think, sufficient. If, because of your affection for me, you feel you should not spend any of mine, there are those strangers here ready to spend money. One of them, Simmias the Theban, has brought enough for this very purpose—Cebes, too, and a good many others. So, as I say, do not let this fear make you hesitate to save yourself, nor let what you said in court trouble you, that you would not know what to do with yourself if you left Athens, for you would be welcomed in many places to which you might go. If you want to go to Thessaly, I have friends there who will greatly appreciate you and keep you safe, so that no one in Thessaly will harm you.

Besides, Socrates, I do not think that what you are doing is just, to give up your life when you can save it, and to hasten your fate as your enemies would hasten it, and indeed have hastened it in their wish to destroy you. Moreover, I think you are betraying your sons by going away and leaving them, when you could bring them up and educate them. You thus show no concern for what their fate may be. They will probably have the usual fate of orphans. Either one should not have children, or one should share with them to the end the toil of upbringing and education. You seem to me to choose the easiest path, whereas one should choose the path that a good and courageous man would choose, particularly when one claims throughout one's life to care for virtue.

I feel ashamed on your behalf and on behalf of us, your friends, lest all that has happened to you be thought due to cowardice on our part: the fact that your trial came to court when it need not have done so, the handling of the trial itself, and now this absurd ending, which will be thought to have got beyond our control through some cowardice and unmanliness on our part, since we did not save you, or you save yourself, when it was possible and could be done if we had been of the slightest use. Consider, Socrates, whether this is not only evil but shameful, both for you and for us. Take counsel with yourself, or rather the time for counsel is past and the decision should have been taken, and there is no further opportunity, for this whole business must be ended tonight. If we delay now, then it will no longer be possible—it will be too late. Let me persuade you on every count, Socrates, and do not act otherwise.

[SOCRATES' INITIAL REPLY TO CRITO]

SOCRATES: My dear Crito, your eagerness is worth much if it should have some right aim; if not, then the greater your keenness the more difficult it is to deal with. We must therefore examine whether we *should* act in this way or not, as not only now but at all times I am the kind of man who listens to nothing within me but the argument that on reflection seems best to me. I cannot, now that this fate has come upon me, discard the arguments I used; they seem to me much the same. I value and respect the same principles as before, and if we have no better arguments to bring up at this moment, be sure that I shall not agree with you, not even if the power of the majority were to frighten us with more bogeys, as if we were children, with threats of incarcerations and executions and confiscation of property. How should we examine this matter most reasonably? Would it be by taking up first your argument about the opinions of men, whether it is sound in every case that one should pay attention to some opinions, but not to others? Or was that well-spoken *before* the necessity to die came upon me, but *now* it is clear that this was said in vain for the sake of argument—that it was in truth play and nonsense? I am eager to examine together with you, Crito, whether this argument will appear in any way different to me in my present circumstances, or whether it remains the same, whether we are to abandon it or believe it. It was said on every occasion by those who thought they were speaking sensibly, as I have just now been speaking, that one should greatly value some people's opinions, but not others. Does that seem to you a sound statement?

You, as far as a human being can tell, are exempt from the likelihood of dying tomorrow, so the present misfortune is not likely to lead you astray. Consider then, do you not think it a sound statement that one must not value all the opinions of men, but some and not others, nor the opinions of all men, but those of some and not of others? What do you say? Is this not well said?

CRITO: It is.

SOCRATES: One should value the good opinions, and not the bad ones?

CRITO: Yes.

SOCRATES: The good opinions are those of wise men, the bad ones those of foolish men?

CRITO: Of course.

SOCRATES: Come then, what of statements such as this: Should a man professionally engaged in physical training pay attention to the praise and blame and opinion of any man, or to those of one man only, namely a doctor or trainer?

CRITO: To those of one only.

SOCRATES: He should therefore fear the blame and welcome the praise of that one man, and not those of the many?

CRITO: Obviously.

SOCRATES: He must then act and exercise, eat and drink in the way the one, the trainer and the one who knows, thinks right, not all the others?

CRITO: That is so.

SOCRATES: Very well. And if he disobeys the one and disregards his opinion and his praises, while valuing those of the many who have no knowledge, will he not suffer harm?

CRITO: Of course.

SOCRATES: What is that harm, where does it tend, and what part of the man who disobeys does it affect?

CRITO: Obviously the harm is to his body, which it ruins.

SOCRATES: Well said. So with other matters, not to enumerate them all, and certainly with actions just and unjust, shameful and beautiful, good and bad, about which we are now deliberating, should we follow the opinion of the many and fear it, or that of the one, if there is one who has knowledge of these things and before whom we feel fear and shame more than before all the others? If we do not follow his directions, we shall harm and corrupt that part of ourselves that is improved by just actions and destroyed by unjust actions. Or is there nothing in this?

CRITO: I think there certainly is, Socrates.

SOCRATES: Come now, if we ruin that which is improved by health and corrupted by disease by not following the opinions of those who know, is life worth living for us when that is ruined? And that is the body, is it not?

CRITO: Yes.

SOCRATES: And is life worth living with a body that is corrupted and in bad condition?

CRITO: In no way.

SOCRATES: And is life worth living for us with that part of us corrupted that unjust action harms and just action benefits? Or do we think that part of us, whatever it is, that is concerned with justice and injustice, is inferior to the body?

CRITO: Not at all.

SOCRATES: It is more valuable?

CRITO: Much more.

SOCRATES: We should not then think so much of what the majority will say about us, but what he will say who understands justice and injustice (the one, that is), and what the truth itself will say. So that, in the first place, you were wrong to believe that we should care for the opinion of the many about what is just, beautiful, good, and their opposites. "But," someone might say, "the many are able to put us to death."

CRITO: That too is obvious, Socrates, and someone might well say so.

SOCRATES: And, my admirable friend, that argument that we have gone through remains, I think, as before. Examine the following statement in turn as to whether it stays the same or not, that the most important thing is not life, but the good life.

CRITO: It stays the same.

SOCRATES: And that the good life, the beautiful life, and the just life are the same—does that still hold, or not?

CRITO: It does hold.

SOCRATES: As we have agreed so far, we must examine next whether it is just for me to try to get out of here when the Athenians have not acquitted me. If it is seen to be just, we will try to do so; if it is not, we will abandon the idea. As for those questions you raise about money, reputation, and the upbringing of children, Crito, those considerations in truth belong to those people who easily put men to death and would bring them to life again if they could, without thinking—I mean the majority of men. For us, however, since our argument leads to this, the only valid consideration, as we were saying just now, is whether we should be acting rightly in giving money and gratitude to those who will lead me out of here, and acting rightly ourselves in helping with the escape, or whether in truth we shall do wrong in doing all this. If it appears that we shall be acting unjustly, then we have no need at all to take into account whether we shall have to die if we stay here and keep quiet, or suffer in another way, rather than do wrong.

CRITO: I think you put that beautifully, Socrates, but see what we should do.

SOCRATES: Let us examine the question together, my dear friend, and if you can make any objection while I am speaking, make it and I will listen to you, but if you have no objection to make, my dear Crito, then stop now from saying the same thing so often, that I must leave here against the will of the Athenians. I think it important to persuade you before I act, and not to act against your wishes. See whether the start of our inquiry is adequately stated, and try to answer what I ask you in the way you think best.

CRITO: I shall try.

[TWO PRINCIPLES OF MORALITY]

SOCRATES: Do we say that one must never in any way do wrong willingly, or must one do wrong in one way and not in another? Is to do wrong never good or admirable, as we have agreed in the past, or have all these former agreements been washed out during the last few days? Have we at our age failed to notice for some time that in our serious discussions we were no different from children? Above all, is the truth such as we used to say it was, whether the majority agree or not, and whether we must still suffer worse things than we do now or will be treated more gently, that nonetheless, wrongdoing or injustice is in every way harmful and shameful to the wrongdoer? Do we say so or not?

CRITO: We do.

SOCRATES: So one must never do wrong.

CRITO: Certainly not.

SOCRATES: Nor must one, when wronged, inflict wrong in return, as the majority believe, since one must never do wrong.

CRITO: That seems to be the case.

SOCRATES: Come now, should one mistreat anyone or not, Crito?

CRITO: One must never do so.

SOCRATES: Well then, if one is oneself mistreated, is it right, as the majority say, to mistreat in return, or is it not?

CRITO: It is never right.

SOCRATES: Mistreating people is no different from wrongdoing.

CRITO: That is true.

SOCRATES: One should never do wrong in return, nor mistreat any man, no matter how one has been mistreated by him. And Crito, see that you do not agree to this, contrary to your belief. For I know that only a few people hold this view or will hold it, and there is no common ground between those who hold this view and those who do not, but they inevitably despise each other's views. So then consider very carefully whether we have this view in common, and whether you agree, and let this be the basis of our deliberation: that neither to do wrong nor to return a wrong is ever right, nor is bad treatment in return for bad treatment. Or do you disagree and do not share this view as a basis for discussion? I have held it for a long time and still hold it now, but if you think otherwise, tell me now. If, however, you stick to our former opinion, then listen to the next point.

CRITO: I stick to it and agree with you. So say on.

SOCRATES: Then I state the next point, or rather I ask you: When one has come to an agreement that is just with someone, should one fulfill it or cheat on it?

CRITO: One should fulfill it.

SOCRATES: See what follows from this: If we leave here without the city's permission, are we mistreating people whom we should least mistreat? And are we sticking to a just agreement, or not?

CRITO: I cannot answer your question, Socrates. I do not know.

[THE SPEECH OF THE LAWS OF ATHENS]

SOCRATES: Look at it this way. If, as we were planning to run away from here, or whatever one should call it, the laws and the state came and confronted us and asked: "Tell me, Socrates, what are you intending to do? Do you not by this action you are attempting intend to destroy us, the laws, and indeed the whole city, as far as you are concerned? Or do you think it possible for a city not to be destroyed if the verdicts of its courts have no force but are nullified and set at naught by private individuals?" What shall we answer to this and other such arguments? For many things could be said, especially by an orator on behalf of this law we are destroying, which orders that the judgments of the courts shall be carried out. Shall we say in answer, "The city wronged me, and its decision was not right." Shall we say that, or what?

CRITO: Yes, by Zeus, Socrates, that is our answer.

SOCRATES: Then what if the laws said: "Was that the agreement between us, Socrates, or was it to respect the judgments that the city came to?" And if we wondered at their words, they would perhaps add: "Socrates, do not wonder at what we say but answer, since you are accustomed to proceed by question and answer. Come now, what accusation do you bring against us and the city, that you should try to destroy us? Did we not, first, bring you to birth, and was it not through us that your father married your mother and begot you? Tell us, do you find anything to criticize in those of us who are concerned with marriage?" And I would say that I do not criticize them. "Or in those of us concerned with the nurture of babies and the education that you too received? Were those assigned to that subject not right to instruct your father to educate you in the arts and in physical culture?" And I would say that they were right. "Very well," they would continue, "and after you were born and nurtured and educated, could you, in the first place, deny that you are our offspring and servant, both you and your forefathers? If that is so, do you think that we are on an equal footing as regards the right, and that whatever we do to you it is right for you to do to us? You were not on an equal footing with your father as regards the right, nor with your master if you had one, so as to retaliate for anything they did to you, to revile them if they reviled you, to beat them if they beat you, and so with many other things. Do you think you have this right to retaliation against your country and its laws? That if we undertake to destroy you and think it right to do so, you can undertake to destroy us, as far as you can, in return? And will you say that you are right to do so, you who truly care for virtue? Is your wisdom such as not to realize that your country is to be honored more than your mother, your father and all your ancestors, that it is more to be revered and more sacred, and that it counts for more among the gods and sensible men, that you must worship it, yield to it, and placate its anger more than your father's? You must either persuade it or obey its orders, and endure in silence whatever it instructs you to endure, whether blows or bonds; and if it leads you into war to be wounded or killed, you must obey. To do so is right, and one must not give way or retreat or leave one's post, but both in war and in courts and everywhere else, one must obey the commands of one's city and country, or persuade it as to the nature of justice. It is impious to bring violence to bear against your mother or father; it is much more so to use it against your country." What shall we say in reply, Crito, that the laws speak the truth, or not?

CRITO: I think they do.

SOCRATES: "Reflect now, Socrates" the laws might say, "that if what we say is true, you are not treating us rightly by planning to do what you are planning. We have given you birth, nurtured you, educated you, we have given you and all other citizens a share of all the good things we could. Even so, we give every Athenian the opportunity, once arrived at voting age and having observed the affairs of the city and us the laws, that if we do not please him, he can take his possessions and go wherever he pleases. Not one of our laws raises any obstacle or forbids it, if you are not satisfied with us or the city, if one of you wants to go and live in a colony or wants to go anywhere else and keep his property. We say, however, that whoever of you remains, when he sees how we conduct our trials and manage the city in other ways, has in fact come to an agreement with us to obey our instructions. We say that the one who disobeys does wrong in three ways, because in us he disobeys his parents, also those who brought him up, and because, in spite of his agreement, he neither obeys us nor, if we do something wrong, does he try to persuade us to do better. Yet we only propose things; we do not issue savage commands to do whatever we order. We give two alternatives, either to persuade us or to do what we say. He [who disobeys] does neither. We do say that you too, Socrates, are open to those charges if you do what you have in mind. You would be among, not the least, but the most guilty of the Athenians."

If I should say "Why so?," they might well be right to upbraid me and say that I am among the Athenians who most definitely came to that agreement with them. They might well say: "Socrates, we have convincing proofs that we and the city were congenial to you. You would not have dwelled here most consistently of all the Athenians if the city had not been exceedingly pleasing to you. You have never left the city, even to see a festival, nor for any other reason except military service; you have never gone to stay in any other city, as people do; you have had no desire to know another city or other laws. We and our city satisfied you. So decisively did you choose us and agree to be a citizen under us. Also, you have had children in this city, thus showing that it was congenial to you. Then at your trial you could have assessed your penalty at exile if you wished, and you are now attempting to do against the city's wishes what you could then have done with her consent. Then you prided yourself that you did not resent death, but you chose, as you said, death in preference to exile. Now, however, those words do not make you ashamed, and you pay no heed to us, the laws, as you plan to destroy us, and you act like the meanest type of slave by trying to run away, contrary to your commitments and your agreement to live as a citizen under us. First then, answer us on this very point, whether we speak the truth when we say that you agreed, not only in words but by your deeds, to live in accordance with us." What are we to say to that, Crito? Must we not agree?

CRITO: We must, Socrates.

SOCRATES: "Surely," they might say, "you are breaking the commitments and agreements that you made with us without compulsion or deceit, and under no pressure of time for deliberation. You have had seventy years during which you could have gone away if you did not like us, and if you thought our agreements unjust. You did not choose to go to Sparta or to Crete, which you are always saying are well governed, nor to any other city, Greek or foreign. You have been away from Athens less than the lame or the blind or other handicapped people. It is clear that the city has been outstandingly more congenial to you than to other Athenians, and so have we, the laws—for what city can please without laws? Will you then not now stick to our agreements? You will, Socrates, if we can persuade you, and not make yourself a laughingstock by leaving the city.

"For consider what good you will do yourself or your friends by breaking our agreements and committing such a wrong. It is pretty obvious that your friends will themselves be in danger of exile, disfranchisement, and loss of property. As for yourself, if you go to one of the nearby cities—Thebes or Megara, both are well governed—you will arrive as an enemy to their government; all who care for their city will look on you with suspicion, as a destroyer of the laws. You will also strengthen the conviction of the jury that they passed the right sentence on you, for anyone who destroys the laws could easily be thought to corrupt the young and the ignorant. Or will you avoid cities that are well governed and men who are civilized? If you do this, will your life be worth living? Will you have social intercourse with them and not be ashamed to talk to them? And what will you say? The same as you did here, that virtue and justice are man's most precious possessions, along with lawful behavior and the laws? Do you not think that Socrates would appear to be an unseemly kind of person? One must think so. Or will you leave those places and go to Crito's friends in Thessaly? There you will find the greatest license and disorder, and they may enjoy hearing from you how absurdly you escaped from prison in some disguise, in a leather jerkin or some other things in which escapees wrap themselves, thus altering your appearance. Will there be no one to say that you, likely to live but a short time more, were so greedy for life that you transgressed the most important laws? Possibly not, Socrates, if you do not annoy anyone; but if you do, many disgraceful things will be said about you.

"You will spend your time ingratiating yourself with all men, and be at their beck and call. What will you do in Thessaly but feast, as if you had gone to Thessaly to attend a banquet? As for those conversations of yours about justice and the rest of virtue, where will they be? You say you want to live for the sake of your children, that you may bring them up and educate them. How so? Will you bring them up and educate them by taking them to Thessaly and making strangers of them, that they may enjoy that too? Or not so, but they will be better brought up and educated here, while you are alive, though absent? Yes, your friends will look after them. Will they look after them if you go and live in Thessaly, but not if you go away to the underworld? If those who profess themselves your friends are any good at all, one must assume that they will.

"Be persuaded by us who have brought you up, Socrates. Do not value either your children or your life or anything else more than goodness, in order that when you arrive in Hades you may have all this as your defense before the rulers there. If you do this deed, it will not be better or more just or more pious for you here, nor for any one of your friends; nor will it be better for you when you arrive yonder. As it is, you depart, if you depart, after being wronged not by us, the laws, but by men. But if you depart after shamefully returning wrong for wrong and mistreatment for mistreatment, after breaking your agreements and commitments with us, after mistreating those you should mistreat least—yourself, your friends, your country, and us—we shall be angry with you while you are still alive; and our brothers, the laws of the underworld, will not receive you kindly, knowing that you tried to destroy us as far as you could. Do not let Crito persuade you, rather than us, to do what he says."

[CONCLUSION]

SOCRATES: Crito, my dear friend, be assured that these are the words I seem to hear, as the Corybants[4] seem to hear the music of their flutes, and the echo of these words resounds in me and makes it impossible for me to hear anything else. As far as my present beliefs go, if you speak in opposition to them, you will speak in vain. However, if you think you can accomplish anything, speak.

CRITO: I have nothing to say, Socrates.

SOCRATES: Let it be then, Crito, and let us act in this way, since this is the way the god is leading us.

---

[4]*Corybants:* priests of the fertility and nature goddess Cybele, whose worship involved frenzied dances. [D. C. ABEL]

Leviathan

Thomas Hobbes

Thomas Hobbes was born in Malmesbury, England, in 1588. He began his schooling at age four and enrolled in Oxford University when he was 14. Upon receiving his bachelor's degree in 1608, Hobbes began working as a private tutor, which remained his occupation for most of his life. After a trip to France and Italy in 1610, he studied classical Greek and Roman culture to gain a greater understanding of life. On a second journey to the Continent in 1629, Hobbes became convinced that all reality consists of matter in motion, and wondered if the powerful deductive method of geometry could be used to explain human nature and human society in terms of matter and motion. During a third trip to the Continent (1634–1637), his interest in philosophy and natural science was fueled by conversations with leading thinkers of the day, including Marin Mersenne, Pierre Gassendi, and Galileo. The England to which Hobbes returned was in political turmoil, and Hobbes, fearing that his political views might cost him his life, fled to France in 1640. During his 11-year exile in France, he worked on his project of explaining human social and political behavior as instances of matter in motion. After returning to England, Hobbes continued to write and publish. He died in 1679 in Derbyshire, England, at the age of 91.

Hobbes's main works are *De Cive* (in Latin, 1642; literally, "On the Citizen," but entitled *Philosophical Rudiments Concerning Government and Society* by Hobbes in his English translation, 1651); *De Corpore Politico* ("On the Body Politic," 1650); *Leviathan; or, The Matter, Form, and Power of a Commonwealth, Ecclesiastical and Civil* (1651); and *The Questions Concerning Liberty, Necessity, and Chance* (1656).

Our reading is from *Leviathan,* Hobbes's masterpiece of political philosophy. Hobbes begins by describing the "state of nature," the condition of human life before the formation of society and government. Each person tries to further his or her own interests by whatever means possible; there is a constant war of "every man against every man." Since there are no laws, there is no such thing as "justice" or "injustice." Life in the state of nature is "solitary, poor, nasty, brutish, and short." Hobbes goes on to explain that the "law of nature" dictates that people do whatever best preserves their lives. Because people in the state of nature would be more secure if they transferred (most of) their rights to a common power, the law of nature requires that they do so. This transferring of rights constitutes a "social contract" and is the foundation of society and government.

With the social contract, justice and injustice are born: To be just is to observe the contract, and to be unjust is to violate it. And justice will be assured only if the common power is a "leviathan"—a "mortal god" with absolute authority to force observance of the contract. According to Hobbes, "Covenants without the sword are but words." Only the terror of punishment by a power with absolute sovereignty will ensure justice and make life secure.

PART I. OF MAN

Chapter XIII. Of the Natural Condition of Mankind as Concerning Their Felicity and Misery

Nature has made men so equal in the faculties of the body and mind, as that though there be found one man sometimes manifestly stronger in body or of quicker mind than another, yet when all is reckoned together, the difference between man and man is not so considerable, as that one man can thereupon claim to himself any benefit to which another may not pretend,[1] as well as he. For as to the strength of body, the weakest has strength enough to kill the strongest, either by secret machination or by confederacy with others that are in the same danger with himself.

And as to the faculties of the mind, setting aside the arts grounded upon words—and especially that skill of proceeding upon general and infallible rules, called science, which very few have, and but in few things, as being not a native faculty born with us; nor attained, as prudence, while we look after somewhat[2] else—I find yet a greater equality among men than that of strength. For prudence is but experience, which equal time equally bestows on all men in those things they equally apply themselves unto. That which may perhaps make such equality incredible is but a vain conceit of one's own wisdom, which almost all men think they have in a greater degree than the vulgar—that is, than all men but themselves and a few others, whom by fame, or for concurring with themselves, they approve. For such is the nature of men, that howsoever they may acknowledge many others to be more witty or more eloquent or more learned, yet they will hardly believe there be many so wise as themselves; for they see their own wit at hand, and other men's at a distance. But this proves rather that men are in that point more equal than unequal. For there is not ordinarily a greater sign of the equal distribution of anything, than that every man is contented with his share.

From this equality of ability arises equality of hope in the attaining of our ends.[3] And therefore if any two men desire the same thing, which nevertheless they cannot both enjoy, they become enemies; and in the way to their end, which is principally their own conservation, and sometimes their delectation only, endeavor to destroy or subdue one another. And from hence it comes to pass that where an invader has no more to fear than another man's single power, if one plant, sow, build, or possess a convenient seat, others may probably be expected to come prepared with forces united to dispossess and deprive him, not only of the fruit of his labor, but also of his life or liberty. And the invader again is in the like danger of another.

And from this diffidence of one another, there is no way for any man to secure himself, so reasonable as anticipation—that is, by force or wiles to master the persons of all men he can, so long, till he see no other power great enough

---

[1]*pretend:* lay claim (to). [D. C. ABEL]
[2]*somewhat:* something. [D. C. ABEL]
[3]*ends:* goals. [D. C. ABEL]

to endanger him. And this is no more than his own conservation requires, and is generally allowed. Also because there be some, that taking pleasure in contemplating their own power in the acts of conquest, which they pursue farther than their security requires; if others, that otherwise would be glad to be at ease within modest bounds, should not by invasion increase their power, they would not be able, [for a] long time, by standing only on their defense, to subsist. And by consequence, such augmentation of dominion over men being necessary to a man's conservation, it ought to be allowed him.

Again, men have no pleasure, but on the contrary a great deal of grief, in keeping company where there is no power able to overawe them all. For every man looks that his companion should value him at the same rate he sets upon himself, and upon all signs of contempt or undervaluing naturally endeavors, as far as he dares (which among them that have no common power to keep them in quiet, is far enough to make them destroy each other), to extort a greater value from his contemners, by damage; and from others, by the example.

So that in the nature of man we find three principal causes of quarrel: first, competition; secondly, diffidence; thirdly, glory.

The first makes men invade for gain; the second, for safety; and the third, for reputation. The first use violence to make themselves masters of other men's persons, wives, children, and cattle; the second, to defend them; the third, for trifles, as a word, a smile, a different opinion, and any other sign of undervalue, either direct in their persons or by reflection in their kindred, their friends, their nation, their profession, or their name.

Hereby it is manifest that during the time men live without a common power to keep them all in awe, they are in that condition which is called *war;* and such a war, as is of every man against every man. For war consists not in battle only, or the act of fighting; but in a tract of time where the will to contend by battle is sufficiently known; and therefore the notion of *time* is to be considered in the nature of war, as it is in the nature of weather. For as the nature of foul weather lies not in a shower or two of rain, but in an inclination thereto of many days together; so the nature of war consists not in actual fighting, but in the known disposition thereto, during all the time there is no assurance to the contrary. All other time is *peace.*

Whatsoever therefore is consequent to a time of war, where every man is enemy to every man; the same is consequent to the time wherein men live without other security than what their own strength and their own invention shall furnish them withal.[4] In such condition, there is no place for industry,[5] because the fruit thereof is uncertain, and consequently no culture[6] of the earth; no navigation nor use of the commodities that may be imported by sea; no commodious building; no instruments of moving and removing such things as require much force; no knowledge of the face of the earth; no account of time; no arts; no letters; no society; and, which is worst of all, continual fear and danger of violent death; and the life of man, solitary, poor, nasty, brutish, and short.

---

[4]*withal:* with. [D. C. ABEL]
[5]*industry:* systematic labor. [D. C. ABEL]
[6]*culture:* cultivation. [D. C. ABEL]

It may seem strange to some man that has not well weighed these things, that nature should thus dissociate and render men apt to invade and destroy one another; and he may therefore, not trusting to this inference made from the passions, desire perhaps to have the same confirmed by experience. Let him therefore consider with himself, when taking a journey, he arms himself and seeks to go well accompanied; when going to sleep, he locks his doors; when even in his house he locks his chests; and this when he knows there be laws and public officers, armed, to revenge all injuries shall be done him; what opinion he has of his fellow subjects, when he rides armed; of his fellow citizens, when he locks his doors; and of his children and servants, when he locks his chests. Does he not there as much accuse mankind by his actions, as I do by my words? But neither of us accuse man's nature in it. The desires and other passions of man are in themselves no sin. No more are the actions that proceed from those passions, till they know a law that forbids them; which, till laws be made, they cannot know; nor can any law be made, till they have agreed upon the person that shall make it.

It may peradventure[7] be thought, there was never such a time nor condition of war as this; and I believe it was never generally so, over all the world. But there are many places where they live so now. For the savage people in many places of America, except the government of small families, the concord whereof depends on natural lust, have no government at all and live at this day in that brutish manner. . . . It may be perceived what manner of life there would be, where there were no common power to fear, by the manner of life which men that have formerly lived under a peaceful government use[8] to degenerate into in a civil war.

But though there had never been any time wherein particular men were in a condition of war one against another; yet in all times, kings and persons of sovereign authority, because of their independency, are in continual jealousies and in the state and posture of gladiators, having their weapons pointing and their eyes fixed on one another; that is, their forts, garrisons, and guns upon the frontiers of their kingdoms, and continual spies upon their neighbors—which is a posture of war. But because they uphold thereby the industry of their subjects, there does not follow from it that misery which accompanies the liberty of particular men.

To this war of every man against every man, this also is consequent, that nothing can be unjust. The notions of right and wrong, justice and injustice, have there no place. Where there is no common power, there is no law; where no law, no injustice. Force and fraud are in war the two cardinal virtues. Justice and injustice are none of the faculties neither of the body nor mind. If they were, they might be in a man that were alone in the world, as well as his senses and passions. They are qualities that relate to men in society, not in solitude. It is consequent also to the same condition that there be no propriety, no dominion, no *mine* and *yours* distinct, but only that to be every man's, that he can get, and for so long as he can keep it. And thus much for the ill condition which man by

---

[7]*peradventure:* perhaps. [D. C. ABEL]
[8]*use:* are accustomed. [D. C. ABEL]

mere nature is actually placed in—though with a possibility to come out of it, consisting partly in the passions, partly in his reason.

The passions that incline men to peace are fear of death, desire of such things as are necessary to commodious living, and a hope by their industry to obtain them. And reason suggests convenient articles of peace, upon which men may be drawn to agreement. These articles are they which otherwise are called the laws of nature, whereof I shall speak more particularly in the two following chapters.

Chapter XIV. Of the First and Second Natural Laws, and of Contracts

The *right of nature,* which writers commonly call *jus naturale,*[9] is the liberty each man has to use his own power as he will himself, for the preservation of his own nature, that is to say, of his own life; and consequently of doing anything which, in his own judgment and reason, he shall conceive to be the aptest means thereunto.

By *liberty* is understood, according to the proper signification of the word, the absence of external impediments, which impediments may often take away part of a man's power to do what he would, but cannot hinder him from using the power left him, according as his judgment and reason shall dictate to him.

A *law of nature, lex naturalis,*[10] is a precept or general rule found out by reason, by which a man is forbidden to do that which is destructive of his life or [to] take away the means of preserving the same, and to omit that by which he thinks it may be best preserved. For though they that speak of this subject use to confound *jus* and *lex, right* and *law,* yet they ought to be distinguished because *right* consists in liberty to do or to forbear, whereas *law* determines and binds to one of them—so that law and right differ as much as obligation and liberty, which in one and the same matter are inconsistent.

And because the condition of man, as has been declared in the precedent chapter, is a condition of war of everyone against everyone, in which case everyone is governed by his own reason; and there is nothing he can make use of, that may not be a help unto him, in preserving his life against his enemies; it follows that in such a condition every man has a right to every thing, even to one another's body. And therefore, as long as this natural right of every man to everything endures, there can be no security to any man, how strong or wise soever he be, of living out the time which nature ordinarily allows men to live. And consequently it is a precept, or general rule of reason, *that every man ought to endeavor peace, as far as he has hope of obtaining it; and when he cannot obtain it, that he may seek and use all helps, and advantages of war.* The first branch of which rule contains the first and fundamental law of nature, which is *to seek peace and follow it.* The second, the sum of the right of nature, which is *by all means we can, to defend ourselves.*

From this fundamental law of nature, by which men are commanded to endeavor peace, is derived this second law: *that a man be willing, when others are so too, as farforth as for peace and defense of himself he shall think it necessary, to lay*

---

[9]*jus naturale:* (Latin) natural right. [D. C. ABEL]
[10]*lex naturalis:* (Latin) natural law. [D. C. ABEL]

down this right to all things; and be contented with so much liberty against other men, as he would allow other men against himself. For as long as every man holds this right of doing anything he likes, so long are all men in the condition of war. But if other men will not lay down their right, as well as he, then there is no reason for anyone to divest himself of his; for that were to expose himself to prey, which no man is bound to, rather than to dispose himself to peace. . . .

To lay down a man's right to anything is to divest himself of the liberty of hindering another of the benefit of his own right to the same. For he that renounces or passes away his right, gives not to any other man a right which he had not before, because there is nothing to which every man had not right by nature: but only stands out of his way, that he may enjoy his own original right without hindrance from him; not without hindrance from another. So that the effect which redounds to one man by another man's defect of right, is but so much diminution of impediments to the use of his own right original.

Right is laid aside, either by simply renouncing it or by transferring it to another—by simply *renouncing,* when he cares not to whom the benefit thereof redounds; by *transferring,* when he intends the benefit thereof to some certain person or persons. . . .

Whensoever a man transfers his right or renounces it, it is either in consideration of some right reciprocally transferred to himself, or for some other good he hopes for thereby. For it is a voluntary act; and of the voluntary acts of every man, the object is some good to himself. And therefore there be some rights which no man can be understood by any words or other signs to have abandoned or transferred. As first a man cannot lay down the right of resisting them that assault him by force to take away his life, because he cannot be understood to aim thereby at any good to himself. The same may be said of wounds and chains and imprisonment; both because there is no benefit conse-quent to such patience,[11] as there is to the patience of suffering[12] another to be wounded or imprisoned; as also because a man cannot tell, when he sees men proceed against him by violence, whether they intend his death or not. And lastly, the motive and end for which this renouncing and transferring of right is introduced, is nothing else but the security of a man's person in his life and in the means of so preserving life, as not to be weary of it. And therefore if a man by words or other signs seem to despoil himself of the end for which those signs were intended, he is not to be understood as if he meant it or that it was his will, but that he was ignorant of how such words and actions were to be interpreted.

The mutual transferring of right is that which men call *contract.*

There is difference between transferring of right to the thing and transferring, or tradition, that is delivery of the thing itself. For the thing may be delivered together with the translation[13] of the right, as in buying and selling with ready money, or exchange of goods or lands; and it may be delivered sometime after.

Again, one of the contractors may deliver the thing contracted for on his part and leave the other to perform his part at some determinate time after, and

---

[11]*patience:* the enduring of something. [D. C. ABEL]
[12]*suffering:* allowing. [D. C. ABEL]
[13]*translation:* transferring. [D. C. ABEL]

in the meantime be trusted; and then the contract on his part is called *pact* or *covenant;* or both parts may contract now, to perform hereafter—in which cases, he that is to perform in time to come, being trusted, his performance is called *keeping of promise* or *faith;* and the failing of performance, if it be voluntary, *violation of faith.* . . .

If a covenant be made wherein neither of the parties perform presently, but trust one another; in the condition of mere nature, which is a condition of war of every man against every man, upon any reasonable suspicion, it is void. But if there be a common power set over them both, with right and force sufficient to compel performance, it is not void. For he that performs first has no assurance the other will perform after, because the bonds of words are too weak to bridle men's ambition, avarice, anger, and other passions, without the fear of some coercive power; which in the condition of mere nature, where all men are equal and judges of the justness[14] of their own fears, cannot possibly be supposed. And therefore he which performs first, does but betray himself to his enemy—contrary to the right, [which] he can never abandon, of defending his life and means of living.

But in a civil estate, where there is a power set up to constrain those that would otherwise violate their faith, that fear is no more reasonable; and for that cause, he which by the covenant is to perform first, is obliged so to do.

The cause of fear, which makes such a covenant invalid, must be always something arising after the covenant made, as some new fact or other sign of the will not to perform; else it cannot make the covenant void. For that which could not hinder a man from promising, ought not to be admitted as a hindrance of performing. . . .

Chapter XV. Of Other Laws of Nature

From that law of nature by which we are obliged to transfer to another such rights, as being retained, hinder the peace of mankind, there follows a third, which is this, *that men perform their covenants made*—without which, covenants are in vain and but empty words; and the right of all men to all things remaining, we are still in the condition of war.

And in this law of nature consists the fountain and original[15] of *justice.* For where no covenant has preceded, there has no right been transferred, and every man has right to every thing; and consequently no action can be unjust. But when a covenant is made, then to break it is *unjust;* and the definition of *injustice* is no other than *the nonperformance of covenant.* And whatsoever is not unjust, is *just.*

But because covenants of mutual trust, where there is a fear of nonperformance on either part, as has been said in the former chapter, are invalid, though the original of justice be the making of covenants; yet injustice actually there can be none, till the cause of such fear be taken away—which, while men are in the natural condition of war, cannot be done. Therefore before the names of *just* and *unjust* can have place, there must be some coercive power to compel men

---

[14]*justness:* reasonableness. [D. C. ABEL]
[15]*original:* origin. [D. C. ABEL]

equally to the performance of their covenants, by the terror of some punishment greater than the benefit they expect by the breach of their covenant; and to make good that propriety[16] which by mutual contract men acquire in recompense of the universal right they abandon—and such power there is none before the erection of a commonwealth. And this is also to be gathered out of the ordinary definition of justice in the schools, for they say that *justice is the constant will of giving to every man his own.* And therefore where there is no *own,* that is, no propriety, there is no injustice; and where there is no coercive power erected, that is, where there is no commonwealth, there is no propriety, all men having right to all things. Therefore where there is no commonwealth, there nothing is unjust— so that the nature of justice consists in keeping of valid covenants. But the validity of covenants begins not but with the constitution of a civil power, sufficient to compel men to keep them; and then it is also that propriety begins. . . .

And though this may seem too subtle a deduction of the laws of nature to be taken notice of by all men (whereof the most part are too busy in getting food, and the rest too negligent to understand), yet to leave all men inexcusable, they have been contracted into one easy sum, intelligible even to the meanest capacity, and that is: *Do not that to another, which you would not have done to yourself*—which shows him that he has no more to do in learning the laws of nature but, when weighing the actions of other men with his own, [and] they seem too heavy, to put them into the other part of the balance, and his own into their place, that his own passions and self-love may add nothing to the weight. And then there is none of these laws of nature that will not appear unto him very reasonable. . . .

PART II. OF COMMONWEALTH

Chapter XVII. Of the Causes, Generation, and Definition of a Commonwealth

The final cause,[17] end, or design of men, who naturally love liberty and dominion over others, in the introduction of that restraint upon themselves, in which we see them live in commonwealths, is the foresight of their own preservation and of a more contented life thereby—that is to say, of getting themselves out from that miserable condition of war, which is necessarily consequent, as has been shown in Chapter XIII, to the natural passions of men, when there is no visible power to keep them in awe and tie them by fear of punishment to the performance of their covenants and observation of those laws of nature set down in the fourteenth and fifteenth chapters.

For the laws of nature, as *justice, equity, modesty, mercy,* and, in sum, *doing to others as we would be done to,* of themselves, without the terror of some power to cause them to be observed, are contrary to our natural passions that carry us to partiality, pride, revenge, and the like. And covenants without the sword are but words, and of no strength to secure a man at all. Therefore notwithstanding the laws of nature, which everyone has then kept, when he has the will to keep

---

[16]*propriety:* private ownership; proprietorship. [D. C. ABEL]
[17]*final cause:* the purpose (end, goal) for which something is done. [D. C. ABEL]

them, when he can do it safely, if there be no power erected, or not great enough for our security; every man will, and may lawfully, rely on his own strength and art for caution against all other men. And in all places where men have lived by small families, to rob and spoil one another has been a trade, and [one that was] so far from being reputed against the law of nature, that the greater spoils they gained, the greater was their honor; and men observed no other laws therein but the laws of honor—that is, to abstain from cruelty, leaving to men their lives and instruments of husbandry.[18] And as small families did then, so now do cities and kingdoms (which are but greater families), for their own security, enlarge their dominions upon all pretenses of danger and fear of invasion, or assistance that may be given to invaders, and endeavor, as much as they can, to subdue or weaken their neighbors by open force and secret arts, for want of other caution, justly—and are remembered for it in after ages with honor. . . .

The only way to erect . . . a common power as may be able to defend [human beings] from the invasion of foreigners and the injuries of one another, and thereby to secure them in such sort, as that by their own industry and by the fruits of the earth they may nourish themselves and live contentedly, is to confer all their power and strength upon one man, or upon one assembly of men, that may reduce all their wills, by plurality of voices, unto one will—which is as much as to say, to appoint one man, or assembly of men, to bear their person; and everyone to own[19] and acknowledge himself to be author of whatsoever he that so bears their person shall act, or cause to be acted, in those things which concern the common peace and safety; and therein to submit their wills, every-one to his will, and their judgments to his judgment. This is more than consent or concord; it is a real unity of them all in one and the same person, made by covenant of every man with every man, in such manner as if every man should say to every man, *I authorize and give up my right of governing myself to this man, or to this assembly of men, on this condition, that you give up your right to him and authorize all his actions in like manner.* This done, the multitude so united in one person is called a *commonwealth,* in Latin *civitas.* This is the generation of that great *leviathan* or rather, to speak more reverently, of that *mortal god,* to which we owe under the *immortal God* our peace and defense. For by this authority, given him by every particular man in the commonwealth, he has the use of so much power and strength conferred on him, that by terror thereof he is enabled to perform the wills of them all, to peace at home and mutual aid against their enemies abroad. And in him consists the essence of the commonwealth, which, to define it, is *one person, of whose acts a great multitude, by mutual covenants one with another, have made themselves every one the author, to the end he may use the strength and means of them all, as he shall think expedient, for their peace and common defense.*

And he that carries this person is called *sovereign* and [is] said to have *sovereign power;* and everyone besides, his *subject.*

---

[18]*husbandry:* agriculture. [D. C. ABEL]
[19]*Own:* accept. [D. C. ABEL]

The Second Treatise of Government

John Locke

A biography of John Locke appears on p. 155.

This reading is from Locke's *Second Treatise of Government,* the treatise following the one in which he criticizes Robert Filmer's defense of the divine right of kings. Locke begins the *Second Treatise* by describing the "state of nature"—the condition that human beings are in before there is any government. People are free to do whatever they wish, provided their actions do not violate the "law of nature." The law of nature forbids harming others or taking their property, except as a way of punishing those who have broken the law of nature. (According to Locke, any transgressor of the law of nature may be punished by anyone.) Positively, the law of nature requires that a person preserve his or her own life and (except when doing so conflicts with self-preservation) the lives of others. People remain in this state of nature "till by their own consents they make themselves members of some politic society."

Political society arises when, through a "social contract," individuals transfer to the community their power to punish transgressors of the law of nature. Members of the community agree to abide by the decisions of the majority. The primary motive for people forming a political society, Locke explains, is to establish a fairer and more reliable way of preserving their property. Anticipating the objection that most people are born into a political society and do not formally enter into a social contract, Locke explains that consent can be tacit as well as explicit. In the final section, he shows how a social contract can be dissolved from without, by foreign conquest, or from within, when the rulers alter the legislature or abuse "the lives, liberties, or fortunes of the people."

CHAPTER II. OF THE STATE OF NATURE

To understand political power aright and derive it from its original,[1] we must consider what state all men are naturally in, and that is a state of perfect freedom to order their actions and dispose of their possessions and persons as they think fit, within the bounds of the law of nature, without asking leave or depending upon the will of any other man.

A state also of equality, wherein all the power and jurisdiction is reciprocal, no one having more than another—there being nothing more evident than that creatures of the same species and rank, promiscuously[2] born to all the same advantages of nature and the use of the same faculties, should also be equal one among another without subordination or subjection, unless the lord and master of them all should, by any manifest declaration of his will, set one above another and confer on him, by an evident and clear appointment, an undoubted right to dominion and sovereignty. . . .

---

[1]*original:* origin. [D. C. ABEL]
[2]*promiscuously:* diversely. [D. C. ABEL]

But though this be a state of *liberty*, yet it is not a state of *license*. Though man in that state have an uncontrollable liberty to dispose of his person or possessions, yet he has not liberty to destroy himself, or so much as any creature in his possession, but where some nobler use than its bare preservation calls for it. The state of nature has a law of nature to govern it, which obliges everyone. And reason, which is that law, teaches all mankind, who will but consult it, that being all equal and independent, no one ought to harm another in his life, health, liberty, or possessions. For men, being all the workmanship of one omnipotent and infinitely wise maker, all the servants of one sovereign master, sent into the world by his order, and about his business—they are his property, whose workmanship they are, made to last during his, not one another's pleasure. And being furnished with like faculties, sharing all in one community of nature, there cannot be supposed any such subordination among us that may authorize us to destroy one another, as if we were made for one another's uses, as the inferior ranks of creatures are for ours. Everyone, as he is bound to preserve himself and not to quit[3] his station willfully, so by the like reason, when his own preservation comes not in competition, ought he, as much as he can, to preserve the rest of mankind and may not, unless it be to do justice on an offender, take away or impair the life, or what tends to the preservation of the life, the liberty, health, limb, or goods of another.

And that all men may be restrained from invading others' rights and from doing hurt to one another, and the law of nature be observed, which wills the peace and preservation of all mankind, the execution of the law of nature is, in that state, put into every man's hands, whereby everyone has a right to punish the transgressors of that law to such a degree as may hinder its violation. For the law of nature would, as all other laws that concern men in this world, be in vain if there were nobody that in the state of nature had a power to execute that law and thereby preserve the innocent and restrain offenders. And if *anyone* in the state of nature may punish another for any evil he has done, *everyone* may do so. For in that state of perfect equality where naturally there is no superiority or jurisdiction of one over another, what any may do in prosecution of that law, everyone must needs[4] have a right to do.

And thus, in the state of nature one man comes by a power over another, but yet no absolute or arbitrary power to use[5] a criminal, when he has got him in his hands, according to the passionate heats or boundless extravagancy of his own will; but only to retribute to him, so far as calm reason and conscience dictate, what is proportionate to his transgression, which is so much as may serve for reparation and restrain—for these two are the only reasons why one man may lawfully do harm to another, which is that we call *punishment*. In transgressing the law of nature, the offender declares himself to live by another rule than that of reason and common equity, which is that measure God has set to the actions of men for their mutual security. And so he becomes dangerous to mankind— the tie which is to secure them from injury and violence being slighted and

---

[3]*quit:* depart from. [D. C. ABEL]
[4]*needs:* necessarily. [D. C. ABEL]
[5]*use:* treat. [D. C. ABEL]

broken by him: which being a trespass against the whole species and the peace and safety of it, provided for by the law of nature, every man upon this score, by the right he has to preserve mankind in general, may restrain—or where it is necessary, destroy—things noxious to them, and so may bring such evil on anyone who has transgressed that law, as may make him repent the doing of it and thereby deter him, and by his example others, from doing the like mischief. And in this case and upon this ground, every man has a right to punish the offender and be executioner of the law of nature. . . .

Besides the crime which consists in violating the law and varying from the right rule of reason, whereby a man so far becomes degenerate and declares himself to quit the principles of human nature and to be a noxious creature, there is commonly injury done to some person or other, and some other man receives damage by his transgression; in which case he who has received any damage, has, besides the right of punishment common to him with other men, a particular right to seek reparation from him that has done it. And any other person who finds it just may also join with him that is injured and assist him in recovering from the offender so much as may make satisfaction for the harm he has suffered.

From these two distinct rights, the one of *punishing* the crime for restraint and preventing the like offense, which right of punishing is in everybody, the other of *taking reparation,* which belongs only to the injured party, comes it to pass that the magistrate, who by being magistrate has the common right of punishing put into his hands, can often, where the public good demands not the execution of the law, remit the punishment of criminal offenses by his own authority, but yet cannot remit the satisfaction due to any private man for the damage he has received. That [satisfaction], he who has suffered the damage has a right to demand in his own name, and he alone can remit. The damnified[6] person has this power of appropriating to himself the goods or service of the offender by right of self-preservation, as every man has a power to punish the crime, to prevent its being committed again, by the right he has of preserving all mankind and doing all reasonable things he can in order to that end. And thus it is, that every man in the state of nature has a power to kill a murderer, both to deter others from doing the like injury, which no reparation can compensate, by the example of the punishment that attends it from everybody; and also to secure men from the attempts of a criminal, who having renounced reason (the common rule and measure God has given to mankind), has, by the unjust violence and slaughter he has committed upon one, declared war against all mankind and therefore may be destroyed as a lion or a tiger, one of those wild savage beasts with whom men can have no society nor security. And upon this is grounded that great law of nature, "Whoso sheds man's blood, by man shall his blood be shed." And Cain was so fully convinced that everyone had a right to destroy such a criminal, that after the murder of his brother, he cries out, "Everyone that finds me shall slay me"[7]—so plain was it writ in the hearts of all mankind.

---

[6]*damnified:* having suffered damage. [D. C. ABEL]
[7]Genesis 4:14. [D. C. ABEL]

By the same reason may a man in the state of nature *punish the lesser breaches* of that law. It will perhaps be demanded,[8] with death? I answer, each transgression may be punished to that degree, and with so much severity, as will suffice to make it an ill bargain to the offender, give him cause to repent, and terrify others from doing the like. . . .

It is often asked as a mighty objection, "Where are, or ever were there, any men in such a state of nature?" To which it may suffice as an answer at present, that since all princes and rulers of independent governments all through the world are in a state of nature, it is plain the world never was, nor ever will be, without numbers of men in that state. I have named all governors of independent communities, whether they are or are not in league with others—for it is not every compact that puts an end to the state of nature between men, but only this one of agreeing together mutually to enter into one community and make one body politic. Other promises and compacts men may make one with another, and yet still be in the state of nature. The promises and bargains for truck,[9] and so on, between the two men in the desert[10] island, mentioned by Garcilaso de la Vega[11] in his history of Peru, or between a Swiss and an Indian in the woods of America, are binding to them, though they are perfectly in a state of nature, in reference to one another—for truth and keeping of faith belongs to men as men, and not as members of society.

To those that say, there were never any men in the state of nature, I . . . affirm that all men are naturally in that state and remain so, till by their own consents they make themselves members of some politic society. . . .

CHAPTER V. OF PROPERTY

Whether we consider natural *reason,* which tells us that men, being once born, have a right to their preservation, and consequently to meat and drink and such other things as nature affords for their subsistence; or *revelation,* which gives us an account of those grants God made of the world to Adam and to Noah and his sons, it is very clear that God, as King David says (Psalms 115:16), "has given the earth to the children of men"—given it to mankind in common. . . .

God, who has given the world to men in common, has also given them reason to make use of it to the best advantage of life, and convenience. The earth and all that is therein is given to men for the support and comfort of their being. And though all the fruits it naturally produces and beasts it feeds belong to mankind in common, as they are produced by the spontaneous hand of nature; and nobody has originally a private dominion, exclusive of the rest of mankind, in any of them, as they are thus in their natural state: yet being given for the use of men, there must of necessity be a means to appropriate them some way or other, before they can be of any use or at all beneficial to any particular man. The

---

[8]*demanded:* asked. [D. C. ABEL]
[9]*truck:* barter. [D. C. ABEL]
[10]*desert:* desolate. [D. C. ABEL]
[11]Garcilaso de la Vega (1539–1616) was a Spanish (Peruvian-born) historian. [D. C. ABEL]

fruit or venison which nourishes the wild Indian, who knows no enclosure and is still a tenant in common, must be his, and so his (that is, a part of him) that another can no longer have any right to it, before it can do him any good for the support of his life.

Though the earth and all inferior creatures be common to all men, yet every man has a property in his own person—this nobody has any right to but himself. The labor of his body and the work of his hands, we may say, are properly his. Whatsoever then he removes out of the state that nature has provided and left it in, he has mixed his labor with, and joined to it something that is his own, and thereby makes it his property. It being by him removed from the common state nature has placed it in, it has by this labor something annexed to it that excludes the common right of other men. For this labor being the unquestionable property of the laborer, no man but he can have a right to what that is once joined to, at least where there is enough, and as good, left in common for others.

He that is nourished by the acorns he picked up under an oak, or the apples he gathered from the trees in the wood, has certainly appropriated them to himself. Nobody can deny but the nourishment is his. I ask then, when did they begin to be his? When he digested? or when he ate? or when he boiled? or when he brought them home? or when he picked them up? And it is plain, if the first gathering made them not his, nothing else could. That labor put a distinction between them and common; that added something to them more than nature, the common mother of all, had done—and so they became his private right. And will anyone say he had no right to those acorns or apples he thus appropriated because he had not the consent of all mankind to make them his? Was it a robbery thus to assume to himself what belonged to all in common? If such a consent as that was necessary, man had starved, notwithstanding the plenty God had given him. We see in commons, which remain so by compact, that it is the taking any part of what is common and removing it out of the state nature leaves it in, which begins the property; without which the common is of no use. And the taking of this or that part does not depend on the express consent of all the commoners. Thus the grass my horse has bit, the turfs my servant has cut, and the ore I have dug in any place, where I have a right to them in common with others, become my property, without the assignation or consent of anybody. The labor that was mine, removing them out of that common state they were in, has fixed my property in them. . . .

CHAPTER VII. OF POLITICAL OR CIVIL SOCIETY

. . . Man being born (as has been proved) with a title to perfect freedom and an uncontrolled enjoyment of all the rights and privileges of the law of nature, equally with any other man or number of men in the world, has by nature a power not only to preserve his property—that is, his life, liberty, and estate—against the injuries and attempts of other men, but [also] to judge of and punish the breaches of that law in others, as he is persuaded the offense deserves, even with death itself, in crimes where the heinousness of the fact, in his opinion, requires it. But because no political society can be nor subsist without having in itself the power to preserve the property, and in order thereunto, punish the offenses of all those of that society—there, and there only, is political society, where every one of the members has quitted[12] this natural power, resigned it up into the hand of the community in all cases that exclude him not from appealing for protection to the law established by it. And thus all private judgment of every particular member being excluded, the community comes to be umpire by settled standing rules, indifferent and the same to all parties; and by men having authority from the community for the execution of those rules, decides all the differences that may happen between any members of that society concerning any matter of right; and punishes those offenses which any member has committed against the society, with such penalties as the law has established. Whereby it is easy to discern who are, and who are not, in political society together. Those who are united into one body and have a common established law and judicature to appeal to, with authority to decide controversies between them and punish offenders, are in civil society one with another. But those who have no such common people (I mean on earth) are still in the state of nature, each being, where there is no other, judge for himself and executioner—which is, as I have before showed it, the perfect state of nature.

And thus the commonwealth comes by a power to set down what punishment shall belong to the several transgressions which they think worthy of it, committed among the members of that society (which is the *power of making laws*), as well as it has the power to punish any injury done unto any of its members by anyone that is not of it (which is the *power of war and peace*), and all this for the preservation of the property of all the members of that society, as far as it is possible. But though every man who has entered into civil society and is become a member of any commonwealth, has thereby quitted his power to punish offenses against the law of nature in prosecution of his own private judgment; yet with the judgment of offenses, which he has given up to the legislative[13] in all cases where he can appeal to the magistrate, he has given a right to the commonwealth to employ his force for the execution of the judgments of the commonwealth, whenever he shall be called to it—which indeed are his own judgments, they being made by himself or his representative. And herein we have the original of the legislative and executive power of civil society, which is to judge by standing laws how far offenses are to be punished when committed within the commonwealth; and also to determine, by occasional judgments founded on the present circumstances of the fact, how far injuries from without are to be vindicated; and in both these to employ all the force of all the members when there shall be need.

Wherever, therefore, any number of men are so united into one society as to quit everyone his executive power of the law of nature and to resign it to the public, there and there only is a political, or civil, society. And this is done wherever any number of men in the state of nature enter into society to make one people, one body politic, under one supreme government; or else when anyone joins himself to, and incorporates with, any government already made. For

---

[12]*quitted:* relinquished. [D. C. ABEL]
[13]*legislative:* legislature. [D. C. ABEL]

hereby he authorizes the society or (which is all one) the legislative thereof to make laws for him, as the public good of the society shall require—to the execution whereof, his own assistance (as to his own decrees) is due. And this puts men out of the state of nature into that of a *commonwealth,* by setting up a judge on earth with authority to determine all the controversies and redress the injuries that may happen to any member of the commonwealth; which judge is the legislative, or magistrates appointed by it. And wherever there are any number of men, however associated, that have no such decisive power to appeal to, there they are still in the state of nature. . . .

CHAPTER VIII. OF THE BEGINNING OF POLITICAL SOCIETIES

Men being, as has been said, by nature all free, equal, and independent, no one can be put out of this estate and subjected to the political power of another without his own consent. The only way whereby anyone divests himself of his natural liberty and puts on the bonds of civil society is by agreeing with other men to join and unite into a community, for their comfortable, safe, and peaceable living one among another in a secure enjoyment of their properties and a greater security against any that are not of it. This any number of men may do, because it injures not the freedom of the rest; they are left as they were in the liberty of the state of nature. When any number of men have so consented to make one community or government, they are thereby presently incorporated and make *one body politic,* wherein the majority have a right to act and conclude[14] the rest.

For when any number of men have, by the consent of every individual, made a community, they have thereby made that community one body, with a power to act as one body, which is only by the will and determination of the majority. For that which acts[15] any community, being only the consent of the individuals of it, and it being necessary to that which is one body to move one way, it is necessary the body should move that way whither the greater force carries it, which is the *consent of the majority*—or else it is impossible it should act or continue one body, one community, which the consent of every individual that united into it agreed that it should. And so everyone is bound by that consent to be concluded by the majority. And therefore we see that in assemblies empowered to act by positive laws, where no number is set by that positive law which empowers them, the act of the majority passes for the act of the whole and of course determines, as having by the law of nature and reason, the power of the whole.

And thus every man, by consenting with others to make one body politic under one government, puts himself under an obligation to everyone of that society to submit to the determination of the majority and to be concluded by it; or else this original compact, whereby he with others incorporates into one society, would signify nothing and be no compact, if he be left free and under no other ties than he was in before in the state of nature. For what appearance would there be of any compact? What new engagement if he were no farther tied by

---

[14]*conclude:* bind, oblige. [D. C. ABEL]
[15]*acts:* actuates; moves to action. [D. C. ABEL]

any decrees of the society than he himself thought fit and did actually consent to? This would be still as great a liberty as he himself had before his compact, or anyone else in the state of nature has, who may submit himself and consent to any acts of it if he thinks fit. . . .

Every man being, as has been showed, naturally free, and nothing being able to put him into subjection to any earthly power but only his own *consent;* it is to be considered what shall be understood to be a sufficient declaration of a man's consent, to make him subject to the laws of any government. There is a common distinction of an *express* and *tacit* consent, which will concern our present case. Nobody doubts but an express consent of any man entering into any society makes him a perfect member of that society, a subject of that government. The difficulty is what ought to be looked upon as a tacit consent and how far it binds—that is, how far anyone shall be looked on to have consented and thereby submitted to any government, where he has made no expressions of it at all. And to this I say that every man that has any possessions or enjoyment of any part of the dominions of any government, does thereby give his tacit consent and is as far forth obliged to obedience to the laws of that government, during such enjoyment, as anyone under it—whether this his possession be of land to him and his heirs forever, or a lodging only for a week, or whether it be barely traveling freely on the highway. And in effect, [this consent] reaches as far as the very being of anyone within the territories of that government. . . .

CHAPTER IX. OF THE ENDS[16] OF POLITICAL SOCIETY AND GOVERNMENT

If man in the state of nature be so free, as has been said; if he be absolute lord of his own person and possessions, equal to the greatest, and subject to nobody, why will he part with his freedom? Why will he give up this empire and subject himself to the dominion and control of any other power? To which it is obvious to answer that though in the state of nature he has such a right, yet the enjoyment of it is very uncertain and constantly exposed to the invasion of others. For all being kings as much as he, every man his equal, and the greater part no strict observers of equity and justice, the enjoyment of the property he has in this state is very unsafe, very unsecure. This makes him willing to quit a condition which, however free, is full of fears and continual dangers—and it is not without reason that he seeks out and is willing to join in society with others who are already united, or have a mind to unite, for the mutual preservation of their lives, liberties, and estates, which I call by the general name *property.*

The great and chief end, therefore, of men's uniting into commonwealths and putting themselves under government is the preservation of their property. To which in the state of nature there are many things wanting:

First, there wants[17] an established, settled, known law, received and allowed by common consent to be the standard of right and wrong, and the common

---

[16]*ends:* purposes, goals. [D. C. ABEL]
[17]*wants:* is lacking. [D. C. ABEL]

measure to decide all controversies between them. For though the law of nature be plain and intelligible to all rational creatures, yet men being biased by their interest, as well as ignorant for want of study of it, are not apt to allow of it as a law binding to them in the application of it to their particular cases.

Secondly, in the state of nature there wants a known and indifferent judge with authority to determine all differences according to the established law. For everyone in that state being both judge and executioner of the law of nature, men being partial to themselves, passion and revenge is very apt to carry them too far, and with too much heat, in their *own* cases—as well as negligence and unconcernedness, to make them too remiss in *other men's*.

Thirdly, in the state of nature there often wants power to back and support the sentence when right, and to give it due execution. They who by any injustice offended, will seldom fail, where they are able, by force to make good their injustice. Such resistance many times makes the punishment dangerous, and frequently destructive, to those who attempt it.

Thus mankind, notwithstanding all the privileges of the state of nature, being but in an ill condition while they remain in it, are quickly driven into society. Hence it comes to pass that we seldom find any number of men live any time together in this state. The inconveniences that they are therein exposed to by the irregular and uncertain exercise of the power every man has of punishing the transgressions of others, make them take sanctuary under the established laws of government and therein seek the preservation of their property. It is this [that] makes them so willingly give up every one his single power of punishing, to be exercised by such alone, as shall be appointed to it among them; and by such rules as the community, or those authorized by them to that purpose, shall agree on. And in this we have the original right and rise of both the legislative and executive power as well as of the governments and societies themselves.

For in the state of nature (to omit[18] the liberty he has of innocent delights) a man has two powers:

The first is to do whatsoever he thinks fit for the preservation of himself and others within the permission of the law of nature—by which law, common to them all, he and all the rest of mankind are one community, make up one society, distinct from all other creatures. And were it not for the corruption and viciousness of degenerate men, there would be no need of any other—no necessity that men should separate from this great and natural community, and by positive agreements combine into smaller and divided associations.

The other power a man has in the state of nature is the power to punish the crimes committed against that law. Both these he gives up when he joins in a private (if I may so call it) or particular politic society and incorporates into any commonwealth, separate from the rest of mankind.

The first power—namely, of doing whatsoever he thought for the preservation of himself and the rest of mankind—he gives up to be regulated by laws made by the society, so far forth as the preservation of himself and the rest of that society shall require, which laws of the society in many things confine the liberty he had by the law of nature.

---

[18]*omit:* disregard. [D. C. ABEL]

Secondly, the power of punishing he wholly gives up and engages his natural force (which he might before employ in the execution of the law of nature, by his own single authority, as he thought fit) to assist the executive power of the society, as the law thereof shall require. For being now in a new state, wherein he is to enjoy many conveniences from the labor, assistance, and society of others in the same community, as well as protection from its whole strength, he is to part also with as much of his natural liberty in providing for himself as the good prosperity and safety of the society shall require—which is not only necessary but just, since the other members of the society do the like.

But though men when they enter into society give up the equality, liberty, and executive power they had in the state of nature into the hands of the society, to be so far disposed of by the legislative as the good of the society shall require; yet it being only with an intention in everyone the better to preserve himself, his liberty, and property (for no rational creature can be supposed to change his condition with an intention to be worse), the power of the society, or legislative constituted by them, can never be supposed to extend farther than the common good, but is obliged to secure everyone's property by providing against those three defects above mentioned, that made the state of nature so unsafe and uneasy. And so whoever has the legislative or supreme power of any commonwealth is bound to govern by established standing laws, promulgated and known to the people, and not by extemporary decrees; by indifferent and upright judges, who are to decide controversies by those laws; and to employ the force of the community at home only in the execution of such laws, or abroad to prevent or redress foreign injuries and secure the community from inroads and invasion. And all this [is] to be directed to no other end but the peace, safety, and public good of the people.

CHAPTER XIX. OF THE DISSOLUTION OF GOVERNMENT

He that will with any clearness speak of the dissolution of government ought in the first place to distinguish between the dissolution of the *society* and the dissolution of the *government*. That which makes the community and brings men out of the loose state of nature into one politic society is the agreement which everyone has with the rest to incorporate and act as one body, and so be one distinct commonwealth. The usual and almost only way whereby this union is dissolved is the inroad of foreign force making a conquest upon them. For in that case (not being able to maintain and support themselves as one entire and independent body), the union belonging to that body which consisted therein must necessarily cease, and so everyone return to the state he was in before, with a liberty to shift for himself and provide for his own safety, as he thinks fit, in some other society. Whenever the society is dissolved, it is certain the government of that society cannot remain. . . .

Besides this overturning from *without,* governments are dissolved from *within.*

First, when the legislative is altered. Civil society being a state of peace amongst those who are of it, from whom the state of war is excluded by the umpirage[19] which they have provided in their legislative for the ending all differences that may arise amongst any of them, it is in their legislative that the members of a commonwealth are united and combined together into one coherent, living body. This is the soul that gives form, life, and unity to the commonwealth; from hence the several members have their mutual influence, sympathy, and connection. And therefore when the legislative is broken or dissolved, dissolution and death follows. . . .

There is . . . , secondly, another way whereby governments are dissolved, and that is when the legislative or the prince (either of them) acts contrary to their trust. . . .

The legislative acts against the trust reposed in them when they endeavor to invade the property of the subject and to make themselves, or any part of the community, masters or arbitrary disposers of the lives, liberties, or fortunes of the people.

The reason why men enter into society is the preservation of their property, and the end why they choose and authorize a legislative is that there may be laws made and rules set as guards and fences to the properties of all the members of the society, to limit the power and moderate the dominion of every part and member of the society. For since it can never be supposed to be the will of the society that the legislative should have a power to destroy that which everyone designs to secure by entering into society, and for which the people submitted themselves to legislators of their own making, whenever the legislators endeavor to take away and destroy the property of the people, or to reduce them to slavery under arbitrary power, they put themselves into a state of war with the people, who are thereupon absolved from any farther obedience and are left to the common refuge which God has provided for all men against force and violence. Whensoever therefore the legislative shall transgress this fundamental rule of society and, either by ambition, fear, folly or corruption, endeavor to grasp themselves, or put into the hands of any other, an absolute power over the lives, liberties, and estates of the people, by this breach of trust they forfeit the power the people had put into their hands for quite contrary ends, and it devolves to the people, who have a right to resume their original liberty and, by the establishment of a new legislative (such as they shall think fit), provide for their own safety and security, which is the end for which they are in society. . . .

In both the forementioned cases, when either the legislative is changed or the legislators act contrary to the end for which they were constituted, those who are guilty are guilty of rebellion. For if anyone by force takes away the established legislative of any society and the laws by them made, pursuant to their trust, he thereby takes away the umpirage which everyone had consented to for a peaceable decision of all their controversies and a bar to the state of war amongst them. They who remove or change the legislative take away this decisive power, which nobody can have but by the appointment and consent of the people; and so destroying the authority which the people did, and nobody else can, set up, and introducing a power which the people has not authorized, they

---

[19]*umpirage:* authority to make a final decision. [D. C. ABEL]

actually introduce a state of war, which is that of force without authority. And thus, by removing the legislative established by the society (in whose decisions the people acquiesced and united, as to that of their own will), they untie the knot and expose the people anew to the state of war. And if those who by force take away the legislative are rebels, the legislators themselves, as has been shown, can be no less esteemed[20] so—when they, who were set up for the protection and preservation of the people, their liberties and properties, shall by force invade and endeavor to take them away.

---

[20]*esteemed:* considered. [D. C. ABEL]

A Vindication of the Rights of Woman

Mary Wollstonecraft

Mary Wollstonecraft was born in London, England, in 1759. When she was 19, she took a job as a companion to an elderly widow in Bath. Two years later she returned to London to care for her dying mother. In 1783 Wollstonecraft helped establish two schools, one in Islington and the other in Newington Green. In 1786 she began working as a governess in County Cork, Ireland, and in the following year published her first book, *Thoughts on the Education of Daughters*. Deciding to make her living as a writer, Wollstonecraft moved back to London. In 1788 she published *Mary: A Fiction* (a largely autobiographical novel), *Original Stories from Real Life* (a children's book), and a translation from the French of Jacques Necker's *Of the Importance of Religious Opinions*. That year she also began working as a translator and reviewer for the journal *The Analytic Review*. Two years later she wrote *A Vindication of the Rights of Men*—a response to British politician Edmund Burke's *Reflections on the Revolution in France*. In 1792 Wollstonecraft published her best-known work, *A Vindication of the Rights of Woman*. That same year she went to France to write a short history of the French Revolution, which was published in 1794. Returning to London, she resumed her job at *The Analytic Review* and also became an active member of the group of radical thinkers that met regularly in the home of Joseph Johnson, the publisher of her books and of *The Analytic Review*. Members of the group included William Blake, William Wordsworth, Thomas Paine, and William Godwin. Wollstonecraft died in London in 1797. (Wollstonecraft married Godwin several months before her death, so she is also known as Mary Wollstonecraft Godwin.)

Our reading is from the Introduction and Chapter IV of *A Vindication of the Rights of Woman*. In the Introduction, Wollstonecraft states the thesis of her book: The misery of women is due primarily to the faulty education they receive—an education designed by men to turn women into "alluring mistresses." In Chapter IV, "Observations on the State of Degradation to Which Woman Is Reduced by Various Causes," Wollstonecraft argues that reason is the distinctively human trait and that the degradation of women is due primarily to the suppression of their rationality and an overemphasis on their feelings and emotions. By denying that women are rational and by maintaining an educational system that develops the rational potential of men only, society prevents women from attaining human perfection. Reason, not pleasure, is the foundation of virtue; by training women to value pleasure and to delight in the trivial attentions and courtesies bestowed by men, society stunts the human development of women. Ironically, by turning women into "creatures of sensation" rather than into fully human beings, men make women less fit to carry out their domestic duties.

INTRODUCTION

After considering the historic page and viewing the living world with anxious solicitude, the most melancholy emotions of sorrowful indignation have depressed my spirits, and I have sighed when obliged to confess that either nature has made a great difference between man and man, or that the civilization which has hitherto taken place in the world has been very partial. I have turned over various books written on the subject of education and patiently observed the conduct of parents and the management of schools. But what has been the result? A profound conviction that the neglected education of my fellow creatures is the grand source of the misery I deplore; and that women, in particular, are rendered weak and wretched by a variety of concurring causes originating from one hasty conclusion. The conduct and manners of women, in fact, evidently prove that their minds are not in a healthy state. For, like the flowers which are planted in too rich a soil, strength and usefulness are sacrificed to beauty; and the flaunting leaves, after having pleased a fastidious eye, fade, disregarded on the stalk, long before the season when they ought to have arrived at maturity. One cause of this barren blooming I attribute to a false system of education, gathered from the books written on this subject by men who, considering females rather as women than human creatures, have been more anxious to make them alluring mistresses than affectionate wives and rational mothers. And the under-standing of the sex has been so bubbled[1] by this specious homage that the civilized women of the present century, with a few exceptions, are only anxious to inspire love, when they ought to cherish a nobler ambition, and by their abilities and virtues exact respect. . . .

My own sex, I hope, will excuse me if I treat them like rational creatures instead of flattering their *fascinating* graces and viewing them as if they were in a state of perpetual childhood, unable to stand alone. I earnestly wish to point out in what true dignity and human happiness consists—I wish to persuade women to endeavor to acquire strength, both of mind and body, and to convince them that the soft phrases, susceptibility of heart, delicacy of sentiment, and refinement of taste, are almost synonymous with epithets of weakness, and that those beings who are only the objects of pity and that kind of love which has been termed its sister, will soon become objects of contempt.

Dismissing, then, those pretty feminine phrases which the men condescend-ingly use to soften our slavish dependence, and despising that weak elegancy of mind, exquisite sensibility, and sweet docility of manners supposed to be the sexual characteristics of the weaker vessel, I wish to show that elegance is inferior to virtue; that the first object of laudable ambition is to obtain a charac-ter as a human being, regardless of the distinction of sex; and that secondary views should be brought to this simple touchstone. . . .

CHAPTER IV. OBSERVATIONS ON THE STATE OF DEGRADATION TO WHICH WOMAN IS REDUCED BY VARIOUS CAUSES

[Women and Reason]

. . . Reason is . . . the simple power of improvement, or (more properly speaking) of discerning truth. Every individual is in this respect a world in itself. More or less may be conspicuous in one being than another, but the nature of reason must be the same in all, if it be an emanation of divinity, the tie that connects the

---

[1]*bubbled:* duped. [D. C. ABEL]

creature with the Creator. For can that soul be stamped with the heavenly image, that is not perfected by the exercise of its own reason? Yet outwardly ornamented with elaborate care and so adorned to delight man, "that with honor he may love,"[2] the soul of woman is not allowed to have this distinction. And man, ever placed between her and reason, she is always represented as only created to see through a gross medium, and to take things on trust. But dismissing these fanciful theories and considering woman as a whole (let it be what it will) instead of a part of man, the inquiry is whether she have reason or not. If she have—which, for a moment, I will take for granted—she was not created merely to be the solace of man, and the sexual should not destroy the human character.

Into this error men have probably been led by viewing education in a false light—not considering it as the first step to form a being advancing gradually towards perfection, but only as a preparation for life. On this sensual error (for I must call it so) has the false system of female manners been reared, which robs the whole sex of its dignity and classes the brown and fair with the smiling flowers that only adorn the land. This has ever been the language of men, and the fear of departing from a supposed sexual character has made even women of superior sense adopt the same sentiments. Thus understanding, strictly speaking, has been denied to woman; and instinct, sublimated into wit and cunning for the purposes of life, has been substituted in its stead.

The power of generalizing ideas, of drawing comprehensive conclusions from individual observations, is the only acquirement . . . that really deserves the name of knowledge. Merely to observe, without endeavoring to account for anything, may (in a very incomplete manner) serve as the common sense of life. But where is the store laid up that is to clothe the soul when it leaves the body?

This power has not only been denied to women, but writers have insisted that it is inconsistent, with a few exceptions, with their sexual character. Let men prove this, and I shall grant that woman only exists for man. I must, however, previously remark that the power of generalizing ideas, to any great extent, is not very common amongst men or women. But this exercise is the true cultivation of the understanding, and everything conspires to render the cultivation of the understanding more difficult in the female than the male world.

I am naturally led by this assertion to the main subject of the present chapter, and shall now attempt to point out some of the causes that degrade the sex and prevent women from generalizing their observations.

[Women and Virtue]

I shall not go back to the remote annals of antiquity to trace the history of woman; it is sufficient to allow that she has always been either a slave or a despot, and to remark that each of these situations equally retards the progress of reason. The grand source of female folly and vice has ever appeared to me to arise from

---

[2]Apparently a reference to John Milton, *Paradise Lost*, Book VIII, lines 57–58: "O when meet now/ Such pairs, in love and mutual Honour join'd?" Milton (1608–1678) was an English poet. [D. C. ABEL]

narrowness of mind, and the very constitution of civil governments has put almost insuperable obstacles in the way to prevent the cultivation of the female understanding. Yet virtue can be built on no other foundation! The same obstacles are thrown in the way of the rich, and the same consequences ensue.

Necessity has been proverbially termed the mother of invention. The aphorism may be extended to virtue. It is an acquirement—and an acquirement to which pleasure must be sacrificed. And who sacrifices pleasure when it is within the grasp, whose mind has not been opened and strengthened by adversity or the pursuit of knowledge goaded on by necessity? Happy is it when people have the cares of life to struggle with, for these struggles prevent their becoming a prey to enervating vices, merely from idleness! But if from their birth men and women be placed in a torrid zone, with the meridian sun of pleasure darting directly upon them, how can they sufficiently brace their minds to discharge the duties of life, or even to relish the affections that carry them out of themselves?

Pleasure is the business of woman's life, according to the present modification[3] of society; and while it continues to be so, little can be expected from such weak beings. Inheriting, in a lineal descent from the first fair defect in nature,[4] the sovereignty of beauty, they have, to maintain their power, resigned the natural rights which the exercise of reason might have procured them, and chosen rather to be short-lived queens than labor to obtain the sober pleasures that arise from equality. Exalted by their inferiority (this sounds like a contradiction), they constantly demand homage as women, though experience should teach them that the men who pride themselves upon paying this arbitrary insolent respect to the sex, with the most scrupulous exactness, are most inclined to tyrannize over, and despise, the very weakness they cherish. . . .

Ah! Why do women (I write with affectionate solicitude) condescend to receive a degree of attention and respect from strangers, different from that reciprocation of civility which the dictates of humanity and the politeness of civilization authorize between man and man? And why do they not discover, when "in the noon of beauty's power,"[5] that they are treated like queens only to be deluded by hollow respect, till they are led to resign, or not assume, their natural prerogatives? Confined then in cages like the feathered race, they have nothing to do but to plume themselves and stalk with mock majesty from perch to perch. It is true they are provided with food and raiment, for which they neither toil nor spin;[6] but health, liberty, and virtue are given in exchange. But where amongst mankind has been found sufficient strength of mind to enable a being to resign these adventitious prerogatives—one who, rising with the calm

---

[3]*modification:* restriction. [D. C. ABEL]

[4]A reference to Milton, who calls woman "this fair defect / Of nature" (*Paradise Lost*, Book X, lines 891–892). [D. C. ABEL]

[5]Apparently Wollstonecraft's paraphrase of a passage in Adam Beuvius, *Henrietta of Gerstenfeld: A German Story*, vol. 2 (London, England: William Lane, 1788), p. 24. Beuvius (flourished 1775–1783) was a German writer. [D. C. ABEL]

[6]An allusion to Jesus' statement, "Consider the lilies of the field, how they grow; they neither toil nor spin, yet I tell you, even Solomon in all his glory was not arrayed like one of these" (Matthew 6:28). [D. C. ABEL]

dignity of reason above opinion, dared to be proud of the privileges inherent in man? And it is vain to expect it while hereditary power chokes the affections and nips reason in the bud.

The passions of men have thus placed women on thrones and, till mankind become more reasonable, it is to be feared that women will avail themselves of the power which they attain with the least exertion and which is the most indisputable. They will smile—yes, they will smile—though told that:

> In beauty's empire is no mean,
> And woman, either slave or queen,
> Is quickly scorn'd when not ador'd.[7]

But the adoration comes first, and the scorn is not anticipated. . . .

I lament that women are systematically degraded by receiving the trivial attentions which men think it manly to pay to the sex, when in fact they are insultingly supporting their own superiority. It is not condescension to bow to an inferior. So ludicrous, in fact, do these ceremonies appear to me, that I scarcely am able to govern my muscles when I see a man start with eager and serious solicitude to lift a handkerchief or shut a door, when the *lady* could have done it herself, had she only moved a pace or two.

A wild wish has just flown from my heart to my head, and I will not stifle it though it may excite a horselaugh. I do earnestly wish to see the distinction of sex confounded in society, unless where love animates the behavior. For this distinction is, I am firmly persuaded, the foundation of the weakness of character ascribed to woman; is the cause why the understanding is neglected, while accomplishments are acquired with sedulous care. And the same cause accounts for their preferring the graceful before the heroic virtues.

Mankind, including every description, wish to be loved and respected by *something;* and the common herd will always take the nearest road to the completion of their wishes. The respect paid to wealth and beauty is the most certain, and unequivocal—and, of course, will always attract the vulgar eye of common minds. Abilities and virtues are absolutely necessary to raise men from the middle rank of life into notice. And the natural consequence is notorious: The middle rank contains most virtue and abilities. Men have thus, in one station, at least an opportunity of exerting themselves with dignity and of rising by the exertions which really improve a rational creature. But the whole female sex are, till their character is formed, in the same condition as the rich—for they are born (I now speak of a state of civilization) with certain sexual privileges, and while they are gratuitously granted them, few will ever think of works of supererogation[8] to obtain the esteem of a small number of superior people.

When do we hear of women who, starting out of obscurity, boldly claim respect on account of their great abilities or daring virtues? Where are they to be found? "To be observed, to be attended to, to be taken notice of with sympathy,

---

[7]Anna Letitia Barbauld, "Song V," lines 16–18. Barbauld (1743–1825) was a British writer and poet. [D. C. ABEL]

[8]*supererogation:* doing more than required by duty or obligation. [D. C. ABEL]

complacency, and approbation, are all the advantages which they seek."[9] "True!" my male readers will probably exclaim. But let them, before they draw any conclusion, recollect that this was not written originally as descriptive of women, but of the rich. In Dr. Smith's *Theory of Moral Sentiments* I have found a general character of people of rank and fortune that, in my opinion, might with the greatest propriety be applied to the female sex.[10] . . . For if, excepting warriors, no great men of any denomination have ever appeared amongst the nobility, may it not be fairly inferred that their local situation swallowed up the man and produced a character similar to that of women, who are *localized* (if I may be allowed the word) by the rank they are placed in, by *courtesy?* Women, commonly called ladies, are not to be contradicted in company, are not allowed to exert any manual strength. And from them the negative virtues only are expected, when any virtues are expected: patience, docility, good humor, and flexibility—virtues incompatible with any vigorous exertion of intellect. Besides, by living more with each other and being seldom absolutely alone, they are more under the influence of sentiments than passions. Solitude and reflection are necessary to give to wishes the force of passions, and to enable the imagination to enlarge the object and make it the most desirable. The same may be said of the rich; they do not sufficiently deal in general ideas, collected by impassioned thinking or calm investigation, to acquire that strength of character on which great resolves are built. . . .

[Women and Sensibility]

In the middle rank of life, to continue the comparison, men in their youth are prepared for professions, and marriage is not considered as the grand feature in their lives; while women, on the contrary, have no other scheme to sharpen their faculties. It is not business, extensive plans, or any of the excursive flights of ambition that engross their attention—no, their thoughts are not employed in rearing such noble structures. To rise in the world and have the liberty of running from pleasure to pleasure, they must marry advantageously, and to this object their time is sacrificed and their persons often legally prostituted. A man when he enters any profession has his eye steadily fixed on some future advantage (and the mind gains great strength by having all its efforts directed to one point), and, full of his business, pleasure is considered as mere relaxation; while women seek for pleasure as the main purpose of existence. In fact, from the education which they receive from society, the love of pleasure may be said to govern them all. But does this prove that there is a sex in souls? It would be just as rational to declare that the courtiers in France, when a destructive system of despotism had formed their character, were not men because liberty, virtue, and humanity were sacrificed to pleasure and vanity—fatal passions, which have ever domineered over the *whole* race!

    The same love of pleasure, fostered by the whole tendency of their education, gives a trifling turn to the conduct of women in most circumstances. For

---

[9]Adam Smith, *The Theory of Moral Sentiments* (London, England: A. Millar, 1759), Part I, Section III, Chapter II, pp. 109–10. Smith (1723–1790) was a Scottish economist. [D. C. ABEL]
[10]Ibid., pp. 117–20. [D. C. ABEL]

instance, they are ever anxious about secondary things, and on the watch for adventures instead of being occupied by duties.

A man, when he undertakes a journey, has, in general, the end[11] in view. A woman thinks more of the incidental occurrences, the strange things that may possibly occur on the road, the impression that she may make on her fellow-travellers. And above all, she is anxiously intent on the care of the finery that she carries with her, which is more than ever a part of herself, when going to figure on a new scene—when, to use an apt French turn of expression, she is going to produce a sensation. Can dignity of mind exist with such trivial cares?

In short, women in general, as well as the rich of both sexes, have acquired all the follies and vices of civilization and missed the useful fruit. It is not necessary for me always to premise that I speak of the condition of the whole sex, leaving exceptions out of the question. Their senses are inflamed and their understandings neglected; consequently they become the prey of their senses (delicately termed *sensibility*) and are blown about by every momentary gust of feeling. Civilized women are, therefore, so weakened by false refinement that, respecting morals, their condition is much below what it would be were they left in a state nearer to nature. Ever restless and anxious, their overexercised sensibility not only renders them uncomfortable themselves, but troublesome (to use a soft phrase) to others. All their thoughts turn on things calculated to excite emotion. And feeling when they should reason [instead], their conduct is unstable and their opinions are wavering—not the wavering produced by deliberation or progressive views, but by contradictory emotions. By fits and starts they are warm in many pursuits. Yet this warmth, never concentrated into perseverance, soon exhausts itself. Exhaled by its own heat, or meeting with some other fleeting passion to which reason has never given any specific gravity, neutrality ensues. Miserable indeed must be that being whose cultivation of mind has only tended to inflame its passions! A distinction should be made between inflaming and strengthening them. The passions thus pampered, while the judgment is left unformed, what can be expected to ensue? Undoubtedly, a mixture of madness and folly!

This observation should not be confined to the *fair* sex. However, at present I only mean to apply it to them.

Novels, music, poetry, and gallantry all tend to make women the creatures of sensation, and their character is thus formed in the mold of folly during the time they are acquiring accomplishments—the only improvement they are excited, by their station in society, to acquire. This overstretched sensibility naturally relaxes the other powers of the mind and prevents intellect from attaining that sovereignty which it ought to attain to render a rational creature useful to others and content with its own station; for the exercise of the understanding, as life advances, is the only method pointed out by nature to calm the passions.

Satiety has a very different effect, and I have often been forcibly struck by an emphatic description of damnation: when the spirit is represented as continually hovering with abortive eagerness round the defiled body, unable to enjoy anything without the organs of sense. Yet, to their senses are women made slaves, because it is by their sensibility that they obtain present power.

---

[11]*end:* purpose, goal. [D. C. ABEL]

And will moralists pretend to assert that this is the condition in which one half of the human race should be encouraged to remain with listless inactivity and stupid acquiescence? Kind instructors! What were we created for? To remain, it may be said, innocent—they mean in a state of childhood. We might as well never have been born, unless it were necessary that we should be created to enable man to acquire the noble privilege of reason, the power of discerning good from evil, while we lie down in the dust from whence we were taken, never to rise again.

It would be an endless task to trace the variety of meannesses, cares, and sorrows into which women are plunged by the prevailing opinion that they were created rather to feel than reason, and that all the power they obtain must be obtained by their charms and weakness:

Fine by defect, and amiably weak![12]

And made by this amiable weakness entirely dependent—excepting what they gain by illicit sway—on man, not only for protection but advice, is it surprising that, neglecting the duties that reason alone points out and shrinking from trials calculated to strengthen their minds, they only exert themselves to give their defects a graceful covering, which may serve to heighten their charms in the eye of the voluptuary, though it sink them below the scale of moral excellence?

Fragile in every sense of the word, they are obliged to look up to man for every comfort. In the most trifling dangers they cling to their support with parasitical tenacity, piteously demanding succor; and their *natural* protector extends his arm or lifts up his voice to guard the lovely trembler—from what? Perhaps the frown of an old cow or the jump of a mouse; a rat would be a serious danger. In the name of reason, and even common sense, what can save such beings from contempt, even though they be soft and fair? . . .

In the regulation of a family, in the education of children, understanding in an unsophisticated sense is particularly required—strength both of body and mind. Yet the men who, by their writings, have most earnestly labored to domesticate women, have endeavored, by arguments dictated by a gross appetite which satiety had rendered fastidious, to weaken their bodies and cramp their minds. But if even by these sinister methods they really *persuaded* women, by working on their feelings, to stay at home and fulfill the duties of a mother and mistress of a family, I should cautiously oppose opinions that led women to right conduct by prevailing on them to make the discharge of such important duties the main business of life, though reason were insulted. Yet— and I appeal to experience—if by neglecting the understanding they be as much, nay, *more* detached from these domestic employments than they could be by the most serious intellectual pursuit (though it may be observed that the mass of mankind will never vigorously pursue an intellectual object), I may be allowed to infer that reason is absolutely necessary to enable a woman to perform any duty properly. And I must again repeat that sensibility is not reason.

---

[12]A nearly verbatim quotation of Alexander Pope, *Moral Essays*, Epistle II, "To a Lady: Of the Characters of Women," line 44 (Pope has "delicately" instead of "amiably"). [D. C. ABEL]

The comparison with the rich still occurs to me. For when men neglect the duties of humanity, women will follow their example; a common stream hurries them both along with thoughtless celerity. Riches and honors prevent a man from enlarging his understanding and enervate all his powers by reversing the order of nature, which has ever made true pleasure the reward of labor. Pleasure—enervating pleasure—is, likewise, within women's reach without earning it. But till hereditary possessions are spread abroad, how can we expect men to be proud of virtue? And till they are, women will govern them by the most direct means, neglecting their dull domestic duties to catch the pleasure that sits lightly on the wing of time.

Manifesto of the Communist Party

Karl Marx and Friedrich Engels

Karl Marx was born in 1818 in Trier, Prussia. He began studying law at the University of Bonn at the age of 17, but soon transferred to the University of Berlin, where he became interested in philosophy. In 1841 he received his doctorate in philosophy from the University of Jena. Unable to get a teaching position because of his association with the politically radical Young Hegelians, Marx in 1842 became editor of the *Rhenish Gazette,* a liberal newspaper in the Rhineland. He then moved to Paris to take a job as coeditor of a new socialist publication, the *German-French Annals.* The *Annals* was soon shut down by the authorities, and Marx was expelled from Paris in 1845. He moved to Brussels, Belgium, where he worked to promote Communism. In 1849 he settled in London, where he lived for the rest of his life. In 1867 he published the first volume of *Capital,* his comprehensive work on economics; the drafts of the second and third volumes were still uncompleted when Marx died in 1883.

Friedrich Engels was born in Barmen, Prussia, in 1820. He attended secondary school but dropped out before graduating. In 1838 he went to Bremen to work in the office of his father's textile company to prepare for a career in business. He soon developed an interest in politics and associated with the Young Hegelians, becoming a Communist in 1842. He then went to Manchester, England, to work as a clerk in a cotton mill owned by his father. In 1844 he went to Paris to visit with Marx, and the two became friends and lifelong collaborators. Engels followed Marx to Brussels when Marx was exiled in 1845; there they coauthored *The German Ideology* (written in 1845, not published in full until 1932) and the *Manifesto of the Communist Party* (1848). Engels later moved back to Manchester and worked again for his father's company. He shared his salary with Marx, who was living in London. After Marx's death, Engels edited and published the second and third volumes of *Capital* (1885, 1894). Engels died in London in 1895.

Our reading is from the *Manifesto of the Communist Party,* a document Marx and Engels wrote as the platform of the Communist League, an international association of workers. Marx and Engels explain that communism interprets the history of society as the history of class struggles. Although the classes vary with the historical epoch, they are always the result of the prevailing economic system. The two classes produced by the industrial revolution are the bourgeoisie (capitalists, who own the means of production) and the proletariat (wage-laborers employed by the bourgeoisie). Under capitalism, workers become just one more commodity, bought and sold at market prices. To earn enough money simply to survive, they must work long hours under increasingly inhumane conditions.

Marx and Engels argue that capitalism, ironically, contains the seeds of its own destruction: On the one hand, its very success leads to overproduction and thus to economic ruin; on the other hand, it drives the oppressed workers to unite to overthrow the entire capitalist system. The fall of capitalism and the victory of the proletariat are therefore inevitable. Marx and Engels explain that the goal of the Communist Party is to hasten the end of capitalism by uniting the workers of all countries and encouraging them to revolt. The revolution will abolish private property (private ownership of the means of production) and shift political power from the bourgeoisie to the proletariat. Eventually the distinction between bourgeoisie and proletariat will disappear, and with it the need for political power.

I. BOURGEOIS AND PROLETARIANS[1]

The history of all hitherto existing society is the history of class struggles.

Freeman and slave, patrician and plebeian, lord and serf, guild master[2] and journeyman, in a word, oppressor and oppressed, stood in constant opposition to one another, carried on an uninterrupted, now hidden, now open fight—a fight that each time ended either in a revolutionary reconstitution of society at large or in the common ruin of the contending classes.

In the earlier epochs of history, we find almost everywhere a complicated arrangement of society into various orders, a manifold gradation of social rank. In ancient Rome we have patricians, knights, plebeians, slaves; in the Middle Ages, feudal lords, vassals, guild masters, journeymen, apprentices, serfs; in almost all of these classes, again, subordinate gradations.

The modern bourgeois society that has sprouted from the ruins of feudal society has not done away with class antagonisms. It has but established new classes, new conditions of oppression, new forms of struggle in place of the old ones.

Our epoch, the epoch of the bourgeoisie, possesses, however, this distinctive feature: It has simplified the class antagonisms. Society as a whole is more and more splitting up into two great hostile camps, into two great classes directly facing each other: bourgeoisie and proletariat.

From the serfs of the Middle Ages sprang the chartered burghers[3] of the earliest towns. From these [burghers] the first elements of the bourgeoisie were developed.

The discovery of America, the rounding of the Cape,[4] opened up fresh ground for the rising bourgeoisie. The East Indian and Chinese markets, the colonization of America, trade with the colonies, the increase in the means of exchange and in commodities generally, gave to commerce, to navigation, to industry, an impulse never before known, and thereby to the revolutionary element in the tottering feudal society a rapid development.

The feudal system of industry, under which industrial production was monopolized by closed guilds, now no longer sufficed for the growing wants of the new markets. The manufacturing system took its place. The guild masters

---

[1]By *bourgeoisie* [the class of bourgeois people] is meant the class of modern capitalists, owners of the means of social production and employers of wage labor; by *proletariat*, the class of modern wage-laborers who, having no means of production of their own, are reduced to selling their labor power in order to live. [F. ENGELS]

[2]*guild master:* a full member of a guild—not a master within, not a head of a guild. [F. ENGELS]

[3]*chartered burghers:* inhabitants of a chartered town who have full municipal rights; citizens. [D. C. ABEL]

[4]*the Cape:* the Cape of Good Hope, at the southern tip of Africa. [D. C. ABEL]

were pushed on one side by the manufacturing middle class. Division of labor between the different corporate guilds vanished in the face of division of labor in each single workshop.

Meantime the markets kept ever growing, the demand ever rising. Even manufacture no longer sufficed. Thereupon, steam and machinery revolutionized industrial production. The place of manufacture was taken by the giant, modern industry; the place of the industrial middle class, by industrial millionaires, the leaders of whole industrial armies, the modern bourgeois.

Modern industry has established the world market, for which the discovery of America paved the way. This market has given an immense development to commerce, to navigation, to communication by land. This development has, in its turn, reacted on the extension of industry. And in proportion as industry, commerce, navigation, railways extended, in the same proportion the bourgeoisie developed, increased its capital, and pushed into the background every class handed down from the Middle Ages.

We see, therefore, how the modern bourgeoisie is itself the product of a long course of development, of a series of revolutions in the modes of production and of exchange. . . .

The bourgeoisie historically has played a most revolutionary part.

The bourgeoisie, wherever it has got the upper hand, has put an end to all feudal, patriarchal, idyllic relations. It has pitilessly torn asunder the motley feudal ties that bound man to his "natural superiors" and has left remaining no other nexus between man and man than naked self-interest, than callous "cash payment." It has drowned the most heavenly ecstasies of religious fervor, of chivalrous enthusiasm, of philistine sentimentalism, in the icy water of egotistical calculation. It has resolved personal worth into exchange value, and in place of the numberless indefeasible[5] chartered freedoms has set up that single, unconscionable freedom—free trade. In one word, for exploitation veiled by religious and political illusions, it has substituted naked, shameless, direct, brutal exploitation.

The bourgeoisie has stripped of its halo every occupation hitherto honored and looked up to with reverent awe. It has converted the physician, the lawyer, the priest, the poet, the man of science, into its paid wage-laborers.

The bourgeoisie has torn away from the family its sentimental veil and has reduced the family relation to a mere money relation. . . .

The bourgeoisie cannot exist without constantly revolutionizing the instruments of production, and thereby the relations of production, and with them the whole relations of society. Conservation of the old modes of production in unaltered form was, on the contrary, the first condition of existence for all earlier industrial classes. Constant revolutionizing of production, uninterrupted disturbance of all social conditions, everlasting uncertainty and agitation, distinguish the bourgeois epoch from all earlier ones. All fixed, fast-frozen relations, with their train of ancient and venerable prejudices and opinions, are swept away; all new-formed ones become antiquated before they can ossify. All that is solid melts into air, all that is holy is profaned, and man is at last compelled to face with sober senses his real conditions of life and his relations with his kind.

---

[5]*indefeasible:* incapable of being annulled or forfeited. [D. C. Abel]

The need of a constantly expanding market for its products chases the bourgeoisie over the whole surface of the globe. It must nestle everywhere, settle everywhere, establish connections everywhere.

The bourgeoisie has through its exploitation of the world market given a cosmopolitan character to production and consumption in every country. To the great chagrin of reactionists, it has drawn from under the feet of industry the national ground on which it stood. All old-established national industries have been destroyed or are daily being destroyed. They are dislodged by new industries whose introduction becomes a life and death question for all civilized nations, by industries that no longer work up indigenous raw material but raw material drawn from the remotest zones—industries whose products are consumed not only at home, but in every quarter of the globe. In place of the old wants, satisfied by the productions of the country, we find new wants, requiring for their satisfaction the products of distant lands and [climates]. In place of the old local and national seclusion and self-sufficiency, we have intercourse in every direction, universal interdependence of nations. And as in material, so also in intellectual production. The intellectual creations of individual nations become common property. National one-sidedness and narrow-mindedness become more and more impossible, and from the numerous national and local literatures there arises a world literature.

The bourgeoisie, by the rapid improvement of all instruments of production, by the immensely facilitated means of communication, draws all, even the most barbarian, nations into civilization. The cheap prices of its commodities are the heavy artillery with which it batters down all Chinese walls, with which it forces the barbarians' intensely obstinate hatred of foreigners to capitulate. It compels all nations, on pain of extinction, to adopt the bourgeois mode of production; it compels them to introduce what it calls civilization into their midst—that is, to become bourgeois themselves. In one word, it creates a world after its own image. . . .

Modern bourgeois society with its relations of production, of exchange, and of property, a society that has conjured up such gigantic means of production and of exchange, is like the sorcerer who is no longer able to control the powers of the nether world whom he has called up by his spells. For many a decade past, the history of industry and commerce is but the history of the revolt of modern productive forces against modern conditions of production, against the property relations that are the conditions for the existence of the bourgeoisie and of its rule. It is enough to mention the commercial crises that by their periodical return put on its trial, each time more threateningly, the existence of the entire bourgeois society. In these crises a great part not only of the existing products, but also of the previously created productive forces, are periodically destroyed. In these crises there breaks out an epidemic that in all earlier epochs would have seemed an absurdity—the epidemic of overproduction. Society suddenly finds itself put back into a state of momentary barbarism; it appears as if a famine, a universal war of devastation, had cut off the supply of every means of subsistence; industry and commerce seem to be destroyed. And why? Because there is too much civilization, too much means of subsistence, too much industry, too much commerce. The productive forces at the disposal of society no longer tend to further the development of the conditions of bourgeois property. On the contrary, they have become too powerful for these conditions by which they are fettered, and so soon as they overcome these fetters, they bring disorder into the whole of bourgeois society, endanger the existence of bourgeois property. The conditions of bourgeois society are too narrow to comprise the wealth created by them. And how does the bourgeoisie get over these crises? On the one hand, by enforced destruction of a mass of productive forces; on the other, by the conquest of new markets and by the more thorough exploitation of the old ones—that is to say, by paving the way for more extensive and more destructive crises and by diminishing the means whereby crises are prevented.

The weapons with which the bourgeoisie felled feudalism to the ground are now turned against the bourgeoisie itself.

But not only has the bourgeoisie forged the weapons that bring death to itself; it has also called into existence the men who are to wield those weapons— the modern working class, the proletarians.

In proportion as the bourgeoisie, that is, capital, is developed, in the same proportion is the proletariat, the modern working class, developed—a class of laborers who live only so long as they find work and who find work only so long as their labor increases capital. These laborers, who must sell themselves piecemeal, are a commodity like every other article of commerce and are consequently exposed to all the vicissitudes of competition, to all the fluctuations of the market.

Owing to the extensive use of machinery and to division of labor, the work of the proletarians has lost all individual character and consequently all charm for the workman. He becomes an appendage of the machine, and it is only the most simple, most monotonous, and most easily acquired knack that is required of him. Hence, the cost of production of a workman is restricted, almost entirely, to the means of subsistence that he requires for his maintenance and for the propagation of his race. But the price of a commodity, and therefore also of labor, is equal to its cost of production. In proportion, therefore, as the repulsiveness of the work increases, the wage decreases. Nay more, in proportion as the use of machinery and division of labor increases, in the same proportion the burden of toil also increases, whether by prolongation of the working hours, by increase of the work exacted in a given time, or by increased speed of the machinery, and so on.

Modern industry has converted the little workshop of the patriarchal master into the great factory of the industrial capitalist. Masses of laborers, crowded into the factory, are organized like soldiers. As privates of the industrial army they are placed under the command of a perfect hierarchy of officers and sergeants. Not only are they slaves of the bourgeois class and of the bourgeois state; they are daily and hourly enslaved by the machine, by the overlooker, and, above all, by the individual bourgeois manufacturer himself. The more openly this despotism proclaims gain to be its end and aim, the more petty, the more hateful, and the more embittering it is.

The less the skill and exertion of strength implied in manual labor—in other words, the more modern industry becomes developed—the more is the labor of men superseded by that of women. Differences of age and sex have no longer any distinctive social validity for the working class. All are instruments of labor, more or less expensive to use, according to their age and sex.

No sooner is the exploitation of the laborer by the manufacturer, so far, at an end and he receives his wages in cash, than he is set upon by the other portions of the bourgeoisie: the landlord, the shopkeeper, the pawnbroker, and so on.

The lower strata of the middle class—the small tradespeople, shopkeepers, and retired tradesmen generally, the handicraftsmen and peasants—all these sink gradually into the proletariat, partly because their diminutive capital does not suffice for the scale on which modern industry is carried on and is swamped in the competition with the large capitalists, partly because their specialized skill is rendered worthless by new methods of production. Thus the proletariat is recruited from all classes of the population.

The proletariat goes through various stages of development. With its birth begins its struggle with the bourgeoisie. At first the contest is carried on by individual laborers, then by the workpeople of a factory, then by the operatives of one trade, in one locality, against the individual bourgeois who directly exploits them. They direct their attacks not against the bourgeois conditions of production, but against the instruments of production themselves. They destroy imported wares that compete with their labor, they smash to pieces machinery, they set factories ablaze, they seek to restore by force the vanished status of the workman of the Middle Ages.

At this stage the laborers still form an incoherent mass scattered over the whole country and broken up by their mutual competition. If anywhere they unite to form more compact bodies, this is not yet the consequence of their own active union but of the union of the bourgeoisie—which class, in order to attain its own political ends, is compelled to set the whole proletariat in motion and is moreover yet, for a time, able to do so. At this stage, therefore, the proletarians do not fight their enemies but the enemies of their enemies: the remnants of absolute monarchy, the landowners, the nonindustrial bourgeois, the petty bourgeoisie.[6] Thus the whole historical movement is concentrated in the hands of the bourgeoisie; every victory so obtained is a victory for the bourgeoisie.

But with the development of industry the proletariat not only increases in number; it becomes concentrated in greater masses, its strength grows, and it feels that strength more. The various interests and conditions of life within the ranks of the proletariat are more and more equalized, in proportion as machinery obliterates all distinctions of labor and nearly everywhere reduces wages to the same low level. The growing competition among the bourgeois and the resulting commercial crises make the wages of the workers ever more fluctuating. The unceasing improvement of machinery, ever more rapidly developing, makes their livelihood more and more precarious; the collisions between individual workmen and individual bourgeois take more and more the character of collisions between two classes. Thereupon the workers begin to form combinations (trade unions) against the bourgeois; they club together in order to keep up the rate of wages; they found permanent associations in order to make provision

---

[6]*petty bourgeoisie:* less wealthy members of the bourgeoisie, especially shopkeepers and artisans. [D. C. ABEL]

beforehand for these occasional revolts. Here and there the contest breaks out into riots.

Now and then the workers are victorious, but only for a time. The real fruit of their battles lies not in the immediate result, but in the ever-expanding union of the workers. This union is helped on by the improved means of communication that are created by modern industry and that place the workers of different localities in contact with one another. It was just this contact that was needed to centralize the numerous local struggles, all of the same character, into one national struggle between classes. But every class struggle is a political struggle. And that union, to attain which the burghers of the Middle Ages, with their miserable highways, required centuries, the modern proletarians, thanks to railways, achieve in a few years.

This organization of the proletarians into a class, and consequently into a political party, is continually being upset again by the competition between the workers themselves. But it ever rises up again, stronger, firmer, mightier. It compels legislative recognition of particular interests of the workers by taking advantage of the divisions among the bourgeoisie itself. Thus the Ten Hours bill in England was carried.[7]

Altogether collisions between the classes of the old society further, in many ways, the course of development of the proletariat. The bourgeoisie finds itself involved in a constant battle—at first with the aristocracy; later on, with those portions of the bourgeoisie itself, whose interests have become antagonistic to the progress of industry; at all times, with the bourgeoisie of foreign countries. In all these battles it sees itself compelled to appeal to the proletariat, to ask for its help, and thus to drag it into the political arena. The bourgeoisie itself, therefore, supplies the proletariat with its own elements of political and general education. In other words, it furnishes the proletariat with weapons for fighting the bourgeoisie.

Further, as we have already seen, entire sections of the ruling classes are, by the advance of industry, precipitated into the proletariat, or are at least threatened in their conditions of existence. These also supply the proletariat with fresh elements of enlightenment and progress.

Finally, in times when the class struggle nears the decisive hour, the process of dissolution going on within the ruling class—in fact within the whole range of old society—assumes such a violent, glaring character, that a small section of the ruling class cuts itself adrift and joins the revolutionary class, the class that holds the future in its hands. Just as, therefore, at an earlier period, a section of the nobility went over to the bourgeoisie, so now a portion of the bourgeoisie goes over to the proletariat, and in particular, a portion of the bourgeois ideologists who have raised themselves to the level of comprehending theoretically the historical movement as a whole.

Of all the classes that stand face to face with the bourgeoisie today, the proletariat alone is a really revolutionary class. The other classes decay and finally disappear in the face of modern industry; the proletariat is its special and essential product. . . .

---

[7]The Ten Hours Act, passed in 1847, limited the labor in industry of women and children to 10 hours a day. [D. C. Abel]

All the preceding classes that got the upper hand sought to fortify their already acquired status by subjecting society at large to their conditions of appropriation. The proletarians cannot become masters of the productive forces of society, except by abolishing their own previous mode of appropriation and thereby also every other previous mode of appropriation. They have nothing of their own to secure and to fortify; their mission is to destroy all previous securities for, and insurances of, individual property.

All previous historical movements were movements of minorities or in the interest of minorities. The proletarian movement is the self-conscious, independent movement of the immense majority, in the interest of the immense majority. The proletariat, the lowest stratum of our present society, cannot stir, cannot raise itself up, without the whole superincumbent strata of official society being sprung into the air.

Though not in substance, yet in form, the struggle of the proletariat with the bourgeoisie is at first a national struggle. The proletariat of each country must, of course, first of all settle matters with its own bourgeoisie.

In depicting the most general phases of the development of the proletariat, we traced the more or less veiled civil war raging within existing society, up to the point where that war breaks out into open revolution and where the violent overthrow of the bourgeoisie lays the foundation for the sway of the proletariat.

Hitherto every form of society has been based, as we have already seen, on the antagonism of oppressing and oppressed classes. But in order to oppress a class, certain conditions must be assured to it under which it can at least continue its slavish existence. The serf, in the period of serfdom, raised himself to membership in the commune, just as the petty bourgeois, under the yoke of feudal absolutism, managed to develop into a bourgeois. The modern laborer, on the contrary, instead of rising with the progress of industry, sinks deeper and deeper below the conditions of existence of his own class. He becomes a pauper, and pauperism develops more rapidly than population and wealth. And here it becomes evident that the bourgeoisie is unfit any longer to be the ruling class in society and to impose its conditions of existence upon society as an overriding law. It is unfit to rule because it is incompetent to assure an existence to its slave within his slavery, because it cannot help letting him sink into such a state that it has to feed him, instead of being fed by him. Society can no longer live under this bourgeoisie. In other words, its existence is no longer compatible with society.

The essential condition for the existence and for the sway of the bourgeois class is the formation and augmentation of capital; the condition for capital is wage-labor. Wage-labor rests exclusively on competition between the laborers. The advance of industry, whose involuntary promoter is the bourgeoisie, replaces the isolation of the laborers, due to competition, by their revolutionary combination, due to association. The development of modern industry, therefore, cuts from under its feet the very foundation on which the bourgeoisie produces and appropriates products. What the bourgeoisie, therefore, produces above all is its own gravediggers. Its fall and the victory of the proletariat are equally inevitable.

II. PROLETARIANS AND COMMUNISTS

In what relation do the Communists stand to the proletarians as a whole?

The Communists do not form a separate party opposed to other working-class parties.

They have no interests separate and apart from those of the proletariat as a whole.

They do not set up any sectarian principles of their own, by which to shape and mold the proletarian movement.

The Communists are distinguished from the other working-class parties by this only: (1) In the national struggles of the proletarians of the different countries, they point out and bring to the front the common interests of the entire proletariat, independently of all nationality. (2) In the various stages of development that the struggle of the working class against the bourgeoisie has to pass through, they always and everywhere represent the interests of the movement as a whole.

The Communists therefore are on the one hand, *practically,* the most advanced and resolute section of the working-class parties of every country, that section that pushes forward all others. On the other hand, *theoretically,* they have over the great mass of the proletariat the advantage of clearly understanding the line of march, the conditions, and the ultimate general results of the proletarian movement.

The immediate aim of the Communists is the same as that of all the other proletarian parties: formation of the proletariat into a class, overthrow of the bourgeois supremacy, conquest of political power by the proletariat.

The theoretical conclusions of the Communists are in no way based on ideas or principles that have been invented, or discovered by this or that would-be universal reformer.

They merely express, in general terms, actual relations springing from an existing class struggle, from a historical movement going on under our very eyes. The abolition of existing property relations is not at all a distinctive feature of Communism.

All property relations in the past have continually been subject to historical change consequent upon the change in historical conditions.

The French Revolution, for example, abolished feudal property in favor of bourgeois property.

The distinguishing feature of Communism is not the abolition of property generally, but the abolition of bourgeois property. But modern bourgeois private property[8] is the final and most complete expression of the system of producing and appropriating products that is based on class antagonisms, on the exploitation of the many by the few.

In this sense, the theory of the Communists may be summed up in the single [phrase]: Abolition of private property. . . .

The first step in the revolution by the working class is to raise the proletariat to the position of ruling class, to win the battle of democracy.

---

[8]*private property:* private ownership of the means of production. [D. C. ABEL]

The proletariat will use its political supremacy to wrest, by degrees, all capital from the bourgeoisie, to centralize all instruments of production in the hands of the state, that is, of the proletariat organized as the ruling class; and to increase the total of productive forces as rapidly as possible.

Of course, in the beginning this cannot be effected except by means of despotic inroads on the rights of property, and on the conditions of bourgeois production—by means of measures, therefore, that appear economically insufficient and untenable but that in the course of the movement, outstrip themselves, necessitate further inroads upon the old social order, and are unavoidable as a means of entirely revolutionizing the mode of production.

These measures will, of course, be different in different countries.

Nevertheless, in the most advanced countries the following will be pretty generally applicable:

1. Abolition of property in land and application of all rents of land to public purposes.
2. A heavy progressive or graduated income tax.
3. Abolition of all right of inheritance.
4. Confiscation of the property of all emigrants and rebels.
5. Centralization of credit in the hands of the state, by means of a national bank with state capital and an exclusive monopoly.
6. Centralization of the means of communication and transport in the hands of the state.
7. Extension of factories and instruments of production owned by the state. The bringing into cultivation of wastelands, and the improvement of the soil generally in accordance with a common plan.
8. Equal liability of all to labor. Establishment of industrial armies, especially for agriculture.
9. Combination of agriculture with manufacturing industries. Gradual abolition of the distinction between town and country, by a more equable distribution of the population over the country.
10. Free education for all children in public schools. Abolition of children's factory labor in its present form. Combination of education with industrial production, and so on, and so on.

When, in the course of development, class distinctions have disappeared and all production has been concentrated in the hands of a vast association of the whole nation, the public power will lose its political character. Political power, properly so called, is merely the organized power of one class for oppressing another. If the proletariat during its contest with the bourgeoisie is compelled by the force of circumstances to organize itself as a class; if, by means of a revolution, it makes itself the ruling class and, as such, sweeps away by force the old conditions of production—then it will, along with these conditions, have swept away the conditions for the existence of class antagonisms and of classes generally, and will thereby have abolished its own supremacy as a class.

In place of the old bourgeois society, with its classes and class antagonisms, we shall have an association in which the free development of each is the condition for the free development of all.

IV. POSITION OF THE COMMUNISTS IN RELATION TO THE VARIOUS EXISTING OPPOSITION PARTIES

... The Communists everywhere support every revolutionary movement against the existing social and political order of things.

In all these movements they bring to the front, as the leading question in each, the property question, no matter what its degree of development at the time.

Finally, they labor everywhere for the union and agreement of the democratic parties of all countries.

The Communists disdain to conceal their views and aims. They openly declare that their ends can be attained only by the forcible overthrow of all existing social conditions. Let the ruling classes tremble at a Communist revolution. The proletarians have nothing to lose but their chains. They have a world to win.

WORKINGMEN OF ALL COUNTRIES, UNITE!

On Liberty

John Stuart Mill

A biography of John Stuart Mill appears on p. 358.

Our reading is from *On Liberty,* Mill's classic defense of the freedom of the individual to do whatever does not harm other people. Mill's thesis is that "the only purpose for which power can be rightfully exercised over any member of a civilized community, against his will, is to prevent harm to others." We may not force people to do or refrain from doing something because we think (rightly or wrongly) that it is for their own good; individuals are sovereign in matters that concern only themselves. (Anticipating an objection, Mill explains that his principle of liberty applies only to rational, mature adults; children, for example, may be prevented from doing things that injure themselves.) A just society, consequently, must preserve freedom of consciousness (thought, opinion, feeling, conscience), freedom of tastes and pursuits, and freedom of association. The exercise of the latter two freedoms is subject to the condition that the actions of the individuals or the group do not harm others.

Mill goes on to give a detailed defense of two liberties he considers especially important: the freedom to express one's opinion and the freedom to live in a way that expresses one's individuality. With regard to the latter, he contends that the free development of individuality is something desirable for its own sake, as an essential part of human well-being. People who cultivate their unique traits live richer and more vibrant lives than those who submerge themselves in uniformity. To the degree that people develop their individuality, they become more valuable to themselves. Society benefits, too, because the more valuable people are to themselves, the more valuable they can be to others.

CHAPTER I. INTRODUCTORY

. . . The object of this essay is to assert one very simple principle, as entitled to govern absolutely the dealings of society with the individual in the way of compulsion and control, whether the means used be physical force in the form of legal penalties, or the moral coercion of public opinion. That principle is that the sole end[1] for which mankind are warranted, individually or collectively, in interfering with the liberty of action of any of their number is self-protection; that the only purpose for which power can be rightfully exercised over any member of a civilized community, against his will, is to prevent harm to others. His own good, either physical or moral, is not a sufficient warrant. He cannot rightfully be compelled to do or forbear because it will be better for him to do so, because it will make him happier, [or] because, in the opinions of others, to do so would be wise, or even right. These are good reasons for remonstrating with him, or reasoning with him, [or] persuading him, or entreating him, but not for compelling him or visiting him with any evil in case he do otherwise. To justify that, the conduct from which it is desired to deter him must be calculated

---

[1]*end:* purpose, goal. [D. C. ABEL]

to produce evil to someone else. The only part of the conduct of anyone for which he is amenable to society is that which concerns others. In the part which merely concerns himself, his independence is, of right, absolute. Over himself, over his own body and mind, the individual is sovereign.

It is perhaps hardly necessary to say that this doctrine is meant to apply only to human beings in the maturity of their faculties. We are not speaking of children or of young persons below the age which the law may fix as that of manhood or womanhood. Those who are still in a state to require being taken care of by others must be protected against their own actions as well as against external injury. For the same reason, we may leave out of consideration those backward states of society in which the race itself may be considered as in its nonage.[2] The early difficulties in the way of spontaneous progress are so great that there is seldom any choice of means for overcoming them; and a ruler full of the spirit of improvement is warranted in the use of any expedients that will attain an end, perhaps otherwise unattainable. Despotism is a legitimate mode of government in dealing with barbarians, provided the end be their improvement, and the means justified by actually effecting that end. Liberty, as a principle, has no application to any state of things anterior to the time when mankind have become capable of being improved by free and equal discussion. Until then, there is nothing for them but implicit obedience to an Akbar or a Charlemagne,[3] if they are so fortunate as to find one. But as soon as mankind have attained the capacity of being guided to their own improvement by conviction or persuasion (a period long since reached in all nations with whom we need here concern ourselves), compulsion, either in the direct form or in that of pains and penalties for noncompliance, is no longer admissible as a means to their own good, and justifiable only for the security of others.

It is proper to state that I forgo any advantage which could be derived to my argument from the idea of abstract right, as a thing independent of utility.[4] I regard utility as the ultimate appeal on all ethical questions—but it must be utility in the largest sense, grounded on the permanent interests of man as a progressive being. Those interests, I contend, authorize the subjection of individual spontaneity to external control only in respect to those actions of each which concern the interest of other people. If anyone does an act hurtful to others, there is a prima facie[5] case for punishing him by law or, where legal penalties are not safely applicable, by general disapprobation. There are also many positive acts for the benefit of others which he may rightfully be compelled to perform, such as: to give evidence in a court of justice; to bear his fair share in the common defense or in any other joint work necessary to the interest of the society of which he enjoys the protection; and to perform certain acts of individual

---

[2]*nonage:* the state of being a minor. [D. C. ABEL]

[3]Akbar (1542–1605) was a Mogul emperor of a territory comprising most of what is now India; Charlemagne (742–814) was king of the Franks and then emperor of the West. [D. C. ABEL]

[4]*utility:* usefulness in promoting good. Mill holds that the good is pleasure and that the ultimate criterion of morality is the promotion of the greatest pleasure of the greatest number of sentient creatures; see pp. 358–366 of this book. [D. C. ABEL]

[5]*prima facie:* on first appearance (literally, in Latin, "at first glance"). [D. C. ABEL]

beneficence, such as saving a fellow-creature's life or interposing to protect the defenseless against ill-usage—things which whenever it is obviously a man's duty to do, he may rightfully be made responsible to society for not doing. A person may cause evil to others not only by his actions but by his inaction, and in either case he is justly accountable to them for the injury. The latter case, it is true, requires a much more cautious exercise of compulsion than the former. To make anyone answerable for doing evil to others is the rule; to make him answerable for not preventing evil is, comparatively speaking, the exception. . . .

This, then, is the appropriate region of human liberty. It comprises, first, the inward domain of consciousness, demanding liberty of conscience in the most comprehensive sense; liberty of thought and feeling; absolute freedom of opinion and sentiment on all subjects, practical or speculative, scientific, moral, or theological. The liberty of expressing and publishing opinions may seem to fall under a different principle, since it belongs to that part of the conduct of an individual which concerns other people; but, being almost of as much importance as the liberty of thought itself and resting in great part on the same reasons, is practically inseparable from it. Secondly, the principle requires liberty of tastes and pursuits; of framing the plan of our life to suit our own character; of doing as we like, subject to such consequences as may follow—without impediment from our fellow creatures, so long as what we do does not harm them, even though they should think our conduct foolish, perverse, or wrong. Thirdly, from this liberty of each individual follows the liberty, within the same limits, of combination among individuals; freedom to unite for any purpose not involving harm to others—the persons combining being supposed to be of full age and not forced or deceived.

No society in which these liberties are not, on the whole, respected is free, whatever may be its form of government; and none is completely free in which they do not exist absolute and unqualified. The only freedom which deserves the name is that of pursuing our own good in our own way, so long as we do not attempt to deprive others of theirs or impede their efforts to obtain it. Each is the proper guardian of his own health, whether bodily, or mental and spiritual. Mankind are greater gainers by suffering[6] each other to live as seems good to themselves, than by compelling each to live as seems good to the rest. . . .

It will be convenient for the argument if, instead of at once entering upon the general thesis, we confine ourselves in the first instance to a single branch of it, on which the principle here stated is, if not fully, yet to a certain point, recognized by the current opinions. This one branch is the liberty of thought, from which it is impossible to separate the cognate liberty of speaking and of writing. Although these liberties, to some considerable amount, form part of the political morality of all countries which profess religious toleration and free institutions, the grounds, both philosophical and practical, on which they rest are perhaps not so familiar to the general mind, nor so thoroughly appreciated by many even of the leaders of opinion, as might have been expected. . . .

---

[6]*suffering:* allowing. [D. C. ABEL]

CHAPTER II. OF THE LIBERTY OF THOUGHT AND DISCUSSION

The time, it is to be hoped, is gone by, when any defense would be necessary of the "liberty of the press" as one of the securities against corrupt or tyrannical government. No argument, we may suppose, can now be needed against permitting a legislature or an executive, not identified in interest with the people, to prescribe opinions to them and determine what doctrines or what arguments they shall be allowed to hear. This aspect of the question, besides, has been so often and so triumphantly enforced by preceding writers that it needs not be specially insisted on in this place. Though the law of England on the subject of the press is as servile to this day as it was in the time of the Tudors,[7] there is little danger of its being actually put in force against political discussion, except during some temporary panic, when fear of insurrection drives ministers and judges from their propriety. And speaking generally, it is not, in constitutional countries, to be apprehended that the government, whether completely responsible to the people or not, will often attempt to control the expression of opinion, except when in doing so it makes itself the organ of the general intolerance of the public. Let us suppose therefore that the government is entirely at one with the people and never thinks of exerting any power of coercion unless in agreement with what it conceives to be their voice. But I deny the right of the people to exercise such coercion, either by themselves or by their government. The power itself is illegitimate. The best government has no more title to it than the worst. It is as noxious, or more noxious, when exerted in accordance with public opinion than when in opposition to it. If all mankind minus one were of one opinion, and only one person were of the contrary opinion, mankind would be no more justified in silencing that one person, than he, if he had the power, would be justified in silencing mankind. Were an opinion a personal possession of no value except to the owner, if to be obstructed in the enjoyment of it were simply a private injury, it would make some difference whether the injury was inflicted only on a few persons or on many. But the peculiar evil of silencing the expression of an opinion is that it is robbing the human race; posterity as well as the existing generation; those who dissent from the opinion, still more than those who hold it. If the opinion is right, they are deprived of the opportunity of exchanging error for truth; if wrong, they lose what is almost as great a benefit, the clearer perception and livelier impression of truth, produced by its collision with error. . . .

The necessity to the mental well-being of mankind (on which all their other well-being depends) of freedom of opinion, and freedom of the expression of opinion, [rests] on four distinct grounds. . . .

First, if any opinion is compelled to silence, that opinion may, for aught we can certainly know, be true. To deny this is to assume our own infallibility.

Secondly, though the silenced opinion be an error, it may, and very commonly does, contain a portion of truth; and since the general or prevailing opinion on any subject is rarely or never the whole truth, it is only by the

---

[7]*Tudors:* the English royal house that ruled from 1485 to 1603. [D. C. Abel]

collision of adverse opinions that the remainder of the truth has any chance of being supplied.

Thirdly, even if the received opinion be not only true but the whole truth, unless it is suffered to be, and actually is, vigorously and earnestly contested, it will, by most of those who receive it, be held in the manner of a prejudice, with little comprehension or feeling of its rational grounds. And not only this, but, fourthly, the meaning of the doctrine itself will be in danger of being lost or enfeebled and deprived of its vital effect on the character and conduct—the dogma becoming a mere formal profession, inefficacious for good, but cumbering[8] the ground and preventing the growth of any real and heartfelt conviction from reason or personal experience. . . .

CHAPTER III. OF INDIVIDUALITY, AS ONE OF THE ELEMENTS OF WELL-BEING

Such being the reasons which make it imperative that human beings should be free to form opinions and to express their opinions without reserve; and such the baneful consequences to the intellectual, and through that to the moral nature of man, unless this liberty is either conceded or asserted in spite of prohibition; let us next examine whether the same reasons do not require that men should be free to act upon their opinions—to carry these out in their lives, without hindrance, either physical or moral, from their fellow men, so long as it is at their own risk and peril. This last proviso is of course indispensable. No one pretends that actions should be as free as opinions. On the contrary, even opinions lose their immunity when the circumstances in which they are expressed are such as to constitute their expression a positive instigation to some mischievous act. An opinion that corn dealers are starvers of the poor, or that private property is robbery, ought to be unmolested when simply circulated through the press, but may justly incur punishment when delivered orally to an excited mob assembled before the house of a corn dealer, or when handed about among the same mob in the form of a placard. Acts of whatever kind which without justifiable cause do harm to others may be, and in the more important cases absolutely require to be, controlled by the unfavorable sentiments and, when needful, by the active interference of mankind. The liberty of the individual must be thus far limited; he must not make himself a nuisance to other people. But if he refrains from molesting others in what concerns them and merely acts according to his own inclination and judgment in things which concern himself, the same reasons which show that opinion should be free, prove also that he should be allowed, without molestation, to carry his opinions into practice at his own cost. That mankind are not infallible; that their truths for the most part are only half-truths; that unity of opinion, unless resulting from the fullest and freest comparison of opposite opinions, is not desirable, and diversity not an evil but a good, until mankind are much more capable than at present of recognizing all sides of the truth, are principles applicable to men's modes of action, not less

---

[8]*cumbering:* cluttering up [D. C. ABEL]

than to their opinions. As it is useful that while mankind are imperfect there should be different opinions, so is it that there should be different experiments of living; that free scope should be given to varieties of character, short of injury to others; and that the worth of different modes of life should be proved practically, when anyone thinks fit to try them. It is desirable, in short, that in things which do not primarily concern others, individuality should assert itself. Where not the person's own character, but the traditions or customs of other people are the rule of conduct, there is wanting one of the principal ingredients of human happiness, and quite the chief ingredient of individual and social progress.

In maintaining this principle, the greatest difficulty to be encountered does not lie in the appreciation of means towards an acknowledged end, but in the indifference of persons in general to the end itself. If it were felt that the free development of individuality is one of the leading essentials of well-being; that it is not only a coordinate element with all that is designated by the terms civilization, instruction, education, culture, but is itself a necessary part and condition of all those things—[then] there would be no danger that liberty should be undervalued, and the adjustment of the boundaries between it and social control would present no extraordinary difficulty. But the evil is that individual spontaneity is hardly recognized by the common modes of thinking as having any intrinsic worth or deserving any regard on its own account. . . .

It is not by wearing down into uniformity all that is individual in themselves, but by cultivating it and calling it forth, within the limits imposed by the rights and interests of others, that human beings become a noble and beautiful object of contemplation. And as the works partake the character of those who do them, by the same process human life also becomes rich, diversified, and animating, furnishing more abundant aliment to high thoughts and elevating feelings, and strengthening the tie which binds every individual to the race, by making the race infinitely better worth belonging to. In proportion to the development of his individuality, each person becomes more valuable to himself and is therefore capable of being more valuable to others. There is a greater fullness of life about his own existence, and when there is more life in the units there is more in the mass which is composed of them. . . .

CHAPTER IV. OF THE LIMITS TO THE AUTHORITY OF SOCIETY OVER THE INDIVIDUAL

What, then, is the rightful limit to the sovereignty of the individual over himself? Where does the authority of society begin? How much of human life should be assigned to individuality, and how much to society?

Each will receive its proper share if each has that which more particularly concerns it. To individuality should belong the part of life in which it is chiefly the individual that is interested; to society, the part which chiefly interests society.

Though society is not founded on a contract and though no good purpose is answered by inventing a contract in order to deduce social obligations from it, everyone who receives the protection of society owes a return for the benefit, and the fact of living in society renders it indispensable that each should be bound to observe a certain line of conduct towards the rest. This conduct consists, first, in not injuring the interests of one another—or rather certain interests which, either by express legal provision or by tacit understanding, ought to be considered as rights; and secondly, in each person's bearing his share (to be fixed on some equitable principle) of the labors and sacrifices incurred for defending the society or its members from injury and molestation. These conditions society is justified in enforcing at all costs to those who endeavor to withhold fulfillment. Nor is this all that society may do. The acts of an individual may be hurtful to others, or wanting in due consideration for their welfare, without going the length of violating any of their constituted rights. The offender may then be justly punished by opinion, though not by law. As soon as any part of a person's conduct affects prejudicially the interests of others, society has jurisdiction over it and the question whether the general welfare will or will not be promoted by interfering with it becomes open to discussion. But there is no room for entertaining any such question when a person's conduct affects the interests of no persons besides himself, or needs not affect them unless they like (all the persons concerned being of full age and the ordinary amount of understanding). In all such cases there should be perfect freedom, legal and social, to do the action and stand the consequences. . . .

Neither one person nor any number of persons is warranted in saying to another human creature of ripe years that he shall not do with his life for his own benefit what he chooses to do with it. He is the person most interested in his own well-being; the interest which any other person, except in cases of strong personal attachment, can have in it is trifling compared with that which he himself has. The interest which society has in him individually (except as to his conduct to others) is fractional and altogether indirect; while, with respect to his own feelings and circumstances, the most ordinary man or woman has means of knowledge immeasurably surpassing those that can be possessed by anyone else. The interference of society to overrule his judgment and purposes in what only regards himself, must be grounded on general presumptions which may be altogether wrong—and even if right, are as likely as not to be misapplied to individual cases by persons no better acquainted with the circumstances of such cases than those are who look at them merely from without. In this department, therefore, of human affairs, individuality has its proper field of action. In the conduct of human beings towards one another, it is necessary that general rules should for the most part be observed, in order that people may know what they have to expect; but in each person's own concerns, his individual spontaneity is entitled to free exercise. Considerations to aid his judgment, exhortations to strengthen his will, may be offered to him, even obtruded on him, by others; but he himself is the final judge. All errors which he is likely to commit against advice and warning are far outweighed by the evil of allowing others to constrain him to what they deem his good.

B. Contemporary Social Issues

READING 47

Letter from Birmingham Jail

Martin Luther King, Jr.

Martin Luther King, Jr., was born in 1929 in Atlanta, Georgia. He attended Morehouse College and during his senior year decided to follow in his father's footsteps and become a Baptist minister. Upon graduating in 1948, he entered Crozer Theological Seminary in Chester, Pennsylvania. There he was deeply influenced by Mohandas Gandhi's philosophy of nonviolence and became convinced that black Americans should use this strategy to attain their civil rights. King received his bachelor of divinity degree in 1951. He then began doctoral studies in theology at Boston University, completing his degree in 1955. While still working on his doctorate, King became pastor at the Dexter Avenue Baptist Church in Montgomery, Alabama. In 1954 he led a boycott of the city transit company to protest segregated seating on buses. Within a year the buses were desegregated. Encouraged by this success, King began to work for civil rights on a national basis by forming the Southern Christian Leadership Conference. In 1960 he moved to Atlanta, where he directed the Conference and served as copastor (with his father) at Ebenezer Baptist Church. In 1963 he and many others were arrested and jailed for participating in a demonstration in Birmingham. Later that year King helped organize a massive demonstration in Washington, D.C., for civil rights legislation. King addressed the crowd, proclaiming "I have a dream"—a dream of interracial equality and harmony. The following year King received the Nobel Peace Prize. In 1968, while in Memphis to support a strike by sanitation workers, he was killed by a sniper's bullet.

King's works include *Stride toward Freedom: The Montgomery Story* (1958), *Why We Can't Wait* (1964), and *Where Do We Go from Here: Chaos or Community?* (1967).

Our reading is from King's "Letter from Birmingham Jail" (published in *Why We Can't Wait*), an essay King wrote in 1963 when in jail for protesting segregation at lunch counters and discrimination in hiring practices. King's essay is a response to eight members of the clergy who had published a statement criticizing his civil rights activities as "unwise and untimely." King explains that blacks in America have waited for more than three centuries to gain their basic human rights—and that they should wait no longer. In answer to the objection that his nonviolent activities sometimes violate laws, King distinguishes between just and unjust laws. Just laws should be obeyed, but unjust laws are not binding because they contradict moral laws and degrade human beings. There are some situations in which even just laws are not binding, however. For example, a law requiring a permit for a parade is just, but it need not be obeyed when it is used for the unjust purpose of denying citizens the right of peaceful assembly and protest. King explains that a person who breaks a just law as a form of protest must do so openly and with a willingness to accept the penalty. Responding to the charge that he is an extremist, King points out that nonviolent protest is certainly less extreme than violence. He admits, however, that in a certain way he is an extremist—an extremist for love and justice.

April 16, 1963

My dear fellow Clergymen:

[INTRODUCTION]

While confined here in the Birmingham city jail, I came across your recent statement calling my present activities "unwise and untimely." Seldom do I pause to answer criticism of my work and ideas. If I sought to answer all the criticisms that cross my desk, my secretaries would have little time for anything other than such correspondence in the course of the day, and I would have no time for constructive work. But since I feel that you are men of genuine good will and that your criticisms are sincerely set forth, I want to try to answer your statement in what I hope will be patient and reasonable terms. . . .

You deplore the demonstrations taking place in Birmingham. But your statement, I am sorry to say, fails to express a similar concern for the conditions that brought about the demonstrations. I am sure that none of you would want to rest content with the superficial kind of social analysis that deals merely with effects and does not grapple with underlying causes. It is unfortunate that demonstrations are taking place in Birmingham, but it is even more unfortunate that the city's white power structure left the Negro community with no alternative. . . .

We know through painful experience that freedom is never voluntarily given by the oppressor; it must be demanded by the oppressed. Frankly, I have yet to engage in a direct-action campaign that was "well timed" in the view of those who have not suffered unduly from the disease of segregation. For years now I have heard the word "Wait!" It rings in the ear of every Negro with piercing familiarity. This "Wait" has almost always meant "Never." We must come to see, with one of our distinguished jurists, that "justice too long delayed is justice denied."[1]

We have waited for more than 340 years for our constitutional and God-given rights. The nations of Asia and Africa are moving with jetlike speed toward gaining political independence, but we still creep at horse-and-buggy pace toward gaining a cup of coffee at a lunch counter. Perhaps it is easy for those who have never felt the stinging darts of segregation to say "Wait." But when you have seen vicious mobs lynch your mothers and fathers at will and drown your sisters and brothers at whim; when you have seen hate-filled policemen curse, kick, and even kill your black brothers and sisters; when you see the vast majority of your twenty million Negro brothers smothering in an air-tight cage of poverty in the midst of an affluent society; when you suddenly find your tongue twisted and your speech stammering as you seek to explain to your six-year-old daughter why she can't go to the public amusement park that has just been advertised on television, and see tears welling up in her eyes when

---

[1]This quotation is attributed to the British politician William Ewart Gladstone (1809–1898). [D. C. Abel]

she is told that Funtown is closed to colored children, and see ominous clouds of inferiority beginning to form in her little mental sky, and see her beginning to distort her personality by developing an unconscious bitterness toward white people; when you have to concoct an answer for a five-year-old son who is asking, "Daddy, why do white people treat colored people so mean?"; when you take a cross-country drive and find it necessary to sleep night after night in the uncomfortable corners of your automobile because no motel will accept you; when you are humiliated day in and day out by nagging signs reading "white" and "colored"; when your first name becomes "nigger," your middle name becomes "boy" (however old you are), and your last name becomes "John," and your wife and mother are never given the respected title "Mrs."; when you are harried by day and haunted by night by the fact that you are a Negro, living constantly at tiptoe stance, never quite knowing what to expect next, and are plagued with inner fears and outer resentments; when you are forever fighting a degenerating sense of "nobodiness"—then you will understand why we find it difficult to wait. There comes a time when the cup of endurance runs over, and men are no longer willing to be plunged into the abyss of despair. I hope, sirs, you can understand our legitimate and unavoidable impatience.

[CIVIL DISOBEDIENCE]

You express a great deal of anxiety over our willingness to break laws. This is certainly a legitimate concern. Since we so diligently urge people to obey the Supreme Court's decision of 1954 outlawing segregation in the public schools, at first glance it may seem rather paradoxical for us consciously to break laws. One may well ask, "How can you advocate breaking some laws and obeying others?" The answer lies in the fact that there are two types of laws: just and unjust. I would be the first to advocate obeying just laws. One has not only a legal but a moral responsibility to obey just laws. Conversely, one has a moral responsibility to disobey unjust laws. I would agree with St. Augustine that "an unjust law is no law at all."[2]

Now, what is the difference between the two? How does one determine whether a law is just or unjust? A just law is a man-made code that squares with the moral law or the law of God. An unjust law is a code that is out of harmony with the moral law. To put it in the terms of St. Thomas Aquinas: An unjust law is a human law that is not rooted in eternal law and natural law.[3] Any law that uplifts human personality is just. Any law that degrades human personality is unjust. All segregation statutes are unjust because segregation distorts the soul and damages the personality. It gives the segregator a false sense of superiority and the segregated a false sense of inferiority. Segregation, to use the terminology of the Jewish philosopher Martin Buber, substitutes an "I–it" relationship for an "I–thou"

---

[2]Augustine, *On Free Choice of the Will*, Book I, Chapter 5. Augustine (345–430) was a North African theologian and philosopher; for a biography, see p. 74. [D. C. ABEL]

[3]Thomas Aquinas, *Summa Theologiae*, Part Two, First Part, Question 95, Second article. Aquinas (about 1224–1274) was an Italian theologian and philosopher; for a biography, see p. 39. [D. C. ABEL]

relationship and ends up relegating persons to the status of things.[4] Hence segregation is not only politically, economically, and sociologically unsound; it is morally wrong and sinful. Paul Tillich has said that sin is separation.[5] Is not segregation an existential expression of man's tragic separation, his awful estrangement, his terrible sinfulness? Thus it is that I can urge men to obey the 1954 decision of the Supreme Court, for it is morally right; and I can urge them to disobey segregation ordinances, for they are morally wrong.

Let us consider a more concrete example of just and unjust laws. An unjust law is a code that a numerical or power majority group compels a minority group to obey but does not make binding on itself. This is *difference* made legal. By the same token, a just law is a code that a majority compels a minority to follow and that it is willing to follow itself. This is *sameness* made legal.

Let me give another explanation. A law is unjust if it is inflicted on a minority that, as a result of being denied the right to vote, had no part in enacting or devising the law. Who can say that the legislature of Alabama which set up that state's segregation laws was democratically elected? Throughout Alabama all sorts of devious methods are used to prevent Negroes from becoming registered voters, and there are some counties in which, even though Negroes constitute a majority of the population, not a single Negro is registered. Can any law enacted under such circumstances be considered democratically structured?

Sometimes a law is just on its face and unjust in its application. For instance, I have been arrested on a charge of parading without a permit. Now, there is nothing wrong in having an ordinance which requires a permit for a parade. But such an ordinance becomes unjust when it is used to maintain segregation and to deny citizens the First Amendment privilege of peaceful assembly and protest.

I hope you are able to see the distinction I am trying to point out. In no sense do I advocate evading or defying the law, as would the rabid segregationist. That would lead to anarchy. One who breaks an unjust law must do so openly, lovingly, and with a willingness to accept the penalty. I submit that an individual who breaks a law that conscience tells him is unjust, and who willingly accepts the penalty of imprisonment in order to arouse the conscience of the community over its injustice, is in reality expressing the highest respect for law.

Of course, there is nothing new about this kind of civil disobedience. It was evidenced sublimely in the refusal of Shadrach, Meshach, and Abednego to obey the laws of Nebuchadnezzar, on the ground that a higher moral law was at stake.[6] It was practiced superbly by the early Christians, who were willing to face hungry lions and the excruciating pain of chopping blocks rather than submit to certain unjust laws of the Roman Empire. To a degree, academic freedom is a reality today because Socrates[7] practiced civil disobedience. In our own nation, the Boston Tea Party represented a massive act of civil disobedience.

---

[4]Martin Buber, *I and Thou,* 2d ed., trans. Ronald Gregor Smith (New York: Scribner, 1958). Buber (1878–1965) was an Israeli (Austrian-born) philosopher. [D. C. ABEL]

[5]Paul Tillich, *Systematic Theology,* vol. 2 (Chicago: University of Chicago Press, 1957), pp. 59–66. Tillich (1886–1965) was an American (German-born) theologian. [D. C. ABEL]

[6]Daniel 3:1–30. [D. C. ABEL]

[7]Socrates (about 470–399 B.C.E) was a Greek philosopher. [D. C. ABEL]

We should never forget that everything Adolf Hitler did in Germany was "legal" and everything the Hungarian freedom fighters did in Hungary was "illegal." It was "illegal" to aid and comfort a Jew in Hitler's Germany. Even so, I am sure that, had I lived in Germany at the time, I would have aided and comforted my Jewish brothers. If today I lived in a Communist country where certain principles dear to the Christian faith are suppressed, I would openly advocate disobeying that country's antireligious laws.

[WHITE MODERATES]

I must make two honest confessions to you, my Christian and Jewish brothers. First, I must confess that over the past few years I have been gravely disappointed with the white moderate. I have almost reached the regrettable conclusion that the Negro's great stumbling block in his stride toward freedom is not the White Citizen's Counciler or the Ku Klux Klanner, but the white moderate, who is more devoted to "order" than to justice; who prefers a negative peace, which is the absence of tension, to a positive peace, which is the presence of justice; who constantly says, "I agree with you in the goal you seek, but I cannot agree with your methods of direct action"; who paternalistically believes he can set the timetable for another man's freedom; who lives by a mythical concept of time and who constantly advises the Negro to wait for a "more convenient season." Shallow understanding from people of good will is more frustrating than absolute misunderstanding from people of ill will. Lukewarm acceptance is much more bewildering than outright rejection.

I had hoped that the white moderate would understand that law and order exist for the purpose of establishing justice and that when they fail in this purpose they become the dangerously structured dams that block the flow of social progress. I had hoped that the white moderate would understand that the present tension in the South is a necessary phase of the transition from an obnoxious negative peace, in which the Negro passively accepted his unjust plight, to a substantive and positive peace, in which all men will respect the dignity and worth of human personality. Actually, we who engage in nonviolent direct action are not the creators of tension. We merely bring to the surface the hidden tension that is already alive. We bring it out in the open, where it can be seen and dealt with. Like a boil that can never be cured so long as it is covered up but must be opened with all its ugliness to the natural medicines of air and light, injustice must be exposed, with all the tension its exposure creates, to the light of human conscience and the air of national opinion before it can be cured.

In your statement you assert that our actions, even though peaceful, must be condemned because they precipitate violence. But is this a logical assertion? Isn't this like condemning a robbed man because his possession of money precipitated the evil act of robbery? Isn't this like condemning Socrates because his unswerving commitment to truth and his philosophical inquiries precipitated the act by the misguided populace in which they made him drink hemlock?[8]

---

[8]Socrates was convicted by the Athenians of impiety and the corruption of youth and was executed by being given hemlock (a poison) to drink. [D. C. ABEL]

Isn't this like condemning Jesus because his unique God-consciousness and never-ceasing devotion to God's will precipitated the evil act of crucifixion? We must come to see that, as the federal courts have consistently affirmed, it is wrong to urge an individual to cease his efforts to gain his basic constitutional rights because the quest may precipitate violence. Society must protect the robbed and punish the robber.

I had also hoped that the white moderate would reject the myth concerning time in relation to the struggle for freedom. I have just received a letter from a white brother in Texas. He writes: "All Christians know that the colored people will receive equal rights eventually, but it is possible that you are in too great a religious hurry. It has taken Christianity almost two thousand years to accomplish what it has. The teachings of Christ take time to come to earth." Such an attitude stems from a tragic misconception of time, from the strangely irrational notion that there is something in the very flow of time that will inevitably cure all ills. Actually, time itself is neutral; it can be used either destructively or constructively. More and more I feel that the people of ill will have used time much more effectively than have the people of good will. We will have to repent in this generation not merely for the hateful words and actions of the bad people but for the appalling silence of the good people. Human progress never rolls in on wheels of inevitability; it comes through the tireless efforts of men willing to be coworkers with God, and without this hard work, time itself becomes an ally of the forces of social stagnation. We must use time creatively, in the knowledge that the time is always ripe to do right. Now is the time to make real the promise of democracy and transform our pending national elegy into a creative psalm of brotherhood. Now is the time to lift our national policy from the quicksand of racial injustice to the solid rock of human dignity.

[THE CHARGE OF EXTREMISM]

You speak of our activity in Birmingham as extreme. At first I was rather disappointed that fellow clergymen would see my nonviolent efforts as those of an extremist. I began thinking about the fact that I stand in the middle of two opposing forces in the Negro community. One is a force of complacency, made up in part of Negroes who, as a result of long years of oppression, are so drained of self-respect and a sense of "somebodiness" that they have adjusted to segregation; and in part of a few middle-class Negroes who, because of a degree of academic and economic security and because in some ways they profit by segregation, have become insensitive to the problems of the masses. The other force is one of bitterness and hatred, and it comes perilously close to advocating violence. It is expressed in the various black nationalist groups that are springing up across the nation, the largest and best-known being Elijah Muhammad's Muslim movement.[9] Nourished by the Negro's frustration over the continued existence of racial discrimination, this movement is made up of people who

---

[9]Elijah Muhammad (1897–1975) was an American religious leader who directed the Black Muslim movement. [D. C. ABEL]

have lost faith in America, who have absolutely repudiated Christianity, and who have concluded that the white man is an incorrigible "devil."

I have tried to stand between these two forces, saying that we need emulate neither the "do-nothingism" of the complacent nor the hatred and despair of the black nationalist. For there is the more excellent way of love and nonviolent protest. I am grateful to God that, through the influence of the Negro church, the way of nonviolence became an integral part of our struggle.

If this philosophy had not emerged, by now many streets of the South would, I am convinced, be flowing with blood. And I am further convinced that if our white brothers dismiss as "rabble-rousers" and "outside agitators" those of us who employ nonviolent direct action, and if they refuse to support our nonviolent efforts, millions of Negroes will, out of frustration and despair, seek solace and security in black-nationalist ideologies—a development that would inevitably lead to a frightening racial nightmare.

Oppressed people cannot remain oppressed forever. The yearning for freedom eventually manifests itself, and that is what has happened to the American Negro. Something within has reminded him of his birthright of freedom, and something without has reminded him that it can be gained. Consciously or unconsciously, he has been caught up by the zeitgeist,[10] and with his black brothers of Africa and his brown and yellow brothers of Asia, South America, and the Caribbean, the United States Negro is moving with a sense of great urgency toward the promised land of racial justice. If one recognizes this vital urge that has engulfed the Negro community, one should readily understand why public demonstrations are taking place. The Negro has many pent-up resentments and latent frustrations, and he must release them. So let him march; let him make prayer pilgrimages to the city hall; let him go on freedom rides— and try to understand why he must do so. If his repressed emotions are not released in nonviolent ways, they will seek expression through violence; this is not a threat but a fact of history. So I have not said to my people, "Get rid of your discontent." Rather, I have tried to say that this normal and healthy discontent can be channeled into the creative outlet of nonviolent direct action. And now this approach is being termed extremist.

But though I was initially disappointed at being categorized as an extremist, as I continued to think about the matter I gradually gained a measure of satisfaction from the label. Was not Jesus an extremist for love: "Love your enemies, bless them that curse you, do good to them that hate you, and pray for them that despitefully use you, and persecute you." Was not Amos an extremist for justice: "Let justice roll down like waters and righteousness like an everflowing stream." Was not Paul an extremist for the Christian gospel: "I bear in my body the marks of the Lord Jesus." Was not Martin Luther an extremist: "Here I stand; I cannot do otherwise, so help me God." And John Bunyan:[11] "I will stay in jail to the end of my days before I make a butchery of my conscience." And Abraham Lincoln: "This nation cannot survive half slave and half free." And Thomas Jefferson: "We hold these truths to be self-evident, that all

---

[10]*zeitgeist:* the cultural and moral climate of an era (literally, in German, "spirit of the time"). [D. C. ABEL]
[11]Bunyan (1628–1688) was an English preacher and author. [D. C. ABEL]

men are created equal . . . " So the question is not whether we will be extremists, but what kind of extremists we will be. Will we be extremists for hate or for love? Will we be extremists for the preservation of injustice or for the extension of justice? In that dramatic scene on Calvary's hill three men were crucified. We must never forget that all three were crucified for the same crime—the crime of extremism. Two were extremists for immorality, and thus fell below their environment. The other, Jesus Christ, was an extremist for love, truth, and goodness, and thereby rose above his environment. Perhaps the South, the nation, and the world are in dire need of creative extremists.

I had hoped that the white moderate would see this need. Perhaps I was too optimistic; perhaps I expected too much. I suppose I should have realized that few members of the oppressor race can understand the deep groans and passionate yearnings of the oppressed race, and still fewer have the vision to see that injustice must be rooted out by strong, persistent, and determined action. I am thankful, however, that some of our white brothers in the South have grasped the meaning of this social revolution and committed themselves to it. They are still all too few in quantity, but they are big in quality. Some—such as Ralph McGill, Lillian Smith, Harry Golden, James McBride Dabbs, Ann Braden, and Sarah Patton Boyle—have written about our struggle in eloquent and prophetic terms. Others have marched with us down nameless streets of the South. They have languished in filthy, roach-infested jails, suffering the abuse and brutality of policemen who view them as "dirty nigger-lovers." Unlike so many of their moderate brothers and sisters, they have recognized the urgency of the moment and sensed the need for powerful "action" antidotes to combat the disease of segregation. . . .

[CONCLUSION]

Never before have I written so long a letter. I'm afraid it is much too long to take your precious time. I can assure you that it would have been much shorter if I had been writing from a comfortable desk, but what else can one do when he is alone in a narrow jail cell, other than write long letters, think long thoughts, and pray long prayers?

If I have said anything in this letter that overstates the truth and indicates an unreasonable impatience, I beg you to forgive me. If I have said anything that understates the truth and indicates my having a patience that allows me to settle for anything less than brotherhood, I beg God to forgive me.

I hope this letter finds you strong in the faith. I also hope that circumstances will soon make it possible for me to meet each of you, not as an integrationist or a civil rights leader but as a fellow clergyman and a Christian brother. Let us all hope that the dark clouds of racial prejudice will soon pass away and the deep fog of misunderstanding will be lifted from our fear-drenched communities, and in some not-too-distant tomorrow the radiant stars of love and brotherhood will shine over our great nation with all their scintillating beauty.

Yours for the cause of peace and brotherhood,
MARTIN LUTHER KING, JR.

A Theory of Justice

John Rawls

John Rawls was born in 1921 in Baltimore, Maryland. He received his undergraduate education at Cornell University and then served in the U.S. Army during World War II. After the war he enrolled in the doctoral program in philosophy at Princeton University, receiving his degree in 1950. He then taught at Princeton for two years. During the following academic year, Rawls was a Fulbright Fellow at Oxford University. In 1953 he accepted a position at Cornell, where he taught for six years. Rawls taught at Harvard University from 1959 to 1960 and at the Massachusetts Institute of Technology for the following two years. In 1962 he returned to Harvard. He was named James Bryan Conant University Professor at Harvard in 1979—a position he held until his retirement in 1997. He died in 2002 in Lexington, Massachusetts.

Rawls's principal works are *A Theory of Justice* (1971); *Political Liberalism* (1993); *The Law of Peoples; with, The Idea of Public Reason Revisited* (1999); *Collected Papers* (1999); *Lectures on the History of Moral Philosophy* (2000); and *Lectures on the History of Political Philosophy* (edited by Samuel Freeman, 2007).

Our selection is from *A Theory of Justice,* the work in which Rawls sets forth his theory about how to assign basic rights and duties to members of a society and how to distribute benefits. Rawls contends that the specific laws and practices in a society will be just if they result from basic principles that are themselves just. To determine which basic principles are just, Rawls uses the device of a hypothetical "original position." In the original position, individuals who are prevented by a "veil of ignorance" from knowing their personal status in their society (for example, whether they are rich or poor, talented or untalented) rationally deliberate about what principles of justice should govern the society in which they will live. Rawls argues that the impartiality and objectivity of the people in the original position would lead them to adopt two basic principles of justice.

The first principle states that each person is to have the maximum basic liberty compatible with a similar liberty for others. (Basic liberties includes such things as the freedom of speech, the right to vote, and freedom from arbitrary arrest.) The second principle is that social and economic inequalities be arranged in a way likely to work to everyone's advantage and that there be equality of opportunity to attain the higher social and economic positions. (An example of a social inequality would be some people having authority and others being subject to them.) Rawls stipulates, however, that this second principle cannot be employed if it violates the first. In other words, social or economic advantages do not justify the violation of anyone's basic liberties, even if the very people whose liberties are curtailed would share in those advantages. A society whose subsequent laws and practices conformed to these two basic principles would, according to Rawls, be a just society.

CHAPTER I. JUSTICE AS FAIRNESS

1. The Role of Justice

Justice is the first virtue of social institutions, as truth is of systems of thought. A theory however elegant and economical must be rejected or revised if it is untrue; likewise laws and institutions no matter how efficient and well-arranged must be reformed or abolished if they are unjust. Each person possesses an inviolability founded on justice that even the welfare of society as a whole cannot override. For this reason justice denies that the loss of freedom for some is made right by a greater good shared by others. It does not allow that the sacrifices imposed on a few are outweighed by the larger sum of advantages enjoyed by many. Therefore in a just society the liberties of equal citizenship are taken as settled; the rights secured by justice are not subject to political bargaining or to the calculus of social interests. The only thing that permits us to acquiesce in an erroneous theory is the lack of a better one; analogously, an injustice is tolerable only when it is necessary to avoid an even greater injustice. Being first virtues of human activities, truth and justice are uncompromising.

These propositions seem to express our intuitive conviction of the primacy of justice. No doubt they are expressed too strongly. In any event I wish to inquire whether these contentions or others similar to them are sound, and if so how they can be accounted for. To this end it is necessary to work out a theory of justice in the light of which these assertions can be interpreted and assessed. I shall begin by considering the role of the principles of justice. Let us assume, to fix ideas, that a society is a more or less self-sufficient association of persons who in their relations to one another recognize certain rules of conduct as binding and who for the most part act in accordance with them. Suppose further that these rules specify a system of cooperation designed to advance the good of those taking part in it. Then, although a society is a cooperative venture for mutual advantage, it is typically marked by a conflict as well as by an identity of interests. There is an identity of interests since social cooperation makes possible a better life for all than any would have if each were to live solely by his own efforts. There is a conflict of interests since persons are not indifferent as to how the greater benefits produced by their collaboration are distributed, for in order to pursue their ends[1] they each prefer a larger to a lesser share. A set of principles is required for choosing among the various social arrangements that determine this division of advantages and for underwriting an agreement on the proper distributive shares. These principles are the principles of social justice: They provide a way of assigning rights and duties in the basic institutions of society and they define the appropriate distribution of the benefits and burdens of social cooperation.

Now let us say that a society is well-ordered when it is not only designed to advance the good of its members but when it is also effectively regulated by a public conception of justice. That is, it is a society in which (1) everyone accepts and knows that the others accept the same principles of justice, and (2) the basic social institutions generally satisfy and are generally known to satisfy these principles. In this case, while men may put forth excessive demands on one another, they nevertheless acknowledge a common point of view from which their claims may be adjudicated. If men's inclination to self-interest makes their vigilance against one another necessary, their public sense of justice makes their secure association together possible. Among individuals with disparate aims and purposes, a shared conception of justice establishes the bonds of civic

---

[1]*ends:* goals. [D. C. ABEL]

friendship; the general desire for justice limits the pursuit of other ends. One may think of a public conception of justice as constituting the fundamental charter of a well-ordered human association.

Existing societies are of course seldom well-ordered in this sense, for what is just and unjust is usually in dispute. Men disagree about which principles should define the basic terms of their association. Yet we may still say, despite this disagreement, that they each have a conception of justice. That is, they understand the need for, and they are prepared to affirm, a characteristic set of principles for assigning basic rights and duties and for determining what they take to be the proper distribution of the benefits and burdens of social cooperation. Thus it seems natural to think of the concept of justice as distinct from the various conceptions of justice and as being specified by the role that these different sets of principles, these different conceptions, have in common. Those who hold different conceptions of justice can, then, still agree that institutions are just when no arbitrary distinctions are made between persons in the assigning of basic rights and duties and when the rules determine a proper balance between competing claims to the advantages of social life. Men can agree to this description of just institutions since the notions of an arbitrary distinction and of a proper balance, which are included in the concept of justice, are left open for each to interpret according to the principles of justice that he accepts. These principles single out which similarities and differences among persons are relevant in determining rights and duties, and they specify which division of advantages is appropriate. Clearly this distinction between the concept and the various conceptions of justice settles no important questions. It simply helps to identify the role of the principles of social justice. . . .

2. The Subject of Justice

Many different kinds of things are said to be just and unjust—not only laws, institutions, and social systems, but also particular actions of many kinds, including decisions, judgments, and imputations. We also call the attitudes and dispositions of persons, and persons themselves, just and unjust. Our topic, however, is that of social justice. For us the primary subject of justice is the basic structure of society, or more exactly, the way in which the major social institutions distribute fundamental rights and duties and determine the division of advantages from social cooperation. By major institutions I understand the political constitution and the principal economic and social arrangements. Thus the legal protection of freedom of thought and liberty of conscience, competitive markets, private property in the means of production, and the monogamous family are examples of major social institutions. Taken together as one scheme, the major institutions define men's rights and duties and influence their life prospects, what they can expect to be, and how well they can hope to do. The basic structure is the primary subject of justice because its effects are so profound and present from the start. The intuitive notion here is that this structure contains various social positions and that men born into different positions have different expectations of life determined, in part, by the political system as well as by economic and social circumstances. In this way the institutions of society favor certain starting places over others. These are especially deep inequalities. Not only are they pervasive, but they affect men's initial chances in life; yet they cannot possibly be justified by an appeal to the notions of merit or desert. It is these inequalities, presumably inevitable in the basic structure of any society, to which the principles of social justice must in the first instance apply. These principles, then, regulate the choice of a political constitution and the main elements of the economic and social system. The justice of a social scheme depends essentially on how fundamental rights and duties are assigned and on the economic opportunities and social conditions in the various sectors of society. . . .

3. The Main Idea of the Theory of Justice

My aim is to present a conception of justice that generalizes and carries to a higher level of abstraction the familiar theory of the social contract as found, say, in Locke, Rousseau, and Kant.[2] In order to do this, we are not to think of the original contract as one to enter a particular society or to set up a particular form of government. Rather, the guiding idea is that the principles of justice for the basic structure of society are the object of the original agreement. They are the principles that free and rational persons concerned to further their own interests would accept in an initial position of equality as defining the fundamental terms of their association. These principles are to regulate all further agreements; they specify the kinds of social cooperation that can be entered into and the forms of government that can be established. This way of regarding the principles of justice I shall call justice as fairness.

Thus we are to imagine that those who engage in social cooperation choose together, in one joint act, the principles that are to assign basic rights and duties and to determine the division of social benefits. Men are to decide in advance how they are to regulate their claims against one another and what is to be the foundation charter of their society. Just as each person must decide by rational reflection what constitutes his good—that is, the system of ends that it is rational for him to pursue—so a group of persons must decide once and for all what is to count among them as just and unjust. The choice that rational men would make in this hypothetical situation of equal liberty, assuming for the present that this choice problem has a solution, determines the principles of justice.

In justice as fairness the original position of equality corresponds to the state of nature in the traditional theory of the social contract. This original position is not, of course, thought of as an actual historical state of affairs, much less as a primitive condition of culture. It is understood as a purely hypothetical situation characterized so as to lead to a certain conception of justice. Among the essential features of this situation is that no one knows his place in society, his class position or social status; nor does anyone know his fortune in the distribution of

---

[2]Social contract theories explain the origin of organized society in terms of an agreement (actual or hypothetical) among individuals. Social contract theorists include the English philosopher John Locke (1632–1704), French (Swiss-born) philosopher Jean-Jacques Rousseau (1712–1778), and German philosopher Immanuel Kant (1724–1804). Locke's and Kant's biographies appear, respectively, on p. 155 and p. 175. [D. C. ABEL]

natural assets and abilities, his intelligence, strength, and the like. I shall even assume that the parties do not know their conceptions of the good or their special psychological propensities. The principles of justice are chosen behind a veil of ignorance. This ensures that no one is advantaged or disadvantaged in the choice of principles by the outcome of natural chance or the contingency of social circumstances. Since all are similarly situated and no one is able to design principles to favor his particular condition, the principles of justice are the result of a fair agreement or bargain. For given the circumstances of the original position, the symmetry of everyone's relations to each other, this initial situation is fair between individuals as moral persons, that is, as rational beings with their own ends and capable, I shall assume, of a sense of justice. The original position is, one might say, the appropriate initial status quo, and thus the fundamental agreements reached in it are fair. This explains the propriety of the name "justice as fairness": It conveys the idea that the principles of justice are agreed to in an initial situation that is fair. The name does not mean that the concepts of justice and fairness are the same, any more than the phrase "poetry as metaphor" means that the concepts of poetry and metaphor are the same.

Justice as fairness begins, as I have said, with one of the most general of all choices that persons might make together, namely, with the choice of the first principles of a conception of justice that is to regulate all subsequent criticism and reform of institutions. Then, having chosen a conception of justice, we can suppose that they are to choose a constitution and a legislature to enact laws, and so on, all in accordance with the principles of justice initially agreed upon. Our social situation is just if it is such that by this sequence of hypothetical agreements we would have contracted into the general system of rules that defines it. Moreover, assuming that the original position does determine a set of principles (that is, that a particular conception of justice would be chosen), it will then be true that whenever social institutions satisfy these principles those engaged in them can say to one another that they are cooperating on terms to which they would agree if they were free and equal persons whose relations with respect to one another were fair. They could all view their arrangements as meeting the stipulations that they would acknowledge in an initial situation that embodies widely accepted and reasonable constraints on the choice of principles. The general recognition of this fact would provide the basis for a public acceptance of the corresponding principles of justice. No society can, of course, be a scheme of cooperation that men enter voluntarily in a literal sense; each person finds himself placed at birth in some particular position in some particular society, and the nature of this position materially affects his life prospects. Yet a society satisfying the principles of justice as fairness comes as close as a society can to being a voluntary scheme, for it meets the principles that free and equal persons would assent to under circumstances that are fair. In this sense its members are autonomous and the obligations they recognize self-imposed.

One feature of justice as fairness is to think of the parties in the initial situation as rational and mutually disinterested. This does not mean that the parties are egoists—that is, individuals with only certain kinds of interests, say in wealth, prestige, and domination. But they are conceived as not taking an interest in one another's interests. They are to presume that even their spiritual aims may be opposed, in the way that the aims of those of different religions may be opposed. Moreover, the concept of rationality must be interpreted as far as possible in the narrow sense, standard in economic theory, of taking the most effective means to given ends. . . .

I shall maintain . . . that the persons in the initial situation would choose two rather different principles: The first requires equality in the assignment of basic rights and duties, while the second holds that social and economic inequalities, for example, inequalities of wealth and authority, are just only if they result in compensating benefits for everyone, and in particular for the least advantaged members of society. These principles rule out justifying institutions on the grounds that the hardships of some are offset by a greater good in the aggregate. It may be expedient but it is not just that some should have less in order that others may prosper. But there is no injustice in the greater benefits earned by a few provided that the situation of persons not so fortunate is thereby improved. The intuitive idea is that since everyone's well-being depends upon a scheme of cooperation without which no one could have a satisfactory life, the division of advantages should be such as to draw forth the willing cooperation of everyone taking part in it, including those less well situated. Yet this can be expected only if reasonable terms are proposed. The two principles mentioned seem to be a fair agreement on the basis of which those better endowed, or more fortunate in their social position, neither of which we can be said to deserve, could expect the willing cooperation of others when some workable scheme is a necessary condition of the welfare of all. Once we decide to look for a conception of justice that nullifies the accidents of natural endowment and the contingencies of social circumstance as counters in quest for political and economic advantage, we are led to these principles. They express the result of leaving aside those aspects of the social world that seem arbitrary from a moral point of view. . . .

4. The Original Position and Justification

I have said that the original position is the appropriate initial status quo that ensures that the fundamental agreements reached in it are fair. This fact yields the name "justice as fairness." It is clear, then, that I want to say that one conception of justice is more reasonable than another, or justifiable with respect to it, if rational persons in the initial situation would choose its principles over those of the other for the role of justice. Conceptions of justice are to be ranked by their acceptability to persons so circumstanced. Understood in this way, the question of justification is settled by working out a problem of deliberation: We have to ascertain which principles it would be rational to adopt given the contractual situation. This connects the theory of justice with the theory of rational choice.

If this view of the problem of justification is to succeed, we must, of course, describe in some detail the nature of this choice problem. A problem of rational decision has a definite answer only if we know the beliefs and interests of the parties, their relations with respect to one another, the alternatives between which they are to choose, the procedure whereby they make up their minds, and so on. As the circumstances are presented in different ways, correspondingly different principles are accepted. The concept of the original position, as I shall refer to it, is that of the most philosophically favored interpretation of this initial choice situation for the purposes of a theory of justice. . . .

One should not be misled, then, by the somewhat unusual conditions that characterize the original position. The idea here is simply to make vivid to ourselves the restrictions that it seems reasonable to impose on arguments for principles of justice, and therefore on these principles themselves. Thus it seems reasonable and generally acceptable that no one should be advantaged or disadvantaged by natural fortune or social circumstances in the choice of principles. It also seems widely agreed that it should be impossible to tailor principles to the circumstances of one's own case. We should ensure further that particular inclinations and aspirations, and persons' conceptions of their good do not affect the principles adopted. The aim is to rule out those principles that it would be rational to propose for acceptance, however little the chance of success, only if one knew certain things that are irrelevant from the standpoint of justice. For example, if a man knew that he was wealthy, he might find it rational to advance the principle that various taxes for welfare measures be counted unjust; if he knew that he was poor, he would most likely propose the contrary principle. To represent the desired restrictions, one imagines a situation in which everyone is deprived of this sort of information. One excludes the knowledge of those contingencies that sets men at odds and allows them to be guided by their prejudices. In this manner the veil of ignorance is arrived at in a natural way. This concept should cause no difficulty if we keep in mind the constraints on arguments that it is meant to express. At any time we can enter the original position, so to speak, simply by following a certain procedure—namely, by arguing for principles of justice in accordance with these restrictions.

It seems reasonable to suppose that the parties in the original position are equal. That is, all have the same rights in the procedure for choosing principles; each can make proposals, submit reasons for their acceptance, and so on. Obviously the purpose of these conditions is to represent equality between human beings as moral persons, as creatures having a conception of their good and capable of a sense of justice. The basis of equality is taken to be similarity in these two respects. Systems of ends are not ranked in value; and each man is presumed to have the requisite ability to understand and to act upon whatever principles are adopted. Together with the veil of ignorance, these conditions define the principles of justice as those that rational persons concerned to advance their interests would consent to as equals when none are known to be advantaged or disadvantaged by social and natural contingencies.

There is, however, another side to justifying a particular description of the original position. This is to see if the principles that would be chosen match our considered convictions of justice or extend them in an acceptable way. We can note whether applying these principles would lead us to make the same judgments about the basic structure of society that we now make intuitively and in which we have the greatest confidence; or whether, in cases where our present judgments are in doubt and given with hesitation, these principles offer a resolution that we can affirm on reflection. There are questions that we feel sure must be answered in a certain way. For example, we are confident that religious intolerance and racial discrimination are unjust. We think that we have examined these things with care and have reached what we believe is an impartial judgment not likely to be distorted by an excessive attention to our own interests. These convictions are provisional fixed points that we presume any conception of justice must fit. But we have much less assurance as to what is the correct distribution of wealth and authority. Here we may be looking for a way to remove our doubts. We can check an interpretation of the initial situation, then, by the capacity of its principles to accommodate our firmest convictions and to provide guidance where guidance is needed.

In searching for the most favored description of this situation we work from both ends. We begin by describing it so that it represents generally shared and preferably weak conditions. We then see if these conditions are strong enough to yield a significant set of principles. If not, we look for further premises equally reasonable. But if so, and these principles match our considered convictions of justice, then so far well and good. But presumably there will be discrepancies. In this case we have a choice. We can either modify the account of the initial situation or we can revise our existing judgments, for even the judgments we take provisionally as fixed points are liable to revision. By going back and forth, sometimes altering the conditions of the contractual circumstances, at others withdrawing our judgments and conforming them to principle, I assume that eventually we shall find a description of the initial situation that both expresses reasonable conditions and yields principles that match our considered judgments duly pruned and adjusted. This state of affairs I refer to as reflective equilibrium. It is an equilibrium because at last our principles and judgments coincide; and it is reflective since we know to what principles our judgments conform and the premises of their derivation. At the moment everything is in order. But this equilibrium is not necessarily stable. It is liable to be upset by further examination of the conditions that should be imposed on the contractual situation and by particular cases that may lead us to revise our judgments. Yet, for the time being, we have done what we can to render coherent and to justify our convictions of social justice. We have reached a conception of the original position. . . .

CHAPTER II. THE PRINCIPLES OF JUSTICE

11. Two Principles of Justice

I shall now state in a provisional form the two principles of justice that I believe would be chosen in the original position. . . .

First, each person is to have an equal right to the most extensive basic liberty compatible with a similar liberty for others.

Second, social and economic inequalities are to be arranged so that they are both (a) reasonably expected to be to everyone's advantage, and (b) attached to positions and offices open to all. . . .

By way of general comment, these principles primarily apply, as I have said, to the basic structure of society. They are to govern the assignment of rights and duties and to regulate the distribution of social and economic advantages. As their formulation suggests, these principles presuppose that the social structure can be divided into two more or less distinct parts, the first principle applying to the one, the second to the other. They distinguish between those aspects of the social system that define and secure the equal liberties of citizenship and those that specify and establish social and economic inequalities. The basic liberties of citizens are, roughly speaking, political liberty (the right to vote and to be eligible for public office) together with freedom of speech and assembly; liberty of conscience and freedom of thought; freedom of the person along with the right to hold (personal) property; and freedom from arbitrary arrest and seizure as defined by the concept of the rule of law. These liberties are all required to be equal by the first principle, since citizens of a just society are to have the same basic rights.

The second principle applies, in the first approximation, to the distribution of income and wealth and to the design of organizations that make use of differences in authority and responsibility, or chains of command. While the distribution of wealth and income need not be equal, it must be to everyone's advantage, and at the same time, positions of authority and offices of command must be accessible to all. One applies the second principle by holding positions open, and then, subject to this constraint, arranges social and economic inequalities so that everyone benefits.

These principles are to be arranged in a serial order with the first principle prior to the second. This ordering means that a departure from the institutions of equal liberty required by the first principle cannot be justified by, or compensated for, by greater social and economic advantages. The distribution of wealth and income, and the hierarchies of authority, must be consistent with both the liberties of equal citizenship and equality of opportunity. . . .

The two principles . . . are a special case of a more general conception of justice that can be expressed as follows:

> All social values—liberty and opportunity, income and wealth, and the bases of self-respect—are to be distributed equally unless an unequal distribution of any, or all, of these values is to everyone's advantage.

Injustice, then, is simply inequalities that are not to the benefit of all. Of course, this conception is extremely vague and requires interpretation.

As a first step, suppose that the basic structure of society distributes certain primary goods, that is, things that every rational man is presumed to want. These goods normally have a use whatever a person's rational plan of life. For simplicity, assume that the chief primary goods at the disposition of society are rights and liberties, powers and opportunities, income and wealth. . . . These are the social primary goods. Other primary goods such as health and vigor, intelligence and imagination, are natural goods; although their possession is influenced by the basic structure, they are not so directly under its control. Imagine, then, a hypothetical initial arrangement in which all the social primary goods are equally distributed: Everyone has similar rights and duties, and income and wealth are evenly shared. This state of affairs provides a benchmark for judging improvements. If certain inequalities of wealth and organizational powers would make everyone better off than in this hypothetical starting situation, then they accord with the general conception.

Now it is possible, at least theoretically, that by giving up some of their fundamental liberties men are sufficiently compensated by the resulting social and economic gains. The general conception of justice imposes no restrictions on what sort of inequalities are permissible; it only requires that everyone's position be improved. We need not suppose anything so drastic as consenting to a condition of slavery. Imagine instead that men forgo certain political rights when the economic returns are significant and their capacity to influence the course of policy by the exercise of these rights would be marginal in any case. It is this kind of exchange that the two principles as stated rule out; being arranged in serial order, they do not permit exchanges between basic liberties and economic and social gains. The serial ordering of principles expresses an underlying preference among primary social goods. When this preference is rational, so likewise is the choice of these principles in this order.

Multiculturalism

Joseph Raz

Joseph Raz was born in 1939 in Haifa, Palestine (now Israel). After completing his master's degree in law at Hebrew University of Jerusalem in 1963, he enrolled in the graduate program in philosophy at Oxford University, where he received his doctorate in 1967. He then accepted an appointment as lecturer in law in philosophy at Hebrew University. In 1970 he returned to Oxford, where he was a research fellow at Nuffield College (1970–1972) and a tutorial fellow at Balliol College (1972–1985). Raz has been professor of the philosophy of Law at Oxford since 1985 and professor at Columbia Law School since 1995. He has held visiting appointments at numerous institutions, including the Australian National University, the University of Toronto, the University of California–Berkeley, Yale University, and the University of Michigan. His book *The Morality of Freedom* received the W. J. M. Mackenzie Book Prize from the Political Studies Association and the Elaine and David Spitz Book Prize from the Conference for the Study of Political Thought. Raz was awarded an honorary doctorate by Catholic University in Brussels, Belgium (1993), and was the first recipient of the International Prize for Legal Research from the National Autonomous University of Mexico (2005).

Raz's publications include *The Concept of a Legal System* (1970; 2d ed., 1980); *Practical Reason and Norms* (1975; 2d ed., 1990); *The Authority of Law* (1979); *Engaging Reason: On the Theory of Value and Action* 1999); *Value, Respect, and Attachment* (2001); *The Practice of Value* (2003); and *The Authority of Law: Essays on Law and Morality* (2009).

Our reading is Raz's 1998 article "Multiculturalism," which was originally presented as a lecture at the University of Bremen, Germany, in 1997. Raz discusses some of the theoretical, political, and practical challenges to multiculturalism. On the theoretical level, how can the universality of multiculturalism be combined with the particularity of human relationships? Politically, can multiculturalism emerge as a political bond that supplements or replaces nationalism? Morally—and perhaps most fundamentally—why is multiculturalism necessary?

Raz contends that we should think of multiculturalism not primarily as an ethical or political theory, but as "a way of marking a renewed sensitivity, a heightened awareness of certain issues and certain needs people encounter in today's political reality." Nonetheless, multiculturalism includes the ethical and political precept that we respect the identity of groups and foster their material and cultural prosperity. To follow this precept, we must conceive of our societies as consisting not of a majority and minorities, but as a plurality of cultural groups. Raz suggests several political policies that would promote this plurality. He argues that multiculturalism is necessary, even in societies in which individuals already have the right to nondiscrimination and other civil and political rights, because these rights do not guarantee the change in sensitivity and awareness that is essential to multiculturalism. For a multicultural society to be unified, members of diverse cultural groups need to be able to identify with the political society, and for this to occur the political society must respect all its diverse groups. We must recognize that universal human values are realized in different ways in different cultures.

1

You will remember the dark and haunting music introducing us to the dungeon where Florestan is languishing.[1] When Leonore first sees him, she is unnerved by her inability to recognize him. Her doubt persists, but after a couple of minutes it no longer troubles her:

> Whoever you are, I will save you.
> By God, you shall not be a victim!
> For sure, I'll loosen your chains.
> I'll free you, poor man![2]

In those few minutes, Leonore turned from a devoted wife struggling to save her husband to a moral volunteer sharing in the struggle of the oppressed wherever they are, and the opera has completed its transformation from the romantic comedy of the opening scene into the political drama that it is.

This journey from love for an individual to sympathy for human beings is a powerful modern narrative. We are often told that morality emerged in this way, as a universalized understanding and universalized sympathy: We come to understand that others have the feelings, hopes, and aches that we and our loved ones have, and we extend our sympathies from our loved ones to all those who, as we now see, are like them.

This Enlightenment[3] narrative provides ammunition to some modern critics of the so-called "Enlightenment project." The Enlightenment, they say, has thrown out the baby with the bath water. In recognizing that morality overcomes people's partiality to themselves, the Enlightenment has—those critics claim—created a monster: a universalized individual who is stripped of everything that makes people human, and is reduced to a sheer abstraction. The Enlightenment project is the morality of this abstract individual, and, like abstract individuals, it is barren of any content.

As a challenge to the universality of morality, such criticism is totally misguided and confused. The universality of morality is rooted in the nature of moral thought—in the fact that generality is of the essence of all conceptual thought, that morality is necessarily knowable, and that moral principles are essentially intelligible, rather than arbitrary givens. But the confused criticism of the universality of morals arises out of comprehensible, even laudable, motives and concerns. It reflects the realization that, in respecting humans as humans, we are in danger of understanding them and their needs as if they were our own clones, as if what is good for us is good for them. From childhood on we are saturated with words of wisdom that emphasize the universality of morality: "Love thy neighbor as thyself," we are told. "Do unto others as you

---

[1]In the opera *Fidelio* by German composer Ludwig van Beethoven (1770–1827), Leonore rescues her husband, Florestan, from death in a political prison. The lyrics are by German librettist Josef Sonnleithner (1776–1835), who based them on the play *Leonore; or, Conjugal Love,* by French dramatist Jean-Nicolas Bouilly (1763–1842). [D. C. ABEL]

[2]Beethoven, *Fidelio,* Act II, no. 12. [D. C. ABEL]

[3]*Enlightenment:* an 18th-century philosophical movement that had great confidence in the use of the power of reason to understand the universe and improve the human condition. [D. C. ABEL]

would be done by." These are, of course, when properly understood, perfectly true words of wisdom. But they are also very dangerous. They are liable to encourage the tendency to understand others by direct reference to oneself: "When I was young I did not have a television. I do not understand why the young today must have television." "I never went to a mosque, why should we give those newcomers mosques just because they want them?"

One of the *theoretical*—rather than merely political—*challenges* multiculturalism gives rise to is how to combine the truth of universalism with the truth in particularism. Multiculturalism is a new word. The *Oxford English Dictionary* traces it back to the late 1950s and early 1960s. But does it designate a new ethical idea? Does it respond to a new social and political reality? The answer to these questions is far from clear. After all, people have lived in societies that were, for much of their history, multicultural. So what is distinctive about the idea? The coexistence of cultural, ethnic, and religious communities within one political society, within one state, has been the condition of European countries long before they knew of themselves as European. Large-scale immigration from one country to another is a more fitful aspect of history, but it is certainly not new. The 19th century in particular saw massive movement of people in Europe, and predominantly out of Europe to Argentina, Canada, the United States, South Africa, and so on. To be sure, many aspects of immigration during the second half of the 20th century are without precedent. But that does not explain why multiculturalism arose in the late 20th century and not before.

You may say that apart from the word there is nothing new in it, that it is simply a return to how we were before the triumph of nationalism and its ideology some 150 years ago. For I believe that it was not until the triumph of nationalism that the thought that seems so natural as to be almost inescapable to us—that is, the thought that only common ethnicity, a common language, and a common culture can constitute the cement that bonds a political community—became the commonplace that it is today. Some of us were brought up to think of nationalism as liable to lead to regrettable extremes, but as essentially a liberating, and therefore an essentially just movement. The ideology of one nation one state was, however, responsible for many of the acts of oppression that Europe has known over the last two centuries, and for much of the misery that parts of Europe experience today. In a way multiculturalism is one of the strands in modern political thought that is trying to undo some of the harm done by nationalism.

I say that it is but one of several political and theoretical moves sharing this aim. The dominant one is of course that of the European Union itself, namely the movement towards political integration of the countries of the Common Market, and others, which will pull aspects of their sovereignty together to create a Federal Europe. Developments in the Union are a product of political fears and economic hopes. Neither are particularly good foundations for a political community. Their theoretical underpinnings are clearer, I suspect, to historians than to philosophers, but the reaction against nationalism is no less evident there than it is in multiculturalism. Both multiculturalism and its big brother, the European Union, reject the thesis that a common nationality is necessary for the viability of a political community. So does another European movement familiar to all of us: the movement whose slogan is "Europe of the Regions." I think that it is a mistake to regard it simply as a revival of the national movements that lost in the battle for nationalist supremacy during the 19th century. Some of the advocates of the ideas of Europe of the Regions did not participate in that struggle. The Scots are an example of such a people. The 18th century was in many ways the golden age of Scotland, and the country did not share in the nationalist fervor of the 19th century. Besides, while Europe of the Regions is advocated by supporters of various nationalist movements, for the most part they do not wish to secede from their countries, and they do not uphold the traditional nationalist ideal of the nation-state. Rather they support devolution of powers to the regions within larger political units, both national and European. Europe of the Regions, along with the movement for a European Union and for multiculturalism, reject common nationality as the common bond on which political units must be based.

All three have to face the same hard challenge: What can replace common nationality as the cementing bond of a political unit? For it cannot be denied that nationalism has proven a very effective political cement for people in the grip of nationalist fervor or anxiety. Those who wish to displace it are inevitably suspected of political naïveté. This is the *political challenge,* as against the theoretical challenge, that multiculturalism—along with the European movement and the ideal of Europe of the Regions—has to face: How do they conceive of the political bond? What will replace nationalism, according to them?

But perhaps the most basic challenge to multiculturalism, the challenge that has to be addressed before any of the others is the *moral challenge:* Why multiculturalism? What is the moral reason for trying to go down this road in the first place? Our countries are, no doubt, far from ideal. But we uphold—I will be assuming—certain ideals, which I will call the ideals of Western liberalism, or, if you prefer, the ideals of Western social democracy. These combine an endorsement of democratic government, individual liberties, a welfare state, and a market-driven economy. These headlines allow for considerable disagreement both about the implementation of these ideals, their precise nature, and their justification. But for my purpose today there is no need to explore those. The basic point is that these ideals give the lie to the charge that anything here is blinkered by a devotion to an abstract and barren conception of a universal Man. Rather, liberal politics arise out of the application of a universal humanistic morality to the conditions of the Western capitalist societies in their postindustrial stage. Within the political frameworks that these principles sanction, and that to a lesser or greater degree do in fact prevail in the Western democracies, cultural institutions can and sometimes do flourish, various churches can and do operate, diversity is unhindered, and no legitimate human interests are ignored. So what is the moral need for a new ideal, that of multiculturalism?

2

In a way, multiculturalism is not a new doctrine. Morality is after all universal, and therefore immutable. Moreover, the fundamentals of morality, inasmuch as they apply to us, are not a mystery. In one way or another they are known.

Rather, multiculturalism brings with it a new way of conceiving an old truth, putting it center stage, not letting us forget about it. It reflects a new sensitivity to the facts that establish this moral truth. And in particular it warns us against the dangers of each one of us understanding the universal in terms of him- or herself, a danger that is particularly great when the other is an alien in our country—when we are at home, and he is not.

I am suggesting that we should not think of multiculturalism *primarily* as an ethical or political theory, but as a way of marking a renewed sensitivity, a heightened awareness of certain issues and certain needs people encounter in today's political reality. The term was used first in, and applied to, Canada. Multiculturalism means—among other things—the coexistence within the same political society of a number of sizable cultural groups wishing, and in principle able, to maintain their distinct identity. Multiculturalism is with us to stay. Insofar as one can discern the trend of historical events, it is likely to grow in size and importance. In its birthplace, Canada, three forms of multiculturalism exist: first, the coexistence of indigenous people—Inuits and various American Indian nations alongside the "old immigrants" of European stock; second, the coexistence of anglophone and francophone communities[4] of "old immigrants"; and third, the coexistence of the immigrants of west European stock, who are mostly "old immigrants," with the mostly new immigrants from Asia and southern Europe. In Britain the situation is very different. We have predominantly two forms of multiculturalism: the coexistence of the four peoples—Scots, Welsh, Irish, and English—whose union created the United Kingdom; and their coexistence with new immigrant communities, mainly Afro-Caribbean, Hindu-Indian, and a variety of Muslim communities—Pakistani, Bangladeshi, Indian, and others.

It is the diverse forms that multiculturalism takes in different countries that makes it difficult to think of multiculturalism as more than a new moral sensitivity. The multicultural policies appropriate in different countries vary greatly, and any useful generalizations one can think of allow for many exceptions. Nevertheless multiculturalism is more than just a new moral sensitivity. I have suggested elsewhere[5] that what we may call *liberal multiculturalism* is a normative precept motivated by concern for the dignity and well-being of all human beings. It is a precept that affirms that, in the circumstances of contemporary Western societies, a political attitude of fostering and encouraging the prosperity, cultural and material, of cultural groups, and respecting their identity, is justified.

This precept has far-reaching ramifications. It calls on us radically to reconceive society, changing its self-image. We should learn to think of our societies as consisting not of a majority and minorities, but as constituted by a plurality of cultural groups. Naturally such developments take a long period to come to fruition, and they cannot be secured through government action alone, as they

---

[4]*Anglophone* communities are English-speaking; *francophone* communities are French-speaking. [D. C. ABEL]

[5]Joseph Raz, "Liberal Multiculturalism," in *Ethics in the Public Domain: Essays in the Morality of Law and Politics,* 2d ed. (Oxford, England: Clarendon Press, 1995), pp. 170–91. [D. C. ABEL]

require a widespread change in attitude. The current attitude of the population at large, and the speed with which it accepts the precepts of multiculturalism, set limits on the practicability and good sense of proceeding with various concrete policies to advance and implement liberal multiculturalism. But we must think long-term to set short-term policies within a sensible context. The size of cultural groups and their viability is another variable affecting the way various concrete measures should be pursued. Where publicly funded programs are called for, relative size is inevitably a consideration. So is viability. There is no point in trying to prop up by public action cultures that have lost their vitality, that have become moribund, and whose communities—usually their young members—drift away from them. Of course multiculturalism changes the prospects of survival for cultures it supports. That is its aim. But it recognizes that deliberate public policies can serve a useful purpose only if they find response in the population they are meant to serve. They can serve to facilitate developments desired by the population, but not to force cultural activities down the throats of an indifferent population.

The more concrete policies, which become appropriate gradually, as developments justify, will be varied and highly dependent on local conditions. They will include measures like the following:

(1) The young of all cultural groups of significant size should be educated, if their parents so desire, in the culture of their groups. But all of them should also be educated to be familiar with the history and traditions of all the main cultures in the country and an attitude of respect for them should be cultivated.

(2) The different customs and practices of the different groups should, within the limits of permissible toleration, be recognized in law and by all public bodies in society, as well as by private companies and organizations that serve the public, be it as large employers, providers of services, and in other ways. At the moment petty intolerance is rife in many countries. In Britain people still have to fight to be allowed to wear traditional dress to school or to work, to give one example.

(3) It is crucial to break the link between poverty, undereducation, and ethnicity. So long as certain ethnic groups are so overwhelmingly overrepresented among the poor, ill-educated, unskilled, and semiskilled workers, the possibilities of cultivating respect for their cultural identity, even the possibility of members of the group being able to have self-respect and to feel pride in their cultures, are greatly undermined.

(4) There should be a generous policy of public support for autonomous cultural institutions, such as communal charities, voluntary organizations, libraries, museums, theater, dance, musical, or other artistic groups. Here (as in education) the policy calls for allocation of public resources. In the competition for them, the size of the groups concerned is an important factor. It works in two ways. By and large it favors the larger groups with a more committed membership. But it also calls for disproportionate support for small groups that are strong enough to pass the viability test. Given that the overheads are significant, the per capita cost of support for small viable cultural groups is greater than for large ones.

(5) Public space, streets, squares, parks, shopping arcades, and so on (as well as air space on television) should accommodate all the cultural groups.

Where they differ in their aesthetic sense, in their preferences for colors, patterns, smells, music, noise, and speed, the way to do so may involve dividing some public spaces between them (as often happens without direction in ethnic neighborhoods), while preserving others as common to all.

Of course all such measures are designed to lead to relatively harmonious coexistence of nonoppressive and tolerant communities. They therefore have their limits. But it is important not to use false standards as tests of the limits of toleration. The fact that the Turkish government does not tolerate certain practices of the Kurds, let us say, in Turkey, is no reason why the Kurds from Turkey should not be allowed to continue with the practices when they settle in Europe.

Similarly, the fact that tolerating certain practices of immigrant communities will lead to a change in the character of some neighborhoods or public spaces in one's country is no reason for suppressing them. It is natural that we should wish to preserve the character of neighborhoods and public spaces. Our lives, and the quality of our lives, are bound up with them. But so are the lives of others, and many of them—be they the younger generation (that is, our children) or members of other cultural groups—may find uncongenial what we find congenial. We owe them what we owe ourselves, that is, the ability to feel at home in their own home, for once they emigrated to a country it has become their home.

Nevertheless there are significant limits to toleration. I will mention four. First, all cultural communities should be denied the right to repress their own members. This applies as much to homophobia among native Germans, as to female circumcision among Somali immigrants. Second, no community has a right to be intolerant of those who do not belong to it. All forms of racism or other manifestations of lack of respect should be discouraged by public policy, though not necessarily outlawed or criminalized. Third, the opportunity to leave one's community must be a viable option for its members. There should be a public recognition of a right of exit from one's community. Finally, liberal multiculturalism will require all groups to allow their members access to adequate opportunities for self-expression and for participation in the economic life of the country, and the cultivation of the attitudes and skills required for effective participation in the political culture of the state.

3

I have mentioned some concrete multicultural policies, not in order to recommend them to any government for immediate implementation; as I mentioned, we have to assess such policies carefully against local conditions and available alternatives. I mentioned them to illustrate the sort of policy consequences I have in mind when discussing multiculturalism. I will say no more of its practical consequences. I hope, however, that what I said begins to address the third challenge, which I called the *moral challenge.* "Why multiculturalism," it asked, "given that we have civil and political rights, including a right to nondiscrimination?" One way in which the challenge can be understood is this: Can all the policies and political attitudes that multiculturalism advocates be encompassed by and derived from doctrines of basic rights and nondiscrimination? The preceding remarks show that the answer is No. Policies such as teaching everyone in a country the language and culture of minority groups cannot be derived from doctrines of nondiscrimination. Moreover, I want to emphasize again that multiculturalism involves more than specific policies. It involves a change in attitudes, and in the ways we understand our societies and think of them. To repeat the point: It involves primarily thinking of our societies as consisting not of a majority and minorities, but as constituted by a plurality of cultural groups. Nothing like this follows from rights against discrimination, or of freedom of religion, or any of the other basic rights.

Not everyone will take the fact that the precepts of multiculturalism cannot be derived from traditional liberal rights as a point in their favor. On the contrary, many will say that this shows that multiculturalism cannot be justified. But that would be a mistake. Those who take this stand are really guilty of a charge leveled by some antiliberal writers: They disregard the fact that people's prosperity and dignity derive their concrete forms from the shared social meanings in the societies in which they live.

People's well-being consists in their success in valuable relationships and activities. Their social and other skills to engage in activities and pursue relationships derive from their own cultures, and their sense of their own dignity is bound up with their sense of themselves as members of certain cultures. Up to a point people can retrain and acquire the skills needed to make a life in another culture. In a multicultural society, it is important to give people the opportunity to do so. This is what I called the right to exit. But not all could do so, and not all would want to do so. The case for letting people have the chance to carry on with their own cultures and ways of life derives in part from the fact that people's ability to retrain and adapt are limited. But it depends on something even more important: on the fact that such demands—that is, *the demand for a forced retraining and adaptation*—is liable to undermine people's dignity and self-respect. It shows that the state, their state, has no respect for their culture, finds it inferior, and plots its elimination.

It is tempting to reply to this that the problem is one of transition. The considerations I mentioned—the difficulty and pain of adapting to a new culture and abandoning one's own, and people's limited capacity for successful adaptation to a new culture—are all factors that affect people who are already conscious of belonging to one culture rather than another. Newborn babies have no such problems. They may just as easily be brought up to be Chinese, as Indonesian, as French or German, or Turks. This is true. But it is not really relevant unless one is willing to contemplate the monstrosity of tearing children away from their parents and bringing them up as prescribed by the state. Given the fact that parents are the most formative influence on children, if the problem is one of transition, then the transition is stretched out over many generations.

So the *moral challenge* "Why multiculturalism?" is answered by our concern for the well-being and dignity of people. Unfortunately, this answer only serves to emphasize the seriousness of the *political challenge:* What, according to multiculturalist views, is the bond that unites a political society, since they reject common nationality as a common bond?

4

I think that we have to admit that this is a serious challenge. It also harbors serious dangers. The truth is that our understanding of the bonds that keep a political society together is very tenuous. There are serious dangers of acting immorally out of exaggerated fears and anxieties. Let me reflect first on the dangers.

One of the most familiar bonds that holds countries together is a common enemy. As we know, most commonly though not exclusively the enemy is a foreign country that represents a threat to one's existence or to one's vital interests. Sometimes it is an ideological enemy: an alien religion or ideology. Sometimes it is an enemy within.

If I may deviate for a moment: The thesis about the advantages of having a common enemy was the first theoretical political thesis I was ever struck by. I was a teenager at an Israeli high school when we had a lecture in a series in which successful people talked about ideas from various aspects of the economy and society. That time the lecturer was a leading Israeli politician, and he explained that the absence of peace between Israel and its neighbors should not be regarded, as official Israeli propaganda and public media presented it, as a tragedy. On the contrary, it was a blessing—a factor that galvanized the national energies. It led Israelis to high achievements in science and technology. It created an educated and alert people, and stopped the assimilation of the country into the Middle East with its Levantine[6] culture of sloth, slovenliness, and sleaze.

I expect you do not need me to argue against the proposition that we should strive for a state of perpetual cold or hot war in order to foster unity. The point I am making is that we reject that proposition not because we believe that the threat of a common enemy cannot bring people together. Everyone I know believes that it can. We reject it as a means of forging unity in spite of the fact that it is an effective means, because it is an immoral means.

So we should be careful in invoking the clarion call of national unity, and of the need for a common bond. We should not let it lead us to policies of oppression against groups living in our countries. Having said that I should immediately add that the question of a political bond is very important. We are all struggling with it at several levels: The enterprise of European unity depends on our ability to forge or to strengthen a sense of European identity as the backbone of the Union. Often the political leaders of Europe seem to be but little aware of this fact. Too often they give the impression that they think that unity depends on institutional ties, and on common economic interests alone. This mistake is even more unforgivable today than it was when it was made by the leaders of the communist movement, if only because we have their mistake to learn from.

As I said before, in various aspects of politics and political theory we are struggling to replace the ideology of nationalism that has dominated Europe for a 150 years. European unity and multiculturalism both raise the same political challenge, for both aim to replace nationalism as the common bond of political society. The need for such a bond cannot be doubted. Political societies are

---

[6]*Levantine:* relating to the Levant, the region bordering on the eastern Mediterranean Sea. [D. C. ABEL]

characterized by the fact that they claim authority over individuals, and in the name of that authority they not infrequently require individuals to make sacrifices for the benefit of other members of the same political society. Redistributive taxation, regional policies, and all the institutions of the welfare state are examples of state institutions imposing sacrifices on some for the sake of others. The willingness to share is not purchased easily. Without it a political society soon disintegrates, or has to rely on extensive use of force and coercion. How is the willingness to share maintained?

Some of the things that can be safely said about this question are true but do not take us far enough. Members of a modern political society need to share a common culture. This is true, but it is easy to read exaggerated conclusions from this harmless observation. We know that a common culture does not mean a common religion, and it does not mean membership of a common ethnic or racial group. It does not even mean a common language, though the absence of a common language can be a nuisance. When I say that none of these is *necessary* for a willingness to share in a common political society I do not mean that they do not help. They certainly do help where they are present. But they are not necessary, and this is just as well, for the thought that political societies must be based on common religion or race is not much more appealing than the suggestion that they must be based on a common enemy.

So what is the truth in the talk of the importance of a common culture? It is not easy to summarize. There are many diverse factors to consider. Here are a few: First, for a country's economy to function well there must be a general knowledge of the basic skills required for it—a more general sharing of the more general skills, and a smattering of understanding and more specialized training in the more specialized skills. Second, a democratic political system depends on literacy, access to information, a certain understanding of political issues and of political processes. Third, willingness to share depends on capacity for empathy: It depends on the ability of people to feel for others and that depends on their ability to understand and empathize with other people's experiences, aspirations, and anxieties.

A variety of factors contribute to the realization of these conditions. Sharing in the same economic system leads to acquisition of similar skills and to a shared understanding of the relatively technical aspect of how things work, and what people's fortunes depend on. The existence of democratic institutions and of free mass media spreads a shared understanding of the nature of political processes, and of the constraints that political action must meet. It also familiarizes people with the lifestyles prevalent in the society, and with other people's points of view and aspirations. The existence of a common education, and of a multicultural syllabus that makes the cultures of all cultural groups familiar to all members of a society, are essential to the spread of mutual understanding and respect.

I have listed some factors that show the truth in the thesis that a common culture is necessary for a political society. But let me repeat again my caution on the matter. For one thing, a common culture is not enough. In some sense all European countries share a common culture; so do all those countries that once belonged to the French Empire or to the British Empire. But this does not make them ready to participate in one political society. Other factors are important as well: Restricting inequalities of income and wealth helps to limit gaps in life expectancy, in health, and in general expectations—gaps that often make people on the opposite sides of the social and economic divide incapable of understanding and empathizing with each other.

But none of this gets to the heart of the matter. And it is our limited understanding of what lies at the heart of the matter that accounts for our uncertainties. Ultimately political unity depends on people's free and willing identification with the political society they belong to—for example, on the fact that they feel German, that their sense of their own identity as German is totally instinctive and unproblematic; and it depends on the fact that they are proud to be German.

Among the things that our very imperfect understanding of the condition of identification teaches us are the following few: First, identification involves a sense of belonging, of being a part of a larger whole. Second, people identify with a variety of groupings and institutions: They belong to a family, to a workplace, to a party, to a sports club, to a religious group, and so on. We know that multiple identifications do not generally conflict with each other. On the contrary, they are often mutually supportive. Third, it is particularly important that identification with a political society does not replace, but incorporates identification with other groups in that society. It is generally agreed that the communist attempt to suppress all other groups has been disastrous, and many studies nowadays emphasize the importance of the coexistence of a multiplicity of foci of identification.

Coming now to points more directly relevant to multiculturalism: It is of vital importance for the ability of one group to be able to identify with the political society that their membership of the smaller group is respected by the political society. This applies to all aspects of identity. A political society that does not respect gays, or Christians, or black people, cannot expect that those it fails to respect will identify with it, and it does not deserve their allegiance. So an important condition of identification with a political society is that that society respects its members. To respect them it has to respect their cultures, their religions, and so on. To that extent multiculturalism, far from being a threat to the common bond that unites a political society, is one of the factors contributing to it.

5

I will say nothing about the *theoretical challenge* that liberal multiculturalism encounters. What I have said so far is sufficient to show how I see the universal and the particular to be complementary rather than antagonistic, and the point has always been clear in the best philosophical tradition—that is, the one descending from Aristotle: The universal must find expression in the particular, and the particular can only get its meaning from the fact that it is subsumed under the universal. In placing multiculturalism in that tradition I am placing it firmly beyond what mere toleration will vindicate.

The thought is not that we must excuse members of other cultures their cultures, for they know no better. That is true too, but it is only part of the truth. Nor is it the thought that one must tolerate cultural minorities or they will destabilize the state. That is true too, but it is not the core concern. At the heart of multiculturalism lies the recognition that universal values are realized in a variety of different ways in different cultures, and that they are all worthy of respect. This, I should emphasize, is not to endorse all aspects of any culture. My culture no less than others is flawed. Many cultures are flawed in similar ways: The suppression of sexuality, at least in some of its forms, is common to many, to give but one example. We should fight superstition, repression, and error wherever we find them, in our culture and in others. When we do so we are of course constrained by principles of toleration and of respect for people. But we should not confuse the fight against error and repression with the condemnation of cultures other than our own. We should recognize that they realize important values, and that they provide a home and a focus of identity that are entirely positive to their members, just as our culture realizes important values and provides a home and a focus of identity for us.

This is why multiculturalism transcends what any principles of toleration can provide. Principles of toleration restrain us regarding what we may do in the elimination of error. Multiculturalism denies that the variety of cultures it enjoins us to protect and support are in error. They are seen essentially as different ways in which universal values are realized.

These comments bring me—at the conclusion of my talk—to the point I started from: the thought that multiculturalism is primarily a matter of a new moral sensibility. I said there that it is a sensibility that takes more seriously the otherness of the other, a sensibility that stops us from forcing our own ways on the other, just because he follows a different style of life, because he comes from a different culture. Think of the point I just made a minute ago: We tend to condemn alien cultures when we find them riddled with error. But we do not condemn our own culture when we find it riddled with error. The idea is not even conceivable for most people. For each person his own culture covers the horizon.

This is well and good, but then nor should we condemn other cultures for their failings; rather we should—as we do with our own—reject the failings but not the culture as a whole. The ability to do so requires more than theoretical knowledge of the right moral principle. It requires understanding and sensitivity. To acquire it we must do more than understand others and the role their own culture plays in their life. We must understand ourselves better, we must acquire the ability not to take our culture for granted, to regard it not as the epitome of human achievement but as no more than one necessarily imperfect manifestation of the human spirit. As I said, there is nothing theoretically new in that. But there is a long way from knowing it, to being able to live by it.

Multiculturalism without Culture

Anne Phillips

Anne Phillips was born in 1950 in Lancaster, England. She completed her bachelor's degree in philosophy and politics at the University of Bristol in 1971. The following year she earned a master's degree in politics of West Africa at the University of London's School of Oriental and African Studies. She subsequently pursued doctoral studies at City University London, receiving her degree in 1982. Phillips was a lecturer in politics at City of London Polytechnic from 1975 to 1988, reader in politics from 1988 to 1989, and senior lecturer in politics from 1988 to 1999. She was concurrently professor of politics at London Guildhall University from 1990 to 1999. Phillips was named director of the Gender Institute at the London School of Economics and Political Science (LSE) in 1999, and five years later she began a joint appointment at the Gender Institute and LSE's Government Department. She is currently professor of political and gender theory at LSE. Phillips's awards include an honorary doctorate from the University of Aalborg, Denmark (1999); election to the British Academy (2003); and a special recognition award from the Political Studies Association for her contributions to political studies (2008).

In addition to numerous journal articles on political theory, feminism, equality, and multiculturalism, Phillips has published 11 books, including *Divided Loyalties: Dilemmas of Sex and Class* (1987); *Engendering Democracy* (1991); *Democracy and Difference* (1993); *Which Equalities Matter?* (1999); *Multiculturalism without Culture* (2007); and *Gender and Culture* (2010).

Our reading is from the Introduction and Chapter 1 of *Multiculturalism without Culture.* In the Introduction, Phillips explains that by advocating a multiculturalism "without culture," she means one that does not exaggerate the homogeneity within a culture, the differences in moral values among cultures, or the extent to which the behavior of individuals is determined by the dictates of their culture. She contends that a multiculturalism without culture is compatible with the principles of gender equality and women's rights.

In the first section of Chapter 1, Phillips argues that a proper multiculturalism must find a middle path between *universalism* (the view that all moral values are valid for all cultures) and *relativism* (the view that the differences among cultures imply that all moral values are relative to culture). We can avoid relativism if we realize that cultures do not exist in mutual isolation, that cultures are composed of subcultures, and that there is a similarity of human experience among persons of all cultures. Phillips then proposes three moral principles that she believes hold for all cultures. The second section of Chapter 1 examines the tension between gender equality and the autonomy of women, and the importance of distinguishing between cultural coercion of women and their own free choices.

INTRODUCTION

. . . My object . . . is a multiculturalism without culture: a multiculturalism that dispenses with the reified[1] notions of culture that feed those stereotypes to which so many feminists have objected, yet retains enough robustness to address inequalities between cultural groups; a multiculturalism in which the language of cultural difference no longer gives hostages to fortune or suste-nance to racists, but also no longer paralyzes normative judgment. I maintain that those writing on multiculturalism (supporters as well as critics) have exag-gerated not only the unity and solidity of cultures but the intractability of value conflict as well, and often misrecognized highly contextual political dilemmas as if these reflected deep value disagreement. Though there are important areas of cultural disagreement, most do not involve a deep diversity with respect to ethical principles and norms, and many are more comparable to the disputes that take place *within* cultural groups.

In developing this argument, I query what I see as one of the biggest prob-lems with culture: the tendency to represent individuals from minority or non-Western groups as driven by their culture and compelled by cultural dictates to behave in particular ways. Culture is now widely employed in a discourse that denies human agency, defining individuals through their culture and treating culture as the explanation for virtually everything they say or do. This some-times features as part of the case for multicultural policies or concessions, but it more commonly appears in punitive policies designed to stamp out what have been deemed inappropriate or unacceptable practices. When, for example, European governments decide that the best way to protect young Moroccan, Turkish, or Bangladeshi women from being forced into unwanted marriages with strangers from their parents' country of origin is to ban marriages with overseas partners for anyone under the age of 18, 21, or 24, they represent young women from these groups as incapable of agency. They operate on the (highly stereotypical) assumption that all parents from these cultural groups are coer-cive and all young women are submissive, and hence, that any marriage arranged with an overseas partner should be regarded as forced. I argue that a more careful understanding of culture provides a better basis for multicultural policy than the overly homogenized version that currently figures in the argu-ments of supporters and critics alike. A defensible multiculturalism will put human agency much more at its center; it will dispense with strong notions of culture.

I focus on areas of contestation where a sensitivity to cultural traditions has been employed to deny women their rights, or principles of gender equality have been used as a reason to ban cultural practices, and I draw on a growing feminist literature that sees the deconstruction[2] of culture as the way forward to addressing tensions between gender equality and cultural diversity. . . . The basic contention throughout is that multiculturalism can be made compatible

---

[1]*reified:* regarded as having concrete existence. [D. C. ABEL]
[2]*deconstruction:* a critical dismantling that questions traditional distinctions and oppositions. [D. C. ABEL]

with the pursuit of gender equality and women's rights so long as it dispenses with an essentialist[3] understanding of culture. I have somewhat polemically described my project as a multiculturalism without culture. . . .

CHAPTER 1. MULTICULTURALISM WITHOUT CULTURE

Cultural Difference and Moral Norms

. . . Anyone advocating policies of multicultural accommodation has to engage with the question of limits: Is there a limit to the practices and behaviors that can be condoned in any given society, and if so, what justifies this limit? Refusing to engage with the question—for example, refusing to make judgments on the permissibility of female genital cutting, or sex between a 10-year-old girl and a 30-year-old man—invites criticism for abdicating moral responsibility. But answering with a supposedly universal principle that turns out to reflect more local norms invites criticism for privileging one group above others. The universalist ignores the contextual nature of principles of justice, the shaping of all norms of right and wrong by the historical circumstances in which they evolved. The relativist goes off in the other direction, presenting norms of justice as if they are always relative to the societies in which they emerge, and arguing that it is inappropriate to take the norms of one culture as the measure against which to assess the practices of another. Between the deception that dresses up the parochial concerns of one group as if these were universal requirements of justice, and the relativism that suspends judgment in the face of oppression and harm, where on Earth is one supposed to go?

This stark opposition is at least partially dissolved when we move away from a bounded understanding of culture. It then becomes less plausible to conceive of cultures as existing in mutual isolation, or to think of their value systems as evolving in unique and distinct ways. As Joseph Carens argues, it is a mistake to equate a moral community with a political one, as if the norms that regulate our lives begin and end at the borders of our state.[4] It is also a mistake to conceive of the larger society or culture as bounded in this way. Cultures are made up of people, and people and their ideas move. Trade, migration, the forcible removal of millions from one continent to another, and the more peaceful exchange of literatures and ideas (all long predating what is currently labeled globalization) mean that there are few societies left in the world that can be described as insulated from contact with outside groups. Cultures are also made up of subcultures, each evolving its own norms of behavior, which means there will always be a range of normative principles being debated (or squashed) within any single cultural group.

The idea that each culture evolves its own distinct norms of justice, with not much overlap and not much hope of mutual reconciliation, only makes sense if,

---

[3]*essentialist:* relating to *essentialism,* the view that there is a distinction between essential and nonessential properties of a thing. [D. C. ABEL]

[4]Joseph H. Carens, *Culture, Citizenship, and Community: A Contextual Exploration of Justice as Evenhandedness* (New York: Oxford University Press, 2000), p. 27. [A. PHILLIPS]

first, there has been no exchange of people or ideas, and second, there is no great similarity in human experience that might lead people in different societies or cultures to formulate similar principles for regulating their collective life. Both assumptions seem misplaced. Gilroy talks of an overwhelming, "almost banal" human sameness, reflecting the predicaments of a common species life.[5] Bhikhu Parekh, more convinced than Gilroy of the salience of cultural difference, still observes the "genuinely universal feel" of the United Nations Declaration of Human Rights, and the way its notions of respect for human life, dignity, and equality of rights speak across cultural difference to human values and needs.[6] . . .

Though I believe, along with many contemporary writers on multiculturalism, that the norms we live by should be subjected to continual scrutiny and can be expected to evolve and change when exposed to a wider variety of ideals, I also think there are some relatively straightforward limiting principles. These are not especially original. I believe that societies should act to protect minors from harm, prevent physical and mental violence, and ensure that men and women are treated as equals. Among those pressing for a more multicultural approach to policy-making, it is commonly alleged that cultural uncertainty stops at the point where a practice causes significant and irreversible harm to a minor. Although this is not usually how people put it, the underlying thought seems to be that it is irrelevant whether the prejudice against causing such harm is culturally induced, for this is one prejudice that is worth defending. Carens describes female genital cutting as a "relatively easy case" because it involves permanent and significant physical harm to young girls. "In the light of this fact, its local meaning and the degree to which that meaning is accepted by people subject to the practice . . . seem to me irrelevant."[7] Parekh also identifies the genital cutting of young girls as an simple case, while noting that it is harder to see why the practice should be banned for adult women.[8]

As Parekh's qualification indicates, we cannot simply extend the protections we regard as appropriate for children to apply equally to adults because of the well-rehearsed risks of paternalism; but cultural uncertainty should also stop at the point where people are being subjected to physical or mental violence. Definitions will always be problematic here, as will the implied distinction between a legitimate harm we inflict on ourselves and violence inflicted by others. But the contestability of definitions should not blind us to the effects of violence or cruelty, which speak to a universal human vulnerability to pain. Nor should the frequent breaking of this norm lead us to think of it as peculiar to particular societies and cultures. Torture, to take one subset of the norm against violence, is employed by many regimes around the world, but the fact that is so widely practiced does not undermine the basic intuition against it.

---

[5]Paul Gilroy, *Against Race: Imagining Political Culture beyond the Color Line* (Cambridge, MA: Harvard University Press, 2000), p. 29. [A. PHILLIPS]

[6]Bhikhu Parekh, *Rethinking Multiculturalism: Cultural Diversity and Political Theory* (Cambridge, MA: Harvard University Press, 2000), p. 134. [A. PHILLIPS]

[7]Carens, *Culture, Citizenship, and Community*, p. 42. [A. PHILLIPS]

[8]Parekh, *Rethinking Multiculturalism*, pp. 278–80. [A. PHILLIPS]

My third principle[9] is equality, which I take to include equality between the sexes. When people say the principle of gender equality is culturally specific, they usually have in mind the fact that status of women varies greatly around the world. But again, variations in practice do not prove differences of principle, and if we are willing (as people increasingly are) to see equality as reflecting a wider shared intuition about all humans having the same rights to dignity and respect, it is incoherent to represent equality between the sexes as requiring separate or additional justification. It is, of course, depressingly apparent that women are not treated as equal to men, but it is also hard to envisage any social group in which no one raises a voice to object to women being treated as intrinsically inferior. Equality between the sexes is not to be regarded as something additional to equality. Nor is it something that can be claimed as the value of a particular kind of society or cultural group.

The ideal of equality is historically, but not geographically, specific. I incline to the view (derived broadly from Karl Marx)[10] that as the evolution of market society made people more interchangeable, this made it more possible to conceive of them as composed of the same sort of stuff. New circumstances enabled new ways of thinking, and a notion that seemed bizarre at one point in time—that all humans are born equal—came to be regarded as relatively commonplace during another. The meaning of *human* equality then had to be fought over and extended via political contestations that spanned many centuries, and only slowly incorporated women as well as men, black people as well as white. The process has been extraordinarily slow, and its achievements remain fragile, but while the norm of equality is rightly understood as historically contingent and contextual, it cannot be seen as peculiar to Western societies. Indian notions of caste differences are sometimes cited as evidence that the idea of a fundamental human equality remains alien to many cultures. Amartya Sen notes, however, that dissident voices have spoken against caste differentiations at least as far back as the *Mahabharata*, as in Bharadvaja's comment that "we all seem to be affected by desire, anger, fear, sorrow, worry, hunger, and labor: How do we have caste differences then?"[11]

I believe we can assert the principle of human equality and its subsequent elaboration to include sexual equality as a widely shared norm, and like Sen, am unconvinced by suggestions that equality is culturally specific. And though this does not constitute proof of universality, it is worth remembering that equality is the official position in all countries that have endorsed the Universal Declaration of Human Rights,[12] and a fortiori,[13] all those that have signed up to the United Nations Convention on the Elimination of All Forms of Discrimination

---

[9]The first two principles were discussed in the previous two paragraphs, respectively. [D. C. ABEL]

[10]Marx (1818–1883) was a German philosopher and socialist; for a biography, see p. 466. [D. C. ABEL]

[11]Cited in Amartya Sen, *The Argumentative Indian: Writings on Indian History, Culture, and Identity* (New York: Allen Lane, 2005), p. 11. [A. PHILLIPS] The *Mahabharata* is an epic of ancient India; Bharadvaja, a Hindu sage, is one of the characters in the epic. [D. C. ABEL]

[12]The General Assembly of the United Nations adopted the Universal Declaration of Human Rights on December 10, 1948. [D. C. ABEL]

[13]*a fortiori:* (Latin, "from the stronger [argument]") with even greater certainty. [D. C. ABEL]

against Women.[14] That people should be treated as equals has become the default position in discourses around the world—something from which people have to justify deviations, rather than something to be defended in its own right. This is now commonly said as regards the general principle of equality. In my view, the same principle also applies to gender equality.

Before the irritated reader throws this book across the room, I hasten to add that this rosy vision of the world, with everyone signed up to the same basic norms, does not mean everyone now endorses the same version of equality. There may be no great division at the level of official declarations, but there is still much disagreement between people; or there may be no great division between people on fundamental principles, but there is still almost endless scope for disagreement when it comes to interpretations. In the case of equality, it is evident that some of the endorsements are cynical, yet there are also heartfelt disagreements about meaning, even among those who genuinely support the ideal. It is often argued, for example, that equality means desegregation and is at odds with separate spheres for women and men or separate enclaves for blacks and whites. But it is possible to make a plausible case about equality also requiring a degree of segregation. In the context of current gender relations, some have argued that girls will get more attention from their teachers or more opportunity to specialize in scientific subjects if they are taught in single-sex schools. In Britain, where pupils of African-Caribbean origin may be stereotyped by their teachers and treated as an inherently disruptive influence, there has been discussion about whether separate classes or schools might provide better opportunities for educational advancement. In many countries, it is alleged that the division of cities between black and white neighborhoods is a major obstacle to citizen equality. But it is also argued that in a context of racist violence and harassment, people may enjoy better security if they are able to concentrate in the same neighborhood than if they are dispersed around the city. These disagreements cannot be settled by a simple invocation of the equality principle. The vexed questions start from that stage onwards, in the competing interpretations of what equality means. . . .

Probably the most widely held understanding of gender equality in contemporary Europe and the United States takes it as referring to an equality of opportunity or choice—the idea being that men and women alike must have the same opportunities to choose their way of life and not be prevented by sexist discrimination or excluded by sexist laws, but that they do not therefore have to end up performing the same social roles or earning the same levels of income. On this understanding, there would be nothing intrinsically inegalitarian about a woman being more likely than a man to become a full-time caregiver for the young, sick, or old; or a man being more likely than a woman to reach positions of high influence in the political and economic world, or to earn an above-average wage. If men and women have the same opportunities but systematically choose different occupations or roles, then, according to this view, no one can really complain of inequality. Many feminists contest this,

---

[14]The General Assembly of the United Nations adopted this convention on December 18, 1979. [D. C. ABEL]

including [Susan Moller] Okin, who argued in much of her work that justice requires an equal division between the sexes not only in terms of incomes but also in relation to the time spent on housework, paid employment, and caring for children.[15] Yet the idea that men and women can be different but equal has continued to exert its appeal. Criticizing Okin's "equal split" scenario, Richard Arneson probably speaks for many when he objects that differences in tastes and talents may make it more efficient for the one to specialize in child care and the other in paid employment (he suggests, somewhat disingenuously, that it might be the man whose tastes and talents lead him to be better at looking after the child and the woman who is the better bet on the job market), in which case surely it is better for everyone if they divide things in this way.[16] Like Okin, I find this complacency about the sexual division of labor unsatisfactory. Like her, I incline to the view that men and women only "choose" systematically unequal outcomes because they live in gender regimes that make it hard for them to do otherwise. But I suspect that Arneson's understanding of what is required by gender equality is closer to the dominant ones than either Okin's or mine. . . .

Equality and Autonomy

At this point, we seem to come back to the questions that underpin much feminist thinking about cultural differences. Who is to say what counts as gender equality? And by what right does someone with one set of cultural experiences comment on and judge the practices and beliefs of someone from a different background? In challenging the distinction between what have been presented as distinct and separate cultures, we seemed to move towards a resolution, because this undermined the notion of distinct worldviews insulated from one another behind impenetrable cultural walls. But if a central part of that challenge is questioning the notion of individuals as driven by cultural dictates, this means taking more seriously than before what people represent as their own choice. Rejecting holistic understandings of culture then promises to ease some of the normative difficulties associated with value differences, but makes it harder to settle some others.

Previous discussions of this have largely revolved around two competing principles. On the one hand, it seems plausible to think that insiders, those who share a belief or engage in a practice, will be better able than outsiders to articulate its social meaning and significance. Of course, people do all sorts of things without even realizing what they are doing, which is why the sociological observer might sometimes be in a better position to explain what is going on than those being observed. But we would be distinctly unimpressed by the sociologist who tried to arrive at an understanding of particular beliefs or practices without engaging with or listening to the people being studied. I, for one, would think this would be a guaranteed way to get things wrong. Lived experience matters, not as a uniquely privileged route to knowledge and understanding.

---

[15]Susan Moller Okin, *Justice, Gender, and the Family* (New York: Basic Books, 1989). [A. PHILLIPS]

[16]Richard Arneson, "Feminism and Family Justice," *Public Affairs Quarterly* 11 (1997): 345–63. [A. PHILLIPS]

but certainly as an important one. The weight attached to this lived experience is, however, commonly set against a second principle, which is that those unconstrained by a particular belief or practice will sometimes be in the better position to identify its limitations. At work here is the human tendency to make the best of a bad job, the capacity to ignore those things we feel we cannot change or undervalue those opportunities we know to be closed to us—what has been described in the literature as the problem of learned or adaptive preferences. Perceptions of what is desirable are formed against a backdrop of what seems possible, and choices are made from what appears to he the available range. Given these constraints, it may sometimes be outsiders rather than insiders who are better able to recognize the injustice of a particular practice or belief. Evidence of internal support cannot be taken as decisive, for it may reflect the poverty of aspirations rather than "genuine" belief.

This uncomfortable conclusion becomes still more problematic in light of arguments against treating culture as the explanation of virtually everything individuals say or do. This has to mean attaching more weight to individual autonomy and taking more seriously what people represent as their choice. In Sawitri Saharso's reading of this, we cannot rule out in principle any practice that offends against gender equality, not because of the disagreements noted above about what constitutes gender equality, but because the value attached to equality may come into conflict with the value attached to autonomy. "How," Saharso asks, "should the autonomy of women be balanced against sexual equality?"[17] What of a situation where a woman seeks to abort a female fetus because her family sees girls as less valuable than boys, and she knows her life will be made a misery if she has yet another girl child? What of the estimated 10 to 15 cases a month in the Netherlands, where young Turkish or Moroccan women request hymen repair surgery because they are about to get married and need to conform (or at least give the appearance of conforming) to a sexist virginity rule? Aborting a female fetus because a girl baby is of less value than a boy clearly offends against principles of gender equality, as does the requirement that young women (but not young men) be virgins on marriage. In societies that pride themselves on applying principles of gender equality, these might then seem easy cases: We should surely treat such operations as unacceptable capitulations to cultural differences and call on medical practitioners to refuse to carry them out. Does it make a difference, however, that it is women who are requesting the operations?

Saharso notes that the tension between equality and freedom is commonly resolved by presuming that women are being culturally coerced into their decisions, that no woman would voluntarily seek either sex-selective abortion or hymen repair surgery, and that when women ask for these operations, they are therefore bowing to illegitimate pressure. "But this seems very much like saying that, if a woman takes a decision that runs counter to the majority culture's sense of what is right and just, it cannot be her decision. It must be imposed by an outsider source—her husband, her culture, her religion."[18]

---

[17]Sawitri Saharso "Feminist Ethics, Autonomy, and the Politics of Multiculturalism," *Feminist Theory* 4 (2003): 205. [A. PHILLIPS]

[18]Ibid., p. 209. [A. PHILLIPS]

This looks a denial of agency, for even if people have been subjected to an oppressive socialization or have imbibed norms that consider women of lesser significance than men, this does not mean they lose all capacity for agency and choice. As a feminist, Saharso is deeply troubled by situations where the principles of women's equality and women's autonomy threaten to collide, but she insists that we cannot resolve such tensions by redescribing the situation such that the conflict disappears. We also, she argues, cannot make gender equality a nonnegotiable principle, for it will sometimes come into conflict with women's freedom of choice.

I am not in complete agreement with the way Saharso frames this issue—I believe, for example, that more than she allows depends on disagreements in the interpretation of gender equality, rather than a standoff between autonomy and equality—but the issue she identifies is central. . . . Arguments from women's rights and women's equality are increasingly employed to override the stated preferences of women from cultural minorities, and particularly to override the stated preferences of young women from cultural minorities. In my reading of culture, which questions the understanding of individuals as at the mercy of cultural dictates, these moves are problematic. It is important to recognize the choices people make, not read these as a reflection of their so-called culture or treat them as a false consciousness that can be set to one side in the promotion of gender equality. Yet the insight about learned or adaptive preferences remains, as does the more standard point about many people not having much of a choice at all. We cannot assume that all is well just because people nod their heads and bear it, or that individuals have consented to the way they are being treated so long as they refuse to leave. In many cases, the issue will be how to differentiate choice from coercion. This has to be approached differently once we drop the misguided understandings of culture.

Much recent literature on multiculturalism has turned towards practices of deliberative democracy as the preferred way of addressing cultural disputes, arguing that intercultural dialogue can generate a more culturally sensitive agreement on core values, while avoiding the appeal to external principles of justice as a deus ex machina[19] to settle the debate." The points of overlap with my own approach are the recognition that principles of justice are formed in particular historical contexts, and the belief that when people are sufficiently open to debate and discussion, they often discover significant common ground. But despite an encouraging view of value resolution, the deliberative approach can still be said to exaggerate the scale of value conflict, while understating the difficulties of what to do next. My own emphasis is not so much on getting agreement across different value systems, for I do not regard this as the major issue in the multicultural societies of contemporary Europe or America, where there already is substantial agreement on fundamentals. The more pressing question is whether—and how—to intervene in practices that may or may not be consensual. To give an example . . . , there is no great value disagreement in contemporary Europe over the acceptability of forced marriage, and you would

---

[19]*deus ex machina:* (Latin, "God from a machine") something introduced suddenly and unexpectedly to solve an apparently unsolvable difficulty. [D. C. ABEL]

be hard-pressed to find a spokesperson for any cultural or religious group prepared to say that this practice is condoned by their culture. The question, rather, is at what point do the familial and social pressures that make arranged marriage a norm turn into coercion, and how, short of banning all arranged marriages, can public agencies act to protect young people from ones that are forced? Differentiating between choice and coercion is central to solving this problem. This means understanding cultural pressures, but not assuming that culture dictates.

Sources and Credits

Reading 43: From John Locke, *Two Treatises on Government*. London, England: R. Butler, 1821 (updated stylistically).

Reading 44: From Mary Wollstonecraft, *A Vindication of the Rights of Woman*. London, England: Walter Scott, 1891 (updated stylistically).

Reading 45: From Karl Marx and Friedrich Engels, *Manifesto of the Communist Party*, trans. Samuel Moore. Chicago: Charles H. Kerr, 1888.

Reading 46: From John Stuart Mill, *On Liberty*, 4th ed. London: Longmans, Green, Reader & Dyer, 1869.

Reading 47: Reprinted by arrangement with The Heirs to the Estate of Martin Luther King, Jr., c/o Writers House as agent for the proprietor New York, NY. Copyright 1963 Dr. Martin Luther King, Jr., copyright renewed 1991 Coretta Scott King.

Reading 48: Reprinted by permission of the publisher from *A Theory of Justice* by John Rawls, pp. 3–7, 11–15, 17–21, 54, 60–63, Cambridge, Mass.: The Belknap Press of Harvard University Press, Copyright © 1971, 1999 by the President and Fellows of Harvard College.

Reading 49: "Multiculturalism" by Joseph Raz from *Ratio Juris*, Vol. 11, No. 3, September 1998, pp. 193–205. Reprinted by permission of Blackwell Publishers.

Reading 50: Phillips, Anne; *Multiculturalism without Culture*. Princeton University Press. Reprinted by permission of Princeton University Press.

Diagram on p. 137: From Samuel Enoch Stumpf and Donald C. Abel, *Elements of Philosophy: An Introduction*, 4th ed. © 2002, 1993, 1986, 1979 by The McGraw-Hill Companies. Reproduced with permission of The McGraw-Hill Companies.

Diagram on p. 139: From *The Great Dialogues of Plato* by Plato, translated by W. H. D. Rouse, copyright © 1956, renewed © 1984 by J. C. G. Rouse. Used by permission of Dutton Signet, a division of Penguin Group (USA), Inc.

Headnotes for Readings 1, 8, 12, 25, 36, 39, 40, 41, and 44 from *Discourses*, a section of McGraw-Hill's *Create* database, edited by Donald C. Abel. Copyright by The McGraw-Hill Companies. Reproduced with permission of The McGraw-Hill Companies.

Index